A

GRAMMAR

OF THE

HINDI LANGUAGE

A GRAMMAR OF THE HINDI LANGUAGE

BY THE

REV. S. H. KELLOGG, M.A.

GYAN

Published by

Gyan Publishing House
5, Ansari Road
Daryaganj, New Delhi-110002
Phone: 011-47034999, 9811692060
E-mail: books@gyanbooks.com

Distribution Network
gyanbooks.com
India, USA, Canada, UK, Australia

ISBN: 978-81-212-7049-6 (PB)
First Published, 1876

2nd Impression 2024

Printed at: Gyan Press, Delhi.

A GRAMMAR OF THE HINDI LANGUAGE
Author: S. H. KELLOGG

A GRAMMAR OF THE HINDÍ LANGUAGE

A GRAMMAR OF THE HINDÍ LANGUAGE

IN WHICH ARE TREATED THE HIGH HINDÍ, BRAJ, AND THE EASTERN HINDÍ OF THE RÁMÁYAN OF TULSÍ DÁS,

Also

THE COLLOQUIAL DIALECTS OF RÁJPUTÁNÁ, KUMÁON, AVADH, RÍWÁ, BHOJPÚR, MAGADHA, MAITHILA, ETC.,

WITH COPIOUS PHILOLOGICAL NOTES.

By the

REV. S. H. KELLOGG, D.D., LL.D.,

With Notes on Pronunciation by

T. GRAHAME BAILEY, M.A., B.D., D.Litt.,

Reader in Hindi. University of London.

ROUTLEDGE & KEGAN PAUL LTD.

Broadway House, 68-74 Carter Lane

London, E.C.4

PREFACE TO THE SECOND EDITION.

At the repeated request of many friends in India, and in view of the fact that Her Majesty's Civil Service Commissioners for India have done the former edition of this Grammar the honour to prescribe it to be studied by selected candidates for the India Civil Service, that edition having been exhausted, I have prepared, and herewith offer to the public, a second edition, revised and enlarged.

To the ten dialects presented in the earlier edition, three more have been added: viz., the Mágadhí, the Maithilí, and the Naipálí, making thirteen which are now exhibited in the Tables. The sections and Tables which exhibit the Bhojpúrí and the Rajputana dialects have also been carefully revised, and amplified with considerable new material. The brief section in the 1st edition (pp. 44–49), on "Dialectic Peculiarities," has been enlarged to a full chapter (pp. 65–80, of the present edition). The philological notes have been thoroughly revised, and to a considerable extent rewritten, in the light of the advance made since 1876 in the scientific investigation of the Áryan languages of India. I have found it impossible, however, having due regard to proper limitations of proportion and space, to work out in detail all of the large number of additional forms given in the Tables. But with the aid of the principles set forth in Chapters III. and IV., and the abundant illustrations of their application which are given, the interested student, it is believed, will be able to investigate intelligently for himself forms which are left unexplained.

In the Syntax, I have substituted for the *Prem Ságar*, to a considerable extent, as a source of illustration, the *Shakuntalá* of *Kálidás*, as translated into Hindí by Rájá Lachhman Sinh, Deputy Collector, N.W.P.; which is now ordered as one of the subjects of examination for the Indian Service. I have also occasionally introduced illustrations from other modern works, as, especially, the drama of *Randhír aur Prem Mohiní*, by Lálá Shrí Nivás Dás, which is to be commended as of special value, for the variety of dialect used by the different characters. I have, however, still retained many illustrative references to the *Prem Ságar*, because, despite its very artificial style and provincial colour, yet, as a favourite authority for Puranic Hindooism of the *Bhakti Márgí* school, it is still, and is likely for some time to continue to be, a most popular religious book among the masses of North India, which therefore can be wisely neglected by no missionary among them.

Very considerable changes will be observed in some parts of the work, in the arrangement of the paragraphs, besides many minor verbal alterations, all which, it is hoped, will be found to conduce to greater clearness and accuracy.

I desire to express here my indebtedness to the authors of the various criticisms of the 1st edition, from which, in the preparation of this new edition, I have derived much valuable help. I have also to acknowledge with thanks the assistance rendered me, in reply to a circular sent out before the revision of the Grammar, by many valuable communications giving suggestions for the improvement of the new edition, from members of the civil and missionary services of North India, and from native *paṇḍits*, who have made helpful annotations on the original work. In this connection, I may specially mention Messrs. F. S. Growse and Wm. Crooke, of the Civil Service; and the Rev. Messrs. Zenker, C.M.S., of Mathurá; Coley, L.M.S., of Almorá; Edwin Greaves, L.M.S., of Mirzapur; and the Rev. Messrs. Robb and Traill, of the Scotch U.P. Mission, Rajputana. My former teacher and friend, Paṇḍit Lakshmí Naráyan, of Allahabad, has again rendered me, as in the former edition, helpful service.

Special acknowledgement is also due, of my indebtedness in the preparation of this edition, to the publications of Messrs. Grierson and Beames, of the Bengal Civil Service, and Dr. A. D. Rudolf Hoernle.

Without the admirable Comparative Grammars of the two last named, and the contributions of Mr. Grierson to our knowledge of the dialects of Eastern India, it would have been impossible for me thus to have enlarged the Grammar in the direction of the treatment of the eastern forms of speech. My resources for the investigation of Naipálí have unfortunately been limited; as, notwithstanding repeated attempts, I was unable to procure more than the Naipálí Gospel of Luke, printed by the Serampúr press, until the Grammar was printed as far as the Tables of Dialectic Conjugation; when, happily, I succeeded in obtaining the "Nepalese Grammar" of the Rev. A. Turnbull, M.A., B.D., of the Church of Scotland Mission, Darjeeling; by the aid of which I was enabled to revise a part of the Naipálí portion of the Tables, and incorporate a number of new forms. I should not omit also an appreciative reference to Mr. Frederic Pincott's Hindí Manual, from which I have taken the liberty, in some instances, to draw valuable illustrations of Hindí construction and idiom, out of the many which enrich its pages.

It may not be amiss to remark, in conclusion, that the revision and enlargement of this Grammar has been carried out under considerable disadvantage, on account of many years' enforced absence from India, and residence in a provincial capital, with little opportunity of access to large libraries, or of conference with other scholars in the languages of North India; while the many duties connected with the charge of a large city church have perforce greatly limited the time which it was possible to give to Hindí studies. Under such conditions, it could hardly be otherwise but that many defects and imperfections should still remain, which under other circumstances might not have appeared. But the flattering reception which was given to the first edition of the Grammar encourages me to hope that, notwithstanding these, the work in its present revised and enlarged form, may meet with a no less kind reception from those to help whom it has been prepared.

S. H. KELLOGG.

TORONTO, CANADA,
September, 1892.

PREFACE TO THE FIRST EDITION.

Of the two hundred and fifty million inhabitants of India, speaking a score or more of different languages, fully one fourth, or between sixty and seventy millions, own the Hindí as their vernacular.* In all the great centres of Hindú faith in North India, alike in populous Benares, Allahabad and Mathurá, and in the mountains about the sacred shrines of Gangotrí, Kedárnáth, and Badrínáth, among the Himalayas; in many of the most powerful independent native states of India, as in the dominions of the Mahárájá Sindhia, and the extensive territories under the Mahárájá of Jaipúr and other Rájpút chiefs; in short, throughout an area of more than 248,000 square miles, Hindí is the language of the great mass of the population. Only where Mohammedan influence has long prevailed, as in the large cities, and on account of the almost exclusive currency of Mohammedan speech in Government offices, have many

* This estimate is probably too low. Mr. Cust says that the Hindí-speaking population of India "cannot fall short of eighty millions" (*Modern Languages of the East Indies*, p. 46), and if the Persianized Hindí called Urdú or Hindustání be reckoned, as by most, a dialect of Hindí, then Hindí must be counted the vernacular of over one hundred millions, and is spoken by more of our race than any language except the Chinese.

Hindús learned to contemn their native tongue and affect the Persianized Hindí known as 'Urdú.'

Of the importance, especially to those who have been called to places of authority in North India, of thoroughly knowing a language so widely diffused, and of the need of a grammar which shall exhibit its chief phenomena, one would think that no doubt could be entertained. But chiefly because Urdú has been adopted by Government as the official language, it has come to pass that although this dialect represents grammatically only a single western form of speech, and is the vernacular only of the Mohammedans of North India, it has been read and studied by foreigners in India, to the great neglect, even almost to the exclusion, of the living Aryan speech which is the actual vernacular of the great mass of the Hindú population. Many, indeed, have even been led to believe that the Urdú with which they are themselves familiar, is essentially the vernacular of the Hindús as well as of the Mohammedans of North India; that the only difference between Urdú and Hindí consists in the use of a different alphabet; and that such a language as Hindí, apart and distinct from Urdú, exists only in name and not in reality. The refutation of such a theory needs no other argument than that which is afforded in the declensional and conjugational tables of this grammar.

Others, again, while rightly asserting for Hindí an individual existence, have still erred in their apprehension of the relation between it and Urdú. Thus when I first entered India, I was repeatedly assured that the main difference between Hindí and

Urdú was one of vocabulary. And this statement, indeed, was quite correct, if it be understood to apply only to that special form of Hindí which is exhibited in those religious and educational works which owe their origin, directly or indirectly, to the foreigner in India. Many foreigners who have written books in Hindí, seem to have imagined that by merely substituting Sanskrit for the Arabic and Persian terms which are found in Urdú, that familiar dialect might be at once transformed into *boná fide* Hindí. Hence, apparently, has arisen the strange but popular notion, that the 'purity' of Hindí is to be measured by the degree to which a writer may have succeeded in excluding from his pages words of Arabic or Persian origin; a standard of purity, according to which the author of the *Rámáyan* has failed, and the gifted *Kabír*, with his free use of Arabic and Persian words, must renounce his claim to be considered a Hindí poet. But the early delusion on this subject was soon dispelled. When we fancied that we were speaking something like 'pure Hindí,' the villagers stared confounded at our sonorous Sanskrit terms, many of which were evidently less familiar to them than even the Arabic and Persian of the Urdú. Still it was equally plain that, although often using Arabic and Persian words, they themselves did not speak Urdú, except, perhaps, in condescension to our ignorance. Their Hindí, indeed, was scarcely more intelligible to us than was ours to them; but it soon became quite plain that the speech of the people differed from Urdú much more notably in grammatical forms than in vocabulary. Similarly, in literature, the difference between the Hindí, e.g. of *Tulsí Dás*, *Súr Dás* or *Kabír*, and modern Urdú, is not by any means merely in their choice of words; it is not that they scrupulously exclude Arabic and Persian terms, for they do not. The special difficulties and peculiarities, for instance, of the *Rámáyan* are of a much more radical and serious nature. They concern, not mere vocabulary, but also the grammatical forms and syntax of the language.

Regarding these distinctive peculiarities of Hindí, the student hitherto has had no adequate help. No grammar, indeed, has hitherto even attempted or professed to exhibit, with any approach to thoroughness or completeness, the actual colloquial and literary language of the Hindús of North India. Mr. Etherington in his grammar has confined his attention to that single modification of Hindí which agrees in grammatical form with the Urdú dialect; only giving, in his last edition, a brief synopsis of the Braj declensions and conjugations. On the other hand, Dr. Ballantyne in his brief Braj Grammar, as also Prof. De Tassy in his 'Grammaire de la Langue Hindouí,' passing by the Urdú dialect, gave only the forms of the Braj; which, indeed, had been previously exhibited in an old Hindí Grammar published by Government in connection with the College of Fort William. All grammarians of the Hindí hitherto, have alike entirely ignored the eastern type of Hindí, as represented, e.g., with some admixture, in the *Rámáyan* of *Tulsí Dás*. Indeed, it is a remarkable fact that although, of all Hindí books, the writings of *Kabír* excepted, none compare with the *Rámáyan* in universal popularity and general influence upon the people, and although this eastern Hindí, even more than the western Braj, may be regarded as *par excellence* the classic dialect of Hindí, yet not a Hindí grammar hitherto published, nor a Hindí dictionary, previous to the late valuable work of Mr. Bate, so much as hints the existence of any grammatical form or construction, peculiar to *Tulsí Dás* or any similar writer.* What Hindí grammarian, for example, has ever noted the future in *b*, so common not only in the *Rámáyan*, but in all the modern eastern Hindí dialects? Or where has the fact been noted in any grammar, that one chief distinguishing characteristic of the Urdú and other western Hindí dialects, viz. the passive construction of the perfects of transitive verbs with the case of the agent in *ne*, does not exist in eastern Hindí? and that this *ne* is never used by *Tulsí Dás*, even when he employs the passive construction?

This absence of the assistance needed by the Hindí student, has doubtless been the occasion of increasing the prevailing indifference of Europeans to classic Hindí, and of turning many to the special study of the more fashionable Urdú, for which helps have become so abundant. Very many civilians in India, instead of seeking the rewards and honours offered by Government to the thorough student of the great Hindí poem of *Tulsí Dás*, have preferred to compete for the prizes

* Happily this is now (1892) no longer true; as witness, e.g., the excellent Hindí Manual of Mr. Pincott, published some years ago; not to speak of the more elaborate works of Mr. Beames, and the grammars of Mr. Grierson and Dr. Hoernle.

which are offered for high proficiency in Arabic and Persian, languages utterly alien to all but the Mohammedan population of India. Too many missionaries, seeking to influence the religious thought of the people, have omitted to make themselves familiar with the one poem which, more than any other, is exerting a present, living influence, direct or indirect, upon the religious thought of the Hindús of North India. And one chief reason of this neglect of their great vernacular epic is to be found in the utter absence of any work which might aid the student in its interpretation. For, as I know by a vexatious experience, it is by no means so easy as might be imagined to obtain, in a small station in India, a trustworthy *paṇḍit*, really competent to guide the student to a thorough critical knowledge of the *Rámáyan* or any similar poetry. No less difficulties have hitherto met him who would acquaint himself with the actual speech of the Hindús in the district where he might be stationed. Most of these dialects have no literature; and whatever the intrinsic merits of some of them may be, the attempt to force any one of them into the field already preoccupied by the Urdú dialect as the *lingua franca* of North India, would doubtless be both unwise and futile. Still it is evidently very desirable that the magistrate in his court should be able to understand the rustic witness, and the missionary disputing in the bazaar, his adversaries, without the aid of a third, and not always disinterested, party. But no effort whatever has yet been made to indicate the actual nature and extent of those dialectic variations, which always perplex, and sometimes discourage, him who really desires a knowledge of the spoken language of the people, as well as that of their books.

Thus it was, that, embarrassed by these difficulties, I was led to take up the Hindí, with such *paṇḍits* as might be procured, and note and arrange, primarily for my own use, and with no thought of writing a book, facts of the class above referred to. In this way, in the course of several years, gradually grew up a considerable body of notes on Hindí, which has finally developed into this Grammar. My aim has accordingly been, not merely to reproduce, under a new arrangement, the matter of grammars previously existing, but rather to supply their omissions and supplement their defects. All existing Hindí and Urdú grammars have been carefully studied, with this particular point in view. Thus, in addition to the fundamental matter pertaining especially to modern standard Hindí, or common to that with other Hindí dialects, the grammar now offered to the public will be found to contain a large amount of matter not to be found in any Hindí Grammar hitherto published. I may be allowed to mention the following particulars.

I. For practical reasons, that variety of Hindí which agrees in grammatical form with the Urdú has been taken as the basis of the Grammar. It is to this form of Hindí, for various reasons, that the student commonly first directs his attention; and, moreover, in virtue of the position of this dialect as a *lingua franca* throughout the whole Hindí area of North India, and its adoption by the educational authorities as the medium of vernacular instruction in all Hindí schools, it has a special claim to our primary consideration;

and, for such reasons only, may be justly termed the 'standard dialect' of Hindí.* But while thus yielding to this 'standard Hindí' a priority in certain respects, I have endeavoured to treat with equal thoroughness the two great dialects of classic Hindí literature as of no less importance to the Hindí scholar. Of these dialects, the *Braj* and the old *Púrbí*,† the former represents the western, as the latter represents the eastern type of Hindí. The very numerous and marked peculiarities of these two typical dialects, in declension, conjugation, and syntax, have been for the first time collected, classified, and compared. It is not indeed claimed that all the various forms of these types which may occur in Hindí, will be found in these pages; nor will this be expected by any one at all familiar with the almost endless vagaries of Hindí writers. It is hoped, however, that the student of the *Prem Ságar*, the *Rájníti*, or the *Rámáyan*, will rarely be disappointed in consulting this work.‡ Outside of these books any variations not noted in this grammar will probably be found but slight and unimportant deviations from some central type herein exhibited.

II. In addition to the various forms of literary Hindí, the declension and conjugation of nine or ten less important colloquial dialects have been exhibited in these

* This form of Hindí has also often been termed *kharí boli*, or the 'pure speech;' and also, by some European scholars, after the analogy of the German, 'High Hindí.'

† That is, 'Eastern;' more precisely called, by Hoernle, the Baiswáṛí, or language of Baiswáṛ, the land of the tribe called the Bais.

‡ A few passages in the *Rámáyan*, however, chiefly in the *Laṅká Káṇḍ* and *Uttar Káṇḍ*, have been written in pure Sanskrit; and I have regarded the explication of such passages as belonging to Sanskrit rather than to Hindí grammar.

pages. This is, I believe, the first attempt to set forth, with any approach to completeness, the actual living speech of the Hindí-speaking population of North India. It is indeed true that local variations may be adduced almost without number, which have not been mentioned in this grammar; but the dialects which have been exhibited, it is hoped, will be found to represent all of the leading varieties of speech, from Bangál in the east to Gujarát and Sindh in the west. Moreover, all these numerous dialects may be readily assigned to two or three general types, so that excessive detail might embarrass, rather than aid, the student. I trust that in this respect this grammar may prove a valuable aid to the foreigner in India, who would learn to understand the special vernacular of the district where he may reside. For although colloquial speech cannot be learned from books alone, yet a grammar, if it indicate the forms for which we are to listen, may assist us in acquiring a knowledge of colloquial speech. Nor are these rude dialects without value in a literary point of view. For very often some unusual form in literature may be explicated by a reference to the colloquial of some rustic district; while for the purposes of the philologist, it is such wild, unpruned dialects as these, which of all others promise and yield the richest harvest of valuable fruit.*

---

* I have ventured for practical reasons to deviate in some cases from the common nomenclature of these dialects, and have preferred generally to indicate them by names indicative of the modern names of the province in which they are used. Thus, *Avadhí*, of course, denotes the dialect of Oude; *Riwáí*, that of the state of *Riwá*; etc., etc. It may be noted here, that the Rajputana dialect of *Mewáṛ*, is also essentially that of the Mairs, and might, perhaps with equal propriety, be designated either *Mairwáṛí* or *Mewáṛí*.

III. Especial attention has been given to the matter of illustration. In grammar, particularly, mere assertion, unsupported by example, is extremely unsatisfactory. And when one undertakes to write a grammar of any language not his own, examples constructed by the author himself to fit his rules, however correct they may be, can hardly inspire a student with perfect confidence in his guide. I have accordingly made it a rule to support every statement of any consequence in etymology or syntax, by one or more illustrations, which, with no exception of any importance, have been culled from native books, or taken down fresh from the lips of the people. Nor have I allowed myself to draw an illustration from any Hindí book written by a foreigner; for even those European scholars who have most thoroughly mastered an Oriental language, cannot be regarded as models so trustworthy as native authors, who write in their own vernacular. Very few, if any, Hindí books have been written by Europeans, which in some casual turn of expression, or occasional peculiarity of idiom, do not betray their foreign origin; while the great majority of such books would prove in many important respects quite misleading to him who should trust them implicitly as guides to a knowledge of Hindí. While the abundant illustration characteristic of this grammar, as will be evident at a glance, has very materially increased the size and expense of the book, it is believed that its practical value to the student has thereby been much enhanced. The illustrations of literary Hindí have been drawn chiefly from the *Prem Ságar* and the *Rámáyan.* To this special use of these works, I have been led, partly by the fact that these books have been chosen by Government,* for the examination of candidates in connection with the civil and military services of India, so that the illustration of their grammar and idiom is especially demanded. And I may venture to express the hope that by all applicants for admission to the Indian services, or contestants in the competitive examinations which are held for Indian civilians, this grammar, with its copious illustrations, may be found to meet a real need. A second consideration which has seemed to justify a prominent reference to these books, is found in their undeniable popularity and influence among all classes of the Hindú population. For, however much may have been said against the Hindí of the *Prem Ságar*, and even of the *Rámáyan*, by critics commonly familiar only with Urdú, and therefore judging everything in Hindí, either by English standards of taste, or from a Mohammedan point of view, the fact remains that the Hindús, from the highest to the lowest, learned and unlearned, greatly admire their style. Crowds, even of the most illiterate rustics, may often be seen listening eagerly to some Brahman intoning the measured rhyming prose of the *Prem Ságar*. And although much has been said of the unintelligibility of the *Rámáyan*, it is the experience of every missionary, at least everywhere in the Ganges valley, that a happy quotation from the *Rámáyan* in preaching or in conversation, is sure to awaken a look of intelligent appreciation from

* Since this was written, the *Prem Ságar* has been dropped from the list of books required for examination.

even the rudest villagers. No civilian, and especially no missionary, can well afford to remain ignorant of a book so popular and influential with the people; and if this grammar shall serve in any degree to aid and stimulate the study of the great poem of *Tulsí Dás*, one great aim of my work will have been accomplished. But while a large proportion of my quotations have been taken from the *Prem Ságar* and the *Rámáyan*, other books have not been ignored. In particular, I have now and then drawn from the sententious Braj prose of the *Rájníti*, the western Hindí of *Kabír*, the *Sukh Bilás*, and the metaphysical *Shaṭ Darsaṇ Darpaṇ* of Pundit *Nílkanth Gore Shástrí*, and, as an excellent example of the modern colloquial style, Kanva Lachhman Siṉh's translation of the Sanskrit drama of Shakuntalá by Kalidása.* Máṛwáṛí can scarcely be called a literary dialect; the only work accessible to me, has been the Máṛwáṛí *Khyàls* or 'Plays,' edited by Rev. Mr. Robson of the Scotch Presbyterian Mission, Beawr.

IV. Another feature peculiar to this grammar will be found in the philological notes, occupying in all about fifty pages, in which I have attempted to indicate the probable origin and derivation of the forms of the Hindí language, and the relation of various dialectic forms to one another, and to the Sanskrit and old Prakrit dialects of India. In a field where, until the late researches of scholars like

* Mr. Frederic Pincott has edited this in an admirable manner, with Lexicon and Grammatical Notes. It should be in the hands of every learner of Hindí.

Mr. Beames and Dr. Hoernle, so little had been done, I cannot venture to hope that I have always succeeded in reducing apparent chaos to order, and in correctly pointing out the lines of derivation. I have only endeavoured, with no little diffidence, to indicate the conclusions to which facts, so far as known, would seem to guide us. And while I have not been able to follow implicitly the guidance of any one individual, it has on several occasions been a satisfaction to find that authorities like the learned scholars mentioned, had been independently led to the same conclusions with myself.

V. Besides the above, much else will be found in this Grammar which is strictly new, both in matter and in arrangement. In the sections, for instance, on pronunciation, I have aimed at more precision and accuracy than has been previously attempted. If some may deem that I have sometimes erred in the way of an over-refinement, I am still glad to know that some of the best practical masters of Hindí have recognised the chief distinctions which I have made in treating of this subject. A nomenclature of the tenses has been presented which is believed to be more uniform and philosophical than any which has been hitherto employed, and which, it is hoped, may commend itself to Hindí scholars. The chapter on Derivation, again, will be found more than a mere arbitrary list of terminations; I have endeavoured rather to group them according to their probable mutual relations and affinities. In the section on Compound Words, all, it is believed, is quite new. Strange to say, no Hindí Grammar that I remember, has dealt with this most characteristic feature of the language, although an understanding of the subject is indispensable to the interpretation of almost any page of Hindí poetry. In the Syntax, attention has everywhere been given to those constructions which are characteristic of poetry, especially in archaic Hindí; and the construction of Compound Sentences, for the first time, has been separately and distinctly treated. The chapter on Prosody, it is hoped, will be found, in completeness and accuracy, all that for any practical purpose the student of Hindí can desire. The Prosody of Hindí deserves and will repay far more study than is commonly bestowed upon it. In no western language is an understanding of the laws of its prosody so essential to the interpretation and comprehension of its literature as in Hindí, where, indeed, a purely native work in prose is a rare exception. Unfortunately, however, until very lately, there has been no English work on Hindí prosody; and the native works upon the subject are so laden with technicalities and an enigmatical symbolism, as without the aid of a rare native prosodian, quite to baffle the student. I shall be glad if I have so cleared away the thorns which have obstructed the entrance, as to tempt my fellow missionaries and others to labour in this attractive field.

Finally, it should be remarked that as this Grammar is intended alike for the beginner and for the advanced student, I have endeavoured to indicate by the use of a large type those important fundamental matters to which chiefly the beginner will do well to confine his attention. Matter less fundamental, and intended rather for the advanced scholar, as, e.g., all in the sections upon dialectic Hindí, has been uniformly printed in smaller type.

It gives me pleasure to express my grateful appreciation of the assistance and encouragement which I have received from many missionaries and members of the civil service, during the years that this grammar has been in progress. In particular, I would express my hearty thanks to the Rev. W. Robb, of the Scotch Presbyterian Mission, Toḍgaṛh, Rajputana, for his invaluable assistance in the compilation of the sections on the Máṛwáṛí and other Rajputana dialects, and afterwards in the correction of the proofs of the same. Indeed, it is only due to this gentleman to say that whatever of value those sections may be found to possess, the merit is chiefly due to him. My thanks are also due to Mr. Beames, C.S., of Cuttack, Orissa, for valuable hints and constant encouragement in the work; and to the Rev. J. D. Bate, of the Baptist Mission, Allahabad, for many a useful suggestion.

S. H. KELLOGG.

ALLAHABAD, N.W.P., INDIA,
December, 1875.

NOTE.

In the preparation of this Grammar, as now published, the following works have been consulted:

Grammaire de la Langue Hindoui: De Tassy.
Hindí Manual: Pincott.
Introduction to the Maithilí Language of North Bihár: Grierson.
Seven Grammars of the Dialects and Sub-Dialects of the Bihárí Language: Grierson.
Hindustání Grammar: Forbes.
Hindustání Grammar: Platts.
Hindustání Grammar: Dowson.
Introduction to Hindustání: Monier-Williams.
Nepálí Grammar: Turnbull.
Panjábí Grammar: Newton.
Gujarátí Grammar: Shápurjí Edaljí.
Maráṭhí Grammar: Stevenson.
Maráṭhí Grammar: Bellairs and Ashkedar.
Sindhí Grammar: Trumpp.
Bangálí Grammar: Sháma Charan.
Sanskrit Grammar: Monier-Williams.
Institutiones Linguæ Pracriticæ: Lassen.
Prákṛita Prakásha: Vararuchi (edited by Cowell).
Comparative Grammar of the A'ryan Languages of India: Beames.
Grammar of the Gauḍian Languages: Hoernle.

The Chapter on Prosody is based upon the study of the following authorities:

Chhandárnava.
Chhandodípaka.*
Shrípingaládarsha:† Kavi Hírá Chand Kánjí.
Also, the Chapter on Prosody, by John Christian, in Etherington's Hindí Grammar.

---

* A small but useful compendium issued by the Government of the N.W.P.

† An exhaustive Treatise on Prosody, in the Braj dialect, with a Gujerátí Commentary.

CONTENTS.

ABBREVIATIONS.

Ap.	Apabhransic.	M.	Maráṭhí.
Ar.	Arabic.	Mair.	Mairwáṛí.
Av.	Avadhí.	Máṛ.	Marwáṛí.
Bang.	Bangálí.	Mg.	Mágadhí.
Bh.	Bhojpúrí.	Mt.	Maithilí.
Br.	Braj.	Mw.	Mewáṛí.
Bú.	Búndelkhaṇḍí.	N.	Naipálí.
E. H.	Eastern Hindí.	O. B.	Old Baiswáṛí.
G.	Gaṛhwálí.	O. H.	Old Hindí.
Guj.	Gujarátí.	Pers.	Persian.
H.	Hindí.	Pr.	Prakrit.
H. H.	High Hindí.	R.	Riwáí.
K., Kan.	Kanaují.	S.	Sindhí.
Kum.	Kumáoní.	Sk.	Sanskrit.
W. H.	Western Hindí.		

NOTES ON PRONUNCIATION.

By

T. GRAHAME BAILEY, M.A., B.D., D.Litt.

(*Reader in Hindi, University of London.*)

Dr. Kellogg's account of Hindi pronunciation was written over sixty years ago, and revised almost fifty years ago. Since then much has been learnt about Hindi sounds. The following notes have been written to bring his account up to date and in some respects to correct it.

a is like the vowel *u* in English *rub*.
ã or *aṉ* is the same vowel nasalized.
á like the middle *a* in English *banana*.
ã́ or *áṉ* is the same nasalized.
i like *i* in English *limb*.
ĩ or *iṉ* is the same nasalized.
í like *i* in English *machine*.
ĩ́ or *íṉ* is the same nasalized.
u like *u* in English *put*.
ũ or *uṉ* the same nasalized.
ú like *oo* in *boon*.
ṹ or *úṉ* the same nasalized.
e rather like *a* in English *pane* as pronounced in Wales, north England, or Scotland.
ẽ or *eṉ* the same nasalized.
o rather like *o* in *mote* as pronounced in Wales, north England, or Scotland.
õ or *oṉ* the same nasalized.
ai in the north and west of the Hindi area is like the vowel *a* in English *hand*; in the south and east it tends towards a diphthong composed of the *u* in *rub* followed by *e* in *met*.
aĩ or *aiṉ* is the same nasalized.
au in the north and west of the Hindi area is like *aw* in *shawl*; in the south and east it tends towards a diphthong composed of the *u* in *rub* followed by *o* in *mote* as pronounced in Wales, etc.
aũ or *auṉ* is the same nasalized.
aí is a diphthong composed of *u* in *rub* followed by *i* in *machine*.
ae is a diphthong composed of *u* in *rub* and *e* in *met*.
aú is a diphthong composed of *u* in *rub* and *oo* in *boon*.

Consonants.

b, g, m, n, s, sh, s͟h, are almost the same as in English.
sh and *s͟h* are pronounced alike. The letter *s͟h* is sometimes used for *kh*; see p. 19.

p and *k* are the same as in English but unaspirated.

ch and *j* are like English, but a little further forward, sometimes almost like *ty* and *dy*; *ch* is unaspirated.

l is like *l* in *holly*, but not like *l* in *whole, peel, pool,* or *mild.*

r is very like *r* in *through, three.* It is like the trilled *r* sometimes heard in Scotland; it is heard too in Italy.

The letter ṛi is pronounced as ri: in speech it is usually pronounced -ir, as kirpā for kripā.

n and *ṇ* are pronounced alike, like English *n*: *ṇ* immediately before *ṭ* and *ḍ* is assimilated to them in position.

ṅ occurs only before *k* and *g*; it is like *ng* in English *sing.*

ñ occurs only before *ch* and *j*; it is like ordinary *n.*

Dental *t* and *d* are like Italian and French *t* and *d*; the tongue touches the upper teeth all round.

ṭ and *ḍ* are called cerebral or retroflex; in making them the tongue strikes or touches the palate a little behind the teeth ridge. English *t* and *d* are actually on the teeth ridge. *ṭ* must be pronounced without aspiration.

Cerebral or retroflex *ṛ* is like a very rapid *ḍ.* It cannot be pronounced without at least a very short vowel before it. It never begins a word.

w varies between a faint English *v* and a very short *u* with or without slight friction.

h in *ph, th, ṭh, chh,* and *kh* is as in English; otherwise it is much more resonant than in English, like the *h* in *childhood.*

y is like English *y,* but fainter. When it occurs between two vowels it is like short *e*; thus *laḍáyá, k͟hoyá, biṭhláyá, ḍuboyá* are pronounced *laḍáeá, khoeá, biṭhláeá, ḍuboeá.*

Nasal vowels are pronounced in the same manner as the nasal vowels in French *allons, fin, engendre.*

On p. 24 are mentioned nine special Hindi letters or signs. The first eight are sounds sometimes heard in borrowed Urdu words. If we read each column from top to bottom we have the following:—

q pronounced in Urdu like a *k* with contact further back than usual. In Hindi it may be pronounced exactly like *k.*

k͟h like *gh* in *lough* or *ch* in *loch.*

g̱ like *kh* but voiced, like the usual sound as *g* in German *sagen.*

z as in English.

ṯ like ordinary Hindi *t.*

f like English *f* but fainter; often tends towards *ph.*

ṣ, s̤ like ordinary Hindi *s.*

ḥ like ordinary Hindi *h.*

h like ordinary Hindi *h.*

HINDÍ GRAMMAR.

CHAPTER I.

OF THE LETTERS.

1. THE Hindí language is commonly written, like the Sanskrit, in the Devanágarí alphabet.* This alphabet, as used in Hindí, has eleven vowels and thirty-three simple consonants. To these we must add the nasal symbols, *Anusvár* and *Anunásik*, and the symbol for a weak aspiration, *Visarg*.† The latter of these, however, is of very rare occurrence in Hindí. The letters are given below, with their equivalents in the Roman character.

2. It will be observed that all the vowels but the short *a* have two forms. Of these, the form first given is used as initial in a word or syllable; the second, as medial or final. It will aid the memory to observe that the alphabetical order of each class of letters, vowels, mutes, semivowels, and sibilants, is the order of the organs of utterance, beginning with the throat, and ending with the lips. The first five classes of consonants are technically known as the five *vargs*.‡ Order of the Alphabet.

---

* More commonly called *Nágarí*.

† In Sanskrit these three words, as also *varg*, below, are pronounced with a final short *a*, inherent in the final consonant, thus, *anusvára*, *anunásika*, *visarga* and *varga*. But this *a* is always silent in prose and colloquial Hindí. Vid. infra, § 10, *a*.

‡ Sansk. वर्ग *varga*, 'a class.'

Rem. Hindí exhibits a large number of dialects, most of which, however, possess no written literature. All of the dialects, like the High Hindí,* which is taken as the basis of this Grammar, are written, as occasion may require, though not exclusively, in the Devanágarí character.†

3. The Devanágarí alphabet is as follows:

VOWELS.

अ *a* आ ा *á* इ ि *i* ई ी *í* उ ु *u* ऊ ू *ú* ऋ ृ *ri* ए े *e*
ऐ ै *ai* ओ ो *o* औ ौ *au*

Nasal symbols, *Anunásik*, ँ, *Anusvár*, ं ṉ. Symbol of the weak final aspirate, *Visarg*, ः ḥ.

CONSONANTS.

Gutturals,	क *ka*	ख *kha*	ग *ga*	घ *gha*	ङ *ña*
Palatals,	च *cha*	छ *chha*	ज *ja*	झ *jha*	ञ *ńa*
Cerebrals,	ट *ṭa*	ठ *ṭha*	ड *ḍa*	ढ *ḍha*	ण *ṇa*
Dentals,	त *ta*	थ *tha*	द *da*	ध *dha*	न *na*
Labials,	प *pa*	फ *pha*	ब *ba*	भ *bha*	म *ma*
Semivowels,	य *ya*	र *ra*	ल *la*	व *va*	
Sibilants,	श *sha*	ष *s̲h̲a*	स *sa*		
Aspirate,	ह *ha*				

---

* By this term, 'High Hindí,' European scholars, of late years, have denoted that dialect of Hindí which essentially agrees, in grammatical forms and constructions, with the Urdú or Hindústání, the vernacular of the Muhammadans of India. This latter, indeed, might be well described as an Arabized or Persianized form of High Hindí. The High Hindí is that dialect which the Government of India recognizes in the business of the courts, and in which, as a *lingua franca* understood by Hindí-speaking people everywhere, have been prepared the Hindí educational works used in Government and Mission Schools, the received translations of the Holy Scriptures, and the largest part of the literature which has been produced by the missionaries of Northern and Central India.

† Other alphabets, sometimes used, are given below, Vid. p. 23.

a. Besides the above, classical Sanskrit had three additional vowels, viz., ॠ *ṛí*, ऌ *lṛi*, ॡ *lṛí*; and the Vedic Sanskrit, one additional cerebral consonant, ळ *ḷa*, which is still preserved in the Maráṭhí. The Panjábí, Gujarátí, and Oṛíya have also preserved the sound, though denoting it by different characters. This same consonantal sound is heard in the Mairwáṛí dialect of Hindí, and in some, at least, of the Himalayan dialects. So also the villagers of the central Doáb sometimes give the final ल of पीपल, 'the sacred fig tree,' an unmistakable cerebral sound. But none of the above letters have any place in literary Hindí. Sounds peculiar to Dialects.

b. In addition to the above vowels, a short *ĕ*, nearly like *ĕ* in 'met,' exists in the colloquial of some districts. It is heard, for example, in the local dialect about Ayodhyá and in Ríwá, chiefly in certain verbal and pronominal forms; as, e.g., in the subst. verb, *ahĕṉuṉ*, 'I am,' *ahĕs*, 'thou art,' etc.* It may also be heard in some words in the Doáb, where it has arisen from the shortening of a previous long *e*; as, e.g., in *bĕṭiyá* for *biṭiya*, dim. from *beṭá*, 'a son.' This sound is also said to be common in the N.W. Himalayas. It may be noticed, as further indicating the existence of this short *e*, that ए, which, according to some books on Prosody, should be uniformly long, in the Rámáyan is sometimes reckoned prosodially short. In these cases, it commonly appears as a substitute, either for short *i*, as in *jĕhi* for *jihi*; or for a short *a*, as in *rákhĕu* for *rákhäu*.†

Rem. Lassen has noted the fact that this same letter also represented a long and a short sound in the literary Prakrit.‡

c. The dialects of Avadh and Ríwá present in certain pronominal forms also a short *ŏ*, as in *ŏn ká* for *un ká*.

* For further illustrations, see the Tables of Declension and Conjugation, and chap. xiii. on Prosody.

† Abundant illustrations of this statement will be found in the Rámáyan. Vid. chap. xiii. on Prosody.

‡ *Inst. Ling. Prac.* § 19, 4.

d. According to Hoernle and Grierson, the colloquial dialects east of Allahabad exhibit not only this short *ĕ*, *ŏ*, but also a short *ăi* and *ău*, differing from the corresponding long sounds simply in quantity.* To represent these four sounds, unknown to the Devanágarí alphabet, Hoernle has introduced four characters from the Bangálí and Panjábí, in which he has been followed by Grierson. These are as follows, the initial form being in each case given first:

ऎ ॆ *ĕ*, ऐ ै *ăi*, ऒ ॊ *ŏ*, औ ौ *ău*.

It will be observed that these differ from the corresponding long vowel characters merely in that the strokes above the line are doubly curved; and that the initial forms of *ĕ* and *ăi* face to the left instead of the right.† These characters will be used for the notation of these short vowels in the following pages.

Vocalization of Consonants.

4. The consonants are all vocalized by the short vowel *a*, which is theoretically inherent in each consonant. Thus, क properly represents, not *k*, but *ka*, प, *pa*; etc. The letters are indicated by adding the word कार *kár*; as, अकार *akár*, 'the letter *a*'; तकार *takár*, 'the letter *t*'; etc. र, when first in a compound consonant, as in र्क *rk*, is indicated as रेफ *reph*. When no particular letter is intended, the term अक्षर *akshar*, often corrupted into अच्छर *achchhar*, is used; as in the phrase, वह कौन सा अक्षर है *wah kaun sá akshar hai*, 'what letter is that?'

a. As a general rule the inherent *a* is silent after a final consonant. But in many words in the eastern dialects it is pronounced, and in such cases in the following pages it will

* Vid. Grierson: *Seven Grammars*, Part i. p. 10; also, Hoernle: *Comp. Gramm.* p. lx.

† In this last particular, I have varied slightly from Hoernle.

be represented by the sign ऽ, as used by Grierson in his 'Seven Grammars.' Thus, घर is *ghar*, but घरऽ, Mt. obl. sing., is *ghara*.

MODE OF WRITING THE DEVANÁGARÍ.

5. अ *a* being inherent in each consonant, is only written when initial in a word or syllable; thus, we write अप *ap*, तुअ *tua*, but प *pa*, त *ta*. The other vowels, when following a consonant, are substituted for the inherent *a*, and, in this case, the second of their two forms, as above given, is used. But when the vowel sound is initial in a word or syllable, the first of the two forms is required; as, उक *uk*, ऊन *ún*, इप *ip*, ईख *íkh*, गाओ *gáo*, दाई *dái*. Of the several non-initial vowel forms, ा *á*, ी *í*, ो *o*, and ौ *au*, are written after, ि *i*, before, े *e* and ै *ai*, over, and ु *u*, ू *ú*, and ृ *ri*, under the consonants which they vocalize. Thus, the several vowel sounds, when they follow क, are written as follows: **Mode of Writing Vowels.**

क *ka*, का *ká*, कि *ki*, की *kí*, कु *ku*, कू *kú*, कृ *kṛi*, के *ke*, कॆ *kĕ*, कै *kai*, कॅ *kăi*, को *ko*, कॊ *kŏ*, कौ *kau*, कॏ *kău*.

When initial, in any syllable, the vowels are all written before the following consonants: as, अत *at*, उद् *ud*, ओर *or*, etc. Instead of ऐ *ai* initial, we sometimes find, in Hindí books, the combination अै; but this is not correct and should never be imitated.

6. The consonants have but one invariable form. Excepting the cerebrals, and ङ, छ, द, र, and ह, they all have one perpendicular, with one horizontal stroke; which latter, again, is broken in three letters, viz., ध *dh*, भ *bh*, and झ, for झ *jh*. **Form of Consonants.**

a. झ *jh* has two alternative forms, झ and झ. The former is often used in many dialects; the latter is the regular form in the Máṛwáṛí dialect. These forms, like स्र, *and all the other consonants*, are used both as initial and as non-initial.

b. In Máṛwáṛí, and often in other dialects, *b* and *v* are distinguished merely by a diacritical point; thus, ब *b*, व *v*. The character व is not commonly used; its place is regularly taken by ब. No sibilant is used but स *s*.

Conjunct Consonants.

7. In addition to the above simple consonants, a great number of compound letters are used. The compound form is used to denote the non-intervention between its elements of the inherent *a*. Thus, सत is *sata*, but स्त is *sta*; तव is *tava*, but त्वा, *tva*. In certain cases, however, to be hereafter mentioned, the elementary forms are regularly used, though no full vowel sound intervene; as, करता, 'doing,' pronounced *kartá*; but the Sk. *karttá*, 'a doer,' is written कर्त्ता.*

a. It may be remarked, for the guidance of the student, that the use of the compound consonants is chiefly confined to the pure Sanskrit words in the language; in words of Prakrit origin, the elementary letters are commonly preferred.

b. Consonants are compounded in three ways: viz., 1stly, by writing one above the other, as, क्क *kk*, ट्ट *ṭṭ*; 2ndly, by writing one after the other, omitting in all but the last the perpendicular stroke,. and uniting the remainder of the character to that next following; as, ब्द *bd*, त्थ *tth*, य्य *yy*; 3rdly, some letters, when in combination, partially or wholly change their form; thus, क + ष becomes क्ष *kṣh*, also written क्ष; ज + ञ, ज्ञ *jñ*.

(1) र takes two different forms, according as it is the first or last letter of a compound. Thus, when initial in a conjunct, it is written as a semicircle above the second consonant, as

* Vid. § 14, *c*.

in सर्प *sarp*; but when non-initial, it takes the form of a short stroke below the preceding consonant, as in ग्रहण *grahaṇ.*

(2) When a conjunct of which र *r* is the first member, consists of more than two consonants, the semicircle *reph* is written over the last letter, as in धर्म्म *dharmm*, सर्व्व *sarvv*. When a conjunct with *r* initial is vocalized by ि *i*, ी *í*, े *e*, ै *ai*, ो *o*, ौ *au*, or is followed by Anusvár, then *reph* is written to the right of them all; thus, धर्म्मी *dharmmí*, मूर्त्ति *múrtti*, सर्व्वं *sarvvam*, etc.

8. Conjuncts are classified as strong, weak, or mixed, according to the character of the letters composing them.* Conjuncts formed of strong letters only, are termed *strong*, and those formed of weak letters only, *weak* conjuncts. Combinations of strong and weak letters are called *mixed* conjuncts. The following list will be found to comprise all the more common combinations, arranged in these three classes. As given below they are all vocalized with *a*. Classification of Conjuncts.

Strong Conjuncts.

क्क *kk*, क्ख *kkh*, क्त *kt*; ग्ध *gdh*; च्च *chch*, च्छ, *chchh*; ज्ज *jj*, ज्झ *jjh*; ट्ट *ṭṭ*, ट्ठ *ṭṭh*; ड्ग *ḍg*, ड्ड *ḍḍ*; त्क *tk*, त्त *tt*, त्थ *tth*, त्प *tp*; द्ग *dg*, द्द *dd*, द्ध *ddh*, द्भ *dbh*; प्त *pt*, प्प *pp*, प्फ *pph*; ब्ज *bj*, ब्द *bd*, ब्ध *bdh*, ब्ब *bb*, ब्भ *bbh*.

Weak Conjuncts.

ण्ण, ण्ण *ṇṇ*, ण्य *ṇy*; न्न *nn*, न्म *nm*, न्य *ny*, न्र *nr*, न्व *nv*, न्स *ns*; म्न *mn*, म्म *mm*, म्य *my*, म्र *mr*, म्ल *ml*, म्ह *mh*; य्य *yy*; र्ण *rṇ*, र्म *rm*, र्य *ry*, र्व *rv*, र्श *rsh*, र्ष *rsh̲*, र्ह *rh*; ल्म *lm*, ल्य *ly*, ल्ल *ll*, ल्ह *lh*; व्य *vy*, व्र *vr*, व्व, व्व *vv*; श्न *shn*, श्य *shy*, श्र *shr*, श्ल *shl*, श्व *shv*, श्न *shn*; ष्म *sh̲m*, ष्य *sh̲y*, ष्व *sh̲v*; स्न *sn*, स्म *sm*, स्य *sy*, स्र *sr*, स्व *sv*, स्स *ss*; ह्म *hm*, ह्य *hy*, ह्र *hr*, ह्ल *hl*, ह्व *hv*.

Mixed Conjuncts.

क्म *km*, क्य *ky*, क्र *kr*, क्ल *kl*, क्व *kv*, क्ष *ksh̲*; ख्य *khy*; ग्न *gn*, ग्म *gm*, ग्य *gy*, ग्र *gr*, ग्ल *gl*, ग्व *gv*; घ्न *ghn*, घ्य *ghy*, घ्र *ghr*; ङ्क *ñk*,

---

* By the strong letters are intended all the five classes of mute letters, both smooth and aspirated; by weak letters, all other consonants.

ङ्ख ñkh, ङ्ग ñg, ङ्घ ñgh; च्य chy; छ्र chhr; ज्ञ jṅ, ज्म jm, ज्य jy, ज्र jr, ज्व jv; ञ्च ṅch, ञ्छ ṅchh, ञ्ज ṅj, ञ्झ ṅjh; ड्र ḍr; ण्ट ṇṭ, ण्ठ ṇṭh, ण्ड ṇḍ; ण्ढ ṇḍh; त्न tn, त्म tm, त्य ty, त्र tr, त्व tv, त्स ts; थ्य thy; द्न dn; ध्य dhy, ध्र dhr, ध्व dhv; न्त nt, न्थ nth, न्द nd, न्ध ndh; प्न pn, प्म pm, प्य py, प्र pr, प्ल pl, प्स ps; ब्य by, ब्र br; भ्य bhy, भ्र bhr; र्क rk, र्ख rkh, र्ग rg, र्घ rgh, र्च rch, र्छ rchh, र्ज ṛj, र्त rt, र्थ rth, र्द rd, र्ध rdh, र्प rp, र्ब rb, र्भ rbh; ल्द ld, ल्प lp, ल्ब lb; श्च shch; ष्क s̲h̲k, ष्ट s̲h̲ṭ, ष्ठ s̲h̲ṭh, ष्प s̲h̲p, ष्म s̲h̲m, ष्य s̲h̲y; स्क sk, स्त st, स्थ sth, स्प sp, स्फ sph.

Additional Signs.

9. *Anunásik* (अनुनासिक) ँ, simply denotes the nasalization of a preceding vowel, and can therefore never begin a syllable. It is written directly over, or to the right of the vowel thus nasalized; thus, कहाँ *kahán̲*, कौँ *kaun̲*. In books edited by foreigners, Anusvár is commonly written instead of Anunásik.

10. *Anusvár* (अनुस्वार) ं, which, in strict accuracy, denotes a stronger nasalization than the above, is written, like Anunásik, over, or to the right of the preceding vowel; as, अंश *an̲sh*, बांह *bán̲h*, सों *son̲*.

11. *Visarg* (विसर्ग), meaning 'rejection,' (i.e., of स् or र्,) indicates a weak aspiration, which has euphonically taken the place of those letters. It is only found in pure Sanskrit words, and even then, though occurring in the original, is commonly omitted in Hindí. It is written thus, ः; as, e.g., in दुःख *duḥkh*, written and pronounced दुख *dukh*, = दुस् + ख *dus* + *kha*; अन्तःकरण *antaḥkaraṇ*.*

Rem. 1. The native grammarians give a different explanation of *visarg*, regarding it, and not *s*, as the original sound, and interpreting it as meaning 'omission' of breath. But I prefer the explanation given above; for the reason that while in the Indo-Aryan languages the weakening of *s* to *h* is very common, the reverse change is at least very rare.†

---

* Colloquially, about Mirzapur, sometimes *s* takes the place of this *visarg*, as in *antaskaran*, for *antaḥkaraṇ*.

† Vid. Monier-Williams: *Sanskrit Grammar*, § 8.

Rem. 2. The retention of *Visarg* in Hindí spelling cannot be justified; as the sound had already disappeared in Prakrit, and does not properly belong to the modern Indo-Aryan vernaculars.*

12. Besides these, several other signs are used in Sanskrit, which, as they occasionally appear in Hindí, may here be explained.

(1) *Virám* (विराम), 'pause,' is written under a consonant, thus, क् *k*, and denotes the absence of the inherent *a* by which the consonant is vocalized.

(2) *Avagrah* (अवग्रह), ऽ, indicates the elision of an initial अ *a* after a final ए *e* or ओ *o*; as, त्रिंशो ऽध्याय *trinsho 'dhyáya*, for त्रिंशोअध्याय *trinsho adhyáya*. It is therefore analogous to the English apostrophe. The *half pause*, ।, is written at the end of the first line of a couplet; the *full pause*, ॥, at the end of the second. These marks are only prosodial, and, besides these, there are no other marks of punctuation. In most native works, indeed, space is not even left between the words.

(3) The symbol २ between two words indicates that the former of the two is repeated; as, वह अपने २ घर गए *wah apne apne ghar gae*, etc.

(4) The mark ॰ is used, like the period in English, to indicate the abbreviation of a word; as, रामायन बा॰ *Rámáyan Bá.*, for रामायन बालकाण्ड *Rámáyan Bál Kánd.*

(5) In some books issued by English publishers the English punctuation marks are used. Of late, native publishers also are beginning to introduce them, but in such works as I have seen they are often used very inaccurately.

13. The orthography of Hindí is as yet in a very unsettled state. न is constantly substituted for ण, even in Sanskrit words, where rule or accurate usage would demand it; as in किरन for किरण, गुन for गुण, etc. The same confusion exists

* Vid. Hoernle: *Comp. Gramm.* p. 26.

with reference to the characters ब and व, and also the sibilants श, ष; the tendency is to substitute स for the other sibilants. ख is also often written for an original ष. The Sanskrit rules of orthography are the only recognized standard at present; but these rules, it should be remembered, apply only, as has been remarked, to the spelling of such Sanskrit words as exist in the language in an unaltered and uncorrupted form.

PRONUNCIATION OF LETTERS.

Pronunciation of Vowels.

14. The vowels, in Hindí, are pronounced, for the most part, nearly as in the continental languages of Europe. अ *a* has no exact counterpart in English, though the *a* in such words as 'hum,' 'up,' or, in unaccented syllables, the last *a* in 'total,' 'America,' very nearly represents it. It is said to correspond exactly to the short *a* in German. Many foreigners in India pronounce this अ *a* as *a* in 'cat,' but the correct sound is quite different.

a. In conversation and in reading prose, अ *a* final, inherent in a consonant, as a general rule, is silent; as in गुण, pronounced *guṇ*, not *guṇa*; रात *rát*, not *ráta*. But to this general rule there are a few important exceptions.

(1) अ *a* final is, of necessity, always distinctly pronounced in a few monosyllables; as, न *na*, त *ta*, छ *chha*.

(2) So, also, it is very slightly sounded after र *r* or व *v* final in a conjunct, and after य *y* final, preceded by इ *i*, ई *í*, or ऊ *ú*; as, शास्त्र *shástra*, इन्द्र *indra*, बिप्र *bipra*,* ईश्वरत्व *íshvaratva*, गुरुत्व *gurutva*; तिय *tiya*, प्रिय *priya*, इन्द्रिय *indriya*, राजसूय *rájasúya*.

---

* It should be noted, that while the Paṇḍits give this pronunciation of these conjuncts with र, yet the common people usually separate the letters, and pronounce *shástar*, *bipar*, etc.

(3) The final inherent *a* of the Denominative Numerals, commonly written चौक, तीन, नम्म, is always pronounced; thus, *chauka, tína, namma*; तीन तीन नौ, pronounced *tín tína nau*, lit., 'three threes nine.'

(4) In poetry, the inherent *a* is always pronounced, even when final, as in the following half stanza: समरथ कहं नहिं दोष गुसाईं, which is read, *samaratha kahan nahin dosha gusáín*. But when the metrical pause falls on this letter, it is commonly silent; thus, झुलत पलना रघुबर । पुलकित माई *jhulata palaná Raghuvar* । *pulakita mái*.

(5) As remarked above, an inherent *a* final is pronounced in some of the eastern dialects, in inflectional terminations, and even in other cases; as, घर, Mt. obl. sing. of घर, 'a house'; रहल, 2nd plur. pret., 'you were'; pronounced, *ghara, rahala*. The final *a* in such cases will be represented in this Grammar, as above, by ऽ; thus, घरऽ, रहलऽ.

(6) When, in prose and in conversation, या *ya* final is preceded by अ *a*, this *aya* differs but slightly, if at all, in sound from ऐ *ai*, which is even occasionally, though inaccurately, written for it; as, समय *samaya*, always pronounced, and sometimes written, समै *samai*; छय *chhaya*, also pronounced, and sometimes written, छै *chhai*. Conversely, it may here be noted, that अय *aya* is sometimes inaccurately written for ऐ *ai*, and अव *ava* for औ *au*; as often in the Rámáyan, बयर *bayar*, for बैर *bair*; and in Chand, किन्नव *kinnava*, for किन्नौ *kinnau*.

b. Observe, that when, in the formation of compound words, a silent final अ *a* becomes medial, it is sounded very faintly. This obscure sound may be illustrated, to Hebrew scholars, by the Hebrew vocal *Sh'vá*, and like that, might be represented by an apostrophe, instead of *a*: thus, अन्न is pronounced *ann*; but in composition, अन्नदाता, *ann'dátá*; फल, *phal*; but फलदायक, *phal'dáyak*.

c. The same obscure sound is given to the inherent *a*, when final in roots or in primitive words, before added heavy terminations. Thus, करना, root, कर *kar*, is pronounced *kar'ná*; चलता, root, चल *chal*, *chal'tá*, etc. So also, पुरवा, for the primitive, पुर *pur*, is pronounced *pur'vá*; कुंआरपन, from कुंआर *kuṉár*, *kuṉár'pan*; मूरखपन, from मूरख *múrakh*, *múrakh'pan*. Before light terminations it is fully vocalized, as, जानत *jánat*.

d. The inherent *a* is attenuated in like manner in the final syllable of dissyllabic verbal roots, before all the terminations beginning with vowels; as in निकला *nik'lá*, from the root निकल *nikal*. But in the same roots, when the termination begins with a consonant, the *a* is fully vocalized, as, e.g., in निकलता *nikal'tá*.*

Rem. 1. Hoernle and Grierson represent this obscure sound, which they term 'the neutral vowel,' by a dot between the Nágarí consonants, and by an apostrophe in the Romanized character, as above. I have, however, thought it sufficient, in the present work, having thus called the attention of the student to the facts, to conform to the usual mode of writing words of the above classes in Nágarí and the Romanized character, in the latter simply omitting the inherent *a*.

Rem. 2. It should be observed that the above remarks refer only to *a* when inherent in a consonant; when non-inherent, it is always distinctly pronounced, whether medial or final; as, तुअ *tua*, हरुअ *harua*.

e. In Eastern Hindí, as might be expected, अ begins to approximate in sound to the broad Bangálí sound of अ *a* as in 'ball.' This broad sound is universal in Northern Maithilí, and is heard in all the Maithilí country in all verbal 2nd plural masculines in अ or अहु, as also in the 3rd sing. of the substantive verb, थ॰. The same sound is given to अ in Bhojpurí in all 2nd masc. plurals, and in the penultimate *a* of the inflected present, as in

* In the 1st edition of this Grammar, this obscure sound of *a*, noted in this section, is not mentioned; but instead, in the cases above named, *a* was said to be 'silent.' My own later observation in India had led me to doubt the accuracy of this statement; and as the representation now given in the text has been since confirmed by the independent observation of Hoernle and Grierson, and other accurate scholars in India, I now make this change from the former edition of the Grammar.

15. आ *á* is pronounced like *a* in 'father'; इ *i*, like *i* in 'pin'; ई *í*, as *i* in 'machine'; उ *u*, like *u* in 'pull'; ऊ *ú*, like *oo* in 'tool'; ऋ *ṛi*, as *ri* in 'brink.'

a. इ *i* and उ *u* final, though, like *a* final, always sounded in poetry, like that, in the colloquial are but very faintly, if at all pronounced; as, मति, pronounced *mati* or *mat*: परन्तु, pronounced *parantu* or *parant*.

b. But some of the dialects, on the other hand, often lengthen a final *i*; as in Kanaují, मती *matí*, for मति *mati*; Kumáoní, चली बेर *chalí ver*, for चलि कर *chali kar*.

Rem. Theoretically, ऋ differs from रि, in that the tongue vibrating, is not allowed to touch the gums, as in the consonant र. But this distinction is never regarded in practice.

16. ए *e*, ऐ *ai*, and ओ *o*, औ *au*, are diphthongs: ए *e* and ऐ *ai* are the diphthongs of इ *i*; ओ *o* and औ *au*, of उ *u*. ए *e* is pronounced nearly like *e* in 'they.'* Its elements are अ + इ *a* + *i*. ऐ *ai* is not quite the English *i* in 'time.' Like this English *i*, a diphthong, it differs from it, in that the short *i*, instead of the long *í*, is the latter element of the diphthong; i.e., ऐ = *á* + *i*, but *i* in 'time' = *á* + *í*. Thus, e.g., the common word, है *hai*, 'is,' is *not* rightly pronounced exactly like the English word 'high.' ओ *o* corresponds to the English *o* in 'go'; it never has the sound of the English *o* in 'top.' Its elements are अ + उ *a* + *u*. औ differs from the English *ou* in 'our,' in the same way that ऐ *ai* differs from *i* in 'fine.' It is composed of आ + उ *á* + *u*; the English *ou*, of *á* + *ú*. Pronunciation of Diphthongs.

17. *Anunásik* (ँ), as has been remarked, simply indicates the nasalization of the preceding vowel. The Anunásik.

---

* A scholarly friend in India suggests as an illustration *ea* in 'great,' as pronounced by a Yorkshireman.

sound is heard in the proper pronunciation of such French words as *bon*, *enfant*, etc. But in many Hindí books, especially those published by foreigners, this sound is represented by the symbol *Anusvár* (ं).

Anusvár.

18. *Anusvár* properly represents a nasal sound stronger than that of Anunásik: it is best heard before the sibilants, as in अंश *an̲śh*, वंश *ban̲śh*. But in words introduced from the Sanskrit, with little or no alteration, the sign Anusvár is very often used, after a short vowel, to express the nasal of the class of a following mute consonant; and may thus represent, as the case may be, any one of the five nasals, ङ, ञ, ण, न, or म. Thus, e.g., we may either write मङ्गल or मंगल *mañgal*, Anusvár having here the power of ङ. Similarly, in संबंध *sambandh*, the first Anusvár, preceding the labial ब *b*, has the power of the labial nasal म *m*; but the second, before the dental ध *dh*, has the power of the dental nasal न *n*.

a. But in the case of words much corrupted from the Sanskrit, after a long vowel, Anusvár, even before a mute consonant, denotes, not a consonant, but a nasalization; as, e.g., सोंठ, pronounced *son̲ṭh*, not *sonṭh*, चांद *chán̲d*, सांड़ *sán̲ṛ*, etc.

Rem. In the cases referred to, Anusvár stands in the place of an original nasal consonant, preceded by a short vowel; as, e.g., in कांटा for कण्टकः. The question has been raised, whether the Anusvár in such cases denotes a consonant or merely a nasalization. But all the Paṇḍits that I have been able to consult insist on the inorganic character of the nasal. Beames, in his Comparative Grammar, takes the same view. As he justly remarks, the lengthening of the preceding vowel, according to all the analogies of the language, argues the loss of a letter from the original conjunct.*

b. Occasionally in poetry, Anusvár, in Sanskrit words, following a final consonant in the end of a line, represents the

---

* Vid. *Comp. Gramm.* vol. i. p. 296.

letter य, and must be so pronounced; as, e.g., गुणमयं *guṇa-mayam*; अयं *ayam*.

19. क *k* and ग *g* are pronounced, respectively, as *k* in 'key,' and *g* in 'give': ग *g* never has the sound of *g* in 'gin.' Pronunciation of Smooth Mutes.

20. च *ch* and ज *j* are pronounced nearly as *ch* in 'church,' and as *j* in 'just,' but are slightly more dental.

21. ट *ṭ* and ड *ḍ*, though often compared to the English *t* and *d*, have no precise equivalents in English. In pronouncing them, the tongue should be thrown well back, so as to strike, not the gums, as in the English *t* and *d*, but the roof of the mouth.

Rem. It is to be observed that in transferring English words into Hindí, these letters, and never त and द, are used in speech and writing by native Hindoos, as the nearest equivalent to the English *t* and *d*.

22. ड is often written with a diacritical point (ड़), and is then represented in the Roman character by *ṛ*. To utter this correctly, place the tongue in the same position as for ड *ḍ*, and try to pronounce the English *r*; the proper sound will then be given. The corresponding aspirate ढ has also the same double sound, which is represented by ढ़ *ṛh*.

N.B. Great care should be taken to acquire the correct pronunciation of this letter, which is, undoubtedly, for western organs, the most difficult of all the Hindí sounds; very few Europeans ever give it correctly. The learner should carefully observe that this is equally distinct from the English *r* and the Hindí र. The sound, when correctly given, much more resembles the cerebral ड, with which, indeed, it is constantly interchanged; many words being written and pronounced indifferently with ड *ḍ*, ढ *ḍh*, or ड़ *ṛ*, ढ़ *ṛh*; as, बुढ़ा *búṛhá*, or बुढा *búḍhá*. The Panjábí distinguishes these two sounds by two separate characters.

23. The sounds of त *t* and द *d* do not exist in English. In pronouncing them, press the tongue, not against the gums, as in the English *t* and *d*, but against the front teeth.

24. प *p* is pronounced like the English *p*. ब *b* differs from the English *b*, only in that the contact of the lips is less firm. Many words thus fluctuate in orthography and pronunciation between ब *b* and व *v*.

Pronunciation of Aspirated Mutes.

25. Each of the above consonants has its aspirate; i.e., it is combined with the *spiritus asper* so as to form but one vocal utterance. The same direction applies to the pronunciation of all the aspirates: viz., utter the smooth consonant with a forcible expiration; the corresponding aspirates will then be given. In the English phrases, 'up-hill,' 'brick-house,' pronounced so that the *p* and *k* shall be closely joined to the following *h*, we have the correct sound. Especial care should be taken that no vowel-sound be interpolated between the smooth consonant and the aspiration; thus, फल is pronounced *phal*, not *pahal*; खाना, *khánú*, not *kahánú*, which has a very different meaning.

Rem. The greatest pains should be taken by the learner to master the pronunciation of these aspirates. A native, however illiterate, never confounds the smooth and aspirated consonants; and, except in the case of फ *ph*, which is often by the uneducated corruptly pronounced as *f*, never fails to give the aspirate its correct pronunciation. He never separates the smooth consonant from the following aspiration.

Pronunciation of Nasals.

26. ङ *ñ* has the sound of the first *n* in 'England'; it is only found immediately before a guttural consonant, and never begins a word or syllable.

ञ *ń* has the sharp sound of *n* in 'pinch.' Like ङ, it is never initial, and is only found before a consonant of its own class.

a. But in Naipálí and some vulgar forms of Eastern Hindí ञ sometimes occurs by itself, both as initial and medial. Thus, in Naipálí, we have the Honorific Pronoun, तपाञि; बडाञि, 'greatness'; पवित्रताञि, 'holiness,' ञाहाँ, 'here'; पाञि, 'I have found.' In Eastern Hindí, Hoernle gives the examples, अगिञा, 'fire,' ञाहि, 'no.'* ञ also occurs alone in Búndelkhaṇḍí, in the series of Local Pronominal Adverbs of Place, याञी, etc.†

Rem. Inasmuch as the guttural and palatal nasals can commonly be known by their position before a mute of their own class, I have thought it sufficient to represent them, like the dental nasal, by the Roman *n* without any diacritical point.

27. ण *ṇ*, like the other letters of the class to which it belongs, has no equivalent in any European language. It is pronounced after the analogy of the other cerebrals; i.e., the tongue should be turned back, as for ट and ड, so as to strike the roof of the mouth; then, with tongue in that position, endeavour to pronounce *n*.

a. This nasal, while the only nasal admissible before a consonant of its own order, is not, like the former two, confined in use to such a position, but may occur separately, as, e.g., in the common words गुण *guṇ* and वर्णन *barṇan*. It never occurs as initial in a word, except in some vulgar dialects of Eastern Hindí, as in णरसिंह, 'man-lion,' णारैण, '*Náráyan*,' where High Hindí and most other dialects have न.

b. The common people in the valley of the Ganges, as well as most foreigners in India, make no distinction between this and the dental न *n*, which is often substituted for it, even in writing. Educated Hindoos, however, carefully distinguish the two letters, and the correct sound should be acquired.

28. न *n* is slightly more dental than the English *n*, being pronounced, like the foregoing nasals, after the analogy of the class to which it belongs, i.e., with the tip of the tongue against the front teeth.

म *m* is sounded like the corresponding English letter.

---

* Vid. *Comp. Gramm.* § 13.

† Vid. *Table* xxiii.

Pronunciation of Liquids.

29. य *y* is generally pronounced like *y* in English.

a. But sometimes it is pronounced like ज *j*, especially when initial in Sanskrit words; as, e.g., युग *yug*, pronounced जुग *jug*; योग्य *yogya*, pronounced *jog*. So also it is pronounced as *j*, when doubled and final; as, सूर्य, pronounced, and occasionally written, सूरज *súraj*. As above remarked,* य final, preceded by short *a*, so blends with it as to approximate closely to the diphthongal sound ऐ *ai*; as, समय *samaya*, pronounced समै *samai*, etc.

30. र *r* has no precise equivalent in English; it has a rolling sound like the German *r*, but much softer.

ल *l* is not quite identical in sound with the English *l*. In its utterance the tip of the tongue touches the front teeth, instead of the gums. The resulting sound is distinctly softer and more dental than the English *l*.

व *v* has a sound intermediate between the English *v* and *w*; *v* has been chosen as the usual Roman equivalent.

a. But in a conjunct, after any consonant but र *r* or त *t*, व has a much softer sound than *v*, more like the English *w*; as, e.g., ह्वै, *hwai*, स्वर्ग, *swarg*. In the common conjunct स्व *sva*, the common people usually soften व still further to its cognate vowel, उ *u*; pronouncing, e.g., स्वर, *swar*, as if it were written सुर, *sur*, etc. Similarly, in some parts of the country, people say ईसुर *ísur* for ईश्वर *íshwar*. व initial in the pronoun वह *wah* generally receives the softer sound. Examples of the harder sound, in the conjuncts र्व *rv* and त्व *tv*, are तत्त्व *tattva*, महत्त्व *mahatva*; पूर्व *púrv*, सर्व *sarv*.† In these conjuncts with र, व is often hardened to ब, so that many pronounce *púrb*, *sarb*.

Pronunciation of Sibilants.

31. श *sh* is pronounced like *sh* in 'shut'; the palatal ष *sh* differs little from श; the lingual contact is slightly further back, as in the cerebral mutes.

---

* Vid. § 14, *a*. (6). † The inherent *a* of र्व is never pronounced.

स *s* is the dental sibilant, and, like the other letters of its class, differs from the corresponding English letter, in that the tongue, in its utterance, touches the teeth instead of the gums.

ह *h* does not differ from the English *h*.

a. ष is very often pronounced exactly like ख *kh*; e.g., दोष *dosh* is pronounced either *dosh* or *dokh*. Accordingly, ष is often inaccurately written for ख; as, दुष, for दुख; राषा, for राखा, etc. This is the uniform usage in Máṛwáṛí, as also in much old Hindí.

32. In pronouncing compound letters, each element should be distinctly articulated, whether the letters be different or the same; e.g., कुत्ता is *kut-tá*, not *kut-á*; पत्थर, *pat-thar*, not *path-ar*. But this should not be exaggerated.

33. *Western Peculiarities.* The following peculiarities of pronunciation occur in Máṛwṛá and Mairwáṛá. The vowel-sound in the plural termination आं *áṉ* is pronounced very nearly as *a* in 'all,' but a little less open. The sound of औ *au* also closely resembles that of आ in this आं. च *ch* and छ *chh* are both pronounced like स; thus, चक्की is pronounced *sakkí*, and छाछ, *sás*. ह is pronounced lightly, and often entirely dropped. The cerebral ळ *ḷ* is common, and is pronounced by rolling the upturned tongue along the palate. It is sometimes indicated by a diacritical point under ल.

34. The grammarians of the Indian languages have not, for the most part, indicated so many distinctions between the pronunciation of the Indian and English letters as have been made in the above sections. But we are none the less confident that a large part of the Hindí letters do differ slightly from their nearest English equivalents. Let the reader, if in India, ask some native who is learning English, to read an English sentence, and it will soon appear to the attentive listener that he pronounces very few of the English letters quite correctly. Perhaps there is no better way than this to train the ear to catch the nice distinctions of pronunciation to which we have adverted. So long as both words and sounds are foreign, the sounds are not so closely noticed; but when the native pronunciation of the vowels and consonants is applied to English words, the difference is instantly apparent.

Accent.

35. It should be observed, before leaving the subject of pronunciation, that Accent, although unquestionably existing in Hindí, is much less strongly marked than in English, and is quite subordinate in importance to Quantity. Even in conversation, the Hindú habitually observes the quantity of each syllable. In the enunciation of sentences, therefore, the student should be careful to avoid that strongly accentuated style, which is so characteristic of English speech, and give to every long vowel in an unaccented syllable its full quantity.

36. It will be apparent from the above sectións, that, with the two exceptions of ष and य, which each represent two sounds, the Devanágarí alphabet is strictly phonetic. The same ambiguity attaches to *y* in Bangálí; but the Bangálís distinguish the two sounds by a diacritical point. So also in the Mahájaní or script alphabet, used in business, *b* and *v* are distinguished in the same way, merely by a dot.* As the pronunciation of words in which ष and य occur varies, even in the same locality, they will be uniformly represented in the present work by the Roman letters *sh* and *y*.

a. To the two exceptions, ष and य, may be added the compound character ज्ञ = ज + ञ, *j* + *ṅ*, which is invariably pronounced in Hindí as if it were *gy*. This conjunct will therefore be represented in this book by the Roman letters *gy*; as, ज्ञान *gyán*, not *jṅán*. Also, in N. Maithila, र्ष *rsh* is pronounced *rkh*, ष *ksh*, *chchh*, and ह्य *hy*, *zhjy*.

Mispronunciation of Foreigners.

37. As above remarked, it is extremely important that the student accurately discriminate in pronunciation between closely related letters. Because the undisciplined ear at first detects little or no difference between, e.g., a smooth and an aspirated consonant, or between the cerebral and dental letters, it is often imagined that a failure to distinguish them in pronunciation cannot be a very serious matter. No mistake

* See *Table* I., pp. 26 and 27.

could be greater or more fatal to one who wishes to understand the people, and be understood by them. As a matter of fact, multitudes of words of different meaning differ only in these similar letters; so that, by the neglect of an aspirate, the substitution of our English *t* for the Hindí dental, or converting the hard ड़ *ṛ* into the Hindí र *r* or English *r*, we may say something so foreign to our intention, if not worse, as to make our speech, if understood at all, a matter only of ridicule.

a. The foreigner is most apt to blunder in the following particulars, viz.: a smooth consonant is substituted for an aspirate; the cerebral *ṭ* and *ḍ*, or the English *t* and *d*, which have a somewhat similar sound, are substituted for the corresponding Hindí dentals; and, especially, the cerebral ड़ *ṛ* is pronounced like the Hindí र *r*, or the English *r*; doubled consonants are indistinctly pronounced. To these common mistakes may be added an English tendency to shorten a final unaccented long vowel; so that, e.g., करता *kartá* is mispronounced *karta*; पानी *pání*, *pány*; माली *málí*, *mály*, etc.

38. As the best means of impressing the above remarks upon the mind, we subjoin a list of common words similar in sound, but differing in meaning.

LIST OF SIMILAR WORDS.

खाना *khánâ*, 'dinner, food, to eat.'	खड़ा (होना) *khaṛá* (*honá*), 'to stand.'
कहाना *kahánâ*, 'to cause to say.'	कड़ा *kaṛá*, 'hard.'
काना *kánâ*, 'a one-eyed man.'	खरा *khará*, 'pure.'
ख़ाना (Pers. خانه) *ḳhánâ*, 'a room.'	खर्रा *kharrá*, 'a curry comb.'
	khaṭṭá, 'sour.'
कीड़ा *kíṛá*, 'a worm.'	कट्टा *kaṭṭá*, 'a large louse.'
खीरा *khírá*, 'a cucumber.'	कटा *kaṭá*, 'cut.'
काटना *káṭná*, 'to cut.'	खपरा *khaprá*, 'a tile.'
कातना *kátná*, 'to spin.'	कपड़ा *kapṛá*, 'a cloth.'

गाओ *gáo*, 'a cow.'
घाओ *gháo*, 'a bruise.'

घड़ा *ghaṛá*, 'a water-jar.'
गड़ा *gaṛá*, 'buried.'
गढ़ा *gaṛhá*, 'a ditch.'

घोड़ा *ghoṛá*, 'a horse.'
गोरा *gorá*, 'white, a European soldier.'

गाड़ी *gáṛí*, 'a carriage.'
गारी *gárí*, 'abuse.'

छुरी *chhurí*, 'a knife.'
चूड़ी *chúṛí*, 'a bangle.'

छूना *chhúná*, 'to touch.'
चूना *chúṇá*, 'to leak.'

जाड़ा लगना *jáṛá lagná*, 'to feel cold.'
झाड़ा लगना *jháṛá lagná*, 'sens. obscœn.'

झाल *jhál*, 'spice, pungency.'
जाल *jál*, 'a net.'

टीका *ṭíká*, 'inoculation ; a sectarial mark.'
ठीका *ṭhíká*, 'hire.'

दाल *dál*, 'a split pulse.'
डाल *ḍál*, 'throw' (*imperat.*).
ढाल *ḍhál*, 'a declivity.'

धो *dho*, 'wash' (*imperat.*).
दो *do*, 'give' (*imperat.*).

बकरी *bakrí*, 'a goat.'
बखरी *bakhrí*, 'a house.'

ताला *tálá*, 'a lock.'
टाला *ṭálá*, 'a quagmire.'

पढ़ना *paṛhná*, 'to read.'
पड़ना *paṛná*, 'to fall.'

पानी *pání*, 'water.'
पाणि *páṇi*, 'hand.'

पुड़िया *puṛiyá*, 'a powder.'
फुड़िया *phuṛiyá*, 'a boil.'
फुरिया *phuriyá*, 'true.'

फल *phal*, 'fruit'
पल *pal*, 'an instant.'

बात *bát*, 'a word, a thing.'
बाट *báṭ*, 'a road.'
भात *bhát*, 'boiled rice.'
भाट *bháṭ*, 'a bard.'

बुढ़िया *buṛhiyá*, 'an old woman.'
बुड़िया *buṛiyá*, 'sens. obscœn.'

बूढ़ा *búṛhá*, 'old.'
बुरा *burá*, 'bad.'

भाई *bháí*, 'brother.'
बाई *báí*, 'rheumatism.'
भई *bhaí*, 'became' (*fem.*).

मोटी *moṭí*, 'fat, thick' (*fem.*).
मोती *motí*, 'a pearl.'

रोती *rotí*, 'crying' (*fem. part.*).
रोटी *roṭí*, 'bread.'

सात *sát*, 'seven.'
साथ *sáth*, 'with.'
साठ *sáṭh*, 'sixty.'

Other Alphabets.

39. Besides the Devanágarí, Hindí is written in three other alphabets, the *Káyathí*, the *Mahájaní* or *Sarráfí*, and the *Baniauṭí*. The word *Káyathí* is from *Káyath*, the name of the writer caste among the Hindús; and the character is so called because certain slight alterations better adapt it to the purpose of rapid writing. Books are printed in this character, but it is by no means as common as the Devanágarí, and is not much used W. of Allahabad. The *Mahájaní* (from the Hindí *mahájan*, 'a banker'), also called *Sarráfí* (from the corresponding Ar. صراف), is only used in business, and is the character in which receipts, drafts, etc., are commonly written. The *Baniauṭí* (from the Hindí *baniyáṉ*, 'a shopkeeper'), differs but little from the *Mahájaní*, and, like that, is used only for business purposes. These alphabets will be found at pp. 26 and 27.

a. It will be noticed that the Káyathí form of र is identical with that which this letter assumes in Devanágarí, when it is the last letter of a conjunct. In Káyathí, a single letter is commonly written for a doubled character, and dissimilar conjuncts are resolved. Thus, for *kuttá* would be written *kutá*; for *gyán*, *gián*; for *pravesh*, *paraves*, etc., etc. The same character is often used indifferently for a long or a short vowel, and *v* is often written for *y*. One character is used, in each case, for ऋ and रि, ख and ष, श and स, and all the nasals.

b. Both the *Mahájaní* and also the *Baniauṭí* alphabets are derived directly from the *Káyathí*, by the omission of the horizontal top-stroke, the perpendicular, or both. Some of the characters, however, have assumed a form widely different from both Káyathí and Nágarí, and in practice they are frequently run together. One sign is used to represent both the long and the short sound of any vowel, whether initial or non-initial. Similarly, no distinction is made between ऋ and रि, or ष, श and स, or in the nasals. Anusvár is never written, and the vowels are very commonly omitted, so that a word is represented only by its consonantal elements, as in unpointed Persian or Arabic, or in English phonographic short-hand. Thus, *kyk* stands for *kyúṉki*; *n*, for *ne*; *kr*, for *kare*, etc. As in English script, the form of the different letters in all these alphabets varies considerably as used in different places and by various persons.

Arabic Letters in Hindí.

40. An attempt has been made to indicate in the Devanágarí character, by means of diacritical points, the various letters peculiar to the Arabic and Persian alphabets, as used in Urdú. A few common Hindí books, as the *Baitál Pachísí* and *Siṇhdsan Battísí*, contain a large admixture of Persian and Arabic words, and are sometimes met with printed in this pointed Nágarí. A point written under any of the vowels indicates that the vowel is followed or preceded by ع 'Ayin; also अ़, occurring alone, represents the consonant ع. The other pointed characters are as follows:

क़ = ق	ज़ = ظ ض ژ ذ ز	स़ = ص ث
ख़ = خ	त़ = ط	ह़ = ح
ग़ = غ	फ़ = ف	ः = ة

Classification of Letters.

41. All the letters, both vowels and consonants, may be classified according to the organ by which they are pronounced, as in the following table:

Class.	Vowels.	Mutes.		Nasals.	Liquids	Sibi-lants.
		Hard.	Soft.			
	I.	II.	III.	IV.	V.	VI.
Gutturals	अ आ	क ख	ग घ	ङ		ह
Palatals	इ ई ए ऐ	च छ	ज झ	ञ	य	श
Cerebrals	ऋ (ॠ)	ट ठ	ड ढ	ण	र ळ	ष
Dentals	(ऌ) (ॡ)	त थ	द ध	न	ल	स
Labials	उ ऊ ओ औ	प फ	ब भ	म	व	

a. In Col. I., ए, ऐ, and ओ, औ, are classified, according to their second diphthongal element, as respectively palatal and labial; but they are also related to the guttural sounds, by their initial element, अ or आ. Letters of the same organ are said to be *cognate* to each other.

42. The letters may again be classified according to the nature of the vocal effort made in their utterance. If, in the utterance of a letter, the breath be completely arrested, the resulting sound is reckoned *hard*; if the breath be partially arrested, or be allowed to escape freely, the resulting letter is called *soft*. Thus, in the above table, the consonants in Col. II., together with the sibilants, are called hard; all the other letters, whether vowels or consonants, are reckoned soft. **Hard and Soft Letters.**

a. The following relations between the letters should be carefully noted. (1) Each hard consonant in Col. II. has its cognate soft consonant in Col. III. and vice versâ. Thus, to the hard क in Col. II. corresponds the soft ग in Col. III.; and to the soft aspirate भ in Col. III. corresponds the hard aspirate फ in Col. II. (2) Each soft consonant in Col. III. and each vowel, except the gutturals, has its cognate semivowel in Col. V. Thus, the labial semivowel व corresponds to the soft labial consonant ब in Col. III. and to the labial vowels उ, ऊ, in Col. I. So also, cognate to the vowels इ and ई, are the soft mute ज and the palatal semivowel य. (3) ह, strictly speaking, is a guttural sibilation, so that it is written in Col. VI. with the sibilants. Each of the consonants, therefore, except the labials, has its corresponding sibilation. The student is now prepared to understand the principles of "*Sandhi.*" **Cognate Letters.**

TABLE I.—HINDI ALPHABETS.

Nágarí	Kâyathí.	Mahájaní.	Baniauṭí.

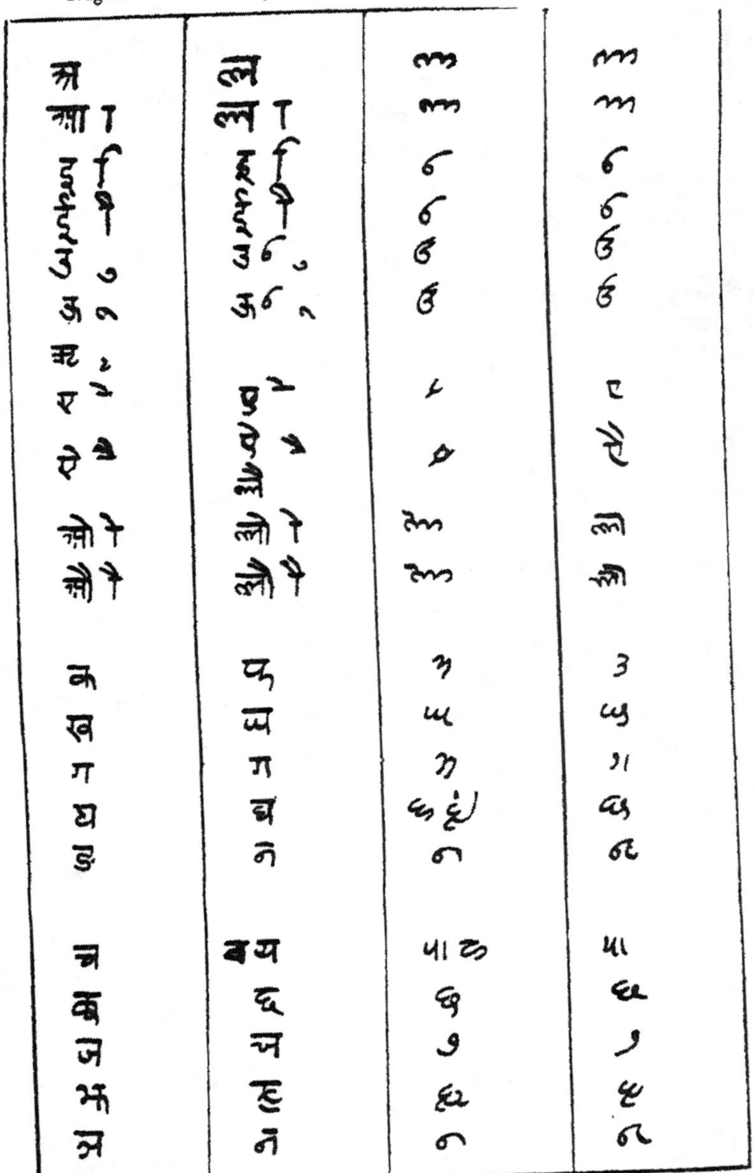

TABLE I. (CONCLUDED).—HINDI ALPHABETS.

Nágarí. Káyathí. Mahájani. Baniauṭí.

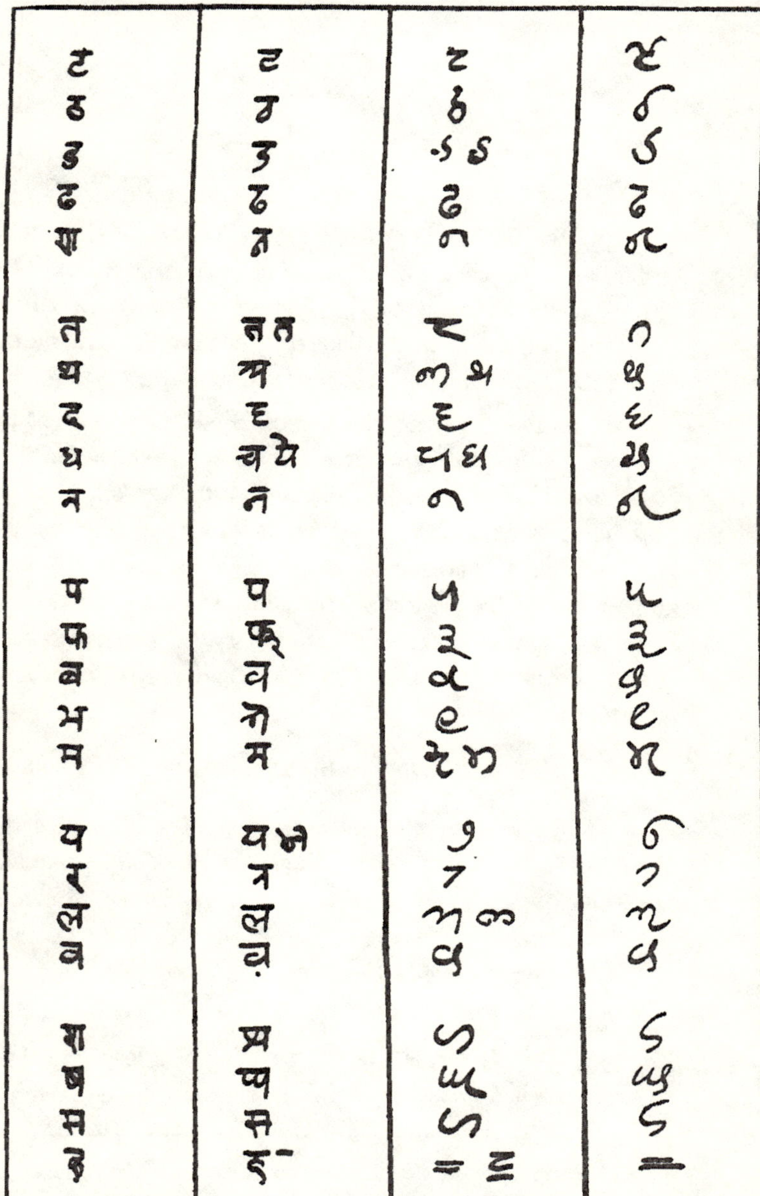

CHAPTER II.

SANDHI.*

43. By the term '*Sandhi*' (सन्धि, 'union') is technically denoted the euphonic combination of concurrent letters. Its laws apply uniformly to the Sanskritic element in Hindí, determining the correct orthography of pure Sanskrit words, and the formation of compounds from such single words.

a. In the Prakritic element of Hindí, in compounding words, the laws of *sandhi* are constantly disregarded. Still, we may observe, even in Prakritic words, the operation of these laws at a former period, in producing the modern forms; and a knowledge of the principles of *sandhi* will thus often enable the student to recognize, without a tedious and perhaps fruitless search in the Dictionary, the various peculiar and corrupted words with which Hindí poetry, especially, abounds.

Guṇ† and Vṛiddhi.

Guṇ defined. **44.** In treating of *sandhi*, we have first to notice the subject of *Guṇ* (गुण) and *Vṛiddhi* (वृद्धि). *Guṇ* essentially consists in the prefixing of a short *a* to the several simple vowel sounds; so that अ + इ or ई = ए; अ + उ or ऊ = ओ; अ + ऋ = अर्. By *guṇ*, therefore, is denoted this change of इ or ई to ए, उ or ऊ to ओ, and ऋ to अर्.

Vṛiddhi defined. **45.** *Vṛiddhi* consists in the prefixing of a long *á* to these same simple vowels; or, which is the same thing, prefixing

* This chapter and the following may be omitted by the beginner.

† In Sanskrit pronounced *guṇa*.

a short *a* to the *guṇ* of those vowels. Thus, by *vṛiddhi*, आ + इ = ऐ; आ + उ = औ; आ + ऋ = आर्: or, अ + ए = ऐ; अ + ओ = औ; and अ + अर् = आर्. By *vṛiddhi*, therefore, is denoted the change of इ or ई to ऐ, उ or ऊ to औ, and ऋ to आर्. अ is technically regarded as itself a *guṇ* vowel, and is therefore susceptible of the *vṛiddhi* modification only.

46. Observe, further, that vowels of the same organ, whether simple or diphthongal, are said to be *similar* to each other. Thus, इ, ई, ए, ऐ, are similar to each other. Vowels of different organs are said to be *dissimilar*; thus, e.g., अ, उ, ऐ, are mutually dissimilar. Mutual Relations of Vowels.

47. Observe, finally, that, according to § 42, *a*, the vowels of each organ, except the gutturals, अ and आ, have their cognate semivowel. Thus, the cognate semivowel of इ, ई, ए, and ऐ, is य; of उ, ऊ, ओ, and औ, the cognate semivowel is व; and of ऋ, र. The following table will present this whole matter at a glance.

Primitive Short Vowel.	Similar Long Vowel.	Guṇ.	Vṛiddhi.	Cognate Semivowel.
अ	आ	अ	आ	
इ	ई	ए	ऐ	य
उ	ऊ	ओ	औ	व
ऋ	(ॠ)	अर्	आर्	र

The following common rules of *sandhi* will be now readily understood.

Sandhi of Vowels.

48. Any simple vowel, long or short, followed by a *similar* simple vowel, long or short, coalesces with it into its own long. In the application of this, and all succeeding rules of Rules of *Sandhi*: Vowels.

sandhi, the inherent *a* is never regarded as silent. Thus, कल्प + अन्त becomes कल्पान्त; पाप + आत्मा, पापात्मा; कृपा + आयतन, कृपायतन; अहि + ईश, अहीश; भानु + उदय, भानूदय.

49. अ and आ, followed by a *dissimilar* simple vowel, long or short, blend with it into the *guṇ* of that vowel; and when followed by a *guṇ* or *vṛiddhi* vowel, blend with it into the corresponding *vṛiddhi*. Thus, परम + ईश्वर becomes परमेश्वर; न + इति, नेति; महा + ईश, महेश; हिम + उपल, हिमोपल; सेल + ऊपरि, सेलोपरि; एक + एक, एकैक; सदा + एव, सदैव; देव + ऋषि, देवर्षि; अमित + ओजस, अमितौजस; महा + औषधि, महौषधि.

50. The simple vowels, इ, ई, उ, ऊ, ऋ, followed by any *dissimilar* vowel, are changed into their cognate semivowels. Thus, इति + आदि becomes इत्यादि; सु + अल्प, स्वल्प; अनु + एषी, अन्वेषी.

51. The *guṇ* diphthongs, ए and ओ, followed by any vowel, are changeable, respectively, to अय् and अव्; and the *vṛiddhi* diphthongs, ऐ and औ, under the same conditions, are changeable to आय् and आव्.

a. This is, in fact, only a special application of the foregoing rule, according to which the *i* and *u*, which are, respectively, the second elements in the above diphthongs, harden into *y* and *v*, leaving the first element, *a* or *á*, unchanged.

b. This rule will chiefly be of service to the Hindí scholar, in enabling him to recognize the roots of those Sanskrit words with which Hindí abounds. Thus, by *guṇ* of the radical vowel, and addition of the affix *a*, we have, from the root जि, 'to conquer,' जे + अ = जय, 'victory'; similarly, from भू, 'to be,' भो + अ = भव, 'existence.' So also, by *vṛiddhi* of the radical vowel, and addition of the termination अक, we have, from the root, नी, 'to guide,' नै + अक = नायक, 'a leader'; similarly from पू, 'to purify,' पौ + अक = पावक, 'fire.'

52. Sometimes, in a few Sanskrit phrases, rarely met, अ initial, following ए or ओ, is elided, and ए or ओ remain unchanged. Thus, in the *Rámáyan* we find तेपि for ते अपि, and तेति for ते अति. But these in Sanskrit would be written with Avagrah,* thus: तेऽपि, तेऽति.

SANDHI OF CONSONANTS.

53. A hard consonant,† before any soft letter, must be changed to its own unaspirated soft. Thus, जगत् + अम्बा becomes जगदम्बा; हनुमत् + आदि, हनुमदादि; भविष्यत् + वक्ता, भविष्यद्वक्ता. In Sanskrit, it is also true that a soft consonant before a hard consonant must be changed to its own unaspirated hard. But Hindí scarcely affords examples of the operation of this rule. Hard Consonants before Soft.

54. If the second consonant be a nasal, the first is changed into the nasal of its own class. Thus तद् + मात्र becomes तन्मात्र; चित् + मय, चिन्मय.

55. त or द final, followed by च or ज, are changed to that following letter. Thus, न before the resulting conjunct being dropped, we have, from सन्त् + चित्, सच्चित्; from सन्त् + जन, सज्जन. Dental Mutes before Palatals.

56. न, before any vowel-sound, or one of the consonants न्, म्, य्, or व्, in all pure Sanskrit words, is changed to ण, when following either of the three cerebral letters, ऋ, र, ष. This rule operates, even though a guttural or labial mute, a semivowel, a nasal, or a vowel, Anusvár, or ह, or any combination of these, intervene between न and the above cerebral letters. Thus, we correctly write ऋण for ऋन, शरण for शरन, आभूषण for आभूषन. So also, e.g., we correctly write रामायण, not रामायन, on account of the initial र, even though the combination आमाय intervene between the र and the nasal. Sandhi of Nasals.

a. This rule is especially to be remembered in order to the correct spelling of pure Sanskrit words in Hindí. But it must be no less carefully observed, that the rule applies to such words only. In all other

---

* Vid. § 12. † Vid. § 42.

words, ण under the above circumstances, in High Hindí, remains unchanged. Thus, although we must write कारण, and not कारन, it would not be correct to write करणा for करना, because करना, unlike कारण, is not an uncorrupted Sanskrit word. In some of the dialects, indeed, as, e.g., Máṛwáṛí, Gaṛhwálí, etc., ण often appears even in these corrupted Prakritic words; but this is to be attributed, not to the operation of the above principle of euphony, but to a fondness for the cerebral nasal, which those dialects everywhere exhibit, preferring it constantly to the dental, in the most unexpected places.

57. म्, before any mute consonant, is changeable to the nasal of that class, which may be always written as Anusvár.* Before all other consonants it becomes Anusvár. The operation of this rule is especially to be noticed in the numerous Sanskrit compounds in which सम्, 'with,' 'together,' is the first element. Thus, e.g., सम् + कल्प = सङ्कल्प or संकल्प; सम् + चित = सञ्चित; सम् + ताप, सन्ताप; सम् + शय = संशय.

Sandhi of Sibilants.

58. Final स्, in composition, when preceded by any vowel other than अ or आ, becomes र्, before all soft letters except र. Instances of this change are common in Sanskrit compounds; as, e.g., आशिस् + वाद = आशीर्वाद; दुस् + जन = दुर्जन. When र follows, स is dropped, and the preceding vowel is lengthened; as in नीरोग, from निस् + रोग.

59. ओ is substituted for अस (or अः) before short अ, or a soft consonant; अ following, is then elided, and the elision marked by Avagrah. This rule is illustrated by such compounds as मनोहर, from मनस् + हर; रजोगुण, from रजस् + गुण; also in the headings of chapters, as, प्रथमोऽध्यायः for प्रथमस् अध्यायस्. So likewise, such Sanskrit phrases in the *Rámáyan* as सोपि, योसि, सोसि, are to be explained; यस् (यः) and सस् (सः), before अपि and असि, have first become यो and सो by the above rule, and then the following initial अ has been elided. Avagrah, in these instances, is often thus inaccurately omitted.

---

* Vid. § 18.

60. In all Sanskrit words, ष must be written for स, not final, after any vowel but अ or आ, and after either क or र. Thus we write, correctly, भविष्य, not भविस्य. But Hindí yields few examples under this rule.

61. स् final, in Sanskrit compounds, is changed to Visarg or ष्, before क, ख, प, and फ. This rule is illustrated by numerous compounds with the negative prefix निस्, and a few other words; as, निष्प्रमाण for निस्प्रमाण; निष्कलंक or निःकलंक for निस्कलंक; प्रातःकाल for प्रातस्काल.

62. In Sanskrit, the number of these euphonic rules is much greater, but those that we have given will be found sufficient to indicate and explain the correct writing of nearly every Sanskrit word ever used in Hindí.

CHAPTER III.

OF THE CONSTITUENT ELEMENTS OF HINDI'.

Aboriginal Indian Languages.

63. WHEN, long before the Christian era, the Aryan, Sanskrit-speaking people entered what is now called Hindústhán, they found it inhabited by people of another race and another tongue. This aboriginal race, as the tide of Aryan invasion rolled on eastward, retreated before it, falling away, some into the mountains on the north, more into the jungles and hills of Central and Southern India, where, under various names, preserving still their ancient dialects, and superstitious demon-worship, they are found to-day. Many, however, doubtless remained in their ancient homes, where the stream of Aryan immigration and Aryan speech soon swept over them, and they became the servants of the invading race. Although the aboriginal speech must thus soon have disappeared for the most part from Northern and Western India, it is scarcely conceivable that it should not, before its disappearance from the scene, have influenced, to some extent, the language of the Aryan invaders. To this external, Turanian influence, we shall probably not err in attributing many peculiarities of those ancient Indian dialects known as *Prakrit*, 'common, vulgar,' which for centuries co-existed with the Sanskrit, much as, in ancient Italy, the various provincial dialects co-existed with the Latin of the court and of the forum.

The Ancient Prakrit Dialects.

64. These Prakrit dialects, in the earliest period of which we can speak, appear to have existed under two leading types, the Shauraseni in the west, and the Mágadhí in the east, with an intermediate dialect called Arddha-Mágadhí (Half-Mágadhí) between them. These two or three, at that early

time—in the 4th century B.C.—divided between them all Continental India from east to west. The Maháráshṭrí, mentioned also by the early Prakrit grammarians, varied little from the Shaurasení; being specially the language of poetry, as the latter was the language of prose. Besides these forms of the Prakrit which assumed a literary character, arose forms of speech still more abraded and removed from classic standards, called by the native grammarians Apabhransha, 'debased,' 'incorrect,' lit., 'fallen.' But the Apabhransha of one region was not the same thing as the Apabhransha of another; it was Shaurasení Apabhransha in the west, and Mágadhí Apabhransha in the east, and so on. Out of these Prakrit dialects, the literary Shaurasení and Mágadhí, and the various Apabhransha colloquial variations of these, arose the modern Aryan languages of India. Their relation to Sanskrit is thus closely similar to that of the modern Romance languages of Europe to the classic Latin.* In number they are commonly reckoned seven, and—proceeding from the west eastward—they are known as Panjábí, Sindhí, Gujarátí, Maráṭhí, Hindí, Oṛiyá and Bangálí. Of these, in order of antiquity, Hindí stands first, along with Panjábí and Gujarátí, dating from about 1000 A.D. The earliest writer whose work is preserved for us is Chand Bardai, who wrote about the end of the 12th century. Closely after these, in order of time, follows Maráṭhí, and, latest of all, the Bangálí.

Prakrit, and Modern Languages of N. India.

65. Of these seven Indo-Aryan languages, the Hindí is undoubtedly the first in importance. In one or other of its numerous dialects, it is spoken from the snowy ranges of the Himalayas on the north to the Vindhya Mountains and the Narmadá River in the south; on the east it is bounded by the Sankhassí River from the Himalayas to the Ganges, and thence by a line drawn south-westerly to the Narmadá;

Relative Importance of Hindí.

---

* An interesting and suggestive note on this subject will be found in Muir's *Sanskrit Texts*, vol. ii. pp. 146-149.

on the west it is bounded by a line drawn from near the head of the Gulf of Kachchh northward and then north-eastward to the Satlaj River near Simla. It thus covers an area of more than 248,000 square miles, containing not less than 70,000,000 of Hindí-speaking people.* Moreover, in that special modification known as Urdú or Hindusthání, Hindí has become the official language in a large part of North India, as the speech of the Mussulman population everywhere, and, in a manner, a lingua franca for the whole Indian Peninsula.

Muhammadan Influence on Hindí.

66. Almost from its very origin Hindí has been subjected to foreign influence. The successive invasions and the final subjugation of the largest part of North India by the Muhammadans, occasioned the rise of the so-called Urdú, or 'camp-speech,' just mentioned, about the close of the 12th century. Although this latter is commonly contrasted with Hindí, in the narrower sense of that word, it is essentially merely a dialect of that language, and differs from others chiefly in the very great extent to which Arabic and Persian words and phrases have been substituted for those of Sanskrit and Prakrit origin. But the effect of Muhammadan influence has not been confined to the development of the Urdú dialect. There is probably no dialect of Hindí, however pure, which has not received at least a few Arabic and Persian words from the Muhammadan element in the population; and through the preference given to Urdú in the governmental administration of the country, and the greatly increased facilities of internal communication, the process of change,

---

* Grierson, with Hoernle, insists that the dialects spoken east of Allahabad as far as Bengal should not be reckoned Hindí, but a separate language, for which he proposes the name of Bihárí. In like manner they both would also exclude from the category of Hindí all Himalayan dialects. See Grierson: *Seven Grammars*, etc. Part I. pp. 1-3; Hoernle: *Comp. Gramm.* pp. i, ii.

in this respect and in others, is going on more rapidly than ever in all the Hindí-speaking populations.

67. From the above brief sketch of the origin and history of modern Hindí, it is apparent that Hindí, though essentially as truly an Aryan tongue as Sanskrit, contains, besides the Aryan,* which constitutes its form and most of its substance, a Turanian and a Shemitic element. Turanian Element in Hindí.

As to the Turanian or aboriginal element preserved in Hindí, little that is satisfactory can be said. We are not aware that any such thorough and systematic comparison of Hindí with the modern aboriginal and Draviḍian dialects of India has been made, as might give much certain information on this question. It would be difficult, probably, to find many scholars competent for such an investigation. But, if we mistake not, modern researches would seem to indicate that Turanian influence in the Hindí and other Indo-Aryan dialects has often been unduly exaggerated.

a. Some have thought that they could trace this influence almost throughout the entire Hindí grammatical system. The indication of the case-relation by certain appended particles, rather than by inflection, or organic additions to the word; the conjugation of the verb chiefly by means of auxiliaries, instead of by tense and modal inflections,—these, among other deviations from the Sanskrit and Prakrit dialects, and corresponding agreements with the Draviḍian languages of S. India, have been attributed to extra-Aryan influence. But all these analogies are more fancied and apparent than real and significant. The relation of the postposition to the Hindí substantive is, in fact, quite another thing from the 'agglutination' of words in the Turanian languages. It may be regarded as demonstrated, that the Hindí particles indicative of case-relation are, in reality, boná fide Sanskrit words greatly corrupted, which were originally apprehended, not as 'agglutinated' to the noun, but as in grammatical construction with it. The correspondence, pointed

---

* Most Aryan words in Hindí are of Sanskrit or Prakrit origin. But a few, brought in by the Muhammadan invasions, have come from the old Zand through the modern Persian.

out by Dr. Caldwell in his Comparative Grammar, between the Dravidian dat. sign *ko* or *ku*, and the Hindí dat. postposition *ko*, is now regarded by the best scholars as only a casual coincidence. As to the difference noted between the Sanskrit and the Hindí conjugation, it is only precisely similar to what we observe, to a greater or less extent, in every European language, where, in consequence of the abrasion and loss of the terminations and inflections which characterized the synthetic languages from which they severally arose, the use of auxiliaries has become a simple necessity of speech. As to vocabulary, it is a notable fact, that as the various Indo-Aryan dialects become better known, and their phonetic laws better understood, many words, which at first resisted all attempts to prove their Aryan origin, and therefore might have been imagined to be aboriginal, have finally been satisfactorily identified as connected with classic Sanskrit terms. Still there can be little reason to doubt that, more especially among the vulgar words of various local dialects, investigation will finally leave a residuum of words unquestionably Turanian.* Prof. Monier-Williams has suggested, in his Sanskrit Grammar, that the cerebral letters, which the Hindí has received from Sanskrit, are probably derived from the aboriginal dialects.† It is, at least, a fact worth noticing in this connection, that, of those Hindí words which begin with a cerebral, much the larger part belong to the Prakritic, rather than the pure Sanskrit element of Hindí. For example, of 89 words in the *Prem-Ságar* beginning with one of the cerebral letters *ṭ, ṭh, ḍ, ḍh*, only 21 are pure Sanskrit, to 68 Prakritic words; whereas, of 128 words beginning with *k*, we find 21 of Prakritic origin to 107 pure Sanskrit words; i.e., in the case of words with initial cerebrals, over three-fourths are Prakritic; while of words with an initial *k*, five-sixths are Sanskrit. And it may be further observed, that the cerebral letters prevail most in those sections of the Hindí country where, as in the Himalayas and the wastes of Rajputana, the aborigines, if not still remaining, may be supposed to have held the ground the longest. Beames and Hoernle, however, hesitate to accept this suggestion of Prof. Monier-Williams, and incline to regard both the cerebrals and the dentals as of Indo-Aryan origin, modifications, probably, of an original semi-cerebral sound, which, to use Hoernle's words, "varied in two directions so as to become the true cerebral and the true dental respectively." ‡

* Vid. Trumpp: *Grammar of the Sindhí*, p. iii.

† Vid. *Sansk. Grammar*, p. xxiv, footnote †.

‡ Vid. Beames: *Comp. Gramm.* vol. i. pp. 232-235; Hoernle: *Comp. Gramm.* § 12.

68. In brief, then, the Turanian element in Hindí must be regarded as, in any case, of very subordinate importance. In grammar and in vocabulary alike, Hindí is emphatically an Aryan language. But some foreigners have gone to the extreme of denying that Hindí, properly so called, contains any other than Sanskrit and Prakrit words; and, in their zeal for what they term '*pure* Hindí,' scrupulously exclude from their writing, if not from their speech, all Arabic and Persian words.* But it should not be forgotten that, in such a matter as this, we have to do, not with theories, but with facts. Now if, to determine this question, we examine classic Hindí works, such as, in prose, the *Prem-Ságar*, and in poetry, the *Rámáyan*, we do not find, in point of fact, that the language which the people of the country call Hindí is thus free from any Arabic and Persian admixture. **Arabic and Persian Element in Hindí.**

a. In proof of this assertion, the student may note the following list of Arabic and Persian words occurring even in the *Rámáyan*. We follow the Hindí spelling. गरीबनिवाज, साहेब, बराबरी, असवार, बकसोस, बजार, लायक, बाग, हाल, फौज, सोर, बन्दीखानः, हवाले, बजाज, सराफ, उमर, सक्र, गुमान, खबर, तरवार, दरबार, गर्द, ताज, जोर, कायद, गनी, गरीब, जिनिस, दाम, जहाज, याद, सलाम, जीन, etc. In other Hindí writers, as, e.g., *Kabír*, and others who, like him, have been much under Muhammadan influence, they are much more numerous. Nor, if we listen to the colloquial of the people, shall we fail to hear, even in the most secluded districts, and from Hindoos living quite apart from the Muhammadans, such Arabic and Persian words as हुकम, सरकार, बन्दोबस्त, वा, साहिब, बखशिश, मजूरी (for مزدوري), जमीन्दार (for زميندار), etc.

b. It may be noted here, with regard to the character and extent of this Arabic and Persian admixture, that in the case of all words having any special reference to government and

---

* See, e.g. Etherington: *Hindí Grammar*, Preface, pp. iv, v.

law, the conquering Muhammadans have succeeded in imposing their own words upon the colloquial Hindí to the exclusion of the Sanskrit. And if any one, in his zeal for 'pure Hindí,' will attempt to use, instead of these, the corresponding Sanskrit words, he will probably find that none but a few Paṇḍits will understand him. As to Arabic and Persian words of other classes, the proportion found in Hindí varies, as might be expected, in different parts of the country; being greatest in the extreme N.W., and gradually diminishing toward the E. and S.

Arabic and Persian Letters in Hindí.

69. Inasmuch as the Arabic and Persian alphabets differ widely from the Devanágarí, all words from those languages containing letters not represented in those alphabets, when received into Hindí, undergo certain modifications. These are, in brief, as follows:—

a. Both ط and ت are pronounced as त, and are so represented; as, طلب, तलब, 'wages'; تکرار, तकरार, 'contention.'

b. The three sibilants, ث, ص, and س, all become स; as, ثابت, साबित, 'proved'; سئیس, सईस, 'a groom'; صاحب, साहिब or साहेब, 'sir, master.' ش often becomes श; but in most sections of the country, (as, for example, through the central Doáb and in Máṛwáṛ,) it is regularly sounded as स; thus, شروع, शुरू or सुरू, 'beginning'; شک, शक or सक, 'doubt.'

c. The letters, ذ, ز, ض, ظ, all pronounced in Urdú as *z*, become ज, *j* in Hindí; as, ذرا, जरा, 'a little'; زمین, जमीन, 'land'; ضامن, जामिन, 'a surety'; ظاهر, जाहिर, 'manifest.' But in Máṛwáṛí and some other forms of Hindí, ذ final becomes द; as in कागद, for کاغذ, 'paper.'

d. ح and ه both become ह; as, حال, हाल, 'state'; هر, हर, 'every.' In Máṛwáṛí, when medial, they commonly disappear; as, e.g., सैर for شهر, 'a city,' साब for صاحب, 'sir.' The gutturals خ and غ become, respectively, ख and ग; as, e.g., in खाक, 'dust,' for خاک; गम, 'grief,' for غم; and गुलाम, 'a slave,' for غلام. ق commonly becomes क; as in हक़, 'right,' for حق; and कौल, 'word,' for قول. But the common people in the central Doáb often oddly change a final ق to त; thus, تحقیق, 'investigation,' becomes तैकीत; موافق, 'like,' माफित. ع is always dropped; thus, عقل becomes अकल, 'intellect'; واقع, वाकि, 'existent, real.' But short *a* before ع, on the rejection of ع, is lengthened; as, मालूम, 'known,' for معلوم. و is ordinarily unchanged; but in Máṛwáṛí, I have found उजीर, 'a minister of state,' for وزیر, where the consonantal *v* has been softened to the cognate vowel.

e. The sound of ف may be regarded as fairly naturalized in most Hindí dialects. Not only is its pronunciation retained in Arabic and Persian words when introduced into Hindí, where it is represented by फ, as in सराफ, 'a banker,' for صراف; but, to a great extent, the common people substitute the foreign sound of *f* for *ph*, even in Indian words; pronouncing, e.g., फल, 'fruit,' *fal*, instead of *phal*; फिर, 'again,' *fir*, etc.

f. Arabic and Persian words not containing any of the above letters, for the most part enter Hindí without change, the Devanágarí furnishing the equivalents of all the other Arabic letters. Occasional changes and corruptions indeed occur which can scarcely be reduced to rule. There seems to be at least a tendency in some parts of the country to reject a consonant following any sibilant; thus we hear, in the Doáb, मजूर, 'a labourer,' for مزدور; मजूद, 'firm,' for مضبوط; and in Máṛwáṛí, मसीत, 'a mosque,' for مسجد. We may also note a decided tendency to substitute *i* for *a*; as in निमक, 'salt,' for نمک; करिन्द॰, 'an agent,' for کرنده.

OF TATSAMA WORDS.

70. We may now pass to the consideration of words of Sanskrit origin, which make up not less than nine-tenths of the language. These have been divided by native writers into *Tatsama* and *Tadbhava* words. The word *Tatsama*, Sanskritic Element in Hindí.

तत्सम, meaning 'the same as that,' appropriately denotes all purely Sanskrit words; i.e., all such as have entered Hindí with no alteration save the loss of the ancient affixes of declension. The word *Tadbhava*, तद्भव, 'of the nature of that,' denotes, on the other hand, all corrupted Sanskrit words, which, by the addition, loss, or change of certain letters, have come to appear in Hindí in a form more or less modified, and often greatly disguised.

71. *Tatsama* words, as is evident from the above definition, appear in every dialect under one and the same form. But inasmuch as pure Sanskrit words in Hindí, like most words of Latin and Greek origin in English, are especially appropriated to the expression of higher or scientific thought, it is evident, that the proportion of these *Tatsamas* actually found in the various Hindí dialects, must needs vary greatly, in proportion to their literary cultivation. Moreover, it must not be forgotten that, to a limited extent everywhere, but more especially in Western Hindí, Arabic and Persian words have often usurped the place of the Sanskrit *Tatsamas*. And so it has come to pass, that, speaking in a general way, the proportion of *Tatsamas* current in Hindí regularly increases as we go eastward, till we reach the Bangálí, in which they reach a maximum. The following remarks will help to indicate the nature and extent of this *Tatsama* element.

Coexistent Tatsamas and Tadbhavas.

72. In very many cases, the *Tatsama* and *Tadbhava* forms of the same word or root coexist in the language. Thus, e.g., we have क्रोध, *Tatsama*, कोह, *Tadbhava*; लाभ, *Tatsama*, लाह, *Tadbhava*. In some cases, the two forms retain the same meaning; thus, क्रोध and कोह both signify 'anger'; योग्य and जोग, 'fit, worthy.' In such cases, one form is often dialectic. Thus, *Tadbhava* forms with ह for an aspirated mute, are especially characteristic of the old Eastern Hindí of the *Rámáyan*, as, e.g., लाह, सोहा, कोह, for लाभ, सोभा, क्रोध. But where *Tatsamas* and *Tadbhavas* co-exist in the same dialect, it often happens that, with the difference in form, we find a difference also in signification; thus, मेघ, *Tatsama*, is 'a rain-cloud'; but the corresponding *Tadbhava*, मेंह, is always 'rain,' 'a shower.' Often, the *Tatsama* is the general term, and the *Tadbhava*, the more specific one; as, स्थान, 'a place,' in general; but ठाना, 'a police-station.' Where the words will admit it, the *Tatsama* form is often appropriated to a higher sense, and the *Tadbhava* is restricted to a lower signification. Thus, the *Tadbhava* देखना is 'to see, seeing,' in general; but the *Tatsama* दर्शन is 'beholding,' in a higher sense, as of a superior in rank, an idol, or a deity. Thus, people say, जगन्नाथ का दर्शन करना, 'to behold Jagannáth,' but never, जगन्नाथ को देखना, 'to see Jagannáth.'

Rem. **The careful regard to etiquette for which the Hindoos are noted, is manifest, not only, as will hereafter appear, in the appropriation of certain pronominal forms and verbal inflections for the indication of various degrees of respect, but also, and very often, in the choice of a *Tatsama* or *Tadbhava* word, the former being commonly the more respectful.**

73. Of purely Sanskrit nouns and adjectives, the case-terminations have been lost, and they regularly appear in Hindí under the form which they assume in the Sanskrit nom. sing., minus the nom. case termination. Thus, the bases यत्न, इच्छा, अपि, धेनु, दातृ, मातृ, सरित, धनवत, नामन, महिमन, तेजस्विन, respectively appear in Hindí as यत्न, इच्छा, अपि, धेनु, दाता, माता, सरित, धनवान, नाम, महिमा, and तेजस्वी. Tatsama Nouns and Adjectives.

a. The only nouns exempted from the operation of this law are crude bases in अस् and उस्, as, e.g., मनस्, चक्षुस्, which, in Hindí, have lost, not only, as in Sanskrit itself, the nom. sing. termination, but also the final radical स्, as found in the Sanskrit nom. sing.; so that the above words appear in Hindí as मन, चक्षु. Also, in a single instance in the *Rámáyan*, *Tulsí Dás* has written (doubtless for the sake of the metre) the root of the strong Sanskrit cases, दातार for दाता, 'a giver.'

b. Sanskrit adjectives in वत्, occurring in Hindí, frequently substitute for the nom. sing., the base in वन्त्, of the strong cases, as, e.g., दयावन्त, 'merciful,' पापवन्त, 'sinful'; so also, छुधावन्त for क्षुधावन्त, 'hungry.'

c. As has been remarked, Hindí nouns exhibit, in their declension, only the scanty remainder of the Sanskrit case-terminations, so corrupted and modified as to be recognized only with difficulty. The unchanged Sanskrit forms are, however, occasionally met with, but are no more organically connected with the Hindí, than such Latin and Greek phrases and words as '*id est*,' '*et cetera*,' '*dogmata*,' are thus connected with English. Examples are, सर्वस्य, gen. sing. of सर्व, 'all'; अर्थात = 'viz.,' abl. sing. of अर्थ; पितरौ, 'parents,' nom. dual of पितृ; वर्षाः, 'the rains,' nom. plur. from वर्ष; सुखेन, 'with pleasure,' instr. sing. of सुख. But the most of these are very rare; and, with few exceptions, are only found in poetry.

Sanskrit Comparatives and Superlatives.

74. Sanskrit comparatives and superlatives occur in Hindí, with the usual loss of the case-terminations, but are by no means common, and, with a few exceptions, they belong rather to literature than to the colloquial. Examples are, of superlatives; श्रेष्ठ, 'most excellent,' from श्री; प्रियतम, 'dearest,' from प्रिय. Comparatives are yet more uncommon; we have noted मन्दतर, 'slower,' from मन्द; पुण्यतर, 'more holy,' from पुण्य. It may be remarked that these Sanskrit comparatives, when they occur in Hindí, very commonly lose the comparative sense and are, in effect, superlatives.

Tatsama Numerals and Pronouns.

75. The numerals and pronouns appear in Hindí, as might be expected of words in such incessant use by all classes, in an extremely mutilated and corrupted form. But the unchanged Sanskrit numerals are occasionally found in Hindí literature, especially in the headings of chapters. So also, we occasionally meet certain cases of the Sanskrit pronouns; more especially, the gen. sing. of the 1st and 2nd personal pronouns, मम and तव, chiefly in poetry.

Tatsama Verbal Forms.

76. The Hindí verbs, without an exception, are *Tadbhava* words. Still, in poetry, parts of Sanskrit tenses are occasionally found; thus, from the root नम्, we have नमामि, 'I salute,' 1st sing. pres. *Parasmai.* But such forms as this have no organic connection with the language. The Hindí, however, besides the regular Tadbhava participles of its verbal conjugation, admits, even in the colloquial, various Sanskrit participles in an unaltered form. Thus, we have the pres. participle *A'tmane* in मान; as, from the root वृत्, वर्तमान, 'existing, present,' and, very rarely, the indecl. past participle, in त्वा; as, in the *Rámáyan,* चित्वा. Much more common is the past part. in त or न (ण); as, e.g., from कृ, कृत, 'done, made'; from वच्, उक्त, 'spoken, said'; from पृ, पूर्ण, 'filled'; from मुह्, मोहित, 'fascinated.' Not uncommon are fut. pass. participles; whether those in तव्य, as, from कृ, कर्तव्य, 'worthy to be done'; or अनीय, as, ग्रहणीय, 'to be received,' from ग्रह्; or in य, as, दृश्य, from दृश्, 'to be seen,' 'visible.' Very rare is the 2nd fut. part. *Parasmai* in स्य; as, from भू, 'to be,' the final consonant त having been rejected, भविष्य, 'future.' Sanskrit also contributes to Hindí many adverbs, prepositions and conjunctions, in an unaltered form. A list of these will be given in the appropriate place.

Of Tadbhava Words.

77. The plan of this work will not allow the space necessary to an exhaustive discussion of the *Tadbhava* words of Hindí; but a brief exhibition of the processes by which they have been formed, will be found of service in the study of the Hindí dialects, and aid the student to an intelligent acquaintance with the language. Accordingly, referring the student elsewhere for a full discussion of this matter,* we

* See the "Comparative Grammar of the Modern Aryan Languages of India," by John Beames, B.C.S., and the "Comparative Grammar of the Gauḍian Languages," by Dr. A. D. F. Hoernle; works which are indispensable to any one who will make a thorough study of this subject.

propose to notice, as briefly as may be, the more important of those phonetic laws which have operated and are still operating in the Hindí dialects of N. India.

Of Vowel Changes.

Changes of Guttural Vowels.

78. As has already appeared, Hindí exhibits a decided tendency to the omission of the short vowels. The inherent *a* is constantly dropped from unaccented syllables, even though its omission be not marked by the use of a conjunct consonant. इ and उ are very commonly silent when final; in other positions they usually remain.

a. But Beames has noted the frequent elision of अ and उ initial, in Sanskrit compounds in which one of the inseparable prepositions अधि, अपि, अभि, उप, etc., is the first member. Among his illustrations are, झांकना, 'to peep,' from Sk. अध्यक्षणं, 'overlooking'; भीगना, 'to be wet,' from Sk. अभ्यंजनं; बैठा, 'seated,' from Sk. उपविष्ट; to which might be added others, as, e.g., पठावना or पठावन, 'to send,' from the Sanskrit causal base, उपस्थापय. अ initial is sometimes omitted in simple words also; as, e.g., in लावू, 'a pumpkin,' for Sk. अलावू.

b. The Sanskrit fem. termination, आ, in *Tadbhava* nouns is reduced to the silent *ă*; as in बात, 'a thing, a word,' Sk. वत्ती; नींद, 'sleep,' Sk. निद्रा. इ or ई final, vanishes, as in feminines in इनी, whence Hindí feminines in न; as, मालिन, 'a gardener's wife,' for मालिनी, from माली; बहिन, 'a sister,' Pr. बहिणी, Sk. भगिनी; सेठन, 'the wife of a Seṭh'; आंख, 'the eye,' Sk. अक्षि, etc. A similar change passes on ऊ and उ; as in तन, 'body,' Sk. तनु; सास, 'mother-in-law,' Sk. सासु.

c. ए final follows the same law in many words now used as adverbs or prepositions, but originally Sanskrit locatives singular; as, समीप, 'near,' Sk. समीपे; संग, 'with,'

Sk. संगे, etc. Sometimes this ए of the locative is weakened to इ; as in लागि, 'till.'

79. अ is often changed to इ, especially in unaccented syllables. Thus स्मरण, 'remembrance,' becomes सुमिरन; पहला, 'first,' is constantly pronounced, and often written, पहिला. Sometimes the same change takes place in accented syllables; as in छिमा, 'pardon,' Sk. क्षमा. In नेवला, 'a weasel,' Sk. नकुला, अ appears to be changed to ए.

The change of अ to उ is less common, and chiefly occurs under the influence of a neighbouring labial; as in खुजली, 'the itch,' Sk. खर्जू; मूंछ, 'moustache,' Sk. श्मश्रु,

a. When इ or उ follow a syllable containing अ, they frequently supersede अ in that syllable, or cause it to be exchanged for the cognate *guṇ* diphthong. Illustrations are; इमली, 'a tamarind tree,' Sk. अम्लिका; उंगली, 'a finger,' Sk. अंगुली; सेंध, 'a hole dug by burglars,' Sk. संधि; चोंच, 'the beak of a bird,' Sk. चंचु.

b. Very often in Sanskrit words, अ, when followed by the semivowels व or य, coalesces with them into the cognate diphthong, commonly the *vriddhi.* Thus, the Sk. नयन, 'eye,' becomes नैन; समय, 'time,' समै or समे; लवण, 'salt,' लोन, but also लून; अपर, 'another,' through the previous substitution of व for प, और.

c. Here may best be noticed the operation of a law by which ओ was regularly substituted in Prakrit for the Sanskrit declensional termination अस् (अः).* Although, in most Tadbhava words, the corruption of this termination in Hindí has proceeded still further, till only अ or उ final is left, yet many illustrations still remain, as in the pronouns, where, e.g., the relative जो and the (Braj) interrogative को, stand respectively for strong Prakrit forms, preserved in Máṛwáṛí, जिको and किको, for the Sanskrit यः and कः.

---

* Cf. Vararuchi: Prakr. Prak. V. (1).

Similarly, we have, from the Sk. परश्वस्, परसों, 'the second day before or after the present.'

Changes of Palatal and Labial Vowels.

80. इ, ई, उ, and ऊ present few instances of change. But इ is changed to ऊ, in सूंघना, 'to smell,' from Sk. शिंघ; and ई to अ, in परखन, 'testing,' for Sk. परीक्षण. उ has become अ in the common word बिजली, 'lightning,' for Sk. विद्युत्. In बाई, 'rheumatism,' for Sk. वायु, the final ई has probably arisen from the cognate य, उ final having been dropped, and य (इ) lengthened in compensation. In बिन्दी, 'a dot,' from Sk. बिन्दु, we have apparently a real change of उ to ई; unless, indeed, after the analogy of many other Tadbhavas in ई, ई represents, in this instance, the इ of a Prakrit stem, बिन्दिक (?). उ has also become इ, in तनिक, 'a little,' for Sk. तनुक. In फफेरा, 'the lungs,' Sk. फुप्फुस, उ has become ए.

Changes of Cerebral Vowels.

81. ऋ undergoes various changes. When initial it always appears in Tadbhava words as रि; as in रिषि for ऋषि. When non-initial, the most common substitution is इ; as in गिद्ध, 'a vulture,' for गृध; बिच्छू, 'a scorpion,' for वृश्चिक. It may be changed to ई; as in सींग, 'a horn,' for शृंग, and मीच, for मृत्यु, 'death'; or even ए, as in गेह, 'a house,' for गृह. It often becomes उ, commonly under the influence of a contiguous labial; as in सुरत, 'remembrance,' for स्मृति; or ऊ, as in मूआ, 'dead,' for मृतः. Less frequently it appears as अ, as in मट्टी, 'earth,' Sk. मृत्तिका; पावस, 'the rainy season,' Sk. प्रावृष. In many cases, even when non-initial, it is represented by the consonant र, in combination with one or more vowels; most commonly रि, as in गिरहस्थ, 'a householder,' for गृहस्थ; or even इरि, as in सिरिजन, 'creating,' for सृजन; or, under the influence of a labial, रु, as in रूख, 'a tree,' for Sk. वृक्ष.

Lengthening of Vowels.

82. अ, इ, and उ, in the penult of Sanskrit or Prakrit words regularly appear as long in Hindí, in all cases where the original ultimate syllable has been dropped. This is most

of all to be noted in a large class of Sanskrit and Prakrit words formed by the suffix क. This includes a few Sanskrit nouns of agency, but especially, a very large number of words, chiefly Prakrit, formed by the addition of an inorganic क to the original Sanskrit base.* This law will be found to cover most Tadbhava masculine nouns in आ final, and feminine nouns in ई, as also many nouns in ई, denoting trades. Examples are: चीता, 'a leopard,' Sk. चित्रकः (Pr. चित्तओ?); घोड़ा, 'a horse,' Sk. घोटकः (Pr. घोडओ?); मक्खी, 'a fly,' Sk. मक्षिका; बालू, 'sand,' Sk. बालुका; घी, 'clarified butter,' Sk. घृतं; all formed after the manner of नाई, 'a barber,' from Sk. नापितः. The ई and ऊ of these words have probably arisen directly from intermediate forms, इयो, उवो,† य and व having been euphonically inserted after the elision of क (as in नापित, त).‡

83. When, in the process of phonetic decay, a Sanskrit conjunct has been reduced in Hindí to a simple consonant, a short vowel, preceding such a conjunct, is regularly lengthened. Thus, the Sk. हस्त, 'hand,' becomes in Hindí, हाथ; अग्नि, 'fire,' आग; इक्षु, 'sugar-cane,' ईख; मिष्टः (मिष्टकः), मीठा; विंशति, 'twenty,' बीस. Lengthening of Vowels.

a. Sometimes, instead of the long vowel, the cognate *guṇ* diphthong is the substitute; as in कोढ़ी, 'a leper,' Sk. कुष्ठी; सोंठ, 'ginger,' Sk. शुण्ठि or शुंठी. ऋ under such circumstances commonly becomes ई, as in पीठ, 'back,' from पृष्ठ; दीठ, 'sight,' from दृष्टि.

b. In such cases, the lengthened vowel is often nasalised, especially where the first member of the conjunct was a nasal. Examples are: चांद, 'the moon,' Sk. चन्द्र; कांटा, 'a thorn,' Sk. कण्टक; also ऊंट, 'a camel,' Sk. उष्ट्र; सांप, 'a snake,' Sk. सर्प; ऊंचा, 'high,' Sk. उच्च. It may be added that very often vowels are optionally nasalised, even where there

---

* Concerning this Prakrit suffix, see Lass. Inst. Ling. Prac. §§ 89, 1; 164, 19; et passim. † Vid. § 88, *a*, *Rem.* 1. ‡ Vid. § 89.

has been no previous conjunct; as, मेह or मेंह, 'rain,' Sk. मेघ; खासी or खांसी, 'a cough,' Sk. कासिका; in which last instance the initial क has been aspirated through the influence of the following sibilant.

c. But in some such cases, chiefly Sanskrit compounds with various prefixes, in which the accent rests on the radical syllable, the accent has prevented the lengthening of the vowel, as in derivatives from Sk. उत्था (उद् + स्था), 'rising,' where Hindí has उठना, etc., and not ऊठना.

Shortening of Medial Vowels:

84. Long vowels are almost invariably changed to their own short, when any long or heavy appendage is added to a word. This occurs especially in the first member of compounds; as in बटमार, 'a highwayman,' where बट is for बाट, 'a road'; पनहारा, 'a water-carrier,' for पानीहारा; फुलवारी, 'a flower-garden,' for फूलवारी; सितकाल, 'winter,' for शीतकाल. So also where heavy terminations have been added; as in बुढ़ापा, 'old age,' from बूढ़ा; मिठाई, 'sweetmeats,' from मीठा, 'sweet,' Sk. मिष्टकः. For the diphthongs the corresponding simple vowel is the substitute; as in बिटिया, dim. from बेटा, 'a son'; छुटका, 'younger,' 'smaller,' from छोटा, 'little.'

Shortening of Final Diphthongs.

85. Diphthongs final in Prakrit and Sanskrit are in Hindí regularly reduced to their simple vowel. Thus the Prakrit nom. sing. termination ओ, for Sk. अः, in archaic Hindí, and among the moderns, in Naipálí, and often in other Himalayan dialects, regularly becomes उ. Thus, Sk. शरः, 'an arrow,' Pr. सरो, is in the *Rámáyan*, सरु; अनुरागः, 'affection,' Pr. अनुरागो, O.H. अनुरागु. It should be observed, however, that in later Hindí,* this short उ also has been dropped, leaving, e.g., अनुराग, *anurág*, for अनुरागु. Similarly, ए or ऐ final, in the conjugation of verbs, often appears as इ; as in होइ for होए, Sk. भवति; चाहि for चाहै, etc.

* Vid. § 78, *b*.

a. But where, in Prakrit, after elision of a final consonant, we have अओ, इओ, उओ final, High Hindí presents आ, ई, and ऊ. In the western and Himalayan dialects, ओ and औ appear for the Pr. अओ. In H.H. गेहूं, 'wheat,' for Sk. गोधूम, ए exceptionally stands for ओ; and औ medial becomes ओ, in मोती, for मौक्तिक.

b. In K. ओ for Br. औ, in the termination of Tadbhava nouns and adjectives, औ medial becomes ओ; so also in पोता, 'a grandson,' for Sk. पौत्र. In केवट, a pilot,' for Sk. कैवर्त्त, ऐ has become ए.

Prefixing of a Vowel.

86. The modern Hindoos, in the colloquial, constantly prefix a short अ to words beginning with a conjunct in which स is the first letter; thus, e.g., स्त्री, 'a woman,' becomes अस्त्री, or, with some, इस्त्री; स्थान, 'a place,' अस्थान, etc. Such forms are occasionally found in literature; as, e.g., in the *Rámáyan*, अस्तुति, for स्तुति, 'praise,' and अस्नान, for स्नान, 'bathing.'

Of Hiatus.

87. When, by the elision of a medial consonant, two vowels have been brought into contact, Hindí, instead of allowing the hiatus to remain, as in Prakrit, very often, though by no means always, seeks to avoid it, either, where the rules of *sandhi* will permit, by uniting the concurrent vowels; or, in other cases, by inserting a consonant, usually य or व, sometimes ह. Thus, the Sk. चरति, 'he walks,' त being elided, becomes in O.H. चलइ, and in many modern dialects, चले or चलै. The Sk. पिपासित, 'thirsty,' प and त being elided, and a य inserted, becomes पियासा; वातुल, 'crazy,' त being elided, and व inserted, becomes बावला, but sometimes बाउला or बाउरा. Occasionally, as in सूई, 'a needle,' Sk. सूची, and कोइल, 'the cuckoo,' Sk. कोकिल, the hiatus is suffered to remain.

Variations from Sanskrit Sandhi.

88. While these combinations often take place in accordance with the Sanskrit rules of *sandhi*, this is by no means always the case. The following exceptions may be especially noted.

(1) A short vowel after a long often disappears; as in रोना, 'to cry,' where रोन is for रोअन, from रोदन. The short vowel, however, sometimes maintains its ground, as, e.g., above, in कोइल, for Sk. कोकिल.

(2) The simple vowels, अ + इ, अ + उ, sometimes coalesce into the *vriddhi*, instead of the *gun*, which the Sanskrit law would require; but often this is dialectic. Examples frequently occur in the conjugation of verbs; as, e.g., हंसै, 'he laughs,' from हसइ, Sk. हसति; and probably चलौ, 2nd plur. imperat., 'walk,' from the old Hindí, चलऊ.

(3) Anomalous is the ऐ or ए in the first syllable of the following numerals, viz.: पैंतीस, 35; सैंतीस, 37; पैंतालीस, 45; सैंतालीस, 47; पैंसठ, 65. The original Sanskrit equivalents of these present no combination which by any phonetic law could give rise to these diphthongs.* But in तैंतीस or तैंतीस, 33, the same diphthongs are derived regularly from the Sk. त्रय in त्रयस्त्रिंशत्; as also the same in तैंतालीस, or तैंतालीस, 43, from Sk. त्रिचत्वारिंशत्. Hence Beames has not unnaturally suggested that these perplexing forms may be due to the fancy of the Hindoos for rhyming related words, which led them to assimilate all these numerals in sound to the perfectly regular derivative, तैंतीस.†

a. The semivowels य and व, after अ or their cognate vowels, इ and उ, are often treated as vowels, so that अ + य, like अ + इ, becomes ऐ or ए; अ + व, like अ + उ, = ओ or औ; इ + य, like इ + इ, = ई, and उ + व, like उ + उ, = ऊ. Thus, as before noted, समय, 'time,' becomes समै; भव, 'existence,' भौ; इन्द्रिय, 'the senses,' इन्द्री.‡

Rem. 1. This principle apparently leads to the explanation of those nouns in ई and ऊ referred to in § 82. The अ of the ultimate being

---

* See Table of Hindí and Sanskrit Numerals.

† *Comp. Gramm.* vol. ii. p. 292. ‡ Vid. § 90.

rejected, य or व was inserted to fill the hiatus, giving us, e.g., for the Sk. घोटिका, 'a mare,' Pr. घोडिआ, first, घोडिया, and then घोड़िय, and, finally, इय becoming ई, घोड़ी. By a similar process, from the Sk. बालुका, Pr. बालुआ, we should have the successive forms, बालुवा, बालुव, बालू.

Rem. 2. It may be noted here, that in the colloquial throughout Oude and the Doáb, the intermediate forms thus postulated as the immediate origin of nouns fem. in ई, still exist. In the dialect of W. Oude, e.g., we have भैंसिया (as if from a Sk. form, महिषिका), for भैंसी, 'a buffalo-cow'; घोड़िया, Sk. घोटिका, 'a mare,' etc.*

b. Hoernle gives the following contractions as peculiar to the modern Indo-Áryan languages, viz.: अ or आ with इ to ऐ, or with उ to औ; as in the 1st and 3rd sing. conting. future, in चलै, for चलइ, and कहौं, for कहउं; इ with अ, to ऐ, ए, ई, or इ; as in डेढ़, 'one and a half,' Pr. दिअड्ढ (?) Mg. दिवड्ढे, etc.; Máṛ. मीनत, for मिहनत, Ar. محنت, 'labour'; उ with अ, to औ, ओ, or ऊ; as, सौंधा, 'perfume,' Sk. सुगंधक, etc.; ए with अ, इ, उ, or ए, to ए, and ओ with अ, to ओ.† Modern Sandhi.

Rem. Anusvár (for Anunásik) is frequently found where it represents, not an organic part of the word, but a local habit of nasalising the vowel. Thus, e.g., in the drama of *Raṇdhír aur Prem Mohaní*, we find constantly नें for ने, the postposition of the case of the agent; also एं for ए in the masc. obl. sing., especially in the inflected infinitive; as, जाननें का for जानने का, कहनेंवाला for कहनेवाला, etc., etc. Inorganic Anusvár.

OF CONSONANTAL CHANGES.

Simple Consonants.

89. Any smooth mute, except ट or ड, also म, य, व, स, and ह, and rarely र and ल, when single and non-initial, may Elision of Medials.

* It is to be remembered, in investigating words of this class, that the suffix क, in Prakrit, was added indifferently to almost any word. Lassen's words are, 'omnibus thematis.' See Lassen: *Inst. Ling. Prac.* passim.

† *Comp. Gramm.* p 48. For additional illustrations, see the same, §§ 94–98.

be elided. The vowels thus brought together, combine, if similar; if otherwise, the hiatus often remains, as in Prakrit; but in the modern dialects, य or व, and occasionally इ, is preferably inserted. Examples are: Sk. मेलकः, 'an assembly,' Pr. मेलओ, H. मेला, for the older Már. मेलो; Sk. भगिनी, 'sister,' H. बहिन, where the medial aspirate, ग being rejected, has arisen from the aspiration of भ; Sk. सूची, 'a needle,' H. सूई; Sk. रजनि, 'night,' H. रैन; Sk. चतुर्थ, 'fourth,' H. चौथा; Sk. हृदय, 'the heart,' H. हिय; Sk. उदय, 'rising of the sun,' O.H. उए; Sk. कूप, 'a well,' H. कूआ; Sk. दीपक, 'a lamp,' H. दिया; Sk. पूर्णिमा, 'the day of new moon,' H. पून्यौं; Sk. विवाह, 'marriage,' H. बियाह or ब्याह, for बिआह; H. पहचान or पहिचान, 'acquaintance,' for Pr. परिचअणं. नाक, 'the nose,' for Sk. नासिका, has probably arisen from a collateral form, नासका.

a. ठ is elided in Máṛ. पोशाल, for H.H. पाठशाला, where the ठ of the root पठ् has disappeared.

b. The elision of ह has taken place in High Hindí, chiefly in verbal forms, before or after इ; as in 3rd sing. pres. or conting. fut. of होना, 'to be,' होई, O.H. होहि, Sk. भविष्यति; चलें, 'they go,' O.H. चलहिं, for Sk. चलन्ति; and sometimes before उ; as in 2nd plur. pres. of करना, 'to do,' करो, O.H. करहु. The chief example in nouns is found in the obl. sing. termination ए of Tadbhava nouns in आ; in which ए has arisen from अहि by *sandhi* of अ and इ, after elision of ह. Hoernle gives a single example of the elision of ह in the stem of a noun, in E.H. बिपै, for Sk. बृहस्पति. But in Máṛwáṛí, such elision is very common, as also in the Himalayan dialects; as in मीनत for मिहनत, and साब for साहिब, etc., etc. Sometimes medial ह is omitted in High Hindí in a verbal stem; as in ठैरना, 'to be established,' for ठहरना, giving such forms as ठैरेगा, ठैरो, etc.

c. स, when elided, appears in most cases to have first passed into ह. The older Hindí generally preserves the form ह, and, rarely, even those in स. Thus, in the futures, we have करहि, 'thou wilt do,' for करसि, 2nd sing. fut.; whence, by elision of ह

and *sandhi*, करइ and करै. But in पछतैहसि, 'thou wilt regret,' 2nd sing. fut., the स is preserved.

d. The chief example of the elision of र is in कइ or कै for करि, in the termination of the conj. part., and in कै, again for करि, in the obl. form, के, of the gen. postposition, का. I have found no case of the elision of ल, except that given by Hoernle, viz., केंचुवा, 'an earth-worm,' Sk. किंचुलक.

90. The labials, प, ब, म, व, when medial after *á* or *a*, very Softening of Labials.
commonly soften into the cognate vowel उ, which then combines with the preceding *a* into the diphthong ओ or औ. Thus the Sk. अपर, 'another,' becomes in Hindí, first, अवर, and then, और; लवण, 'salt,' becomes लोन; गमन, 'going,' गौना, for the more frequent गवना, 'the going home of a bride'; वामन, 'a dwarf,' बौना; प्रभाव, 'excellency,' प्रभौ. In such cases, the nasal element of म is often retained, in the form of an Anusvár attached to the diphthong, as in H. चौंरी, 'a whisk,' from Sk. चमर. So also, the palatal य, under Softening of य.
similar conditions, passes into the cognate vowel इ, whence, by *sandhi*, arises the diphthong, ए or ऐ; as, e.g., in सैन, 'sleeping,' for Sk. शयन; समै or समै, 'time,' for समय. When इ precedes य, the य combines with it into the cognate long vowel; as in इंद्री, 'an organ of sense,' for इंद्रिय. So also, उव becomes ऊ.

91. A final consonant is usually rejected. Thus, यशस्, Elision of Finals.
'renown,' becomes यश and जस; आत्मन्, 'self,' becomes आप. By the same law, न final is dropped in all numerals; as, e.g., in आठ, 'eight,' दस, 'ten,' for अष्टन्, दशन्.

92. Initial consonants commonly remain unchanged. The Treatment of Initials.
exceptions occur, for the most part, in the case of the sibilant स, initial in a conjunct;* or if in other letters, they may be traced to the disturbing influence of a neighbouring sibilant or aspirate. Thus the Sk. विभूति, 'superhuman power,'

---

* Vid. § 108.

becomes भबूत; बुस, 'chaff,' भूसा; पाश, 'a noose,' फांस; वाष्प, 'vapour,' भाफ. But in Naipálí, a hard mute is sometimes softened, even when initial. A common example is गरनु = H.H. करना, 'to do'; with which may be compared the Mairwáṛí gen. postposition, गो, for H.H. का, from the same root, कृ.

Softening of Hard Mutes.

93. Hard mutes, when medial or final, as in other Áryan languages, are frequently softened. Examples are: काग, 'a crow,' Sk. काक; सूजो, 'a small awl,' Sk. सूची. The change is especially common with the cerebrals, as, e.g., in घोड़ा, a 'horse,' Sk. घोटक; पढ़न, 'reading,' for पठन. प more commonly passes through ब or व into the cognate vowel उ, and thus loses its consonantal character entirely. But occasionally it stops at व; as in ताव, 'heat,' for Sk. ताप, and in the fifties; as, e.g., बावन, 'fifty-two'; चौवन, 'fifty-four'; सत्तावन, 'fifty-seven,' etc., where व is for the प of पांच, which remains in some other numbers of the same series; as, e.g., तिरपन, 'fifty-three.' I should therefore suppose that such forms as बापन, चौपन, etc., must have preceded the forms now in use, but hitherto I have not met with them in Hindí. Maráṭhí preserves the form चौपन; but the other forms of this series agree with Hindí. Naipálí furnishes an example of the reverse change, in the hardening of ब to प in जुवाप, H.H. जवाब, Ar. جواب. Rarely, a nasal is substituted for a cognate mute; as in पसीना, 'sweat,' for Sk. प्रस्वेद.

Changes of Palatals.

94. Letters of one organ are often substituted for those of another. Thus, palatals are often exchanged for dentals or cerebrals. Beames has noted a large number of examples involving the apparently cognate roots, चप्, डप्, टप्, दब्, etc., from the Sk. चि (?)*

Rem. But in the numerals, 41, 43, 45, 47, and 48, त is not, in reality, a substitute, as might appear, for च; for, e.g., in इकतालीस, 'forty-one,'

* Vid. *Comp. Gramm.* vol. i. § 57.

for Sk. एकचत्वारिंशत्, the त represents the त्व of the Sk. चत्वारिंशत्, which in Prakrit became चत्तालीसा.*

a. The cognate languages present numerous instances of the change of the palatals to the sibilants, but this is scarcely found in Hindí outside of the Rajputana and Himalayan dialects. In the Máṛwáṛí dialect, the rule is universal, in respect to च and छ, which, although still written, are always pronounced as *s.*

Interchange of Dentals with Cerebrals, र and ल.

95. Very common is the substitution of the cerebrals, whether initial or medial, for the dentals. Examples are numerous: as, e.g., डर, 'fear,' Sk. दर्; डाह, 'burning, envy,' from Sk. दह्; पड़ना, 'to fall,' from Sk. पत्; टीका, 'a sectarial mark,' for तिलक, which is also used; बूढ़ा, 'old,' for Sk. वृद्ध. Here may be noted a large class of words from the Sk. root, स्था; as, ठां, 'a place,' for Sk. स्थान; ठाना, 'a police-station,' as if from a form, स्थानकः, etc.

a. But in some cases a Sanskrit cerebral is changed to a dental; as in the Hindí दबना, 'to be pressed down,' from Sk. डप्, etc.; but, H. डंक, Sk. दंश्, etc.

b. Through the change of ड to ड़, the cerebrals, and, through the cerebrals, the dentals, modulate into र. This is especially characteristic of the Eastern Hindí, which constantly substitutes र for ड़, as also for ल. Thus, पड़ना, 'to fall,' from Sk. पत्, becomes, in E. Hindí, परन; so also the regular form, लड़की, 'a girl,' from the root लट्, appears in the *Rámáyan* as लरकि. In तालाव, 'a tank,' for Sk. तडाग, the cerebral ड is changed to ल.

c. Sometimes ल is thus the substitute; as, H.H. चेला, E.H. चेरा, 'a servant, disciple,' for Sk. चेट, and Máṛ. खुटबो, 'to open,' for खुलना, where ल is for ट. In कुल्हारी, 'an axe,' for Sk. कुठार, ल्ह is the substitute for ठ. In the numerals, from eleven to eighteen, the द of दशन् regularly becomes ṛ, except

* Vid. Comparative Table of Hindí and Prakrit Numerals.

in सोलह, 'sixteen,' where ल is the substitute. But the dialects give also सोरह, after the analogy of the other numbers in question.

Changes of Nasals.

96. In High Hindí, the Sanskrit cerebral nasal is regularly changed to the dental nasal in all Tadbhava words, as, e.g., in गुन, 'virtue,' for गुण; पुन, 'merit,' for पुण्य; and universally in the infin. termination of verbs, wherever the laws of *sandhi* would require णा; as in करना, 'to do, make,' instead of करणा; मरना, 'to die,' for मरणा. But in the Himalayan and Rajputana dialects, Naipálí excepted, the reverse tendency is exhibited, the cerebral nasal being constantly preferred to the dental.

Changes of Semivowels.

97. य initial is regularly changed to ज, in all Tadbhavas; as in जुग, 'an age,' for युग. य is also hardened when doubled and final; as in सूरज, 'the sun,' for सूर्य्य. But in these and other words, even when thus pronounced, the original spelling is more commonly retained. र is changed to ल in सलिता, 'a river,' Sk. सरित्; as also in बाल, 'hair,' if from वृ, 'to cover.' But this is far less common than the reverse change of ल to र, which is very frequent throughout the Hindí country. व initial very frequently becomes ब; in Eastern Hindí this is an invariable rule.

Changes of Sibilants.

98. The sibilants are all prone to change. श is pronounced, throughout the Doáb and the East, as स; as, e.g., in दिसा, 'region,' for दिशा, etc., etc. ष very commonly becomes ख; as in मनुख, 'a man,' for मनुष्य; दोख, 'a fault,' for दोष, etc. But in writing, ष is generally retained, and in some districts, as in Máṛwáṛ, has usurped the character ख in all words whatever. ष becomes छ in छ, 'six,' and छठा, 'sixth,' for Sk. षष्, षष्ठ. स becomes च or छ in लालच, 'covetousness,' for लालसा. Similarly, we find छोभा, 'beauty,' for Sk. शोभा. The tendency of the sibilants to pass into the pure aspirate, of which the cognate languages afford so many examples, is abundantly illustrated in Hindí. Thus the श of दशन is changed to ह in all the numerals from eleven to eighteen inclusive, as also the स of सप्तति in the seventies throughout, except in सत्तर, 'seventy,' and उनासी, 'seventy-nine,' which is from another root. Thus the Sk. त्रयोदशन्, 'thirteen,' becomes तेरह; एकसप्तति, 'seventy-one,' becomes इकहत्तर, etc., etc. This change, as regards these numerals, is found in all dialects alike; but, except in some of the Rajputana and Himalayan dialects, it is rarely met with in other words. Certain pronominal and verbal forms of extensive or universal use, are, however, to be explained by reference to this principle. These will be noted in another place.

99. Very common is the substitution of the pure aspirate ह for any of the aspirated mutes, ख, घ, थ, ध, or भ. Examples are: मुंह, 'mouth,' 'face,' for मुख; मेंह, 'rain,' from मेघ; कहना, 'to speak,' from the root कथ्; दही, 'curdled milk,' for दधि: बहरा, 'deaf,' for बधिर. If initial, however, the letter commonly remains unchanged. I have only found instances of such a change of an initial aspirate in the case of भ. A notable example is found in the verb होना, 'to be,' from the Sk. भू. To this may be added हांडी, 'a pot,' and हुंडी, 'a cheque,' for Sk. भांड, भुंड. This change of these aspirated letters is more common in old Eastern Hindí than in modern literature; additional examples will be found in the chapter on the dialects. Treatment of Aspirated Mutes.

a. Naipálí sometimes substitutes the aspirated, where High Hindí has the smooth consonant; as in आफनु, 'own,' H.H. आपना; बालख, 'child,' H.H. बालक, But, on the other hand, more instances occur, where it prefers the smooth, where H.H. has the aspirated mute; as in दुद, 'milk,' for H.H. दूध; सिकाउनु, H.H. सिखाना, 'to teach'; तोरो, H.H. थोरा, 'little.'

100. Before leaving this subject of the changes affecting single letters we should note an old Prakrit habit of adding to various words the affix क. This Prakritic क is not to be confounded with the Sanskrit affix क, which is added to roots to The Prakritic affix क.

form adjectives and nouns of agency. Unlike that, this Prakrit क is wholly unmeaning.* Although, in modern Western Hindí, this affix has for the most part disappeared, yet its former existence is to be noted, as having influenced the form of a great number of modern words. In Eastern Hindí, Tulsí Dás, *cir.* 1600 A.D., frequently uses nouns, pronouns, and numerals, with the old Prakrit affix; and in the Maithilí and Mágadhí colloquials, it has maintained its place to this day in many words. We shall have frequent occasion hereafter to refer to this usage.

a. In Máṛwáṛí, besides this क, various other unmeaning letters or syllables are attached to words at the fancy of the speaker or writer. Of these the most common are ज, झ, र, स, सी, and सन. They appear to be added at pleasure to all parts of speech. From the *Khyáls* and *Raṇdhír aur Prem Mohaní*, I have taken the following examples: इसीर मर्जी होय, 'if such be (your) pleasure,' where इसोर is for ऐसी; ज़कम दिया है कंपनीस, 'the Company (i.e. the East India Company) has ordered'; पांवां आई आप कैस; 'I have come to your honour's feet'; षबरज लेणो जाय, (where षबरज is for Ar. خبر), 'go and get news.'

Inversion of Syllables.

101. The Hindús have an odd habit of inverting syllables, which should be remembered in the investigation of obscure words. Thus, in the west, people say मतबल for मतलब, 'object'; in the Doáb, नहान, 'bathing,' for इनान, Sk. स्नान, and बीराम for बीमार, 'sick'; in Tirhút and Gaṛhwál, पहुंपना, for पहुंचना, 'to arrive'; in Nepál, निसाफ़, for H.H. इनसाफ़, 'justice,' where also we have, by transposition of vowels, भोरस, 'trust,' for H.H. भरोसा.

* Even Sanskrit contains many words thus formed; as, e.g., घोटक, 'a horse'; कण्टक, 'a thorn'; मेलक, 'an assemblage,' etc. But in Prakrit the use of this affix was greatly extended. On this subject, which is of much etymological importance, the student may consult Vararuchi, Prakr. Prak. iv. (25); Lassen, Inst. Ling. Prac. pp. 288, 434, 461, 475.

OF CONJUNCT CONSONANTS.

102. This subject of the treatment of conjunct consonants in Hindí, is so extensive and complicated, that the limits of this work will not allow us more than to indicate general principles which have operated in the case. We shall enter into detail only so far as may be necessary briefly to illustrate these general laws, and refer the student for a full discussion of the subject to the Comparative Grammars of Beames and Hoernle.*

103. The general principles which regulate the treatment of conjunct consonants in Tadbhava words, may be briefly summed up under two heads, viz.: Rules for Changes in Conjuncts.

(1) Where the members of the conjunct are of equal or nearly equal strength, Hindí, in older words, rejects the first of the two consonants; in those of later formation, it separates them by a vowel.

(2) Where the members of the conjunct are of unequal strength, as a general rule, the stronger remains, and the weaker is dropped. In some cases, however, the remaining consonant, under the influence of the vanishing letter, is itself modified, and often transferred to another order.

a. Prior to the rejection of one element of a conjunct, there was, in the Prakrit period, an assimilation, in the case of strong conjuncts, of the first to the second consonant; and, in the case of mixed conjuncts, of the weaker to the stronger. Not a few examples of this earliest process are

---

* It is proper that I should here express my indebtedness to Mr. Beames for much in this chapter, more especially in the present section. Although the substance of this chapter was written prior to the appearance of Mr. Beames' work, I have derived from him many additional examples, and have modelled this section, with a view to greater brevity and clearness, somewhat after the plan of his chapter on 'Compound Consonants.'

preserved in Hindí; as, e.g., in पत्थर, 'a stone,' मक्खी, 'a fly,' and the old form, हत्थ, 'hand,' for the Sk. प्रस्तर, मक्षिका, and हस्त. Further illustrations will be found below.

b. When, under the application of these rules, a conjunct has been reduced to a simple consonant, a short vowel, originally preceding the conjunct, is usually lengthened in compensation. But when long and heavy syllables follow, and in a few other cases, this compensatory lengthening of the vowel is sometimes neglected.

c. For the interpretation of these general principles, it is to be remembered that the first four letters of the five '*vargs*' are called *strong*, and all the others *weak* letters.* It is further to be noted, that in the practical application of these principles, the strong letters are regarded as of equal strength, but the weak letters vary in strength among themselves.†

104. The following examples and remarks will illustrate the above rules. In the following strong conjuncts, the first consonant is rejected: मोती, 'a pearl,' for Sk. मौक्तिकं; दूध, 'milk,' Sk. दुग्ध; सात, 'seven,' Sk. सप्तन्. The vowel commonly remains short when an accented syllable has in Sanskrit followed the conjunct; as in उठना, 'rising,' from Sk. उत + स्था. Most strong conjuncts, in words written as Tatsamas, are by the common people among the modern Hindús, divided in pronunciation. Thus, शब्द, 'a word,' in the common speech, becomes सबद; तृप्त, 'satisfied,' becomes त्रिपत, and then तिरपत; कर्म, 'work,' करम, etc.

105. In the following conjuncts, the elements being of

---

* Vid. § 8.

† Beames arranges the weak consonants in the order of their strength, as follows, viz.: first, the nasals, then the sibilants, and, last of all, the semivowels. The nasals and the sibilants he regards as of equal strength. The semivowels he arranges in the following order, beginning with the strongest; viz., व (with the power of ब), य (with the power of ज), ल, र, व (softened to उ), य (softened to इ). Vid. *Comp. Gramm.* vol. i. p. 360.

unequal strength, the weaker is rejected, and a preceding vowel is lengthened or gunated: viz., अग्नि, 'fire,' H. आग; ऊर्ण, 'wool,' H. ऊन; गर्भिणी, 'pregnant,' H. गाभिन; ज्योतिष, 'astrology,' H. जोतिष; प्रावृष, 'the rains,' H. पावस; मूल्य, 'price,' H. मोल; स्नेह, H. नेह; स्त्री, 'a woman,' H. तिया. For मज़दूरी, 'wages,' 'work,' Pers. مزدوری, rustic Hindí has मजूरी.

a. र following प in a conjunct is very often separated from it by *a*; as in परछाईं, 'shade,' Sk. प्रतिच्छाया; प्रकाश, 'brightness,' H. परगास; प्रसाद्, 'favour,' H. परसाद्, etc.

b. The root ज्ञा, 'to know,' becomes जा, as in जानना, 'to know'; this is further weakened to य, in सियाना, 'wise,' and अयान, 'foolish,' for सज्ञान, अज्ञान.

106. A nasal initial in a conjunct with a mute usually vanishes, leaving Anusvár, and lengthening a preceding short vowel. This class of words is very numerous. Examples are: कांटा, 'a thorn,' Sk. कण्टक; चांद, 'the moon,' Sk. चन्द्र; तांबा, 'copper,' Sk. ताम्र, etc. Nasals in Conjuncts.

107. य, र, and व, in a conjunct with a dental, disappear, transferring the dental to their own organ. Thus the conjunct त्य becomes च in सच, 'true,' for Sk. सत्य, and मीच, 'death,' Sk. मृत्यु. द्य becomes ज in आज, 'to-day,' Sk. अद्य; ध्य becomes झ in सांझ, 'twilight,' Sk. सन्ध्या. र very often modifies the dental, if first, and more rarely, if second in the conjunct. Examples are: बाट, 'a road,' Sk. वर्तन; पाट, 'cloth,' Sk. पत्र. The vowel ऋ, in Hindí becoming रि and अर्, has the same effect; as in बूढ़ा, 'old,' for Sk वृद्धः. This assimilation, in the case of the labial, is much more rare. The chief examples are afforded by the numerals, in the combinations of द्वि, 'two'; as, बारह, 'twelve,' for Sk. द्वादशन्; बाईस, 'twenty-two,' Sk. द्वाविंशति, etc. Analogous is the derivation of आप, 'self,' from the Sk. आत्मन्. Semivowels in Conjuncts.

108. A sibilant, in a conjunct with a stronger letter, disappears, commonly aspirating the remaining consonant. Thus, Sibilants in Conjuncts.

we have हाथी, from Sk. हस्तिन्, 'an elephant'; पच्छिम, 'west,' Sk. पश्चिम; थन, 'an udder,' Sk. स्तन; सूखा, 'dry,' Sk. शुष्क; आठ, 'eight,' Sk. अष्टन्. In some cases the aspirate assumes a separate existence, and is even transferred to the beginning of a syllable; as in हड्डी, 'a bone,' Sk. अस्थि; हनान, 'bathing,' Sk. स्नान; पुहुप, 'a flower,' Sk. पुष्प. For a conjunct formed by क, त, or प preceding a sibilant, the regular substitute is छ. Thus, क्षय, 'destruction,' becomes छय; अक्षर, 'a letter,' अछर; मत्स्य, 'a fish,' मछ; ईप्सित, 'desired,' इच्छित,—unless, with Weber, we derive it from the Prakrit root, इष.

a. But, in conjunction with क, the sibilant often merely leaves an aspiration, without changing the *varg*; as, in Old Hindí, आखर, 'a letter,' for Sk. अक्षर; and मक्खी, or माखी, 'a fly,' for Sk. मक्षिका.

b. In a large class of words beginning with स्थ, chiefly derivatives of the root स्था, 'to stand,' the dental has been transferred to the cerebral *varg*. Such are, e.g., the words, ठाँ, 'a place'; ठाँणा, 'a police-station'; ठाढ़ा, 'erect'; Már. कठा, 'where,' etc., etc. With a weaker letter the sibilant remains; as in अवसि, 'necessary,' for Sk. अवश्य, etc.

109. While the foregoing exposition of the phonetic laws which have operated in the development of the Hindí, is necessarily but brief and incomplete, it is hoped that it may at least indicate the path of research to the student; and aid him in interpreting the various strange and irregular forms which one often encounters in Old Hindí books, and in the diverse local dialects of modern Hindí.

CHAPTER IV.

THE DIALECTS OF HINDÍ.

110. Hindí, as already remarked, is spoken and written in a great variety of dialects, which it is difficult to enumerate with precision. While some of these, as Braj and Kanaují, differ from each other but slightly, others, again, as those of Rajputana, in the West, and of the region about Benares and eastward, differ so widely that it may at least be regarded as an open question, whether we should not, with Hoernle, Grierson, and some others, regard them rather as distinct languages than as dialects. Without entering into the present discussion on this point, I have used the word "Hindí," in this Grammar, in the more customary sense, as including the speech of the whole region from the lower ranges of the Himalaya mountains, in the north, to the Narmadá river and the Vindhyá mountains, in the south; and from the Panjáb, Sindh, and Gujerát, in the west, to Bengál and Chutía Nágpur, in the east and south-east.

111. Within this region, the dialects of Hindí may be enumerated as follows, beginning in the west and proceeding eastward, namely: (1) The dialects of Rajputana: Máṛwáṛí, Mewáṛí, Mairwáṛí, Jaipurí, and Háṛotí; (2) The Himálayan dialects: Gaṛhwálí, Kumáoní, and Naipálí; (3) The dialects of the Doáb: Braj, and Kanaují; (4) The Púrbí or Eastern dialects: Avadhí, Riwáí, Bhojpurí, Mágadhí, and Maithilí; to which may be added, because of the literary and religious importance of the chief poem in the dialect, the Old Baiswáṛí of the *Rámáyan* of *Tulsí Dás*, and, finally, High Hindí, which is the basis of the Urdú or Hindustání. It is, of course, Enumeration of Dialects.

impossible to indicate the boundaries of these with absolute precision, as dialects are never limited by sharply defined lines; but, with this reservation, the regions to which these severally belong may be indicated as follows:

Limits of Dialects.

112. *The Máṛwáṛí is spoken from the extreme western* boundary of Hindí, as far eastward as the Aravallí Hills, through a region of which Jodhpur and Jayanagar may be taken as the centre. In the northern part of the Aravallí Hills, is spoken the Mairwáṛí; and to the south and east of these hills, about the head waters of the Banás and the Chambal, in the state of Mewáṛ or Udaipur, the Mewáṛí. Next come the dialects of East Rajputana, from the Aravallí Hills to the Betwa River; in the north, the Jaipurí, and in the south, in Kotáh, Bundí, and the states to the south-east, the Háṛotí.* On the north-east of these Rajputana dialects, throughout the upper Doáb, in the valley of the Ganges and Jamná, the Braj is spoken; and in the lower Doáb, to the east and south, the Kanaují, so called from the ancient city of Kanauj, near the centre of that region. Parallel with these dialects of the Doáb, in the Himalayas, are found the Gaṛhwálí, spoken from the Satlaj River to the Ganges; the Kumáoní, from the Ganges to the Gogarí River, and the Naipálí, from the Gogarí to the Sankhassí River on the extreme east. Returning to the plains, as we approach Allahabad from the west, we begin to meet a type of speech differing widely from that in the north and west. Northward is the Avadhí,† or dialect of Avadh (Oude), and to the south, the Riwáí, so called from the native state of that name—also called Baghelkhaṇḍí

* These dialects of Rajputana are sometimes still further subdivided. Thus, according to an enumeration adopted by the Government of India in a recent paper, to the north and west of the Máṛwáṛí, we have the Bikanírí; to the north and east of the Jaipurí, the Alwarí; to the south of the Háṛotí, the Ujjainí.

† Also called Kosalí and Baiswáṛí.

from the old name of that region (the land of the Baghels).* Bordering these on the east, and extending from the foot of the Himalayas to about the 22nd parallel of latitude, and to Chutiá Nágpur, the Son river, and the district of Muzaffarnagar in the east, the dialect is Bhojpurí. The Mágadhí is spoken in its purity in a small triangular area east of the Son and south of the Ganges, in the centre of which are the cities of Patná and Gayá. Maithilí occupies the region immediately east of Bhojpurí and north-east of Mágadhí, extending to the east as far as the districts of Purniá and Bhagalpúr, where, on the east, the Bangálí, and on the south-east, the Sonthálí, begin to be spoken. The Old Baiswáṛí of the *Rámayan* is closely related, as a more archaic type of speech, to the modern colloquials of Avadh and Riwá. All the dialects thus far mentioned, with the exception of the last, are the living colloquials of the Hindoo population in the several regions named.

113. There remains to be mentioned one dialect, the most modern of all, understood more or less through all the Hindí-speaking country, but in no place the language of the home, which has latterly been called, after the analogy of German, High Hindí.† Of the living Hindí colloquials, it stands in closest connection with the Braj and Kanaují, and is still more nearly related to the Urdú of the Muhammedan population, with which it agrees in declension, conjugation, etc.; differing chiefly in the exclusion, to a great degree, of the Arabic and Persian words and phrases which are so largely employed in Urdú. It has come into existence as the result High Hindí.

* These two, which differ but slightly, are grouped together by Grierson, under the name Baiswáṛí, from Baiswáṛ, the land of the Bais, a Rajpút tribe.

† In the former edition of this work, this was called 'standard Hindí;' but as this term is liable to occasion misapprehension as to the relation of this dialect to others, I have in the present edition conformed, as above, to an extending usage.

of the political influence of the English Government of India, and the missionary activity of the present century. It is the dialect in which the Government, and, for the most part, English and American missionaries, publish their Hindí books, and which is used in communication with the Hindí-speaking people. And yet, though understood more or less by a multitude of Hindí-speaking people, this High Hindí is nowhere the household speech of the Hindoos.* Still, under the stimulus of English influence, a considerable literature is already springing up in this dialect, and, if one might venture to predict, it seems probable that the language of the future in North India will be a form of High Hindí, less highly Arabized and Persianized than the Urdú, but yet containing less of the Sanskrit and Prakrit element than much of the Hindí of to-day.

Classification of Dialects.

114. The dialects enumerated may be classified under two general heads, as *Western* and *Eastern* Hindí. Under the

---

* The following description of the state of the case in North India, given by Mr. Grierson, B.C.S., before the Seventh International Congress of Orientalists, will be readily recognized as having in it much of truth, by all who have had any experience of life among the village populations of India: "The literary or Government language of any tract is widely different from the language actually spoken by the people. In some cases, this is only a question of dialect, but in others, the polite language learned by Europeans, and by natives who wish to converse with Europeans, is totally distinct, both in origin and construction, from that used by the same natives in their homes. . . . The fact is, and it is one that should be faced, that nowhere in Hindustan is the language of the village the same as the language of the court, and before a poor man can sue his neighbour in the court, he has to learn a foreign language, or to trust to interpreters, who fleece him at every step; and before a boy can learn the rule of three, he has to learn the foreign language in which it is taught. In some parts of Hindustan this difficulty exists in greater degrees than in others, but it is always more or less present."—Proceedings of the Asiatic Society of Bengal, No. iv. April, 1887, p. 132.

former head, are included all the Rajputana dialects, together with those of the Himalayas, Gaṛhwálí, Kumáoní, and Naipálí, and those of the valley of the Ganges and Jamná, Braj and Kanaují. To Eastern Hindí belong Avadhí, Riwáí, the Old Baiswáṛí of the *Rámáyan*, Bhojpurí, Mágadhí, and Maithilí. The dialects comprehended in each of these divisions present common points of agreement among themselves, and of difference from those of the other family, which, as will appear, abundantly justify this classification.

a. Hoernle sets apart the Himalayan dialects named, as also the Eastern Hindí dialects, as forming each a separate language. Without entering into the discussion, it may be remarked that the affinity between these Himalayan dialects and those of Rajputana is so close, that if the differences between them and Braj and Kanaují forbid us to classify them with the latter, as dialects of one language, similar reasons will compel us also to deny that Braj and Maṛwáṛí are dialects of one language,—an opinion to which Hoernle seems indeed to incline.*

But, as the name 'Hindí' is also denied by him and by Grierson to the Eastern dialects,† this will limit its application to the Braj and Kanaují. And yet, if I am rightly informed, the Braj literature throughout all this region is exposed for sale, and freely read by those generally who are able to read at all. As for Naipálí, in particular, it is so very like the contiguous Kumáoní and Gaṛhwálí, that its relation to Hindí must be regarded as the same as theirs, whatever that may be. And as to the claim of Naipálí to be regarded as Hindí, the writer may refer to the fact that meeting some years ago a company of Naipálese pilgrims near the source of the Ganges, he found that they perfectly understood him in

* See *Comp. Gramm.* p. xxxv, note.

† Grierson regards the Bhojpurí, Mágadhí, and Maithilí, as constituting a distinct language, to which he gives the name 'Bihárí.'

speaking simple High Hindí, such as is chiefly used by missionaries in their preaching. So also, the Gaṛhwálí coolies who were with me, conversed freely with these Naipalese in the local patois of the mountains. In like manner, it may be added, throughout Gaṛhwál, notwithstanding the comparatively infrequent intercourse of the natives with Europeans, I have found no difficulty in conversing with the villagers in a simple form of High Hindí.

How this question regarding the claim of the Himalayan dialects and those of the extreme east to be regarded as varieties of Hindí, should be decided, I leave to the judgment of the student, placing their phenomena before him in these pages.

Lexical Differences in Dialects.

115. The differences between the two classes of Hindí dialects, and, to a lesser extent, between different dialects in each class, are both *lexical* and *grammatical*. Totally different words are often used to express the most common ideas. Thus, 'to send,' in High Hindí, is **भेजना**; in Máṛwáṛí, **भेलवो**; in Baiswáṛí, **पठावन**. 'To call,' is, in High Hindí, **बुलाना**; in the *Rámáyan*, **बोलब**; in Riwáí, **गोहराउब**. In Riwáí, again, **रेंगब**, which in High Hindí, under the form **रेंगना**, has only the sense 'to creep,' regularly takes the place of the H.H. **चलना**, 'to go.' These differences are strikingly illustrated in the substantive verb. Thus, 'is,' H.H. **है**, in Máṛwáṛí is **छै**, and in Bhojpurí, **बा** or **बटे**. But the indication of these lexical differences belongs to a dictionary rather than to a grammar.

Grammatical Differences in Dialects.

116. The *grammatical* differences which pertain to the different dialects and types of Hindí, pertain to *pronunciation*, to *etymology*, and to *syntax*. In detail, they will be set forth under their respective heads hereafter. In this place, we have only to note the chief dialectic distinctions of a general character; and, first, those which mark, respectively, the two great families of the Eastern and Western Hindí.

117. The following peculiarities pertain to *pronunciation* in the Eastern dialects. As a general rule, any vowel or diphthong in any syllable before the penult, is shortened. This rule governs all the modifications which any word may undergo in processes of derivation or inflection.* The exceptions are as follows: Pronunciation in Eastern Dialects.

(1) Any long vowel in the antepenultimate but आ, when followed by अ, or a euphonic या or वा, remains long.

(2) The rule never takes effect in a causal root.

(3) In Northern Maithilí, these rules do not operate in the inflection of verbs.

(4) In the Bhojpurí present indicative, a vowel is not shortened except it be one syllable further back than the above rule requires.

118. In Eastern Hindí it must be noted, in the application of this rule, that we have the short vowels *ĕ*, *ŏ*, *ăi*, *ău*, which, with the exception of *ĕ*, are not known to exist in Western Hindí. Thus we hear बेटिया, *bĕṭiyá*, 'daughter;' परोसिया, *parŏsiyá*, 'neighbouring;' करतैं, *kartăin̲*, 'if they did,' etc. Eastern Short Vowels.

Rem 1. Both Hoernle† and Grierson ‡ make the above statement without the exception noted. But the existence of a short ĕ in the colloquial of the Dóab, and in the Hindí of the N.W. Himalayas, had already been noted in the 1st edition of this Grammar.§

Rem. 2. According to Hoernle, ‖ the use of these short vowels is restricted, except in the case of a few frequently used words, to the following cases:—

(1) In an antepenultimate syllable where they stand for a long *é*, *ó*, *ai*, *au*, shortened by the operation of the rule above given.

(2) Optionally, in the gen. postpositions *ké* and *kai*, also *kĕ* and *kăi*.

* This rule was first pointed out by Grierson: *Maithilí Gram.* pp. 77, 78; and by Hoernle: *Comp. Gram.* pp. 4, 5, et passim.

† *Comp. Gram.* pp. ix, 5.
‡ *Seven Grammars*, Pt. I. p. 10.
§ Vid. 1st ed. § 1, *b*.
‖ *Comp. Gram.* § 5, *b*.

(3) In the short obl. forms of pronouns in *h*; as in the relative, *jĕh*, *jĕhi*; the demonstrative, *ĕh*, etc., etc.*

(4) Also in the inflections of verbs, in the terminations *ĕs*, *ĕn*, and *ăin̲*; and in one form of the conjunctive participle; as *kahĕ kĕ*, where Western Hindí would have *kahi kai*.

Hiatus in E. Hindí.

119. In case of *concurrent vowels*, E.H. constantly retains the hiatus which W.H. removes by *sandhi*. Illustrations are, from the *Rámáyan*: करइ, 'he does,' for W.H. करे; भयउ, 'became,' for K. भयो; पिअ, 'husband,' for W.H. पिय; जिअत, 'living,' for जियत. But E.H. sometimes avoids the hiatus by the insertion of a consonant, though it shows an aversion to य, which W.H. constantly uses in such cases, and prefers ह instead; as in E.H. दिहल, 'gave,' for W.H. दिया, etc.

Consonants in E. and W. Hindí.

120. As regards *consonants*, Eastern Hindí exhibits a preference for dentals, where Western Hindí, following the Prakrit tendency, retains cerebrals. Illustrations are, from the *Rámáyan*: तरे, 'under,' from W.H. तले; दूबरि, 'thin,' 'lean,' for H.H. दुबला; and, from modern Eastern colloquials: घोर, 'horse,' for H.H. घोड़ा; तोरै, 'he breaks,' for W.H. तोड़े; परब, 'to fall,' for H.H. पड़ना. Reference has already been made to the aversion of E.H. to य; it may be added, that it never allows either य or व to stand as initial. On the other hand, the aversion of W.H. to ह, which is shown by the avoidance of its use in a hiatus, reaches an extreme in the dialects of Rajputana and the Himalayas, in which medial ह is very commonly dropped, and the concurrent vowels combined. Thus, H.H. कहना, 'to say,' E.H. कहब, in Máṛwáṛi becomes कैबो; चाहिये, 'ought,' becomes चैये; E.H. पहिल, 'first,' H.H. पहिला, becomes पैलो; साहिब, साब;† H.H. मिहनत, मीनत, etc. But it should be noted that in S. Rajputana, ह is very commonly substituted for स; as, e.g., in हमझ, 'understanding,' for समझ. Illustrations of the same aversion to ह,

* Cf. also this Grammar, 1st ed. § 1, *b*.

† For this *sandhi*, vid. § 88, (1).

from the Himalayan dialects, are: in Gaṛhwálí, चोलो, 'he will be,' instead of होलो, H.H. होगा, E.H. होब, etc.; and, in Kumáoní; यां, 'here,' and कां, 'where,' for E.H. and H.H. यहां, कहां; and कौणो, 'to say,' for H.H. कहना, E.H. कहब, etc.

a. Grierson mentions as also characteristic of Eastern, as contrasted with Western Hindí, the change of ल to न.* But this is not peculiar to the Eastern dialects; the same tendency is observable in Máṛwáṛí, where we have, e.g., नानत, 'a curse,' for लानत, Ar. لعنت; and नन्दन, for 'London;' and in Naipálí; as in नुन, H.H. लोन, 'salt;' also in the fut. 3rd plur. termination. -नन; as in देखनन, for देखलन, H.H. देखेंगे.

121. Before indicating *etymological* distinctions between Eastern and Western Hindí, it is necessary to advert to the different forms under which Hindí nouns and adjectives occur. These have been classified as *short*,—including (1) *weak*, and (2) *strong* forms,—*long*, and *redundant*.† Those are called 'weak' which present the shortest form of the word; they commonly end in a short vowel or a silent consonant. Those are called 'strong,' in which the final vowel, vocalized or silent, is lengthened. 'Long' forms are those in which a suffix, commonly या or वा, is added to the weak form; 'redundant' forms are those in which this suffix is duplicated. Thus, for 'horse,' the weak form is घोड़, the strong, घोड़ा; the long, घोड़वा; the redundant, घोड़ौवा, or, as in Av., घोड़ौना. Any noun in Eastern or Western Hindí may take either the long or the redundant form, but the redundant is vulgar, and even the long is rarely used in High Hindí. When used, it often gives to the noun a diminutive sense, and hence is sometimes used to express endearment; as, e.g., in बेटिया, from बेटी, 'daughter,' etc. A long vowel in the ultimate or penultimate syllable, is shortened before the long and redundant termina- Etymological Differences in Dialects; Nouns classified.

---

* *Seven Grammars*, Part I. p. 9.

† See Grierson: *Seven Grammars*, Part I. pp. 8, 9; and Hoernle: *Comp. Gramm.* §§ 195-201.

tions; as in गुलबवा, from गुलाब, 'a rose;' बतिया, from बात, 'a word,' etc., etc. But in Braj, at least, the final long vowel may sometimes remain. Thus we not only have पुटरिश्रा, 'a little bundle,' from पोटरी, but टट्टूश्रा, 'a pony,' long form of टट्टू.

122. Of these various forms of nouns and adjectives, Western Hindí shows a preference for the strong, and Eastern Hindí, for the weak forms.

Thus, where W.H. has घोड़ा, 'a horse,' E.H. prefers, though not exclusively, घोड़ or घोर; for W.H. नारी, 'a woman,' E.H. has नारि; for W.H. बड़ा, बड़ो, or बड़ौ, 'great,' E.H. has बड़ or बर. In E.H., where the strong form is used, the termination श्रा is preferred to श्रो or श्रौ. In the use of the long forms, while W.H. uses either those in या (ऐ), or वा (श्रौ),—preferably, the latter,—E.H., in accordance with the above law, prefers वा and श्रौ. But after *ī* or *ĭ* final, या is used as well as वा; as, from नारि, 'a woman,' E.H. नारिया or नारीवा, but W.H., preferably, नारिया. In the pronouns, where W.H. has a final श्रो in the termination of the strong forms, E.H. has ए; as in जे, for W.H. जो, etc. The long form of the pronouns—restricted in the west, for the most part, to the H.H. कौन, 'who?' for Br. को—is commonly employed in E.H. also in the relative pronoun, जौन, and the correlative, तौन, both of which are rare in the west.

Dialectic Variations in Inflection.

123. The following contrasts appear between Eastern and Western Hindí in regard to *inflection*. In W.H., nouns ending in a consonant are never inflected before the postpositions; but in some of the Eastern dialects, such nouns are inflected to ए *ĕ* or श्र; and verbal nouns in ल, to ला. Thus, while घर, 'house,' in W.H. is unchanged in the obl. sing., in E.H. it sometimes takes an obl. sing. inflection, becoming घरे or घरउ; and देहल, 'giving,' = H.H. देना, takes an obl. form, दिहला. The postpositions of declension are radically the same in the east and the west, with the important exception, that ने, distinguishing the case of the agent, is unknown in the Eastern dialects, the construction with which it is used being never employed.

a. Grierson adds, as another contrast, that W.H. "declines its nouns entirely with the aid of postpositions, while E.H. has in some dialects true inflectional forms for the instrumental and locative singular." This is qualified in a foot-note by the remark that "in some of the more vulgar forms of the Hindí dialects a locative in ए is found." But the exception might be extended to the instrumental case also, for which the Márwáṛí dialect regularly uses a true inflected form in ए, identical with the corresponding form in E.H.

124. The conjugational system in Eastern Hindí is distinguished, in general, from that of the West, by the retention of a larger proportion of inflected forms. Thus while High Hindí, for instance, has but three inflected tenses, Eastern Hindí, besides these, has also an inflected present imperfect, indefinite perfect, and past contingent imperfect. This comparatively archaic character of the Eastern dialects is further illustrated, especially in Maithilí, by the preservation of old Prakritic terminations; as, e.g., in the past contingent imperfect, which in Western Hindí has lost the terminations throughout, but retains them in Eastern Hindí, as in the Mt. 1st and 3rd sing., देखितहुँ, देखितथि, 'had I seen,' 'had he seen,' where H.H. has in both persons simply, देखता. This remark is further strikingly illustrated by the retention in verbal forms, as also in various pronominal themes, of the Prakritic क, which seems to have had so much influence in determining the forms of many modern Hindí Tadbhava words, but which, except occasionally in the rude dialects of Rajputana, has almost entirely disappeared from Western Hindí. Of these remarks the conjugational Tables will afford abundant illustration. Conjugation in E. and W. Hindí.

125. Again, as regards individual tenses, while Western Hindí presents three types of the future, characterised severally by the letters ह (Máṛ. स) ग, and ब (N. न), the Eastern dialects all use a future with the characteristic, ब (व), showing only occasional fragments of any other type. The Western dialects exhibit in the perf. participle and its tenses, forms in आ, ओ, or औ; but the Eastern dialects are distinguished by the formation of the corresponding parts of the verb by means of suffixes with ल. Peculiar also to the east, is an inflected present with ल as the characteristic letter, in Bhojpurí, Mágadhí, and Maithilí. Both Eastern and Western Hindí add the auxiliaries to the participle, conjugating fully only the latter. But many dialects of Eastern Hindí, in the present and past perfect often reverse this, adding the auxiliary to an inflected preterite, and then conjugating only this first member, and retaining the auxiliary unchanged. Other minor points of difference between Western and Eastern Hindí will be learned from the Tables of conjugation: the above are the most important.

Dialectic Differences in Syntax.

126. As regards *syntax*, the chief contrast between the two families of speech is found in the construction of the tenses of the perfect in transitive verbs. All the Western dialects, in such cases, use an indirect passive construction, placing that which in English idiom is the subject nominative, in a special case, the case of the agent, which is only used in this construction. In the Eastern Hindí dialects, this construction, as also the case appropriated to it, is wholly unknown.

127. The specific differences between the various dialects in each family will be indicated as they come up in the following pages. The following remarks of a general character, however, may well be made here.

Braj Peculiarities.

128. In the Braj, the inflectible आ final of High Hindí (for Pr. ओ, Sk. अः), in adjectives and verbs, commonly appears as औ; but in nouns, the Prakritic ओ has become आ. Often in verbs, and more rarely in nouns, ए final is *vriddhied* to ऐ. Anusvár is used much more freely than in High Hindí. Short *a* in close roots is very often lengthened; as, e.g., in राखनौं,

for रखना, 'to keep;' चालबौं, 'to walk,' for चलना; साँच, 'true,' for सच. The Kanaují is related closely to the Braj. Kanaují. Where the Braj, as above, has औ, the Kanaují retains the Prakrit ओ. ए final remains unaltered. Anusvár is used with great freedom.

129. The Márwáṛí and Mairwáṛí agree with the Kanaují in presenting ओ in adjectives, instead of the inflected आ; but extend this usage so as to include nouns, saying, e.g., घोड़ो, instead of घोड़ा, 'a horse,' etc. आ is preferred to a medial *a*, as in Braj; as in लागणो, 'to adhere,' for लगना; माटी, for मट्टी, 'earth,' etc. इ is very commonly preferred to अ, in an unaccented syllable before a verbal termination. I have obtained no written examples, but it is evident that the *sandhi* ऐ, in the cases given in § 120, must have arisen from अ + इ. Occasionally, य or व is inserted between the concurrent vowels; as in कवाबो, for कहाबो (कहाना); सायब, for साहिब, etc. In Márwáṛ, स very commonly becomes ह; as in हमझ, for H.H. समझ, 'understanding;' हाब, for साहिब, etc. These dialects, and, it is said, the Rajputana dialects generally, agree in that, unlike those of the Ganges valley, they constantly prefer the cerebral nasal, ण, to the dental न. Thus, the H.H. forms, अपना, 'own,' होना, 'to be,' are, in Márwáṛí, अपणो, होणो. Other changes peculiar to the Rajputana dialects are illustrated by the Máṛ. तगत, for Ar. تخت, 'a throne,' and बाछा, 'a king,' for Pers. بادشاه.

Rajputana Dialects.

130. Inasmuch as the Kumáoní, Gaṛhwálí, and Naipálí, so far as I know, possess little or no literature, our materials for the illustration of these dialects are but scanty. But it will be abundantly evident from the sequel that their affinities are very close—not with the contiguous dialects of the Ganges valley—but with those of Rajputana. The important qualification must be made regarding Naipálí, that although it possesses a case of the agent, like the Western dialects, it yet makes the verb, in the tenses of the perfect, to agree in gender and number with the subject, as in Eastern Hindí, and thus

The Himalayan Dialects.

occupies a position intermediate between the two families. As agreements of these Himalayan dialects with those of Rajputana, we may note specially the frequent preference of the cerebral to the dental nasal; as in G. अपणो, 'own,' for H.H. अपना; and बणायो, 'made,' for H.H. बनाया; and in infinitives generally; as in G. रोणो, 'to cry,' for H.H. रोना. A common aversion to ह is also to be observed, as in Ku. कौणो, 'to say,' for H.H. कहना, where Máṛ. has कैबो. The *sandhi* in such cases indicates a preference of उ to the Máṛ. इ, as union-vowel. Again, स, in both, often becomes ह; as, e.g., in G. हांखिला, 'a honey-comb,' H.H. सांखिला; and also, च becomes स; as in G. निस्तो, 'under,' H.H. नीचे. Many nouns and adjectives, in all these dialects, present the archaic termination, उ or ऊ, the last remainder of the Prakritic ओ, before its final total disappearance in H.H. nouns ending in the silent inherent *a*. The Himalayan dialects, as will appear from the tables of conjugation, are further contrasted with those of Rajputana, as with other forms of Western Hindí, by their great abbreviation, especially in verbal forms. Naipálí, however, as above remarked, has other features in common with the Eastern type of Hindi, and thus occupies an intermediate position. Illustrations are found in the absence of the Rajputana aversion to ह, and the preference of र् to ड़ and of न to ण; as in पक्रनु, 'to seize,' H.H. पकड़ना; and in नु, for the Máṛ. णो, in all infinitives.

Dialect of the *Rámáyan*. **131.** Among the Eastern dialects, the Old Baiswáṛí of the *Rámáyan* of Tulsi Dás deserves special attention, on account of the literary importance and religious influence of this poem. It should be observed, however, that Tulsí Dás has allowed himself the utmost freedom in drawing grammatical forms from various Hindí dialects, and even from the Prakrit and Sanskrit, as the exigencies of the metre or his own fancy might suggest. The student should, of course, carefully discriminate between such foreign elements, and those which are distinctive of that form of Hindí in which the poet wrote.

Although, e.g., the Braj. perf. part. in यौ, and the K. in ओ, are often found in the *Rámáyan*, as also the Bhoj. perf. in ल, neither of these are to be regarded as belonging to the Old Baiswáṛí, in which the poem is written.

a. All the peculiarities of Eastern Hindí which have been mentioned above, appear in the *Rámáyan*, and need no further illustration. As peculiarities of orthography, it may be noted that for ई, इय is sometimes written; as in जियव, for जीव, 'living creature.' Some words are written indifferently with आव, आउ, or औ; as, e.g., रावरे, राउरे, and रौरे, used as an honorific pronoun, 'your Excellency.' For अय, we sometimes find written, ऐ; as in ऐन, for अयन, 'a place.' Before affixes and suffixes, ए is very often substituted for अ or इ. Thus we have, बारेक, 'a child,' for H.H. बालक; भयेउ, 'was,' 'became,' for भयउ; कहेहु, 'say,' for कहहु, etc., etc. This ए, thus used, is prosodially common, but oftener short than long. The semi-vowels य and व are often softened to इ and उ, producing a hiatus which is suffered to remain; as in दुआरे, 'at the door,' for द्वारे, etc. Many nouns which in High Hindí terminate in the silent *a*, in the *Rámáyan* end in उ, often lengthened, *metr. grat.*, to ऊ. Examples are numerous: as, सरु, 'an arrow;' सिरु, 'the head;' मुहु, 'the face;' for the H.H. सर, सिर, मुंह.

Rem. This final *u* is the characteristic vowel of the final diphthong *o* of the Prakrit nom. sing. This termination represents a stage of the language immediately preceding the modern forms, in which, the *u* being no longer sounded, it is no longer written, so that all words of this class are reduced to the form of nouns ending in a silent *a*.

b. Quite characteristic is the very frequent substitution of the simple aspirate ह for an aspirated mute.* Thus we find, लाह, 'gain,' for लाभ; कोह, 'anger,' for क्रोध; नाह, 'lord,' for नाथ, etc., etc. Instances of this change occur in every dialect, but it is especially common in the *Rámáyan*.

---

* Vid. § 99.

c. The unmeaning Prakritic suffix, क, is of frequent occurrence, as it is also in modern Maithilí.* The following instances may be noted: of nouns; दारिका, 'a wife,' मुठिका, 'the fist,' नौका, 'a ship;' for दारा, मुट्ठो, and नौ; of numerals; चारिक, 'four,' पचासक, 'fifty,' कोटिक, 'a crore;' of pronominals, etc.; कितिक, 'how much,' कछुक, 'some,' बहुतक and बहुतेक, 'much,' कबहुंक, 'ever.'

132. The modern Eastern colloquials call for no further remark in this place, further than the observation that among them the Northern Maithilí presents the most archaic type, corresponding, in this respect, to the remote dialects of Rajputana in Western Hindí.

* Vid. § 124, and the Maithilí Conjugation in the Tables.

CHAPTER V.

OF SUBSTANTIVES (संज्ञा).

Gender.

133. Hindí substantives are affected by gender, number, and case. We have first to consider the subject of gender. Only two genders, masculine (पुंलिंग) and feminine (स्त्रीलिंग), are recognized. The neuter of Sanskrit, (which has been retained in the Maráṭhí,) the Hindí, as well as the closely related Panjábí, has lost, so that the gender of many nouns is of necessity ambiguous, being apparently determined solely by popular usage.

134. As a general principle, Sanskrit nouns, introduced into Hindí, if masculine or feminine, retain their original gender; or if neuter, become masculine in Hindí. But there are many exceptions to this principle. Hindí follows Sanskrit Gender.

a. Among the most common exceptions may be noted the following words, which, although masculine in Sanskrit, have become feminine in Hindí: viz., आग (Sk. अग्नि), 'fire;' आंच (Sk. अर्चि), 'flame;' घाम (Sk. घर्म्म), 'heat of the sun;' झंकार, 'a tinkling;' धूप, 'incense;' बास (Sk. वास), 'odour.' बयार, 'a strong wind,' if derived, as some say, from the Sk. masculine, वायु, would furnish another illustration; but the original identity of the two words is not certain.

b. The following Sanskrit masc. nouns are in Hindí commonly reckoned fem., though occasionally masc.: viz., जय or जै, 'victory;' तान, 'a tune;' दाह, 'burning,' and from the same Sanskrit root, डाह, 'envy,' 'malice.' आंख, 'the eye,' वस्तु, 'a thing,' and गात, 'the body,' from the Sk. neuters, अर्चि, वस्तु, and गात्र, have become feminine. So also देह, 'the body,' and पुस्तक, 'a book,' in Sanskrit, masc. or neut., are feminine in Hindí. मृत्यु, 'death,' masc. or fem. in Sanskrit, in Hindí is always feminine, as also is the derived Tadbhava, मीच.

c. In some cases, the reason of the change of gender may probably be found in the influence of co-existing Urdú equivalents. Thus, e.g., the words बयार, बस्तु, पुस्तक, may have become feminine through the influence of the Urdú هوا, چیز, and كتاب. In like manner देह often retains the masculine gender, possibly under influence of not only the Sanskrit original, but also the masc. Urdú بدن. In the case of some Tadbhavas, the words may possibly not be, in fact, descended directly from the Sanskrit, but from similar Prakrit words, which have not been preserved in literature.

135. Although, as thus appears, the gender of a Hindí word often seems to be quite arbitrary, yet there are certain practical rules by which the gender of most nouns may be known. These rules respect, either the *signification* of nouns, or their *terminations*.

Nouns Masc. by Signification.

136. Nouns of the following significations are *masculine*:—

(1) All names of males.

(2) Names of large, or coarse and roughly made objects, as contrasted with small, or more finely made objects of the same kind: as, गाड़ा *gáṛá*, 'a cart,' in contrast with गाड़ी *gáṛí*, 'a carriage,' fem.; रस्सा *rassá*, 'a heavy rope;' पोथा *pothá*, 'a tome;' in contrast, respectively, with रस्सी *rassí*, 'a small rope,' and पोथी *pothí*, 'a book.'

(3) Names of metals, alloys, precious stones, and rocks generally: as, सोना *soná*, 'gold;' रूपा *rúpá*, 'silver;' जस्ता *jastá*, 'pewter;' हीरा *hírá*, 'a diamond;' कंकर *kaṇkar*, 'nodular limestone.'

Exc. The following are feminine: viz., चांदी *chándí*, 'silver;' and compounds in which मृत्तिका or मक्खी (मक्षिका) is the last member; as, पांडुमृत्तिका *páṇḍumṛittiká*, 'opal;' सोनामक्खी *sonámakkhí*, 'goldstone.'

(4) Names of the year, of the months, of the days of the week, and of the astrological *karaṇs*: * as, संवत *samvat*, 'a year;' बुध *budh*, 'Wednesday.'

(5) Names of mountains and seas, whether common or proper: as, पहाड़ *pahár*, 'a mountain;' सागर *ságar*, 'the ocean;' गिरि *giri*, 'a mountain;' विंध्य *vindhya*, 'the Vindhya mountains.'

(6) Names of the heavenly bodies: as, सूर्य (pronounced *súraj*), रवि *ravi*, etc., 'the sun;' शुक्र *shukr*, 'the planet Venus;' केतु *ketu*, 'a comet.'

(7) Most words denoting affections of the mind: as, प्रेम *prem*, 'love;' कोप *kop*, 'anger;' लोभ *lobh*, 'avarice.'

Exc. All Sanskrit nouns of this class in आ *á* final are feminine: as, इच्छा *ichchhá*, 'desire;' also the three following: viz., अड़ंच *araiṉch*, 'enmity;' क्रुध *krudh*, and occasionally, क्रोध *krodh*, 'anger.'

(8) All nouns denoting agency or relationship. These include the following:—

a. Many nouns in ता *tá*, from Sanskrit bases in तृ *tṛi*: as, दाता *dátá*, 'a giver;' योद्धा *yoddhá*, 'a warrior,' from युध् *yudh*, 'to fight;' where the final ता *tá*, for the sake of euphony, has been changed to धा *dhá*.

b. Some nouns in ई *í*, from Sanskrit bases in इन् *in*: as, कारी *kárí*, 'a doer,' and its compounds.

c. A large class of Sanskrit nouns in क *ka*: as, उपदेशक *upadeshak*, 'an instructor;' रचक *rachak*, 'a maker.'

---

* The Paṇḍits reckon eleven *karaṇs*, seven moveable, and four fixed, of which two equal a lunar day (*tithi*).

d. Another large class of Sanskrit nouns in न *na* (ण *ṇa*), especially common in poetry, as the last member of compound words: as, हरण *haraṇ*, 'a remover;' दुखभंजन *dukhabhañjan*, 'a destroyer of grief;' पतितपावन *patitapáwan*, 'purifier of the guilty.'

e. A large class of compounds, in which the last member is a Sanskrit root, either unchanged, or affected with *guṇ*: as, रजनीचर *rajníchar*, 'a demon,' lit. 'night-walker;' धरनीधर *dharnídhar*, 'supporter of the earth;' पापहर *pápahar*, 'remover of sin.'

f. A numerous class of Tadbhava substantives in या *yá* (इया, ईया, and ऐया): as, गवैया *gawaiyá*, 'a singer;' लेवैया *lewaiyá*, 'a taker;' ढंढोरिया *ḍhanḍhoriyá*, 'a crier.'

Nouns Fem. by Signification.

137. The following are *feminine*; viz.:—

(1) All names of females.

(2) Names of the lunar days: as, दूज *dúj*, 'the second;' अष्टमी *ashṭamí*, 'the eighth;' अमावस *amávas*, 'the day of new moon.'

(3) Most names of rivers: as, गंगा *gangá*, 'the Ganges;' लवना *lavaná*, 'a river in Tirhut.'

Exc. सोन *son*, 'the Sone,' सिंधु *sindhu*, 'the Indus,' and ब्रह्मपुत्र, 'the Brahmaputra,' are masculine.

138. As to the gender of trees, plants and flowers, no general rule can be given, further than this, that the majority of such names, especially of large trees, are masculine. The many various names of the lotus, as *jalaj*, *saroruh*, *kamal*, etc., are all masculine. But the names of a large number of plants and fruits are feminine. As the most of these are rarely used, it is not necessary to enter into further detail here.

139. It would not be easy to assign a reason for these rules in every case. In some instances, doubtless, the gender of the prevailing common term has determined the gender of the individuals included under it.

Thus, names of mountains are probably masc., because the generic terms, *parbat, giri*, etc., signifying 'mountain,' are masc. So, probably, names of metals, stones, etc., are masc., because the common terms, *dhátu*, 'a metal,' *patthar, páshán*, etc., 'a stone,' *ratn*, 'a jewel,' are masc. In the case of the exceptions, *chándí*, and the compounds of *mṛittiká* and *makshiká*, the fem. terminations, *á* and *í*, have occasioned the deviation from the rule. So, also, the days of the week are reckoned masc., because the words, *din, divas*, etc., 'a solar day,' are masc.; but the names of the days of the month are fem., as following the gender of *tithi*, 'a lunar day.' Still, the ultimate reason for these rules must be found in the imagination of the people, which assigned the gender of inanimate objects, according as masculine or feminine attributes were fancied to be predominant in them.

140. The following rules have respect to the *terminations* of nouns. **Nouns Masc. by Termination.**

Nouns having the following terminations are *masculine*; viz.:—

(1) Most Tadbhava nouns in आ *á* or आं *án* final: as, घड़ा *ghaṛá*, 'an earthen jar;' डेरा *ḍerá*, 'a tent;' झोला *jholá*, 'a wallet;' धूआं *dhúán*, 'smoke.'

Exc. Diminutives ending in इया are feminine: as, e.g., थैलिया *thailiyá*, 'a small bag;' चिड़िया *chiṛiyá*, 'a small bird;' फुड़िया *phuṛiyá*, 'a boil.' The following are also feminine: viz., गूआ *gúá*, 'betel nut;' झींगा *jhíngá*, 'a shrimp;' टोआ *ṭoá*, 'the act of feeling;' बिरियां *biriyán*, 'time.' ठां *ṭhán*, 'a place,' is masc. or fem.

N.B. Tadbhava masc. nouns in *á* may be recognized as such, by their uniform inflection of *á* to *e* in the oblique cases of the singular.

(2) Most nouns in उ *u* or ऊ *ú*, in their diphthongs, ओ *o* or औ *au*, or in the cognate semivowel व *v*, whether with or without Anusvár: as, मधु *madhu*, 'honey;' कलेऊ *kaleú*, 'a luncheon;' चढ़ाओ *chaṛháo*, 'an ascent;' मह्यौ *mahyau*, 'buttermilk;' भाव *bháv*, 'an emotion;' गांव *gánw*, 'a village.'

The following lists comprise all common exceptions.

a. Nouns fem. in उ *u.*

अचक्षु *achakshu*, 'spectacles.'
आयु *áyu*, 'age.'
इक्षु *ikshu*, 'sugarcane.'
चंचु *chanchu*, 'the beak of a bird.'
जंबु *jambu*,* 'the rose-apple.'
तर्कु *tarku*,* 'a spindle.'
बस्तु *bastu*,* 'a thing.'
मृत्यु *mrityu*,* 'death.'
रेणु *renu*, 'sand.'

b. Nouns fem. in ऊ *ú*, ऊं *ún.*

आफू *áphú*, 'opium.'
उलू or ऊलू *ulú* or *úlú*, 'a kind of grass.'
गू *gú*, 'excrement.'
चमाऊ *chamáú*, 'shoes fixed to pattens.'
चमू *chamú*, 'an army.'
चंपू *champú*, 'a work in alternate prose and verse.'
जागू *jágú*, 'a place.'
जूं *jún*, 'a louse.'
दारू *dárú*, 'ardent spirits.'
बालू or बारू *bálú* or *bárú*, 'sand.'
भू *bhú*, 'the earth.'
रेहू पेहू *rehú pehú*, 'abundance.'
लावू *lávú*, 'a pumpkin.'
लू *lú*, 'the hot wind.'
सारू *sárú*, 'a starling.'

आंसू, 'a tear,' is both masculine and feminine. In the *Shákuntalá* it is masculine.

c. Nouns fem. in ओ *o*, ओं *on.*

छाओं *chháon*, 'shade.'
जोखों *jokhon*, 'risk.'
बाओ *báo*, 'wind.'
भों *bhon*,† 'the eyebrow.'
सलनो *salno*, 'the full moon in Sáwan.'
सरसों *sarson*, 'a kind of mustard.'
सों *son*, 'an oath.'

d. Nouns fem. in औ *au*, औं *aun.*

गौं *gaun*,‡ 'opportunity.'
दौं *daun*, 'flame.'
पौ *pau*, 'the ace in dice.'
लौ *lau*, 'the flame of a candle.'

e. The following in व *v*, are feminine: viz., नेव *nev*, 'a foundation;' टेव *ṭev*, 'habit, custom;' राव चाव *ráv cháv*, 'merriment.'

---

* Also, rarely, masculine. † Also *bhaun* and *bhaunh*.
‡ Occasionally masc.

f. The following are of either gender: viz., खराऊं *kharáún*,* 'wooden sandals;' ठाओं *tháon*, 'a place;' सहाऊ *saháú*, 'help.'

Rem. Many words are written indifferently with one or another of these cognate letters: as, e.g., बाओ or बाव; भाव or भाऊ; सौं or सूं; भौं or भौं, etc.; but as this does not affect their gender, it has not been thought necessary to repeat them under each list.

(3) Abstract nouns in त्व *tva* and य *ya* final are all masculine: as, ईश्वरत्व *íshvaratva*, 'godhead,' from ईश्वर *íshvar*, 'God;' राज्य *rájya*, 'a kingdom,' from the base राजन् *rájan*.

a. These are all Tatsamas and are all derived from concrete nouns. When, in any case, a Tadbhava form exists, derived from such a Tatsama, its gender is commonly determined by that of the Tatsama, according to § 134; as, e.g., *ráj*, for *rájya*, masc.

(4). Nouns formed with the suffixes पन *pan*, पना *pana*, or पा *pá*, = English, '-hood,' '-ness;' also, आउ or आव, and आन, are all masc.: as, लड़कपन *larakpan*, 'childhood;' बुढ़ापा *burhápá*, 'old age;' मूरखपन *múrakhpan*, 'foolishness;' ऊंचाव or ऊंचाउ, 'height;' लम्बान, 'length.'

Rem. 1. A few of these are sometimes used as feminines; probably as following the analogy of most abstract nouns. Also, the anomalous form लुच्चपनी *luchchpani* is fem.

Rem. 2. These terminations are all corruptions of the Sk. suffix त्व (Ved. त्वन्), used to form neuter nouns; whence, like the Tatsama forms in उ, they become masculine in Hindí.

(5) Nouns formed with the suffix ज *ja*, 'born,' are masculine: as, जलज *jalaj*, 'a lotus,' from जल *jal*, 'water,' lit., 'the water-born;' उखमज *ukhamaj*, for उष्मज *ushmaja*, from उष्मन् *ushman*, 'heat,' lit., 'heat-born,' a general term, comprehending gnats, mosquitoes, and all other insects of that class.

---

* In the E. always fem.

(6) Nouns in न *n* (ण *ṇ*) are both masc. and fem.; but the majority are masc. Among masculines in न *n* may be particularly noted the following; viz.:—

a. All nouns of agency: as, दहन *dahan*, 'a consumer;' गंजन *gañjan*, 'a destroyer,' etc.

b. A large class of Tatsamas (Sanskrit neuters): as, अयन *ayan*, 'a place;' दान *dán*, 'a gift,' 'alms;' दर्पण *darpaṇ*, 'a mirror;' ज्ञान (pronounced *gyán*), 'knowledge.'

c. A few abstract nouns from Sanskrit nouns in *n* final in a conjunct: as, यत्न *yatn*, commonly pronounced, and often written, as a Tadbhava, जतन *jatan*, 'labor;' स्वप्न *svapn*, 'sleep.'

d. Add to these a large class of verbal nouns in न *n* (Tadbhavas): as, चलन *chalan*, 'going,' 'walk;' करन *karan*, 'action,' 'deed;' मारन *máran*, 'slaughter.'

Exc. The following list comprehends most common feminine nouns in न *n*:—

अदवान *adván*, 'braces for tightening a bedstead.'

आनबान *ánván*, 'spirit,' 'proper pride.'

आवनआवन *ávanávan*, 'tidings of arrival.'

उतरन *utran*, 'fragments,' 'cast-off clothes.'

ऊन *ún*, 'wool.'

कान *kán*, 'shame.'

केन *kain*, 'a bamboo twig.'

खिरकिन *khirkin*, 'a window.'

घिन *ghin*, 'disgust.'

छान *chhán*, 'a bamboo frame for a thatch.'

धरन *dharan*, 'a beam,' 'accent.'

धुन *dhun*, 'propensity,' 'ardor.'

फूटन *phúṭan*, 'a quarrel.'

बकायन *bakáyan*, 'the name of a tree.'

रहन *rahan*, 'method.'

रैन *rain*, 'night.'

सुटकुन *suṭkun*, 'a rod.'

सूंघन *súnghan*, 'act of smelling.'

सूथन *súthan*, 'drawers.'

सैन *sain*, 'a hint,' 'a wink.'

हुन *hun*, 'name of a coin.'

To which may be added all feminines in इन, which fall under the specifications found in §§ 145, *a.*, 147, 148, 150.

141. Nouns which have the following terminations are *feminine*; viz. :— Nouns Fem. by Termination.

(1) Pure Sanskrit nouns in आ *á* final. Under this head, we may note especially:

a. Nouns in आ *á* and ना *ná* (णा *ṇá*), from roots either unaltered or affected with *guṇ*: as, from the root इच्छ्, इच्छा *ichchhá*, 'desire;' from तृष्, तृष्णा *triṣhṇá*, 'thirst;' from लिख्, लेखा *lekhá*, 'a line.'

b. Abstracts in ता *tá*, derived from nouns and adjectives: as, from नम्र, 'courteous,' नम्रता *namratá*, 'courtesy;' प्रभु, 'lord,' प्रभुता, *prabhutá*, 'lordship.' These are very numerous.

Exc. A few Tatsama nouns in आ *á*, from bases in अन् *an*, are masculine, according to § 134. The principal of these are: अणिमा *aṇimá*, 'the faculty of becoming invisible;' मूर्द्धा *múrddhá*, 'the head;' यक्ष्मा *yakṣhmá*, 'pulmonary consumption;' श्लेष्मा *shleṣhmá*, 'the phlegmatic humor.'

Rem. But the following, from bases in अन् *an*, have become fem. in Hindí: viz., प्लीहा *plíhá*, 'the spleen;' महिमा *mahimá*, 'majesty.' तारा *tárá*, 'a star,' is sometimes masc. and sometimes fem.

(2) Many nouns in इ *i* final are feminine.

a. Under this head are to be noted, especially, all abstract nouns in ति *ti* and नि *ni*: as, मति *mati*, 'the mind:' संगति *saṅgati*, 'intercourse;' ग्लानि *gláni*, 'weariness.' Under this class come also such nouns as वृद्धि *vriddhi*, 'increase;' बुद्धि *buddhi*, 'wisdom;' where the final affix ति *ti* has become धि *dhi* by *sandhi*.

Exc. But the following nouns in इ *i* are masc.; viz. :—

a. Names of animals: as, कपि *kapi*, 'a monkey;' कृमि *krimi*, 'a worm.'

b. All compounds with धि *dhi*: as, परिधि *paridhi*, 'circumference;' निधि *nidhi*, 'a treasure;' वारिधि *váridhi*, 'the ocean.'

c. To these add all nouns in the following list, viz.:

अतिथि *atithi*, 'a guest.'
अक्षि *akshi*, 'the eye.'
अग्नि *agni*, 'fire.'
अणि *aṇi*, 'the edge of a weapon.'
अर्चि *archi*, 'a flame.'
असि *asi*, 'a sword.'
अस्थि *asthi*, 'a bone.'
आराति *áráti*, 'an enemy.'
दधि *dadhí*, 'curd.'
ध्वनि *dhvani*, 'sound.'

पाणि *páṇi*,* 'the hand.'
मणि *maṇi*,* 'a jewel.'
यष्टि *yashṭi*, 'a stick.'
राशि *ráshi*, 'a heap,' quantity.'
वह्नि *vahni*, 'fire.'
वारि *vári* or बारि *bári*, 'water.'
व्रीहि *vríhi*, 'rice.'
शालि *sháli*, 'rice.'
सचि *sachi*, 'intimacy.'
सुरभि *surabhi*, 'nutmeg.'

(3) Most nouns in ई *í* final are feminine: as, रोटी *roṭí*, 'bread;' बिन्ती *bintí*, 'supplication;' गाली *gálí*, 'abuse.'

Exc. Except those included under § 136, (8) *b*, and the following;

अमी *amí*, 'nectar.'
अरी *arí*, 'an enemy.'
घी *ghí*, 'clarified butter.'
जी *jí*, 'life,' 'soul.'

दही *dahí*, 'curdled milk.'
पानी *pání*, 'water.'
मोती *motí*, 'a pearl.'
हाथी *háthí*, 'an elephant.'

Rem. These exceptions can all be explained as corruptions of Sanskrit masc. or neut. nouns. Thus, अमी and घी are corruptions of अमृतं and घृतं; अरी and दही, of अरि (अरिकः) and दधि (दधिकं); जी and पानी, of जीवं and पानीयं; मोती, of मौक्तिकं. They thus all come under the general principle laid down at the beginning of this chapter (§ 134).

(4) All nouns in हट *haṭ*, वट *waṭ*, or वत *wat*, are feminine: as, चनचनाहट *chanchanáhaṭ*, 'a throbbing;' बुलाहट *bulaháṭ*, 'a calling;' बनावट *banáwaṭ*, 'a fabrication;' सगावत *sagáwat*, 'relationship.'

* Sometimes also fem.

Rem. 1. It may be observed (1) that these nouns in *haṭ* are all derived from verbal roots in *á* final, and are, for the most part, alliterative and imitative words: and (2) that the व and the ह are in some dialects frequently dropped.

Rem. 2. The original of these terminations is the Sanskrit fem. noun, वृत्ति, 'state,' 'condition;' which has determined the gender of these derivatives.

N.B. It is to be observed, in the application of the above rules, that each rule is to be regarded as limited by all that has gone before, even though words thus excepted be not expressly mentioned. Thus, *e.g.*, *dhobí*, 'a washerman,' is masc., though not explicitly excepted from § 141 (3), because it is already included under § 136 (8) *b*.

142. The above rules have especial reference to those words of Sanskrit origin, which make up the chief part of the Hindí language. With regard to the gender of such Arabic and Persian words as occasionally appear in Hindí, the following principles will enable the student, in most cases, to determine their gender. Gender in Arabic and Persian Words.

(1) Most Arabic and Persian words in आ *á* or ह *h* (*Ar.* ا or ة, ح), are masc.: as, दरया *daryá* (دریا), 'a river;' खानः *khánaḥ* (خانه), 'a room;' गुनाह *gunáh* (گناه), 'sin.'

Exc. The following common words are fem.: viz., खता *khatá* (خطا), 'a fault;' तरह *tarah* (طرح), 'manner;' दवा *dawá* (دوا), 'medicine;' दुआ *duá* (دعا), 'a prayer;' दुनया *dunyá* (دنیا), 'the world;' बला *balá* (بلا), 'a calamity;' रूह *rúh* (روح), 'spirit;' सलाह *saláh* (صلاح), 'counsel;' सुबह (صبح), 'morning.'

(2) A large class of Arabic trisyllables, in which त *ta* is the first syllable, and उ *u*, the vowel of the last syllable, and which have the medial radical doubled, or the vowel preceding it in the second syllable lengthened, are masc.: as, तअल्लुक *taalluq* (تعلق), 'connexion;' तलावत *taláwat* (تلاوت), 'reading.' The word तवज्जुह

tawajjuh (توجہ), is an exception. But words of this form, though common in Urdú, are quite rare in Hindí.

(3) Most Arabic and Persian words in त *t* (ت) and श *sh* (ش) are fem.: as, हुकूमत *hukúmat* (حکومت), 'government;' नालिश *nálish* (نالش) 'a complaint.'

Exc. The most common exceptions to the above rule are the following: viz., गोश्त *gosht* (گوشت), 'meat;' तख़्त *takht*, Máṛ. तगत (تخت), 'a throne;' दरख़्त *darakht* (درخت), often mispronounced *darakhat*, and even *darkhat*, 'a tree;' दस्त *dast* (دست), 'a hand;' दोस्त *dost* (دوست), 'a friend;' नक़्श *naksh* (نقش), 'a picture,' 'a print;' बुत *but* (بت), 'an idol;' वक़्त *wakt* (وقت), often mispronounced *wakat*, and even *wakht*, 'time;' शर्बत *sharbat* (شربت), 'a drink.'

(4) Arabic dissyllables (infinitives) with त *ta* (ت) for the first syllable, and ई *í* as the vowel of the last syllable, are generally fem.: as, तद्बीर *tadbír* (تدبیر), 'an expedient;' तज्वीज़ *tajwíj* (تجویز), 'a plan.' तावीज़ *táwíj* (تعویذ), 'an amulet,' is masc., but will scarcely be met with in Hindí, except, possibly, in the extreme west.

143. Most compound words follow the gender of the last word: as, ईश्वरेच्छा *íshwarechchhá*, fem., 'the will of God;' गोपीनाथ *gopínáth*, masc., 'lord of the milk-maids.'

Exc. But the following Tadbhava copulatives, most frequently take the gender of the first word: viz., चालचलन, चालव्यवहार, fem., 'walk,' 'behaviour.'

144. In the Naipálí Gospel, many nouns which, according to the above rules, are feminine, are masculine. This is especially to be noted as regards a large number of Tatsama nouns in आ. Examples are: कृपा, 'kindness;' आज्ञा, 'command;' इच्छा, 'desire;' etc., etc.; all which, although by the above rules feminine, are masculine in the Naipálí Gospel.

Formation of Feminine Nouns.

145. Tadbhava masc. nouns in आ *á* final * usually form their feminines by the substitution of ई *í* for आ *á*.† Thus घोड़ा *ghoṛa*, 'a horse,' makes घोड़ी *ghoṛí*, 'a mare;' बेटा *beṭá*, 'a son,' बेटी *beṭí*, 'a daughter.'

a. A few such nouns, chiefly names of occupations or trades, make the fem. in इन *in*; as, e.g., कसेरा *kaserá*, 'a brazier,' fem. कसेरिन *kaserin*; दूल्हा *dúlhá*, 'a bridegroom,' fem. दुल्हिन *dulhin*, 'a bride.' But ठठेरा *ṭhaṭherá*, 'a brazier,' makes the fem. ठठेरी *ṭhaṭherí*; and भटियारा *bhaṭiyárá*, 'an innkeeper,' makes its fem. भटियारी *bhaṭiyárí* or भटियारिन *bhaṭiyárin*.

146. Many nouns ending in a consonant, both Tatsamas and Tadbhavas, also form their feminine by adding the termination ई *í*. Examples are, of Tatsamas:—देवी *deví*, 'a goddess,' from देव *dev*; पुत्री *putrí*, 'a daughter,' from पुत्र *putra*; ब्राह्मणी *bráhmaṇí*, 'a Bráhman woman,' etc.: of Tadbhavas:—भेड़ी *bheṛí*, 'a ewe,' from भेड़ *bheṛ*; बंदरी *bandarí*, 'a female monkey,' from बंदर *bandar*, etc.

147. Masc. nouns in ई *í* commonly form their feminine by adding न *n*, the final vowel being previously shortened; as, धोबी *dhobí*, 'a washerman,' fem., धोबिन; माली *málí*, 'a gardener,' fem., मालिन *málin*; नाई *náí*, 'a barber,' fem., नाइन *náin*. Nouns of this class are all Tadbhavas, and commonly denote professions and occupations.

148. Other masc. nouns denoting occupations or trades, if ending in a consonant, form the fem. by the

* Vid. § 140 (1) *N.B.*

† Always, where the *a* represents an original *akaḥ*.

suffix इन *in* or नी *ní*: as, e.g., सोनार *sonár*, 'a goldsmith,' fem., सुनारिन *sunárin* or सुनारनी *sunární*; कलार *kalár*, 'a distiller,' fem., कलारिन *kalárin* or कलारनी *kalární*.

a. So, also, some Tatsama and Tadbhava names of animals form their fem. in न *n* or नी *ní*: as, सिंहनी *siṉhaní*, 'a lioness,' from सिंह *siṉh*; बाघनी, *bághaní*, 'a tigress,' from बाघ *bágh*, Sk. व्याघ्र.

Rem. In some cases, *i* takes the place of *a* before the termination: as from नाग, 'a serpent,' the fem., नागिन. पति, 'a husband,' makes its fem., पत्नी.

b. In like manner is formed (a final vowel being shortened) the fem. of Tatsama nouns of agency in ई *í*: as, हितकारी *hitkárí*, 'a friend,' fem., हितकारिणी *hitkáriṇí*.

149. The suffix आनी *ání* is added to Sanskrit nouns, to denote 'the wife of': as, e.g., पंडितानी *paṇḍitání*, 'the wife of a paṇḍit,' from पंडित *paṇḍit*; इंद्राणी *indráṇí*, 'the wife of Indra.' This usage is extended to a very few Persian words; as, especially, मिहतरानी *mihtarání*, 'the wife of a sweeper,' from मिहतर (مہتر).

150. A few family and class names, much corrupted, form their fem. by adding the suffix आइन *áin*, a final long vowel being rejected. Thus, दुबे *dube*, 'a class of Brahmans,' makes its fem., दुबाइन *dubáin*; पाँड़े *páṉṛe*, 'a brahmanical title,' fem., पड़ाइन *paṛáin*.

151. As in other languages, the feminine noun is, in many instances, quite a different word from the corresponding masc. term. Examples are: साँड़ *sáṉṛ*, 'a bull,' fem., गाओ *gáo*, 'a cow;' पुरुष *puruṣh*, 'a man,' fem., स्त्री *strí*, 'a woman;' भाई *bháí*, 'a brother,' fem., बहिन *bahin*, 'a sister;' पिता *pitá*, 'a father,' fem., माता *mátá*, 'a mother.'

152. Nouns of agency in या retain the same form in either gender: as, e.g., गवैया *gawaiyá*, 'a singer;' लपतिया *lapatiyá*, 'a liar,' masc. or fem.

153. In the fem. term., *í*, as found in Tatsama nouns, we have simply the regular Sanskrit fem. termination. But the same termination in the fem. of Tadbhava nouns in *á* will be found to represent the Sanskrit fem. term., *iká*. Thus, as, e.g., *ghoṛá*, 'a horse,' is for the Sanskrit *ghoṭakaḥ*; *ghoṛí*, 'a mare,' is for the Sanskrit *ghoṭiká*, through an intermediate form, *ghoṛiyá*. Tadbhava feminines in *n*, *in*, *ní*, have, in most cases, arisen from Sanskrit masc. bases in *in*, fem., *iní*. Thus, e.g., *málin*, 'a gardener's wife,' from *málí* (Sk. *málin*, nom. sing., *málí*), is for *máliní*; *dhobin*, 'a washerman,' masc., *dhobí*, for a form, *dhávini*; *sunárin* or *sunární*, 'a goldsmith's wife,' points to a Sk. masc. base, *svarṇakáriṇ* (fem. *svarṇakáriṇí*), for the more common *svarṇakára*. Origin of Fem. Terminations.

Declension of Nouns.

154. Declension (विभक्ति) respects those modifications of the noun by which are expressed the relations of number (संख्या) and case (कारक).

a. Hindí, in common with all the Indo-Aryan languages, has lost the dual, and only recognizes a singular (एकवचन), and plural (बहुवचन). If, very rarely, we meet a Sanskrit dual form, as, e.g., पितरौ *pitarau*, 'parents,' from पितृ, 'father,' such forms have no organic connection with the language.

155. The distinctions of number and case are marked, in part, and in a limited and imperfect degree, by certain inflectional changes; and in part, and more precisely, by the addition of certain particles to the base. Practically, Hindí has but one declension, from which certain classes of nouns exhibit slight variations, to be noted below. The following four rules cover all the inflectional changes to which substantives are subject in High Hindí. Method of Declension.

(1) Most Tadbhava *masc.* nouns in आ *á*, inflect the final vowel to ए *e*, and those in आँ *áṉ*, to एँ *eṉ* or ए *e*, Inflection in Obl. Sing.

throughout the oblique singular; all other nouns, masc. or fem., are inflected in the singular. Examples of inflected nouns are the following: कुत्ता *kuttá*, 'a dog,' obl. sing., कुत्ते *kutte*; घोड़ा *ghoṛá*, 'a horse,' obl. sing., घोड़े *ghoṛe*; ताम्बा *támbá*, 'copper,' obl. sing., ताम्बे *támbe*; बनियां *baniyáṉ*, 'a shopkeeper,' obl. sing., बनियें *baniyeṉ* or बनिये *baniye*; धूत्रां *dhúáṉ*, 'smoke,' obl. sing., धूएं *dhúeṉ*. Examples of uninflected nouns are: माली *málí*, 'a gardener,' घर *ghar*, 'a house,' लड़की *laṛkí*, 'a girl,' माता *mátá*, 'a mother,' बिरियां *biriyáṉ*, 'time,' रात *rát*, 'night,' etc., all which forms are used alike in the nom. and obl. sing. Similarly all Tatsama masc. nouns in आ *á*, as, राजा *rájá*, 'a king,' आत्मा *átmá*, 'spirit,' पिता *pitá*, 'father,' etc., retain the same form unchanged throughout the singular.

a. A few Persian nouns, ending in the obscure ه *h*, follow the analogy of inflected Tadbhavas and make the obl. sing. in ए *e*, as, e.g., बन्दः *bandah*, 'a servant,' obl. sing., बन्दे *bande*.

Exc. 1. The following Tadbhava masc. nouns remain unchanged in the sing.: viz., काका *káká*, 'a paternal uncle;' चचा *chachá*, 'a maternal uncle;' लाला *lálá*, 'a schoolmaster;' 'a title of respect;' and a few other nouns expressive of relationship.

Exc. 2. Occasionally the voc. sing., even of inflected Tadbhava masc. nouns, remains uninflected. Thus, 'son!', is either बेटे *beṭe* or बेटा *beṭá*.

Rem. It is difficult to give any rule or rules, by which the beginner, unacquainted with Sanskrit, may be able infallibly to distinguish Tadbhava masc. nouns in आ, from Tatsama nouns having the same termination. It will, however, be of service to observe, that

1st, All nouns of agency and relationship in ता, and

2nd, All abstract nouns in आ, including especially a large

number of common fem. nouns in ता, and a few in ना (णा), are pure Sanskrit and are never inflected; while, on the contrary, most common concrete terms in आ are Tadbhava and masc., and are inflected, as above, to ए throughout the obl. sing.

For example, the following, viz.: दाता *dátá*, 'a giver,' कोमलता *komaltá*, 'softness,' इच्छा *ichchhá*, 'desire,' तृष्णा *trishṇá*, 'thirst,' are thus indicated as Tatsama nouns and uninflected. But, on the contrary, the concrete terms, घड़ा *ghaṛá*, 'an earthen jar,' लड़का *laṛká*, 'a boy,' घुटना *ghuṭná*, 'the knee,' are Tadbhavas, and are inflected to ए in the obl. sing.

Inflection in Masc. Nom. Plur.

(2) All such *masc.* nouns as are inflected by the above rule to ए *e* or एं *eṉ* in the obl. sing., retain the same inflection in the nom. plur. In all other masculine nouns, the nom. sing. and plur. are alike. Thus, लड़का *laṛká*, 'a boy,' obl. sing., लड़के *laṛke*, makes its nom. plur. also लड़के *laṛke*, 'boys;' गढ़ा *gaṛhá*, 'a ditch,' obl. sing., गढ़े *gaṛhe*, nom. plur., गढ़े *gaṛhe*, 'ditches.' रूपिया *rúpiyá*, 'a rupee,' makes the obl. sing. and nom. plur., रूपिये *rúpiye*, or रूपए *rúpae*. On the other hand, घर *ghar*, 'a house,' योद्धा *yoddhá*, 'a warrior,' भाई *bháí*, 'a brother,' have in the nom. plur. also, घर *ghar*, 'houses,' योद्धा *yoddhá*, 'warriors,' भाई *bháí*, 'brothers.'

Rem. Although, thus, in many nouns the number is not apparent from the termination, yet, practically, this will be found to occasion no ambiguity. As in the use of such English words as 'deer,' 'sheep,' etc., the number is generally quite evident from the context.

Inflection in Fem. Nom. Plur.

(3) All *fem.* nouns in इ *i* and ई *í*, make the nom. plural in आं *áṉ*; all other fem. nouns, in एं *eṉ*. It is to be observed, that fem. nouns in आ *á*, occasionally, and those in इ *i*, or ई *í*, commonly, insert a euphonic य *y* before all such added terminations, ई *í* final before this

य being regularly shortened. Examples are, of the first class: लड़की *laṛkí*, 'a girl,' nom. plur., लड़कियां *laṛkiyán̲*; विधि *vidhi*, 'a divine law,' nom. plur., विधियां *vidhiyán̲*: of the second class: बात *bát*, 'a word,' भेड़ *bheṛ*, 'a sheep,' बस्तु *bastu*, 'a thing;' nom. plur., बातें *báten̲*, भेड़ें *bheṛen̲*, बस्तुएं *bastuen̲*.

a. ऋचा *ṛichá*, 'a sacred ode,' and घटा *ghaṭá*, 'a heavy cloud,' make the nom. plur. either ऋचाएं *ṛicháen̲*, घटाएं *ghaṭáen̲*, or ऋचायें *ṛicháyen̲*, घटायें *ghaṭáyen̲*. जोरू, 'a wife,' makes the nom. plur. जोरुआं.

b. व *v* is rarely inserted as the euphonic letter instead of य *y*; chiefly after a labial vowel, as in भौंवें *bhauwen̲*, 'eye-brows,' nom. plur. of भौं *bhaun̲*; and, very rarely, after ई *í*, as in पुतलिवां *putliwán̲*, for पुतलियां *putliyán̲*, 'dolls,' 'puppets,' from पुतली *putlí*.

c. A number of fem. nouns in इया *iyá*, chiefly diminutives, form the plur. by the addition of Anusvár only; as, टिलिया *ṭiliyá*, 'a young hen,' nom. plur., टिलियां *ṭiliyán̲*; डिबिया *ḍibiyá*, 'a small box,' nom. plur., डिबियां *ḍibiyán̲*; चिड़िया *chiṛiyá*, 'a bird,' nom. plur., चिड़ियां *chiṛiyán̲*. Similarly, विधवा *vidhvá*, 'a widow,' makes the nom. plur., विधवां *vidhván̲*.

d. गाए *gáe* or गाओ *gáo*, 'a cow,' and रोम *rom*, 'fine hair,' 'down,' both reject the final letter before the plural terminations; as in the nom. plur., गोएं *gáen̲*, रोएं *roen̲*.

Rem. 1. The nom. plur. termination of feminine nouns is sometimes omitted, and the tendency to this omission seems to be increasing.

Rem. 2. The numerals, when used collectively, either as substantives or adjectives, make the nom. plur. in ओं; otherwise, the nom. plur. and sing. are alike;* as, तीनों *tínon̲*, nom. plur., 'the three;' चारों घोड़े *cháron̲ ghoṛe*, 'the four horses;' but चार घोड़े *chár ghoṛe*, 'four

---

* These numeral forms in *on̲* are all Aggregatives, and the termination is not to be identified with the affix of the obl. plural, with which it has no connection. The form is explained in the chapter on Numerals.

horses,' चार आए, 'four came.' But दो *do*, 'two,' used collectively, makes the nom. plur., दोनों *donon*, 'the two,' 'both.'

(4) All nouns whatever, masc. and fem., terminate in ओं *on*, throughout the oblique plural; Anusvár being dropped in the vocative only. Inflection in Obl. Plur.

In the case of nouns inflected to ए *e* in the obl. sing., this termination ओं *on* is substituted for the final vowel. If the noun end in ई *í* or इ *i*, the vowel, if long, is shortened, and a euphonic य *y* is inserted before the termination. A long final ऊ *ú* is shortened. In all other cases the termination is simply added to the nom. sing.

Examples are, of nouns inflected to ए in the sing.: घोड़ा *ghoṛá*, 'a horse,' obl. plur., घोड़ों *ghoṛon*, voc. plur., घोड़ो *ghoṛo*; कुत्ता *kuttá*, 'a dog,' obl. plur., कुत्तों *kutton*, voc. plur., कुत्तो *kutto*; of nouns in ई and इ: बिल्ली *billí*, 'a cat,' obl. plur., बिल्लियों *billiyon*, voc. plur., बिल्लियो; धोबी *dhobí*, 'a washerman,' obl. plur., धोबियों *dhobiyon*; विधि *vidhi*, 'a law,' obl. plur., विधियों *vidhiyon*; of other nouns: पुस्तक *pustak*, 'a book,' obl. plur., पुस्तकों *pustakon*; रात *rát*, 'night,' obl. plur., रातों *ráton*: जोरू *jorú*, 'a wife,' obl. plur., जोरुओं *joruon*; पिता *pitá*, 'a father,' obl. plur., पिताओं *pitáon*.

a. Occasionally we meet with the obl. plurals, देवतों *devton*, राजों *rájon*, आत्मों *átmon*, from देवता *devtá*, 'a deity,' राजा *rájá*, 'a king,' आत्मा *átmá*, 'the spirit;' but these forms are incorrect, and have not the sanction of good usage. They, correctly, follow the usage of all Tatsama nouns, and for the obl. plur. add the termination to the nom. sing., making देवताओं *devtáon*, राजाओं *rájáon*, आत्माओं *átmáon*. Irregular Obl. Plural.

b. But the following nouns, viz., गाए *gáe*, 'a cow,' रोम *rom*, 'down,' गांव *gánw*, 'a village,' नांव *nánw*, 'a name,' दांव *dánw*, 'a time,' पांव *pánw*, 'the foot,' drop the final letter before the obl. plur. termination. In the last four, the Anusvár before the final consonant is also often dropped, so that the obl. plur. of these nouns becomes गाश्रों *gáoṉ*, रोश्रों *rooṉ*, गाश्रों *gáoṉ*, नाश्रों *náoṉ*, दाश्रों *dáoṉ*, पाश्रों *páoṉ*.

Postpositions of Declension. **156.** The elaborate inflectional system of the Sanskrit having become reduced to the few inflections above noted, the necessity for a more precise definition of the various relations of the noun than these could afford, was met by the addition to the oblique form of the noun of certain particles, commonly called *postpositions.** Although the relation of the noun to these postpositions is less intimate than that of the Latin or Sanskrit case-terminations to the stem, still reasons of practical convenience have led grammarians to arrange the declension of the Hindí noun after the Sanskrit model, in eight cases, as follows: Nominative (कर्त्ता), Accusative (कर्म्म), Dative (संप्रदान), Agent (करण),† Ablative (अपदान), Genitive (संबंध), Locative (अधिकरण), and Vocative (संबोधन). No postpositions are used with the Nominative and Vocative. Those which are assigned to the remaining cases, in High Hindí, are as follows: Acc. and Dat. को, Agt. ने, Abl. से, Gen. का (के, की), Loc. में, पर, तक or तलक. All of these are appended to the oblique form of the noun, where such a form exists.

Rem. The same postpositions are used for the several cases, whether the noun be in the singular or plural. तईं is sometimes substituted for को in the accusative of the reflexive pronoun, अपने तईं.

* These are similar in character to prepositions in English; but as they always follow their noun, they are more accurately termed '*post*positions.'

† What we have termed the case of the Agent, has usually been called, after the terminology of Sanskrit grammars, the Instrumental case. But as, in Hindí, this case never denotes the instrument, but the agent only, it seems better to drop a term which can only mislead.

157. The accusative appears in Hindí under two forms, the one identical with the nominative, the other consisting of the noun in its oblique form with the appended postposition को. In this last case, when the accusative is the object of a transitive verb, को is incapable of translation, and merely gives a certain definiteness to the noun. But with an accusative preceding a verb of motion, it is to be rendered 'to;' and when the accusative denotes the time at which, it will be translated 'at;' as, घर को चलो, 'go to the house;' रात को, 'at night.' को is also used as the postposition of the dative, when it is always rendered 'to.' **Formation of Accusative and Dative.**

158. Strictly speaking, ने is the English 'by,' but in rendering into English idiom, it will be found necessary to translate the case of the agent precisely as the nominative. The full exposition of the use of this case is of necessity deferred to the chapter on Verbs. **Formation of Case of the Agent.**

159. The ablative postposition, से, is sometimes to be translated 'from,' but sometimes also, 'by' or 'with.' **Formation of Ablative.**

160. The genitive postposition, का, is, accurately speaking, an adjective particle, equivalent to such English phrases as 'belonging to,' 'pertaining to,' etc.* The noun, by the addition of this particle, is in reality converted into a possessive adjective; hence this postposition, as will hereafter appear, follows the regular rules for the inflection of Tadbhava adjectives in *á*, **Formation of Genitive.**

* The following remarks of Lassen, concerning the corresponding Maráṭhí genitive in *chá*, apply equally to the Hindí genitive in *ká*. "*Mahraṭṭhi nimirum non dicunt 'patris equum,' 'oppidi cives,' sed 'paternum equum,' 'oppidanos cives.' Adjectivum autem quum sit, facile apparet cur terminatio pro vario regiminis genere varietur.*"—Inst. Ling. Prac. p. 54.

and is made to agree with the noun which the genitive defines, in gender, number, and case.

Inflection of Gen. Postposition.

161. The following rules regulate the use of the three forms of the genitive postposition.

(1) का *ká* is used before all masc. nouns in the nom. sing., or in that form of the acc. which is the same as the nom. sing.

(2) के *ke* is used before all masc. nouns when in any case but the nom. sing. The only exception has been stated under rule (1).

(3) की *kí* is used before all fem. nouns in any case whatever, singular or plural. The following examples will illustrate these rules. Thus we say:

धोबी का बेटा *dhobí ká beṭá*, 'the washerman's son.'
माली के बेटे *málí ke beṭe*, 'the gardener's sons.'
बढ़ई के लड़के पर *baṛhaí ke laṛke par*, 'on the carpenter's child.'
राजा के गाओं में *rájá ke gáoṉ meṉ*, 'in the king's villages.'
पंडितों का घर *paṇḍitoṉ ká ghar*, 'the house of the pundits.'
ब्राह्मण की पोथी *bráhmaṉ kí pothí*, 'the Brahman's book.'
राजा की आज्ञा पर *rájá kí ágyá par*, 'on the king's command.'
ईश्वर की बातें *íshwár kí báteṉ*, 'the words of God.'
पहाड़ों की चोटियों पर *paháṛoṉ kí choṭíoṉ par*, 'on the peaks of the mountains.'

N.B. The student will carefully observe that the gender or number of the noun to which the gen. particle is attached, has nothing whatever to do with the inflection of the particle. It is determined solely by the gender, number, and case of the *following* noun.

The Locative Postpositions.

162. Of the various postpositions commonly assigned to the locative case, में is the English 'in;' पर is 'on;' तक and तलक alike denote the limit to which, 'up to,' 'as far as.' For तक, the Sk. पर्यन्त is occasionally used, as in the *Shakuntalá*; thus, समुद्र पर्यन्त, 'as far as the ocean.'

a. It should be observed, that, in fact, the locative, like the accusative, has two forms, the one consisting of the oblique form of the noun, singular or plural, with one of the locative postpositions attached; and the other form consisting of such oblique form only, the postpositions being omitted. In the case of uninflected singular nouns, the latter form will of course be identical with the nom. sing. Thus we may say, उस समय में, or उस समय, 'at that time;' नगर के बीच, or, more rarely, नगर के बीच में, 'in the midst of the city.' This latter form is used in cases where the noun has almost or quite lost its substantive character, and has become practically equivalent to a preposition or adverb.

Rem. That the oblique form alone, in this last instance, is a true locative case, is plain from the fact that the *á* final of the genitive postpositions and of adjectives, is always inflected to *é* before the form in question, even when it is identical with the nominative singular. Nor is it correct, with some, to represent the postposition as in such cases arbitrarily omitted. In reality, we have herein a remaining trace of the old inflectional system of declension. The inflectional ending has indeed, in all nouns except Tadbhavas in *á*, entirely disappeared, leaving the noun in form like the nominative, but the real character of such words is still discernible from their power to occasion the inflection of an attributive adjunct.

163. The word लोग *log* (Sk. and Gaṛh. लोक) is appended to plural nouns when it is desired to indicate the plural as a class. The plural inflection and the several postpositions are then added, not to the noun itself, but to this appended लोग. In the case of inflected Tadbhavas in *á*, the noun is inflected to *e* before लोग, whether in the nom. or the obl. plur. In all other cases the noun before लोग remains uninflected. Periphrastic Plural.

Examples are the following: nom. plur., राजा लोग *rájá log*, 'kings,' as a class; धोबी लोगों में *dhobí logon̲ men̲*, 'among washermen;' कवि लोगों को *kavi logon̲ ko*, 'to poets;' बनियें लोगों से *baniyeṉ logoṉ se*, 'by shopkeepers.' To illustrate further, such a phrase as 'ten kings came,' we must render, दस राजा आए *das rájá áe*, since there is no reference to kings as a class; but the phrase 'kings are wealthy,'—a general statement with regard to the class 'kings,'—must be translated, राजा लोग धनी होते हैं *rájá log dhaní hote haiṉ*.

a. This usage of the word लोग is properly confined to nouns denoting persons, though it is occasionally used, somewhat jocosely, in reference to animals, by the common people, who might say, e.g., बंदर लोग *bandar log*, much as we would say, 'the monkey folk.' It has indeed been denied that लोग is ever used except with nouns denoting persons; but exceptions occur to this general rule, even in literature, as in the following phrase from the *Rámáyan*: मृग लोग सरेन हिए, '(they) killed deer with the arrow.'

b. The word लोग is often used alone, where in English we have 'they' in the sense of 'people, in general;' as, लोग कहते हैं, = French, 'on dit,' 'they say.' But often, in such cases, लोग is omitted and the verb stands alone.

Rem. लोग has also a feminine form, लुगाई, 'woman,' but this is never appended as a sign of plurality to other nouns.

164. Besides लोग, the word गण or गन, 'a host,' is also often added to nouns to denote a class; as, e.g., देवतागण, 'the gods;' तारागन, 'the stars,' etc. Many other words are appended to nouns in like manner, in prose as well as in poetry, as indicative of plurality or multitude. Among these, the most common are the following, viz.: वृंद, as, भूधर वृंद, 'mountains;' जन, as, भक्त जन, 'worshippers;' निकर, as, रविकर निकर, 'sunbeams;' संकुल, as, जंतु संकुल, 'animals;' व्रात, as, ऋषि व्रात, 'sages;' समूह, as, पाप समूह, 'sins,' i.e., 'the whole of my sins;' समाज, as, संत समाज, 'the good,' i.e., 'the assemblage of the good;' बरूथ, as, भट बरूथ, 'warriors;' समुदाई, as, बटु समुदाई, 'young Brahmans;' ठात, as, कपि

ठाट, 'the monkeys;' ओघ, as, अघ ओघ, 'sins.' The word आवली is added to a few nouns to connote order in a line; as, रोमावली, 'the line of hair along the breast bone;' बलाकावली, 'a flock of cranes,' as always flying in a line. Two nouns of plurality are occasionally appended to a word; as, निसचर निकर बरूथ, 'a multitude of demons.'

Rem. In many cases the noun of plurality may be translated, 'assemblage,' 'multitude,' 'flock,' etc., but very often it will be found that English idiom will only admit the translation of the noun as a simple plural. The above words are by no means all equivalent to लोग, nor are they all used interchangeably among themselves.

165. As Hindí has no article, the distinction indicated in English by the definite and indefinite article, cannot always be expressed in Hindí. घोड़ा may be either 'a horse' or 'the horse;' स्त्रियां may be 'women' or 'the women.' The indefinite article may be sometimes rendered by the numeral एक, 'one,' or the indefinite pronoun, कोई, 'some,' 'any;' but it is oftener incapable of translation. The definite article, occasionally, when strongly demonstrative, may be expressed by the remote demonstrative pronoun, वह. In the case of nouns in the accusative, the force of the definite article may be often expressed by the use of the form with को; as, घोड़े को, which may mean, '*the* horse.' But the student must not therefore understand that the acc. with को is always to be rendered with the definite article. **The Article Wanting.**

166. In exhibiting the declension of nouns according to the foregoing rules, it will be convenient to classify them according to gender in two declensions, each of which has two varieties. **Classification of Declensions.**

I. (1) The *First Declension* will comprise all masculines. Of this declension the *First variety* will include all Tadbhava * nouns in आ or आँ which are inflected in **Masc. Declension: 1st Variety.**

* For definition of 'Tadbhava' nouns, see § 70.

the obl. sing. to ए or एं, and the *Second variety*, all other masculine nouns. Nouns of the first variety are declined like

घोड़ा *ghoṛá*, 'a horse.'

Singular.	Plural.
N. घोड़ा *ghoṛá*, 'a horse.'	N. घोड़े *ghoṛe*, 'horses.'
Ac. घोड़ा *ghoṛá* or घोड़े को *ghoṛe ko*, 'a horse,' or 'to a horse.'	Ac. घोड़े *ghoṛe* or घोड़ों को *ghoṛoṇ ko*, 'horses,' or 'to horses.'
D. घोड़े को *ghoṛe ko*, 'to a horse.'	D. घोड़ों को *ghoṛoṇ ko*, 'to horses.'
Ag. घोड़े ने *ghoṛe ne*. 'by a horse.'	Ag. घोड़ों ने *ghoṛoṇ ne*, 'by horses.'
Ab. घोड़े से *ghoṛe se*, 'from a horse.'	Ab. घोड़ों से *ghoṛoṇ se*, 'from horses.'
G. घोड़े का (के or की), *ghoṛe ká* (*ke* or *kí*), 'of a horse,' 'horse's.'	G. घोड़ों का (के or की) *ghoṛoṇ ká* (*ke* or *kí*), 'horses,' or 'of horses.'
L. घोड़े में, पर, तक, तलक, *ghoṛe meṇ, par, tak, talak*, 'in, on, to a horse.'	L. घोड़ों में, पर, तक, तलक *ghoṛoṇ meṇ, par, tak, talak*, 'in, on, to horses.'
V. हे घोड़े *he ghoṛe*, 'O horse.'	V. हे घोड़ो *he ghoṛo*, 'O horses.'

Masc. Declension: 2nd Variety. (2) The *Second variety* of masculine declension includes all other masculine nouns of whatever termination, and may be represented by घर *ghar*, 'a house.' It differs from the above, only in that the inflection of the noun is confined to the oblique plural. As the postpositions are the same with all nouns, it will be unnecessary to give the remaining paradigms in detail. It will be remembered that the second form of the loc. is like the nom.

घर *ghar*, 'a house.'

SINGULAR.	PLURAL.
N. घर *ghar*, 'a house.'	N. घर *ghar*, 'houses.'
Ac. घर *ghar* or घर को *ghar ko*, 'a house,' or 'to a house.'	Ac. घर *ghar* or घरों को *gharon̤ ko*, 'houses,' or 'to the houses.'

So also is declined the Tatsama* noun,

राजा *rájá*, 'a king.'

SINGULAR.	PLURAL.
N. राजा *rájá*, 'a king.'	N. राजा *rájá*, 'kings.'
Ac. राजा *rájá* or राजा को *rájá ko*, 'a king.'	Ac. राजा *rájá* or राजाओं को *rájáon̤ ko*, 'kings.'

So also decline masc. nouns ending in any other vowel, as the following:

माली *málí*, 'a gardener.'

SINGULAR.	PLURAL.
N. माली *málí*, 'a gardener.'	N. माली *málí*, 'gardeners.'
Ac. माली *málí* or माली को *málí ko*, 'a gardener.'	Ac. माली *málí* or मालियों को *máliyon̤ ko*, 'gardeners.'

बिच्छू *bichchhú*, 'a scorpion.'

SINGULAR.	PLURAL.
N. बिच्छू *bichchhú*, 'a scorpion.'	N. बिच्छू *bichchhú*, 'scorpions.'
Ac. बिच्छू *bichchhú* or बिच्छू को *bichchhú ko*, 'a scorpion.'	Ac. बिच्छू *bichchhú* or बिच्छुओं को *bichchhuon̤ ko*, 'scorpions.'

167. II. (1) The *Second Declension* comprises all feminine nouns. The *First variety* includes all feminines in इ *i*, ई *í*, उ *u*, or ऊ *ú*; the *Second variety*, all other feminines. **Fem. Declension: 1st Variety.**

---

* For definition of 'Tatsama' nouns, see § 70.

As an example of the *First variety*, we may take

पोथी *pothí*, 'a book.'

SINGULAR.	PLURAL.
N. पोथी *pothí*, 'a book.'	N. पोथियां *pothiyán*, 'books.'
Ac. पोथी *pothí* or पोथी को *pothí ko*, 'a book.'	Ac. पोथियां *pothiyán* or पोथियों को *pothiyon ko*, 'books.'

Like पोथी is declined

सारू *sárú*, 'a starling.'

SINGULAR.	PLURAL.
N. सारू *sárú*, 'a starling.'	N. सारुआं *sáruán*, 'starlings.'
Ac. सारू *sárú* or सारू को *sárú ko*, 'a starling.'	Ac. सारुआं *sáruán* or सारुओं को *sáruon ko*, 'starlings.'

And after the analogy of the accusative are declined the remaining cases in these and all similar nouns.

Fem. Declension: 2nd Variety.

(2) The *Second variety* of feminine declension may be illustrated by the word

रात *rát*, 'night.'

SINGULAR.	PLURAL.
N. रात *rát*, 'night.'	N. रातें, *ráten*, 'nights.'
Ac. रात *rát* or रात को *rát ko*, 'night.'	Ac. रातें *ráten* or रातों को *ráton ko*, 'nights.'

As an example of fem. nouns in आ we take

माता *mátá*, 'a mother.'

SINGULAR.	PLURAL.
N. माता *mátá*, 'a mother.'	N. माताएं *mátáen* or माता *mátá*,* 'mothers.'
Ac. माता *mátá* or माता को *mátá ko*, 'a mother.'	Ac. माताएं *mátáen* or माताओं को *mátáon ko*, 'mothers.'

* The more common form in both nom. and uninflected acc.

In like manner are declined all other nouns of this class.

N.B. For the indefinite article, the definite article may be substituted throughout the above tables.

DIALECTIC SUBSTANTIVE DECLENSION.

The Western Dialects.

168. In the Braj dialect, ऐ is rarely substituted for ए in the obl. sing. of Tadbhava nouns in आ; as in मेरै for मेरे; more commonly the inflection of the singular agrees with High Hindí. A voc. sing. in आ, from masc. nouns in ई, is occasionally found; as, मालिआ, 'O gardener;' स्वामिआ, 'O Lord,' from माली, स्वामी. In the nom. plur. of Tadbhava masc. nouns in आ, the termination is ए, as in High Hindí. An irregular nom. masc. plur., मरद्दनियाँ, 'a class of servants,' occurs in the *Prem Ságar.* In the nom. plur. of fem. nouns, ऐं often appears for H.H. एं, as in रातैं for रातें, 'nights.' The nom. plur. of fem. nouns in ई is often formed by the simple addition of Anusvár; as in पोथीं, for पोथियाँ, 'books;' अलीं, for अलियाँ, 'friends.' In the obl. plur., ओं is sometimes *vriddhied* to औं, as in घरौं, for घरों, 'houses;' but more commonly the obl. plur. is formed by the termination न or नि. A final long vowel is shortened before this न, and a euphonic य is sometimes inserted after a final इ. Examples are, पापी, 'a sinner,' obl. plur., पापिन, पापिनि, or पापियन; नारी, 'a woman,' obl. plur., नारिन, or नारियन; पेड़, 'a tree,' obl. plur., पेड़न; पाए, 'a foot,' obl. plur., पायन. The Kanaují does not differ from High Hindí in its inflections, except in the obl. plur., which terminates in न. **Braj and Kanaují inflections.**

169. The Márwárí, as also the other Rajputana dialects, exhibits ओ, instead of आ, as the sign of the nom. sing. of strong Tadbhava masc. nouns; which, again, is inflected in the obl. sing. to आ, instead of ए, in all the dialects in question. Thus, e.g., for the High Hindí, घोड़ा, 'a horse,' we have घोड़ो, **Inflection in Rajputana.**

obl. sing., घोड़ा. All other nouns agree with the High Hindí throughout the singular.

a. But the case of the agent, in Máṛwáṛí nouns *of this class*, ends in ए, and to this form no postposition is affixed. Thus we have घोड़े = घोड़े ने. In all other nouns, the case of the agent sing. is like the nom. It never takes a postposition. All Máṛwáṛí nouns have also an inflected loc. sing. in ए; as, e.g., घरे, 'in the house,' घोड़े, 'on the horse.'

b. So also, according to Beames,* Chand sometimes uses an inflected form in ए, or occasionally अय, for the case of the agent. Gujarátí and Maráṭhí also both preserve this inflected case of the agent, the former making it in ए, the latter in एं.

c. The nom. plur. of all Máṛwáṛí Tadbhava masc. nouns in ओ, ends in आ. Thus, from घोड़ो, 'a horse,' we have the nom. plur., घोड़ा, 'horses.' Other masc. nouns are unchanged in the nom. plural. All Máṛwáṛí fem. nouns make the nom. plur. in आं; ई final, before this termination, is hardened to य. Examples are: घोड़ी, 'a mare,' nom. plur., घोड़्यां; बात, 'a word,' nom. plur., बातां. The obl. plur. form of all Máṛwáṛí nouns terminates in आं, ई final being hardened to य; as in माळ्यां रो = H.H. मालियों का, 'of the gardeners.' The above rules for Máṛwáṛí declension apply to all the Rajputana dialects.

Inflection in Himalayan Dialects.

170. The Gaṛhwálí and Kumáoní dialects agree with the Rajputana dialects in the inflection of the sing., except that, so far as I know, they have not the inflected case of the agent and the locative.† In the nom. sing. also, like Máṛwáṛí, they have the termination आ; but differ from the Rajputana dialects in inflecting the obl. plur. to आँ instead of आं. In Naipálí, all nouns have the same form in the nom. and

---

* *Comp. Gramm.* vol. ii. p. 212.

† I am surprised that I have not found such forms, as, from the archaic character of these dialects, I should have expected such survivals of the old inflections. Very possibly they may yet be discovered.

obl. sing., with the exception, as in High Hindí, of strong Tadbhava nouns in ओ (H.H. आ) which inflect the obl. sing, to आ. Both the nom. and obl. plur. in Naipálí are formed by adding to the nom. sing. the termination हेरु or हरु; as बालख, 'a child,' nom. and obl. plur., बालखहेरु or बालखहरु. But often this plural termination is omitted, and the noun appears in form like the singular; thus, अर्का कांड़ा मा परे, 'other fell among thorns,' and in the Gospel, *passim*.

Rem. This plural termination is sometimes added to participles used adjectively, and even to whole phrases. Examples are given in the section on Naipálí conjugation.

171. The remarks made above as to the meaning and use of the postpositions, apply, for the most part, equally to the corresponding postpositions in the western dialects, as exhibited in Table II. कौं, or कुं, and कूं, is used as the postposition of the accusative and dative. The abl. postposition, ते, or तें, used in the Braj and other dialects, must always be translated 'from' or 'by,' never, 'with.' The Braj form, पै, is almost always rendered 'on,' but is occasionally used in the sense of 'by,' where, in High Hindí, we would have से. सौं or सों are exactly equivalent to सच. The Braj Postpositions.

172. The Máṛwáṛí forms call for little remark. The gen. postpositions, रो, रा, री, correspond in usage respectively to का, के, की, in High Hindí; with the single exception, that when the gen. denotes possession or duty, रै is used before masc. nouns in the obl. sing., instead of रा. The same remarks apply to the use of को, का, की, etc., in Mewáṛí. Examples are: बठोठ रो सिरदार डूंग जी है, 'the ruler of Baṭhoṭh is Ḍúng Jí;' ऊ ब्राह्मण रै घर गीयो, 'he went to the Brahman's house;' दस हजार री रोकड़, 'ten thousand of treasure.' कुं, for को (= का), is occasionally found; as, देवन कुं देव, 'the god of gods.' The gen. postpositions, तणो and हंदो (= का), so far as we are aware, are used only in poetry. Examples are, धूवां हंदो जाम्ब = धूएं का जहाज, 'a steamer;' दिल्ली तणो नवाब, 'the Nawáb of Delhi.' तणी (for तणो) Postpositions in Rajputana Dialects.

occurs, in one instance only, in the *Prem Ságar*, with the 2nd pers. pron., तुमतणो, 'your,' for तुम्हारा. माँहि, often माँई (=में), 'in,' in Máṛ. is regularly used as a postposition, as, धूल पगड़ी माँहि, 'dust on the turban'; but it more rarely occurs in its primitive sense as a substantive, in construction with a preceding genitive; as, मुलक के माँहि, 'in the country,' for मुलक माँहि = मुल्क में; कैद रे माँहि, 'in captivity,' = कैद में. The same usage with the dialectic equivalents of में occasionally occurs in the *Rámáyan* and other archaic Hindí poetry. In the colloquial, सूधी (= तक) is often treated as a predicative adjective, and is then made to agree with the subject of the sentence in gender and number. Thus they say, बाणो गाम सूधो गयो, 'the shopkeeper went as far as the village;' धोबिन ताल सूधी गयी, 'the washerwoman went as far as the lake.' The following sentences illustrate the remaining Máṛ. postpositions: डूंगर सिंगनि पकड़ लेगयो, 'he has seized and carried off Ḍúngar Sing;' चढ़ि किला ऊपरै, 'having climbed upon the fort.' ऊपरै is sometimes construed with the genitive, like माँहि; as, घोड़ा कै ऊपरै, 'on the horse.' सूं is used like से; as, अंगरेज सूं करी लड़ाई, 'he fought with the English.'

173. In Western Hindí, I have met an acc. and dat. postposition ना = H.H. को. It is evidently connected with the corresponding Máṛ. नै, Panj. नूं. दा as the gen. postposition, the regular substitute for का, in Panjábí, is also found, very rarely, in Western Hindí. Beames gives from Chand an instance of an inflected instr. singular of a feminine noun in नूपुरया, from नूपुरा.

a. करके, although in reality a conjunctive participle from करना, 'to do,' or 'make,' is colloquially used as a postposition with the inflected forms of both nouns and pronouns, throughout the Ganges Valley. It is nearly equivalent to से in the sense of 'from' or 'by;' it is never to be rendered 'with.' Thus we may say, पाप करके रहित, 'free from sin,' for पाप से रहित or पाप रहित. But in the following from the

Rámáyan, पारखे is equivalent to में, 'in;' सर सम लगे मातु उर पारखे, 'fastened like arrows in (his) mother's breast.'

b. सेइ and सन are sometimes found for the abl. postposition से. ले is sometimes colloquially added to से, thus, से ले; it emphasizes the idea of 'source,' 'beginning;' thus, पहाड़ से ले नदी तक, 'quite from the mountain to the river.' तोड़ी very rarely occurs as a dialectic substitute for तक; it properly belongs to Háṛotí.

c. The Himalayan postpositions, as will be seen in Table II., differ very considerably from those used elsewhere, but call for little special remark in this connection. It is well, however, to note the very frequent use, in Naipálí, at least, of the conjunctive participle, देखि, of the verb देखणु (H.H. देखना), 'to see,' as a postposition, in many instances where High Hindí would have से.* Thus, जुनसुकै मठ देखि लाज़ मानला = H.H., जो कोई मुझ से लजावे, 'whosoever shall be ashamed of me.' The gen. postposition in all the Himalayan dialects is को, which is inflected to का for the masc. obl. sing. and the plur., and to की for the fem. throughout. The use of the postposition ले, assigned to the ablative, is confined to those cases in which से, in High Hindí, bears an instrumental sense.

The Eastern Dialects.

174. In the dialect of the *Rámáyan*, as in many eastern dialects, a short vowel takes the place of a final long vowel in Tadbhava nouns, masc. and fem. Thus, for दूलहा, 'a bridegroom,' we have दूलह; for घड़ा, 'an earthen jar,' घट; for नारी, 'a woman,' नारि; etc., etc. Also for the inherent *a* final of nouns in High Hindí, we often find *u*, sometimes lengthened, *metri gratiá*; as, देहु, for देह, 'body;' बीरु or बीरू, for बीर, 'a hero;' etc., etc. Declension in the Rámáyan.

* Compare the analogous use of *karke*, above referred to, § 173, *a*.

175. All nouns whatever, in this dialect, are declined in precisely the same way. The class of (High Hindí) Tadbhava substantives in आ does not exist, and all nouns are unchanged in the sing., except that for the acc. or dat. the termination हि or हिं is often added to the uninflected base; thus, रामहि or रामहिं, '*Rám*,' or 'to *Rám*;' मुनिहि or मुनिहिं, 'the sage,' or 'to the sage.' In the following, this form is apparently used as an abl.: गुरहि पूछ, करि कुलविधि राजा, 'the king, having made inquiry of his *Guru* and performed the family rites.' Occasionally, at the end of a line, in old Hindí poetry, we find the termination म्, commonly represented by *Anusvár*. It may be added (1) to a nom. sing.: as, आजु न संसयं, 'to-day there is no doubt,' in which case it is to be regarded as a neuter termination; or (2) to an acc. sing.: as, समेत सुग्रीवं, 'together with *Sugrív*,' where it represents the masc. acc. sing. termination. But it is often added only for the sake of metre or rhyme. The voc. sing. is regularly like the nom.

176. The nom. plur. of all nouns, masc. and fem., is like the nom. sing.; the obl. plur. is formed by adding न, न्ह or न्हि, to the nom. sing.: as, from मुनि, 'a sage,' obl. plur., मुनिन्ह; सुर, 'a god,' obl. plur., सुरन्हि; नारि, 'a woman,' obl. plur., नारिन. In some instances, अन्ह is added after a vowel-termination, the euphonic य being characteristically omitted: as in कौतुकिअन्ह, 'to the eager,' dat., from कौतुकि.

a. In a single instance, we find in the *Rámáyan* a masc. nom. plur. in आं, in बजनियां, 'musicians;' thus, सेवक सकल बजनियां नाना। पूरन किये दान सनमाना, 'the servants all, and the different musicians, he loaded with gifts and honour.'*

* Compare the similar form from the *Prem Ságar*, मरदनियां.

177. The following Sanskrit case-forms occur: viz., masc. instr. sing., सरेन, 'with an arrow;' also सुखेन, used adverbially, 'joyfully;' neut. acc. sing., ब्रह्मं, '*Brahma*;' masc. abl. sing., पदाद्, 'from (their) rank;' neut. loc. sing., मनसि, 'in the heart;' masc. nom. plur., नरा (for Sk. नराः), 'men;' masc. voc. sing., राजन्, 'O king!'; fem. voc. sing., सीते, 'O *Sítá!*'.

178. In many instances, we find in the *Rámáyan* the termination औ, added to substantives and words used substantively: as, अधमौ, अंधौ, एकौ, etc. This, however, is not a case-ending, but serves merely to emphasize the noun, and is therefore equivalent to the High Hindí emphatic particle, ही;* e.g., अंधौ बधिर न अस कहहि, 'even one blind or deaf would not speak thus.'

179. In the *Rámáyan* the postposition for the acc. and dat. is कहं: thus, तुम कहं बिपति बीज बिधि बयउ, 'for you *Brahma* has sown the seed of trouble.' Variant forms are कांह, काह, and काऊ (काहू); कु and कुं also occur. None of these, however, are of frequent employment; the obl. form in हि or हिं, mentioned above, is very commonly preferred. Postpositions in the Rámáyan.

180. The gen. postposition appears in the *Rámáyan* under three different forms: viz., केर or केरा, obl. masc., केरे, fem., केरि; कर, inflected, before fem. nouns only, to करि; and क, to which we may assign the fem. inflected form, कि. As these are apt to confuse the beginner, we give the following examples of the use of each form: प्रभु कह गरल बंधु ससि केरा, 'the Lord said, It is the poison of the moon, brother;' मिटै न जीवन्ह केर कलेसा, 'the pain of the creatures is not removed;'

---

* This form has apparently arisen from the Braj form of this particle, *hú*, by the elision of *h*, and *sandhi* of the then concurrent vowels; so that, e.g., *ekau* is for *ekahu*.

परहितहानि लाभ जिन्ह केरे, 'whose gain is the injury of others' well-being;' सीता केरि करहु रखवारी, 'guard *Sítá*,' or 'keep a watch of *Sítá*;' प्रथम भक्ति संतन्ह कर संगा, 'the first (form of) devotion is association with the good.' कर is also used before masc. nouns or pronouns in an oblique case: हम काहु कर मरहिं न मारे, 'I may not be killed by any one,' lit., 'die, killed by any one;'* जाकरि तैं दासी सो अबिनासी, 'that immortal One, whose handmaid thou art;' नीको तुलसी क, 'the welfare of *Tulsí*;' उमा संत कइ इहइ बड़ाई, '*Umá*, this is the greatness of the good.' Besides the above, the regular inflections, के and की, are also found in the *Rámáyan*; so also, rarely, the Kanaují gen. sign, को, and the Braj, कौ; but all these are foreign to the dialect.

181. The usual form of the abl. postposition in the *Rámáyan* is तें. The loc. postposition is महं, with seven variant forms, given in Table II., all of which = H. H. में. The other postpositions assigned to the locative call for no special remark. The Sanskrit पर्यन्त, corrupted to प्रजंत, is occasionally used in the sense of the H.H. तक, 'up to;' as, योजन एक प्रजंत, 'for as much as one *yojan*.' पर्यन्त also becomes परयन्त and परजन्त.

Declension in Eastern Colloquials.

182. In Avadhí, Bhojpúrí, Mágadhí, and Maithilí, strong Tadbhava masc. nouns in आ are uninflected in the obl. sing. But in the gen. sing., before the postposition क, a final आ, ई, or ऊ, is shortened, giving, e.g., घोड़क, मालिक instead of घोड़ाक, मालीक. In S. Bhagalpúr, however, a final long vowel is retained in this case also. Weak nouns ending in a silent consonant, as घर *ghar*, may be inflected to ĕ in the obl. sing.

* मारे is here the nom. plur., agreeing with हम, as plural in form, though singular in sense.

in Mágadhí, or to ă in the Maithilí of S. Bhagalpúr, giving घरे gharĕ, घरऽ ghara. In the other eastern dialects, nouns of this class are unchanged in the obl. sing.

Inflection of Verbal Nouns.

a. Verbal nouns in ब, in Bhojpúrí, Mágadhí, and Maithilí, make the obl. sing. in बा; as, देखब, 'seeing,' obl. sing. देखबा. Verbal nouns which consist of the root, either alone or with an added इ, make the obl. sing. in ए ĕ in all these dialects; as देख or देखि, obl. sing, देखे. But in the centre and extreme east of the Maithilí country ऐ ăi is sometimes used for this ĕ, and on the border of the Mágadhí, ă; as in the Mt. देखै, Mg. देखऽ. The verbal noun in ब् in the central part of the S. Maithilí area, makes the obl. sing. in बा; as देखब, obl. sing. देखबा. In Bhojpúrí, the nom. and obl. plur. terminate in न, नि, or न्ह. Besides these, in Sáran and Champáran is used a non-honorific plural in सऽ sa. Avadhí, Riwáí, and Mágadhí have न in the nom. and obl. plur., and Mágadh-Maithilí, नि. The other Maithilí sub-dialects make the plural throughout like the singular, or use a periphrastic form with सभ, etc. Sufficient illustrations will be found in the Tables.

Inflectional Cases.

b. Bhojpúrí, Mágadhí, and Maithilí present in the singular true inflectional instrumental and locative cases, which terminate respectively in एं and ए. Variant forms of the instr. are, in W. Bhojpúrí, आन, and in S.E. Maithilí, ऍ and हैं. In general, these inflectional cases are confined to weak nouns, except in Bhojpúrí, where they occur in strong nouns also, a final á being first rejected. Other final long vowels are shortened, and the cognate semi-vowel is inserted before these terminations. Illustrations are: from घोड़ा, instr. घोड़ें and घोड़न; from माली, instr. मलियें; from पोथी, loc. पोथिये.

Eastern Periphrastic Plural.

183. In all the Eastern Hindí dialects लोग is added to the noun, as in High Hindí, to form a periphrastic plural. But when the noun denotes other than rational beings, सभ is used instead of लोग. In the Maithilí dialects, spoken on the border of Bangál, occur the following variants: in S. Bhagalpúr, सब and सभे, and in Central and Western Puraniyá, सब, सिबी, सिभी, and सी. In the former district, बारहिन and सब्ही, and in the latter, बार, are used in like manner. Usually, the plural

termination of the noun is omitted before these appended words, as before लोग in High Hindí; but in Bhojpúrí, Mágadhí, and some forms of Maithilí, it is pleonastically retained, giving, e.g., such forms as, पोथियन सब, 'books,' घरन सभ, 'houses.' But the postpositions only follow the second word.

Postpositions in Eastern Colloquials.

184. The several cases are formed in all the Eastern dialects, as in High Hindí, by means of postpositions added to the oblique form of the noun, sing. or plur. These are given for the several cases in Table II., and for the most part require no special remark. It should be noted, however, that of the acc. and dat. postpositions, the क forms are used both for the acc. and dat.; the remainder for the dative only. The gen. postpositions lack for the most part the inflections which they take before nouns masc. and fem. in High Hindí. The following statements indicate usage in the various Eastern dialects.

Gen. Postpositions in Eastern Dialects.

185. In Avadhí and Riwáí, कर *kar* is used unchanged before all nouns. In Bhojpúrí, क् *k*, के *kĕ*, and कै *kaï*, are used without inflection before both masc. and fem. nouns in the direct form, about as H.H. का and की; before masc. nouns in the obl. sing. and the plur., the inflected form का is used, nearly as H.H. के. In Mágadhí and Maithilí, क्, के, केर, *k*, *kĕ*, and *ker*, are used before all nouns without change for gender or number. In the Mágadhí near Patná, केरा is rarely used before masc. nouns, and केरी before fem. nouns in all cases. In Avadhí, Riwáí, and Maithil-Mágadhí, कर, as also, in the last named, कठ and केर, are used without change before all nouns. In the Maithilí of South Bhagalpúr, केरठ is used without change for number before all masc. nouns, and केरी before all fem. nouns.

Case of Agent Wanting.

186. The remaining postpositions call for no remark. It will be observed that the case of the Agent is wanting in all the modern eastern dialects. The construction of the verb with the case of the Agent in ने is distinctively a western idiom, and is not found in the local speech much east of Cawnpore. The instr. case, mentioned § 182, *b*, takes a different construction from that of the case of the agent with ने in High Hindí.

187. It should be noted that in most Hindí poetry the postpositions, though sometimes used, are oftener omitted, and the oblique form of the noun, if there be such, or if not, the nom. form, may represent any one of the cases. The same peculiarity appears, though to a more limited extent, in some Braj prose. This omission of the postpositions is not to be regarded as mere poetical or rhetorical license. The classic poetry, which is still held as the model of poetical composition, presents the language at a much earlier stage than the modern High Hindí. *Tulsí Dás,* whose *Rámáyan* is regarded by the people as a model of poetic merit, wrote in the latter half of the sixteenth century. *Kabír,* whose writings are also highly esteemed, wrote over a hundred years earlier. In its last stage of decay the ancient case-terminations had been almost all lost, so that one form—commonly the ancient genitive—had to express all the various relations formerly distributed among six cases. It was out of this state of things that the modern system of declension by the aid of post-positions gradually arose, as it was felt to be demanded by the progressive abrasion of the old forms. The old Hindí poetry presents the language to us near the beginning of this period of grammatical reform. Postpositions are indeed used, but sparingly, as compared with modern Hindí prose, and the Prakrit system of declension still to some extent maintains its ground. But this latest form of Prakrit declension, so worn out as scarcely to deserve the name, is accurately represented, not by eight, but by two, or—if we count a vocative, which now and then appears,—three cases only. The recognition of this state of things is essential to the grammatical understanding of classic Hindí poetry. **Omission of Postpositions.**

188. The following tables present a comparative view of the chief peculiarities of declension in fourteen dialects, so far as I have been able to ascertain them. Table II. gives the postpositions to be severally appended to the oblique form of the nouns in the different dialects. Table III. gives the declension of a strong masc. Tadbhava noun, with the postpositions properly appended. A few are omitted for lack of space, but they may be readily supplied from Table II. It has been judged sufficient in the other three Tables to give, with the nominative, only that form of the noun in the oblique cases, to which the postpositions are added, and the inflectional cases which occur in a few dialects. Those stems are called 'close,' which terminate in a consonant, or the silent *a*; those which end in a vocalized vowel, are called 'open.' In Table VI. the Naipálí is omitted, as the word बात does not occur in the only Naipálí that I have seen, the translation of Luke's Gospel; in which, for बात, we always have the masc. Tadbhava कुरो, obl. sing., कुरा. But if the word बात is used in Naipálí, we may infer from analogy that its declension will not differ from that of other masculine and feminine nouns uninflected in the singular. In fact, in Naipálí, all nouns, except masc. Tadbhavas in ओ, are declined exactly alike. In all the dialects the accusative may have the same form as the nominative, even though this is not always given in the Table. Where alternative forms are given for the nom. sing. or plur., either may be declined throughout.

TABLE II. POSTPOSITIONS.

	High Hindi.	*Kanauji.*	*Braj.*	*Mârwârî.*	*Mewârî.*	*Garhwâlî.*	*Kumâonî.*	*Naipâlî.*	*Old Baiswârî.*	*Avadhî.*	*Riwâî.*	*Bhojpûrî.*	*Mâgadhî.*	*Maithilî.*
Acc. Dat.	को, तईं.	को.	कौं, कूं, कुं.	कै.	पै.	सणि.	कणि, कैं. ऊणि.	लाई, लाइ.	कहं, कंह, काऊ,* कु, कुं.	क.	कहं.	के, को.‖ लाग, ला, ले. खातिर.	के.‖ लागी, लेल, ला. खातिर.	के, कें, कै, कैं, कौं.‖ लागी, लेल, ले, ले. खातिर.
Ag.	ने.	ने.	नें.	......	......	ने.	ले.	ले.	*Wanting.*	*Wanting.*	*Wanting.*	*Wanting.*	*Wanting.*	*Wanting.*
Abl.	से.	से, सेती.	सौं.	सूं.	सं.	....	है.	संग.	सन, सु.	से, सेंती, सेन.	....	सौं, सें. संती, करते.	से, सें. सतीं.	से, सें, सै, सैं. सौं, सठ, सं.
„	......	तें, ते.	तें.	......	......	ते.	थें, थै.	बाट.	तें.	....	तन, ते.	......	......	......
„	......	करि, करके.	....	......	......	....	ले.	ले.	......	....	....	......	......	......
Gen.	का, *infl.* के, की.	को, *infl.* के, की.	कौ, *infl.* के, की.	रो, *infl.* रा, री, रै.	को, *infl.* का, की, कै.†	को, *infl.* का, की.	को, *infl.* का, (की?)	को, *infl.* का, कि.	केर, केरा, केरो, *infl.* केर, केरे, केरि.	कर, *infl.* के.	कर.	......	.....	कर्, कैर.
„	......	......	....	तणो, तणूं, *fem.* तणी, *pl.* तणां.	ऌो, *infl.* ऌा, ऌी, ऌै.	....	....	....	कर, *fem.* करि.	....	....	......	केर, केरा, *fem.* केरी.	केरठ.¶
„	......	......	....	हंदो, *f.* हंदी.	......	....	....	....	क, *fem.* कि.	....	....	कै, के, कि, क्, *infl.* का.	के, क्.	के, कठ, क्.
Loc.	में.	में, मों.	में.	माहै, मांहे, मांय.	माहै.	मा.	में, मों.	मा.	मह, मई, माहि, माहिं, मांझ, मुई, मुझ, मझारी.‡	में.	म.	में, मों.	मे, में, मों.	में, मों.
„	पर, प.	पर.	पै.	ऊपरै.	ऊपरै.	पर.	पर.	माथि.	पै, परि, ऊपरि.	पर.	पर.	परि.	......	......
„	तक, तलक.	लों.	लौं.	सूधी, ताईं.	सूधी, ताईं.	तलक.	लों.	सम्म.	प्रयन्त, लगि.§	....	....	......	......	......

* Also, in the Bhaṭṭi dialect of Chand, काऊँ. † Among the Mairs, also को, का, etc. ‡ Also, in Chand, मंझ, मंझं, मझ, मझं, मधि, and मध्य. § Also, among the moderns, लग.

‖ The क forms are dat. or accusative; the others dative only. ¶ In S. Bhagalpúr inflected to केरी, only before names of female living creatures.

To face page 120.]

TABLE III. DIALECTIC DECLENSION: STRONG MASCULINE NOUN.

घोड़ा, 'a horse.'

		High Hindí.	Kanaují.	Braj.	Márwárí.	Mewárí.	Gaṛhwálí.	Kumáoní.	Naipálí.	O. Bais.	Avadhí.	Riwáí.	Bhojpúrí.	Mágadhí.	Maithilí.
SINGULAR.	N.	घोड़ा.	घोड़ा.	घोड़ा.	घोड़ो.	घोड़ो.	घोड़ो.	घोड़ा.	घोड़ो.	*Nouns of this type do not occur in the Rámáyan.*	{घोड़वा, घोड़. / घोड़ौना.	घ्वाड़.	घोड़ा, घोरा.	घोड़ा.	घोड़ा.
	Ac.	घोड़े को.	घोड़े कों.	घोड़े कौं.	घोड़ा नै.	घोड़ा ऐ.	घोड़ा सणि.	घोड़ा कणि.	घोड़ा लाई.		घोड़वा क.	घ्वाड़ कहं.	घोड़ा {के. / को.	घोड़ा के.	घोड़ा {कें, के. / कँ, कै.
	D.	घोड़े को.	घोड़े कों.	घोड़े कौं.	घोड़ा नै.	घोड़ा ऐ.	घोड़ा सणि.	घोड़ा कणि.	घोड़ा लाई.		घोड़वा क.	घ्वाड़ कहं.	घोड़ा {के. / ले.	घोड़ा {के. / किल.	घोड़ा {के. / लै.
	Ag.	घोड़े ने.	घोड़े ने.	घोड़े नें.	घोड़ै.	घोड़ै.	घोड़ा ने.	घोड़ा ले.	घोड़ा ले.		*Wanting.*	*Wanting.*	घोड़ें.	*Wanting.*	*Wanting.*
	Ab.	घोड़े से.	घोड़े तें.	घोड़े {सौं. / तें.	घोड़ा सूं.	घोड़ा ऊं.	घोड़ा ते.	घोड़ा है, etc.	घोड़ा {बाट. / से.		घोड़वा से.	घ्वाड़ ते.	घोड़ा {सें, सीं. / संति.	घोड़ा {सें, से. / सतीं.	घोड़ा {से, सै. / सऽ, सं.
	G.	घोड़े का.	घोड़े को.	घोड़े कौ.	घोड़ा रो.	घोड़ा {को, नो. / ळो.	घोड़ा को.	घोड़ा को.	घोड़ा को.		घोड़वा कर.	घ्वाड़ कर.	{घोड़क. / घोड़ा {के, के. / कि.	घोड़क. / घोड़ा {केर, केरा. / के.	घोड़क, घोड़ाक† / घोड़ा {के, कऽ. / केर, कर.
	L.	घोड़े {में. / पर.	घोड़े {में. / पर.	घोड़े {में. / परि.,	{घोड़ा / घोड़ै. {माहे. / ऊपरे	{घोड़ा माए. / घोड़ै.	घोड़ा मा.	घोड़ा मा.	घोड़ा {मा. / माथि.		घोड़वा {म. / मा.	घ्वाड़ म.	{घोड़ा / घोड़े. {में, मों. / परि.	घोड़ा {में, मे. / मों.	घोड़ा {में. / मों.
	V.	घोड़े.	घोड़े.	घोड़े.	घोड़ा.	घोड़ा.	(घोड़ा.)	(घोड़ा.)	(घोड़ा.)		घोड़वा, etc.	घ्वाड़.	घोड़ा, घोड़वा.	घोड़ा.	घोड़ा, घोड़वा.
PLURAL.	N.	घोड़े.	घोड़े.	घोड़े.	घोड़ा.	घोड़ा.	घोड़ा.	(घोड़ा.)	घोड़ाहेरु.		{घोड़वन. / घोड़ौनन.	घ्वाड़ें.	घोड़न.*	घोड़न.	घोड़नि. ‡
	Ac.	{घोड़े. / घोड़ों को.	{घोड़े. / घोड़न को.	{घोड़े. / घोड़ौं / घोड़नि} कौं.	{घोड़ा. / घोड़ां नै.	{घोड़ा. / घोड़ां ऐ.	{घोड़ा. / घोड़ौं सणि.	{घोड़ा. / घोड़ां कणि.	घोड़ाहेरु लाई.		घोड़वन क.	{घ्वाड़ें. / घ्वाड़न कहं.	घोड़न {के. / को.	घोड़न के.	घोड़नि {कि, कें. / कै, कै.
	D.	घोड़ों को.	घोड़न को.	घोड़ौं / घोड़नि} कौं.	घोड़ां नै.	घोड़ां ऐ.	घोड़ौं सणि.	घोड़ां कणि.	घोड़ाहेरु लाई.		घोड़वन क.	घ्वाड़न कहं.	घोड़न {के. / ले.	घोड़न {कि. / किल.	घोड़नि {कि. / लै.
	Ag.	घोड़ों ने.	घोड़न ने.	घोड़ौं / घोड़नि} नें.	घोड़ां.	घोड़ां.	घोड़ौं ने.	घोड़ां ले.	घोड़ाहेरु ले.		*Wanting.*	*Wanting.*	*Wanting.*	*Wanting.*	*Wanting.*
	Ab.	घोड़ों से.	घोड़न से.	घोड़ौं / घोड़नि} सौं.	घोड़ां सूं.	घोड़ां ऊं.	घोड़ौं ते.	घोड़ां है, etc.	घोड़ाहेरु {बाट. / से.		घोड़वन से.	घ्वाड़न ते.	घोड़न {सें, सीं. / संति.	घोड़न {सें, से. / सतीं.	घोड़नि {से, सै. / सऽ, सं.
	G.	घोड़ों का.	घोड़न को.	घोड़ौं / घोड़नि} कौ.	घोड़ां रो.	घोड़ां {को, नो, / ळो.	घोड़ौं को.	घोड़ां को.	घोड़ाहेरु को.		घोड़वन कर.	घ्वाड़न कर.	{घोड़नक. / घोड़न {के, के. / कि.	{घोड़नक. / घोड़न {केर, केरा / के.	{घोड़नक. / घोड़नि {के, कऽ. / को, कर.
	L.	घोड़ों {में. / पर.	घोड़न {में. / पर.	घोड़ौं / घोड़नि} में. / परि.	{घोड़ां / घोड़ां. {माहे. / ऊपरे.	{घोड़ां माए. / घोड़ां.	घोड़ौं मा.	घोड़ां {मा. / पर.	घोड़ाहेरु {मा. / माथि.		घोड़वन {मा. / मऽ.	घ्वाड़न मऽ.	घोड़न {में, मों. / परि.	घोड़न {में, मे. / मों.	घोड़नि, में, मों.
	V.	घोड़ो.	घोड़ो.	घोड़ौ.	घोड़ा.	घोड़ा.	(घोड़ौ.)	(घोड़ा.)	घोड़ाहेरु.		घोड़वन.	घ्वाड़े.	घोड़न.	......	घोड़नि.

* Also *ghŏrani, ghŏranh, ghŏrdsa.* † In S. Bhagalpúr. ‡ In several sub-dialects, plur. like sing.; and in all, the periphrastic plural with *sabh*, etc., is preferred.

To face page 121.]

TABLE IV. DIALECTIC DECLENSION: WEAK MASCULINE NOUN.

घर, 'a house.'

	H. H.	Kan.	Braj.	Már.	Mew.	Gaṛh.	Kum.	Naip.	Old Bais.	Avadh.	Riwá.	Bhoj.	Mág.	Maith.
SINGULAR.														
Nom.	घर.	घर.	घर.	घर.	घर.	घर.	घर.	घर.	घर.	घर.	घर.	घर.	घर.	घर.‡
Obl. form	घर.	घर.	घर.	घर.	घर.	घर.	घर.	घर.	घर. घरहि.	घर.	घर.	घर.	घर. घरे.	घर. घर०.
Infl. Inst.				घर.*	घर.*							घरें. घरन.	घरें.	घरें, घरैं. घरहिं.
Infl. Loc.				घरे.	घरे.							घरे.	घरे.	घरे.
PLURAL.														
Nom.	घर.	घर.	घर.	घर.	घर.	घर.	घर.	घरहेरू. घर.	घर.	घरन. घरने.	घरें.	घरन, घरनि. घरन्ह. घरसभ०.†	घरन.	घरन.§
Obl. form	घरों.	घरन.	घरौं. घरनि.	घरां.	घरां.	घरौं.	घरां.	घरहेरू. घर.	घरन्हि. घरन्ह. घरन.	घरन.	घरन.	घरन.	घरन.	घरन.§

* Used alone for the case of the Agent; = H. H. *ghar ne*. † In Sáran and Champáran. ‡ In S. Maithilí, also *ghaur* throughout.

§ Several of the Maithilí sub-dialects have no separate form for the plural; and in all the periphrastic plural with *sabh*, etc., is preferred.

TABLE V. DIALECTIC

नारी,

	SINGULAR.						
	H. Hindí.	*Kan.*	*Braj.*	*Már.*	*Mew.*	*Gaṛh.*	*Kum.*
Nom.	नारी.	नारी.	नारी.	नारी.	नारी.	नारी.	नारी.
Obl. form.	नारी.	नारी.	नारी.	नारी.	नारी.	नारी.	नारी.
Infl. Inst.				नारी.*	नारी.*		
Infl. Loc.							
	PLURAL.						
Nom.	नारियां.	नारीं.	नारीं. नारियां.	नार्यां.	नार्यां.	नारी.	नारियां.
Obl. form.	नारियों.	नारिन.	नारिन. नारियन. नारियनि. नारियौं.	नार्यां.	नार्यां.	नारियौं.	नारिन.

* Used without a postposition, = H. H. *nárí ne.*

† In Sáran and Champáran.

‡ An inflected loc. form occurs in a few words only, especially in phrases.

DECLENSION : Open Feminine Noun.

'a woman.'

Naip.	*Old Bais.*	*Avadh.*	*Riwá.*	*Bhoj.*	*Mág.*	*Maith.*
नारी.	नारि.	नारिया. नारीआ.	नारी.	नारी.	नारी.	नारी.
नारी.	नारि. नारिन्हि.*	नारिया. नारीआ.	नारी.	नारी. नरियें. नरिये.	नारी.	नारी. (नारियें)‡
नारी. नारीहरु.	नारि.	नारिन. नारियन.	नारी.	नारिन. नारिन्ह. नारीस०.†	नारिन.	नारिन.§
नारी. नारीहरु.	नारिन. नारिन्ह. नारिन्हि.	नारिन. नारियन.	नारिनि.	नारिन. नरिन्हि. नारीस०.†	नारिन.	नारिन.

§ Several Maithilí sub-dialects have no separate form for the plural; but the periphrastic plural is preferred in all.

TABLE VI. DIALECTIC DECLENSION: Close Feminine Noun.

बात, 'a word.'

	H. H.	Kan.	Braj.	Máṛ.	Mew.	Gaṛh.	Kum.	Old Bais.	Avadh.	Riwá.	Bhoj.	Mág.	Maith.
SINGULAR.													
Nom.	बात.	बात.	बात.	बात.	बात.	बात.	बात.	बात.	बात.	बात.	बात.	बात.	बात.
Obl. form	बात.	बात.	बात.	बात.	बात.	बात.	बात,	बात.	बात. बातहि.	बात.	बात.	बात.	बात.
Infl. Inst.				बात.*	बात.*						बतें.		बतें.
Infl. Loc.											बते.		बते.
PLURAL.													
Nom.	बातें.	बातें.	बातें.	बातां.	बातां.	बातऽ.	बात.†	बात.†	बात.	बात.	बातन. बातन्ह. बतनि. बातसऽ.‡	बातन.	बातन.§ बतियनि.
Obl. form	बातों.	बातन.	बातन. बातनि.	बातां.	बातां.	बातु.	बातन.	बातन. बातनि. बातन्ह.	बात.	बात.	बातन. बातन्ह. बातसऽ.	बातन.	बातन. बतियनि.

* Used alone = H. H. *bát ne.*

† So in the only book I have seen; I should suppose, from analogy of contiguous Gaṛhwálí, it would be pronounced *báta.*

‡ In Sáran and Champáran.

§ Several Maithilí sub-dialects have no distinct plural form. But the periphrastic plural is preferred in all.

ORIGIN OF THE DECLENSIONAL FORMS.

189. In all Tatsama nouns and many Tadbhavas, the distinctive termination of the Sanskrit nom. sing. has entirely disappeared from modern High Hindí. But in archaic and poetic Hindí, as also in Naipálí and other Himalayan dialects, *u* final often remains in masc. nouns, where it represents the Prakrit termination *o*, for the Sk. *aḥ*; as, e.g., in *desu*, for Pr. *deso*, Sk. *deshaḥ*, H. H. *desh*; and *láhu*, Pr. *láho*, Sk. *lábhaḥ*, H. H. *lábh*.* This form is common in the *Rámáyan*, with the final vowel often lengthened *metr. grat.*; as in *láhú* for *láhu*, H. H. *lábh*. Origin of Nom. Sing.

a. Tadbhava masc. nouns in *á*, Máṛ. *o*, inflected to *e* in the sing., usually represent Sanskrit or Prakrit nouns formed by adding the affix *ka* to bases in *a*.† This added *k* was first rejected, and then the concurrent vowels were combined. Thus, e.g., for the Sk. *ghaṭa*, we have a Prakrit theme, *ghaṭaka*, nom. sing., *ghaṭakaḥ*, whence, by §§ 79, *c.*, 89, *k* being rejected, and the final *aḥ* changed to *o*, we have a form *ghaṛäo*, which by *sandhi*, yields first a form in *au*, the common Braj termination; which, again, is softened to *o* in *ghaṛo*, as in Máṛwáṛi and in most western dialects, and is finally reduced to *á* in the High Hindí form, *ghaṛá*. By a similar process, we obtain in succession from the Sk. *melakaḥ*, for *melaḥ*, the forms, *meläo*, Máṛ. *melo*, H. H. *melá*.

---

* See §§ 79, *c.*, 85, *a.*, 99; the change had already taken place in the Apabhransic Prakrit. In the dialect of the *Rámáyan* of *Tulsí Dás*, this final *u* is added, from analogy, even to Arabic and Persian nouns, where it does not belong; as, e.g., *niwáju*, for the Pers. *niwáz*; *tarwáru*, for *talwár*; and in the Baghelkhaṇḍi N.T., in *shaksu*, *shahru*, for Ar. *shakhs*, *shahr*.

† See § 100, and foot-note. Lassen (*Inst. Ling. Pracr.*, p. 475) explains this termination as due to the elision of the affix *k*, 'of very frequent use' in the Apabhransic Prakrit. Beames, while accepting, in general, with Hoernle, this theory as to the origin of these Hindí nouns in *o* and *á*, adds the suggestion that an original accent of the ultimate in such words may have had much to do in the preservation of this Prakritic *o*. (*Comp. Gramm.* vol. ii. pp. 4-15.) But the lists of words which he gives will hardly warrant us in assigning to this factor a universal influence, and I am inclined still to regard the addition and subsequent elision of this Prakritic *k* as at least the chief cause of the conservation of the long termination in this class of Hindí nouns.

b. Tadbhava fem. nouns in *í* commonly stand for Sanskrit or Prakrit nouns ending in the fem. affix *iká*, whence have arisen, successively, forms in *iá* and *iyá*.* By a similar process are explained the Avadhí fem. nouns in *ívá*; as, e.g., *nadívá* (H. H. *nadí*), which presupposes a Prakrit theme, *nadiká*. After the same analogy are derived fem. nouns in *ú*, as, e.g., *bálú*, for Sk. *báluká*, whence the Pr. *bálua*, Av. *báluyá*, H. H. *bálú*. Similarly we explain many Tadbhava masc. nouns in *í* and *ú*; as, e.g., from Sk. *dhávikaḥ*, H. H. *dhobí*, through intermediate forms, *dhávio*, *dhobiyá*; *motí*, masc. from Sk. neut. *mauktikam*, through Pr. *mottiam*; and also, H. H. *bichchhú*, for a Prakrit form, *viñchhuo*, for vulgar Sk. *vṛishchukaḥ* (?), for *vṛishchikaḥ*. The Sk. fem. termination, *á*, has disappeared; as, e.g., in *bát*, for Sk. *vártá*.

Origin of Obl. Sing.

190. In the *hi*, *hiṉ*, which mark the obl. sing. of all nouns in O. B. and other archaic Hindí, we have a last surviving remnant of the Sk. sing. declensional system. These appear to stand respectively for the gen. sing., *he*, and the loc. sing., *hiṉ*, of the Apabhransic Prakrit. Of these, the former is derived from the termination of the Sk. gen. sing., *sya*;† the latter from that of the Sk. loc. sing. in *smin*, which in Sk. appears only in certain pronouns, but in Apabhransic Prakrit was transferred also to nouns. In archaic Hindí, the case distinctions were so far obliterated that these terminations stand not only for the gen. and loc., but also for the dat., acc., and abl. as well.

a. From this obl. sing. form in *hi*, when added to Prakritic themes in *ako*, *äo*, by the common elision of *h* we should have *äi*, which by contraction gives us the *e* which in High Hindí marks the obl. sing. of nouns of this class. In unaugmented themes, as in *ghar* (Sk. *gṛiha*), the *hi* has wholly disappeared, leaving the obl. form like the nom.

b. The Máṛ., Mw., Kan., and G. (also Guj.) obl. sing. of this class of nouns, points back to another Pr. gen. sing., in *ssa*, for Sk. *sya*; whence Prakrit terminations, *ha*, *aho*, which, added to stems of this type, by a similar elision of *h*, and *sandhi* of concurrent vowels, would yield the obl. sing. termination, *á*, of these dialects. Hence also the Avadhí form in *vá*, where, however, *v* has been inserted because of the hiatus caused by the loss of the original suffix, *k*.

---

* Vid. §§ 82, 88, *a.*, *Rem.* 1.

† Vid. Lassen: *Inst. Ling. Pracr.* § 175, 6.

‡ Vid. ib. §§ 175, 7; 106, 6.

c. The Máṛwáṛí and Mewáṛí have preserved an inflected case of the agent, in *ai*, derived apparently from the Sk. instr. case termination *ina*, Ap. Pr. *eṇa* and *eṉ*, whence, with the loss of the nasal, the form in question. The same termination is to be recognized in the Bhojpúrí, Mágadhí, and Maithilí inflected instr. case in *eṉ*, as in *baleṉ*, 'by force;' in which, as also in the same case-ending in Maráṭhí, Anusvár represents the original *n* of *ina*. Gujerátí retains this same case-ending, though Anusvár has been lost, as in the Rajputana dialects. The same Hindí dialects retain also an inflected loc. sing. in *e* or *ai*, in which we have the Sk. loc. termination *i*. Inflected Instr. and Loc. Sing.

191. The nom. plur. termination, *e*, of Tadbhava nouns in *á*, as also the dialectic termination, *á*, finds a parallel in the same termination in the nom. plur. masc. of the Mágadhí Prakrit,* and one might be inclined to adopt this view of their origin, except that the Mágadhí was an eastern form of Prakrit, whereas these terminations are chiefly found in the western dialects of Hindí. The western Apabhransic Prakrit, which so often helps in the elucidation of Western Hindí forms, apparently furnishes the original of the Máṛwáṛí (also Kum., G., Mw.) nom. plur. in *á*, as a weakening of the Apabhransic termination *áö*, *áu*; but this gives no light as to the termination *e*. As regards this last termination, therefore, I still incline to prefer Hoernle's suggestion that the inflected nom. plur. of these nouns is in fact identical with the obl. sing.; i.e., it is originally a gen. sing., and thus an elliptical expression, leaving *log*, *vṛind*, or some such noun of multitude, to be understood. This hypothesis would not only explain both of these nom. plurals, but also explicate such rare and now vulgar idioms as *kutte log*, etc. An analogy to this supposed transfer of a gen. to the nom. is found in the Baghelkhaṇḍí N. T., where the gen. plur. form of the 2nd personal pronoun, *tiháṉre*, similarly appears as a nominative. In the archaic nom. plur. in *n* or *ni*, still preserved in Avadhí, we have the Sk. neut. nom. plur. termination, transferred to masc. and fem. nouns. This change had already taken place in Prakrit.† Origin of Nom. Plur.

a. The various fem. nom. plur. terminations, *aiṉ*, *áṉ*, *eṉ*, and *ṉ*, have arisen from the same neut. termination, *ani*, by contraction from the

* Vid. Lassen: *Inst. Ling. Prac.* p. 430. So also Beames: *Comp. Gramm.* vol. ii. p. 205.

† Vid. Lassen: *Inst. Ling. Prac.* p. 309.

Prakrit *äiṉ*, or by rejection of the final *i* and softening of *ṉ* to Anusvár; *áṉ*, indeed, already appears as nom. plur. in Shaurasení Prakrit.*

b. Nouns not included under the above heads, have lost the nom. plur. termination, and thus become in form like the singular.

Origin of Obl. Plur. Forms. **192**. Of the oblique plural, the earliest Hindí form that I have found is given by Beames from Chand, in *ánaṉ*, Pr. *áṇam*; from which last are readily derived, through Prakrit gen. forms in *huṉ* and *hüṉ*, the Hindí terminations, *auṉ*, *oṉ*, and *áṉ*. In the obl. plur. forms in *an* and *ani*, we must again recognize the Sanskrit termination, *ani*, of the nom. and acc. neut. plural, which, not unnaturally, appears to have been confused with that of the gen. plural.

a. I am unable to account for the *hi* which is added to this final *n* in some Eastern Hindí dialects, except it be that, from the need of a clearer indication of the oblique than this *an* alone could give, the termination *hi* (Sk. *sya*), already the sign of the oblique in the singular,† was made to serve the same purpose in the plural also. The plural termination, *nh*, is probably to be explained, with Hoernle,‡ as representing the *ṇṇ* of the Prakrit gen. plural, which already in some Prakrit dialects had become *nh*.§

193. The Naipálí termination, *heru* or *haru*, of the nom. and obl. plur., is made up of two elements; the first, *he* (or *ha*) is the termination of the Ap. Prakrit gen. sing., for Sk. *sya*;‖ to which has been added, in the second place, the affix *kerako*, whence *keräo*, *kero*, *keru*, giving, e.g., such a form as *ghoḍahakeru*, whence by elision of *k*, etc., *ghoṛáheru*.

Origin of the Postpositions of Declension.

194. The origin of the genitive postposition has long been one of the vexed questions of Hindí philology; but Dr. Hoernle, of Benares, may be regarded as having at last reached a solution of the problem.¶ For the

* Vid. Lassen: *Inst. Ling. Prac.* p. 379.

† Vid. § 18. ‡ *Comp. Gramm.* p. 211.

§ Vid. Lassen: *Inst. Ling. Prac.* p. 271. ‖ Ib. p. 462.

¶ Vid. op. cit. § 377. Since the first edition of this work, Beames has published his acceptance of essentially the same theory; see his *Comp. Gramm.* vol. ii. pp. 276-287.

exhibition of his argument we refer the reader to his Comparative Grammar, and here briefly note the conclusions to which his investigation leads.

a. The various forms of the Hindí gen. postposition, viz. *ká, kau, ko, ka, kar, kará, kerau, kero, kerá, ker, go, ro, ḷo,* are all corruptions or Prakrit modifications of *kṛita,* the Sk. past part. of *kṛi,* 'to do.' This participle received in Prakrit the addition of the common affix *ka,* so that by the elision of *t,* and change of *ṛi* to *er,* it assumed the form *keraka* or *kerika.* In Prakrit, this participle was often used after a gen. noun, with which it was made to agree, but without any modification of the sense. Thus it came at last to supplant the gen. termination, and became itself a sign of the gen. case, as it is to-day in Hindí. From *kerakaḥ* we obtain the Hindí postpositions, *kero, kerá, ker, kĕ,* precisely as we have *ghoṛo, ghoṛá,* and *ghor,* from *ghoṭakaḥ*; and—*ar,* instead of *er,* being substituted for the *ṛi* of *kṛita*—through shorter Prakrit forms, *karito, kario,* may be derived the eastern colloquial forms, *kara, kar, ka.* These are thus the oldest forms of the Hindí gen. postposition. In the case of the 1st and 2nd pers. pronouns in High Hindí, and in Máṛwáṛí and Mewáṛí universally, the initial *k* and the final *k* of *karako* or *kerako* having both been elided, the forms *räo, rau, ro,* and *rá* remained. From the forms above given may easily be derived the Braj, Kanaují and High Hindí forms, *kau, ko,* and *ká,* as also the Márwáṛí, *go.* The Mewáṛí, *ḷo,* in like manner, points back to another Prakrit form of this same word, *kelako,* for *kerako,* as its original; unless, indeed, it be connected with the Máṛwáṛí *dá* (?). Origin of Gen. Postpositions.

b. The Máṛ. gen. postposition *dá,* G. *do,* I now regard as abbreviated from the archaic Máṛ. gen. postposition, *hando.** This last has been connected by Beames, through the common Máṛwáṛí change of *s* to *h,* with the Sindhí gen. postposition, *sando,* and thus with the Sk. pres. part., *santa,* from the root *as.*† Thus, e.g., the Máṛ. *ghoṛá dá* (archaic, *ghoṛá hando*) would be, lit., 'being of the horse,' i.e., 'that which is of the horse.'

c. The rare Máṛ. gen. postposition, *tanau* (Guj. *ṇo*), already appears, as *taṇo,* in the Apabhransic Prakrit, and later, in Old Gujeráti. It is connected by Beames with the Sk. affix, *tana,* as in *sanátana, purátana,*

* Vid. § 172. Hoernle, however, would connect it with *diyá,* 'given,' perf. part. of *dená.* See *Comp. Gramm.* p. 239.

† *Comp. Gramm.* vol. ii. pp. 290, 291.

nútana, from *saná, purá, nú* (*nava*).* If this origin be granted, then the heavy termination in *o* would seem from analogy to point toward a Prakritic form of this affix, *tanako*, whence *tanäo*, etc.; a supposition the more probable in this case, that to this day the Máṛwáṛís are specially fond of adding *k* and other meaningless letters to various words. Yet in view of the fact that the postpositions generally are demonstrably Prakrit forms of individual words, originally regarded as in grammatical construction with the preceding noun, some doubt would seem to attach to the above derivation, as making this *tanau* unlike other postpositions, and an exception to this rule. On this we must wait for more light.

Origin of Dat. and Acc. Postpositions.

195. In the former edition of this work I was inclined, with Trumpp, to seek the origin of the objective postpositions, *ko, kauṉ*, etc., in this same Sk. participle, *kṛita*, which has been the original of the gen. postpositions, *ká*, etc. Further study of the matter, however, has led me to accept the theory suggested by Hoernle,† and worked out also by Beames,‡ which connects the various objective postpositions which have an initial *k*, with the Sk. loc. sing., *kákshe*, from *káksha*, 'armpit,' 'side,' whence the loc. Bang. form, *káchhe*, 'near.' From this word comes the O. H. *kákh*, acc. *kákham*; whence, by the common attenuation of *kh* to *h*, and its subsequent elision, may easily be derived the various forms of this postposition, *káhaṉ, kahaṉ, káhuṉ* or *kahuṉ, kauṉ*, and *ko*. An apposite instance of an identical series of phonetic changes is given by Beames, in the case of the Sk. *paksha*, 'side,' which has become, in Hindí, *pákhaṉ, páhuṉ, pahuṉ*.§ This accounts in a simple way for the medial *h* in the archaic forms of this postposition, as the older theory does not; while the meaning, 'to,' 'towards,' may be easily derived from the earlier sense of the word, as illustrated in the Bang., *káchhe*, 'near.'

a. The origin of the objective postpositions, *neṉ, nai*, and *na*, used in Western Hindí, is suggested by the Naipálí substitute, *leṉ*, which, by a simple and common phonetic change, has probably arisen from *lagi* (from the root *lag*), still used in dialectic Hindí, as a postposition meaning 'to,' 'up to.'‖ This change of *l* to *ne* is well illustrated by the Máṛ., *nánat*,

* *Comp. Gramm.* vol. ii. p. 287. † See *Comp. Gramm.* § 375, 1.

‡ *Comp. Gramm.* vol. ii. pp. 252-259. § Ib. vol. ii. p. 258.

‖ Another possible derivation, however, is that suggested by Hoernle, from Sk. *labdha* (H. H. *liyá*), 'received,' 'obtained,' loc. sing., *labdhe*, 'for the benefit of.' See *Comp. Gramm.* § 375, 2.

for Ar., *la'nat*, 'curse,' and *Nandan*, for 'London,' as found in the Máṛ. *Khyáls*.

b. Of the Himalayan objective postpositions, *kaṇi* is an old loc. sing., from the Sk., *karṇe*, 'at the ear,' or 'side.' It is to be identified with the Br. and Kan., *kane*, used in a distinct prepositional sense, as in *mere kane áo*, 'come to me.' *Saṇi*, found also in other Western Hindí dialects, is derived by Hoernle from the Sk. *sañge*, in the sense, 'in attachment to.' With this he also connects the abl. postpositions, *san*, *sen*, *san*, *sane*, and *sent*. The origin of the Kum. *huni* is not so clear; but I am inclined to connect it with the noun of agency, *hunyá* (from *hunu*, 'to be'), in the contiguous Naipálí, the usage of which sometimes closely approaches that of an objective postposition, as in the following: *mero hunyá aṇs*, 'the part which is for me' (Luke xv. 12.)

c. *Taiṇ*, sometimes used for *ko*, as in *apne taiṇ* for *apne ko*, is from the Sk. loc. sing., *sthâne*.*

196. The facts brought to light by Beames† since the former edition of this Grammar was published, appear to settle the long-debated question of the origin of the postposition *ne*, in the case of the agent, and demonstrate its connection with the *n* forms of the objective postposition. Origin of the Postpositions of the Agent.

a. Against the old theory of the connection of this *ne* with the Sk. instr. affix, *ina*, stand the following facts. First, unlike that, it is but loosely connected with the noun, in which respect, however, it evidently resembles the other postpositions, as *meṇ*, *par*, etc., which are known to have been originally separate words. In the second place, it is impossible thus to account for the final *e*. The natural effect of long use, as in all similar cases, would be to shorten, rather than to lengthen, the affix. Thirdly, its very late appearance is against such an origin; it cannot be traced back further than two or three hundred years. Lastly, in older authors, where the subject is a pronoun, and the construction in modern High Hindí would require the case of the agent with *ne*, they often use simply the obl. form of the pronoun, thus showing that already the distinctive termination of this case had been lost. And so in the Rajputana dialects, where a relic of the Sanskrit termination of this case has been demonstrably preserved, as in Máṛ., *ghoṛai*, for *ghoṛe ne*, the *n* has already disappeared.

b. The clue to the real origin of this postposition is furnished by the

---

* See, however, § 198, *b*.

† *Comp. Gramm.* vol. ii. pp. 262-272.

Gujeráti, which, in many cases where High Hindí would use the case of the agent with *ne*, employs instead the dative, which case, in Gujeráti, is formed by the postposition *ne*. Remembering now that the use of *ne* for the agent belongs exclusively to Western Hindí, with which Gujeráti is historically and geographically connected, one cannot well resist the conclusion that the *ne* of the agent in Hindí, is identical with the *ne* of the dative in Gujeráti and Panjábí. But while Gujeráti used this particle for both the object and the agent, Hindí, having already an objective postposition, *ko*, naturally restricted the use of *ne* to the case of the agent. If, now, we inquire further what was the origin of this *ne*, we are thus at once led to connect it,—like the *nai*, *naiṉ*, and *ná*, which in some Western Hindí dialects are substituted for *ko*,—through the Naipálí *le*, with the root *lag*; the order of derivation being as follows: Sk. past part. act., *lagya*, Pr. *laggio*, H. *lagi*, *lai*, *le*, *ne*. The Anusvár, which sometimes occurs, appears to be inorganic.

Origin of the Abl. Postpositions.

197. The postposition, *se*, with its variants, *saṉ*, *seṉ*, *saiṉ*, *sane*, *san*, and *sení*, as already suggested, may be connected with the Sk. loc. sing., *sañge*. The form *hai*, is easily explained by the familiar change of *s* to *h*. The forms *soṉ* and *sauṉ*, however, are more naturally explained as having arisen from the Sk., *sam*, 'with,' the *m* of which would account for the labial diphthongs, *o* and *au*.

a. *Teṉ*, *te*, and *tan*, may *possibly* be connected, as has been suggested,* with the Sk. abl. affix, *tas*, which may be added to any noun in Sanskrit, giving it an ablative sense. It may be noted that under the form *to*, this *tas* had become the regular abl. termination in Prakrit. But the analogy of the other postpositions as being separate words, requiring the inflection of the stem of the noun to which they are attached, casts doubt upon this derivation, and suggests that the origin of these postpositions also must be sought in some individual word. I am thus inclined to accept the suggestion of Hoernle† that the original of *te* and *teṉ* is the loc. of a Sk. past part., *tarite*, root *tṛí* (for the regular form *tírṇa*), 'to pass over.' From this would come a Pr. form, *tarie*, or *täie*, whence, *te*. The Anusvár would then be inorganic.

Origin of the Loc. Postpositions.

198. The various forms of the loc. postposition, *meṉ*, are all referable to the loc. sing., *madhye*, of the Sk. *madhya*, 'middle.' The various forms, *madhya*, *madhi*, *mahi*, *máhi*, *mah*, all exhibit successive processes

* Beames: *Comp. Gramm.* vol. ii. p. 273.

† *Comp. Gramm.* pp. 225, 226.

of derivation, *dh* becoming *h*, and *y*, by § 90, first becoming *i* and then disappearing. In the forms *máṉjh*, *majhi*, *jh* is substituted for the conjunct *dhy* (§ 107). The long form, *máhai*, suggests an increased Prakritic form, *madhyake*. The various forms with Anusvár, *máhiṉ*, *mahaṉ*, *meṉ*, *moṉ*, *majjham*, are possibly to be referred to the acc. form, *madhyam*. *Meṉ* or *maiṉ* has arisen from *máhiṉ*, and *máṉ* from *mahaṉ*, by rejection of *h*, and *sandhi* of the concurrent vowels.*

a. The other loc. postposition, *par*, in all its variations, is derived from the Sk. *upari*, 'on.' The Máṛwáṛí, always tenacious of old forms, has retained the initial vowel to the present day. From this original have proceeded in succession, the Bh. *pari*, H. H. *par*, Br. *pai*, and Urdú *pa*.

b. The postposition *tak* is connected by Prof. Monier-Williams† with the Sanskrit affix, *daghna*, used in the same sense; thus, we may compare the Hindí, *ghuṭne tak*, 'up to the knee,' with the Sk. *jánu-daghna*, of the same meaning. But the analogy of the other postpositions again leads us rather to seek for the original of *tak* in some separate word; and I am inclined to accept the opinion of Hoernle‡ that it is to be found in the Sk. past part., *tarita*,—from the root *tṛí*,—'passed to,' hence, 'up to;' to which has been added the dat. affix, *ku*, *r* and *t* having suffered elision. In the form *talak*, the *l* would represent the *r* of *tarita*, which in the shorter form has disappeared. With *tarita* Hoernle also connects *te* and *taiṉ*.

c. The postposition *lagi* or *lági*, having the same meaning as the above, is to be identified with the Sk. indecl. past part., *lagya*, Pr. *laggio*, from the root *lag*, 'to be attached.' The forms *loṉ* and *lauṉ*, may be derived from the other Prakrit form of the same participle, viz. *lagiúṇa*, for the Sk. *lagitvá*, whence, by the rejection of the medial *g*, and *sandhi* of the vowels, *ṇ* final passing into Anusvár, we have the forms, *lauṉ* and *loṉ*. Unless, indeed, with Hoernle,§ we trace it to the Ap. Pr. loc. sing. *läiahuṉ*, for the Sk. loc. *labdhe*, lit., 'for the benefit of' (?).

* Notwithstanding the high authority of Professor Weber, with this series of forms before me, I cannot agree with him when (*Jena Literatur Zeitung*, 1877, Nr. 33), he would derive *meṉ* from the Sk. loc. affix, *smin*. Still less can I accept his alternative suggestion that, when used in comparisons, *meṉ* may represent the Ar. *min*. Arabic particles are very rarely used in modern Hindí, and *min*, I think, never. Moreover, when *min* is used, even in Urdú, it is not found by itself, but always in Arabic phrases, like *min jumla*, *min jánib*, etc., and is never transposed from its proper place at the beginning of a word.

† *Sansk. Gramm.* 80, xx.

‡ *Comp. Gramm.* pp. 225, 226.

§ *Comp. Gramm.* p. 224.

CHAPTER VI.

ADJECTIVES (गुणवाचक).

199. The Hindí adjective is exceedingly simple, and presents little requiring special explanation. Adjectives fall into two classes, viz., *uninflected* and *inflected*. Uninflected adjectives, as the term implies, remain unchanged before all nouns and under all circumstances, like the English adjective, and require no explanation. Inflected adjectives all terminate in आ *á*, and correspond in all respects to Tadbhava nouns of the same termination, inflected to ए *e* in the oblique singular. The rules for the inflection of such Tadbhava adjectives are the same as those given for the inflection of the genitive postposition, का, viz. :—

Inflection of Adjectives. (1) Before a masc. noun in the nom. sing., आ *á* final is unchanged.

(2) Before a masc. noun in any other case, आ *á* final is changed to ए *e*.

(3) Before a fem. noun in any case, sing. or plur., आ *á* final is changed to ई *í*.

The following examples will illustrate the construction of adjectives :—

UNINFLECTED ADJECTIVES.

सुंदर फूल *sundar phúl*, 'a beautiful flower,' or 'beautiful flowers.'

सुंदर फूल पर *sundar phúl par*, 'on a beautiful flower.'

सुंदर फूलों का *sundar phúloṉ ká*, 'of beautiful flowers.'
सुंदर लड़की *sundar laṛkí*, 'a beautiful girl.'
सुंदर लड़कियां *sundar laṛkiyáṉ*, 'beautiful girls.'
सुंदर लड़की का *sundar laṛkí ká*, 'the beautiful girl's.'
सुंदर लड़कियों को *sundar laṛkiyoṉ ko*, 'to beautiful girls.'
धर्म्मी पुरुष *dharmmí purush*, 'a virtuous man,' or 'virtuous men.'
धर्म्मी पुरुष का *dharmmí purush ká*, 'a virtuous man's.'
धर्म्मी पुरुषों में *dharmmí purushoṉ meṉ*, 'among virtuous men.'
धर्म्मी स्त्री *dharmmí strí*, 'a virtuous woman.'
धर्म्मी स्त्रियां *dharmmí striyáṉ*, 'virtuous women.'
धर्म्मी स्त्री को *dharmmí strí ko*, 'to a virtuous woman.'
धर्म्मी स्त्रियों को *dharmmí striyoṉ ko*, 'to virtuous women.'

Inflected Adjectives.

काला घोड़ा *kálá ghoṛá*, 'a black horse.'
काले घोड़े *kále ghoṛe*, 'black horses.'
काले घोड़े का *kále ghoṛe ká*, 'the black horse's.'
काले घोड़ों पर *kále ghoṛoṉ par*, 'on black horses.'
काली बिल्ली *kálí billí*, 'a black cat.'
काली बिल्लियां *kálí billiyáṉ*, 'black cats.'
काली बिल्ली पर *kálí billí par*, 'on a black cat.'
काली बिल्लियों को *kálí billiyoṉ ko*, 'to black cats.'

a. Very rarely, adjectives in ई *í* are inflected to इया *iyá*, for the feminine: as in दुखिया *dukhiyá*, from दुखी *dukhí*, 'afflicted.'

200. A very few adjectives terminate in आं *áṉ*; these follow the analogy of Tadbhava masc. nouns of the same termination, and are inflected to एं *eṉ*, obl. masc. and ईं *íṉ*, fem., according to the rules above given for adjectives in आ *á*.* The same rule applies to all ordinal numeral adjectives ending in वां *wáṉ*. Examples

* Vid. § 199.

are: बायें हाथ *báyen̲ háth*, 'on the left hand;' दसवीं घड़ी पर *daswín̲ gharí par*, 'at the tenth hour;' बीसवें महीने में *bíswen̲ mahíne men̲*, 'in the twentieth month.'

Rem. Adjectives do not, as a rule, assume the plural terminations, एं, आं, ओं. When the adjective comes last, in the poetic style, they are very rarely added. The perfect and imperfect participles of verbs, when used adjectively, are subject to the same rules as inflected adjectives.

Affixes of Likeness.

201. The affix सरीखा *saríkhá* (also सरीका and सारिखा) Sk. सदृश, Pr. सरिच्छं, is sometimes added to the inflected base both of substantives and pronouns, to express likeness. It is then inflected according to the rules for the inflection of Tadbhava adjectives in आ *á*; as, तुम सरीखे पुरुषों का *tum saríkhe purushon̲ ká*, 'of men like you;' उस सरीखे को मत मानो *us saríkhe ko mat máno*, 'do not mind the like of him.'

202. The affix सा *sá* is added to adjectives to express resemblance, with the accessory idea of a lesser degree of the quality.

a. This affix is inflected to ए *e* and ई *í* according to the rules for the inflection of Tadbhava adjectives in आ. The adjective preceding सा *sá*, if capable of inflection, must also be inflected. Examples are: लाल सा फूल *lál sá phúl*, 'a reddish flower;' नीली सी चिड़ियां *nílí sí chiṛiyán̲*, 'blueish birds;' पीले से पत्ते *píle se patte*, 'yellowish leaves.'

b. The same particle may also be added to a noun or pronoun, converting it into an adjective expressing likeness; the pronoun must be put in the oblique form. Thus, e.g., we may say: खड्ग सा हथयार *khaṛag sá hathyár*, 'a sword-like weapon;' मुझ सा पापी *mujh sá pápí*, 'a sinner like me;' तुम सा मित्र *tum sá mitr*, 'a friend like you.'*

---

* With such expressions as the above, compare such English colloquial forms as 'sick-like,' 'weak-like,' etc.

Rem. These compounds with सा are sometimes used in a substantive sense; in which case सा is inflected to agree with the noun to which it is appended; as, पिघा सी छाई जाती है, 'something like a sorrow is overspread.'

c. सा *sá* is also added to the genitive both of nouns and pronouns, when the likeness intended is not, as in the previous case, to the person or thing itself, but to something pertaining to the person or thing. Both the genitive and the appended सा are then inflected to agree with the following noun.

Thus we say: पंडित की सी बोली *paṇḍit kí sí bolí*, 'speech like that of a pundit;' हाथी का सा मुंह *háthí ká sá muṇh*, 'a face like an elephant's;' बाघ के से दांत *bágh ke se dáṇt*, 'teeth like those of a tiger.'

d. This idiom is to be explained by supposing an ellipsis of the substantive after the genitive. Thus, *háthí ká sá muṇh* is for *háthí ká muṇh sá muṇh*; as we say in English, 'a face like an elephant's,' for 'a face like an elephant's face.'

e. Sometimes the noun qualified is omitted, as in the following: *parbat kí kundalá sí dikhái paṛtí hai*, 'something like a mountain cave appears.' Here we must evidently supply some feminine noun, as, e.g., *bastu*.

203. Identical in form, but of different origin and meaning, is the particle सा *sá*, which is added in like manner to adjectives, to denote intensity or excess. Affix of Intensity.

Examples of this usage are: बहुत सा आटा *bahut sá áṭá*, 'a great deal of flour;' थोड़ी सी रोटी *thoṛí sí roṭí*, 'a very little bread;' ऊंचा सा पहाड़ *úṇchá sá paháṛ*, 'a very high mountain;' बड़े से घोड़े *baṛe se ghoṛe*, 'very large horses.'

a. *Sá*, as used in this sense, is derived from the Sanskrit affix, *shas*, '-fold,' through the Braj *so*. *Sá*, the affix denoting likeness, has come from the Sanskrit *sama*, 'like,' through the intermediate Braj form, *saun*, as the H. H. inf., *karná*, has come through the Braj *karnaun*.

204. The dialectic forms of adjectives call for little remark. Tadbhava High Hindí adjectives in आ, inflected, in Dialectic Forms of Adjectives

Braj have the termination औ, and in Kanaují, the Rajputana and Himalayan dialects, ओ. The inflection of such adjectives in each of these dialects is the same as that of the corresponding class of nouns. Occasionally Anusvár is added to the Braj obl. masc. inflection. Examples are the following: for H.H., थोड़ा, Br., थोड़ौ, Máṛ., Mew., Kan., etc., थोड़ो, 'little;' Br. मीठे बचन सौं or मीठें बचन सौं, 'with a pleasant word,' for H.H., मीठे बचन से. Máṛwáṛí illustrations are: बड़ो घोड़ो, 'a large horse;' बड़ी घोड़ी, 'a large mare;' बड़ा घोड़ा, 'large horses' (H.H. बड़े घोड़े); बड़ा बाद्शा री तगत, 'the throne of the great king.' Kanaují forms of the adjective occasionally occur in poetry; as, in the *Rámáyan*, सांवरो, for H.H., सांवला, 'sallow.'

a. In all the Himalayan dialects, these same adjectives have in the nom. sing. the termination ओ, inflected, as in nouns of this class, to आ, in the masc. obl. sing. and the plur.; and to ई, for the fem., throughout: as, N. ठुलो, 'great,' infl. masc. ठुला, fem. ठुली. But the possessive adjective, H. H., अपना, appears in Naipálí in the weak form, आफनु; it is inflected, however, after the analogy of the strong forms, to आफना and आफनी.

205. In the dialect of the *Rámáyan*, the class of Tadbhava adjectives in आ is wanting, and all adjectives alike are uninflected; except that, as noted below, they occasionally assume the Sanskrit fem. nom. sing. terminations. But sometimes इ is added for the fem. Thus, we have बर राऊ, 'a great king,' and बर हानि or बरि हानि (fem.), 'a great injury.' सम is the usual substitute for सा; as, e.g., दसरथ सम राऊ, 'a king like *Dasarath*.'

a. In the modern eastern colloquials, adjectives of every type remain uninflected before masc. nouns in the oblique singular and nom. plural. The only exception mentioned by Grierson is in the case of Tadbhava adjectives in आ, in A'zamgaṛh and Benares, which are inflected to ए, as in High Hindí. These Tadbhavas in आ are inflected before feminine nouns to ई, as in High Hindí, except in the Maithilí of S. Bhagalpúr, in which they suffer no change for gender. In this dialect, however, they have a strengthened form in ă, which is inflected to ई before feminine

nouns. In N. Maithilí, some close adjectives are inflected before feminine nouns to इ, as in the Old Baiswáṛí of the *Rámáyan*.

206. Occasionally, in poetry, some adjectives, chiefly *Tatsamas*, assume certain Sanskrit terminations, indicative of case and gender. Thus we often meet adjectives with the Sanskrit fem. terminations, ई (after bases in अन् or इन्,) and आ. Such forms occur most frequently in the latter part of compound words. The final ई is often shortened for the sake of the metre. Examples are: कामिनी . . . . . . रतिमदमोचनी 'beautiful women, destroyers of the pride of *Rati*;' भगति अति पावनि, 'devotion most holy;' सीता पुनीता, '*Sítá*, the pure;' गरुड़ कै गिरा बिनीता, 'the modest speech of *Garuṛ*.' More rarely, we meet with the termination म(ं) of the Sk. acc. sing., masc. or neut.; as, e.g., अजं नित राम नमामि, '*Rám*, the unborn, I ever adore;' निकंदय द्वंद घनं, 'destroy all my doubt.'

Comparison.

207. The Hindí adjective has no separate form to indicate the degrees of comparison. The *Comparative* degree is expressed by simply putting the noun or pronoun with which comparison is made, in the ablative case, thus: यह घर उस से बड़ा है *yah ghar us se baṛá hai*, 'this house is larger than that;' वह वृक्ष आम के पेड़ से ऊंचा है *wah vṛiksh ám ke peṛ se úṉchá hai*, 'that tree is higher than a mango tree;' शहद से मीठा *shahad se míṭhá*, 'sweeter than honey.' The Comparative Degree.

a. Comparison may also be expressed by prefixing the words और *aur* and अधिक *adhik*, 'more,' and sometimes, with the same signification, the Persian *ziyáda*, corrupted in Hindí to जियादः *jiyáda*, or, colloquially, in the Doáb, जास्ती *jástí*, N. ज्यास्ती.

208. The *Superlative* degree is expressed by using with the adjective, the abl. of सब *sab*, 'all;' thus, सब The Superlative Degree.

से बड़ा *sab se baṛá*, 'the greatest;' i.e., 'great with all;' सब से नीच *sab se ních*, 'the lowest;' यह मछली सब मछलियों से सुंदर है *yah machhlí sab machhliyon̤ se sundar hai*, 'this fish is the most beautiful of all fishes.'

a. Where no comparison is intended, a high degree of any quality is expressed by prefixing various words to the adjective, as in English and other languages. Most commonly, the word बहुत *bahut*, 'much,' 'very,' is prefixed; as, बहुत गहरी नदी *bahut gahrí nadí*, 'a very deep river.' Sometimes, colloquially, बड़ा *baṛá*, 'great,' is used instead of बहुत; as, बड़ा भारी पत्थर *baṛá bhárí patthar*, 'a very heavy stone;' but this use of बड़ा is not considered elegant. The intensive affix, सा *sá*, (§ 203) has the same force. Other words thus employed, especially in literary Hindí, are अति *ati*, 'very,' अत्यन्त *atyant*, 'extremely;' as, अति सुंदर *ati sundar*, 'very beautiful;' अत्यन्त भयानक *atyant bhayának*, 'exceedingly terrible.' The word परम *param* (cf. Lat. *primus*), is often prefixed to Tatsama adjectives in the same sense as the above; as, e.g., परम अद्भुत *param adbhut*, 'very wonderful;' परमशुद्ध *paramshuddh*, 'supremely holy.'

b. Sometimes the superlative degree of comparison is elegantly expressed by placing the noun or pronoun with which comparison is made, in the loc. case with में *men̤*, either with or without सब *sab* prefixed; as, e.g., वह सब बुद्धिमानों में बुद्धिमान था *wah sab buddhimánon̤ men̤ buddhimán thá*, 'he was the wisest of the wise;' इन पेड़ों में बड़ा यही है *in peṛon̤ men̤ baṛá yahí hai*, 'of these trees this is the greatest.' Compare the similar English idiom, 'brave among the brave.'

Sanskrit Forms. **209.** A few Sanskrit comparatives and superlatives occur, the former often in a superlative sense; as, e.g., पुण्यतर *puṇyatar*, from पुण्य *puṇya*, 'more holy,' or 'very holy.' But superlative forms are much more common; as, उत्तम *uttam*, 'best;' श्रेष्ठ *shresh̲ṭh*, 'most excellent,' from श्री; प्रियतम *priyatam*, 'dearest,' from प्रिय; पापिष्ठ *pápish̲ṭh*, 'most sinful,' from पापी *pápí*.

a. Persian comparatives and superlatives have found no place in Hindí, unless we except the word बिहतर (بہتر), which one occasionally hears from Hindoos who are in the habit of using much Urdú.

210. In Naipálí, the *comparative* degree is expressed by affixing to the oblique form of the noun with which comparison is made, the word भन्दा, which is the oblique form of भन्दो, the imperfect participle of the verb भन्नु (H. H. भनना), 'to say.' Practically, in this instance, it is used as a postposition. Examples are: तिम्हेरु धेरै चरा भन्दा ठुला मोल का छौ, 'ye are of more value than many sparrows;' यो कंगाली विधुवा ले उन्हेरु भन्दा ज्यास्ति हाली, 'this poor widow cast in more than they.' Much more rarely, चाँहि, conj. participle of चाहनु, takes the place of भन्दा with the inflected form of the noun or pronoun; as in उस चाँहि धर्म्मी, 'more righteous than that (man).' The *superlative* degree is expressed by prefixing to the adjective the adjective सबै, 'all,' with चाँहि: thus, सबै चाँहि असल लूगा, 'the best garment;' कुन सबै चाँहि ठुलो गनिन्या छ, 'who is to be accounted the greatest?' Comparison in Naipálí.

211. The same general principles of derivation which have been indicated (§§ 189-192) in explanation of substantive forms, apply equally in regard to adjectives. Thus Tadbhava adjectives in *á*, *o*, and *au*, have always arisen from Prakritic bases increased by the addition of a consonant, usually *k*; and all Tatsamas ending in *u* or the silent *a*, from the simple Sanskrit base. Thus the adjective *kálá*, 'black,' must be derived, not directly from the Sk. *kála*, but from an increased Prakritic base, *kálaka*. On the other hand the Tatsama, *sundar*, 'beautiful,' has arisen directly from the Sk. *sundara*, with only the loss of the case-termination. Tatsamas in *í* commonly represent Sk. bases in *in*, as *dhaní*, from the base *dhanin*.*

---

* Vid. § 153.

CHAPTER VII.

NUMERALS (संख्या).

212. The Hindí numerals are quite irregular in their formation, and it will be necessary for the student to commit them all to memory as far as 100. The Sanskrit numerals are also in common use in books, especially in numbering chapters and sections.

Both the Hindí and Sanskrit numerals, with the figures corresponding, are given in the following table:

TABLE VII. NUMERALS.

		Hindí.		Sanskrit.	
0	०	शून्य	*shúnya.*	शून्य	*shúnya.*
1	१	एक	*ek.*	एक	*ek.*
2	२	दो	*do.*	द्वि	*dwi.*
3	३	तीन	*tín.*	त्रि	*tri.*
4	४	चार	*chár.*	चतुर्	*chatur.*
5	५	पांच	*pánch.*	पंचन्	*panchan.*
6	६	छ	*chha.*	षष्	*shash.*
7	७	सात	*sát.*	सप्तन्	*saptan.*
8	८	आठ	*áṭh.*	अष्टन्	*ashṭan.*
9	९	नौ	*nau.*	नवन्	*navan.*
10	१०	दस	*das.*	दशन्	*dashan.*

		Hindí.		Sanskrit.	
11	११	ग्यारह	*gyárah.*	एकदशन्	*ekadashan.*
12	१२	बारह	*bárah.*	द्वादशन्	*dwádashan.*
13	१३	तेरह	*terah.*	त्रयोदशन्	*trayodashan.*
14	१४	चौदह	*chaudah.*	चतुर्दशन्	*chaturdashan.*
15	१५	पन्द्रह	*pandrah.*	पंचदशन्	*pańchadashan.*
16	१६	सोलह	*solah.*	षोडशन्	*shoḍashan.*
17	१७	सत्रह	*satrah.*	सप्तदशन्	*saptadashan.*
18	१८	अठारह	*aṭhárah.*	अष्टादशन्	*ashṭádashan.*
19	१९	उनीस	*unís.*	ऊनविंशति	*únavinshati.*
20	२०	बीस	*bís.*	विंशति	*vinshati.*
21	२१	इक्कीस	*ikkís.*	एकविंशति	*ekavinshati.*
22	२२	बाईस	*báís.*	द्वाविंशति	*dwávinshati.*
23	२३	तेईस	*teís.*	त्रयोविंशति	*trayovinshati.*
24	२४	चौबीस	*chaubís.*	चतुर्विंशति	*chaturvinshati.*
25	२५	पचीस	*pachís.*	पंचविंशति	*pańchavinshati.*
26	२६	छब्बीस	*chhabbís.*	षड्विंशति	*shaḍvinshati.*
27	२७	सताईस	*satáís.*	सप्तविंशति	*saptavinshati.*
28	२८	अठाईस	*aṭháís.*	अष्टाविंशति	*ashṭávinshati.*
29	२९	उन्तीस	*untís.*	ऊनत्रिंशत्	*únatrinshat.*
30	३०	तीस	*tís.*	त्रिंशत्	*trinshat.*
31	३१	इकतीस	*iktís.*	एकत्रिंशत्	*ekatrinshat.*
32	३२	बतीस	*batís.*	द्वात्रिंशत्	*dwátrinshat.*
33	३३	तेंतीस	*tentís.*	त्रयस्त्रिंशत्	*trayastrinshat.*
34	३४	चौंतीस	*chauntís.*	चतुस्त्रिंशत्	*chatustrinshat.*
35	३५	पैंतीस	*paintís.*	पंचत्रिंशत्	*pańchatrinshat.*

		Hindí.		Sanskrit.	
36	३६	छत्तीस	*chhattís.*	षट्त्रिंशत्	*shaṭtrinshat.*
37	३७	सैंतीस	*saintís.*	सप्तत्रिंशत्	*saptatrinshat.*
38	३८	अड़तीस	*arṭís.*	अष्टात्रिंशत्	*ashṭátrinshat.*
39	३९	उन्तालीस	*untálís.*	ऊनचत्वारिंशत्	*únachatvárinshat.*
40	४०	चालीस	*chálís.*	चत्वारिंशत्	*chatvárinshat.*
41	४१	इकतालीस	*iktálís.*	एकचत्वारिंशत्	*ekachatvárinshat.*
42	४२	बयालीस	*bayálís.*	द्विचत्वारिंशत्	*dwichatvárinshat.*
43	४३	तेंतालीस	*tentálís.*	त्रिचत्वारिंशत्	*trichatvárinshat.*
44	४४	चौआलीस	*chauálís.*	चतुश्चत्वारिंशत्	*chatushchatvárinshat.*
45	४५	पैंतालीस	*paintálís.*	पंचचत्वारिंशत्	*pañchachatvárinshat.*
46	४६	छियालीस	*chhiyálís.*	षट्चत्वारिंशत्	*shaṭchatvárinshat.*
47	४७	सैंतालीस	*saintálís.*	सप्तचत्वारिंशत्	*saptachatvárinshat.*
48	४८	अड़तालीस	*arṭálís.*	अष्टचत्वारिंशत्	*ashṭachatvárinshat.*
49	४९	उनचास	*unchás.*	ऊनपंचाशत्	*únapañcháshat.*
50	५०	पचास	*pachás.*	पंचाशत्	*pañcháshat.*
51	५१	इकावन	*ikáwan.*	एकपंचाशत्	*ekapañcháshat.*
52	५२	बावन	*báwan.*	द्वापंचाशत्	*dwápañcháshat.*
53	५३	तिरपन	*tirpan.*	त्रिपंचाशत्	*tripañcháshat.*
54	५४	चौवन	*chauwan.*	चतुःपंचाशत्	*chatuḥpañcháshat.*
55	५५	पचपन	*pachpan.*	पंचपंचाशत्	*pañchapañcháshat.*
56	५६	छप्पन	*chhappan.*	षट्पंचाशत्	*shaṭpañcháshat.*
57	५७	सतावन	*satáwan.*	सप्तपंचाशत्	*saptapañchásha*
58	५८	अठावन	*aṭháwan.*	अष्टपंचाशत्	*ashṭapañcháshat.*
59	५९	उनसठ	*unsaṭh.*	ऊनषष्टि	*únashashṭi.*
60	६०	साठ	*sáṭh.*	षष्टि	*shashṭi.*

		Hindí.		Sanskrit.	
61	६१	इकसठ	*iksaṭh.*	एकषष्टि	*ekashashṭi.*
62	६२	बासठ	*básaṭh.*	द्वाषष्टि	*dwáshashṭi.*
63	६३	तिरसठ	*tirsaṭh.*	त्रिषष्टि	*trishashṭi.*
64	६४	चौंसठ	*chaunsaṭh.*	चतुःषष्टि	*chatuḥshashṭi.*
65	६५	पैंसठ	*painsaṭh.*	पंचषष्टि	*pañchashashṭi.*
66	६६	छियासठ	*chhiyásaṭh.*	षट्षष्टि	*shaṭshashṭi.*
67	६७	सरसठ	*sarsaṭh.*	सप्तषष्टि	*saptashashṭi.*
68	६८	अड़सठ	*aṛsaṭh.*	अष्टषष्टि	*ashṭashashṭi.*
69	६९	उनहत्तर	*unhattar.*	ऊनसप्तति	*únasaptati.*
70	७०	सत्तर	*sattar.*	सप्तति	*saptati.*
71	७१	इकहत्तर	*ikhattar.*	एकसप्तति	*ekasaptati.*
72	७२	बहत्तर	*bahattar.*	द्वासप्तति	*dwásaptati.*
73	७३	तिहत्तर	*tihattar.*	त्रिसप्तति	*trisaptati.*
74	७४	चौहत्तर	*chauhattar.*	चतुःसप्तति	*chatuḥsaptati.*
75	७५	पछत्तर	*pachhattar.*	पंचसप्तति	*pañchasaptati.*
76	७६	छिहत्तर	*chhihattar.*	षट्सप्तति	*shaṭsaptati.*
77	७७	सतहत्तर	*sathattar.*	सप्तसप्तति	*saptasaptati.*
78	७८	अठहत्तर	*aṭhhattar.*	अष्टसप्तति	*ashṭasaptati.*
79	७९	उनासी	*unásí*	ऊनाशीति	*únáshíti.*
80	८०	अस्सी	*assí.*	अशीति	*ashíti.*
81	८१	इकासी	*ikásí.*	एकाशीति	*ekáshíti.*
82	८२	बयासी	*bayásí.*	द्व्याशीति	*dvyáshíti.*
83	८३	तिरासी	*tirásí.*	त्र्यशीति	*tryashíti.*
84	८४	चौरासी	*chaurásí.*	चतुरशीति	*chaturashíti.*
85	८५	पचासी	*pachásí.*	पंचाशीति	*pañcháshíti.*

		Hindí.		Sanskrit.	
86	८६	छियासी	*chhiyásí.*	षडशीति	*shaḍashíti.*
87	८७	सतासी	*satásí.*	सप्ताशीति	*saptáshíti.*
88	८८	अठासी	*aṭhásí.*	अष्टाशीति	*ashṭáshíti.*
89	८९	नवासी	*navásí.*	नवाशीति	*naváshíti.*
90	९०	नब्बे	*navve.*	नवति	*navati.*
91	९१	इकानवे	*ikánave.*	एकनवति	*ekanavati.*
92	९२	बानवे	*bánave.*	द्वानवति	*dwánavati.*
93	९३	तिरानवे	*tiránave.*	त्रिनवति	*trinavati.*
94	९४	चौरानवे	*chauránavė.*	चतुर्नवति	*chaturnavati.*
95	९५	पचानवे	*pachánave.*	पंचनवति	*pañchanavati.*
96	९६	छियानवे	*chhiyánave.*	षण्णवति	*shaṇṇavati.*
97	९७	सतानवे	*satánave.*	सप्तनवति	*saptanavati.*
98	९८	अठानवे	*aṭhánave.*	अष्टानवति	*ashṭánavati.*
99	९९	निनानवे	*ninánave.*	नवनवति	*navanavati.*
100	१००	सौ	*sau.*	शत	*shata.*
1000	१०००	{ सहस्र { हजार*	*sahasra.* *hajár.*	सहस्र	*sahasra.*
100000	१०००००	लाख	*lákh.*	लक्ष	*laksha.*
1000000	१००००००	नियुत	*niyut.*	नियुत	*niyuta.*
10000000	१०००००००	करोड़ †	*karoṛ.*	कोटि	*koṭi.*

a. The following are of less frequent occurrence, viz.: अर्ब *arb* or अर्बुद *arbud*, 'one hundred millions;' खर्ब *kharb*, 'one hundred *arb*,' = 'ten thousand millions;' नील *níl*, 'one

* This is a Persian word, but it is common in Hindí. Etymologically it is identical with the Sanskrit form, *sahasra*. † Also, करोड़.

hundred *kharb*,' = 'one million millions;' पद्म *padm*, 'one hundred *níl*,' = 'one billion;' शंख *sankh*, 'one hundred *padm*,' = 'one hundred billions.'

213. A special notation is employed to denote the subdivisions of the rupee. It is to be observed that the rupee is subdivided into sixteen *áne*, and each *áná* again into four *paise*. These are denoted as follows:—One *paisá*,)।; two *paise*,)॥; three *paise*,)।॥; one *áná*, –); two *áne*, =); three *áne*, ≡); four *áne*, ।); eight *áne*, ॥); twelve *áne*, ।॥). These, again, are combined, after the following manner:—Five *áne* and one *paisá*, ।–)।; six *áne* and two *paise*, ।=)॥; eleven *áne* and three *paise*, ॥≡)।॥; fourteen *áne* and one *paisá*, ।॥=)।; one rupee, १); thirty rupees and four *áne*, ३० ।); two hundred and thirty-five rupees, seven *áne* and two *paise*, २३५ ।≡)॥.

Dialectic Variants of the Cardinals.

214. In the Braj, we find, for दो, 'two,' द्वै, द्वौ, and दोऊ; and for चार, 'four,' चारि. Kanaují presents the following: for चार, 'four,' चौ; for उनीस, 'nineteen,' and इकीस, 'twenty-one,' उनईस and इकईस; and for सौ, 'one hundred,' सै. Braj and Kanaují Cardinals

215. In Máṛwáṛí the cardinals are the same as in High Hindí, except that स is characteristically changed into ह. Thus, for सोलह, 'sixteen,' Máṛwáṛí has होलह; for बीस, 'twenty,' बीह; for साठ, 'sixty,' हाठ; etc. This ह, when final, is sounded very lightly. In *Raṇdhír aur Prem Mohaní*, we find पनरा, for H.H. पंद्रह, 'fifteen.' Márwáṛí Cardinals.

216. The Mewáṛi Cardinals present many peculiarities. ग्र is regularly used for स, initial, medial, or final: as in ग्रात, 7; ग्राट, 60; बाग्रट, 62; बीग्र, 20; चालीग्र, 40; etc. But for ग्रात, 7, the common people often say दात. In the twenties, thirties, and forties, this final ग्र often disappears, so that, e.g., for बीग्र, 20, चोतीग्र, 34, चमालीग्र, 44, we have बी, चोती, चमाली, etc., etc. For the क of एक, ग is substituted in the following: अगतीग्र, 31; अगतालीग्र, 41; अगग्रट, 61; अगोतर, Mewáṛí Cardinals.

(also अक्योतर,) 71. The same substitution has taken place in the ninth of each decade after नो, 9, except in नव्याशी, 89, and नन्याणुं, 99; where the ग represents the क of the full Sanskrit form (as, e.g., एकोनचिंशत्, 29,) from which the forms of High Hindí, etc., have been derived. Thus we have the following series: उगणीस, 19; गुणतीस, 29; गुणचालीश, गुणतालीश, or गुणालीश, 39; गुणचाश, 49; गुणशट, 59; गुणंतर, 69; गुणियाशी, 79. In the sixties, ठ final is changed to ट throughout; as in चेशट, 63, चोशट, 64, etc. Other Mewáṛí forms, the most of which are peculiar to that dialect, are as follows:

4, च्यार.	24, चोईश.	74, चोतर.	92, बाणुं.
6, छ.	26, छाईश.	75, पच्योतर.	93, तराणुं.
9, नो.	34, चोतीश.	76, छियोतर.	94, चोराणुं.
10, दश.	42, बिंयालीश.	77, शत्योतर..	95, पच्याणुं.
11, ग्यारा.	43, तिंयालीश.	78, अठ्योतर.	96 { छन्नूं.
12, बारा.	44 { चमालीश.	80, अशी.	छियाणुं.
13, तेरा.	चंवालीस.	81, अक्याशी.	97, शत्याणुं.
14, चवदा.	51, अक्यावन.	82, बिंयाशी.	98, अठ्याणुं.
15, पनरा.	54, चोपन.	83, तिंयाशी.	99, नन्याणुं.
16 { सोला.	55, पचावन.	84, चोराशी.	100 { शो.
होला.	66, छाशट.	85, पच्याशी.	शेकड़ो.
17 { शतरा.	67, शतशट.	87, शत्याशी.	1,000, हजार.
हतरा.	70, शतर.	88, अठ्याशी.	100,000, लाख.
18, अठारा.	72, बोतर.	90, नेउवे.	10,000,000 { करोड़.
21, अकीश.	73, तेतर.	91, अक्याणुं.	कोड़.

Himalayan Cardinals.

217. The cardinals in the Himalayan dialects do not in general diff… much from those in High Hindí. The following variants occur in th… Naipálí Gospel: viz., तिन, 3; एघारठ, 11; and बाह्र, 12. In the obl. sing. of एक, 'one,' we find एका, apparently when it is desired to give special definiteness: as, एका घर का पांच जना आपस मा बिरोध गर्नेन, 'of (the) one house, five persons shall be at enmity among themselves;' and so especially in contrast with अर्को, 'the other:' as, एका को शत्रु होला र अर्का को मित, 'he will be an enemy of the one, and a friend of the other.'

a. In Naipálí, a series of numerals is formed from the cardinals by the addition of the affix उटो, infl. आ, ई: thus, येउटो or येवोटो, 'a certain one,' दुवोतो, 'certain two,' सातोटो, 'certain seven.' These appear to be used when it is desired to designate a number with a certain definiteness, as in the following: सातोटो भाई थिया, 'there were seven brethren;' Luke xx. 29, where the reference is to a particular seven.

218. The following variant forms occur in the *Rámáyan*: Cardinals in Rámáyan.

1, एक.	4, चारि.	16, सोरह.
2, दुइ.	9, नव.	25, पचवीस.
3, त्रय.	14, चारिदस.	1000, सहस.

To these may be added the anomalous form, नवसप्त, lit., 'nine-seven,' i.e., 'sixteen.' The Prakritic form, षोडश or षोडष, for सोलह, 'sixteen,' also occurs in the *Rámáyan*, and even in High Hindí. It is chiefly used in certain phrases of a technical character: as, षोडश कला, 'the sixteen digits' (of the sun's or moon's diameter). दह is occasionally substituted for दस, 'ten,' as in the phrase, दहदिसि, 'the ten points of the compass.' Many of the above forms merely present differences of orthography.

219. The following are the cardinals in Bhojpúrí, Mágadhí, and Maithilí, so far as they differ from High Hindí, up to 18. Cardinals in Eastern Colloquials.

	Bhojpúrí.	*Mágadhí.*	*Maithilí.*
1,	एगो.	एक, एगो.	एक, एकै, ऐगो.
2,	दू, दूइ.	दू.	दुइ, दूइ, दुगो.
3,	तीनि.	......	दू.
4,	चारि.	......	चारि.
6,	छौ, छव.	छौ.	छव, छौ.
8,	आठ.	......	......
9,	......	नौ.	नौं, नउ.
11,	इगारह, इग्यारह.	.....	एगारह.
15,	पनरह.	पनरह.	पनरह.
16,	सोरह.	सोरह.	सोरह.

a. By the operation of the law, mentioned § 117, a short vowel in an initial syllable, not penultimate, is often, though not invariably, shortened; as also in some other cases, given below. Illustrations are: in Bhojpúrí, एकइस, 21; एकतिस, 31; एकसठि, 61; in Mágadhí, एक, 1; एकहत्तर, 71; in Maithilí, एक, 1; एगारह, 11; एकैस, 21; एकतिस, 31; एकतालिस, 41; बेआलिस, 42; एकौन, 51; तेरपन, 53; बेआसी or बेरासी, 82. In like manner, ओ becomes ओ; ऐ, ऐ; and औ, औ; as in the following: in Maithilí, तेंतालिस, 43; पेंतालिस, 45; सेंतालिस, 47; चौरासी, 84; चौरानवे, 94; in Mágadhí, नोआसी, 89; चौहत्तर, 74; and in Bhojpúrí, चौरांवे, 94.

b. In Bhojpúrí and Maithilí all compounds of बीस, 20, तीस, 30, and चालीस, 40, shorten the vowel of the ultimate, giving, e.g., such forms as उनइस, 19, तेंतिस, 33, चवालिस, 44, etc. But in some Maithilí sub-dialects, this *ĭ* is combined with the preceding vowel, as in the following: एकैस, 21, तैस, 23, सतैस, 27.

c. In Bhojpúrí, the penultimate *á* in साठि, 60, is shortened in all its compounds: as, e.g., एकसठि, 61, बासठि, 62, etc. In the nineties, the न of नबे, in all its compounds is softened to Anusvár: as in बांवे, 92, etc. In Mágadhí, the त्त of सत्तर, in all its compounds, becomes न्त: as in बहन्तर, 72, etc.

d. The following Maithilí forms of the cardinals are also to be noted: viz., सतैस, 27; अठैस, 28; उनचालिस, 39; ब्यालिस, 42; एकौन, 51; बौन, 52; सतौन and संतावोन, 57; अंठौन and अंठावोन, 58; तिरेसठ and तिरेसठ, 63; चौसठ, 64; छिअरसठ, 66; सउ, 100.

e. In the eastern dialects, in the numerals, as in many other words, अव is optionally written for औ; and sometimes, again, the diphthong is resolved: as in चवबिस or चउबिस, for H. H., चौबीस, 24; चौअन or चउअन, for H. H., चौवन, 54.

Miscellaneous Variants.

220. The following forms also occur, many of which are to be regarded as presenting, not dialectic variations, but merely differences of spelling.

1, एक.	43, तैंतालीस.	61, एकसठ.	90, नवे.
2, दोन.	44, चवालीस.	63, चेसठ.	91 { इक्यानवे.
6, छः.	46, छत्तालीस.	68, अठसठ.	एक्यानवे.
11, एग्यारह.	48, अठतालीस.	71, एकहत्तर.	एकानवे.
19, उन्नीस.	49, उनंचास.	73, तिरहत्तर.	95 { पंचानवे.
21, एकीस.	51 { एकावन.	75, पचहत्तर.	पचानवे.
27, सत्ताईस.	इक्यावन.	76, छहत्तर.	96, छानवे.
31, एकतीस.	53, चेपन.	81, इक्यासी.	97, सत्तानवे.
32, बत्तीस.	54, चौपन.	82, बासी.	99 { निन्यानवे.
33, तैंतीस.	55, पचावन.	87, सत्तासी.	निन्नावे.
38, अठतीस.	57, सत्तावन.	88, अट्ठासी.	100, सय.
41, एकतालीस.	58, अट्ठावन.		

221. The numbers above one hundred proceed as in English, except that the copulative conjunction is omitted. Thus, एक सौ एक *ek sau ek*, 'one hundred and one;' तीन सौ साठ *tín sau sáṭh*, 'three hundred and sixty;' एक हजार बीस *ek hajár bís*, 'one thousand and twenty.' Numbers above 100.

a. But the copulative is sometimes inserted in poetry, even in the lower numbers: as, बीते कल्प सात अरु बीसा, 'seven and twenty *kalpas* passed.'

b. The numbers between 100 and 200 are sometimes expressed by writing the smaller number first, with the affix *á*: as, e.g., चालीसा सौ, 'a hundred and forty.' Other modes of expression will be noticed in the sections concerning fractional and denominative numerals.

222. The numeral एक is added to other numerals in the sense of the English 'about:' as, e.g., चालीस एक, 'about forty;' सौ एक, 'about a hundred,'—not एक सौ एक, which is 'one hundred and one.' But to एक itself the word आद (Sk. आदि) is added to give this sense: as, एक आद सेर आटा, 'a *seer* or so of flour.' Idioms with एक.

a. एक is also sometimes used where in English we would have the indefinite article. But the English student must beware of thus using it too freely. It should only be so employed, where there is a distinct emphasis on the idea of unity: thus, एक आधा सेर आटा, 'a half *seer* of flour;' एक आधा कोस, 'a half *kos.*'

Aggregatives. **223.** Ordinarily the numerals are not used in the inflected plural form. But when they are used to denote a totality, as Aggregatives, they may take, both in the nom. and obl. cases, the termination ओं.* Thus, चार पेड़ *chár peṛ* is 'four trees,' but चारों पेड़ *cháron̲ peṛ*, 'the four trees;' so also बीस आए *bís áe* is 'twenty came,' but बीसों आए *bíson̲ áe*, 'the twenty came.' In दोनों *donon̲*, 'the two,' दोन *don* is the substitute for दो *do.*

a. This termination ओं *on̲*, added to the numbers 'one hundred,' 'one thousand,' etc., always denotes an indefinite number of these aggregates. In this idiom, सैकड़ा *saikṛá* is substituted for सौ *sau*, 'one hundred.' Examples are: सैकड़ों पेड़ *saikṛon̲ peṛ*, 'hundreds of trees;' हजारों *hajáron̲*, 'thousands;' लाखों रुपए *lákhon̲ rupae*, '*lákhs* of rupees.'

Dialectic Aggregatives. **224.** For ओं in these aggregative forms, Braj has औं; Márwáṛí, Bíkanerí, and Háṛotí have आं. Special Braj forms are also: for दोनों, 'the two,' 'both,' दूनौं, दोन्यौं, दुऊ; for तीनों, 'the three,' तीन्यौं, तिऊ; and for चारों, 'the four,' चारौ and चऊ. In Naipálí, these forms terminate in ऐ or ै; as in दुवै, 'both,' 'the two;' सातै, 'the seven;' दसै, 'the ten;' etc. But the form एकै, 'one,' for एक, is emphatic, by elision and contraction, for एकहि. In Bhojpúrí and Mágadhí, aggregatives terminate in ओ; in Maithilí, in ओ or ओं. In the *Rámáyan*, for दोनों, 'the two,' we have दौ, दुअनि, and दुओ; in Bhojpúrí, दूनू, दूनो; in Mágadhí, दुन्नों, दूनों; and in Maithilí, दूनों and दुन्नों.

* For the origin of these terminations, *on̲, ain̲*, etc., see § 239.

a. When an indefinite number of such aggregates is denoted, Bhojpúrí adds अन to the series, 100, 1000, etc., and हां to other numerals; as, हजारन, 'thousands;' सत्तरहां, 'seventies.' Mágadhí, in such cases, adds ओ or ओं, before which, सौ, 'one hundred,' is hardened to सय; and Maithilí adds either ओं or अन.

b. एक exceptionally takes the obl. plur. form एकन्ह, in a few places in the *Rámáyan.*

225. The Hindí idiom in such indefinite expressions as 'one or two,' 'four or five,' differs slightly from the English. The numbers, except in the case of 'one' and 'two,' are rarely taken consecutively, and the larger very often precedes the smaller. The disjunctive conjunction is always omitted. Thus we say, दो एक, 'one or two;' दो चार, 'two four,' = 'two or three;' दस बीस, 'ten or twenty.'

ORDINALS.

226. The *Ordinals*, up to 'sixth,' are as follows, viz:—

पहला, पहिला *pahlá, pahilá*, 'first.'
दूसरा *dúsrá*, 'second.'
तीसरा *tísrá*, 'third.'
चौथा *chauthá*, 'fourth.'
पांचवां *páñchwáñ*, 'fifth.'
छट्ठा, छठवां *chhaṭṭhá, chhaṭhwáñ*, 'sixth.'

The ordinals above 'sixth' are all formed by adding वां *wáñ* to the cardinal numbers. Both the आ *á* and आं *áñ* final of the ordinals are inflected, like Tadbhava adjectives of the same terminations, to ए and एं for the obl. masc., and ई *í* and ईं *íñ* for the fem. Thus, from दस *das*, 'ten,' is formed दसवां *daswáñ*, 'tenth;' from पचास *pachás*, 'fifty,' पचासवां *pacháswáñ*, 'fiftieth,' etc.

Further examples of the use of the ordinals are: पहिली पुस्तक *pahilí pustak*, 'the first book;' सातवें पर्ब्ब में *sátweñ parbb meñ*, 'in the seventh chapter;' दसवां महीना *daswáñ mahíná*, 'the tenth month.'

13

Rajputana and Naipálí Ordinals.

227. In Máṛwáṛí, the ordinals are as follows:—पैलो, 'first;' दूजो and बीजो (this last peculiar to Máṛwáṛí), 'second;' तीजो, 'third;' चौथो, 'fourth,' पांचमो, 'fifth;' छठो and छठमो, 'sixth.' From 'sixth' onward, the ordinals are formed by adding to the cardinals the termination मो. The Mewáṛí forms essentially agree with the Máṛwáṛí. Before the termination मो, a final आ is shortened; as in बारमो, 12th, etc. Bíkanerí agrees with the above, except in पैलडो, 'first;' as also Háṛotí. All these inflect ओ to आ for the obl. masc. sing., and the plural; and to ई for the fem. sing. and plur., except Háṛotí, which has ए. In Naipálí, the series runs, पहिलो, 'first,' दुसरो, 'second,' तेस्रो, 'third,' चौथो, 'fourth,' पाचौं, 'fifth,' छैटौं, 'sixth;' from which onward, with the exception of नउं, 'ninth,' the ordinals are formed by adding to the cardinal, औं. The inflection throughout, for the obl. masc. sing. and the plur., is, आ, and for the fem., ई.

Ordinals in E. Hindí.

228. The eastern colloquials, so far as I have been able to ascertain, present the following variations. For पहला, 'first,' Bh., Mg., and Mt. have पाहल; for दूसरा 'second,' Bh. and Mt., दूसर, and Mg. and Mt., दोसर; for तीसरा, 'third,' Bh. and Mt., तीसर, Mg. and Mt., तेसर; for चौथा, 'fourth,' Bh. and Mg. चौठ, Bh. also चौथ, Mt., चौठ and चारिम. In all these, except on the border of Bangál, the forms for 'first,' 'second,' and 'third,' are inflected to आ before nouns, in an obl. case; in S. Bhagalpúr the inflection is to ă. Bhojpúrí inflects to आई for the fem. All three dialects present alternative forms with the pleonastic suffix का; as पहिलका, दुसरका, तेसरका or तिसरका. For 'sixth,' छठवां, Bh. has छट्ठां or छठां; Mg. छठौं or छठवां; Mt., छठवां, छठम, छठमा, or छठमठ. All other ordinals in these dialects are formed by adding to the cardinal, in Bh., वां or वां; in Mg., औं or वां; in Mt., औं, म, अम, इम, अमा or अमठ. Thus, दसवां, 'tenth,' is in Bh., दसां; in Mg., दसौं; in Mt., दसम, दसिम, etc. In all the E. Hindí country a long final vowel is very commonly shortened before these terminations.

229. The following dialectic variations occur in the *Rámáyan*, viz., सातव, 'seventh,' अठव, 'eighth,' नवम, 'ninth.'

230. When referring to the lunar days, another set of ordinals is used. The month is reckoned as consisting of two parts, each of 15 lunar days, corresponding to the waxing and waning half of the moon. The waning half is commonly called कृष्णपक्ष or बदी; the waxing half, शुक्लपक्ष or सुदी. The month is reckoned to begin with the full moon, and the lunar days are counted twice in a month from one to fifteen. Although the names of these days are, strictly speaking, numeral adjectives in the feminine gender, agreeing with तिथि, 'a lunar day,' this noun is rarely written, and they are practically used as nouns. They are as follows, the Máṛwáṛí variants being given in the second column:— Names of Lunar Days.

Names of the Days of the Month.

H. H.	*Máṛ.*	*H.H.*	*Máṛ.*
1st, परिवा *pariwá.*	एकम.	8th, अष्टमी *ashṭamí.*	आठम.
2nd, दूज *dúj.*	दूज or बीज.	9th, नौमीं *naumíṉ.*	(नवम?).
3rd, तीज *tíj.*	तीज.	10th, दसमीं *dasmíṉ.*	दस्सम.
4th, चौथ *chauth.*	चोथ.	11th, एकादसी *ekádasí.*	ग्यांरस.
5th, पंचमी *pañchamí.*	पांचम.	12th, द्वादसी *dwádasí.*	बारस.
6th, छट्ठ *chhaṭṭh.*	छठ.	13th, तेरस *teras.*	तेरस.
7th, सत्तमी *sattamí.*	सातम.	14th, चौदस *chaudas.*	चौदस.

15th, अमावस *amávas*, or मावस *mávas.*

a. The days of the second fortnight are reckoned in the same way, except that the fifteenth, or day of full moon, is called पूर्णमासी, पूनो or पून्या, Br. पून्यौं or पून्यौ, Máṛ. पूनम or पूंन्यूं.

b. Mewáṛí employs not only the forms above given for Máṛwáṛí, but, as alternative, the following: एकें, 1st; दोज, 2nd; चोथ, 4th; पांचे, 5th; छठ, 6th, साते, 7th; आठे, 8th; नोमी, 9th; दशो or दशमी, 10th; ग्यारश, 11th; बारश, 12th; तेरश, 13th; चवदश, 14th; अमावश, 15th; and for the 15th of the 1st fortnight, full moon, पुनम. To the final vowel of these forms Anusvár is occasionally added; as in सातें, 7th, etc.

c. Sometimes the lunar days are denoted by the Sanskrit ordinals throughout. In so far as these differ from the above, they are as follows:—

1st, प्रथमा *prathamá.*	7th, सप्तमी *saptamí.*
2nd, द्वितीया *dwitíyá.*	9th, नवमी *navamí.*
3rd, तृतीया *tṛitíyá.*	10th, दशमी *dashamí.*
4th, चतुर्थी *chaturthí.*	13th, त्रयोदशी *trayodashí.*
6th, षष्ठी *shashṭí.*	14th, चतुर्दशी *chaturdashí.*

Fractional Numbers.

231. The fractional numbers are very irregular. The more common are the following:—

¼, { पाओ *páo.* / चौथाई *chauthái.* }	−¼, पौने *paune*, lit., 'a quarter less than.'
	1¼, सवा *savá.*
⅓, तिहाई *tihái.*	1½, डेढ़ *ḍeṛh.*
½, आधा *ádhá.*	2½, अढ़ाई *aṛhái*, or ढाई *ḍhái.*
¾, पौन *paun.*	+½, साढ़े *sáṛhe.*

Usage of Fractionals.

232. Of the above, पाओ *páo* is often used by itself to denote 'a quarter of a *seer*;' so that चौथाई *chauthái* should be preferred where there is any chance of ambiguity from the use of the former word. पौने *paune,* prefixed to any number, or noun of measure, denotes a quarter less than that number or measure; सवा *savá,* similarly prefixed, denotes a quarter more than that number or measure. डेढ़ *ḍeṛh* is similarly used, to denote one and a half times such number or measure. When either of these three stand alone, unity is to be understood; but in this case पौन *paun* is the substitute for पौने; it is used with units only. अढ़ाई *aṛhái,* used alone, is 2½; prefixed to any numeral or noun of measure, it denotes two and a half times that number or measure. साढ़े *sáṛhe* is never used alone. Prefixed, as above, to a noun or number, it denotes one half more than the following number or measure. It is never used with 'one' or 'two,' where डेढ़ and अढ़ाई take its place. आधा *ádhá,* 'half,' is very commonly shortened to

आध *ádh* before numerals; as आध सौ *ádh sau*, 50. For आध, the Sk. अर्द्ध is sometimes used.

a. The following examples will illustrate the use of these fractional numbers:—

$\frac{1}{2}\times\frac{1}{4}=\frac{1}{8}$,	आध पाओ *ádh páo.*	250,	अढ़ाई सौ *aṛhái sau.*
$1\frac{1}{4}\times\frac{1}{4}=\frac{5}{16}$,	सवा पाओ *savá páo.*	375,	पौने चार सौ *paune chár sau.*
$1\frac{1}{2}\times\frac{1}{4}=\frac{3}{8}$,	डेढ़ पाओ *ḍeṛh páo.*	450,	साढ़े चार सौ *sáṛhe chár sau.*
$2\frac{1}{2}\times\frac{1}{4}=\frac{5}{8}$,	अढ़ाई पाओ *aṛhái páo.*	1225,	सवा हजार *savá hajár.*
$2\frac{1}{4}$,	सवा दो *savá do.*	1500,	डेढ़ हजार *ḍeṛh hajár.*
$5\frac{1}{2}$	साढ़े पांच *sáṛhe pánch.*	1725,	पौने दो हजार *paune do hajár.*
$7\frac{3}{4}$,	पौने आठ *paune áṭh.*	2500,	अढ़ाई हजार *aṛhái hajár.*
75,	पौने सौ *paune sau.*	3500,	साढ़े तीन हजार *sáṛhe tín hajár.*
150,	डेढ़ सौ *ḍeṛh sau.*	150,000,	डेढ़ लाख *ḍeṛh lákh.*

b. They are used with nouns of measure, quantity, etc., as follows: डेढ़ कोस *ḍeṛh kos*, 'a *kos* and a half;' पौने दस गज *paune das gaj*, '$9\frac{3}{4}$ yards;' अढ़ाई मन *aṛhái man*, '$2\frac{1}{2}$ *mans*;' पाओ छित्ताक *páo chitták*, '$\frac{1}{4}$ *chitták*;' साढ़े बारह हाथ *sáṛhe bárah háth*, '$12\frac{1}{2}$ *cubits*;' सवा बरस *savá baras*, 'a year and a quarter.'

233. Máṛwáṛí presents but few and unimportant variations in the fractionals. For the inflected ए final of some of the forms, it has आ, as in nouns and adjectives; as in पौणा, $\frac{1}{4}$, H.H. पौने. But for साढ़े, $2\frac{1}{2}$, I have met, not only साढ़ा, as above, but also, with the added Prakritic क, साढ़ीक; thus, साढ़ीक बारा बर्ष, 'two years and a half.' Dialectic Fractionals.

234. Mewáṛí exhibits the following forms: पाव, $\frac{1}{4}$; आदो, $\frac{1}{2}$; पूंण, $\frac{3}{4}$; सवा, $1\frac{1}{4}$; डोढ़, $1\frac{1}{2}$; पूंणा दो, $1\frac{3}{4}$; सवा दो, $2\frac{1}{4}$; अढाई, $2\frac{1}{2}$; साढ़ा तीन, $3\frac{1}{2}$, etc.

235. Grierson gives the following variant forms of the Fractionals as occurring in the eastern colloquial dialects.

$\frac{1}{4}$, Bh., पा, पौवा, पउवा; Bh., Mg., पाव; Mt., पौ, पा, पौआ.

$\frac{1}{3}$, Bh., तिसरी; Mg., Mt., तेहाई; Mt., तेहाइ, तिहाइ, तिहै, तेसरो तेसरो, तिरभाग.

½, Bh., आध, आंड़ा; Bh., Mg., अधिया; Mt., अद्धा, आधे, अध, आधउ.

¾, Bh., पौना; Mg., गंउठ; Mt., पौना, पौने, तोन पा.

−¼, Bh., पौना, पवन्ने; Mg., गंउठ.

1¼, Bh., Mg., Mt., सावा, सवाइ; Bh., सवाइया.

1½, Mt., डेढ़ा, डेर.

2½, Bh., आढ़ा; Bh., Mg., अढइया; Mg., Mt., अढाइ, अढ़ै, अराइ, अढ़िया.

+½, Mt., सारेह.

PROPORTIONALS.

236. To express proportion, गुना *guná* or गुन *gun* is added to the numerals, some of which then assume forms slightly different. Illustrations are the following: दुगुना *duguná*, 'two-fold;' चौगुना *chauguná*, 'four-fold;' तिगुना *tiguná*, 'three-fold;' सतगुना *satguná*, 'seven-fold;' दसगुना *dasguná*, 'ten-fold;' सौगुना *sauguná*, 'a hundred-fold.'

a. Besides गुना the affix हरा is also sometimes added to a few numerals, in a similar sense: as, दोहरा, 'double;' तिहरा, 'three-fold.'

b. When, either in a literal or metaphorical sense, the idea of a string or cord is involved, लड़ा may be similarly added: as, तिलड़ा, 'triple;' चौलड़ा, 'quadruple.'

DENOMINATIVES.

237. Multiplicatives, such as the English 'twice,' and 'thrice,' are not found in Hindí. The Hindí idiom is illustrated in such phrases as the following, viz.: दो सत्ते चौदह *do satte chaudah*, lit. 'two sevens, fourteen;' तीन पंजे पन्द्रह *tín panje pandrah*, 'three fives, fifteen;' which correspond to the English idioms, 'twice seven is fourteen,' and 'three times five is fifteen.' Numbers thus used may be termed *Denominative* numerals. They have, in many cases, a form slightly different from that of the Cardinals. These special forms are as follows:—

1,	एकं *ekam.* / कं *kam.*	4,	चौक *chauka.* / चौका *chauká.*
1¼,	सम *sama.*	4½,	ढोंचा *ḍhon̲chá.*
1½,	डौढा *ḍauṛhá.* / डेओढा *ḍeoṛhá.*	5,	पंजे *panje.*
2,	दूना *dúná.*	5½,	पोंचा *pon̲chá.*
2½,	ढाम *ḍháma.* / ढामा *ḍhámá.*	6,	छक्का *chhakká.*
3,	ती *tí.* / तीन *tína.*	6½,	खोंचा *khon̲chá.*
3½,	हूंटा *hún̲ṭá.* / होंटा *hon̲ṭá.*	7,	सत्ते *satte.*
		7½,	सतोंचा *saton̲chá.*
		8,	अट्ठे *aṭṭhe.*
		9,	नम *nama.* / नम्मा *nammá.*

10, दहाम *dahám.*

238. The above are the only numbers which present peculiar forms, and even these forms are not substituted in every case. The only way to master their idiomatic use, is to commit the multiplication-table to memory. Meantime the following remarks will suffice. कम, commonly written कं, is substituted for एक, in the series of 'one' only: as, चार कं चार, lit., 'four ones four,' i.e., 'once four is four.' In the first of the series, however, we have simply एकम एक, 'once one is one,' probably a contraction for एक कं एक; and in the second, दो कं दो. In all other places in the table एकं is the substitute, as, e.g., दस एकं दस, 'ten times one is ten.' From the series of 'two' onwards, दूना is used as the Denominative numeral for दो; compare the Maráṭhí form of the numeral, दोन. From twos to tens, the fem. form, दूनी, is used; from tens onward, the masc. Thus, सात दूनी चौदह, $7\times2=14$, but बारह दूना चौबीस, $12\times2=24$. ती is substituted for तीन from threes to tens only; in all other cases, तीन is used. Thus, चार ती बारह, $4\times3=12$; ग्यारह तीन तेंतीस $11\times3=33$. From threes onward, चौक (pronounced *chauka* before consonants), is the substitute for चार; in the twos, the longer form, चौका, is preferred. Thus, पांच चौक बीस, 5×4=20; दो चौका आठ, 2×4=8. पंजे is the substitute for पांच throughout: as, दस पंजे पचास, 10×5=50. The sing. form, छक्का, 'six,' is used from eleven on; from two to eleven, the plur., छक्के, is preferred; as, चार छक्के चौबीस, 4×6=24; बारह छक्का बहत्तर, 12×6=72. सत्ते, 'sevens,' (as if plur. of सत्ता), is used throughout, except in the elevens, where सात is employed; e.g., छ सत्ते बयालीस, 6×7=42; but ग्यारह सात सतहत्तर, 11×7=77. Similarly अट्ठे is used for 'eight,' except in the elevens, where we have आठ; e.g., पांच अट्ठे चालीस, 5×8=40; ग्यारह आठ अठासी, 11×8=88. नम्म is used for nine in the twos only; नम्मा, from the threes to the tens; नौ is retained in the elevens; नम is used from the twelves onward. Thus, दो नम्म अठारह, 2×9=18; चार नम्मा छत्तीस, 4×9=36; ग्यारह नौ निनानवे, 11×9=99; बारह नम एक सौ आठ, 12×9=108. दहाम is substituted for दस in every instance. Above ten the cardinal numbers are employed as Denominatives.

a. In the multiplication table the word *utar*, 'over,' is sometimes added to the smaller number in the numerals from 100 to 200. In this case the word *sau* always comes last, as, e.g., *bisotar sau*, 120. Observe that *bisotar* = *bisa* + *utar*.

b. The fractional Denominatives from $3\frac{1}{2}$ to $7\frac{1}{2}$ are chiefly used in surveying. Sometimes डोढ़ा is used for डोढ़ा, and झंठा, हौंठा, for झंटा, हौंटा.

c. In numeration the words एकाई, दहाई and सैकड़े are used respectively for 'units,' 'tens,' 'hundreds.' In the headings of the multiplication-table, for $1\frac{1}{4}$, and $2\frac{1}{2}$, सवाया and अढ़ैया are the forms employed; i.e.,—to imitate English idiom,—'the one-and-a-quarters,' 'the two-and-a-halfs.'

239 The following are the Máṛwáṛí and Mewáṛí forms of the Denominatives:— Dialectic Denominatives

	Máṛ.	*Mew.*		*Máṛ.*	*Mew.*		*Máṛ.*	*Mew.*
1,	एकूं.	एक.	5,	पंजे, पाण.	पंजा.	8,	अट्ठे.	अठां.
2,	दूणो.	दूणा.	6,	छक, छके.		9,	नै.	नमां.
3,	ती, तोया.	तोण.		छंग.	छंगे.		नम्मे.	
4,	चौक.	चोकु.	7,	सत्ते.	सता.	10,	धाम.	दा.

a. The following forms of the Fractional Denominatives are used in Mewáṛí: 1¼, सवाया; 1½, डोडा; 2½, ढिया; 3½, हुटा; 4½, हूचा.

240. The eastern dialects present the following forms of the Denominatives:—

	Bhojpúrí.	*Mágadhí.*	*Maithilí.*
1,	का, एक्का, एकाई, के. एकं,* एकै.*	एक्कां.	का, कां, काइ.
1¼,	सवा.	सवा, सवैया.	*As Mg. and* सवठ, सवैएं, सवैये, समठ, समां.
1½,	डेढ़ा, डेढ़े, डेयढ़, डेढ़ो.	ड्योढा.	डेउढ़ा, डेउढे, डेयोढ़ा, डौढ़ा, दोबर.
2,	दूनी, दूना, दुगुनी, दो.	दूनी, दोबरी, दूगुना.	दुन्ना, दूनी, दून, दोबरा, दोबर.
2½,	अढ़ां, अढाई, अढइया, अढैया.	अढाई, अढैया.	*As Mg. and* अढ़ैएं, ढाम.
3,	तियां, तियाई, तिरिका. ति, चिका, चिके, तिरिके, तिन.	तीया, तीना.	तो, तिया, तियाइ, तेबरा, तिरि.
3½,	हुंठा, अंगूठा, अंगूढ़ा.	अंठा, अठा.	हुंठा, हुंठे, अण्ठा, अड्ढा, अड्ढे.
4	चौक, चौके, चर.	*As Bh.*	चौका, चौके, चौप, चौपरा.
4½,	धमूचा, धंगूचा.	धौंचा, ढौंचा.	धौंचा, धौंचे, ढोंचे, ढौंचठ, ढोंचा.

* Only used in एकं एक or एकै एक, 'once one is one.'

	Bhojpúrí.	*Mágadhí.*	*Maithilí.*
5,	पच, पाच, पचा,* पचे, पुरे.†	पचे, पंचे.	पचे, पांचबरा, पंजा. पंजे.
5½,	पऊंचा.	पऊंचा.	पऊंचा, पऊंचे, पोंचा.
6,	छह, छक, छका, छके, छाक.	छक, छक्का, छट्टे.	*As Mg.*, छके, छाक.
6½,	खिछिया.	खौंचा.	खौंचा, खोंचा, खौंचे.
7,	सात, सते, सत.	सते.	*As Mg.*, *and* सत्ते, सतें, सातबरा.
7½,	चखौसा.	*Wanting.*	सतौंचा.
8,	आठ, आठे, अट्ठे.	अट्ठे.	अट्ठे, अट्ठें, अट्ठा, आठबरा.
9,	नवां, नवांई, नउका.	नवांई.	नमऊ, नम, नमा, नवां, नमां, नाम, नवें, नव॰, नौबरा.
10,	दहां, दहांई, दसका.	दहांई.	दहम, दहांए, दहाए, दहिएं, दांहों, दहां, धां, दसबरा.

241. In Eastern Hindí, the numbers above 100 assume peculiar forms when used in the Multiplication Table, as follows. For सौ, 100, सो is substituted throughout. From 100 to 120, the smaller number is prefixed to the larger with the word उतर, 'above,' intervening as in High Hindí, उ with *a* preceding becoming ओ by *sandhi*; as in एकोतरसो, 101; चौदहोतरसो, 114, etc. From 120 to 160, and optionally from 110 to 120, and from 160 to 170, the two numbers are connected by the vowel आ instead of उतर, as in तीसासो, 130; छपन्नासो, 156, etc. In all these forms it is to be remembered that the rules for the shortening of antepenultimate vowels commonly take effect; also in the 2nd, 3rd and 4th decade, in most cases, the penultimate short vowel is lengthened; as in पनराहासो, 115; छब्बीसासो, 126, etc.

* Only used in the phrase पचा पचीस, 'five times five are twenty-five.'

† Only used when in the product we have the words पच or पें, 'five;' excepting however, पंद्रह, 15, and पचीस, 25.

a. In the first decade ल is inserted before उतर in the following:— द्लोतरसो, 102; तिलोतरसो, 103; चलोतरसो, 104; छिलोतरसो, 106; सतलोतरसो, 107. For 109, the form is निगरोतरसो, and for 110, दहोतरसो. In the nineties, व becomes ब; as in नब्बेसो, 190.

Collectives.

242. The terminations आ *á* and ई *í* are added to some of the cardinals, to denote collective numbers; as, बीसा *bísá*, 'a score;' बत्तीसी *battísí*, 'a thirty-two;' चालीसा *chálísá*, 'a forty.' Besides these, the following words are used as collective numbers, viz.:—

जोड़ा *joṛá*, जोड़ी *joṛí*, 'a pair.'
गंडा *gaṇḍá*, 'a four' (chiefly of cowries).
गाही *gáhí*, पंजा *pañjá*, 'a five.'
कोड़ी *koṛí*, 'a score.'
सैकड़ा *saikṛá*, 'a hundred.'

a. The cardinal numbers are often used as collectives, without any change of form.

Derivation of the Numerals.

243. The Hindí numerals are all derived from the Sanskrit, through intermediate Prakrit forms; and by referring to the column of Hindí and Prakrit numerals given below, and the general principles set forth in Chap. III., the student will be able himself to demonstrate the origin of most of the various forms. We only note a few particulars.

The data for the Prakrit numerals are far from complete. I am indebted to Beames for the collection of the forms given in the following table:—

Prakrit.	Hindí.	Prakrit.	Hindí.
1. *ekka.*	*ikka, ik, ek.*	5. *pañcha.*	*pánch.*
2. *do,* (Sk. *dva, dvi*).	*doya, doí, dúí, do.*	6. *chha* (Sk. *shash*).	*chha, chhe.*
		7. *satta.*	*sát.*
3. *tiṇṇi* (neut. *tríṇi*).	*tin, tín.*	8. *aṭṭha.*	*áṭh.*
4. *chattári,* (for Sk. neut. *chatvári*).	*chári, chár.*	9. *ṇüa,* (Sk. *nava*).	*nava, nau.*
		10. *dasa.*	*das.*

Prakrit.	Hindí.	Prakrit.	Hindí.
11. *eáraha.*	*igárah, gyárah.*	19. *ekúnavisái, únavisái.*	*unáís, unís.*
12. *váraha.*	*bárah.*	20. *visái.*	*bís.*
13. *teraha.*	*terah.*	30. *tísá.*	*tís.*
14. *chauddaha.*	*chárídasa, chaudah.*	40. *chattálísá.*	*chális.*
		50. *paṇṇásá.*	*pachás.*
15. *paṇṇaraha.*	*panara, pandrah, panarah.*	60. *saṭṭhi.*	*sáṭhi, sáṭh.*
		70. *sattari.*	*sattar.*
16. (*soraha*).*	*sorah, solah.*	80. *asíi.*	*assí.*
17. *sattaraha.*	*satturah, satrah.*	90. *näüe.*	*nave.*
		100. *sata, saya, säa.*	*saye, sai, sau.*
18. *aṭṭharaha.*	*aṭhárah.*		

Derivation of Cardinals.

244. Sanskrit presents for 'two,' *dva* and *dvi*, the former of which yields the High Hindí *do*, and the latter, the dialectic forms, *doya*, *doi*, *dui*, and *dvai*. In *tín*, 'three,' the *n* represents the *ṇ* of the Sk. neut. form, *tríṇi*; † O.B. retains the masc. form in *traya*. In like manner the final *ri* and *r* of *chári* and *chár* points to the Sk. neut. *chatvári*; while the Kanaují *chau* represents the Sk. masc. *chatur*. This preference for the neut. plur. termination, reminds one of the common use of the same in the plural of substantives.

245. In the series from 'eleven' to 'eighteen' inclusive, the *d* of the Sk. *dashan* becomes *r* in High Hindí, except in *chaudah*, 14, and *solah*, 16. A similar substitution of *r* for a dental, occurs in the compounds with *sattar*, 70, where *r* is for the last *t* of the Sk. *saptati*. In *chaudah*, the retention of the original *d* is due to the influence of the *r* of *chaturdashan*, still retained in the archaic Hindí form, *chárídasa*, in which, however, the *u* of *chatur* has disappeared. In *solah*, *d* has suffered a further change,

* Conjectural: Beames gives the conjecture, *solaha*, but as *soraha* is found uniformly in the older Hindí, and the *r* seems to be sustained by other Prakrit analogies, I prefer to regard the change to *l* as the later of the two.

† A similar neut. form, *don* for *do*, regularly used in Maráṭhí, is retained in Hindí, as the base of the Aggregative form, *donon*, § 223.

through *r* to *l*. The regular form, *soraha*, is however used by *Tulsí Dás*, and other writers in Eastern Hindí. *Tulsí* also uses an archaic form, *shoḍasha*, in which *d* has become *ḍ*, through the influence of the initial cerebral.

246. In the twenties, the labial *b*, for *v* of the Sk. *vinshati*, has disappeared in all compounds except *chaubís*, 24, and *chabbís*, 26; so also *p* has vanished in *unchás*, 49, for the older *únapañchás*. On the other hand, the labial element of *dvi* is preferred to the dental in *bís*, 20, and the whole series, *báís*, 22, *battís*, 32, etc., to *búnave*, 92; as also in *bárah*, 12, for Sk. *dvádashan*.

247. The numbers of the series, *unís*, 19, *untís*, 29, *untális*, 39, etc., have arisen from the combination of the Sk. *úna*, 'lessened,' with the next higher number. Thus even in Sanskrit, we have for *navatrinshat*, the alternative form, *ekonachatvárinshat*, = H.H., *untalís*, lit., 'forty less one;' and already in Sanskrit this *eka* was dropped, as in Sk. *únavinshati*, for *navadashan*, H. *unäis* or *unís*. *Navási*, 89, and *ninánave*, 99, are exceptions to this rule for the series, and follow the same law as the preceding numbers of each series.

248. The *l* which appears in the compounds with *chális*, 40, is explicated by a reference to the Prakrit form of this numeral, *chattálísá*, wherein the *l* has been substituted for the *r* of the Sk. *chatvárinshat*. It is therefore inaccurate to say that *l* is substituted in these cases for the *ch* of *chalís*, which letter in all this series has disappeared entirely; the hiatus, caused by its elision being marked by the inserted *y* in *bayális*, for *dvichatvárinshat*. In the fifties, the *p* of the Sk. *pañchásha t* has been softened to *w* in *ikáwan*, 51, *báwan*, 52, *chauwan*, 54, *satáwan*, 57, and *aṭháwan*, 58, though retained in the remainder. Beames is inclined to regard the *r* of *tirpan*, 53, as also of *tirsaṭh*, 63, *tirási*, 83, and *tiránawe*, 93, as merely euphonic. But I prefer to see in it a survival of the *r* of the original Sanskrit forms, *tripañchásha t*, etc., just as in *chaurási*, 84, is retained the *r* of the Sk. *chaturashíti*.

249. *Sau* or *sai*, 100, has arisen from the Sk. *shatam*; the former through the Pr. *säu*, the latter through the Pr. *sayan*, in which *y* has been inserted to fill the hiatus after elision of *t*. The *l* of E.H. *sala* represents the *d* of the Mg. Pr. *sadan*, for Sk. *shatam*.

250. The termination *on*, dial., *ún*, *ain*, etc., added to the numerals to form aggregatives, as in *donon*, 'the two,' *bíson*, 'the twenty,' *lákhon*, 'hundreds of thousands,' represents the termination *yam*, added in Derivation of Aggregatives.

Sanskrit to form aggregratives; so that *bísoṇ*, e.g., presupposes a Sanskrit form, *viṇshatayam*. It is thus quite inaccurate to say, with some, that in these cases the regular termination *oṇ* of the H.H. obl. plural, has been assumed into the nominative. The coincidence of this form with that of the obl. plural, is purely accidental.

Derivation of Fractionals.

251. The irregular fractional numbers are probably derived as follows: *Páo*, '¼,' with its equivalents, comes from the Sk. *páda*, Pr., *páu*, *páo*. *Paun*, ¾, and *paune*, −¼, are derived from the Sk. *pádona*, *páda* + *úna*, Pr. *páona*, 'a quarter less.' *Adhá*, '½,' is from *arddhaka*, secondary form of Sk. *arddha*; *savá*, '¼' or, as a prefix, '+ ¼,' Pr. *saváu* is from the Sk. *sapáda* (*sa* + *páda*) 'with a quarter.' *Sáṛhe*, '+ ½,' (obl. of *sáṛhá*, not used, (is regularly formed from the Pr. *saḍḍhao*, Sk. *sárdhaka*, *sa* + *ardhaka*, 'with a half.' The more difficult problem of the origin of the series, 2½, 3½, 4½, is explicated by the aid of the intermediate Prakrit forms furnished by Dr. Hoernle in his Grammar,* by which he makes it clear that they have arisen from the combination of the Sk. *ardha* with the ordinal next higher. Thus the immediate antecedent of *ḍeṛh*, '1½,' and its variants, is the Pr. *divaḍḍhe*, derived, through transposition, from Pr. *aḍḍhadiaie*, easily connected with the Sk. *arddha* + *dvitíya*, lit., 'half-second.' *Aṛhái*, '2½,' has in the Pr. the antecedent form, *aḍḍháijjá*, (for *aḍḍháia*), a form which has arisen through contraction from Pr. *aḍḍha* + *täijjá* = Sk. *arddha* + *tṛitíyá*. Similarly, *húṇṭá*, etc. '3½' has for its antecedents, Pr. *addhuṭṭha*, presupposing forms, *addhoṭṭha* = *addha* + *auṭṭha* = *addha* + *chäuṭṭha*, for Sk. *ardha* + *chaturtha*. Again, '4½,' *ḍhoṇchá*, etc. is traced back to a similar Sk. combination, through the Pr. *aḍḍhauñchäu*, for *aḍḍhavañchäu*, in which *v* is for Sk. *p*, as in several of the fifties, etc., pointing thus to a Sk. original, = *arddha-pañchama*. It is impossible, however, to carry this system of derivation further in this series, as evidently in *póṇchá*, '5½,' *khoṇchá*, '6½,' and *satoṇchá*, '7½,' the first element is the numeral preceding. This is plain at sight in *poṇchá*, *satoṇchá*; and in *khoṇchá*, evidently the *kh*, as often, is for the Sk. *sh* of *shash*. With the derivation of *ḍhoṇchá* so clearly made out by Hoernle, I now reject my former suggestion of a combination with *uchcha*, and see no reason to doubt Hoernle's theory that these are simply 'anomalous forms,' ignorantly made up by the common people, after the analogy of the foregoing *ḍhoṇcha*. The forms of the Collectives and Multiplicatives with a *k* termination, are directly descended from the

* Grammar of the Gauḍian Languages: pp. 269, 270.

Sanskrit, which forms Collectives by adding the suffix *ka*, or sometimes, *kará*, which latter is illustrated by the Hindí *saikṛá* and its equivalents. The forms in *á* (except *dúná*, Sk. *dviguṇaka*) are formed by the addition of the suffix *á* used to form abstract nouns.

Derivation of Ordinals.

252. Most of the ordinals are derived from the corresponding Sanskrit ordinals through intermediate Prakrit forms. Thus, e.g., *daswáṉ*, *pacháswáṉ*, have respectively arisen from the Sk. *dashama* and *pancha-shattama*. *Pahilá*, 'first,' is connected with the Sk. *prathama* through the Mg. Pr. *paḍhamille*, *ḍh* having (exceptionally) become *h*, after the analogy of other aspirates; the *l* is simply a pleonastic suffix. The derivation of the peculiar forms *dúsra* and *tísrá* is not so clear. Hoernle explains the *srá* of the termination as having arisen from the Sk. *sṛita*, 'moved;' assuming, e.g., a Sk. form, *dvissṛita*, antecedent to the Pr. *dusaliye*.

a. The ordinals used to denote the days of the lunar fortnight are derived directly from the feminine of the Sanskrit ordinals; the fem. noun, *tithi*, 'a lunar day,' being understood. Thus, e.g., *pariwá*, 'the first (day),' is for *prathamá*, through resolution of the original conjunct, elision of *th*, and softening of *m* to *w*. *Dúj* and *tíj*, 'the second' and 'the third,' come respectively from *dvitíyá* and *tṛitíyá*, *t* in both cases becoming elided, and *y* being hardened to *j*.

CHAPTER VIII.

PRONOUNS (सर्वनाम) AND PRONOMINALS.

253. The pronouns in Hindí, as in all other languages, exhibit many irregularities in their forms of declension. Old inflectional case-endings which have quite vanished from the noun, except in certain dialects, here appear in the regular system of declension; although, indeed, the analytical forms, even in pronominal declension, largely prevail over the inflectional. The Hindí pronoun, except in some of the Rajputana dialects, has quite lost the distinction of gender, which was still retained in the Prakrit. There is no distinctive pronoun for the third person; the demonstratives (निश्चयवाचक सर्वनाम), यह *yah*, 'this,' वह *wah*, 'that,' and, after a relative pronoun (संबंधवाचक सर्वनाम), expressed or implied, the correlative pronoun, सो *so*, supply its place.

Rem. The Hindí technical terms for *person* are: for the 1st person, उत्तम पुरुष; the 2nd person, मध्यम पुरुष; the 3rd person, अन्य पुरुष.

Pronominal Genitives.

254. In the pronouns of the 1st and 2nd persons, मैं *maiṉ* and तुम *tum*, रा *rá* appears as the sign of the genitive, instead of का *ká*, and is appended to a stem different from that which we find in any other case. The Reflexive pronoun, आप *áp*, is peculiar in retaining a purely inflectional gen., अपना *apná*, for the Sk. आत्मनः. In none of the pronouns, except in the case of the ag. sing. of the 1st and 2nd persons, is the base in the oblique cases identical in form with the nom. sing.

255. It will aid the memory to observe the close analogy in the declension of the different pronouns. In both Demonstratives, the Relative, Correlative, and Interrogative pronouns, स appears as the inflective sign of the oblique singular throughout; and न *n*, or, in the longer forms, न्ह *nh*, as the sign of the oblique plural. A similar analogy will be found to run through each of the dialectic systems of declension. Observe, further, that throughout all the varieties of declension, an initial *palatal*, viz., इ, (rarely अ,) its long vowel, ई, or its *gun* diphthong, ए, or the cognate semi-vowel, य, marks the Proximate Demonstrative; an initial *labial*, viz., उ, its long vowel, ऊ, its *gun* diphthong, ओ, or its cognate semi-vowel, व, marks the Remote Demonstrative; ज initial marks the Relative; स or त initial, the Correlative; and क, the Interrogative pronoun. Thus the declension of any one of these five pronouns may be transformed into that of any other, by simply substituting the proper pronominal initial. Thus, to tabulate the above, we have, in High Hindí, the following pronominal bases:— Pronominal Elements.

	P ox. Dem.	*Rem. Dem.*	*Rel.*	*Correl.*	*Interr.*
Nom.	य	व	ज	स	क
Obl.	इ	उ	जि	ति	कि

a. The idea of indefiniteness is expressed by adding to the interrogative inflected base, in High Hindí, ई *í*, in other dialects, इ, उ, or ऊ, or with the aspirate, हि, ही, or हू.

b. After the same analogy are formed from these pronominal bases six classes of adverbs, which will be noticed in Chap. XI.

256. The First Personal pronoun is declined as follows:

मैं *main̲*, 'I.'

	SINGULAR.	PLURAL.
N.	मैं *main̲*, 'I.'	हम *ham*, 'we.'
Ac.	मुझे *mujhe*, 'me,' 'to me.'	हमें *hamen̲*,
D.	मुझ को *mujh ko*,	हम / हमों } को *ham* or *hamon̲ ko*, 'us,' 'to us.'
Ag.	मैंने *main ne*, 'by me.'	हम / हमों } ने *ham* or *hamon ne*, 'by us.'
Ab.	मुझ से *mujh se*, 'from me.'	हम / हमों } से *ham* or *hamon̲ se*, 'from us.'
G.	मेरा *merá* (-रे, -री) (*-re, -rí*), 'my,' 'mine.'	हमारा *hamárá* (-रे, -री) (*-re, -rí*), 'our,' 'ours.'
L.	मुझ { में, or पर, *mujh men̲*, or *par*, 'in' or 'on me.'	हम / हमों } में, or पर, *ham, hamon̲ men̲*, or *par*, 'in' or 'on us.'

257. After the same model is declined the Second Personal pronoun,

तू *tú*, 'thou.'

	SINGULAR.	PLURAL.
N.	तू *tú*, 'thou.'	तुम *tum*, 'you.'
Ac.	तुझे *tujhe*, 'thee,' 'to thee.'	तुम्हें *tumhen̲*
D.	तुझ को *tujh ko*,	तुम / तुम्हों } को *tum* or *tumhon̲ ko*, 'you,' 'to you.'
Ag.	तू ने *tú ne*, 'by thee.'	तुम / तुम्हों } ने *tum* or *tumhon̲ ne*, 'by you.'
Ab.	तुझ से *tujh se*, 'from thee.'	तुम / तुम्हों } से *tum* or *tumhon̲ se*, 'from you.'
G.	तेरा *terá* (-रे, -री) (*-re, -rí*), 'thy,' 'thine.'	तुम्हारा *tumhárá* (-रे, -री) (*-re, -rí*), 'your,' 'yours.'
L.	तुझ { में, or पर, *tujh men̲*, or *par*, 'in' or 'on thee.'	तुम / तुम्हों } में, or पर, *tum, tumhon̲ men̲*, or *par*, 'in' or 'on you.'

258. For तुम्हारा, we sometimes find तुमारा; as in *Randhír aur Prem Mohiní*, passim. In the dat. and acc. sing., we occasionally find the forms, मेरे तईं, तेरे तईं; and in an example in Pincott's Hindí Manual, also तेरे को; thus, तेरे को क्या चाहिये सो मांग लेओ, 'ask for yourself what you may desire.' But this employment of the genitive in रे as an oblique stem, although the common usage in the eastern dialects, is rare in High Hindí, and is not to be imitated.

259. In the above pronouns, the plural forms, हम and तुम, as in the corresponding English pronouns, are often used for the singular. The singular of the 1st person is to be preferred, in High Hindí, to the plural used in a singular sense; although herein usage varies. The sing. of the 2nd Personal pronoun is used to express familiarity, chiefly by women among themselves, and by a man to his wife and children. Used by a *guru** to his disciples, or by a man to his servants and dependents, it seems to connote with this also a suggestion of the inferior position of the person addressed; and hence, as used by men to equals and superiors, it easily becomes expressive of aversion and contempt. Indeed, it so readily suggests this, that one should be very cautious about using it, even to one's servants. Use of Sing. and Plur.

260. The usage of the 2nd Personal pronoun in addressing the Deity seems to be as yet somewhat unsettled. There can be, I think, little doubt that, strictly speaking, the *Honorific* pronoun, आप,† would be regarded by Hindoos as the proper form in this case, but the pronoun requires words which are in regimen with it to be in the plural. But, in the Urdú, on the contrary, under the powerful influence of the Muhammedan monotheism, the singular of the 2nd Personal pronoun is employed, as in English; and hence it has come to pass, that Address to the Deity.

* A Hindoo religious guide.

† Vid. infra, § 270.

under this Urdú influence, missionaries and native Christians in India address God with तू, even in Hindí. It seems likely that this latter usage will prevail, if indeed it has not prevailed already, as correct in Christian Hindí.

a. It may be remarked, however, that when the reference is to the historic appearance of our Lord Jesus Christ, in narrating the incidents of his earthly life, आप is certainly to be greatly preferred. It is inconceivable, from a Hindoo point of view, that the mass of the people of that day, regarding Jesus as an eminent Rabbi, should have addressed him as तू; and I thus decidedly endorse the usage on this point, of the Baptist Missionary Society's admirable version of the Gospels.

261. The longer forms, हमों, तुम्हों, are restricted to a plural signification. They are not, however, extensively employed, but instead of these, when a plural is intended, the word लोग *log*, duly inflected for the several cases is added to the bases हम and तुम. Thus, in a plural sense, instead of the forms given in the paradigms, in High Hindí we preferably have, N., हम लोग, तुम लोग; Ac., हम लोगों को, तुम लोगों को; G., हम लोगों का, तुम लोगों का; etc., etc.

262. When these pronouns are used appositively with any noun or adjective in the gen. case, instead of the gen. forms given above, the base of the oblique cases must be used, and the postposition, का, के, or की, be appended to the following noun only. Thus we must translate, 'of unlucky me,' मुझ अभागी का; 'of us carpenters,' हम बढ़इयों का; 'of you wise men,' तुम बुद्धिमानों का; etc. हमारे बढ़इयों का would mean, 'of *our* carpenters;' तुम्हारे बुद्धिमानों का, 'of *your* wise men.'

263. The genitives of the personal pronouns are occasionally used substantively, with the obl. plur. inflection, in which case the objects denoted must be determined from the context. The following example is from the *Bhágavat Purán*: आन देशों में तुम्हारों से बड़े सुर बीर ऊए हैं, 'in other countries there have been heroes and braves greater than yours.'

264. The close analogy between the next six pronouns will best appear by exhibiting their declension in a tabulated form, as follows.

TABLE VII. High Hindí

		Prox. Demonst.	Rem. Demonst.	Relative.
		यह *yah*, 'this.'	वह *wah*, 'that.'	जो *jo*, 'who,' 'which.'
Singular.	N.	यह यिह *yah, yih.*	वह, वुह† *wah, wuh.*	जो *jo.*
	Ac. D.	यह *yah*, इसे *ise*, or इस को *is ko.*	वह *wah*, उसे *use*, or उस को *us ko.*	जो *jo*, जिसे *jise*, or जिस को *jis ko.*
	Ag.	इस ने *is ne.*	उस ने *us ne.*	जिस ने *jis ne.*
	Ab.	इस से *is se.*	उस से *us se.*	जिस से *jis se.*
	G.	इस का§ *is ká.*	उस का§ *us ká.*	जिस का§ *jis ká.*
	L.	इस { में, पर } *is men, par.*	उस { में, पर } *us men, par.*	जिस { में, पर } *jis men, par.*
Plural.	N.	ये,‖ यह *ye, yah.*	वे, वह *we, wah.*	जो *jo.*
	Ac. D.	इन्हें *inhen*, { इन, इन्हों } को *in* or *inhon ko.*	उन्हें *unhen*, { उन, उन्हों } को *un* or *unhon ko.*	जिन्हें *jinhen*, { जिन, जिन्हों } को *jin* or *jinhon ko.*
	Ag.	{ इन, इन्हों } ने *in* or *inhon ne.*	{ उन, उन्हों } ने *un* or *unhon ne.*	{ जिन, जिन्हों } ने *jin* or *jinhon ne.*
	Ab.	{ इन, इन्हों } से *in* or *inhon se.*	{ उन, उन्हों } से *un* or *unhon se.*	{ जिन, जिन्हों } से *jin* or *jinhon se.*
	G.	{ इन, इन्हों } का§ *in* or *inhon ká.*	{ उन, उन्हों } का§ *un* or *unhon ká.*	{ जिन, जिन्हों } का§ *jin* or *jinhon ká.*
	L.	{ इन, इन्हों } { में, पर } *in* or *inhon men, par.*	{ उन, उन्हों } { में, पर } *un* or *unhon men, par.*	{ जिन, जिन्हों } { में, पर } *jin* or *jinhon men, par.*

* Except in the nom., the Remote Demonstrative is very commonly preferred to
belongs to Braj. ‡ कौन is often colloquially used for किस, and कोई for
की according to § 161. ‖ ये is sometimes used, though less elegantly, for

?RONOMINAL DECLENSION.

CORRELATIVE.	INTERROGATIVE.	INDEFINITE.
सो *so*, 'that.'*	कौन *kaun*, 'who.'	कोई *koí*, 'anyone.'
सो *so.*	कौन *kaun.*	कोई *koí.*
सो *so,* तिसे *tise* or तिस को *tis ko.*	किसे *kise,* or किस को ‡ *kis ko.*	किसी को ‡ *kisí ko.*
तिस ने *tis ne.*	किस ने *kis ne.*	किसी ने *kisí ne.*
तिस से *tis se.*	किस से *kis se.*	किसी से *kisí se.*
तिस का § *tis ká.*	किस का § *kis ká.*	किसी का § *kisí ká.*
तिस { में / पर } *tis meṉ, par.*	किस { में / पर } *kis meṉ, par.*	किसी { में / पर } *kisí meṉ, par.*
सो *so.*	कौन *kaun.*	*Plural Wanting.*
तिन्हें *tinheṉ,* तिन / तिन्हों } को *tin* or *tinhoṉ ko.*	किन्हें *kinheṉ,* किन / किन्हों } को *kin* or *kinhoṉ ko.*	
तिन / तिन्हों } ने *tin* or *tinhoṉ ne.*	किन / किन्हों } ने *kin* or *kinhoṉ ne.*	
तिन / तिन्हों } से *tin* or *tinhoṉ se.*	किन / किन्हों } से *kin* or *kinhoṉ se.*	
तिन / तिन्हों } का § *tin* or *tinhoṉ ká.*	किन / किन्हों } का § *kin* or *kinhoṉ ká.*	
तिन / तिन्हों } में / पर *tin* or *tinhoṉ meṉ, par.*	किन / किन्हों } में / पर *kin* or *kinhoṉ meṉ, par.*	

the Correlative. † वो is also found in High Hindí books, but properly किसी, but the forms are inaccurate. § का is of course inflected to के or the nom. sing.; see *Raṇdhír aur Prem Mohiní*, passim.

265. Observe, that the Relative pronoun, जो, does not precisely correspond to the English Relative, 'who,' 'which.' It is rather 'the one who' or 'which,' 'that which.' Thus, जो आदमी आया, 'the man who came;' मैं ने जो कहा सो किया, 'what I said, that I have done.'

266. The plural of the Indefinite pronoun, कोई, is often expressed by repeating the pronoun; thus, कोई कोई आया, 'some (persons) came;' मैं ने किसी किसी को देखा, 'I saw some, (*or* several) persons.' This often has an intensive force, i.e., 'some few.' For the plural of कोई, कितने may be the substitute; as, कितने कहते थे, 'some (a number) were saying.'

Rem. कितने is in fact an interrogative pronominal, meaning 'how many,' and its use as a plural indefinite pronoun rests upon this fact. Compare the English idioms, 'how many go?' and 'how many go!'

267. कौन, as also, still more rarely, कोई, is occasionally uninflected in the oblique singular, as in the following from the *Prem Ságar*; कौन रीति से कृष्ण उपजे, 'in what manner *Krishna* was born.'

The Emphatic Affix.

268. The emphatic particle ई *í* or ही *hí* is sometimes added to all the above pronouns. In the oblique plural, ईं *iṉ* is substituted for the final ओं *oṉ*.

Examples are, यही *yahí*, 'this very;' मैं ही *maiṉ hí*, 'I myself;' उसी को *usí ko*, 'to that very person;' उन्हीं ने कहा *unhíṉ ne kahá*, 'those same persons said.' But, rarely, ही also follows the plur. inflection; as, e.g., उन्हों ही से *unhoṉ hí se*, 'from those very persons,' or 'that very person.'

Substantive and Adjective Use.

269. When any of the pronouns are used substantively, they take the proper postpositions as given in the tables. When they are used adjectively, i.e., with a noun, if in any oblique case, the inflected form of the pronoun, sing. or plur., is placed before the noun, and the postposition is added to the noun only.

Thus we say, उस पर *us par*, 'on that,' or 'on him;' but उस घोड़े पर *us ghoṛe par*, 'on that horse;' किस के घर को गया *kis ke ghar ko gayá*, 'to whose house did he go;' but, किस घर को *kis ghar ko*, 'to what house;' उस के देश के लोग *us ke desh ke log*, 'the people of his country;' but, उस देश के लोग *us desh ke log*, 'the people of that country;' जिन का *jin ká*, 'of whom;' but, जिन बनियों का *jin baniyoṉ ká*, 'the shop-keepers whose;' तिन कवियों को *tin kaviyoṉ ko*, 'to those poets,' etc. etc.

270. Observe, that the longer plural forms, in हों, can only be used in a substantive sense; the shorter forms may be used either adjectively or substantively. Thus, 'of those horses,' is उन घोड़ों का,—never उन्हों घोड़ों का; but, on the other hand, we may say either उन ने कहा, or उन्हों ने कहा, 'he' or 'they said.'

a. But the longer forms are much to be preferred when an honorific sense is intended. Colloquially, about Mathurá the ह of these forms is often dropped.

271. The plural forms of these pronouns are used for the singular, whenever it is intended to express respect. The longer forms are considered more respectful than the shorter. Since, thus, ambiguity might sometimes arise, the word लोग is preferably added to the pronoun, to denote plurality. In the oblique cases, this word, with the plural inflection, is inserted between the shorter form of the inflected base and the postposition. Thus, 'they' is वह लोग; 'in their village,' उन लोगों के गांव में; 'those who came,' जो लोग आए; etc. Respectful Forms.

272. It will be observed that all the pronouns hitherto considered, except the Indefinite, present two forms of the acc. and dat. in both the sing. and plur.; the one, purely inflectional, in ए (sing.) or एं (plur.); the other, analytic, consisting of the base of the oblique cases with को. These may both be used as either dative or accusative; but the forms with को are preferred for the accusative, and the others, for the dative. Sometimes the employment of one or the other is determined merely by a regard to euphony, as, e.g., मैं ने उसे माली को दिया, 'I gave it to the gardener;' where the immediate repetition of को would have been unpleasant to the ear.

273. All the above pronouns, when used adjectively with a noun in the accusative without को, take the nom. form.

Thus, we may say, जो घर मैं देखता हूं, 'the house which I see;' यह बात कहकर, 'saying this thing.' So also, when used substantively, the nom. form of the accusative may be employed, but only when the reference is to things: as, मैं यह कहता हूं, 'I say this;' जो हम सुनते हैं सोई कहते हैं, 'we say those very (things) which we hear.' But with कौन and कोई this usage is not considered elegant.

Neuter Indef. and Interrog. Pronoun.

274. Besides the Interrogative, कौन *kaun*, 'who,' and the Indefinite pronoun, कोई *koí*, 'any one,' 'some one,' etc., it will be observed that another interrogative pronoun, क्या *kyá*, 'what,' and another indefinite pronoun, कुछ *kuchh*, 'some,' 'any,' 'something,' 'anything,' is employed. The following principles regulate the usage of the two *Interrogative* pronouns (प्रश्नवाचक सर्वनाम).

Usage of the Interrog. Pronoun.

(1) कौन *kaun* may be applied both to persons and to things; क्या *kyá*, to things only, except in expressions denoting surprise, as, e.g., क्या मूरख *kyá múrakh*, 'what a fool!' More commonly, in such a case, the emphatic particle, ही *hí*, is added to the pronoun, as, क्या ही बड़ा राजा *kyá hí baṛá rájá*, 'what a great king!'

(2) कौन *kaun* is used both substantively and ad-

jectively, in both the nom. and obl. cases, but when used substantively, it refers to persons only.

Examples are: कौन है *kaun hai*, 'who is it?;' तुम ने किस को बुलाया *tum ne kis ko buláyá*, 'whom did you call?;' किस का है *kis ká hai*, 'whose is it?;' किस लड़के का *kis larke ká*, 'what boy's?;' तुम ने किस महाजन से पूछा *tum ne kis mahájan se púchhá*, 'of what banker did you inquire?;' किस घर में *kis ghar men*, 'in what house?.'

a. For the plural कौन कौन is often used; as, कौन कौन आए, *kaun kaun áé*, 'who came?'

(3) क्या *kyá* can be used adjectively in the nom. only: in the oblique cases it is always used substantively.

a. The dat., काहे को *káhe ko*, 'for what,' is commonly used as the equivalent for the English 'why.' The gen., काहे का *káhe ká*, 'of what,' usually denotes the material. Examples are: तुम काहे को आए *tum káhe ko áe*, 'why have you come?;' यह क्या है *yah kyá hai*, 'what is this?;' यह काहे का बना है *yah káhe ká baná hai*, 'of what is this made?.'

275. The two *Indefinite* pronouns (अनिश्चयवाचक सर्वनाम), Usage of the Indef. Pronoun
कोई *koí* and कुछ *kuchh*, are both used either substantively or adjectively, and of both persons and things. But when used substantively, कोई *koí*, like कौन, refers to persons only, and कुछ *kuchh*, to things only. When used adjectively, each may be used to denote both persons and things.

a. The distinction between these two pronouns, when used adjectively, appears to be this; that कुछ *kuchh* always conveys, more or less distinctly, a partitive sense. Examples of their use are: कोई है *koí hai*, 'is there any one?,' or 'there is some one;' but, कुछ है *kuchh hai*, 'there is some;' मैं ने किसी को देखा *main ne kisí ko dekhá*, 'I saw some one;' कुछ लड़के आए *kuchh larke áe*, 'some boys came.'

276. क्या *kyá* is declined in the singular only: कुछ *kuchh* is indeclinable.

a. The obl. form *kisú*, which many grammarians have assigned to *kuchh*, is properly a dialectic variation of the old form of *koí*. It will be found in the tables of dialectic declension. Prof. De Tassy similarly assigns to *kuchh*, obl. plur. forms, *kinhún*, *kinhún*,* but these are to be regarded as mere variations of *kinhon*, the obl. plur. of *koí*.

क्या *kyá* is declined as follows:

क्या *kyá*, 'what?'

SINGULAR.

N. क्या *kyá*, 'what?'	Ab. काहे से *káhe se*, 'from what?'
Ac. D. } काहे को *káhe ko*, 'for what?'	G. काहे का *káhe ká*, 'of what?'
Ag. *Wanting.*	L. काहे { में *káhe men*, 'in' or पर or *par*, 'on what?'

The Honorific Pronoun.

277. The *Honorific* pronoun, आप *áp*, is used instead of the 2nd personal pronoun, तू *tú* or तुम *tum*, whenever it is intended to show respect to the person addressed. In the singular it is declined exactly like a masculine noun of the second variety of declension; i.e., Nom., आप *áp*, Acc. Dat., आप को *áp ko*, Gen., आप का, etc.

a. But when more than one person is addressed, the plural is denoted by affixing the word लोग *log*, which is then regularly declined throughout the plural, the word आप remaining unchanged: as, आप लोग देखिये *áp log dekhiye*, 'your Excellencies will please to see;' मैं आप लोगों से कहता हूं *main áp logon se kahtá hún*, 'I say to your Excellencies.'

b. The Honorific pronoun आप is also, much more rarely, used for the person spoken of, when that person is present,

---

* Rudiments de la Langue Hindouí, p. 35.

so that the reference will be evident. But in such cases it is better to use, instead of आप, the proper title of the person addressed, as, साहिब, पंडित, लाला, etc.

278. The *Reflexive* pronoun, आप *áp*, 'self,' although, like the foregoing, derived from the Sanskrit आत्मन्, is differently declined. The singular number is declined as follows:— The Reflexive Pronoun.

आप *áp*, 'self.'

SINGULAR.

N.	आप *áp.*	Ab.	आप से *áp se.*
Ac. D.	आप } को *áp ko,* अपने } *apne ko* or	G.,	अपना (-ने, -नी,) *apná (-ne, -ní.)*
	अपने तईं *apne taiṉ.*	L.	आप } में *áp* or *apne* अपने } पर *meṉ, par.*
Ag.	आप ने *áp ne.*		

a. The plural forms are the same as the singular, with the exception of the gen., आपस का *ápas ká*, and the loc., आपस में *ápas meṉ*, 'among themselves.'

Examples of their use are: आपस की बातचीत *ápas kí bátchít*, 'mutual conversation;' वे आपस में झगड़ा करते हैं *we ápas meṉ jhagṛá karte haiṉ*, 'they are quarrelling among themselves.'

279. The genitive of the Reflexive pronoun must always be substituted for the genitive of the other pronouns, when the pronoun refers to the subject of the verb, and also in certain other cases, which will be duly noted in the chapter on Syntax. For the present one or two examples will suffice. The Reflexive Genitive.

Thus, वह अपने घर को जाता है *wah apne ghar ko játá hai*, 'he is going to his own house;' but, वह उस के घर को जाता है *wah us ke ghar ko játá hai*, 'he is going to his house,' i.e., the house of another person. Similarly, स्यार अपने बिल में छिपा रहा *syár apne bil meṇ chhipá rahá*, 'the jackal remained hid in his hole.'

280. The genitive अपना sometimes assumes the plural termination ओं, and is then used as a noun, in the sense 'one's own people.' Thus, वह अपनों के पास आया, 'he came to his own (people).' It sometimes is thus used elliptically in the singular, when the reference is clear: as, उस ने अपने को मारा, 'he struck his own (child, body, etc.),' as the connection may indicate.

281. It will be noticed that all the shorter forms of the Reflexive pronoun are identical with those of the Honorific pronoun, आप. Thus, उस ने आप को मारा may mean, 'he struck you,' (honorific form), or 'he struck himself.' Whenever, therefore, the sense might be ambiguous, the longer form of the Reflexive is to be preferred combined with आप; thus, उस ने अपने आप को मारा can only mean, 'he struck himself.'

Dialectic Pronominal Declension.

282. The tables annexed to this section exhibit the pronominal declension of thirteen dialects. Preliminary to the tables, the following remarks upon the forms current in the more important of these, may be found of service. The Braj forms are so uniform and regular as to demand little illustration. The tables exhibit all the common Máṛwáṛí colloquial forms. The remarks in the following paragraphs refer especially to the Máṛwáṛí of the 'Plays.'

Braj Pronouns. **283.** Rarely, in Braj, मो and तो are used for the genitive instead of मेरी and तेरी: thus, तो मन की जानति नहीं, 'thy mind I know not;' भक्ष करत पै मो हियो, 'but he consumes my heart.' For मोहि, I have also met मोए. Of the Relative and Correlative pronouns, gen. sing. forms, जासु and तासु, frequently occur in literature.

284. The aspirated and unaspirated bases of the 1st Personal pronoun are indifferently employed: thus, म्हारी अरज सुनूं, 'hear my supplication;' सुण मारी बात, 'hear my word.' मैं is used alone, as ag. sing., in the following: गुरु की आग्या मैं पाई, 'I have received the command of my *Guru*.' Instead of the regular base, थ, of the Máṛ. obl. sing. of the 2nd personal pronoun, तौ (Braj, तो) is sometimes used; as, तौ नै गोरख नाथ भरमयो, '*Gorakh Náth* has led thee astray.' Rajputana Pronouns.

285. ईं and ओ are the common nom. sing. forms of the two Demonstratives, यह and वह. Thus we read: ओ रुक्को लिख, 'he, writing a note;' ईं दगो कियो अंगरेज, 'this treachery has the Englishman committed.' But यो is found for ईं (यह) and वो for ओ (वह): as, यो जोगी बण आयो, 'this *jogí* has come into the jungle;' वोईं नाथ राणी, 'that same lord, O queen!' Besides the forms given in the tables, the 'Plays' often use the Braj वा (H.H. उस) in the obl. sing.: as, e.g., वा नु पायो, '(he) has found that;' where नु is for नै (H.H. को). The base वुण also occurs in the (honorific) plur. in the following, the postposition नै of the agent being regularly omitted: अमर कियो वुण, 'he has made (me) immortal.' वे occurs in the same case, as in वे ब्रह्म ग्यान सुणायो मा नै, 'he declared to me the knowledge of *Brahma*.' Finally, उ also is used as a base in the obl. sing., as in पींगला उरी लुगाई, '*Píngalá* his wife.' Márwáṛí Demonstratives.

a. In both *colloquial* Mewáṛí and Máṛwáṛí, ओ (masc.) and आ or या (fem.) are uniformly employed for यह, 'this,' and वो (masc.) and वा (fem.) for 'that.' The distinction of gender is preserved in the nom. sing. only. Of the former pronoun, the regular obl. sing. is ईं in both these colloquial dialects. In the colloquial of Máṛwáṛ and Mewáṛ the Relative is very commonly used for the Correlative pronoun.*

* The student will note the difference here indicated between colloquial Máṛwáṛí and that of the 'Plays.'

b. In the gen. sing. of the 1st and 2nd pers. pronouns, besides the forms given in the Tables, the Mairs use म्हौळो and थौळो.*

Már. Relative & Correlative.

286. Besides ज्यो, जो and जे are also used for the Relative. The most common sing. inflection is ज्यां; as, वोही थावंद तेरो ज्यां मे वसि, 'in whom dwells that lord of thine.' This inflected form alone expresses the case of the agent, but ने is occasionally borrowed from the Braj in this and other cases; as, ज्यां ने धर्‌यो सीस पर हात, 'he who placed (his) hand upon (my) head.'

287. Besides the forms of the Interrogative given in the tables, किण and कोण are found in the obl. sing.: thus, in the case of the ag., किण पापी भरमायो, 'what sinner has led (him) astray?;' कोण राज त्याग तपस्या कीनी, 'who, leaving his kingdom, has practised austerities?.' So also the regular form, कौन, occurs in the case of the agent: as, कौन उस्ताद नें ग्यान दिया, 'what teacher hath given (thee) knowledge?.' काहा, for क्या, 'what?,' occurs in the 'Plays,' but this is Braj. The regular Már. form, काँईं, occurs in the following: म्हारे काँईं सराय सूं काम, 'what business of mine in the *saráe*?.' कां is used in the following, merely as a sign of a question, like the corresponding क्या in H.H.; विना पवन कां पाणी, 'is there rain without wind?'

Mewárí Peculiarities.

288. Mewáṛí, it will be observed, is distinguished from all other Hindí dialects in retaining separate forms for the masc. and fem., in all except the two Personal pronouns. It should be further observed, that the Mewáṛí pronominal genitives in ळो are less common than those in को. The longer plural forms of the Personal pronouns, in थां and वरां, are preferred to the shorter for the true plural.

289. In the colloquial of both Máṛwáṛ and Mewáṛ, the reflexive genitive, अपना, is rarely used. The genitive of the

* For the pronunciation of the first diphthong औ, in these forms, see § 33.

several pronouns commonly takes its place, even when referring to the subject of the sentence. Thus the Máṛwáṛís would usually say, म्हूं म्हारो काम करहूं, = मैं अपना काम करूंगा, 'I shall do my work;' ऊ वीं के गाम गीयो, = वह अपने गांव गया, 'he went to his village;' वै वां का घोड़ा चढ्या, = वे अपने घोड़ों पर चढ़े, 'they mounted their horses,' etc.

290. In the Himalayas, so far as my observation has gone, people are not particular about using the Honorific pronoun, and frequently address their superiors with तुम, when no disrespect is intended, in a way that sounds very strange to one used to the speech of the Ganges Valley on the plains. Indeed, आप is very rarely heard from the Himalayan mountaineers, except from individuals who may have mingled much with the people of the plains. So also they freely use the 2nd pers. sing., तु, where in the Ganges Valley we should only hear the plur. तुम. Himalayan Pronouns.

a. But in Naipálí, occurs a Honorific pronoun, तपाञि, which is used exactly as आप in High Hindí, and takes the regular postpositions without inflection throughout; as, तपाञि का इच्छा छ भन्या, H.H., जो आप की इच्छा हो, 'if it be the will of your Excellency.' The Reflexive pronoun, in Naipálí, is आफु or आफैं. It is uninflected in the obl. sing.; in the plural, for H.H. loc. plur., आपस में, is used the form, आपस्त मा. For the High Hindí, आप से आप, or अपने आप, 'of one's self,' 'of one's own accord,' Naipálí has आफु आफै.

291. In the archaic Ḥindí of *Chand*, according to Mr. Beames, मो and तो, like other obl. pronominal stems, are used for all cases more frequently without than with the postpositions. Among his examples are: किम उधार मो होइ, 'how shall there be salvation for me?;' नाथ मो नाम चंद, 'lord, my name is *Chand*;' सुनिय बात तो तात 'hearing this word, thy father.'*

292. In the archaic Baiswáṛí of the *Rámáyan* all the postpositions, excepting that of the agent, which has no existence in the eastern dialects, are often employed with the pronouns as in High Hindí. But they are much more Pronouns in the Rámáyan.

* Vide Journal As. Soc. of Bengal, Part I. No. II. 1873.

frequently omitted, and the inflected base of the pronoun, sing. or plur., may then represent any oblique case whatever. This is indicated in the tables by placing the postpositions in a parenthesis.

a. This remark as to the use of the oblique forms of the pronouns, applies not only to the old eastern Hindí, but, more or less, to all archaic Hindí poetry, as, e.g., to the writings of the Rájpút bard, *Chand*, *Kabír* and others. Abundant illustrations will be found in the Syntax.

Personal Pronouns in Rámáyan.

293. In the *Rámáyan* मैं is used, instead of मो or मोहि, in the case of the agent; as, जो मैं पूछा नहि होई, 'that which I may not have asked.' The same remark applies to तू or तैं.*

294. Observe, that while the longer oblique forms, मोहि, तोहि, of the Personal pronouns, are constantly used in the *Rámáyan*, both with and without the postpositions, on the other hand, the shorter oblique forms, मो and तो, always take the postpositions.

a. हम is occasionally used in the gen. plur., for हमारा, as in the following; ते पुन्यपुंज हम लेखे, 'in my esteem, they are treasuries of merit.'

b. Besides the more common oblique forms of the 1st Pers. pron., given in the tables, a form मह, in the compound, मह सम, (= मुझ सा,) 'like me,' occurs in one place only in the *Rámáyan*. Analogous to this, is an obl. sing. form, तह, of the 2nd Pers. pron., noted by Prof. De Tassy in his Hindouí Grammar.

c. The Sanskrit genitive sing. of the Personal pronouns, मम, तव, 'my,' 'thy,' frequently occur in the *Rámáyan*, as in other Hindí poetry, but they cannot be accounted Hindí, and are therefore omitted from the tables.

* It should be observed, however, that the *Rámáyan* exhibits great confusion in the use of the direct and passive construction.

295. In the dialect of the *Rámáyan*, the regular forms of the Demonstrative pronouns, are इह, ईह, or एह, 'this,' and ओ, 'that.' But for एह, a form येह (for येऊ, metr. grat.) also occurs; as, राम भक्त कर लच्छन येह, 'this is a mark of devotion to *Rám*.' In the obl. sing., the Proximate Demonstrative is inflected to इहि or एहि; the remote, to ओहि, or, rarely, वोहि. Examples are, इहि विधि भरत मज्जन करि, 'in this manner *Bharat*, bathing;' पुनि पुनि पूछति ओहि, 'again and again she asks him;' मोर अभाग्य जिआवत वोही, 'my evil fortune keeps him alive;' एहि के हृदय, 'in the heart of this (demon);' इहिं मह रघुपति नाम, 'in this, the name of the lord of *Raghu*.' Demonstrative Pronouns in Rámáyan.

a. In the plural, we most commonly meet the inflected forms, इन्ह, उन्ह, which, like the obl. sing. forms, are used, after the manner of the dialect, either with or without the postpositions. Thus, राखिय इन्ह आँखिन माहीं, 'keep these (two) in your eyes.' For the dat. and acc. plur., forms उनहिं and इनहिं exist: as, जगदीस इनहिं बन दीन्हा, 'the lord of the world gave a wilderness to these.' For these, इहैं and उहैं also occur.

b. In the *Rámáyan* we meet a form, ओऊ, of the Remote Demonstrative pronoun; the final ऊ is commonly not an essential part of the word, but an emphatic particle, = Br. ऊ, H.H., ही. But sometimes it seems to be added merely metri gratiâ, as, e.g., in the following: लोचन सजल जोरि कर दोऊ। प्रभु सन कछु कहि सकत न ओऊ॥ 'his eyes full of tears, joining both hands, to the lord nothing could he say.'

c. Similarly, in other archaic Hindí, we find the emphatic nom. sing. forms, इहौ, इहै, (for यही,) of the Prox. Demons. pronoun, इह (यह). Thus, निज लोकहिं विरंच गये देवन्ह इहै सिखाइ, '*Brahmá*, having delivered this instruction to the gods, went to his own world;' इहौ कहत, 'saying just this.' The final ऐ or औ has arisen from the *sandhi* of the final inherent अ of इह with the emphatic particle ई or ऊ, = H.H., ही. In the forms एहा, एहू, of the same pronoun, the final vowel is simply lengthened metri gratiâ.

d. In the *Rámáyan* and other Hindí poetry, we occasionally meet the Sanskrit Demonstrative अयं, 'this;' as, पापौघमय तव तनु अयं, 'pervaded by sin and impurity is this body of thine.'

Relative and Correlative in Rámáyan.

296. The most common forms of the obl. sing. of the Relative and Correlative pronouns in the *Rámáyan* and similar poetry, are जिहि or जेहि and तिहि or तेहि. जाहि and ताहि also occur, but are not so common as in Braj. All these forms, as above remarked, are used in any case, either with or without the postpositions: as, e.g., जेहि दिस नारद बैठे, 'in what quarter *Nárad* was seated;' तिहि गिरि पर बट बिसाला 'on that mountain was a large fig-tree.' Instead of these longer forms, the Braj obl. forms, जा and ता, are often used, but generally with the postpositions.

Rem. Like मो and तो, however, these are also sometimes used substantively without the postpositions, as in the following line from the *Sabhá Bilás*; जा घट प्रेम न बसे ता घट जानु मसान, 'in whose body love dwells not, regard his body as a burning-ground (of the dead).'

a. The genitive of these pronouns is thus commonly expressed in the *Rámáyan* by जिहि, जेहि, and तिहि, तेहि, or जाकर, etc.; as, जेहि सुमिरत, 'by remembering (of) whom;' जा करि तैं दासी, 'whose handmaid thou art.' But the Braj inflected genitives, जासु, तासु, occasionally occur, and, still more rarely, जास; as, e.g., यह संबाद जास मन आवा, 'into whose heart this conversation enters.' A form ताऊ, for तिहि, is found in a few places; as, सरन गये प्रभु ताऊ न त्यागा, 'the lord hath not forsaken him (who) hath taken refuge with him,' lit., 'gone to his feet.'

b. जेइ is found in the obl. sing. for जेहि: as, जेइ मातु कीन्ही बावरी, 'who hath made (his) mother crazy.' In the phrase, सेउ मन समुझि, 'thinking this in his mind,' सेउ is an emphatic form of the acc. sing., = H.H., सोही. Very rarely, the Correlative, सो, is treated as if indeclinable; as, e.g., राम परायन सो परि होई, 'over him, *Rám* is chief.'

c. Instead of the oblique forms, जिन्ह and तिन्ह, जे and ते also sometimes occur, with the direct construction, after the manner of modern Eastern Hindí: as, e.g., धन्य जे जाये, 'blessed are they who bore (them);' ते देखे दोउ भ्राता, 'they beheld the two brothers.'

d. The Sanskrit forms of the Relative and Correlative pronouns, are occasionally used: thus, निरखंति तवानन सादर ये, 'who behold thy face with reverence;' पश्यंति यं योगी, 'whom ascetic saints behold.'

297. The most common form of the first Interrogative pronoun, कौन, in the *Rámáyan*, is कवन. To this, the fem. termination, ई, is sometimes added, as in the following: कवनि बस्तु असि प्रिय मोहि लागी, 'what thing has been so dear to me?.' The Braj को is also occasionally used; as, बेष अगनित को गनै, 'who can enumerate (their) countless disguises?.' Interrogatives in Rámáyan.

a. In the obl. sing. the regular forms, किहि, केहि (*kĕhi*), are preferred to others when the pronoun is used substantively: as, केहि सन करहिं बिरोध, 'with whom do they cherish enmity?.' The medial ह is sometimes dropped: as, धनुष केइ तोरा, 'who broke the bow?.' But when the pronoun is used adjectively, the nom. more commonly remains unchanged: as, मिलै कवन बिधि बाला, 'in what way may I obtain the maiden?;' but may take the fem. termination: as, बरनि कवनि बिधि जाइ, 'in what way can (all the wonders) be recounted?.' An obl. sing. form, कवने, also occurs: thus, भगतहीन सुख कवने काजा, 'of what use is pleasure to one destitute of religion?.' This may be contracted to कौने; as, आवै कौने काज, 'of what use can it be?.' The Braj obl. sing., काहि, is also found; as, सेइय काहि, 'whom wouldst thou serve?.' The plur. forms, nom. कवन, obl. किन्ह, किन्हहिं, etc., call for no special remark or illustration.

298. For the second Interrogative, क्या, when used substantively, काह (काहा) is the usual substitute in the *Rámáyan*. The Braj forms, का and काहा, also occur. In the obl. sing., काहा is found; as, दूषन काहा, 'for what fault?.' कि or किं is used for क्या as a mere sign of interrogation: thus, होहि निरामिष कबहुं कि कागा, 'will a crow ever live without meat?.'

Indefinite Pronouns in Rámáyan.

299. For कोई, the first Indefinite pronoun, कोउ, कवनउ, कवनिउ, and कौनो, are the common substitutes in the *Rámáyan.* Thus, कवनिउ सिद्ध कि बिनु बिस्वासा, 'was there ever any saint without faith?.' I should suppose a nominative कवनिहु or कवनहु must exist, but have not noticed it. The ह of हु is however certainly preserved in the obl. form, कवनेहु, for कवनेउ, which is also used; as in कवनेहु काल, 'at any time.' Besides the above nom. forms, केहु and केहि also occur, as in the following: अनुचित कहब न पंडित केही, 'no wise man will call it wrong;' जानि न पाव बात यह केहू 'let no one know this thing.' We also find केउ and कियौ.

a. In the obl. sing. a variety of forms exist. काहू, (in the dat. and acc. काहूहि) is used: as, काहूहि दोष जनि देहू, 'do not impute blame to any one;' and also केहिं; as, कहि न जात बिधि केहीं, 'it cannot in any way be told;' where इ is lengthened metri gratiâ. An obl. plur. form, काहून, exists; thus, पान सब काहून पाये, 'every one received *pán.*' The fem. कवनिहु occurs in the following: कवनिहु भांति बोध नहिं आवा, 'in no way did he comprehend.'

300. The second Indefinite pronoun, कुछ, is used in archaic Baiswáṛí poetry, but कछु is preferred, often in the augmented Prakritic form, कछुक. It is always indeclinable, as in High Hindí. Thus, राम ...... कछुक दिन बास करहिंगे आइ, '(after) some days *Rám* will come and dwell (here).'

301. The Reflexive pronoun commonly appears in the *Rámáyan* as आपु or आपुन: as, आपुन होइ न सोई, '(but) that same himself is not;' नरेस आपु चढ़ेउ, 'the lord of men himself mounted.' The genitive of the Reflexive in the same dialect is आपन; as in the following, where आपन, 'one's own,' is contrasted with पर, 'another's;' आपन पर कछु सुनै न कोई, 'no one heard at all his own (or) another's (voice).' The fem. form is आपनि; as, आपनि दिस, 'toward myself.'

The penultimate vowel is sometimes lengthened metri gratiâ; thus, अपाना, अपानि.

a. Sometimes, in the *Rámáyan* and other poetry, the Sanskrit indeclinable Reflexive pronoun, स्वयं, is substituted for आप; thus, दहन पावक हरि स्वयं, '*Hari*, himself a consuming fire.' Similarly, for the possessive, आपन, the Sanskrit inseparable possessive particle, स्व, is often prefixed to a word; as, स्वकर काटि सीस, 'cutting off (his) head with his own hand.'

Honorific Pronoun in Rámáyan.

302. For आप का, the gen. of the Honorific pronoun, आप, the usual substitute in old Baiswáṛí poetry is राउर; as, भरत कि राउर पूत न होहीं, 'is not *Bharat* your Majesty's son?.'

Pronouns in E. Colloquials.

303. The modern eastern dialects, and especially the Maithilí, are characterised by a remarkable variety of inflectional forms. In all the dialects east of Allahabad, the Demonstratives, the Relative and Correlative, and the Interrogative pronouns, have an honorific and a non-honorific form of declension, in each of which, again, there is a longer and a shorter form. In this fulness of honorific forms, it will be observed, these dialects stand in contrast with those of the west, which only use the plural for the singular, to express respect, and have an Honorific pronoun only in the 2nd person. In the following tables, the honorific forms are given in the second line of case forms in each dialect. Although the 2nd Personal pronoun has no honorific declension based on the same theme as the non-honorific, the place of such a declension is taken by the words अपने, रौवां, and their equivalents, = H.H. आप.

Use of Long and Short Forms, etc.

304. Of the longer and shorter forms, it is to be observed that in Maithilí, at least, the longer is used only as a substantive; the shorter may be used both in an adjective and in a substantive sense when referring to inanimate objects, but only in an adjective sense when referring to animate objects.

305. The student will note in the Bhojpúrí, Mágadhí, and Maithilí, the use of the gen. formation in रा as a theme for all the obl. cases. I have found the postpositions में and पर, even in High Hindí, in construction with the genitive of pronouns, as in मेरे में, तेरे पर, and even ता के पर, but this usage is exceptional and must be regarded as foreign to the idiom of Western Hindí.

Variations in Pronoun Forms

306. Numerous variations from the eastern forms given in the Tables occur, as follows. In some districts in the east, the final consonant झ, of मुझ and तुझ, is changed by the rustics to स, giving such forms as मुस को, तुस से, etc. In all plural forms, the ह of the conjunct न्ह in all plural bases, may be optionally dropped in Bhojpúrí, Mágadhí, and Maithilí; thus we may have इन्ह or इन; जिन्ह or जिन, etc. The same option obtains place in the termination of the plural; so that we may have हमन्ह or हमन, 'we;' इन्हन्ह or इन्हन, 'these,' etc. Also in Bhojpúrí, to demonstrative forms in इन्ह and उन्ह (इन and उन) initial, ह is optionally prefixed, giving, e.g., हुन्हका or उन्हका, 'these;' इन्हके or हिन्हके, 'their,' etc.; and also to the bases of the sing. of the same pronouns, giving, e.g., हे, for एह, 'this;' हो, for ओह, 'that;' for ओकरनके, 'theirs,' होकरनके; हेकर, for एकर, 'of this,' etc. In this same dialect, again, as also in Maithilí, the syllable का may be added to any form of the nom. plur. of the Demonstrative, Relative, Correlative, and Interrogative pronouns; giving thus either इहाँ or इहाँका, 'these' (hon.); केकनी or केकनीका, 'who?' etc.

Increased Pronom. Forms.

307. For the Proximate and Remote Demonstrative, the Relative, Correlative, and Interrogative pronouns, the Bhojpúrí and the Maithilí, of the extreme east and south-east, also use, for things only, another series derived from the same pronominal bases, as follows: Bh. इत्यू or इथुआ, 'this;' ओत्यू or ओथुआ, 'that;' जित्यू or जिथुआ, 'who?'; तित्यू or सित्यू, and तिथुआ or सिथुआ, 'that;' कित्यू or किथुआ, 'who?' These are all declined as substantives, making their plurals, इत्युअन, ओथुअन, etc.

a. To these, as to the other pronouns, ह is sometimes prefixed to an initial इ or उ; giving such forms as हित्यू, होथुआ, etc.

b. The Maithilí of Central and Western Purniyá, exhibits a variation of the same series, thus: इथी, उथी (जिथी or जथी, तिथी or तथी),* किथी or कथी. In S. Bhagalpúr, this series is again slightly varied, thus: ईथि, ऊथि (जथि, तथि),* कथि.

c. In Bhojpúrí a variant, एथी, for इत्यू of the above pronominal series, is used for 'this,' when one cannot call the name of that which is

* These forms are not given in Grierson's Grammars, though he states that the series is carried out. I supply them therefore from the analogy of the other forms.

referred to. In the Doáb, the phrase क्या नाम, 'what (is) the name?' is used under similar circumstances.

308. In Bhojpúrí, Mágadhí, and Maithilí, the genitive singular of all the pronouns after the Personal pronouns, may be formed, not only by adding to the stem the regular genitive postposition, as in High Hindí; but also by adding to the stem the affix कर, which is inflected to करा for the oblique form, a long vowel in the penult of the direct form being then always lengthened. Thus, we have in Maithilí either एहि के or एकरा के (= H.H. इसका) or एकर, obl. एकरा; Bh. ओह के or ओकर, obl. ओकरा, etc. Bh. Mg. and Mt. Pronom. Genitives.

309. In the Serampore translation of the N. T. into Baghelkhaṇḍí Hindí,* the following pronominal forms occur. The nom. plur. of the 1st Personal pronoun is हमारे, and the obl. plur., हमनु. Of the 2nd Personal pronoun, the nom. plur. is तिहारे, and the obl. plur., तिहारेनु. ये and यहे are each found in both the nom. and obl. plur. of the Proximate Demonstrative; यहे also occurs as nom. sing. The nom. plur. of the Remote Demonstrative, वहे, is वे, and the obl. plur., always वाङ्गन. The Relative and Correlative make the obl. plur., respectively, जिननु and तिननु. The Interrogative is कोनु; the nom. and obl. sing. are alike. All the obl. forms above given are used with the postpositions, which are, for the most part, the same as in Braj; but मों is used for में. The periphrastic plur. is sometimes formed with सब, as in other eastern dialects; thus, ये सबरेनु तें = H.H. इन लोगों से. Baghelkhaṇḍí Pronouns.

310. For the indication of a true plural, the eastern dialects all prefer the periphrastic form to the inflectional; and in pure Maithilí, this is the only form employed, the original inflectional plurals being only used in an honorific sense. For this periphrastic plural the eastern dialects all prefer to the word लोग, thus used in western Hindí, the word सब and its variant forms, सभ, सबहि, सभी, सभे, and सबे. Besides सब, Maithilí also employs, in the north, लोकनि, and in the south and east, सी, सिबी, आरहिन, आर, and सम्ही; appending these preferably to the base of the obl. cases. According to Beames, in Bhojpúrí, the longer plural forms, as इन्हकरा, उन्हकरा, etc., are preferred to the shorter, when emphasis is intended. For the plural of कोइ = H.H. कोई, 'some one,' कितेक is commonly employed; as, कितेक घर जरत बा, 'some houses are burning.' Pronom. Plur. in E. H.

* Baptist Mission Press, Serampore, 1821.

Direct and Obl. Pronom. Genitives.

311. Of the genitive forms, those in आ are oblique and the others direct. Thus we have, e.g., Bh. मोरे घोड़ा, 'my horse;' Mt. उन्हकेर घीरक, 'of their house,' etc. But exceptions are found in the Mágadhí gen. postposition, केरा (fem. केरी), used about Patna, which is both masc. direct and oblique, and in W. Bhojpúrí and Avadhí, where the masc. obl. of the gen. in र, रे, and the postposition के, ends in ए, as in High Hindí.

Emphatic Pronom. Forms in E.H.

312. Analogous to the emphatic forms in औ in the *Rámáyan*, we find in Bhojpúrí, Mágadhí, and Maithilí, emphatic forms of the obl. sing. of the 1st and 2nd pers. pronoun in ओ; as, e.g., मोरो, 'me also,' तोहरो, 'thee also.' Besides these, Bhojpúrí also has the forms, मोरे, हमरे, 'even me,' and तोरे, तोहरे, 'even thee.'

Honorific Pronouns in E.H.

313. While the Honorific pronoun, आप, will be heard in the eastern Hindí country wherever Muhammedan influence is felt, as also among the Mágadhí-speaking people in the districts of Patna and Gayá, yet through the largest part of this region the longer form अपने—in Ríwá, अपना—is preferred. As a rule, this is declined regularly as a noun, unchanged throughout the singular. But in the dialect of Ríwá, the nom. sing. अपना is sometimes inflected to अपने, in the obl. cases; and in Mágadhí, when used reflexively, forms of the gen. sing., अप्पन, आपन, are used. In the Maithilí of S. Bhagalpúr, occur the variants, for the nom. sing., अपनै and आपने; also, for the regular obl. sing., अपने, अपना, and अपनउ. The plural is formed by the addition of सभ, लोग, etc., to the base of the singular. But in Mágadhí, अपनन and अपनन्ही are also used throughout the plural. In Avadh, the usual form is आपु.

314. In Bhojpúrí, not only अपने, but also another word, रौवाँ, with variants, रवाँ, रौरा, and रउरा, is used as an Honorific pronoun. This is declined regularly as a noun, except that in the gen. sing. and in the voc. we have variant forms, राउर, रउरे, रौरे. The plural is regular; nom. sing. रौवन or रौरन,* etc., throughout. A variant of this same theme is heard in W. Mágadhí, रौआँ, nom. plur. रौअन्ह. In W. Maithilí also, रौरा and रउरा, plur., रौरन, are used.

315. Besides the above, Maithilí also employs as an Honorific pronoun of the 2nd person, in the north, अहाँ, in the west, also आहाँ; these are declined regularly as nouns in the sing. In the north, an instrumental inflected form, अहँ, is used. The plural is formed periphrastically, after the manner of the dialect. Along the north bank of the Ganges, from

---

* Also न्ह final.

near Patna, to the Kosí River, yet another form, आइस, is used, also declined regularly throughout.

316. In Bhojpúrí, Mágadhí and Maithilí, the *Reflexive* pronoun is अपने, with variations as follows:—Bh., अपना, अपुए, आपु and आप; Mt., in the north, अपनहि; in the east, अपन्हिँ; in the south, अपनैं, and also आइस; in S. Bhagalpúr, आपने, अपनै. These exhibit certain irregularities of declension, as follows. In Bhojpúrí, अपने makes the obl. sing. अपना; but in the west, also आपन and अपनै; the gen. sing. is आपन, अप्पन, or अपने (obl. अपना). The nom. plur. is अपनन्ह; the gen. plur., in N. Muzaffarpúr, आपुस के. In Mágadhí, the Reflexive is declined regularly throughout, except in the gen. sing., अप्पन, आपन. In Maithilí, the Reflexive, under all the above forms, makes the obl. sing., अपना; but in S. Bhagalpúr, also अपनठ and अपनहि, or like the nominative. The gen. sing. is variously अपन, अप्पन, and आपन. In S. Bhagalpúr is also used a gen. plur., आपुसठ केरठ, and a loc. plur., आपुसठ में. Reflexive Pronoun in E.H.

317. In the following Tables the inflected form of the genitive is not always given, but may be readily known from the rules for the inflection of the genitive postpositions in the several dialects. A bracket between the pronominal bases and the postpositions indicates that either of the postpositions may be added to any of the bracketed forms. Alternative postpositions, where not given, may be supplied for the different dialects from Table II. The Pronominal Tables.

Remarks on the Pronominal Tables.

318. Observe, that whenever, in the pronominal tables, we have a final short vowel, in poetry this vowel may, metri gratiâ, be optionally lengthened, so that we may have, e.g., such forms as ओही, केही, काहू, for ओहि, केहि, काहु.

319. Observe, further, that in many dialects *Anusvár* is freely inserted or omitted in all the above pronouns, both in the terminations and, less frequently, in the pronominal base. Thus, e.g., we have जौंन, कौनों, केहिं, याँ, for जौन, कौनो, केहि, या, etc., etc. It has not been thought necessary to give all such trifling variations in detail.

320. Occasionally, for the acc. postposition, को, the postposition तईं, (also written ताईं, तांईं, ताईं, and ताहीं,) is used in construction with pronominal genitives. Thus we find मेरे तईं, उस के तईं, for the acc., मुझ को, उस को. ताईं is also sometimes added, like को, directly to the inflected base. Thus in the Máŗwáŗí play of *Hírá* and *Ranjá*, we have देंगे भेद . . . . तुझ ताईं, '(they) will give thee the secret.'

Additional Bhojpúrí Forms.

321. In Bhojpúrí the following forms are given by Grierson in addition to those exhibited in the tables.*

(1) Of the first Pers. pronoun :—nom. and obl. plur., हमन, हमहन; in the west, nom. sing., में; nom. and obl. sing., मों; nom. and obl. plur., हम्मन, हमहन, हमने; in N. Muzaffarpúr, हमरहिन; in Sáran, हमे; elsewhere, nom. and obl. plur., हमन, हमनिन्ह, † हमहन.†

(2) Of the 2nd Pers. pronoun :—in the west, nom. sing., तैं, तुंह; obl. sing., तूंह, तो, तुहरा, (obl. form, तुहरे); nom. and obl. plur., तूंहन, तुहने, तुहरन; in N. Muzaffarpúr, तोहरहिन; elsewhere, तुम्हन, तोह्निन, तोरन.

(3) Of the two Demonstratives :—in obl. sing., एहि, ओहि; in Sáran, nom. sing., for ई, हे; for ऊ, हेऊ, हुचए, होचहे, ऊहे; in nom. and obl. plur., इन्हन, इन्हनी,† एकनी, *hon.* इहन; उन्हन; उन्हनी,† ओकनी,

* The option indicated in § 306 applies throughout all plural forms, where not otherwise indicated.

† Also in Mágadhí.

TABLE VIII. DIALECTIC PRONOMINAL DECLENSION: 1st Personal Pronoun.

मैं, etc., 'I.'

		High Hindí.	Kanaují.	Braj.	Márwárí.	Mewárí.	Gaṛhwálí.	Kumáoní.	Naipálí.
Singular.	N.	मैं.	मैं.	मैं, हौं, हौं.	हूं.	म्हूं.	मैं.	मैं.	मैं, मठ. मौं.
	Ac. D.	मुझे. मुझ को.	मोहि. मो को.	मोहि, मुहि.[1] मो } कौं. मुज }	म्ह } ने. म }	म्हो } ऐ, ए. म्ह } ने.	मैं. मैं सणि.	मैं { कणी. ऊणि.	मठ लाइ.
	Ag.	मैं ने.	मैं ने.	मैं ने. हौं.	म्हैं. मैं.	म्हैं.	मैं ने.	मैं ले.	मठ ले.
	Ab.	मुझ से.	मो { से. तें.	मो } सौं. मुझ } तें.	म्हैं } सूं. मैं }	म्हो म्हां } ऊं. मारा } सूं.	मैं तें.	मैं { हि. थिं.	मठ { बाट. ले.
	G.	मेरा.	मेरो.	मेरौ.	मारो. म्हारो.	म्हा } को, रो. ळो.	मेरो.	मेरो.	मेरो.
	L.	मुझ { में. पर.	मो { में. पर.	मो } मैं. मुज } परि, पै.	म्हैं } माहि. मैं } ऊपरै.	म्हां म्हो } मांऐ. मारा } ऊपरे, परे.	मैं { मां. पर.	मैं मां.	मठ { मा. माथि.
Plural.	N.	हम.	हम.	हम.	म्हे.	म्हैं.	हम.	हम.	हामि हामिहेरु. हामेरु.
	Ac. D.	हमें. हम को.	हमें. हम को.	हमैं. हम, हमौं } कौं. हमन, हमनि }	मां } नै. म्हां }	म्हां, म्हांयां } ऐ, ए. म्हांवरां } ने.	हमुं. हम } सणि. हमुं }	हमन { कणी. ऊणि.	हामि } लाइ. हामेरु }
	Ag.	हम ने.	हम ने.	हम, हमौं } ने. हमन, हमनि }	म्हां.	म्हां.	हम } ने. हमुं }	हमन ले.	हामि } ले. हामेरु }
	Ab.	हम से.	हम { से. तें.	हम, हमौं } सौं. हमन, हमनि } तें.	मां } सूं. म्हां }	म्हां, म्हांयां } सूं. म्हांवरां } ऊं.	हम } तें. हमुं }	हमन { हि. थिं.	हामि } बाट. हामेरु } ले.
	G.	हमारा.	हमारो.	हमारौ.	मांरो. म्हांरो.	म्हां, म्हांयां } को, रो. म्हांवरां } ळो, णो.	हमारो.	हमरो.	हामरो. हामि } को. हामेरु }
	L.	हम { में. पर.	हम { में. पर.	हम, हमौं } मैं. हमन, हमनि } परि, पै.	मां } माहि. म्हां } ऊपरै.	म्हां, म्हांयां } माऐ. म्हांवरां } ऊपरे, परे.	हम } मां. हमुं } पर.	हमन मां.	हामि } मा. हामेरु } माथि.

		Old Baiswárí.	Avadhí.	Ríwáí.	Bhojpúrí.	Mágadhí.	Maithilí.
Singular.	N.	मैं.	मैं.	मंयं.	मैं, मौं. हम.	हम.	हम, हमे, हमठ. हम्मे, हम्मी.
	Ac. D.	मो मोहि } (कहं). मुहि	मो का.	म्वहि. म्वहि म्वा } का, कहं.	मोरा; मोरा } के. हमरा; हमरा } ला.	मोरा; मोरा } के. हमरा; हमरा } सिल.	मोरा; मोरा } कें. हमरा; हमरा } सिल.
	Ag.	मैं.	*Wanting.*	*Wanting.*	*Wanting.*	*Wanting.*	*Wanting.*
	Ab.	मो मोहि } (सन). मुहि	मो } से. मे } ते, तन.	म्वहि } से. म्वा } तन.	मोरा } सें. हमरा }	मोरा } सें. हमरा }	मोरा } सें. हमरा }
	G.	मोर.	मोर.	म्वार.	मोर, मोरे; मोरा.[2] हमार, हमरे; हमरा.[2]	मोर, मोरा.[3] हम्मर, हमरा.[3] हमार, हमरे.	मोर; मोरे, मोरठ. हमर, हमरठ, हमरे.
	L.	मो मोहि } (माहिं). मुहि	मो { म. पर.	म्वारे म.	मोरा } में. हमरा }	मोरा } में. हमरा }	मोरा } में. हमरा }
Plural.	N.	हम, हमन.	हम.	हम्ह.	हमनीका. हमरन.	हमनी. हमरनी.	हमनी, हमें, हम, (-सभ).[4] हमरा सभ के.
	Ac. D.	हमहिं. हम (कहं).	हम का.	हम्ह कहं.	हमनी; हमनी } के. हमरन; हमरन } ला.	हमनी; हमनी } के. हमरनी; हमरनी } सिल.	हमरा सभ { कें. सिल.
	Ag.	हम.	*Wanting.*	*Wanting.*	*Wanting.*	*Wanting.*	*Wanting.*
	Ab.	हम (सन).	हम { से. ते, तन.	हम्ह { से. तन.	हमनी } सें. हमरन }	हमनी } सें. हमरनी }	हमरा सभ सें.
	G.	हम. हमार.	हमार.	हम्हार.	हमनी } के; का. हमरन }	हमनी } के. हमरनी } केर, केरा.[3]	हमरा सभ के.
	L.	हम (माहिं).	हमरे म.	हम्ह म.	हमनी } में. हमरन }	हमनी } में. हमरनी }	हमरा सभ में.

[1] These forms are also used, more rarely, with the postpositions. [2] Oblique form. [3] Fem. in ी. [4] Instead of सभ, any of the nouns of plurality given in § 183, may be used throughout with any of these themes.

TABLE IX. DIALECTIC PRONOMINAL DECLENSION: 2ND PERSONAL PRONOUN.

तू, etc., 'thou.'

		High Hindí.	Kanaují.	Braj.	Márwárí.	Mewárí.	Garhwálí.	Kumáoní.	Naipálí.	Old Baiswárí.	Avadhí.	Riwáí.	Bhojpúrí.	Mágadhí.	Maithilí.
SINGULAR.	N.	तू.	तू.	तू. तै तैं.	तूं. थूं.	थूं.	तू. तुइन, तिन.	तू.	तउ, तं.	तू, तूं, तैं.	तयं.	तंयं.	तैं, तूं.	तूं, तों.	तोंह, तोंहें. तों, तूं.
	Ac. } D. }	तुझे. तुझ को.	तोहि. तो को.	तोहि. तो कौं.	त / थ } नै.	थो (ए, ऐ). थे नै.	तोई. तोई { कू, / सणि.	ली { कणी. / ऊणि.	तं / तैं } लाई.	तो कहं. तोहि / तुहि } (कहं).	तो का.	त्वां / त्वहि } कंहं.	तोरा; तोरा / तोहरा; तोंहरा } के. / ला.	तोरा; तोरा / तोहरा; तोहरा } के. / लेल.	तोरा; तोरा / तोहरा; तोहरा } कें. / लेल.
	Ag.	तू ने.	तू ने.	तू / तैं } नें.	तै. थें.	थें.	तोई न.	त्वी { ले. / ली { ई.	तं / तैं } ले.	तू. तैं.	*Wanting.*	*Wanting.*	*Wanting.*	*Wanting.*	*Wanting.*
	Ab.	तुझ से.	तो { से. / तें.	तो { सौं. / तें.	तैं / थें } सूं.	थो / था / थारा } ऊं, सूं.	तोई ते.	ली { हैं. / थैं.	तं / तैं } बाट. / ले.	तो सन. तोहि / तुहि } (सन).	तो { से. / तन.	त्वां / त्वहि } तन.	तोरा / तोहरा } सें.	तोरा / तोहरा } सें.	तोरा / तोहरा } सें.
	G.	तेरा.	तेरो.	तेरी.	थारो.	था { को, रो. / ळो.	तेरो.	तेरो.	तेरो.	तोर.	तोर.	त्वार.	तोर, तोरे; तोरा.[2] तोहार, तोहरे; तोहरा[2]	तोर, तोरा.[3] तोहर, तोहार. तोहरे, तोहरा.[3]	तोर; तोर०, तोरे. तोहर, तोहर०, तोहरे.
	L.	तुझ { में. / पर.	तो { में. / पर.	तो { में. / पर, पै.	तैं / थें } माहे. / ऊपरै.	थो / थारा { माएं, / परे.	तोई मां.	ली में.	तं / तैं } मा. / माथि.	तो माहि. तोहि / तुहि } (माहि).	तोरे { म. / पर.	त्वहि / त्वारे } म.	तोरा / तोहरा } में.	तोरा / तोहरा } में.	तोरा / तोहरा } में.
PLURAL.	N.	तुम.	तुम.	तुम.	थे.	थें.	तुमू, तुमन.	तुम.	तिमि. तिम्हेरु.	तुम, तुम्ह. तुमह.	आप.	तुम्ह.	तोहनीका. तोहरन.	तोहनी. तोहरनी.	तोंह, तोंहें, तों / तोहरा, तोरा } सभ.[4]
	Ac. } D. }	तुम्हें. तुम को.	तुम्हें. तुम को.	तुम्हें. तुम / तुम्हों } कौं.	थां नै.	थां. थांया / थांवरां } नै, ने.	तुमुं. तुम / तुमुं } सणि.	तुमन. तुम / तुमन } कणी. / ऊणि.	तिमि / तिम्हेरु } लाई.	तुमहिं. तुम्ह (कहं).	तुम सब / आप } का.	तुम्ह कंहं.	तोहनी; तोहनी / तोहरन; तोहरन } के. / ला.	तोहनी / तोहरनी } के. / लेल.	तोहरा सभ } कें. / लेल.
	Ag.	तुम ने.	तुम ने.	तुम / तुम्हों } नें.	थां.	थां.	तुम / तुमुं } न.	तुमौं / तुमन } ले.	तिमि / तिम्हेरु } ले.	तुम्ह.	*Wanting.*	*Wanting.*	*Wanting.*	*Wanting.*	*Wanting.*
	Ab.	तुम से.	तुम से.	तुम / तुम्हों } सौं. / तें.	थां सूं.	थां, थांणा[1] / थांया / थांवरां } ऊं.	तुम / तुमुं } ते.	तुम / तुमन } हैं. / थैं.	तिमि / तिम्हेरु } बाट. / ले.	तुम्ह सन.	तुम सब / आप } से. / तन.	तुम्ह तन.	तोहनी / तोहरन } सें.	तोहनी / तोहरनी } सें.	तोहरा सभ सें.
	G.	तुम्हरा.	तुम्हारो.	तुम्हारी. तिहारी.	थांरो.	थां / थांया / थांवरां } को, रो. / ळो. / णो.	तुमारो.	तुमारो. तुमरो.	तिमरो. तिमि / तिम्हेरु } को.	तुम्हार. तुमर.	तुमार. आप कर.	तुम्हार.	तोहनी / तोहरन } के; का.[2]	तोहनी / तोहरनी } के, केर. / केरा.[3]	तोहरा सभ के.
	L.	तुम { में. / पर.	तुम { में. / पर.	तुम / तुम्हों } में. / पर, पै.	थां { माहे. / ऊपरे.	थां / थांया / थांवरां } माएं. / परे.	तुम / तुमुं } मां.	तुम / तुमन } में.	तिमि / तिम्हेरु { मा. / माथि.	तुम्ह { माहिं. / ऊपरि.	तुम सब / आप } में. / पर.	तुम्हारे म.	तोहनी / तोहरन } में.	तोहनी / तोहरनी } में.	तेहरा सभ में.

[1] This form my Paṇḍit only gives in this case; I should infer it would be used also in other cases. [2] Oblique form. [3] Fem. in े. [4] Instead of सभ, any of the words denoting plurality given in § 183, may be used throughout with any of these themes.

TABLE X. DIALECTIC PRONOMINAL DECLENSION.—PROXIMATE DEMONSTRATIVE PRONOUN; यह, etc., 'this.'

		H. Hindí.	Kanaují.	Braj.	Márwárí.	Mewárí.	Garhwálí.	Kumáoní.	Naipálí.	Old Baiswárí.	Avadhí.	Riwáí.	Bhojpúrí.	Mágadhí.	Maithilí.
SINGULAR.	N.	यह.	यिऊ, इऊ.	यह.	ओ, यो, *m.* आ, या, *f.*	ओ, यो, *m.* आ, या, *f.*	यो, या.	यो, यों.	यो, ई.	इह, ईह. एह, येऊ.	ई.	या.	ई, एहि,[5] ए.[5] इहां.	ई.	ई, इ, इऋं, ऐ, ऐं, एं. इहे, है, इहै, इहाय.
	Ac. D.	इसे. इस को.	इहि या } को.	याहि. या कौं.	इण, इणी अणी इय, ई } नै.	अणी, इणी } ऐ. ई } नै.	एइ. एइ सणि.	ये ए } कणी.	यस[2] ए } लाई.	इहि,एहि (कहं).	ए का.	या यहि } कंहं.	एह, एकरा इहां, इन्हका } (के).	एक एकरा } के. लेल.	एहि, एई, ए, ई } के. एकरा, हेकरा } लेल.
	Ag.	इस ने.	इहि या } ने.	या नें.	इण, इणी. अणी. ई.	अणी, इणी. ई.	एइ न.	ये ए } ले.	यस[2] ए } ले.	इहि, एहि.	*Wanting.*	*Wanting.*	*Wanting.*	*Wanting.*	*Wanting.*
PLURAL.	N.	यह, ये.	ऊ.	ये, ये.	ए, ऐ.	ऐ, ई.	ये.	ये.	इन, इन्हेरु. इन्ह.[4]	ये.	इन, ए.	ए, एन्ह.	इन्हका,[6] एकरन. इहांका.[6]	ई. इन्हकनी.	इन्ह, इन.[7] हिन्हि, हिनि.
	Ac. D.	इन्हें. इन इन्हों } को.	इन्हें. इन इन्हों } को.	इन्हें, इहें. इनि इन्हीं } कौं.	इणां, अणां यां, आं } नै.	अणां, इणां } ऐ. आं, यां } नै.	यूं. यूं सणि.	युनू इनू इनो } कणी.	इन[3] इन्हेरु } लाई.	इनहिं, इहें. इन इन्ह } (कहं).	इन का.	यन यन्ह } कंहं.	इन्ह, एकरन इहां सभका } के.	इन्ह इन्हकरा } के. लेल.	इन्ह, हिन्ह इन्हकरा, इनका हिन्हकरा, हिनका } के. लेल.
	Ag.	इन इन्हों } ने.	इन इन्हों } ने.	इनि इन इन्हीं } नें.	इणां, अणां. यां, आं.	अणां. आं, यां.	यू न.	युनू इनू इनो } ले.	इन इन्हेरु } ले.	इन. इन्ह.	*Wanting.*	*Wanting.*	*Wanting.*	*Wanting.*	*Wanting.*

REMOTE DEMONSTRATIVE PRONOUN; वह, etc., 'that,' 'he,' 'she,' 'it.'

		H. Hindí.	Kanaují.	Braj.	Márwárí.	Mewárí.	Garhwálí.	Kumáoní.	Naipálí.	Old Baiswárí.	Avadhí.	Riwáí.	Bhojpúrí.	Mágadhí.	Maithilí.
SINGULAR.	N.	वह, वुह.	वुहि, उहि.	वो, वह.	ऊ, *m.* वा, *f.*	ऊ, वू, *m.* वा, *f.*	वह.	वी.	ऊ, उ.	ओ.	ऊ, टेकनवा. फुलनवा.	वह.	ऊ, ओहि,[1] ओ.[1] उहां, उन्हां.	ऊ.	ऊ, उ, उऋं, ओ, ओ.[7] हऊ, हौ, वें, वें, वहाय.
	Ac. D.	उसे. उस को.	उहि वा } को.	वाहि, विसे. वा विस } कौं.	उण, उणी वणी, वीं } नै.	उणी, वणी } ऐ. वों } नै.	वे. वे सणि.	वी वि } कणी.	उस वे } लाई.	ओहि वोहि } (कहं).	ओ का.	वहि कंहं.	ओह, ओकरा उहां, उन्हका } (के).	ओह ओकरा } के. लेल.	ओहि, ओई, ओ, ऊ } के. ओकरा, होकरा } लेल.
	Ag.	उस ने.	उहि वा } ने.	वा विस } नें.	उण, उणी. वणी, वीं.	उणी. वणी. वीं.	वे न.	वी वि } ले.	उस वे } ले.	ओहि. वोहि.	*Wanting.*	*Wanting.*	*Wanting.*	*Wanting.*	*Wanting.*
PLURAL.	N.	वह, वो, वे.	वे.	वे, वै.	वै.	वे, वी.	से.	वूं, वे, ऊं, वी.	उन, उन्हेरु. उन्ह.[4]	ओ.	ओ, ओ सब. फुलाने, टेकाने.	उन्ह.	उन्हका,[6] ओकरन. उहांका.[6]	ऊ. उन्हकनी.	उन्ह, उन. ऊन्हि, ऊनि.
	Ac. D.	उन्हें. उन उन्हों } को.	उन्हें. उन उन्हों } को.	उन्ह, विन्हें. उनि, विन[1] उन्हौं, विन्हौं } कौं.	उणां, वणां वां, व्यां } नै.	वणां } ऐ. वां } नै.	ऊं. ऊं सणि.	उनन उनू उनो } कणी.	उन उन्हेरु } लाई.	उनहि, उहें. उन उन्ह } (कहं).	ओन ओन सब } का.	उन्ह कंहं.	उन्ह, ओकरन उहां सभका } (के).	उन्ह उन्हकरा } के. लेल.	उन्ह, ऊन्ह उन्हकरा, उनका ऊन्हकरा, ऊनका } के. लेल.
	Ag.	उन उन्हों } ने.	उन उन्हों } ने.	उनि, विन उन्हौं, विन्हौं } नें.	उणां, वणां. वां, व्यां.	वणां. वां.	ऊं न.	उनन उनू } ले.	उन उन्हेरु } ले.	उन. उन्ह.	*Wanting.*	*Wanting.*	*Wanting.*	*Wanting.*	*Wanting.*

[1] This is still used about Mathurá and Agra, but is regarded as obsolete. [2] Or यो, or like Kum. [3] Or like Kum. [4] Optional throughout. [5] Either of these forms may be used as the stem in all the obl. cases.
[6] The periphrastic plur. with सभ may be used with इन्ह, इहां, and उन्ह, उहां. The forms in the 2nd line, sing and plur., are honorific. [7] The plural honorific; non-honorific plural formed by adding सभ, etc.

TABLE XI. DIALECTIC PRONOMINAL DECLENSION. — Relative Pronoun; जो, etc., 'who,' 'which.'

		High Hindi.	Kanauji.	Braj.	Márwárí.	Mewárí.	Garhwálí.	Kumáoní.	Naipálí.	Old Baiswárí.	Avadhí.	Ríwáí.	Bhojpúrí.	Mágadhí.	Maithilí.
Singular.	N.	जो.	जौन.	जो, जौन.	ज्यो, जिको, जको. *m.* जिका, जका. *f.*	ज्यो, जो, जिको. *m.* जका. *f.*	जो.	जो, जै.	जुन, जो, ज्या.	जो, जू, जवन.	जे, जवन, जौन.	जऊनंयं.	{जे. {जौन, जवन.	जे. जऊन, जौन.	जे, जं, जै.
	Ac. D.	जिसे. जिस को.	जेहि जा } को.	जाहि. जा जाहि } कौं.	जिकण जिण, जण, जणी } नै. जों.	जणी जों } ऐ. नै.	जद. जद सणि.	जै कणी.	जठ, जो, ज्या. जस[1] जुन } लाई.	जिहि, जेहि जोहि } (कहं).	जे का.	जऊनि ज्या ज्यहि } कहं.	जेह जेकरा, जौना } (के). ला.	जेह जेकरा } (के). लेल.	जेहि, जाहि, जे जकरा, जेकरा } के. लेल.
	Ag.	जिस ने.	जेहि जा } ने.	जा जाहि } नें.	जिकण, जिणै. जिण, जण, जणी, जों.	जणी. जों.	जद न.	जै ले.	जस[1] जुन } ले.	जिहि, जेइ. जेहि.	*Wanting.*	*Wanting.*	*Wanting.*	*Wanting.*	*Wanting.*
	G.	जिस का.	जेहि जा } के.	जासु. जा जाहि } को.	जिकण जिण, जण, जणी } रो. जीं.	जणी जीं } को, रो. ठो. जंडो.	जद को.	जै को.	जस[1] जुन } को.	जिहि, जेहि. जा कर. जासु, जास.	जे कर.	जऊनि ज्या ज्यहि } केर.	जेह के. जेकर. जेकरे (*obl.*), जेकरा.	जेह के. जेकर, जेकरा (री, *f.*)	जेहि, जाहि, जे (के). जेकर, जकर, जेकरo.
Plural.	N.	जो.	जौन.	जो.	ज्यो, जिके, जके.	ज्यो, जके.	जो.	जो, जै.	जुन, जुन्हेरु. जिन्ह, जिन्हेरु.	जे.	जे.	जेन्ह.	जे, जौन, जवन. जिन्हन.	जे, जिन्हकनी.	जिन, जिन्ह. जिन्हि, जिन्ही.
	Ac. D.	जिन्हें. जिन जिन्हों } को.	जिन जिन्हों } को.	जिन्हें. जिनि जिन्हों } कौं.	जियां, जणां जां, ज्यां, जिकां } नै.	जणां जां ज्यां } ऐ. नै.	ज्यूं. ज्यूं सणि.	जनन जनू } कणी.	जुन, जुन्हेरु जिन्ह,[2] जिन्हेरु } लाई.	जे, जिनहिं. जिनहहिं. जिन, जिन्ह (कहं).	जेन जेन्ह } का.	जेन्ह जन ज्यन्ह } कहं.	जेकरन जिन्ह, जिन्हका } (के). ला.	जिन्ह जिन्हकरा } (के). लेल.	जिन्ह, जिन्हकरा जनिका } के. लेल.
	Ag.	जिन जिन्हों } ने.	जिन ने.	जिनि जिन्हों } नें.	जियां, जणां. जां, ज्यां.	जणां. जां. ज्यां.	ज्यूं न.	जनन जनू } ले.	जुन, जुन्हेरु जिन्ह,[2] जिन्हेरु } ले.	जिन, जिन्ह. जे.	*Wanting.*	*Wanting.*	*Wanting.*	*Wanting.*	*Wanting.*
Correlative Pronoun; सो, etc., 'that,' 'the same.'															
Singular.	N.	सो.	सो.	सो.	सो, तिको. *m.* तिका. *f.*	जो, सो, तिको. *m.* तिका. *f.*	सो.	सो.	तुन, त्यो.	सो, सु, से, तवन.	से, तवन, तौन.	तऊनंयं.	{ते, से. {तवन, तौन.	से. तऊन, तौन.	से, ते, तैं.
	Ac. D.	तिसे. तिस को.	तिहि ता } को.	ताहि. ता ताहि } कौं.	तिण तिणो } नै.	तणी तीं } ऐ. नै.	तद. तद सणि.	तै कणी.	तुन, तठ, तो, ताहि.[3] तस त्यो } लाई.	तिहि, तेहि ताहि, ताऊ } (कहं).	ते का.	तऊनि त्या त्यहि } कहं.	तेह तेकरा, तौना } (के). ला.	तेह तेकरा } (के). लेल.	तेहि, ताहि, ते तकरा, तेकरा } के. लेल.
	Ag.	तिस ने.	तिहि ता } ने.	ता नें.	तिण. तिणी.	तणी.	तद न.	तै ले.	ति तस त्यो } ले.	तिहि. तेहि.	*Wanting.*	*Wanting.*	*Wanting.*	*Wanting.*	*Wanting.*
	G.	तिस का.	तिहि ता } को.	तासु. ता ताहि } को.	तिण तिणी } रो.	तणी तीं } को, रो. ठो.	तद को.	तै को.	ति तस त्यो } को.	तिहि, तेहि. ता कर. तासु, तास.	ते कर.	तऊनि त्या त्यहि } केर.	तेह के. तेकर. तेकरे (*obl.*), तेकरा.	तेह के. तेकर, तेकरा (री, *f.*)	तेहि, ताहि, ते (के). तेकर, तकर, तेकरo.
Plural.	N.	सो.	सो.	सो, ते.	सो, तिके.	ज्यो, सो.	ते.	तौं.	तुन, तुनहेरु. ती, ति.	ते.	ते.	तेन्ह.	से, ते, तौन, तवन. तिन्हन.	से, तिन्हकनी.	तिन, तिन्ह. तिन्हि, तिन्ही.
	Ac. D.	तिन्हें. तिन तिन्हों } को.	तिन तिन्हों } को.	तिन्हें. तिनि तिन्हों } कौं.	तियां ने.	तणां तां त्यां } ऐ. नै.	त्यूं. त्यूं सणि.	तनन तनू } कणी.	तिन्ह, तिन्हेरु. तिन्ह,[2] तिन्हेरु (लाई).	से, तिनहिं. तिनहहिं. तिन, तिन्ह (कहं).	तेन तेन्ह } का.	तेन्ह तन त्यन्ह } कहं.	तेकरन तिन्ह, तिन्हका } (के). ला.	तिन्ह तिन्हकरा } (के). लेल.	तिन्ह, तिन्हकरा तनिका } के. लेल.
	Ag.	तिन तिन्हों } ने.	तिन तिन्हों } को.	तिनि तिन्हों } नें.	तियां.	तणां. तां. त्यां.	त्यूं न.	तनन तनू } ले.	तिन्ह[2] तिन्हेरु } ले.	तिन, तिन्ह. ते.	*Wanting.*	*Wanting.*	*Wanting.*	*Wanting.*	*Wanting.*

[1] Or as Gaṛh. [2] Or as Kum. [3] Also with postpositions.

TABLE XII. DIALECTIC PRONOMINAL DECLENSION.—1st Interrogative Pronoun; कौन, etc., 'who,' 'what.'

		High Hindī.	*Kanaujī.*	*Braj.*	*Mārwāṛī.*	*Mewāṛī.*	*Gaṛhwālī.*	*Kumāonī.*	*Naipālī.*	*Old Baiswāṛī.*	*Avadhī.*	*Rīwāī.*	*Bhojpūrī.*	*Māgadhī.*	*Maithilī.*
Singular.	N.	कौन.	को.	को, कौ.	कुण, कण. कोन.	कुण, कूण. कण.	कौ.	को, कौ.	को, कुन.	को. कवन, कवनि.	के.	कउन.	के. कवन, कौन.	के, को. कऊन, कौन.	के, कौन.
	Ac. D.	किसे. किस को.	किहि का } को.	काहि. का कौं.	कुण, कुणी कण, कणी } ने. कौं	कुणी, कणी कौं. } ऐ.	कइ सणि.	कै कणि.	कुन. कस लाई.	किहि, केहि, केइ. कवन, कवनि. कवने, कौने.	के का.	केहि क्या क्वहि } कंहं.	केह, केहि, के } (कें). केकरा, कोना } ला.	केह } (के). केकरा } लेल.	केहि, के } (के). केकरा, ककरा } ले.
	Ag.	किस ने.	किहि का } ने.	का नें.	कुण, कुणी, कोन कण, कणी. कौं.	कुणी, कणी. कौं.	कइ न.	कै ले.	कुन कस } ले.	किहि, केहि. कवन, कोइ.	*Wanting.*	*Wanting.*	*Wanting.*	*Wanting.*	*Wanting.*
Plural.	N.	कौन.	को.	को, कौ.	कुण, कण.	कुण, कूण. कण.	कौ.	को.	को, कुन.	कवन.	के.	कउन.	के. कवन, कौन.	के, किन्हकनी.	किन, किन्ह. किन्हि, किन्ही.
	Ac. D.	किन्हें. किन किन्हों } को.	किन को.	किन्हैं. किनि किन्हौं } कौं.	कुणां कणां } ने.	कुणां कणां } ऐ.	कुं सणि.	कनन कनू } कणि.	कुन्ह कुन्हेरु } लाई.	किनहिं, किनहहिं. किन, किन्ह (कहं).	केन { क०. का.	केन्ह क्वन क्वन्ह } कंहं.	केकरन } (के). किन्ह } ला.	किन्ह } (के). किन्हकरा } (लेल).	किन्ह, किन्हकरा } (के). कनिका } ले.
	Ag.	किन किन्हों } ने.	किन ने.	किनि किन्हौं } ने.	कुणां. कणां.	कणां.	कुं न.	कनन कनू } ले.	कुन्ह कुन्हेरु } ले.	किन. किन्ह.	*Wanting.*	*Wanting.*	*Wanting.*	*Wanting.*	*Wanting.*
1st Indefinite Pronoun; कोई, etc., 'any,' 'any one,' etc.															
Singular.	N.	कोई.	कोऊ, कौनी.	कोऊ, कोइ. कोय.	कोइ.	कोइ. कोह, कणो.	कोई.	को, कै.	कोहि.	केऊ, कौनौ, कवनिउ. काऊ, केऊ, केउ, कैयौ.	केह, केऊ. कौनौ, कवनी.	कोऊ, कौन्हो.	केह, केऊ, केऊ. कौनो.	केह, केऊ, कोई. कउनों, कौनों.	केऊ, कोइ, कोय. केश्रो, कउनो, कौनो.
	Ac. D.	किसी को.	कौनौ किसू } को.	काहू कौं.	कुणी ने.	कणी कौं } ऐ.	कई सणि.	कै कणि.	कोहि कसै } लाई.	कौने, कवनिउ. काऊहिं. केहि, काऊ (कहं).	केउ केह } क०.	कोऊ कौन्हो } कंहं.	*As Nom. or* केकरो } (के) कथियो, केथियो } ला.	केकरो } (के). कौनों } (लेल).	*As Nom. or* केकरो, केकरौ, ककरऊ, केकरहौ } (के) किथियो } (ले)
	Ag.	किसी ने.	कौनौ किसू } ने.	काहू नें.	कुणी.	कणीं. कौं.	कई न.	कै ले.	कोहि कसै } ले.	काहू.	*Wanting.*	*Wanting.*	*Wanting.*	*Wanting.*	*Wanting.*
2nd Interrogative and 2nd Indefinite Pronouns; क्या, etc., 'what?' कुछ, 'any,' 'some.'															
Plural.	N.	क्या.	कहा.	कहा, का.	कंई, कांई.	कंई, कांई.	क्या.	क्या.	क्या, कि.	कहा, काह, का. कि, किं.	का, काय.	काह.	का.	का, की. कौंची.	का, की. कथी, केथी.
	Ac. D.	काहे को.	काहे को	काहे कौं.	कुणी ने.	खा ऐ. हाई, साई.	...	क्या.	क्या.	काहा.	कयि कइ } का.	कई कथी } कंहं.	*As Nom. or* काहे, का } के. केथी } ला.	काहे } के. कौंची } लेल.	*As Nom. or* काहे, कहि, किथे } के. किथी, केथी, कथी } ले.
	Indecl.	कुछ.	कछु.	कछु.	कंई, कांई. कर.	कांई, कंई. कांईक.	कुछ.	के.	केहि.	कछु, कछुक.	कुछ.	कुछ.	कछु, कुछो, किछु. कुछुवो, कुछुओ.	कुछ, कुछो. कुछ्ओ.	कुछ, कुछ. कयुछ, किछु, किछिओ.

hon. उहन; in N. Muzaffarpúr, एकरहिन, ओकरहिन, obl. plur. only. In the W., especially, the forms beginning with a vowel are often written and pronounced with an initial ह; thus, हेकरा, होकरा, हम्ह, and हऊ, for ऊ, etc.

(4) Of the Relative, Correlative, and Interrogative:—in the W., obl. sing. (of things only), जाहे, ताहे, काहे, also, जौने, तौने, कौने, elsewhere, जेहि, तेहि, केहि, or जे, ते, के; nom. and obl. plur., जिन्हनी,* तिन्हनी,* किन्हनी;* जिन्हन, तिन्हन, किन्हन; जेकनी, तेकनी, केकनी; जिन्हकारा, तिन्हकारा, किन्हकारा; obl. plur., in the west, जौनन, तौनन, कौनन; जौनने, तौनने, कौनने; in N. Muzaffarpúr, जेकरहिन, तेकरहिन, केकरहिन.

(5) Of the neut. Interrogative:—in the W., nom. sing., कित्यु, कियुआ; in N. Muzaffarpúr, obl. sing., काथी; also very common, an inflected instr. sing., केथिएं, in sense of 'why.'

(6) Of the neut. Indefinite:—in the W., किछ, किछऊ; in N. Muzaffarpúr, किछिओ; in Sáran, किछु.

322. In Mágadhí we have additional forms as follows. Additional Mágadhí Forms.

(1) Of the 1st Pers. pronoun:—nom. and obl. plur., हमनिन, हमरन्ही, हमरन्ह.

(2) Of the 2nd Pers. pronoun:—nom. and obl. plur., तोहनिआ, तोहरन्ही, तोहरन्ह, or तोहरा सब, etc.

(3) Of the two Demonstratives:—nom. and obl. plur., इखनिन, अखनी, एखनी; उखनिन, ओखनी; obl. plur. only, इन्हका, उन्हका.

(4) Of the Relative, Correlative, and Interrogative:—nom. and obl. plur., जिन्ह, जिन्हन; तिन्ह, तिन्हन; किन्ह, किन्हन; in Gayá, for gen. sing., तेकर, तेकरा, सेकर and सेकरा.

(5). Of the personal Indefinite pronoun:—obl. sing., कौनें, कोई, केह.

323. The following additional Maithilí forms may be noted. Additional Maithilí Forms.

(1) Of the Personal pronouns:—nom. sing., हमें, हमीं, तोंहे; obl. sing., मोहि, तोहि, (poetic).

(2) Of the Demonstrative pronouns:—obl. sing., इन्हकेरा, उन्हकेरा.

* Also in Mágadhí.

(3) Of the Relative, Correlative, and Interrogative pronouns:—obl. sing., जिन्हकेरा, तिन्हकेरा, किन्हकेरा.

(4) In the Maithilí, the 1st Indef. pronoun, केउ, has an obl. plur. base, किनकरो; the 2nd Indefinite, कुछ, adds the postpositions either to the nom. form., or to an inflected base, काहू, कथियो; the plural is wanting. The 1st Indefinite makes the gen. sing., केकरो, केकरहो, केकरो, कथियो; the gen. plur., in S. Maithilí, किनकरो. In Central and S. Muzaffarpúr, कनिक and तनिक are also used for कुछ.

Miscellaneous Dialectic Forms.

324. To the forms above given may be added the following, some of which I am unable to assign to any particular time or place.

(1) ऊं, = मैं, 'I,' is evidently a shortened form of the Márwárí हूं.* An abbreviated form, मुह, for the obl. sing., मोहि, is sometimes used by *Chand*. *Chand* makes the obl. plur. of the 1st and 2nd Personal pronouns, हमहि and तुमहि. But हम and तुम with the postpositions, are also employed.

(2) तैन and तें are sometimes substituted for तै or तू, 'thou.' In western Hindí, I have met with a gen. sing. of this pronoun, तैंड़ा, for तेरा; as, e.g., पकड़े मुगलाणी तैंड़ा हाथ, 'let the wife of the Mogul take thy hand.' A Prakritic gen. sing., तुम्म, (for Sk. तव,) is now and then used in archaic Hindí.

(3) In the nom. sing. of the Proximate Demonstrative, यह, the following variant forms occur, viz.:—यौह, येह, जिह, ईह, ईऊ, ईहि, ईहै, एई. Of these, the last three appear, in some cases at least, to be merely emphatic forms. In the obl.

* हूं is said by Prof. Eastwick, (Vocabulary to *Prem Ságar*, sub. voc.), to be used in the obl. sing. with the postposition कै, in the following Arrdh Chaupái: क्यौं हूं कै पति रही हमारी. But हूं, in this place, is, in fact, the Braj emphatic particle, = ही; and कै is a Braj form of the Conjunctive participle, कर (from the verb करना), which is in High Hindi added directly to क्यौं, making क्यौंकर. We therefore render,—'*how* (then) remained my honor?' *Krishṇá* to *Rukminí*, P.S.: Ch. LXI.

plur., we find इनि and इन्ह. In Braj, जा is sometimes spoken and written for या.

(4) In the declension of the Remote Demonstrative, वह, ओह occurs in the nom. sing., and, in the obl. sing., वौ is sometimes found for वा, and वाऊ, for वाहि. For the obl. sing., उस, rustic Muhammedans sometimes substitute वुस. It occurs also in the following from the Márwárí Play of *Gopí Chand*; धरो वुसी कै ध्यान, 'fix (your) thoughts on him.' In the obl. plur., उने, वुने and उनवों are found for the dat., उन्हें; and उने, in the case of the agent, for उन ने.

(5) Variant forms of the Correlative pronoun are, in the nom. sing., सोव, सोच and सौंच, for सो. The latter two are emphatic forms. In the obl. sing., ति and तिऊ occur, for तिहि; I have also met with a gen. sing., तातनौ, = तिस का, which evidently belongs to the S.W. ता alone is used as gen. sing. in the following from the *Prem Ságar*: कहा नाम ता आहि, 'what is his name?'. जाइ occurs in Braj for जाहि, and जिननि, for the obl. plur., जिन्हों, of the Relative. तिने, for तिन्हें, and तान, for the obl. plur., तिन, of the Correlative, also occur in literary Hindí.

(6) For the nom. sing. of the Interrogative, कौन, we find in the 'Chrestomathie' of Prof. De Tassy, कौणु, कौने and कौनें. An obl. sing. and plur., काय, for किस, is found in western Hindí. कोइय and काउ occur, for the Indefinite, कोई, and काछुव, कहि and काऊ, for कुछ. कहि and काऊ belong to the west. For the Braj Interrogative, कहा, = क्या, we sometimes have काहो, and in the obl. sing., काहै, for काहे.

(7) As the nom. sing. of the Reflexive pronoun, आप, I have met with आपे. With this same pronoun, is evidently to be connected a Máṛ. nom. plur. form, आपां. In the only place, however, where I have met with it, हम would have been used in High Hindí. In the obl. forms of this pronoun, उ is often substituted for अ after प, as, e.g., in आपुस, obl. plur., for आपस.

PRONOMINAL ADJECTIVES.

325. Besides the above pronouns, many pronominal adjectives occur. They may nearly all be used either as adjectives or as pronouns. Two series, the one expressive of quantity, the other of kind, are formed from the five pronominal elements noted in § 255. When used substantively, they all follow, in High Hindí, the first variety of masculine declension; when used adjectively, they follow the laws for the inflection of *Tadbhava* adjectives in आ, and are thus inflected to ए, masc., and ई, fem. The following tables exhibit, first the High Hindí forms, and then the dialectic forms of each series:—

TABLE XIII.: PRONOMINAL ADJECTIVES.

Pron. Base.	ADJECTIVES OF QUANTITY.		ADJECTIVES OF KIND.
अ इ य	इतना *itná*, इत्ता *ittá*,	'this much.'	ऐसा *aisá*, 'such,' 'like this.'
उ व	उतना *utná*, उत्ता *uttá*,	'that much.'	वैसा *waisá*, 'such,' 'like that.'
जि	जितना *jitná*, जित्ता *jittá*,	'as much.'	जैसा *jaisá*, 'like which,' 'as.'
ति	तितना *titná*, तित्ता *tittá*,	'so much.'	तैसा *taisá*, 'like that,' 'so.'
कि क	कितना *kitná*, कित्ता *kittá*,	'how much?'.	कैसा *kaisá*, 'like what?', 'how?'.

TABLE XIV. DIALECTIC FORMS OF THE PRONOMINAL ADJECTIVES.

	H. Hindí.	Kanaují.	Braj.	Márwárí.	Mewárí.	Garhwálí.	Naipálí.	O. Bais.	Avadhí.	Riwáí.	Bhojpúrí.	Mágadhí.	Maithilí.	
ADJECTIVES OF QUANTITY.	इतना. इत्ता.	इतनो.	इतनौ.[1] इतौ.	इतरो.	यतरो. यतरड़ो.	एतका.	यति. येत्तिकि.[2]	इता. ईता. एता.	एतना, एतत. एतिक.	यतना, यत्ताम. इतिक.	यतेक, यतहत. यतिना.	एत्तेक. एतना.	एतेक, एतबाय,[3] एतबे,[4] एते.[3] एतना.	
	उतना. उत्ता.	उतनो.	उतनौ.	उतरो.	उतरो, वतरो. उतरड़ो.	ओतका.	उति. उत्तिकि.[2]	अता. ओता.	ओतना, ओतत. ओतिक.	वतना, वत्ताम. वातिक.	ओतेक, ओतहत. ओतिना.	ओत्तेक. ओतना.	ओतबाय,[3] ओतबे,[4] ओते.[3] ओतना.	
	जितना. जित्ता.	जितनो.	जितनौ.	जतरो.	जतरो. जतरड़ो.	जतका.	जति. जेत्तिकि.[2]	जेता.	जेतना, जेतत. जेतिक.	ज्यतना, ज्यत्ताम. ज्यातिक.	जतेक, जतहत. जतिना.	जेत्तेक. जेतना.	जेतबाय,[3] जेतबे,[4] जेते.[3] जेतना.	
	तितना. तित्ता.	तितनो.	तितनौ.	ततरो.	ततरो. ततरड़ो.	ततका.	तति, तेति. (तेत्तिकि).[2]	तेता.	तेतना, तेतत. तेतिक.	त्यतना, त्यत्ताम. त्यातिक.	ततेक, ततहत. ततिना.	तेत्तेक. तेतना.	तेतबाय,[5] तेतबे,[4] तेते.[3] तेतना.	
	कितना. कित्ता.	कितनो.	कितनौ.	कतरो.	कतरो. कतरड़ो.	कतका.	कति. (केत्तिकि).[2]	केता.	केतना, केतत. केतिक.	क्यतना, क्यत्ताम. क्यातिक.	कतेक, कतहत. कतिना.	केत्तेक. केतना.	केतबाय,[3] केतबे,[4] केते.[3] केतना.	
ADJECTIVES OF KIND.	ऐसा.	ऐसो.	ऐसौ.	इस्यो. ऐरो.	यस्यो. ऐड़ो.	एनो, एनु. यनू.	यस्तो.	अस.	अस, यस.	ऐसन, ऐस.	अइसन.	अइसन.	ऐसन, एहिनठ,[3] एहनु,[4] एहन.[5] ऐन्हठ,[3] एन्ह,[4] एना, इना,[5] अहिन.[4]	ईरंग.
	वैसा.	वैसो.	वैसौ.	उस्यो. वैरो.	उस्यो, वस्यो. वैड़ो.	वनो. वनू.	उस्तो.	. . .	ओस.	वैसन, वैस.	वइसन.	ओइसन.	वैसन, ओहिनठ,[3] ओहनु,[4] ओहिन.[4] औसन, औन्हठ,[3] ओहन,[5] ओना.[5]	उरंग.
	जैसा.	जैसो.	जैसौ.	जिस्यो, जिसो. जैरो.	जस्यो. जैड़ो.	जनो. जनू.	जस्तो.	जस.	जस.	जैसन, जैस.	जइसन.	जइसन.	जैसन, जौहिनठ,[3] जेहनु,[4] जहिन.[4] जेहन,[5] जैन्हठ,[3] जिना,[5] जेना.	जेरंग.
	तैसा.	तैसो.	तैसौ.	तिस्यो. तैरो.	तस्यो. तैड़ो.	तनो. तनू.	तस्तो.	तस.	तस.	तैसन, तैस.	तइसन.	तइसन.	तैसन, तौहिनठ,[3] तेहनु,[4] तहिन.[4] तेहन,[5] तैन्हठ,[3] तिना,[5] तेना.	तेरंग.
	कैसा.	कैसो.	कैसौ.	किस्यो. कैरो.	कस्यो. कैड़ो.	कनो. कनू.	कस्तो.	कस.	कस.	कैसन, कैस.	कइसन.	कइसन.	कैसन, कौहिनठ,[3] केहनु,[4] कहिन.[4] केहन,[5] कैन्हठ,[3] किना,[5] केना.	कीरंग.

[1] Anusvár optionally added. [2] I have only met with these in this obl. form; commonly with the postposition मा. [3] In S.E. [4] In extreme E. [5] S. of Ganges.

To face page 200.]

326. Besides the dialectic forms given in Table XIV., the following modifications of some of these pronominals also occur, viz.:—for उतना; वितना, वेतना, वुतना; for कित्ता; कित, किता, केत्ता, किते; and for जित्ता, जिता. The following forms also are occasionally used in literature, viz.:—जै, तै, कै. They are respectively equivalent to जितना, तितना, कितना. **Dialectic Pronominals.**

a. The Sanskrit forms, ईदृश, एतादृश, = ऐसा, यादृश = जैसा, तादृश, = तैसा, and कीदृश, = कैसा, are occasionally used in poetry. For ईदृश and कीदृश we also find एदृश and कादृश.

327. Besides the above, the following words also are used as pronominal adjectives. Those which terminate in आ follow the declension of *Tadbhava* nouns or adjectives inflected to ए. The others, when used substantively, are declined like the second variety of masc. nouns; when used adjectively, they are indeclinable. **Additional Pronom. Adjectives.**

एक	*ek,*	'one.'	हर	*har,*	'every.'
दूसरा	*dúsrá,*	'another,' 'the other.'	और	*aur,*	'other,' 'more.'
दोनों	*donon,*	'both.'	बहुत	*bahut,*	'much,' 'many.'
सब	*sab,*	'all,' 'the whole.'	कई	*kaï,*	'several,' 'how many?'.
सारा	*sárá,*		कै	*kai,*	
सकल	*sakal,*		निज	*nij,*	'self,' 'own.'
समस्त	*samast,*		पराया	*paráyá,*	'another (person).'
समूचा	*samúchá,*				

328. एक *ek*, strictly speaking, is a cardinal numeral, and दूसरा *dúsrá*, an ordinal. एक, 'one,' when used pronominally, is usually followed by दूसरा, 'the other,' in the succeeding clause; as, एक हंसता दूसरा रोता था *ek hanstá, dúsrá rotá thá*, 'one was laughing, the other was crying.'

a. Sometimes एक itself follows in the second clause,

when the first एक should be rendered 'one,' the second, 'another.' Thus, एक यह एक वह कहता था *ek yah, ek wah kahtá thá*, 'one was saying this, another, that.'

b. When दूसरा follows एक in the same clause, the two have a reciprocal force; as, वे एक दूसरे को मारते हैं *we ek dúsre ko márte hain̲*, 'they are beating one another.' एक is indeclinable in the plural.

329. दोनों *donon̲*, 'both,' is declinable in the plur. only: thus, Nom. दोनों *donon̲*, Acc. दोनों को *donon̲ ko*, etc.

330. सब *sab*, 'all,' 'every,' often aspirates the final ब in the oblique plural; thus, Acc. सभों को *sabhon̲ ko*, Gen. सभों का *sabhon̲ ká*, etc. सबों, also, rarely occurs.

a. When used in the singular, as, सब को *sab ko*, 'to all,' it denotes 'all' considered as a unity, 'the whole;' in the plural, सभों को, *sabhon̲ ko*, 'to all,' it represents 'all' as a plurality, 'every,' 'every one.'

Rem. These forms in ओं are not now regarded as quite elegant, and सब is preferably uninflected throughout. As it contains in itself the idea of plurality, the plural termination is regarded as superfluous.

331. The words सकल *sakal* (Sk. स + कल), समस्त *samast*, and समूचा also signify 'all,' 'the whole.' They are rarely, if ever, used as nouns.

332. The Persian adjective हर *har*, 'every,' though not very common in classic Hindí, is found even in the *Prem Ságar*, and is freely used in the colloquial. It may therefore be fairly regarded as belonging to the language. It is never used substantively. Compounded with एक *ek*, it means 'every one' or 'every single,' and is used either as a substantive or adjective, thus: हर एक आया *har ek áyá*, 'every one came;' हर एक घर *har ek ghar*, 'every single house.'

333. ऋौर *aur*, when used substantively, and followed by no other pronominal in the next clause, always signifies 'more;' as, मुझे ऋौर दो *mujhe aur do*, 'give me more.' But when used adjectively, it may mean either 'more' or 'another,' as the context may determine. Thus, मुझे ऋौर ऋनाज दो *mujhe aur anáj do*, 'give me more grain;' but, यह ऋौर बात है *yah aur bát hai*, 'this is another matter.'

a. When ऋौर is repeated in two successive clauses, the first is to be rendered 'one,' and the second, 'another.' Thus, यह बात ऋौर है वह ऋौर है *yah bát aur hai, wah aur hai*, 'this is one thing, that is another.'

334. Besides बहुत, 'much,' we meet the intensive forms, बहुतेरा *bahuterá*, and बहुत सा *bahut sá*, 'very much,' 'very many.'

a. Colloquially, सारा is also added to बहुत, 'many,' with an intensive force; thus, बहुतसारा is equivalent to the colloquial English idiom, 'a great deal.' This use of सारा is only colloquial. In Panjábí it is employed much more extensively.

335. कई *kaí* or कै *kai* as an adjective means 'several;' when used as a pronoun, it must be rendered 'how many?'. It cannot take the postpositions. Thus, कई पुरुष ऋाए *kaí purus͟h áe*, 'several men came;' कै ऋाए *kai áe*, 'how many came?'. Where in English 'several' has a pronominal force, it must be rendered in Hindí by कई एक *kaí ek* or कितने एक *kitne ek*; as, कई एक हैं *kaí ek hain̠*, 'there are several.' But, कई हैं *kaí hain̠*, would be interrogative,—'how many are there?'. कई एक *kaí ek*, and कितने एक *kitne ek*, however, may also be used adjectively in the same sense; as, कितने एक पेड़ हैं *kitne ek peṛ hain̠*, 'there are several trees.'

a. The pronominal adjective कितने *kitne* is also used in the sense of 'some,' 'several,' both substantively and adjectively. Thus, वहां कितने भाट भी आए *wahán̲ kitne bháṭ bhí áe*, 'several bards also came there;' कितनों का मत है *kitnon̲ ká mat hai*, 'it is the opinion of some.'

336. निज *nij*, 'own,' may be used as a pronoun, the person and thing referred to being determined by the context; as, निज पर आना *nij par áná*, 'to come to one's own (house);' निज बुद्धि भरोस मोहि नाही *nij buddhi bharosa mohi náhí*, 'I have no confidence in my own wisdom.' Or it may be added to possessive genitives of both nouns and pronouns, in the sense of the English 'own;' as, वह राजा का निज पुत्र है *wah rájá ká nij putra hai*, 'he is the king's own son;' यह मेरी निज पुस्तक है *yah merí nij pustak hai*, 'this is my own book;' वह अपने निज घर गया *wah apne nij ghar gayá*, 'he went to his own house.' Also we have such idioms with the genitive of निज as, निज का माल *nij ká mál*, 'private property;' निज का नौकर *nij ká naukar*, 'a personal servant,' etc.

337. पराया *paráyá*, 'another's,' is properly a possessive adjective. It may be used either with or without a noun; thus, यह पराये का है *yah paráye ká hai*, 'this is another's;' पराई स्त्री *parái strí*, 'another's wife.'

Dialectic Pronom. Adjectives.

338. The following dialectic variations of the above pronominals occur, viz.:—for एक, इक and यक; for दूसरा, Br. दूसरौ, K. दूसरो, N. अर्कों; O.B. दूसर, दूज, दूजा; for दोनों, Br. दोनौं, M. दोन्युं, N. दुवै, O.B. दुहं, दूनौं, दुओं; for सारा, Br. सारौ, K. सारो; for सब, Br. सबै, सबरे, O.B. सबरि; for और, N. अर्कों, O.B. अवर; for बहुत, Br. बहौत, O.B. बहुतेक, बहुत, Garh., भिंडो, N. धेर, emph. धेरै, M. घोत, घोदी, घोला, घोहोत, and मोकलो. For कई, Már. has केई.

For सकल, Br. gives सिगरौ, M., झगरो, सगळो, O.B., सगरे (nom. plur.). For कितने एक, the Márwárí has कितोक.

339. The following pronominal adjectives are Sanskrit. The most of them, as compared with the foregoing, are of rare occurrence in the colloquial, but are more frequent in literature, especially in poetry. Sanskrit Pronominal Adjectives.

अन्य	*anya,*	'other.'	बहु	*bahu,*	'much.'
अपर	*apar,*	'another.'	भूरि	*bhúri,*	
अमुक	*amuk,*	'a certain one.'	युग	*yug,*	
उभय	*ubhaya,*	'both.'	युगल	*yugal,*	'both.'
किमपि	*kimapi,*	'any.'	युग्म	*yugma,*	
पर	*par,*	'another,' 'other.'	सर्व	*sarv,*	'all.'
प्रत्येक	*pratyek,*	'each.'			

340. अन्य, as also the more common corrupted form, is 'another,' in the sense of 'a different one,' like the Greek, ἕτερος; but अपर is 'another,' numerically, like the Greek ἄλλος. Thus, अन्य देश गया, 'he went to another country;' नहिं आन उपाऊ, 'there is no other expedient;' but, अपर हेतु सुनु, 'hear another reason.' For अपर, पर is more commonly used; it is often compounded with the noun it qualifies. Examples are: पर दोष, 'another's fault;' परदेश, 'a foreign country;' परलोक, 'the other world.'

341. The related words, युग, युगल, युग्म 'both,' 'the two,' strictly speaking, are all nouns, meaning 'a pair;' but they are practically pronominal adjectives, as will appear from the following examples: युग भूपति, 'the two kings;' युगल नयन जलधार बही, 'from both eyes a stream of water flowed;' स्वपाणि युग्म जोरिके, 'joining (my) two hands.' Examples of the use of the other Sanskrit pronominals are the following: उभय अपार उदधि, 'both a boundless ocean;' किमपि प्रयोजन नाहीं, 'there is not any need;' अमुक कहता है, 'a certain person says;' प्रत्येक दिन, 'every day.'

342. प्रति, (indeclinable), is occasionally used as a pronominal adjective; thus, प्रति अवतार कथा प्रभु केरी, 'the story of each incarnation of the Lord.' बहु and भूरि, 'much,' are both equivalent to बहुत, and, like most of these Sanskrit pronominals, are chiefly used in poetry.

COMPOUND PRONOUNS.

Compounds with Relative Pronoun.

343. The relative pronoun may be compounded with the correlative or the indefinite pronouns. Each member is then inflected, but the postposition is added to the last only.

Thus, with सो, we have जिस तिस का *jis tis ká*, 'whosesoever;' with कोई, जो कोई *jo koí*, 'whoever;' जिस किसी को *jis kisí ko*, 'whomever;' with कुछ, जो कुछ *jo kuchh*, 'whatever.'

a. For जो कोई, Naipálí has जुनसुकै, 'whosoever.'

b. In the *Rámáyan* a similar Sanskrit compound occurs, in the phrase जेन केन विधि, 'in whatever way,' where जेन केन, (for येन केन,) is in the instr. sing.

Compounds with *aur*.

344. Other compounds are formed with और *aur*, 'other;' as, और कुछ *aur kuchh*, 'something else;' और कोई *aur koí*, 'some one else;' और कौन *aur kaun*, 'who else?'. और क्या *aur kyá*, 'what else?,' is colloquially used as a reply of strong affirmation.*

a. Sometimes और occupies the second place, but the compound has then a different meaning; as, कोई और *koí aur*, 'some other;' कुछ और *kuchh aur*, 'some more.'

b. The pronominal, अन्य, 'other,' is compounded with itself in the form अन्योन्य (Sk. अन्योन्य), 'each other,' 'mutual;' but this is rare in Hindí. The two are occasionally written separately, thus: अन्यो अन्य प्रीति तें, 'with mutual love.'

---

* In Gaṛhwál, *aur* alone is used, with a peculiar intonation, in the same sense of a strong affirmative.

Compounds with Interrogative.

345. The particle सा *sá*, (infl. से *se*, सी *sí*,) may be added to the nom. form of कौन, thus: कौन सा *kaun sá*, lit., 'what like?;' वह कौन सा पेड़ है *wah kaun sá per̤ hai*, 'what tree is that?,' i.e., 'what kind of a tree?'.

a. The same affix is added, colloquially, in the east at least, to the relative, जौन, and correlative, तौन, making जौन सा, तौन सा; and in the Doáb to the demonstratives, यह and वह, making यह सा, वह सा. But I have never met these forms in literature.

b. In old eastern poetry, however, the equivalent affix सम is added to the inflected base of the demonstratives, thus: इन सम, इन्ह सम, 'like this;' उन सम, उन्ह सम, 'like that,' or 'like him.'

c. For कौन सा, Mewáṛí has खोयो, fem. खी, as in the following: खोयी मनष थां ऐ कोयो, = कौनसे मनुष्य ने तुम को कहा, 'what man told you?'.

Compounds with Indefinite Pronom.

346. The indefinite pronouns are also compounded with सब *sab*; as, सब कोई *sab koí*, 'every one,' सब कुछ *sab kuchh*, 'everything.' Before कोई, हर *har* may be used instead of सब, in the same sense.

347. A peculiar Indefinite is formed by repeating the indefinite pronoun with the negative particle, न *na*, interposed; as, कोई न कोई *koí na koí*, 'some one or other;' कुछ न कुछ *kuchh na kuchh*, 'a little,' 'somewhat,' more rarely, 'some thing or other.' In the former case, both members are inflected in the oblique cases, but the postposition is added only to the second; as, किसी न किसी का खेत *kisí na kisí ká khet*, 'the field of some one or other.'

348. कुछ is idiomatically added to various pronouns and pronominals to give them an indefinite sense; it is then often scarcely capable of translation. Thus, हम क्या कुछ होंगे, 'what we shall be;' बहुत कुछ, 'a great deal,' 'ever so much.' Similar are, यह कुछ, कितना कुछ, etc. So also we find कुछ बहुत; as, कुछ बहुत स्मरण न रहेगा, 'no *great* remembrance will remain.'

Urdú Pronominals.

349. The following pronominals belong rather to Urdú than to Hindí, but as they will be found in some modern Hindí books, they are enumerated here.

बाज	بعض,	'some.'	फुलाना	فلانا,	'a certain one.'
बाजे	بعضے,		कुल	كلّ,	'the whole.'
गैर	غیر,	'other,' 'different.'	चंद	چند,	'many,' several.'

350. Of these, all are Arabic, except चंद, which is Persian. गैर is sometimes used as a negative prefix, especially in the compound, गैर हाजिर (غیر حاضر), 'absent,' 'not present.' फुलाना is always pronounced *fuláná.* Although it belongs rather to Urdú than to Hindí, still it is often heard from Hindí-speaking people, especially in some parts of Oude, where, in a dialectic form, फुलनवा, it is often used, instead of the remote demonstrative, for a third personal pronoun. Besides फुलनवा, the people of Avadh also use ढेकनवा, plur., ढेकाने, in the same way.

Origin of the Pronominal Forms.

Personal Pronouns Nom. Sing.

351. It is impossible, within the limits of the present work, to discuss in every detail, all the very numerous variations of the Hindí pronouns. I can only briefly indicate the probable origin of the more common forms. In the nom. sing., *maiṉ* or *meṉ*, of the 1st personal pronoun, we have the Sk. instr. sing., *mayá*, Prak. *mai*, Ap. *mäiṉ*, transferred to the nom.* The *ne*, therefore, which is added to *maiṉ*, in the case of the ag., in High Hindí, is really superfluous, and in Máṛwáṛí, Old Baiswáṛí, and other

* Vid. Lassen: *Inst. Ling. Prac.*, p. 480. In Gujarátí, *meṉ* is still used for the case of the Agent, assigned to a nom. sing., *huṉ*, for Sk. *aham.*

archaic Hindí, *maiṉ*, alone, and properly, denotes that case. The same remarks, *mutatis mutandis*, apply to *taiṉ*, the Braj nom. sing. of the 2nd personal pronoun. The transfer is clearly due to a confusion in the minds of the ignorant of the two constructions of the subject with the verb.*

a. Besides the 1st pers. nom. sing., *maiṉ*, from a labial theme, the Braj presents a form, *hauṉ* or *hoṉ*, which has arisen from the corresponding Sk. *aham*, through Prakrit forms, *ahamum*, Ap. *hamuṉ*.† In the Máṛ. *húṉ* or *huṉ*, we have the same word, with the common reduction of the diphthong (§ 85). The corresponding Mw. *mhúṉ*, I would attribute to the theme *sma*, which appears in the Sk. base, *asmad*, and is also the base of the Sk. plur. declension of this pronoun. It presupposes a Prakrit form, *asmakam*, after the analogy of the Pr., *tusmakam*, for Sk. *tvam*, H. *tú*. This theme, *sma*, in Prakrit, regularly became *mha* (§ 108); so that from *asmakam*, *k* being rejected, we would have *amhaam*, and thence, as above, *mhauṉ*, *mhúṉ*. With the same theme, *sma*, I would connect the E.H. nom. sing., *ham*, *m* and *h* having been transposed and *a* inserted between them.

352. The nom. sing., *tú*, of the 2nd person, has arisen from the Sk. nom. sing., *tvam*. The final nasal is preserved in the Máṛwáṛí and Old Baiswáṛí, *túṉ* or *tuṉ*. But I am inclined to regard the *tú* in *tú ne*, ag., as a gen., from Sk. *tava*, through the Pr. *tua*. The Av. and R. nom. sing., *tayaṉ*, as also the R. loc. sing., *mayaṉ*, present merely a variant orthography of *taiṉ*, *maiṉ*.

a. The Bh. nom. sing., *tuṉh*, is a weakened form of *tumh*, for *tus͟hma*, the base of the plur. in High Hindí, where the theme *tu* has received, like the pronominal themes, *a* and *yu*, in Sanskrit, the increment *sma*. In the Mw. and Máṛ. *thúṉ*, we have apparently a transfer of the aspirate of *tumh* from the end to the beginning of the syllable, as in § 108.

353. The obl. sing. forms, *mujh*, *tujh*, have their immediate origin in the Prakrit genitives sing., *majjha*, *tujjha*, for *mah*, *tuh*. Prof. Lassen gives an apposite example of this change in the Prakrit root, *lijjha*, for Sk. *liha*.‡ The form *maha* occurs in the *Rámáyan*, and must be referred to a Pr. gen. sing., *masya* (?) for Sk. *mama*; and, by analogy, *tuha*, to a Pr. gen., *tusya* (?) for Sk. *tava*, formed after the analogy of the other Personal Pronouns: Obl. Sing.

* Vid. infra: § 357.

† Lassen: *Inst. Ling. Prac.* § 176, 2.

‡ Ib. § 50.

Sanskrit pronominal genitives. *Muha,* as also *tuha,* is found in the Apabhransic Prakrit.

a. Braj, Kanaují, Avadhí and some other dialects, present, in the Personal pronouns, the obl. sing. themes, *mo, to.* These also are true genitives, and are so used by *Chand, et al.** Their immediate original is to be found in the Prakrit genitives sing., *mahuṉ* and *tuhuṉ,*† which again, through the common change of *s* to *h,* may be compared with the Br. pron. genitives, *jásu, tásu.* In this *su,* Prof. Lassen judges that we have the Sk. possessive, *sva.*‡ The analogy of the Braj leads us to ascribe a similar origin to the Mw. obl. sing. themes, *mho, tho,* from Prakrit bases, *asmaka, tusmaka,* to which, as above suggested, we may suppose that the possessive *sva,* (or the abl. plur. term., *bhyas,* Ap. *ho,*) was originally added.

b. The R. obl. sing. forms, *mvá, tvá,* are, I think, to be explicated by the supposition that, as the suffix *ka* was in Prakrit added to the themes *asma, tus̱hma,* so it may have been added to the shorter themes, *ma* (*mu*), and *tu,* of these same pronouns, giving new themes, *muka, tuka.* Of these the original genitives would have been *mukasya, tukasya,* whence would arise Pr. forms, *muáha, tuáha,* and thence, by familiar changes, at last, *mvá, tvá.*

354. The genitives, *merá, terá,* have been formed by the addition to an old genitive, *maha,* of *kerá* or *kero,* for *kerako,* (Sk. *kṛita*). Beames gives, from the vulgar Prakrit, the form *mahakero,*§ from which *mero,* and *merá* are readily derived by the common elision of *k* and the *sandhi* of the then concurrent vowels. The Máṛ. and Mw. gen. forms, *mháṉro, mháṉḻo,* etc., as also the eastern gen., *mora,* are similarly derived, through the combination of the same suffix with another Ap. Pr. gen. sing., *mahuṉ.* In the gen., *mhárau,* the long *á* presupposes *karako,* instead of *kerako,* as the original form of the suffix. But in the dat. and acc. forms, *ma nai, mha nai, ta nai, tha nai,* the *a* of the base remains short because the retention of the initial *n* of the suffix prevented the concurrence and union of the vowels. The original form of these genitives is further illustrated by such E.H. obl. plur. forms of other pronouns as *inkará, unhkará,* etc., in which, again, a Prakrit genitive has been taken as a new base, to which is appended the usual gen. postposition in a fuller form.

* Vid. supra: §§ 283, 291. † Sindhí retains the form *mahuṉ.*

‡ *Inst. Ling. Prac.,* § 175, 6. But Hoernle derives it from the Sk. abl. plur. term., *bhyas,* Ap. *ho.* *Comp. Gramm.* p. 211.

§ *Comp. Gramm.,* vol. ii. p. 314.

a. In the *hi* of *mohi, tohi,* etc., we have the same suffix which marks the obl. sing. of nouns in archaic Hindí, derived, as has been shown,* from the Ap. Pr. gen. sing. suffix, *he* (for Sk. *sya*). As in the case of nouns, so here, again, it is added to old genitive forms. In like manner *mujhe* and *tujhe* have arisen from the addition of this *hi* to other Prakrit genitives, *majjha, tujjha,* giving *majjhahi* or *mujjhahi,* and *tujjhahi,* whence, by elision of *h* and *sandhi* of *a* and *i*, the modern forms. The final *e* in these datives is thus identical with the final *e* in the obl. sing. of Tadbhava nouns in *á*. Regarding the use of these (originally) genitive forms as datives and accusatives, it may be remarked that already in many Prakrit dialects, the dative having been lost, its place was often supplied by the genitive; and from the dative, as the case of the indirect object, it is but a step to the accusative as the case of the direct object.

355. In the Máṛ. obl. forms, 1st pers., *mhaiṉ*, 2nd pers., *taiṉ* or *thaiṉ*, we have a true instr. sing., with which the abl. postposition, *súṉ*, must be regarded as in grammatical construction, as would be its original, *sam*, in Sanskrit. I should suppose, however, that the same forms in the loc., *mhaiṉ máhai, thaiṉ úpari,* etc., must be regarded as genitives, for I have found no instance of the Sk. *madhye* and *upari* in construction with the instr. case, but only with the gen. or acc. In the later Prakrit, the pronominal termination *aiṉ* is found in the gen., instr. and loc. Thus the analogous Prakrit forms, *taiṉ, maiṉ,* are either gen., instr., or loc. After the same analogy, probably, may be explained the G. and Ku. obl. forms, *maiṉ, meṉ, tvai,* as Prakrit instr. or gen. sing. forms in grammatical construction with the postpositions.

356. In the E.H. obl. sing. forms, *hamará, tuhará,* etc., we have a plural form transferred to the singular. We would have expected, as in other dialects, *hamárá, tuhárá*; the shortening of the vowel is possibly to be explained by reference to the accent (?). The *h* of *tuhará*, as in all the plur. forms of the pers. pronouns, represents the *s* of *sma*; by which is formed from *tu*, the increased base, *tusma*.

357. Most of the dialects present *ham*, as the nom. plur. of the 1st personal pronoun. This has arisen, by transposition of the consonants and loss of the plur. termination, from the regular Prak. nom. plur., *mhe*, which is still retained in Máṛwáṛí. This Prakrit nom., *mhe* (*amhe*), evidently stands for an earlier form, *asme*, for the regular Sk. nom. Personal Pronouns, Nom. Plur.

---

* Vid. § 190.

plur., *vayam*, in which the theme, *asma*, of the Sk. obl. plur., *asmán*, *asmábhiḥ*, etc., was assumed also into the nom., and the plur. termination, *i*, added after the analogy of all the other pronouns; so that *asme* (= *asma* + *i*) corresponds precisely to the Sk. nominatives plur., *te*, *ime*, *ye*, etc. In the R. nom. plur., *hamh*, I suspect that the *h* has been ignorantly added to make the form correspond to the 2nd pers. nom. plur., *tumh*, of the same dialect. The Mw. nom. plur., *mhaiṉ*, as I conjecture, stands for the acc. plur., *amhäiṉ*, of the western Prakrit, which has been assumed into the nom., after the manner of the English objective, in the vulgar phrase, 'it is me.'

358. The most common form of the nom. plur. of the 2nd person, is *tum*. For this, in archaic Hindí, we have the form *tumh*, (also *tumah*,) which is but one step removed from the Pr. nom. plur., *tumhe*, for the Sk. *yúyam*. The sing. theme, *tu* (*tva*), increased by the pronominal element, *sma*, was, for the sake of regularity, substituted for the increased theme, *yuṣhma*, of the Sk. plur., and, as in the case of the 1st pers., *asme* (*amhe*), a nom. plur., *tuṣhma*, was also formed from the theme of the obl. cases, after the analogy of the other pronouns, making *tuṣhme*. It would therefore appear that besides the classic Sk. irregular plur., *yúyam*, *yuṣhmán*, *yuṣhmábhiḥ*, etc., a more regular plural, *tuṣhme*, *tuṣhmán*, etc., was also formed from the base of the sing.

359. In the Máṛ. nom. plur., *the*, the aspirate of *tumh* has been transferred to the beginning of the previous syllable, (giving *thume?*). The nasal thus left alone, has been weakened to *Anusvár*, and then lost, and the labial has disappeared before the diphthong, as in the sing., *taiṉ*, for *tvayá*, etc. In the Mw. *thaiṉ*, we have probably an acc. transferred to the nom., as in the 1st pers. *mhaiṉ*, so that *thaiṉ* stands for the Pr. acc. plur., *tumhäiṉ*.

Personal Pronouns: Obl. Plur.

360. The acc. and dat. forms, *hameṉ*, *tumheṉ*, etc., of the personal pronouns, have arisen immediately from the Prakrit accusatives plur., *amhäiṉ*, *tumhäiṉ*. The hiatus points to the loss of an *h*, so that the forms in question really stand for *amhahiṉ*, (*hamahiṉ*,) and *tumhahiṉ*,—Prakrit forms which occur frequently even in archaic Hindí. This *hiṉ* I take to be identical with the same termination in the acc. and dat. sing. of nouns in old Hindí, already noticed in § 190; i.e., it is probably identical with the Sk. loc. sing. termination, *smin*, or the Sk. dat. plur. term. *bhyam*.

361. Most of the dialects present a longer and shorter theme in the obl. plur.; as, e.g., *ham* or *hamoṉ*, *tum* or *tumhoṉ*, etc. All these themes in all their varieties were originally genitives plur. The longer forms refer us, perhaps, to the increased Prakrit themes, *asmaka, tus̲h̲maka;* the shorter forms to the simple themes, *asma, tus̲h̲ma. Ham* and *tum* or *tumh* are both used as genitives in old Hindí,* as also are the equivalent *amha, tumha,* in the later Prakrit, where the gen. termination, *áṇam,* of the earlier Prakrit, has quite disappeared. The longer forms, *hamon̲, hamani, tumhon̲, tumani, tuhani,* are to be explained by reference to the Pr. gen. plurals, *amháṇam, tumháṇam,* which were formed on the model of the gen. plur. of the 1st decl. of Sk. masc. nouns. The terminations, *on̲, ani,* etc., have therefore arisen in the same way as the same terminations in the declension of substantives.† In the short *u,* of the G. *tumun̲, hamun̲,* we have a still further reduction of *o* to *u.*‡

362. In the Máṛwáṛí and Mewáṛí, the Pr. gen. plur. termination, *áṇam,* for Sk. *ánám,* has become *án̲,* as in the substantive declension, giving *mhán̲, thán̲,* for *amháṇam, tumháṇam.* The inserted *y* in the longer Mewáṛí forms, *mhán̲yán̲, thán̲yán̲,* distinctly points, as in substantive declension, to the elision of the Prakrit suffix, *k,* which, according to Lassen, was sometimes added to these pronominal bases; so that these longer forms represent Prakrit genitives, *amhakáṇam, tumhakáṇam.* The nasal before *y* must be regarded as inorganic and unessential. As to the origin of the still longer forms, *mhán̲vará n̲, thán̲varán̲,* I am uncertain. Baghelkhaṇḍí presents a modern gen. form, *tihán̲re,* as nom. plur.; apparently some such word as *log* is to be understood.

363. The genitives plur., *hamárá, tumhárá,* have arisen from the combination of the Pr. *karakaḥ* with the bases *amhu* and *tumha,* giving *amha karako, tumha karako,*§ from both of which, *k* having been elided, the forms *amhaarao, tumhaarao,* must have arisen; whence, by *sandhi,* and the usual transposition of *m* and *h* in the 1st person, we have, first the Braj *hamárau, tumhárau,* then the K. *hamáro, tumháro,* whence, finally, the H.H. forms, *hamárá, tumhárá.* In the case of the shorter forms, *hamár, tumhár,* analogy leads us to believe that the suffix was first added to the base, not in its increased form, *karakaḥ,* but without the added *ka.*

* Vid., § 294, *a.* † Vid., § 192. ‡ Vid., § 85.

§ Hoernle in the 'Essays' previously referred to, cites from the *Mṛichchhakati,* a passage containing the analogous form, *amhakelake* (for *amhakerake*).

a. If, in the Máṛwáṛí and Mewáṛí forms, *mhánro, thánro, mhánlo, thánlo*, the *Anusvár* be organic, it follows, that, in this case, the affix was pleonastically added, not to the base, as in the above forms, but to the gen., so that the original of these Rajputana forms must have been *amhánam karako, amhánam kalako*, etc. Otherwise they must be explained like the regular forms.

Prox. Dem. Pronoun: Nom. Sing.

364. The various forms of the nom. sing. of the Prox. Demonstrative, which contain *h*, viz., *yah, yih, yihu, ih, eh, ehu, he*, have probably all arisen from the Sk. *eshah*. The final *u* of *yihu, yehu, ehu*, as in the case of nouns,* represents the Pr. *o*, for the final *ah* of *eshah*. Lassen gives a form, *ehe*, which looks like the original of the Bh. *he*. It appears to presuppose a nom. plur., *eshe*, from the stem *esh*. The loss of the final aspirate from *eh* and *ih*, has left the forms *e, í*. The remaining forms, *yo, yá, yon*, masc. *o*, fem. *á*, I would connect with the base *im*, which, although having a defective declension in Sanskrit, was fully declined in Prakrit. *Yo* and *yá* have apparently arisen from the Pr. nom. masc. sing., *imo*, which, by elision, yields *io*, whence *yo*, and *ya*. The final nasal of *yon* points to the Prakrit neut., *imam*, whence, *iam, yon*. The Mw. *o*, fem., *á*, must, similarly, be ascribed to *imo*, fem. *imá*.†

Rem. Dem. Pronoun: Nom. Sing.

365. The perfect analogy between the two demonstrative pronouns seems to justify the hypothesis, that, as in the case of the Prox. Demonstrative, we have a variety of forms from *eshah* (*esho*) and *imah*, (*imo*), all resting ultimately upon the pronominal base *i*; so there must have been in the ancient vulgar speech, analogous pronouns, *oshah, umah*, resting on the pronominal base *u*, from which, precisely as above, we must derive the various nom. forms of the Remote Demonstrative, *wah*. But, although the existence of this base is abundantly attested by such Sanskrit prepositions as *ut, upa, upari*, etc., yet I have met no instance of a declension resting on this labial, either in Sanskrit or the Prakrit dialects. But it is quite possible that further investigation of these dialects may furnish such examples, and verify the above hypothesis.

Rel., Correl., 1st Interrog., Pronouns: Nom. Sing.

366. The next three pronouns, *jo, so*, and *kaun*, are so closely analogous that we may consider them all together. Each of them presents two general forms in the nom. sing.; the one form terminating in a vowel, *e, o*, or *u*, the other, in *n*. We first consider the group in *o*. It has been formerly assumed that the pronouns *jo, so* and *ko*, are

* Vid. § 189. † But on the dem. forms, see Hoernle: *Comp. Gramm.* § 438.

derived immediately from the Sk. *yaḥ*, *saḥ* and *kaḥ*. But it is to be noticed that we have no proven instance of the preservation of this Prakrit termination, *o*, in modern Hindí, in any monosyllable, but only under the influence of a preceding consonant, commonly *ka*, appended to the Sanskrit base. It is therefore more reasonable to postulate, as the original of these three forms, Prakritic bases, formed by the addition of this *ka* (§ 100). Now in the archaic Hindí spoken in Mewáṛ and Máṛwáṛ, we find precisely the increased form required by this hypothesis, in the relative pronoun, *jako* or *jiko*. From this latter form, again, by elision, and consequent hardening of *i* to *y* before *o*, we have another Máṛwáṛí form, *jyo*, of this same pronoun.* This last form, thus derived, or a form *jao*, from the other base, I therefore regard as the immediate original of the common Hindí *jo;* and by analogy would suppose that similar forms, *sako* or *siko*, *kako* or *kiko*, must have existed, or may exist still, as the originals of *so* and *ko*. Although I can adduce no example of these forms, their actual existence is, I think, intimated in the R. obl. forms of the pronouns, *jyá*, *tyá*, and *kyá*, which are precisely analogous to the Máṛ. *jyo*, and may be held to presuppose as their originals, the bases, *jiá*, *jiká*, *tiá*, *tiká*, and *kiá*, *kiká*.

367. From these we now turn to consider other forms of the three pronouns under discussion. Besides the forms, *jo*, *so*, *ko*, several dialects exhibit *je* or *jai*, *se*, *ke* or *kai*, in the nom. sing. The analogies of the language lead us to infer that, probably, these have arisen from the euphonic insertion of *y* in the place of the lost *k*, giving, therefore, from the above themes, first, *jayo*, *sayo*, *kayo*, and then, *o* having been at last reduced to *a*, as in all Tatsama nouns, *jaya*, *saya*, *kaya*, whence the forms in question immediately arise.† An incidental corroboration of this theory is afforded by the archaic eastern form, *kayau*, of the indefinite pronoun. The base of the indefinite pronoun is always identical with that of the interrogative; and in this instance exhibits the very form postulated as the original of *ke* or *kai*. For the Sanskrit bases, *ja*, *ta*, *ka*, the Prakrit substitutes *ji*, *ti*, *ki*. From *ki* might be formed a theme *kiko*, whence, as above, would proceed the forms, *kiyo*, *kiya*, and thus, finally, the G. interrogative, *ki*.

a. The archaic forms, *ju* and *su*, found in the *Rámáyan* and other Hindí poetry, I would derive immediately from the Sk. *yaḥ* and *saḥ*

---

* Vid., § 50.

† Vid., § 90.

through the Pr. *yo, so.* We have already noted the existence of this final *u*, as the last remnant of the Sk. nom. masc. case-ending, in Tatsama nouns in old Hindí, and it needs no further illustration.*

368. As to the remaining nom. forms, *jaun, taun, kaun,* the interrogative will lead us to the explanation of the rest. To the interrogative *ko,* the word *uṇa,* for Sk. *punaḥ,* was, in Prakrit, pleonastically added, giving for *ko, ko uṇa,* whence by an evident process, *kavan, kaun, käún, kuṇ* and *kaṇ.* This derivation being established, we are naturally led to the conclusion that *jaun* and *taun* must also have had their origin from similar Prakrit forms, as *jo uṇa* and *to uṇa.* The analogies already exhibited seem to justify us in assuming, as the original of the R. forms, *jaúnayaṉ, taúnayaṉ, jaúnai, taúnai,* increased Prakritic forms, *jo punaraka, to punaraka.*

Dem., Rel., Correl., 1st. Interrog.: Obl. Sing.

369. The analogy between the obl. forms of the demonstrative, relative, correlative and interrogative pronouns is so close that the explication of the forms of any one of these pronouns will apply, with the change of the theme, to all the others. As in the case of the personal pronouns, most, if not all, of these obl. forms, sing. or plur., are in fact true genitives. Thus for the Sk. gen. sing., *yasya = jis ká,* Prakrit exhibits *jassa* or *jissa,* whence, by the loss of the last syllable, the modern *jis.* Similarly, *tis* stands for the Pr. *tissa,* Sk. *tasya*; *kis* = Pr. *kissa.* Sk. *kasya*; and, by analogy, *is* presupposes a Prakrit form, *issa,* for Sk. *asya*; and *us, ussa* for *usya* (?).† Again, by the common change of *s* to *h,* and lengthening of the penultimate vowel in compensation for the loss of the conjunct, from the Sk. *yasya,* Pr. *jassa,* we derive the forms, *jáha, jáa,* whence, the Braj. obl. form, *já.* Similarly, *tá* and *ká* may be derived from the Sk. *tasya, kasya,* through intermediate forms, *táha, káha*; while *yá* presupposes the forms, *imasya, iáha, yáa*; and *wá, umasya, uáha, wáa.*

a. The obl. forms, *jáhi, táhi, káhi,* etc., are formed, like *mohi, tohi,* and the obl. sing. of substantives, by the addition of the Prakritic affix, *hi,* (Ap. *he,* Sk. *sya,*) to old genitives taken as themes for a new declension. By the elision of this *h* from *ehi, jáhi,* etc., we get the forms *ei, jai, tai,* etc., and by subsequent *sandhi, e, je, te,* etc. The Av. *e, je,* etc., are probably identical in origin with these Himalayan genitives. In the R. *iyá, jyáhi,* etc., we again have the same genitives. The *y* has probably arisen from the elision of *k* from the increased theme, *jika,* still existent

* Vid., §§ 79, *c.,* 189.

† Or assume prolonged themes in *ka.*

in Máṛwáṛí and some eastern dialects, so that *jyá* and *jyáhi* stand for *jikasya*, and so on.

b. In the Braj genitives, *jásu* and *tásu*, we have the same termination as in the gen. of nouns in the Apabhransic Prakrit, as e.g., in *vachchhasu* = *bachche ká*.*

c. In the Bh. obl. sing., *jikar*, etc. the Pr. *karakaḥ* was apparently added to the theme for a new genitive, which, as in other dialects, became a new secondary base for the obl. sing. throughout.

370. The Máṛ. and Mw. obl. sing. forms in *ṇ*, *ṇi*, or *ṉ*, present some difficulty. Possibly we may identify them with the Pr. instr. sing. of these same pronouns, which terminates in *ṇá*, fem., *e*; but this has little support from analogy, nor have I met with any such intermediate forms as might throw light upon the case. More probably a plur. form has been ignorantly transferred to the sing., as in some other cases.

371. The nom. plur. forms of the five pronouns under discussion may apparently be reduced to two heads, viz., those which correspond with the sing., and those which assume a special plur. termination. In the case of such forms as *wuh*, *yih*, *jo*, *so*, *kaun*, etc., the sing. form has evidently been assumed into the plural. The original model of most of the other forms is to be found in the Máṛ. *jakai*, whence, by elision of *k* and *sandhi* of the vowels, we have *jai*. Similar are the other forms in question. The final *e* (or *ai*) may be identified with the same termination in the Sk. nom. plur. of these same pronouns, where it has resulted from the *sandhi* of the final radical *a* with the *i* which is the affix of the nom. plur. The analogy of *tumh* for *tumhe* leads us to suppose such a form as *jenhe* or *jinhe*, as the original of the R. nom. plur., *jenh*. The analogy is strengthened by the Bh. nom. plur., *jihe*. The same remark applies, *mutatis mutandis*, to the other pronouns.

Dem., Rel., Correl., 1st Interrog.: Nom. Plur.

372. The bases of the obl. plur. of these pronouns present several different forms;—(1) the simple radical, as in the H.H. forms, *un*, *in*, *jin*, etc.; (2) a theme in *anáṉ* or *náṉ*, as in the Máṛ. *uṇáṉ*, *iṇáṉ*, *jaṇáṉ*, etc.; (3) an increased theme in *k*, as in the Máṛ. *jakáṉ*, *tikáṉ*, etc.; (4) another strengthened form in *nh*, as in E.H. *inh*, *unh*, *jinh*; and (5) also forms still further increased to *nhan*, *nhani*, *nhoṉ*, and *nhakará*, as in H.H. *unhoṉ*, *inhoṉ*, and E.H., *jinhan*, *tinhani* and *tinhakará*. Of these, the first needs no explanation. In the second, we have an old acc. plur. in *an*

Dem., Rel., Correl., 1st Interrog.: Obl. Plur.

---

* Vid. Lassen: *Inst. Ling. Prac.* § 175, 6.

to which the gen. plur. termination *áṉ* (for Sk. *ánám*) was added for a new base. The bases with *k* have been already explained;* as also those in *nh*,—which occur also in subst. declension,—and the terminations *an, ani,* and *oṉ*.† Such E.H. forms as *inhakará, kinhakará,* etc., are strictly analogous in their origin to the H.H. forms *inhoṉ*, etc. As in the case of these last, a new obl. plur. base has been formed by adding the old gen. plur. termination *oṉ* (for Sk. *ánám*), so in these eastern forms, the still more modern gen. sign, *kará*, has been added to the same effect.

373. The various terminations of the obl. plur. in the several dialects, are of course identical in their origin with the same terminations in the substantives and personal pronouns; i.e., the long forms are various modifications of the Sk. gen. plur. term., *ám* or *ánám*; like the short forms, through the Pr. neut. obl. plur. in *áṇam*. The dat. and acc. forms, *jinheṉ, tinheṉ*, come immediately from the archaic forms, *jinhahiṉ, tinhahiṉ*, and therefore justify the hypothesis of corresponding forms in the other pronouns of the series. This *hiṉ*, in the dat. and acc. plur., may possibly be identified with the termination *siṉ*, of the Pr. gen. plur. forms, *jesiṉ, tesiṉ*, etc., or else be connected with the Sk. dat. plur. term., *bhyam*.

Forms of 1st Indef. Pronoun.

374. The various modifications of the indefinite pronoun, *koí*, have arisen from the combination of the interrogative in one or another of its various forms, with the Sk. affix, *api*. Thus, *koí* or *koi* stands for the Sk. *ko'pi*, Pr. *kobi*. In *koú* and *kou*, the *i* has disappeared, and the *b* has been softened to the cognate vowel. In *kaunau* and *kaṇo*, the affix *api* has been originally added to the compound form; thus, *ko punar api*, and *api* has been reduced to *au* or *o*. The obl. sing. forms are to be similarly explicated. Thus, from the base *ki*, for Sk. *ka*, come *kisí* and *kisú*, both for *kisyápi*, (*kisyaäpi*) for the Sk. gen. sing., *kasyápi*; and by the change of *s* to *h*, from the base *ka*, we have *káhú* = *kasyápi*. The forms *kehi* and *kehu* probably stand for *kihi, kihu*, or *kahi, kahu*, still other corruptions of the genitive in question; and from these, or similar forms in *h*, proceed the Av. *keú* and the G. *kaí*, K. *kai*. Several of these forms in *h* are found in the nom., but they must be regarded as genitives transferred by the ignorant to that case. The R. form, *kaunko*, I have met but once, and suspect that we have here but an orthographic variation of *kauno*.

Of Forms of 2nd Interrog. Pronoun.

375. In the Baiswáṛí interrogative, *káh*, for *kasya*, we have again a genitive taken as a nom., and as the base of a new declension. This

---

* Vid. § 366. † Vid. §§ 192, 192, *a*.

secondary theme, according to Lassen,* was already declined in Prakrit. All the analogies of the language lead us to regard the longer form, *kahá*, having proceeded from a theme *káhaka*, derived from *káh* by the addition of the Prakritic *k*, as, e.g., in the Hindí *kuchchhuk* for *kuchh*. This *k* being elided, and the long *á* shortened before the heavy termination, we have by *sandhi* the Braj *kahá*. The shorter form, *ká*, was evidently derived from *káha* by the elision of *h*. The regular form, *kyá*, for *kiá*, presupposes a base *kihá* from the theme *ki*. Granting that *kahá*, stands for a secondary base, *káhaka*, it is plain that in the obl. sing. *káhe*, we have a secondary genitive from this base, after the analogy of Tadbhava nouns in *á*, so that *káhe* presupposes a Prák. gen. *káhaäha*, whence, as in nouns, *káháya*, *káhe*.

376. The Máṛ. and Mw. *kaiṉ*, *káiṉ*, etc., appear to be derived from an increased Prakritic neuter form, *kakim*, for the Sk. *kim*. The final *Anusvár* therefore represents the Sk. neut. term., *m*. The first *Anusvár*, of *káṉiṉ*, is, I suspect, merely inorganic. The obl. sing., *khá*, is connected with the secondary themes, *káh*, (*káhaka*,) so common in other dialects. The aspirate has been transferred from the second to the first syllable; the final *á*, instead of *e*, represents the Pr. gen. term., *äáha*, after the analogy of the obl. sing. of substantives in the same dialect.

377. *Kuchh*, *kachhu*, *kichhu*, are all corruptions of the corresponding Sk. *kashchit*. *Kachchhuk*, has already been noticed. The corresponding Máṛ. and Mw. forms, *kani*, *káṉiṉ*, are to be connected with the Sk. neut. of the same pronoun combined with the suffix *api*, viz., *kimapi*, through a similar form, *kamapi*, whence, *m* having become *Anusvár*, and *p* being elided, *káṉi*, or *káṉiṉ* remains. The final *ṉ* has, I judge, been added through a popular misapprehension confounding this word with the interrogative *kaiṉ*. Or these forms may be connected with the Sk. *kiñchana*. Of Forms of 2nd Indef. Pronoun.

378. Of the pronominal series derived from the five pronominal elements (Tables XIII. and XIV.), those expressing quantity are all to be connected with the corresponding Sanskrit series, *iyat*, *kiyat*, etc., or rather with their Prakrit equivalents, viz., *ettiá*, *kettiá*, etc. This hiatus marks the place of a *k*, originally added to these Sanskrit forms, which is still preserved in several dialects noted in Table XIV., as, e.g., Bh. *atek*, *jatek*, G. *etaká*, *tataká*, etc. From the above Prakrit pronominals have immediately proceeded the O.B. *etá*, *jetá*, and the H.H. Of the Pronom. Adjectives.

* *Inst. Ling. Prac.*, § 106, 5.

ittá, *jittá*, etc. The peculiar R. forms, *jyátik*, *tyattán*, etc., have evidently been formed from the secondary bases *jika*, *tika*, etc., like the similar forms in the Riwái and Máṛwáṛí pronouns. The *no* (*nu*, *ná*, *na*, or *n*), which is added to these pronominals, Beames is probably right in regarding as originally a diminutive affix which has now lost, as in many other words, its special significance.* Such certainly seems to be the explanation of the Rajputana pronominals in *ro* or *ṛo*, which represents the Sk. diminutive affix *ra*. Their use is well illustrated by the Sindhí addition of *ṛo* to adjectives, to signify some small degree of the quality expressed by the primary word,† like "ish" in the Eng. "black-ish;" and still further by the Máṛwáṛí practice of adding this same *ṛo* to participles when used as adjectives.

a. The dialectic forms, *jai*, *tai*, *kai*, = *jitná*, etc., are derived from the Sanskrit series, *yati*, *tati*, *kati*.

379. The various forms of the pronominal series expressive of likeness, as, e.g., *jaisá*, *jas*, *jaisan*, are all to be connected through the Pr. series, *járiso*, etc., with the Sk. series formed with the affix *dṛisha*, as, *yádṛishaḥ*. The dialectic affixes, *no*, *nu*, *ná*, *n*, *ro*, *ṛo*, are evidently identical with those in the quantitative series. In the Rajputana and Gaṛhwálí series the absence of the characteristic *s* is to be explained by the custom in those dialects of changing *s* to *h* and then dropping it entirely.‡ Thus, e.g., G. *eno* = H.H. *aisá*, presupposes a form *esano*, similar to R. *aisan*; and Mw. *jaiṛo*, a form *jaisaṛo*.

380. The Reflexive pronoun, *áp*, is derived from the Sk. *átman*, which is used in the same sense. The obl. forms, *apná*, *apne*, point to a Prak. form, *átmanaka*, with an adjective sense. The derivation of the obl. plur. form, *ápas*, is uncertain. Beames with high probability regards it as pointing toward a Prakrit genitive *ápassa*, which, however, is not preserved in literature.

381. The Honorific pronoun, *áp*, is also derived from *átman*, through the intermediate dialectic forms, *ápun*, *ápu*. The dialectic Honorific pronoun, *raur*, or *raurau*, etc., is to be regarded as a gen. formed from the noun, *ráu*, with the affix *rá*. This *ráu* is derived from *rájaḥ*, a form which the base *rájan* assumes in Sk. at the end of compounds; *j* being elided, and *aḥ* changed to *o*, *ráo* remains, whence *ráu*.§

---

* Comp. Gramm., vol. ii. pp. 116, 332.

† Trumpp, Sindhí Gramm., p. 78.

‡ Vid. §§ 98, 120.

§ Vid. §§ 85, *c*, 89.

CHAPTER IX.

OF THE VERB (क्रिया).

382. The Hindí verb is very simple. There is but one conjugation, and all verbs whatever, both in High Hindí, and in the local dialects, take the regular terminations belonging to the several tenses. Conjugation.

a. Seven verbs only in High Hindí present an irregularity in the Respectful form of the Imperative, and in the Perfect Participle and the tenses formed with it. But this irregularity consists only in the substitution of another root, slightly different from that which appears in the other tenses, and will give no trouble. To this root the regular terminations are appended. The same verbs are irregular in the same way in most dialects.

383. The Hindí verb is affected by the distinctions of voice, mood, tense, gender, number, and person. The voices are two, Active and Passive. The moods, properly speaking, are four only, Indicative, Subjunctive, Imperative, and Infinitive. The Infinitive simply expresses the abstract and unrestricted verbal idea; it is indeed, strictly speaking, a Gerund or Verbal noun. The participles are three, viz., Imperfect, Perfect, and Conjunctive.* From every verb may also be formed a Noun of Agency.

---

* The appropriateness of this nomenclature, of necessity, cannot be shown, until we come to examine the use of these participles. We can, in this place, only express our conviction that the terms 'present' and

Rem. The Imperfect and Perfect Participles are sometimes termed 'Adjective Participles.' The Conjunctive Participle is peculiarly characteristic of the Indian languages; its functions will be explained in due order.

384. Reckoning the Imperative as a variety of the Future, we have, in High Hindí, fifteen tenses.* Three of these tenses are formed by inflection of the verbal root; the remaining twelve are all formed by means of the participles, combined, in all the tenses but two, with an auxiliary verb.

385. The distinction of Number is made by inflection in all the tenses. The distinction of Gender is expressed in all the tenses, except the Contingent Future and the Imperative. As in the noun and adjective, आ is everywhere the sign of the masc. singular; ए of the masc. plural; ई of the fem. singular; ईं, or, rarely, इयाँ, of the fem. plural. The distinction of Person is marked by inflection in the three tenses of the future, viz., the Contingent and the Absolute Future, and the Imperative. In the Indefinite, Past, and Past Contingent tenses, both Perfect and Imperfect, the distinction of person is not expressed; in the remaining tenses, the person is indicated by the auxiliary.

'past,' commonly applied to these participles, are not philosophically accurate. These participles, with their dependent tenses, represent action in different stages of *progress*, not necessarily at different points of time. Since the above was written, I have noticed that Mr. Platts, in his excellent Hindustání Grammar, has adopted for the adjective participles these same terms, 'perfect' and 'imperfect.' He has failed, however, to carry out an analogous nomenclature in the tenses.

* The number differs in some dialects; in particular, the number of inflected tenses is larger in some more archaic types of Hindí. Illustrations will be found in the sections on Dialectic Conjugation.

Rem. In none of the tenses, however, is the scheme of personal endings complete in High Hindí. Except in the Imperative, which has a separate form for the 2nd sing., the same terminations everywhere denote both the 2nd and 3rd person sing., and, in the plural, the 1st and 3rd person also have the same terminations.

N.B. The above remarks are to be understood as applying without restriction to High Hindí only. The peculiarities of the dialectic conjugations will be noticed in detail below.

386. In High Hindí the *Infinitive* of all verbs terminates in ना. It is under this form that the verb will always be found in the dictionary; as, e.g., बोलना, 'to speak;' जाना, 'to go,' etc. Formation of the Infinitive.

a. The Hindí infinitive is, strictly speaking, a *Gerund* or *Verbal Noun*, and is so used. It denotes abstractly the action or state signified by the verb. As thus employed, it is inflected to ए throughout the obl. sing., and takes the usual postpositions after the manner of Tadbhava masc. nouns in आ. It is never used in the plural. Thus we have, e.g., लड़ना, 'to fight,' 'fighting;' Gen., लड़ने का, 'of fighting;' Loc., लड़ने में, 'in fighting,' etc.

b. Besides this Verbal Noun in ना and its dialectic variants, High Hindí verbs all form a second Verbal Noun in आ; before which, य is inserted after a vowel. Thus, from मरना, 'to die,' is formed a second verbal noun, मरा, 'dying;' from जाना, जाया, 'going.' This second verbal noun is chiefly restricted in use to the formation of Frequentative and Desiderative Compounds, where it has been erroneously identified with the Perfect Participle.

387. Rejecting the final ना of the infinitive, we obtain the *Root* of the verb, from which, except in the case of seven verbs to be hereafter noted, all the parts of the verb may be derived in a regular and orderly manner. The Root.

Thus, e.g., the root of चलना is चल; of गिरना, गिर; of कहना, कह, etc.

N.B. The root of the verb, in High Hindí, is always identical in form with the 2nd pers. sing. of the Imperative.

Rem. The roots of verbs may be conveniently distinguished as *close* and *open*. By a *close* root is denoted a root terminating in a consonant; by an *open* root, a root terminating in a vowel. Verbs which have *open* roots are often termed *pure* verbs, and those which have *close* roots, *mixed* verbs. Thus, आ, बुला, and सो, the roots of the verbs आना, बुलाना, and सोना, are *open* roots, and their verbs, *pure* verbs; but चल, मार, and पढ़, the roots of चलना, मारना, पढ़ना, are *close* roots, and their verbs, *mixed* verbs.

Formation of Imperf. and Perf. Participles.

388. From the root of the verb, the *Imperfect* and *Perfect* participles in High Hindí are respectively derived as follows :—

(1) The *Imperfect* participle is formed by adding to the root the syllable ता.

(2) The *Perfect* participle is formed by adding to the root the syllable आ.

The following examples illustrate the above :—

Inf.	*Root.*	*Imperfect Part.*	*Perfect Part.*
बोलना, 'to speak.'	बोल.	बोलता, 'speaking.'	बोला, 'spoken.'
डरना, 'to fear.'	डर.	डरता, 'fearing.'	डरा, 'feared.'
मिलना, 'to meet.'	मिल.	मिलता, 'meeting.'	मिला, 'met.'
मारना, 'to strike.'	मार.	मारता, 'striking.'	मारा, 'struck.'

389. Observe, that before the termination आ of the perfect participle,

(1) य is inserted after all roots ending in आ, ए, or ओ;

(2) If the root end in the long ई, this vowel is shortened. Examples are :—

Verb.	*Root.*	*Imperfect Part.*	*Perfect Part.*
लाना, 'to bring.'	ला.	लाता, 'bringing.'	लाया, 'brought.'
पीना, 'to drink.'	पी.	पीता, 'drinking.'	पिया, 'drank.'
बोना, 'to sow.'	बो,	बोता, 'sowing.'	बोया, 'sown.'

390. The participal terminations, ता and आ, are inflected to ए (masc.) and ई (fem.) according to the rules for the inflection of Tadbhava adjectives (§ 199). The fem. plur. is sometimes inflected to ईं, or, rarely, to इयां. Inflection of Participles.

a. Verbs which insert य before आ in the perfect participle, optionally insert य before the inflection ए, and occasionally before ई. But if the root of the verb in the perfect participle terminate in इ or ई, the ई of the fem. termination sometimes combines with this radical vowel, by § 48. Thus we have, e.g., from पीना, 'to drink,' (perf. part. masc., पिया,) the perf. part. fem., पी, for पिई. Examples of these inflected participles are as follows :—

	Nom. Masc.	*Obl. Masc.*	*Fem. Sing.*	*Fem. Plur.*
From डालना, 'to throw.'	डालता,	डालते,	डालती,	डालतीं.
" " " "	डाला,	डाले,	डाली,	डालीं.
" सोना 'to sleep.'	सोता,	सोते,	सोती,	सोतीं.
" सोना, " "	सोया,	सोए or सोये,	सोई,	सोईं.
" देना, 'to give.'	दिया,	दिये,	दी,	दीं.
" करना, 'to do.'	किया,	किये,	की,	कीं.

b. Observe, that in dissyllabic roots with a short vowel in the first syllable, and short *a* in the second, this *a* very commonly, though not invariably, becomes silent before all terminations beginning with a vowel. Thus from निकलना, 'to come out,' we have the perf. part., निकला, commonly pronounced *niklá*. Similarly, in the contingent future, the 3rd sing., समझे, and the 2nd plur., समझो, from समझना, *samajhná*, are respectively pronounced *samjhe* and *samjho*.* But this rule is not to be applied in reading poetry.†

Seven Irregular Verbs.

391. In the following seven common verbs, the perfect participle is formed from a root different from the root of the Infinitive, viz:—

होना,	'to be;'	*Perf. Part.*	हुआ,	*Root.*	हु.
मरना,	'to die;'	„ „	मुआ,	„	मु.
करना,	'to do;'	„ „	किया,	„	की.
देना,	'to give;'	„ „	दिया,	„	दी.
लेना,	'to take;'	„ „	लिया,	„	ली.
जाना,	'to go;'	„ „	गया,	„	ग.
ठानना,	'to determine;'	„ „	ठया.	„	ठ.

a. Of the above, करना and मरना also form their perfect participles regularly from the root of the infinitive; thus, करा, मरा. But although करा occurs in the *Shakuntalá* in a woman's talk, these forms belong rather to Kanaují and other local dialects than to High Hindí.

b. The Sanskrit past participle neuter, समाप्तम्, 'finished,' is very commonly found at the end of Hindí books, where it is used precisely as the Latin *finis* in English books. The corresponding verb has not found a place in Hindí.

Adjective Use of Participles.

392. When the perfect and imperfect participles are used as attributive adjectives, the perf. part., हुआ, of the verb होना, 'to be,' inflected, if necessary, to agree with the participle and noun qualified, is very often added. The participle हुआ, in this idiom, is strictly pleonastic and cannot be translated.

Examples are:—बोया हुआ गेहूं, 'sown wheat;' दौड़ते हुए घोड़े, 'running horses;' गाती हुई लड़की, 'a singing girl.'

---

* But see § 14, *c*, *d*.

† Vid. § 14, *a*. (4).

393. The *Conjunctive* participle consists either of the root alone, or adds to the root the syllable कर or के. The following are examples:— The Conjunctive Participle.

Verb.	*Root.*	*Conjunctive Participle.*
करना.	कर.	कर, कर के, or कर कर, 'doing,' 'having done.'
हंसना.	हंस.	हंस, हंस के, or हंस कर, 'laughing,' 'having laughed.'
जाना.	जा.	जा, जा के, or जा कर, 'going,' 'having gone.'
सीना.	सी.	सी, सी के, or सी कर, 'sewing,' 'having sewed.'

a. Sometimes either कर or के is repeated after कर; thus, चल कर के or चल कर कर, 'having walked;' गा कर के or गा कर कर, 'having sung.' But this is colloquial and scarcely elegant.

394. The verbal *Noun of Agency* is formed by adding to the inflected infinitive the affix वाला or हारा. Thus, to illustrate:— Noun of Agency.

Infinitive.		*Noun of Agency.*		
गाना,	'to sing;'	गानेवाला	or गानेहारा,	'a singer.'
दौड़ना,	'to run;'	दौड़नेवाला	or दौड़नेहारा,	'a runner.'
बोना,	'to sow;'	बोनेवाला	or बोनेहारा,	'a sower.'

a. Of these two suffixes, वाला is everywhere used; हारा is more common in the east than in the west. These nouns are declined in the masc., like घोड़ा (*p.* 106); and in the fem., like पोथी (*p.* 108). The final *á* of these affixes, especially of हारा, is occasionally shortened; but this, again, is an eastern usage.

395. The fifteen tenses of High Hindí may be distributed into three groups. The first group will include such tenses as are formed immediately from the *Root*, by means of certain terminations; the second group, such tenses as are formed by means of auxiliaries combined with the *Imperfect Participle*; the third Classification of Tenses.

group, such tenses as are formed by means of auxiliaries combined with the *Perfect Participle.* As thus distributed, the tenses stand as follows :—

GROUP I.

TENSES FROM THE ROOT.

1. Contingent Future. 2. Absolute Future. 3. Imperat. (Future).

GROUP II. TENSES FROM THE IMPERFECT PARTICIPLE.	GROUP III. TENSES FROM THE PERFECT PARTICIPLE.
1. Indefinite Imperfect.	1. Indefinite Perfect.
2. Present Imperfect.	2. Present Perfect.
3. Past Imperfect.	3. Past Perfect.
4. Contingent Imperfect.	4. Contingent Perfect.
5. Presumptive Imperfect.	5. Presumptive Perfect.
6. Past Contingent Imperfect.	6. Past Contingent Perfect.

396. The above arrangement and nomenclature differs somewhat from any given in earlier Hindí or Hindustání grammars; but it is believed to rest on sound philosophical principles, and to give a more precise expression to the distinctive characteristics and mutual relations of the several tenses. Not only do these several groups have an outward individual character, in respect of their derivation respectively from three different parts of the verb, but one distinctive radical conception will be found to underlie all the tenses of each group, with which all their various usages may be connected. Every action or state, whether actual or contingent, may be conceived of under three different aspects, relatively to its own progress, i.e., (1) as not yet begun; (2) as begun, but not completed; or (3) as completed. It is believed that these are the essential ideas which severally pervade these three groups of tenses. In *Group I*, all these tenses represent the action as *not begun*, i.e., as future. The *Absolute Future* represents this futurition as a reality; the *Contingent Future* and *Imperative* represent it as a possibility. The *Contingent Future* represents the futurition as contingent, in a general way, whether desired or not; the *Imperative* represents it as an object of desire or will. The tenses of *Group II* represent the action of the verb, under various phases, as *imperfect*, i.e., as not yet completed; the tenses of *Group III* represent it, in different aspects, as *perfect*, or completed.

Rem. **Of these three Groups of tenses, the first, as formed immediately from the root, may be called the *radical* tenses; the second and third the *periphrastic* or *participial* tenses.**

397. The three tenses of the Future, in Group I, are formed by adding certain terminations to the root, as follows:— **Tenses of the Future.**

(1) The *Contingent Future* is formed by adding to the root the terminations given in the following table.

TERMINATIONS OF THE CONTINGENT FUTURE.

Sing.	1. ऊं.	2. ए.	3. ए.
Plur.	1. एं.	2. ओ.	3. एं.

Thus, from कहना, 'to say,' root, कह, we have कहूं, 'I may say;' from लिखना, 'to write,' root, लिख, लिखें, 'we (or 'they') may write,' etc.

(2) The terminations of the *Imperative* are identical with the above, except in the 2nd sing., in which no affix whatever is added to the root; thus, from कहना, 'to say,' कह, 'say thou,' etc.

a. In the place of the above affixes for the 2nd and 3rd plur., other terminations are added to the root to form what is commonly known as the *Respectful* or *Precative* Imperative. These terminations are as follows:— 2nd plur., इयो; 3rd plur., इये, or, more rarely, इयेगा. Of these, the form इयो is commonly used with the plur. of the 2nd Pers. pronoun, तुम; that in इये or इयेगा with the Honorific pronoun, आप, or some equivalent word; thus तुम चलियो, 'please go;' आप लिखिये or लिखियेगा, 'your honour will please write.'

b. Verbs of which the root ends in ई or ए insert य before the above affixes. In this case the radical ए is changed to ई.

Thus लेना, 'to take,' makes the resp. imper., लीजियो, लीजिये, 'have the goodness to take;' देना, 'to give,' resp. imper., दीजियो, दीजिये, 'please give,' 'be so good as to give;' सीना, 'to sew;' resp. imper., सीजियो, सीजिये; पीना, 'to drink;' resp. imper., पीजियो, पीजिये, or पीजियेगा, etc.

c. To the verbs included under *b.* may be added three verbs from the list in § 391, which irregularly form the Respectful Imperative from the root of the perfect participle; viz. करना, 'to do,' मरना, 'to die,' and होना, 'to be,' of which the respectful forms of the imperative are, कीजियो, कीजिये; मूजियो, मूजिये; हूजियो, हूजिये. But करिये and मरिये, common in the dialects, are also occasionally used in High Hindí.

d. Observe that इयो and इये, after ज in these respectful forms, are very often contracted to ओ and ए; giving, instead of the above, दीजे, कीजो, पीजे, etc.

Rem. In Braj, Kanaují, and other local dialects, as intimated, the Respectful Imperative of करना and मरना is regularly formed from the root. The regular form also occurs, even in the High Hindí of the *Shakuntalá*; as where *Mátali* says to *Dushyant*, आप . . . . छाया में विश्राम करिये, 'your excellency will please sit in the shade.' But this is not to be imitated in High Hindí.

e. The Sk. 3rd sing. imp. of the substantive verb, अस्तु, is occasionally met with in the formula, तथास्तु (तथा + अस्तु), 'so let it be.'

(3) The *Absolute Future* is formed from the Contingent Future, by adding to each person of that tense, in the sing., गा, masc. (fem. गी); and in the plur., गे, masc. (fem. गीं). The full terminations, therefore, as added to the root, are as follows:—

TERMINATIONS OF THE ABSOLUTE FUTURE.

Sing.	1. ऊंगा, fem. ऊंगी.	2. एगा, fem. एगी.	3. एगा. fem. एगी.
Plur.	1. एंगे, fem. एंगीं.	2. ओगे, fem. ओगीं.	3. एंगे, fem. एंगी.

398. In the 2nd and 3rd sing. and the 1st and 3rd plur., य is very often substituted for ए after *open* roots (§ 387, *Rem.*), in all three tenses of the future. In this case the *Anusvár* in the plural is added, not to the initial ए of the termination, but to the final vowel of the root. Thus, होना, 'to be,' makes the 2nd and 3rd sing. in these tenses होए or होय; होएगा or होयगा; and the 1st and 3rd plur., होएँ or होंय, होएंगे or होंयगे.

399. After roots ending in आ, ई, ए, or ओ, व is optionally inserted before ए and एं in the tenses of the Future. Thus, for बताए, पीए, होए, we very commonly hear बतावे, पीवे, होवे.

a. But in the case of roots ending in ए, educated moderns very often reject that vowel before all the terminations of the three tenses of the future.

Thus, from देना, 'to give,' we may have in the Contingent Future, 1st sing., दूं, for देऊं; 3rd sing., दे, for देवे; 2nd plur., दो, for देओ. Similarly, from लेना, 'to take,' we have, in the Absolute Future, 1st sing., लूंगा, 1st plur., लेंगे, etc.

Rem. The addition of this गा (for Sk. गतः, 'going')* to form from the contingent an absolute future, appears to have been one of the latest developments of the language. This is indicated by the fact that even yet the union of this suffix with the preceding part of the verb is not so close but that occasionally it is found separated from the rest of the verb by the emphatic particle ही. Thus in the *Shakuntalá* we find such forms as कहूंहीगा, मानेहींगे, etc. In one instance, where two verbs follow in immediate succession, the suffix is added only to the last of them, thus: जो यह मोर चले फिरेगा और उड़ेगा, 'if this peacock will walk around and fly.' But it is to be observed, that in this case the verbs चलना, फिरना, are combined after the manner of a Copulative Compound.†

---

* Vid. *Monier-Williams*: *Sansk. Gramm.*, § 896, a.

† Vid. Chapter on 'Compound Nouns.'

Tenses of the Substantive Verb.

400. Before proceeding to explain the formation of the remaining tenses of the verb, it will be necessary, as a preliminary, to exhibit certain tenses of the auxiliary verb **होना**, 'to be,' or 'become.' Besides the regular tenses common to all verbs, two other tenses, viz., a Present and an Indefinite Past, are usually, though inaccurately, assigned to this verb.* These must be considered first in order. They express simple existence, and answer, respectively, to the English 'am' and 'was.' These tenses are conjugated in High Hindí as follows:—

PRESENT.

SINGULAR.		PLURAL.	
मैं हूं,	'I am.'	**हम हैं,**	'we are.'
तू है,	'thou art.'	**तुम हो,**	'you are.'
वह है,	'he is.'	**वे हैं,**	'they are.'

PAST.

SINGULAR.		PLURAL.	
मैं था,	'I was.'	**हम थे,**	'we were.'
तू था,	'thou wast.'	**तुम थे,**	'you were.'
वह था,	'he, she, *or* it was.'	**वे थे,**	'they were.'
Fem. **मैं थी,** etc.		*Fem.* **हम थीं,** etc.	

401. We add the three radical tenses of the verb **होना**, 'to be' or 'become.'

* Though conveniently treated here, it should be understood that, in reality, these tenses have no organic connexion with the verb *honá*, which is derived throughout from the Sanskrit *bhú*; while of these two tenses, the Present is derived from the root *as*, and the Past from the root *sthá*.

Contingent Future.

Singular.	Plural.
मैं होऊं or हूं, 'I may be.'	हम होएं, होवें, होंय or हों, 'we may be.'
तू होए, होवे, होय or हो, 'thou mayst be.'	तुम होओ or हो, 'you may be.'
वह होए, होवे, होय or हो, 'he may be.'	वे होएं, होवें, होंय, or हों, 'they may be.'

Absolute Future.

Singular.	Plural.
मैं होऊंगा or हूंगा, 'I shall be.'	हम होएंगे, होवेंगे, होंयगे or होंगे, 'we shall be.'
तू होएगा, होवेगा, होयगा or होगा, 'thou wilt be.'	तुम होओगे or होगे, 'you will be.'
वह होएगा, होवेगा, होयगा or होगा, 'he will be.'	वे होएंगे, होवेंगे, होंयगे or होंगे, 'they will be.'
Fem. मैं होऊंगी, तू होएगी, etc.	*Fem.* हम होएंगीं, तुम होगीं, etc.

Imperative.

2nd sing. तू हो. The rest like the Contingent Future.

Respectful Imperative, हूजियो or हूजो, हूजिये or हूजे, हूजियेगा, 'be pleased to be.'

402. We are now prepared to explain the formation of the tenses of the Imperfect and Perfect Participles, as enumerated in Groups I and II. Inasmuch as between each of the six tenses in each group, taken in pairs, there is the closest analogy, we may most conveniently treat the tenses of both participles together. The verb आना, 'to come,' is taken as an illustration. The Participial Tenses.

403. The *Indefinite Imperfect* represents an action simply as *incomplete*, without reference to any particular

18

time, and may thus refer either to the past, present, or future; the *Indefinite Perfect* represents the action as *complete*, but also with no definite reference to time. These agree in grammatical form, as consisting simply of the Participle without any auxiliary; e.g., मैं आता, 'I come,' 'I would come;' मैं आया, 'I came.'

a. The Indefinite Imperfect has no one precise equivalent in English, which might of itself express all its various uses. It is most commonly employed as a contingent, as, e.g., *jo tum sach bolte*, 'were you speaking the truth.'*

404. The second pair consists of the *Present Imperfect* and *Present Perfect.* These both agree in referring the action to the present time; the former represents the action as *unfinished* at the present time; the latter as *finished* at the present time. As thus both referring to the present, they are both formed by adding to the participles, the Present of the auxiliary substantive verb; e.g., मैं आता हूं, 'I come,' or 'am coming;' मैं आया हूं, 'I have come,' or 'am come.'

405. The third pair consists of the *Past Imperfect* and *Past Perfect.* The former represents the action of the verb as *in progress* at some past time; the latter as *completed* at some past time. The agreement in time is represented by the Past tense of the auxiliary substantive verb; e.g., मैं आता था, 'I was coming;' मैं आया था, 'I had come.'

---

* In an earlier form of the language this was an inflected tense. In this form it occurs in the *Rámáyan*, and is heard in some of the rustic dialects of Eastern Hindí; in all which it is used in the sense of a past contingent. Vid. § 124, and Tables of Conjugation, infra; also Beames, *Comp. Gramm.* iii. pp. 131, 132; and Grierson: *Seven Grammars*, passim.

406. The fourth pair consists of the *Contingent Imperfect* and the *Contingent Perfect.* These tenses again differ in that we have, in the former, the action in *progress*; in the latter, the action *completed.* But both alike represent the action merely as a *possibility.* The characteristic auxiliary is the Contingent Future of the substantive verb; e.g., **मैं आता होऊं**, 'I may be coming;' **मैं आया होऊं**, 'I may have come.'

407. The fifth pair embraces the *Presumptive Imperfect* and the *Presumptive Perfect.* These exhibit the same contrast of *incompleteness* and *completion*, and agree in representing the action, under these two phases, as a *probability.* The auxiliary common to both is the Absolute Future of the substantive verb; the Future tense indicating the positive presumption of the occurrence of the action; e.g., **वह आता होगा**, 'he must be coming;' **वह आया होगा**, 'he must have come.'

408. In the sixth Group we have two tenses which I have called the *Past Contingent Imperfect*, and *Past Contingent Perfect.* These are formed by adding to the two participles of the verb, the Indefinite Imperfect of the substantive verb; as, e.g., **जो तुम आते होते**, 'had you been coming;' **कदाचित किसी ने बतलाया न होता**, 'if perchance any one had not pointed (it) out.'

a. Grammarians have found much difficulty in defining the precise scope of these infrequent tenses, or assigning them a name. In truth, the former of the two, especially, is so very rarely met, that it is difficult to gather examples enough to form the basis of a judgment. While by no means confident that the name chosen is the best possible, it is so far expressive of the usage of these tenses that they alone are never found except in conditional clauses implying a contingency in the past. It is indeed true that such conditional clauses are also often and more commonly expressed by the Indefinite tenses, perfect and imperfect; but this is not, by any means, in the Indefinite tenses, as in these, their exclusive function.

b. The last three pairs of tenses have sometimes been arranged by themselves, as 'the six uncommon tenses.' But, apart from the fact, that some of these tenses are by no means 'uncommon,' it is certainly not philosophical thus to set off tenses in a class by themselves, on the sole ground of their comparatively infrequent occurrence. They are accordingly made to take their proper place under the tenses of the participles.

The 'Adverbial Participle.'

409. In addition to the above verbal forms, grammarians have usually enumerated a so-called '*Adverbial* participle,' which is formed by adding the emphatic particle, ही, to the obl. form of the imperfect participle; as, e.g., from जाना, जाते ही, 'immediately upon going.' But as this is not in truth an additional formation from the verb, but merely a special grammatical construction of the Imperfect participle, there seems to be no sufficient reason for giving it a separate place in the paradigm of the verb. The same idiom, indeed, occurs with the perfect participle also; as, e.g., उस के गये ही, 'immediately upon his having gone;' but this is practically obsolete.

Six Participial Tenses of होना.

410. The three tenses of the future of the verb होना, 'to be,' have already been exhibited. We now add six tenses of the participles; the remaining six, with the exception of the Contingent Perfect, are much less frequent.

a. Observe, that in all the compound tenses of the Imperfect participle, and in the Indefinite perfect, this verb has the signification, not of 'being,' but 'becoming.' In the other tenses, it may have either sense, but the compound verb, हो जाना, is to be preferred in the sense of 'becoming.'

Imperfect Participle,	होता,	'becoming.'
Perfect Participle,	हुआ,	'been.'
Conjunctive Participle,	हो, होकर, होके, होकरके,	'having been' or 'having become.'
Noun of Agency,	होनेवाला or होनेहारा,	'that which is to be.'

Indefinite Imperfect.

Singular.		Plural.	
मैं होता,	'I would be,'* etc.	हम होते,	'we would be,' etc.
तू होता,	'thou wouldst be,' etc.	तुम होते,	'you would be,' etc.
वह होता,	'he would be.'	वे होते,	'they would be,' etc.

Present Imperfect.

Singular.		Plural.	
मैं होता हूं,	'I am becoming.'	हम होते हैं,	'we are becoming.'
तू होता है,	'thou art becoming.'	तुम होते हो,	'you are becoming.'
वह होता है,	'he is becoming.'	वे होते हैं,	'they are becoming.'

Past Imperfect.

Singular.		Plural.	
मैं होता था,	'I was becoming.'	हम होते थे,	'we were becoming.'
तू होता था,	'thou wast becoming.'	तुम होते थे,	'you were becoming.'
वह होता था,	'he was becoming.'	वे होते थे,	'they were becoming.'

Indefinite Perfect.

Singular.		Plural.	
मैं हुआ,	'I became.'	हम हुए,	'we became.'
तू हुआ,	'thou becamest.'	तुम हुए,	'you became.'
वह हुआ,	'he became.'	वे हुए,	'they became.'

Present Perfect.

Singular.		Plural.	
मैं हुआ हूं,	'I have been' or 'become.'	हम हुए हैं,	'we have been' or 'become.'
तू हुआ है,	'thou hast been' or 'become.'	तुम हुए हो,	'you have been' or 'become.'
वह हुआ है,	'he has been' or 'become.'	वे हुए हैं,	'they have been' or 'become.'

---

* This is only one of many possible renderings of this tense.

Past Perfect.

Singular.		Plural.	
मैं हुआ था,	'I had been' or 'become.'	हम हुए थे,	'we had been' or 'become.'
तू हुआ था,	'thou hadst been' or 'become.'	तुम हुए थे,	'you had been' or 'become.'
वह हुआ था,	'he had been' or 'become.'	वे हुए थे,	'they had been' or 'become.'

a. Observe, that by changing आ final to ई in the singular, and ए final to ईं in the plural, the above will be transformed into the feminine conjugation. In the compound forms of the verb, however, *Anusvár* in the plural is commonly added to the second member only. Thus we say, हम होती थीं, not होतीं थीं; similarly, हुई हैं, etc. These remarks apply to all verbs whatever.

b. हुआ is commonly Romanized, *húá*, but this is incorrect; in the Nágarí orthography, the first syllable is always short.

411. From what has been said, it will be evident that the conjugation of the Hindí verb, as respects terminations, is perfectly regular. In High Hindí and in all other western dialects,* however, there is a peculiar idiom in the construction of the tenses of the *Perfect Participle* in *Transitive* verbs, which demands especial notice. The following rules should therefore be carefully studied.

412. In the use of all the tenses of the Perfect Participle of Transitive verbs, the case of the *Agent* must be substituted for the nominative of the subject. Two constructions are then admissible, viz.:—

Passive and Impersonal Constructions. (1) That which, in English idiom, is the object of the action, may be put in the nominative case, with which the verb is inflected to agree in gender and number.

---

* With the exception of Naipálí. See § 130.

(2) That which, in English idiom, is the object of the action, may be put in the dative, and the verb, irrespective of the gender or number of either the subject or object, is then put in the masc. sing.

These two may be termed, respectively, the *Passive* and *Impersonal* constructions.

Thus, with the Present Perfect of देखना, 'to see,' we have, instead of the English construction, either, e.g., मैं ने वह गाड़ी देखी, 'I saw that carriage;' or, मैं ने उस लड़की को देखा, 'I saw that girl.' In the former case the real nominative to the verb is गाड़ी, with which therefore the verb agrees in the 3rd fem. sing. In the second, there is no nominative expressed; that which in English is the nominative of the verb, appears here in the dative, and the verb is used impersonally in the 3rd masc. sing.

Rem. 1. The beginner should carefully observe, (1) that this construction is used with *transitive* verbs *only*; and (2) with such verbs, *only* in the tenses of the *perfect* participle. Thus, although we must say, उस ने अपने भाई को मारा, 'he beat his brother,' we must use the *active* construction with the same verb in the tenses of the *imperfect* participle, even when referring to past time. Thus we say, e.g., वह अपने भाई को मारता था, 'he was beating his brother;' not, उस ने मारता था, which would be nonsense.

Rem. 2. It will be observed that there are thus in High Hindí three constructions of that which is in English the subject with its verb. Firstly, there is that which precisely corresponds to the English idiom, which is used throughout with all intransitive verbs, and in transitive verbs in all tenses except those which are formed by the aid of the Perfect Participle. Secondly and thirdly, in these tenses of transitive verbs, we may have either the passive or impersonal constructions as explained above. These three are by Hindoo grammarians respectively called the *kartari, karmaṇi,* and *bhávi prayogas.**

* Naipálí, like all Eastern Hindí, does not use the *kartari* and *bháve prayogas*, but instead has a construction peculiar to itself.

413. It is to be noted that all Hindí perfect participles are in fact corrupted forms of the Sanskrit perfect passive participle, and the idiom under consideration has its origin and explanation in the Sanskrit construction of such participles, according to which, under the above conditions, the passive participle is made to agree in gender and number with that which in English idiom is the object of the verb, and the logical subject is put in the instrumental case. Thus, to illustrate, the English phrase 'he said,' may be rendered in Sanskrit, तेन कथितं, *lit.*, 'by him said,' Hindí, उस ने कहा. Similarly, the Sanskrit तेन मूषिकशावको दृष्टः, 'he saw a young mouse,' becomes in Hindí, उस ने मूसे का बच्चा देखा.

414. The following common verbs, viz., बकना, 'to talk idly,' बोलना, 'to speak,' भूलना, 'to forget,' and लाना, 'to bring,' although transitive in sense, taking an object after them, are exceptions to the above rule, and are never construed with the case of the agent.

a. लड़ना, 'to fight,' takes the passive construction if the object is mentioned; otherwise it is construed as an intransitive verb.

b. With जानना, 'to know,' 'to suppose,' most educated Hindoos use the case of the agent if the object is a single word, but the nominative when the object is a sentence.

c. The perfect tenses of समझना, 'to understand,' are also sometimes construed with the nominative of the subject; but it is considered better to use the case of the agent.

d. The verb, पाना, in Acquisitive Compounds only, always takes the subject in the nominative: as, उस ने उस को पाया, 'he found it;' but, वह जाने पाया, 'he was permitted to go.' So also देना is treated as an intransitive verb in a few Nominal Compounds, in which a verbal noun in आई is the first member; as, वह दिखाई दिया, 'he appeared,' etc.

Accent of Verbal Forms.

415. Observe, that in the pronunciation of all primitive or causal verbs with monosyllabic roots, the accent everywhere remains upon the radical syllable. But in Causal verbs formed

by adding a syllable, as, आ, ला, आल, वा, etc., to the root of the primitive, the accent rests throughout upon this causal affix. In the following examples, the accent is indicated by the italic letters: *kar*úngá, kar*áú*ngá; *kah*tá, kah*lá*tá: *baná*, ban*á*; etc. Many words identical in form, but different in meaning, are thus distinguished only by the accent; thus, *paṛhá*, is 3rd sing., indef. perf., from *paṛhná*, '(he) read;' but paṛh*á*, with the accent on the second syllable, is 2nd sing. imp. from *paṛháná*, 'cause thou (him) to read.' Similarly, *suná*, is 'heard;' but sun*á*, 'tell thou;' etc., etc. In no case, however, must the accent be exaggerated, or an unaccented long syllable shortened.

416. The following tables exhibit the conjugation of three verbs. Table XV illustrates the conjugation of a regular *intransitive* verb, with a *consonant* final in the root; Table XVI that of an *intransitive* verb with a *vowel* final in the root. Table XVII exhibits the conjugation of the *transitive* verb करना, 'to do.' So slight are the differences in the conjugation of pure and mixed verbs, that it has not been thought necessary to give more than one paradigm of a regular verb. On the other hand, as will appear, the slightly irregular verbs, आना and करना, in various combinations, are so very common that it has seemed desirable to exhibit their conjugation in full. Exactly like करना, perf. part., किया, are also conjugated the transitive verbs, देना, 'to give,' perf. part., दिया, and लेना, 'to take,' perf. part., लिया. All regular pure verbs, as, e.g., दिखाना, 'to shew,' perf. part., दिखाया, are conjugated exactly as आना, except that the root of the infinitive is preserved throughout. Conjugational Tables.

TABLE XV: CONJUGATION OF AN INTRANSITIVE VERB, (*Close Root*;) गिरना, 'to fall.'

INFINITIVE OR GERUND,	गिरना, 'to fall,' 'falling;' Gen., गिरने का, 'of falling,' etc.
IMPERFECT PARTICIPLE,	गिरता, 'falling;' Adjective form, गिरता हुआ.
PERFECT PARTICIPLE,	गिरा, 'fallen;' Adjective form, गिरा हुआ.
CONJUNCTIVE PARTICIPLE,	गिर, गिरके, गिरकर, गिरकरके, or गिरकरकर, 'having fallen.'
NOUN OF AGENCY,	गिरनेवाला or गिरनेहारा, 'one who falls,' 'a faller.'

TENSES OF THE FUTURE. (*From the Root.*)

	SINGULAR.			PLURAL.		
CONTINGENT FUTURE, 'I may fall,' etc,	1. मैं गिरूं.	2. तू गिरे.	3. वह गिरे.	1. हम गिरें.	2. तुम गिरो.	3. वे गिरें.
ABSOLUTE FUTURE, 'I shall fall,' etc.	1. मैं गिरूंगा.*	2. तू गिरेगा.	3. वह गिरेगा.	1. हम गिरेंगे.	2. तुम गिरोगे.	3. वे गिरेंगे.
IMPERATIVE, 'let me fall,' etc.	1. मैं गिरूं.	2. तू गिर.	3. वह गिरे.	1. हम गिरें.	2. तुम गिरो.	3. वे गिरें.
DO. RESPECTFUL FORMS, 'be pleased to fall,' etc.		...	...	...	2. तुम गिरियो.	3. आप गिरिये, गिरियेगा.

* For the fem., inflect आ to ई in the sing., and ए to ईं in the plural.

TABLE XV, *Continued*: TENSES OF THE IMPERFECT PARTICIPLE.*

	Singular.	Plural.
INDEF. IMP., 'I would fall,' 'I fall,' etc.	1. मैं गिरता. 2. तू गिरता. 3. वह गिरता.	1. हम गिरते. 2. तुम गिरते. 3. वे गिरते.
PRES. IMP., 'I fall,' 'am falling,' etc.	1. „ गिरता हूं. 2. „ गिरता है. 3. „ गिरता है.	1. „ गिरते हैं. 2. „ गिरते हो. 3. „ गिरते हैं.
PAST IMP., 'I was falling,' etc.	1. „ गिरता था. 2. „ गिरता था. 3. „ गिरता था.	1. „ गिरते थे. 2. „ गिरते थे. 3. „ गिरते थे.
CONT. IMP., 'I may be falling,' etc.	1. „ गिरता होऊं.* 2. „ गिरता हो. 3. „ गिरता हो.	1. „ गिरते हों. 2. „ गिरते होओ. 3. „ गिरते हों.
PRESUM. IMP., 'I must be falling,' etc.	1. „ गिरता हूंगा.* 2. „ गिरता होगा. 3. „ गिरता होगा.	1. „ गिरते होंगे. 2. „ गिरते होगे. 3. „ गिरते होंगे.
PAST CONT. IMP., 'Were I falling,' etc.	1. „ गिरता होता. 2. „ गिरता होता. 3. „ गिरता होता.	1. „ गिरते होते. 2. „ गिरते होते. 3. „ गिरते होते.

* For the forms of the auxiliaries given in these tables, any of the alternative forms given in § 401 may be substituted at pleasure.

Table XV, *Completed*: Tenses of the Perfect Participle.*

	Singular.			Plural.		
Indef. Perf., 'I fall,' etc.	1. मैं गिरा.	2. तू गिरा.	3. वह गिरा.	1. हम गिरे.	2. तुम गिरे.	3. वे गिरे.
Pres. Perf., 'I have fallen,' etc.	1. „ गिरा हूं.	2. „ गिरा है.	3. „ गिरा है.	1. „ गिरे हैं.	2. „ गिरे हो.	3. „ गिरे हैं.
Past Perf., 'I had fallen,' etc.	1. „ गिरा था.	2. „ गिरा था.	3. „ गिरा था.	1. „ गिरे थे,	2. „ गिरे थे.	3. „ गिरे थे.
Cont. Perf., 'I may have fallen,' etc.	1. „ गिरा होऊं.	2. „ गिरा हो.	3. „ गिरा हो.	1. „ गिरे हों.	2. „ गिरे होओ.	3. „ गिरे हों.
Presum. Perf., 'I must have fallen,' etc.	1. „ गिरा हूंगा.	2. „ गिरा होगा.	3. „ गिरा होगा.	1. „ गिरे होंगे.	2. „ गिरे होगे.	3. „ गिरे होंगे.
Past Cont. Perf., 'Had I fallen,' etc.	1. „ गिरा होता.	2. „ गिरा होता.	3. „ गिरा होता.	1. „ गिरे होते.	2. „ गिरे होते.	3. „ गिरे होते.

* For the fem., inflect final आ to ई in the sing., and ए to ई in the plur., both in the participles and auxiliary throughout. But see § 410 *a*.

TABLE XVI: CONJUGATION OF AN INTRANSITIVE VERB, (*Open Root;*) जाना, 'to go.'

INFINITIVE OR GERUND,	जाना, 'to go,' 'going;' Gen., जाने का, 'of going,' etc.
IMPERFECT PARTICIPLE,	जाता, 'going;' Adjective form, जाता हुआ.
PERFECT PARTICIPLE,	गया, 'gone;' Adjective form, गया हुआ.
CONJUNCTIVE PARTICIPLE,	जा, जाकर, जाके, जाकरके or जाकरकर, 'having gone.'
NOUN OF AGENCY,	जानेवाला or जानेहारा, 'one who goes,' 'a goer.'

TENSES OF THE FUTURE. (*From the Root.*)

	SINGULAR.			PLURAL.		
CONT. FUT., 'I may go,' etc.	1. मैं जाऊं.	2. तू {जाए, जावे, / जाय.}	3. वह {जाए, जावे. / जाय.}	1. हम {जाएं, जावें. / जांय.}	2. तुम जाओ.	3. वे {जाएं, जावें. / जांय.}
ABS. FUT., 'I shall go,' etc.	1. " जाऊंगा.*	2. " {जाएगा, जावेगा. / जायगा.}	3. " {जाएगा, जावेगा. / जायगा.}	1. " {जाएंगे, जावेंगे. / जांय.}	2. " जाओगे.	3. " {जाएंगे, जावेंगे. / जांयगे.}
IMPERATIVE, 'let me go,' etc.	1. " जाऊं.	2. " जा.	3. " {जाए, जावे. / जाय.}	1. " {जाएं, जावें. / जांय.}	2. " जाओ.	3. " {जाएं, जावें. / जांय.}
Do. RESP. FORMS, 'be pleased to go,' etc.	...	...	...	...	2. " जाइयो.	3. आप {जाइये. / जाइयेगा.}

* For the fem., inflect आ to ई in the sing., and ए to ईं in the plur., throughout the absolute future.

Table XVI, *Continued*: Tenses of the Imperfect Participle.*

	Singular.			Plural.		
Indep. Imp., 'I would go,' 'I go,' etc.	1. मैं जाता.	2. तू जाता.	3. वह जाता.	1. हम जाते.	2. तुम जाते.	3. वे जाते.
Pres. Imp., 'I go,' 'am going,' etc.	1. „ जाता हूं.	2. „ जाता है.	3. „ जाता है.	1. „ जाते हैं.	2. „ जाते हो.	3. „ जाते हैं.
Past Imp., 'I was going,' etc.	1. „ जाता था.	2. „ जाता था.	3. „ जाता था.	1. „ जाते थे.	2. „ जाते थे.	3. „ जाते थे.
Cont. Imp., 'I may be going,' etc.	1. „ जाता होऊं.	2. „ जाता होय.	3. „ जाता होय.	1. „ जाते होंय,	2. „ जाते होओ.	3. „ जाते होंय.
Presum. Imp., 'I must be going,' etc.	1. „ जाता होऊंगा.	2. „ जाता होयगा.	3. „ जाता होयगा.	1. „ जाते होंयगे.	2. „ जाते होगे.	3. „ जाते होंयगे.
Past Cont. Imp., 'Were I going,' etc.	1. „ जाता होता.	2. „ जाता होता.	3. „ जाता होता.	1. „ जाते होते.	2. „ जाते होते.	3. „ जाते होते.

* Inflect चा final to ई, and ए to ईं, for the feminine throughout these tenses.

TABLE XVI, *Completed*: TENSES OF THE PERFECT PARTICIPLE;* (गया for जाया, *Vid.* § 391).

	SINGULAR.			PLURAL.		
INDEF. PERF., 'I went,' etc.	1. मैं गया.	2. तू गया.	3. वह गया.	1. हम गये.†	2. तुम गये.	3. वे गये.
PRES. PERF., 'I have gone,' etc.	1. ,, गया हूं.	2. ,, गया है.	3. ,, गया है.	1. ,, गये हैं.	2. ,, गये हो.	3. ,, गये हैं.
PAST PERF., 'I had gone,' etc.	1. ,, गया था.	2. ,, गया था.	3. ,, गया था.	1. ,, गये थे.	2. ,, गये थे.	3. ,, गये थे.
CONT. PERF., 'I may have gone,' etc.	1. ,, गया होऊं.	2. ,, गया होय.	3. ,, गया होय.	1. ,, गये होंय.	2. ,, गये होओ.	3. ,, गये होंय.
PRESUM. PERF., 'I must have gone,' etc.	1. ,, गया होऊंगा.	2. ,, गया होयगा.	3. ,, गया होयगा.	1. ,, गये होंयगे.	2. ,, गये होगे.	3. ,, गये होंयगे.
PAST CONT. PERF., 'Had I gone,' etc.	1. ,, गया होता.	2. ,, गया होता.	3, ,, गया होता.	1. ,, गये होते.	2. ,, गये होते.	3. ,, गये होते.

* Inflect everywhere आ final to ई, and ए to ईं, for the feminine. † Also गए, throughout these plurals.

TABLE XVII: CONJUGATION OF THE TRANSITIVE VERB, (*Close Root;*) करना, 'to do.'

INFINITIVE OF GERUND,	करना, 'to do;' Gen., करने का, 'of doing,' etc.
IMPERFECT PARTICIPLE,	करता, 'doing;' Adjective form, करता हुआ.
PERFECT PARTICIPLE,	किया, 'done;' Adjective form, किया हुआ.
CONJUNCTIVE PARTICIPLE,	कर or करके, 'having done.'
NOUN OF AGENCY,	करनेवाला or करनेहारा, 'a doer.'

TENSES OF THE FUTURE. (*From the Root.*)

	SINGULAR.			PLURAL.		
CONTINGENT FUTURE, 'I may do,' etc.	1. मैं करूं.	2. तू करे.	3. वह करे.	1. हम करें.	2. तुम करो.	3. वे करें.
ABSOLUTE FUTURE, 'I shall do,' etc.	1. „ करूंगा.	2. „ करेगा.	3. „ करेगा.	1. „ करेंगे.	2. „ करोगे.	3. „ करेंगे.
IMPERATIVE, 'Let me do,' etc.	1. „ करूं.	2. „ कर.	3. „ करे.	1. „ करें.	2. „ करो.	3. „ करें.
DO. RESPECTFUL FORMS,	...	...	...	...	2. „ {कीजियो. / कीजो.	3. आप {कीजिये. / कीजे.

TABLE XVII, *Continued*: TENSES OF THE IMPERFECT PARTICIPLE.

	Singular.			Plural.		
INDEF. IMP., 'I would do,' 'I do,' etc.	1. मैं करता.	2. तू करता.	3. वह करता.	1. हम करते.	2. तुम करते.	3. वे करते.
PRES. IMP., 'I do,' 'am doing,' etc.	1. „ करता हूं.	2. „ करता है.	3. „ करता है.	1. „ करते हैं.	2. „ करते हो.	3. „ करते हैं.
PAST IMP., 'I was doing,' etc.	1. „ करता था.	2. „ करता था.	3. „ करता था.	1. „ करते थे.	2. „ करते थे.	3. „ करते थे.
CONT. IMP., 'I may be doing,' etc.	1. „ करता होऊं.	2. „ करता होवे.	3. „ करता होवे.	1. „ करते होवें.	2. „ करते होओ.	3. „ करते होवें.
PRESUM. IMP., 'I must be doing,' etc.	1. „ करता होऊंगा.	2. „ करता होवेगा.	3. „ करता होवेगा.	1. „ करते होवेंगे.	2. „ करते होगे.	3. „ करते होवेंगे.
PAST CONT. IMP., 'Were I doing,' etc.	1. „ करता होता.	2. „ करता होता.	3. „ करता होता.	1. „ करते होते.	2. „ करते होते.	3. „ करते होते.

TABLE XVII, *Completed*: TENSES OF THE PERFECT PARTICIPLE; किया (for करा).

		Singular.		Plural.	
INDEF. PERF.,	'I did,' etc.	मैं ने, तू ने, or उस ने	किया.*	हम ने, तुम ने, or उन्हों ने	किया.*
PRES. PERF.,	'I have done,' etc.	"	किया है.*	"	किया है.*
PAST PERF.,	'I had done,' etc.	"	किया था.*	"	किया था.*
CONT. PERF.,	'I may have done,'	"	किया हो.*	"	किया हो.*
PRESUM. PERF.,	'I must have done,' etc.	"	किया होगा.*	"	किया होगा.*
PAST CONT. PERF.,	'Had I done,' etc.	"	किया होता.*	"	किया होता.*

* Inflected throughout to agree with the object in gender and number, when used in the passive construction; in the impersonal construction, the form given is always used unchanged. Vid. sup., § 412.

OF THE PASSIVE VOICE.

417. The *Passive* Voice is much less used in Hindí than in English. Its place is largely taken by neuter verbs. It is to be remembered, however, that the construction of the past tenses of transitive verbs with ने is, in reality, a passive construction. Still in certain cases, which will be duly noticed in the Chapter on Syntax, the Hindí verb admits of a Passive Voice.*

Passive Conjugation.

418. Any verb may be conjugated passively by adding to its Perfect participle the verb जाना, 'to go,' which verb is then conjugated after the manner exhibited in Table XVI. The participle is inflected to agree with the subject; आ final becoming ए, for the masc. plur., and ई, for the fem., sing. or plur.

Thus, from the verb मारना, 'to strike,' we have the passive मारा जाना, 'to be struck;' from देना, 'to give,' pass., दिया जाना, 'to be given;' from दिखाना, 'to show,' pass., दिखाया जाना, 'to be shown.' Other examples are as follows: वह पत्र लिखा गया, 'that letter was written;' कोई स्त्री मारी जाती थी, 'some woman was being beaten;' वे नहीं देखे जाते हैं, 'they are not seen;' i.e., 'they are invisible.'

a. Sometimes even neuter verbs are conjugated passively; as, e.g., from आना, 'to come,' pass., आया जाना. But this idiom is scarcely transferable to English.

N.B. This use of जाना with the perfect participle, as an auxiliary, to form a passive, must not be confounded with its use, as added to a verbal

---

* It is strange that some should have denied the existence of this passive with *jáná*. The illustrations given in the Syntax under this head, taken from classic writers, are sufficient to settle the question. Moreover, during years of constant intercourse with Hindí-speaking natives of India, I have been wont to hear this passive freely used, under the restrictions indicated in the Syntax, in the colloquial of all classes.

root to form an intensive compound. Thus, खाया जाना is 'to be eaten,' but खा जाना is 'to eat up,' etc.

419. As the passive conjugation presents no difficulties, it will be quite sufficient to present a mere synopsis of the more common tenses. We take, as an example, the verb लिखना, 'to write,' perf. part., लिखा.

Synopsis of the Passive Conjugation of लिखना.

Infinitive,	लिखा जाना, 'to be written.'
Conjunctive Participle,	लिखा जाकर, 'having been written.'
Contingent Future, 3rd sing.,	लिखा जाए, 'it may be written.'
Absolute Future, ,, ,,	लिखा जाएगा, 'it will be written.'
Imperative, ,, ,,	लिखा जाए, 'let it be written.'
Indefinite Imperfect, ,, ,,	लिखा जाता, 'it is, or would be, written.'
Present Imperfect, ,, ,,	लिखा जाता है, 'it is being written.'
Past Imperfect, ,, ,,	लिखा जाता था, 'it was being written.'
Indefinite Perfect, ,, ,,	लिखा गया, 'it was written.'
Present Perfect, ,, ,,	लिखा गया है, 'it has been written.'
Past Perfect, ,, ,,	लिखा गया था, 'it had been written.'

a. The remaining tenses are extremely rare; if, indeed, many of them ever occur at all. In general, the student will need to guard against the too free use of any of these passive forms.

Causal Verbs.

420. From every primitive verb in Hindí, may be derived a *Causal* and a *Second Causal* verb. The First Causal expresses *immediate* causation, and the Second Causal, the *mediate* causation, of the act or state of the primitive. Thus, from the primitive बनना, 'to be made,' we have the First Causal, बनाना, 'to make,' and the Second Causal, बनवाना, 'to cause (another person) to make.'

Rem. If the primitive be a neuter verb, it is plain that the 1st Causal will be the corresponding active verb. It is thus evident that the Causal may often be translated into English by a single verb having no etymological connexion with the word which properly translates the primitive. Illustrations will be found below.

421. The rules for the formation of Causal verbs are as follows: Formation of Causal Verbs.

(1) Add to the root of the primitive, आ for the First Causal, and वा for the Second Causal. The usual infinitive termination, ना, added to the root of the primitive thus modified, will give the infinitive of the corresponding Causal. Thus, from जलना, 'to burn,' we have the root जल; whence we derive, as above, the root of the First Causal, जला, and of the Second Causal, जलवा; from which again, we have the causal infinitives, जलाना, 'to set on fire,' and जलवाना, 'to cause to set on fire.' Similar are the following examples:—

Primitive.	*First Causal.*	*Second Causal.*
उठना, 'to rise.'	उठाना, 'to raise.'	उठवाना, 'to cause to raise.'
छिपना, 'to be hidden.'	छिपाना, 'to hide.'	छिपवाना, 'to cause to hide.'
पकना, 'to be ripe,' or 'cooked.'	पकाना, 'to cook.'	पकवाना, 'to cause to cook.'
मिलना, 'to meet.'	मिलाना, 'to cause to meet,' 'to mix.'	मिलवाना, 'to cause to mix.'
सुनना, 'to hear.'	सुनाना, 'to tell.'	सुनवाना, 'to cause to tell.'

a. A short *a* in the second syllable of dissyllabic roots which have a short vowel in the first syllable, takes the obscure sound* in the causal. But before

* Vid. supr., § 14, *d.*

the affix of the second causal, the *a* is fully pronounced. Examples are :—

Primitive.	*First Causal.*	*Second Causal.*
चमकना *chamakná*, 'to shine.'	चमकाना, pron. *cham'káná*.	चमकवाना *chamakwáná*.
पिघलना *pighalná*, 'to melt,' *intr.*	पिघलाना, „ *pigh'láná*.	पिघलवाना *pighalwáná*.
भटकना *bhaṭakná*, 'to wander.'	भटकाना, „ *bhaṭ'káná*.	भटकवाना *bhaṭakwáná*.
पकड़ना *pakaṛná*, 'to seize.'	पकड़ाना, „ *pak'ṛáná*.	पकड़वाना *pakaṛwáná*.
परखना *parakhná*, 'to be tried.'	परखाना, „ *par'kháná*.	परखवाना *parakhwáná*.

Rem. But when the second consonant is म, even this obscure sound often vanishes; as, from समझना, 'to understand,' समझाना, 'to cause to understand,' 'to explain,' pronounced *sam'jháná* or *samjháná*.

b. Monosyllabic roots containing a long vowel, shorten that vowel before the causal and second causal affixes. Open roots then insert ल between the shortened vowel and the causal affixes.

N.B. In the application of this rule, observe that *a* is the short substitute for आ; इ, for ई, ए, ऐ, and occasionally for आ; उ, for ऊ, ओ, and औ, in the primitive.

Under this head, the following are examples of close roots :—

Primitive.	*First Causal.*	*Second Causal.*
घूमना, 'to go around.'	घुमाना, 'to turn around.'	घुमवाना.
जागना, 'to awake.'	जगाना, 'to awaken.'	जगवाना.
जीतना, 'to conquer.'	जिताना, 'to cause to conquer.'	जितवाना.

The following are examples of open roots :—

खाना, 'to eat.'	खिलाना, 'to feed.'	खिलवाना, 'to cause to feed.'
पीना, 'to drink.'	पिलाना, 'to give to drink.'	पिलवाना, 'to cause to give drink.'
सोना, 'to sleep.'	सुलाना, 'to put to sleep.'	सुलवाना, 'to cause to put to sleep.'

a. Verbs of this class with monosyllabic roots enclosing ऐ or औ, commonly retain the long vowel, and form their Causals according to (1); as, e.g.,

पैरना, 'to swim.' पैराना, 'to cause to swim.' *2nd Causal,* पैरवाना.
दौड़ना, 'to run.' दौड़ाना, 'to cause to run.' „ „ दौड़वाना.

b. But बैठना, 'to sit,' makes the First Causal बैठाना or बिठाना, 'to seat.' It also often follows the example of open roots, and admits an ल before the causal affix, making बिठलाना. Similarly कहना, 'to say,' सीखना, 'to learn,' and देखना, 'to see,' make their Causals either कहाना, सिखाना and दिखाना, or कहलाना, सिखलाना and दिखलाना. कहाना and कहलाना are peculiar in having a passive sense, viz., 'to be called,' 'to be named.' जानना, 'to know,' makes the First Causal either जनाना or जतलाना.

c. बताना, 'to show,' 'to point out,' though causal in form, has no primitive in Hindí.

(2) Many primitive neuter verbs having a monosyllabic root enclosing a short vowel, form the First Causal by simply lengthening that vowel. The Second Causal is formed in the usual way. Thus, e.g. :—

कटना,	'to be cut.'	काटना,	'to cut.'	कटवाना,	'to cause to cut.'
बंधना,	'to be fastened.'	बांधना,	'to fasten.'	बंधवाना,	'to cause to fasten.'
लदना,	'to be loaded.'	लादना,	'to load.'	लदवाना,	'to cause to load.'
खिंचना,	'to be pulled.'	खींचना,	'to pull.'	खिंचवाना,	'to cause to pull.'

a. Sometimes in such words, instead of the cognate long vowel, the *guṇ* or *vṛiddhi* of the primitive vowel is the substitute, as in the following :—

खुलना, 'to be open.'	खोलना, 'to open.'	खुलवाना, 'to cause to open.'
घुलना, 'to be dissolved.'	घोलना, 'to dissolve.'	घुलवाना, 'to cause to dissolve.'
खिंचना, 'to be pulled.'	खींचना, 'to pull.'	खिंचवाना, 'to cause to pull.'

b. निकलना, 'to come out,' make its First Causal, निकालना, after the analogy of the above.

c. A few primitive roots ending in ट, change this ट to the cognate ड़ in the Causals. Some of these present other irregularities. The most common are the following:—

छूटना, 'to be separated.'	छोड़ना, 'to leave.'	छुड़ाना,	'to liberate.'
टूटना, 'to break,' *intr.*	तोड़ना, 'to break,' *tr.*	तोड़वाना, तोड़ाना.	'to cause to break.'
फटना, 'to tear,' „	फाड़ना, 'to tear.' „	फड़वाना, फड़ाना,	'to cause to tear.'
फूटना, 'to burst,' „	फोड़ना, 'to burst,' „	फुड़वाना,	'to cause to burst.'

d. बिकना, 'to be sold,' changes the final guttural of the root to the corresponding palatal, in the First Causal only, making बेचना, 'to sell.' रहना, 'to remain,' changes ह to the hard guttural aspirate, ख, making रखना, 'to keep.'

e. Two verbs, viz., डूबना, 'to be immersed;' and भीगना, 'to be wet,' make their First Causals, respectively, डुबोना, and भिगोना.* Sometimes, however, they assume the regular causal affixes.

f. निबड़ना, 'to be ended,' makes the First Causal निबाड़ना or निबेड़ना, 'to finish.' The verb बैठना, mentioned at (1) *b.*, makes yet another form, बैठालना; and, similarly, पैठना, 'to enter,' makes पैठालना. लेना, 'to take,' makes लिवाना.

---

* The *o* in these cases has arisen by a common phonetic process from the archaic form of the causal affix, *âva*, the original also of the common H.H. causal affix, *â*.

422. Of a few verbs, the Neuters have become obsolete in High Hindí, though still in use in some dialects. Thus, the common word, देखना, 'to see,' is the causal of the dialectic K. दीखना, 'to appear.' On the other hand, a few neuters are commonly used in High Hindí, of which the causal forms are rarely heard. A common example is पड़ना, 'to fall,' the causal of which, पाड़ना, is very rare in High Hindí, though under the form पारन it frequently occurs in the *Rámáyan*. Obsolete forms.

423. Many verbs form their Causals both according to Rules (1) and (2). Usually, with such difference in form, there is also a difference in signification, and often one form is dialectic. A good illustration is found in the verb दबना, 'to be pressed,' which makes one causal, दबाना, 'to press down,' and another, दाबना, having the special meaning, 'to shampoo.' So also, from मिलना, 'to meet;' High Hindí makes the causal, मिलाना, 'to mix;' but the Máṛwáṛí, following the second rule, makes the causal, मेलणो, 'to send.' बुलाना, 'to call,' is commonly reckoned a causal from बोलना, 'to speak;' but बोलन is invariably used in the *Rámáyan* instead of बुलाना, in the same sense. Duplicated Causals.

424. We may note in conclusion the existence of a class of Causal Verbs derived from abstract nouns, which denote the causation of that which is expressed by the noun. Thus, from रिस, 'anger,' comes रिसियाना, 'to be angry;' from तेवर, 'vertigo,' तेवराना, 'to be giddy.' Under this head also come a great number of onomatopoetic words; as, e.g., छनछनाना, 'to simmer,' 'to chink,' i.e., 'to make the sound *chhan-chhan*;' चिचमिचाना, 'to twitter as a bird,' etc. Causals derived from Nouns.

Of Compound Verbs.*

425. These have been commonly enumerated as of twelve varieties, viz., Intensives, Potentials, Completives,

* It is important to observe that some of these combinations are only conjugated in certain tenses. See Syntax.

Frequentatives, Desideratives, Continuatives, Staticals, Inceptives, Permissives, Acquisitives, Reiteratives, and Nominals.

a. Although, for convenience of reference, common usage has been followed in the above heading, it should be observed that, properly speaking, none of these are true compounds, but grammatical combinations of a conjunctive participle, a verbal noun, or a substantive, with a verb. Strictly speaking, therefore, the explanation of these forms belongs to Syntax. As, however, all these idioms have usually been explained at this point, and as acquaintance with them will greatly facilitate the understanding of many illustrations used in the Syntax, we give the subject a place in this section.

Classification of Compound Verbs. The above-named combinations may be conveniently distributed into the following classes:—

Class I.

Formed with the Conjunctive Participle.

1. Intensives.
2. Potentials.
3. Completives.

Class II.

Formed with Verbal Nouns in á.

1. Frequentatives.
2. Desideratives.

Class III.

Formed with the Infinitive.

1. Inceptives.
2. Permissives.
3. Acquisitives.

Class IV.

Formed with the Imperfect and Perfect Participles.

1. Continuatives.
2. Progressives.
3. Staticals.
4. Reiteratives.

Class V.

Formed with Substantives and Adjectives.

Nominals.

CLASS I. *Combinations formed with the Conjunctive Participle.*

426. In all these, the Conjunctive participle regularly stands first, and, in High Hindí, always in close verbs, and optionally in open verbs, is used in that form which is identical with the root; as in बना देना, दिखा सकता, etc. But in many pure verbs, especially causals in आ, the form in य is often preferred; as, e.g., बताय देना, दिखाय देना, खिला चुका, etc. In many dialects, this becomes the rule for such verbs.

Rem. Because the conjunctive participle in these combinations, in Urdú and High Hindí, is used in that form which is the same as the root, it has been usual to say these 'compounds' were formed 'with the root.' But that we have not in these cases really the root, but the conjunctive participle, is plain at once from a comparison with other dialects of the Hindí, in which, after a vowel final in the root, य, (as optionally in High Hindí) and after a consonant, इ, is added, thus decisively indicating the true nature of the word. Thus in the Braj we have constantly such forms as, बाँटि देगौं, कहि सकतु, काढ़ि लियौ, etc., and in the *Rámáyan*, तजि जाय, कहि सक, Maith., बोलि सकब, etc.

427. *Intensive* Compounds intensify or otherwise modify the meaning of the verb whose conjunctive participle stands first in the combination. Intensive Compounds.

They are formed by adding to this participle one of certain other verbs, which latter verb in combination with this participle is then conjugated as usual. This second conjugated member does not, however, retain its separate character and significance; but only modifies, in accordance with the general idea which it embodies, the meaning of the participial element of the combination. Hence English idiom will sometimes require us to render the Intensive by a different word from that used for the simple verb; as in some of the following examples:—

फेंकना,	'to throw.'	फेंक देना,	'to throw *away*.'
तोड़ना,	'to break.'	तोड़ डालना,	'to break *to pieces*.'
काटना,	'to cut.'	काट डालना,	'to cut *off*.'
बनना,	'to be made.'	बन आना,	'to be *quite* made, to *succeed*.'
गिरना,	'to fall.'	गिर पड़ना,	'to fall *down*.'
गिराना,	'to cause to fall.'	गिरा देना,	'to throw *down*.'
जानना,	'to know.'	जान पड़ना,	'to be found out,' 'appear.'
खाना,	'to eat.'	खा जाना,	'to eat *up*.'
होना,	'to be.'	हो जाना,	'to become.'
पीना,	'to drink.'	पी लेना,	'to drink *down*.'
रोना,	'to weep.'	रो बैठना,	'to despair.'
करना,	'to do.'	कर दिखाना,	'to realize.'
लेना,	'to take.'	ले लेना,	'to take *away*.'
बैठना,	'to sit.'	बैठ रहना,	'to sit *still*.'
देखना,	'to see.'	देख रहना,	'to look *on*,' 'to gaze.'
बोलना,	'to speak.'	बोल उठना,	'to speak *up*.'
चढ़ना,	'to ascend.'	चढ़ बैठना,	'to attack.'
सौंपना,	'to deliver.'	सौंप रखना,	'to entrust.'

Usage of Intensives.

428. The above list comprises about all the verbs which are combined with the conjunctive participles of other verbs to form Intensive Compounds. It is evident that, in most cases, the modification of the meaning of the verb may be expressed in English by a preposition adverbially used with the verb. It may be difficult to find a term which shall exactly express the idea added by the secondary verb in every case, but the following is an approximation.

बैठना, Permanence.	डालना, Violence.
देना, Intensity.	पड़ना, Chance.
आना, Reflexion.	लेना, Reflexion, appropriation.
जाना, Finality, completeness.	रहना, Continuance.
उठना, Suddenness.	

a. Of the above eight verbs, it may be further observed that देना, (except in the compound, चल देना, 'to go away,') and डालना, can only be used with Transitive verbs; आना and उठना, with Intransitives only; the remainder with either Transitives or Intransitives. Such combinations as कर आना, देख आना, etc., can hardly be reckoned proper Intensives; since each of the two words maintains its distinctive significance: as, देख आना, न्हाय आना, lit., 'having seen, to come,' 'having bathed, to come.'

b. It may be also noted that देना is the compound which is most frequently used with Causal Verbs: as, बता देना, 'to show;' समझा देना, 'to explain;' निकाल देना, 'to take out.' But with a few Causals it cannot be used; thus, from बुलाना, 'to call,' we never have बुला देना, but always बुला लेना, 'to call here,' i.e., 'to one's self.'

c. जाना is the verb which is most commonly found combined with Intransitives: as, टूट जाना, 'to be broken;' मिल जाना, 'to meet,' 'to unite;' पहुँच जाना, 'to arrive;' but it is also used with Transitives: as, खा जाना, 'to eat up;' कह जाना, 'to tell.'

d. Occasionally, आना takes the place of जाना in Intensives, when the action of the verb is regarded as directed toward, instead of away from, the speaker: as, कंधे झुक आये हैं, '(thy) shoulders have become stooping;' आज यह चोर यम के घर से बच आया, 'to-day this thief has come back safe from the house of Yama (the God of death).'

e. Compounds with रहना are common, but for the most part are used in the tenses of the perfect participle. As above remarked, these compounds exhibit the action of the verb, emphatically, as continuing or permanent. Thus, बैठ रहो, 'sit still;' दोनों लड़के खेलते थे, 'the two children were playing;' but, दोनों लड़के खेल रहे थे, 'the two children were engaged in play;' वह सुनता है, 'he hears,' 'is hearing;' वह सुन रहा है, 'he is occupied in hearing,' etc.

Rem. It has been questioned by good authority whether these combinations with रहना should be classified under these Intensive forms. The Pandits certainly regard the present and past perfect forms of this combination as distinct tenses, respectively called *tatkálik varttamán, kál*, 'the present tense of that time,' and *tatkálik apúrna bhút kál*, 'the imperfect past tense of that time.'

f. लेना when thus combined with a conjunctive participle, represents the action of the verb as terminating with, upon, near, or to the advantage of the agent. In many cases, therefore, this compound is equivalent to the Middle Voice in Greek. Thus, बुलाना, is 'to call,' in general; but बुला लेना, is 'to call one's self;' रखना, 'to place;' रख लेना, 'to lay by;' i.e., for one's self. Thus in the *Shakuntalá*, *Dushyant* says, उसको अब मैं अपने मन की कल्पना से पूरा कर लेता हूं, 'when by my imaginative power I complete it for myself.' लेना, in compounds, thus stands in absolute contrast with देना, emphasizing the action as terminating upon, or to the advantage of one's self; while देना represents it emphatically as terminating upon or to the advantage of another. Compare, e.g., समझ लेना, 'to understand,' i.e., for one's self; and समझा देना, 'to cause another to understand.' आना approaches to a reflexive sense, but is of much less extensive application than लेना.

g. पड़ना, although used with both transitive and intransitive verbs, cannot be combined with causals. The idea of 'causation' necessarily excludes that of 'chance.' Thus while we can say, देख पड़ा, 'it appeared,' we cannot say दिखा पड़ा.

h. In many cases, the same conjunctive participle may be combined with different secondary verbs. A few such examples will further elucidate this matter. Thus, from खाना, 'to eat,' we have खा जाना, 'to eat up;' खा लेना, 'to eat down;' खा रहना, 'to be engaged in eating.' Similarly from मारना, 'to strike,' we have both मार देना, 'to beat,' and मार डालना, 'to strike down,' 'to kill.'

429. While the modification of the first verb by the secondary member may often be expressed in English either by the addition of certain particles, or by the use of another verb from that employed to represent the simple Hindí verb, in many cases, again, it will be found quite impossible to indicate in English the slight distinction between the simple verb and the combination. Indeed, it is to be remarked, that combinations in which देना is the last member, even in Hindí, are often scarcely to be distinguished in meaning from the simple verb. Thus, such forms as समझाना and समझा देना, दिखाना and दिखा देना, etc., are often used interchangeably, with no apparent intention of greater emphasis in the one case than in the other. But where a distinction is intended, it is undoubtedly that indicated above. The compound form is much more common colloquially.

430. Frequently, both in prose and in the colloquial, a particle, especially a negative, is interposed between the conjunctive participle and the secondary verb; thus, कुछ देख नहीं पड़ता है, 'nothing appears;' टूट तो गया, '(it) is indeed broken.' Sometimes several words are thus interposed, as in the following from the *Shakuntalá*; हो तो एसा ही गया हूं, 'exactly such have I indeed become.' The words interposed are thus made more emphatic. Also, rarely, in the colloquial, the participle is made to follow the secondary verb; thus, वह गया है भाग, 'he has fled away.' This inversion is never found in dignified prose, but like the previous idiom, is not unusual in poetry.*

431. The learner must not confound with these Intensive Compounds other combinations with the conjunctive participle in the same form, in which the final verb retains its individuality and separate signification. Examples of this idiom are: उस गांव को देख आओ, lit., 'having seen that village, come;' मैं माली के घर हो आया हूं, lit., 'having been at the gardener's house, I have come;' i.e., 'I have come from the gardener's house.'

* For other examples, see the section on *Dialectic Conjugation*.

a. ले आना may be explained either on this principle, as 'having taken, come,' or as if a compound, 'to bring.' Similar are, कह सुनाना, 'to announce,' आ मिलना, 'to come and meet,' etc., etc.

432. A number of combinations occur in which चढ़, the conj. part. of चढ़ना, 'to ascend,' is the first member, and a verb of motion, the second. But in these the leading idea is in the second member, to which चढ़ adds the idea of 'hostility.' Examples are, चढ़ धाना, 'to run up hostilely;' चढ़ आना, 'to attack;' चढ़ बैठना, 'to attack' (where बैठना seems to give the idea of *irresistible* attack); चढ़ दौड़ना, 'to rush up hostilely.' Thus, e.g., वह सब कटक ले चढ़ धाया, 'he hastened up with all (his) army;' एक और भी काशी राजा चढ़ दौड़ा, 'one more also, the king of *Káshí*, made an assault.'

Potential Compound Verbs.

433. *Potentials* are formed by adding to the conjunctive participle of any verb, the verb सकना, 'to be able,' which may then be conjugated throughout. This combination denotes *ability* to do the action expressed by the primary member. It thus often takes the place of the potential mood in English.

The following are examples:—बोल सकना, 'to be able to speak;' वह दौड़ सकता है, 'he can run;' मैं जा सकूंगा, 'I shall be able to go;' वे आ सकें, 'they may be able to come.'

a. Sometimes the verb सकना takes the verb which it modifies in the oblique form of the infinitive, instead of the conjunctive participle, thus; मैं नहीं आने सकता हूं, 'I am not able to go.' But this, although often heard, is regarded as less elegant, and about Mathura is called incorrect.

Completive Compound Verbs.

434. *Completives* are formed by adding to a conjunctive participle, the verb चुकना, which may then be conjugated in all its parts. The imperfect participle, चुकता, is rare. This combination denotes the *completion* of the act denoted by the primary member of the compound. It is never identical in sense with the perfect participle, but denotes the completeness of the action in a more emphatic manner. Thus, e.g., उस ने खाया, 'he ate,' but, वह खा चुका, 'he has done eating.'

a. Very often the force of चुकना will be expressed in English by the word 'already;' as, वह तो आ चुका है, 'he is indeed already gone.' When in the absolute future, this combination often nearly corresponds to the English future perfect; as, जब वह खा चुकेगा 'when he shall have eaten,' or, 'shall have done eating.'

CLASS II. *Combinations formed with Verbal Nouns.**

435. *Frequentatives* are formed by combining with the verbal noun in आ, the verb करना, which may then be used in any tense. These denote the *habitual* or *repeated* performance of the action expressed by the first Frequentative Compounds.

* It has been customary to speak of compounds of this class as formed with the perfect participle. This, however, is not accurate. What we have in these combinations is not a perfect participle, but a gerund or verbal noun in *á*, equivalent to the common Hindí gerund or infinitive in *ná*. The coincidence in form with the perf. part. masc. is purely accidental. This form of the gerund, restricted in High Hindí to this combination, occurs in Bangálí, where we have, as three equivalent and alternative forms, e g., *chalan*, = H.H., *chalná*; *chalibá* = Braj, *chalivau*; and *chalá*. This same gerund in its inflected form in *ai* is constantly used in E. Hindí in these compounds: as, e.g., E. H. *chalai laga* = H. H. *chalne lagá*; *sunai chaha* = H. H. *suná cháhá*. There is no reason, therefore, to doubt that such forms as *chalá* and *chalai* in these combinations are true gerunds or verbal nouns, exactly equivalent, respectively, to *chalná* and *chalne*, which latter *n* forms are indeed sometimes substituted in them for the more usual form in *á*. This view, first suggested in the 1st ed. of this Grammar, has been abundantly confirmed by the writer's more recent studies. It has since been maintained and supported by many apposite illustrations from the cognate languages, by Hoernle: *Comp. Gramm.* pp. 388, 326, 147.

member of the compound: thus, पढ़ा करना, 'to read often;' आया करो, 'come often;' वह कहा करता है, 'he is in the habit of saying.'

a. Thus, whenever in an English phrase, the adverb 'always' denotes, not duration, but repeated or customary action, it must be expressed in Hindí by using the verb which it qualifies, in the frequentative form. For example, the phrase, 'he always bathes in the morning,' must be rendered in Hindí, वह तड़के स्नान किया करता है. But, on the contrary, 'we shall be always happy,' is in Hindí, हम सदा आनन्द में रहेंगे. Other examples are: मैं शास्त्र को पढ़ा करता हूं, 'I am in the habit of reading the *Shástra*;' तुम मेरी बातें माना करो, 'always obey my words;' तुम क्यों ऐसा किया करते हो, 'why do you always do so?' The idiom may be illustrated by such English expressions as 'he does washing,' 'he does much talking,' etc.

Desiderative Compounds.

436. *Desideratives* are formed, like Frequentatives, with a verbal noun in आ, combined with the verb चाहना as the second and conjugated member. These denote, primarily, *desire* to do the action expressed by the participial member; secondarily, the *immediate futurition* of that action. It can only be known from the context which of these may be intended in any particular case, but there is not often ambiguity. Thus, वह बोला चाहता है, 'he wishes to speak,' or 'is about to speak;' घड़ी बजा चाहती थी, 'the clock was about to strike.'

a. Frequently the first verb is put in the inflected infinitive, as, वह जाने चाहता है, 'he wishes to go.' The *uninflected* infinitive is also, rarely, used in this combination, even with the perfect tenses of चाहना, though this has been denied. But this form occurs in the *Shakuntalá*: as, मैं ने तपस्वी की कन्या को चलने से रोकना चाहा, 'I wished to hinder the hermit's daughter from going (away).'

Rem. In these cases the infinitive is to be regarded as a verbal noun under the regimen of चाहना, and, like the analogous combinations under Class III., they cannot with strict accuracy be called Compounds.

437. The Desiderative compound, in the respectful form with चाहिये, is idiomatically used to express *obligation* or *duty*: as, इस पुस्तक को पढ़ा चाहिये, '(one) ought to read this book;' or, with a noun or pronoun expressed, तुम्हें वहां जाया चाहिये, 'you ought to go there.' The construction of this idiom will be explained in the Syntax. In this combination, the direct form of the infinitive is very commonly substituted for the verbal form in आ. Thus we may say, वहां जाना चाहिये, '(one) ought to go there.'

Class III. *Combinations formed with the Inflected Infinitive.*

438. *Inceptives* consist of an inflected infinitive in construction with the verb लगना, and denote, primarily, the action of the infinitive as *beginning*. They are also used when that action is interrupted. In this way is to be explained the common use of the phrase, कहने लगा, lit., 'he began to say,' in the narration of conversation. Examples of these combinations are abundant: as, मारने लगना, 'to begin to beat;' खाने लगा, 'he began to eat,' etc., etc. This use of लगना is almost, if not wholly, confined to the tenses of the perfect participle. Inceptive Compounds.

439. *Permissives* are formed by combining with an inflected infinitive, the verb देना, 'to give,' and express *permission* to do the act denoted by the infinitive. Thus, मुझे जाने दो, is 'let me go;' मुझे बोलने दीजिये, 'have the goodness to allow me to speak;' उस ने उस को खाने दिया, 'he allowed him to eat.' Permissive Compounds.

Acquisitive Compounds.

440. *Acquisitives* are the exact converse of the preceding, and are formed in the same way, substituting पाना for देना. Thus, तुम वहां जाने नहीं पाओगे, 'you will not obtain permission to go there;' मैं बैठने नहीं पाया, 'I was not allowed to sit.' It is to be observed that in this idiom, with पाया, as also in the frequentative combination with किया, the case of the agent is never used.

441. In all these combinations of infinitives or verbal nouns, the latter element is to be regarded as governed by the verb, in the same way that a noun would be in the same place. Thus, not only the verbs लगना, देना and पाना, but other verbs may be combined with infinitives in a similar way: as, e.g., in such expressions as जाने मांगना, 'to ask leave to go;' देने चाहना, 'to wish to give;' मैं नहीं जाने सकता हूं, for मैं नहीं जा सकता हूं, 'I cannot go,' etc. The use of the inflected infinitive in the last two cases, however, although heard in the colloquial in many places, is not regarded as elegant.

CLASS IV. *Combinations formed with the Imperfect and Perfect Participles.*

Continuative Compounds.

442. Of these combinations, those have been called *Continuatives* in which the imperfect participle of any verb is connected with the verb रहना, 'to remain.' The participle, which is really a predicative adjunct of the subject, agrees with it in gender and number. This combination denotes the continuance of an incomplete action: as, वह गाती रहती है, 'she continues singing;' तुम क्यों हंसते रहते हो, 'why do you keep laughing?'; नदी की धार बहती रहती है, 'the stream of the river keeps flowing on.'

Rem. 1. जाता रहना very commonly means 'to die;' thus, मेरा पिता जाता रहा है, would be, in English idiom, 'my father has passed away.' It is also used of things: as, सब कुछ जाता रहा, 'every thing is gone.'

Rem. 2. It will be instructive to compare these forms with others closely similar. Thus, वह पढ़ता है is simply, 'he is reading;' वह पढ़ रहा है is, 'he is engaged in reading;' वह पढ़ता रहता है is, 'he continues reading.' बहता जाना is, 'to flow *away*,' from the speaker; बहता रहना is, 'to flow *on*,' continually, as it were, *before* the speaker.'

443. Although combinations with जाना and रहना have always been grouped together as *Continuatives*, they cannot be interchangeably used, and should be separately classified. The combinations with जाना may be more accurately termed *Progressives*. The action of the participle is thus exhibited as steadily progressing or advancing. Thus we may say: वह लिखता जाता है, 'he is going on writing;' वे लड़कियां पढ़ती जाती थीं, 'those girls were going on reading;' पानी बहता जाता है, 'the water keeps flowing away.' Progressive Compounds.

444. Closely analogous to the above, is a common combination in which the perfect participle, instead of the imperfect, takes the first place, and a verb of motion the second place: as, भागा जाना, 'to flee away;' चला जाना, 'to go along;' चला आना, 'to come along,' etc. As in the case of the above combinations of the imperfect participle, the perfect participle agrees with the subject of the verb in gender and number; as, लौंडी चली जाती थी, 'the girl was going along.'

a. Sometimes in these combinations the perfect participle apparently takes the obl. sing. inflection, as in the Statical Compounds mentioned below. Thus, we have, कहे जा, 'say on.' But the form is probably emphatic, contracted as above, e.g., from कहहि जा.

Rem. It is perhaps impossible in all cases to give in English idiom the force of this combination. But it will be found to lie in the distinctive idea of the perfect participle; i.e., the subject is represented as having *completely* come into a certain state, in which state it is then represented as remaining or moving. Thus, in the phrase एक बाघ पड़ा फिरता था, the compound, (from पड़ना, 'to fall,' and फिरना, 'to move around,') represents the lion as first '*crouched*,' and then in this state moving around; hence we render, 'a lion was prowling about.' Hence these may be termed *Perfect Progressives*, and those with the imperfect participle, *Imperfect Progressives*.

Statical Compounds.

445. The verbal combinations which are called *Staticals* denote motion while in the act or state of doing any thing. They are formed by combining a verb of motion with an imperfect participle in the inflected masc. sing. The participle suffers no change for gender and number. Thus, वह रोते हुए आता है, 'he comes weeping;' एक स्त्री गाते आती थी, 'a woman was coming singing.'

Reiteratives.

446. The so-called *Reiteratives* scarcely need a special mention. In these, two verbs of the same or similar meaning, and often similar in sound, are conjugated together in the tenses of the participles, and in the conjunctive participle; as, e.g., बिन समझाए बुझाए, 'without having explained;' सब छोड़ छाड़, 'having left everything;' देख भाल कर,* 'having seen,' etc. The latter word adds little or nothing to the former; but, in accordance with the taste of the Hindoos for rhyme in sense or sound, is added simply to please the ear.

447. With regard to all the above Compound Verbs, as well as these other various combinations, it is to be remarked, that when several roots, infinitives, or participles, thus succeed one another in the same construction, the finite verb is written only with the last. Thus, जब वे सब कुछ खा पी गए, 'when they had eaten and drank everything up;' मैं न पढ़ न लिख सकता हूं, 'I am able neither to read nor to write;' वह आया जाया करता था, 'he was in the habit of coming and going;' वे गा पढ़ चुके हैं, 'they have done singing and reading;'

* भालना, so far as I know, is only used in this combination with देखना.

मैं पढ़ा और लिखा भी चाहता हूं, 'I wish both to read and to write;' वह नाचता गाता चला जाता था, 'he was going along, dancing and singing;' वह मुझे आने जाने देगा, 'he will allow me to come and go.'

Class V. *Combinations formed with Substantives or Adjectives.*

448. Sometimes a substantive or adjective is so combined with a verb as to form, conjointly with it, but one conception. Such combinations as these have been called *Nominal Compounds*. Of these, the largest part are formed with the verbs, करना, 'to do,' or 'to make,' and होना, 'to be;' but several other verbs are also employed in the same way. These may often be rendered into English by a single word: as, e.g., खड़ा होना, 'to stand' (intr.); खड़ा करना, 'to stand' (trans.); प्राप्त करना, 'to obtain;' समाप्त होना, 'to be completed;' मोल लेना, 'to buy,' etc., etc. Nominal Compounds.

a. In many cases, a passive sense is given to these Nominal verbs by substituting for करना, in the compound, the verb होना, 'to be.' Thus, as above, 'to obtain,' is, in Hindí, प्राप्त करना, but, 'to be obtained,' is प्राप्त होना. Other examples will be noted in the study of the following lists.

Rem. Very commonly, when it is intended to express especial respect, or when, as in poetry, an elevated diction is desired, a Nominal verb, formed by the combination of a Sanskrit noun or participle with होना, करना, or some other Hindí verb, is preferred to the corresponding simple verb. In such cases, the slight modification of the meaning may often be well expressed by the use in English of different words. Examples are: दर्शन करना, 'to behold,' for देखना, 'to see;' भोजन करना, for खाना, 'to eat;' गमन or गवन करना, 'to go,' for जाना; प्रस्थान करना, or प्रस्थित होना, 'to depart,' for the more colloquial चला जाना, 'to go away;' etc., etc. This matter is deserving of special attention by the student both in Hindí conversation and composition.

449. These Nominal Compounds present peculiarities of construction which it is impossible to classify under any general rule; so that, as the best aid to the student, we give the following lists of the most frequent combinations. It will be observed, on inspection of these, that not infrequently the compound takes a different meaning, according as it is used in regimen with one or another case.

Combinations with करना.*

450. The following are preceded by a noun with को:—

अंगीकार क॰, 'to agree to.'
आच्छादन क॰, 'to cover.'
आलिंगन क॰, 'to embrace.'
आहार क॰, 'to eat, consume.'
उद्धार क॰,† 'to save.'
उपदेश क॰, 'to instruct.'
गुण क॰, 'to benefit.'
ग्रहण क॰, 'to accept.'
चिन्तन क॰, 'to contemplate.'
छेदन क॰, 'to cut.'
ताड़न क॰, 'to punish.'
त्यागन क॰, 'to forsake.'
पालन क॰, 'to protect.'
पीछे क॰, 'to cast behind.'
प्रणाम क॰, 'to do obeisance to.'
प्रबोध क॰, 'to instruct.'
बस क॰, 'to be done with, stop.'
विदा क॰, 'to dismiss.'
भंग क॰, 'to break,' 'to violate.'
भला क॰, 'to do good to.'
भर्त्ता क॰, 'to support.'
भोग क॰, 'to enjoy.'
भोजन क॰, 'to eat.'
मर्दन क॰,‡ 'to rub.'

---

* The words in this and the following lists have been furnished me by Paṇḍit Lakshmí Naráyaṇ, of Allahabad, with the exception of a few which I have myself added, in part from the full lists in Pincott's *Hindí Manual*. In particular I have added a few Urdú words, because, while purists may deny that they are Hindí, Hindoos everywhere use them. A very few differences regarding the construction of certain words will be found, on comparison with Mr. Pincott's lists. I have followed my Paṇḍit's authority, but the differences indicate variant usage.

† In a religious sense: when referring to deliverance in general, the person saved is put in the gen. So my Paṇḍit.

‡ Preceded by an acc. with को of direct object, and an abl. of that with which the rubbing is done. Or, when the direct object is omitted, then a gen. with का may precede. Thus, *us ne tel se deh ko mardan kiyá*, 'he rubbed his body with oil;' or *us ne tel ká mardan kiyá*, 'he applied oil.'

दहन क०, 'to consume.'
नष्ट क०, 'to destroy.'
निवारण क०, 'to prevent.'
परिपालन क०, 'to protect.'
पसंद क०, 'to approve.'

मोह क०, 'to infatuate.'
वध क०, 'to kill.'
वश क०, 'to subdue.'
शासन क०, 'to chastise.'
सहन क०, 'to tolerate.'

451. The following are commonly preceded by a noun in the genitive, in regimen with the substantive member of the compound:—

अधीनताई क०, 'to be humble.'
अध्ययन क०, 'to peruse.'
अनादर क०, 'to show disrespect to.'
अनुमान क०, 'to infer.'
अनुष्ठान क०, 'to observe.'
अपकीर्ति क०, 'to defame.'
अपमान क०, 'to treat with contempt.'
अपेक्षा क०, 'to wait for.'
अभ्यास क०, 'to study,' 'to practise.'
अभिमान क०, 'to be proud, haughty.'
अवलंबन क०, 'to rely upon.'
आचरण क०, 'to behave.'
आग्रह क०, 'to favour.'
आतिथ्य क०, 'to show hospitality to.'
आदर क०, 'to treat with respect.'
आरंभ क०, 'to begin.'
आशंका क०, 'to suspect.'
आश्रय क०, 'to depend upon.'

इच्छा क०, 'to desire;' (neut.), 'to be ambitious.'
उद्धार क०, 'to remove.'
उपकार क०, 'to aid.'
उपार्जन क०, 'to acquire.'
खेद क०, 'to pain.'
चिंता क०, 'to be anxious about.'
चेष्टा क०, 'to strive after.'
चौकसी क०, 'to watch,' 'guard.'
तारण क०, 'to save' (*sens. relig.*).
दाह क०, 'to burn.'
दोहाई क०, 'to make complaint.'
धन्यवाद क०, 'to thank,' 'bless.'
ध्यान क०, 'to give thought to.'
निग्रह क०, 'to restrain.'
निंदा क०, 'to revile.'
न्याय क०, 'to decide,' 'judge.'
परीक्षा क०, 'to test,' 'try.'
पीछा क०, 'to pursue.'
पूजन क०, 'to worship (the gods and idols only).'
पूजा का०, 'to worship (idols).'
प्रकाश क०, 'to reveal.'

प्रतिपाल क॰, 'to cherish,' 'to provide for.'
प्रतिष्ठा क॰, 'to dedicate.'
प्रतीक्षा क॰, 'to await.'
प्रतीति क॰, 'to confide in,' 'rely upon.'
प्रदक्षिण क॰,* 'to pass round (to the right).'
प्रमाण क॰, 'to assent to.'
प्रशंसा क॰, 'to extol.'
प्रार्थना क॰, 'to pray.'
बखान क॰, 'to describe.'
बड़ाई क॰, 'to magnify.'
बाधा क॰, 'to distress.'
बिगाड़ क॰, 'to injure,' 'spoil.'
बिनती क॰,† 'to supplicate,' 'entrust.'
भला क॰, 'to do good to.'
रक्षण क॰, 'to take care of.'
रखवाली क॰, 'to protect.'
लालन क॰, 'to caress.'
लोभ क॰, 'to covet.'
वध क॰, 'to kill.'
विचार क॰, 'to consider,' 'reflect.'
विवरण क॰, 'to describe.'
विश्वास क॰, 'to trust,' 'believe in.'
विस्तार क॰, 'to develop.'
व्योपार क॰, 'to trade in.'
शिक्षा क॰, to teach.'
शिष्टाचार क॰, 'to treat with honour.'
शोक क॰, 'to grieve.'
शोधन क॰, 'to justify,' 'clear.'
संचय क॰, 'to collect,' 'gather.'
संपादन क॰, 'to acquire.'
सम्मान क॰, 'to honour.'
संयम क॰, 'to hold in restraint.'
सत्कार क॰, 'to treat respectfully.'
सलाह क॰, 'to take counsel.'
साम्हना क॰, 'to oppose.'
सुध क॰, 'to call to mind.'
सेवन क॰, 'to serve,' 'worship.'
सेवा क॰, 'to serve,' 'worship.'
स्तुति क॰, 'to praise.'
स्थापन क॰, 'to establish.'
स्वीकार क॰, 'to confess.'
हत्या क॰, 'to kill.'
हानि क॰, 'to injure.'

452. The following are preceded by a noun either with का (की) or को:—

---

* Used of a certain religious ceremony.

† Requires gen. of person with की; as, *maiṉ terí bintí kartá hún*, 'I entreat thee;' that which is asked then follows in an objective clause.

उपदेश क०, 'to instruct.'
घात क०, 'to waylay,' 'kill.'
त्याग क०, 'to leave,' 'forsake.'
निश्चय क०, 'to ascertain.'
निवारण क०, 'to prevent.'
परित्याग क०, 'to abandon.'
प्रतिपादन क०, 'to enunciate.'
वर्जन क०, 'to avoid.'
वर्णन क०, 'to describe.'
स्पर्श क०, 'to touch.'

453. The following are preceded by a noun either with का (की) or से:—

भेद क०, 'to distinguish.'
ठट्ठा क०, 'to deride.'
पूछ पाछ क०, 'to investigate.'
पूछी गछी क०, 'to investigate.'

454. The following are preceded by a noun either with का (की) or पर:—

अचभा क०, 'to wonder at.'
हठ क०, 'to insist upon.'

455. The following are preceded by a noun in the ablative with से:—

आचरण क०, 'to act towards.'
आनंद क०, 'to enjoy.'
क्षमा क०, 'to forbear.'
गुजारा क०, 'to subsist on.'
द्रोह क०, 'to be hostile to.'
प्रश्न क०, 'to inquire.'
प्रार्थना क०, 'to pray.'
प्रीति क०, 'to display affection.'
बैर क०, 'to be at enmity with.'
भय क०, 'to be afraid of.'
भलाई क०, 'to exercise kindness towards.'
मित्रता क०, 'to form friendship with.'
मेल क०, 'to become intimate with.'
संगम क०, 'to join with.'

456. The following are preceded by a noun either with से or पर:—

वाद क०, 'to discuss,' 'dispute.'
अनीति क०, 'to do injustice to.'

457. The following are preceded by a noun with पर or ऊपर:—

अनुग्रह क०, 'to show grace to.'
अन्याय क०, 'to oppress.'
असर क०, 'to take effect on.'
कृपणता क०, 'to deal niggardly with.'
कृपा क०, 'to show favour to.'

कोप क०, 'to be angry with.'
क्रोध क०, 'to be angry with.'
क्षमा क०, 'to pardon.'
घमंड क०, 'to be proud of.'
दया क०, 'to show mercy to.'
पछतावा क०, 'to regret.'
भरोसा क०, 'to trust in.'
विस्मय क०, 'to be dismayed at.'

458. The following are preceded by a noun in the genitive with साथ or संग:—

कपट क०, 'to deal deceitfully with.'
ठट्ठा क०, 'to make sport of.'
गमन क०, 'to have sexual intercourse with.'
दातव्यता क०, 'to deal generously by.'
प्रीति क०, 'to make friends with.'
भलाई क०, 'to be beneficent to.'
मेल क०, 'to be intimate with.'
समागम क०, 'to associate with.'

459. The following are preceded by a noun with में:—

प्रवृत्ति क०, 'to engage in.'
प्रवेश क०, 'to enter.'
रति क०, 'to be attached to.'
संदेह क०, 'to doubt.'

460. The following are preceded by a noun in the genitive with ओर. Note that ओर, as feminine, requires the genitive in की.

ध्यान क०, 'to give thought to.'
दृष्टि क०, 'to look towards.'
पीठ क०, 'to turn the back to.'
मुख क०, 'to face.'

Combinations with खाना.

461. In these the passive construction, § 412, (1), is employed with the tenses of the perfect participle; so that the verb in these tenses is inflected to agree with the noun of the combination.

कोड़ी ख०, 'to be whipped.'
गम * ख०, 'to be patient.'†
घाम ‡ ख०, 'to bask.'
घूस ‡ ख०, 'to take a bribe.'
टक्कर ‡ ख०, 'to stumble.'
डाह ‡ ख०, 'to be jealous.'
धोखा * ख०, 'to be deceived.'
भय * ख०, 'to be afraid.'

* Masc. † Lit., 'to eat (one's) sorrow.' ‡ Fem.

मार * खा॰, 'to be beaten.'

मूर्छा † खा॰, 'to faint away.'

सौंह † खा॰, 'to take an oath;' with gen., 'to swear by.'

हवा † खा॰, 'to take the air.'

a. Many of the above combinations with खाना. may be converted into Causals by substituting for खाना, its Causal, खिलाना. Thus we have, e.g., मार खिलाना, 'to cause (one) to be beaten;' धोखा खिलाना, 'to deceive,' etc.

Combinations with देना.

462. These all take the passive construction, like the combinations with खाना.

उधार द॰, 'to lend.'

कष्ट द॰, 'to afflict.'

क्लेश द॰, 'to trouble.'

दोहाई‡ द॰, 'to make appeal.'

माथा द॰, § 'to devote one's self to.'

463. Many of the above can scarcely be called Compounds. The combinations with देना, however, in the following list, more closely approach this character. They are all peculiar in that the verbal element is construed as intransitive, and therefore in the tenses of the perfect always takes the *direct*, instead of the *passive* or *impersonal* construction. Thus we say, not उस ने दिखाई दी, but वह दिखाई दिया, 'he appeared;' वह सुनाई दिया, 'it was heard,' etc.

कुलाई देना, 'to be felt.'

दिखाई देना, 'to appear,' 'seem.'

पकड़ाई देना, 'to be seized.'

बंधाई देना, 'to be bound.'

सुनाई देना, 'to be heard.'

Combinations with मारना.

464. The verb in all these may take the passive construction, and is thus determined in form by the noun of the combination.

* Masc. † Fem.

‡ Takes noun with *kī*. § Takes noun with *meṉ*.

झपट्टा म॰, * 'to snatch,' 'to spring upon.'

ठट्ठा म॰, * 'to deride.'

डींग म॰, * † 'to boast.'

डुबकी म॰, ‡ 'to dive.'

बुड़की म॰, ‡ 'to splash.'

कूद § म॰, 'to jump.'

चिंघार § म॰, 'to scream.'

फलांग § म॰, 'to leap.'

465. The following list includes a number of additional combinations of frequent occurrence, arranged according to the alphabetical order of the several verbs.

निश्चय आना, 'to seem certain.'

याद आना, || 'to come to mind.'

हाथ आना, ¶ 'to be found.'

बात § चलाना, 'to start a subject.'

मुक्की § चलाना, 'to beat with the fist.'

मुंह † चलाना, * 'to bite at.'

हल † जोतना, 'to plough.'

बाट † जोहना, ** 'to look for,' 'expect.'

सौंह § डालना, 'to conjure.'

स्मरण † दिलाना, †† 'to remind.'

राह § देखना, ** 'to expect,' 'look for.'

कान † धरना, ‡‡ 'to listen.'

ध्यान † धरना, ‡‡ 'to apply the mind to.'

हाथ † धोना, §§ 'to resign,' 'relinquish.'

जड़ § पकड़ना, 'to take root.'

दिखाई पड़ना, 'to appear.'

सुनाई पड़ना, 'to be heard.'

निश्चय पड़ना, 'to be ascertained.'

पता † पूछना, ** 'to make inquiry about one.'

दया § विचारना, ** 'to take pity upon.'

प्यार † विचारना, ** 'to feel love.'

भय † विचारना, §§ 'to feel fear.'

खेद † मानना, 'to grieve.'

बुरा मानना, 'to take (something) ill.'

---

* Requires the loc. with पर. † Masc. ‡ Requires loc. with में. § Fem.
|| Construction either *yah mujhe yád átá hai*; or *is ká yád mujhe áta hai.*
¶ Requires the gen. with के. ** Preceded by the gen.
†† Preceded by the dat. ‡‡ Preceded by the loc. with पर.
§§ Preceded by the abl.

भला मानना,* 'to take in good part.'

मुंह मोड़ना,† 'to turn away from.'

सांस‡ भरना, 'to sigh.'

ध्यान रखना,‖ 'to think upon.'

प्रेम रखना,† 'to love.'

मुख रखना, 'to end,' 'result.'

सुध रखना,§ 'to remember,' 'look after.'

निश्चय रहना, 'to be certain.'

हाथ लगना,¶ 'to be found.'

जाड़ा लगना,¶ 'to feel cold.'

गर्मी‡ लगना, 'to feel warm.'

ताक लगाना,‖ 'to take aim.'

दांव लगाना,‖ 'to bet.'

दोष लगाना,¶ 'to accuse,' 'blame.'

पता लगाना,** 'to make inquiry about any one.'

टक्कर लड़ना, 'to butt.'

उधार लेना,† 'to borrow.'

मोल लेना,†† 'to buy.'

दम लेना, 'to rest.'

सांस लेना,‡ 'to breathe.'

नाश होना,** 'to be destroyed'

प्रकाश होना, 'to be made clear.'

बिदा होना, 'to take leave.' 'to be known.'

लोप होना, 'to disappear.'

DIALECTIC CONJUGATION OF VERBS.

The Defective Auxiliary Substantive Verb.

466. As a preliminary to the consideration of dialectic conjugation, are exhibited the various dialectic forms and substitutions for the present and past tenses of the auxiliary substantive verb, answering respectively to the High Hindí, हूं and था, etc. *It is thought unnecessary to exhibit the* variations for gender which occur in the past tense, as they are identical with those which occur in the same dialects in nouns and adjectives of the same termination. Nor has it been thought necessary to repeat the pronoun in each dialect. This the student can easily supply for himself from the pronominal tables.

---

* Preceded by the acc. with को. † Requires the abl. with से. ‡ Fem.
‖ Requires the loc. with पर or ऊपर. § Requires the gen. with की.
¶ Preceded by the dat. with को. ** Requires the gen. with का.
†† Requires the abl. of the person, and the acc. of the thing.

Braj. Conjugation of Subst. Verb.

467. The Braj forms in Table XVIII will be found on almost every page of the *Rájníti* and similar books. In the present they differ but slightly from the High Hindí forms, and in the 1st sing. and 2nd plur. only. Thus, हौं लछमी हौं, 'I am *Lakshmí*;' तुम को हौ, 'who are you?.' आहि is used as 2nd plur. in one passage in the *Prem Ságar*, viz., तुम दोउ मेरी कला जु आहि, 'you two who are parts of me.' But this properly belongs to E. Hindí. Of the Braj forms of the past, the following are examples of the use of हो (fem. ही): तहां सुदर्शन नाम राजा हो, 'in that place was a king named *Sudarshan*;' ता को पार्वती नाम पत्नी ही, 'he had a wife named *Párvatí*.' This form of this Braj past tense is the more common in books; but हुतौ also occasionally occurs,* as in the following: मेरौ मुख जैसौ हुतौ तैसौ ही देखिहै, 'thou shalt see my face just as it was;' हुती घर मांझ रानी, 'in the house was the queen.' Closely connected are the Bagh. हथो and K. हतो.

Kanaují Conjugation.

468. The various Kanaují forms of the present of the subst. verb, in गा or गो, etc., are colloquial throughout the central Doáb, but the High Hindí forms are no less common. Panjábí has analogous forms also in the pres. 1st sing., होंगा, 'I am,' and 2nd plur., होवे, 'you are.'

Subst. Verb in Rajputana Dialects.

469. Of the two Rajputana forms of these two tenses, the present, हूं, etc., and हो, past, etc., are used throughout Mewáṛ and Máṛwáṛ; and east of Mewáṛ, through Kotáh, Bundá, Jaipúr, etc., the forms with छ are used. But in literature and correspondence, it is said that छूं, छो, etc., are used much more extensively. Thus the forms in छ constantly occur in the 'Plays,' as in the following examples: मैं छूं बाण्यो, 'I am a shopkeeper;' म्हे छां किस्या अजाण, (plur. for sing.) 'how am I ignorant?;' नाम हमारा लोटणो छै, 'my name is *Loṭno*;' तू छै राजकुमार, 'thou art a prince,' etc., etc.

---

* This word is erroneously explained in Prof. Eastwick's *Prem Ságar*, p. 194, as a Braj form of the imperfect participle, होता.

a. It should be noted that the Máṛwáṛí forms of these and other verbs are often disguised by the addition of various unmeaning letters and syllables, such as क, ज, स, सन, etc. Thus in the 'Plays' we find वोई छोस, 'you are that same,' where छोस is for छो = H.H. हो. These letters are added, indeed, not only to verbs, but to all other parts of speech.*

470. The Gaṛhwálí forms given in Table XVIII are those which prevail in and about Tírí, the capital of native Gaṛhwál, and are commonly understood (though not exclusively used) throughout that province. The form लो is used for the present tense in some villages of Gaṛhwál, both alone and as an auxiliary. Thus I have often heard कोई लो = H.H. कोई है; तुइन औंदा ला = H.H. तुम आते हो, 'are you coming?,' etc. The longer छ forms given in the pres. plur. belong east of Tírí. Subst. Verb in Gaṛhwálí.

471. In the archaic Baiswáṛí of the *Rámáyan*, as in poetry generally, the copula is very commonly omitted, both in the present and the past tense. When the copula is necessary, in the past tense the indef. perf., भयउ, of the verb होन, 'to be,' is often thus used. But occasionally in the *Rámáyan*, as regularly in all the modern eastern dialects, the indef. perf. of the verb रहना, 'to remain,' is used both as a copula and as an auxiliary, instead of the H. H. था. Thus we read in the *Rámáyan*, जो कछु उचित रहा सो कीन्हा, '(*Brahmá*) has done whatever was proper;' सती नाम तब रह तुम्हारा, 'then your name was *Satí*.' Subst. Verb in the *Rámáyan*.

472. With the Avadhí and old Baiswáṛí forms of the present may be compared the almost identical Maráṭhí conjugation, viz., Sing. आहें, आहेस, आहे; Plur. आहों, आहां, आहेत. The common negative, नहीं, Br. नाहि, has arisen from the combination of the negative न, with the 3rd sing., आहि, of the subst. verb. Subst. Verb in Avadhí.

473. Bhojpúrí has two forms of the present and past tense of the substantive verb, answering to H.H. हूं, है, etc.; derived respectively from the roots बाट् and हो or हव. Fragments from the root अछ्, also occur on the borders of the Maithilí. The preterite auxiliary of this verb is taken from the root रह्, as in Avadhí and Riwáí. The indefinite Bhojpúrí Auxiliaries.

---

* See § 100, *a.* (Or is स here, possibly, an old inflectional ending?).

perfect from the root हो, भइलों, etc., is never used as an auxiliary. It is conjugated as the inflected perfect of other neuter verbs. With this exception, the forms derived from the root हो, are used in all their tenses as auxiliaries; those from बाट् only occur in the present.

a. Connected however with this root बाट्, is an emphatic conjugation, formed by prefixing to the present throughout, an inflected verbal noun, बड़ले, from the same root; thus:

Sing.	1. m. बड़ले बाटों,	2. m. बड़ले बाटे,	3. m. बड़ले बाटस,
	1. f. बड़ले बाट्यूं,	2. f. बड़ले बाटिस,	3. f.. बड़ले बटसि,
Plu.	1. m. बड़ले बाटों,	2. m. बड़ले बाटऽ,	3. m. बड़ले बाटन,
	1. f. बड़ले बाट्यूं,	2. f. बड़ले बाटू,	3. f. बड़ले बाटिन.

This tense may be used as a present, conting. future, or an imperative.

Rem. The root बाट् often becomes बाड़् and बार्.

b. Besides the auxiliary होब = H.H. होना, Bhojpúrí also uses a strengthened form from the same root, होखब. This is regularly conjugated throughout, and may be substituted for the other auxiliaries at pleasure.

c. In the region west of Bhojpúr, हे is used for है, 'is.' बा is not confined to Bhojpúr, but is used for all persons in both numbers, both in W. Bhojpúr and as far west as Allahabad. Thus, ऊ आवत बा, 'he is coming;' तुम केहि को गोहरावत बा, 'whom are you calling?' According to Beames, the Bhojpúrí declinable forms, बारीं, बारऽ and बारन, are used in questions and replies, while the other forms given are preferred in narrative.

Bh. Negative Auxiliary.

474. Besides the above, Bhojpúrí also possesses a negative auxiliary subst. verb, assigned to the root नइख् or नहिंख्. This is conjugated only in one tense, which follows the inflection of the inflected present given in Table XXI, and, like the emphatic form of the verb, may be used either as a present, a conting. future, or an imperative.

475. For the past tense of the auxiliary substantive verb, Bhojpúrí uses the root रह् instead of Sk. स्था, as in the H.H. था. There is no difference in meaning between the longer and the shorter forms of this tense given in the Table.

476. Mágadhí presents two auxiliary verbs, the one defective, the other complete in conjugation. Mágadhí Auxiliaries.

(1) Of these, the former is derived from the root अछ्, Sk. अस्. In the present, a few fragments also occur, from a root छक्, formed from अछ् by the elision of the initial अ, and the addition of the Prakritic क. Unlike H.H., Mágadhí forms also its preterite from this same root, by the addition of the usual terminations of the inflected indefinite perfect, giving छलूँ, etc., = H.H. था.

(2) The second auxiliary verb is होएब, = H.H. होना, and is conjugated in all tenses. The only deviation from regularity is found in the inflected indefinite perfect, where, beside the regular form, होलूँ, etc., an older form, भेलूँ, etc., is also used. As in Bhojpúri, this inflected perfect is never used as an auxiliary.

477. In the various Maithilí dialects, five different roots are used for the different forms of the auxiliary verb. Maithilí Auxiliaries.

(1) The first of these is अछ्, which appears only in a present and preterite, = H.H. है and था; the initial अ is lost, except in the 3rd sing. अछ, N.Mt. अछि, 'he is.' In the present only, appears a strengthened form of this root, छिक्, whence, छिकूं, etc., conjugated regularly throughout.

(2) The root अह्, for Sk. अस्, in most parts of the Maithilí area, appears only in certain fragments of the 3rd sing. masc. present, viz., अहि, हो, है, एह, येह, यउ and हउ. But on the borders of Bangál, in Central and Western Puraniya, is heard also a future from this root, which is conjugated as follows:

Sing. 1. हैबै, हैबी, हैबों; 2. हैबा, हैबैं, हैबे,* हैमें, हैमें; 3. हैत, हैतौ, हैती.
Plur. 1. हैब, हैबी; 2. हैबउ, हैबहक. 3. *Not in use.*

a. In the W. also occurs a form of this root strengthened by the addition of त, which is conjugated after the analogy of बाड़ू, Table XVIII, with the addition of some alternative forms with Maithilí terminations: thus, sing. 1. हतु, हतों, हतौं; 2. हतस, हते, हत; 3. हते, हती, हतीक, etc.

(3) In N. Maithilí is used also a present from the root थिक्, strengthened from थि, for Sk. स्था. This is regularly conjugated, थिकऊँ or थिकों, etc., as in Table XVIII.

* Anusvár optional.

(4) Besides a preterite auxiliary derived from the root अछ्, Maithilí very generally uses, like other eastern dialects, a form from the root रह्. This is conjugated both in the form of the present and the perfect tense, रहौं or रहिऔं, etc.; but always has a preterite sense, = H.H. था, 'was.' All these various auxiliaries, present and preterite, are used interchangeably, with no difference of meaning; and two or three different forms will be heard even in the same district.

(5) Besides the above, Maithilí, like all the Hindí dialects, uses as an auxiliary, certain tenses of the verb होएब = H.H. होना. As in other eastern dialects, the भ of the original root, भू, is still preserved in one form of the inflected perfect, भेलौं, etc., as also in the perfect participle, भेल, and the conjunctive participle, भै के. This inflected perfect, however, in none of these dialects, is used as an auxiliary.

478. The very numerous forms of these two auxiliary tenses are presented in Table XVIII.

Conjugation in the Western Dialects.

Braj Conjugation.

479. The tense system in Braj corresponds essentially with that in High Hindí. For final आ and ए, the Braj characteristically exhibits औ and ऐ (§ 101). Thus, e.g., for मारे, we have मारै; for चलेगा, चलैगौ; for कहा, कह्यौ, etc. ऊं, in the 1st sing., and ओ in the 2nd plur. of the future tenses, are also *vriddhied* to औ; as, e.g., in गिरौं, मारौंगौ, चहौ, for H. H. गिरूं, मारूंगा and चहो. But for ऊं, we occasionally find ओं; and after a vowel ऊं is sometimes retained. After roots ending in आ, ई, or ओ, we commonly have व; not only, as in High Hindí, before ए, but also before ओ, occasionally before आ, and regularly before all terminations beginning with a consonant. Thus, e.g., we have खावो, खावनौ, पावतु, ऊवो, मुवो, for H. H. खाओ, खाना, पाता, ऊआ, मुआ. Similarly, व is inserted after roots in ऊ; as, e.g., कौन छुवैगो, 'who will touch (it)?.'

The Braj Infinitive.

480. The Braj Infinitive or Gerund has two forms, the one in नौ or नौं, the other in बौ or बौं. Before the latter termination, य is often inserted. This latter form is especially common in the oblique singular. For the common inflection,

ए, of the infinitive, the Braj, after न has not only ऐ, but इ, which, again, is often dropped, leaving न as the final letter. To illustrate, for H. H. करना, Braj has करनौं or करनो, करबौं or करिबो; inflected forms, करने, करनि or करन, and करबे or करिबे. The vowel of union, इ, after आ is often hardened to य, as in मिलायबो, = H. H. मिलाना. But still more commonly it combines with the preceding आ, forming ऐ, whence such common Braj forms, as, e.g., ऐबे कौ, for आइबे कौ, = H. H. आने का, 'of coming;' बतैबो, for बतायबो or बताइबो, = H. H. बताना, 'to show,' दैन or देनौं, for देना, 'to give,' etc. etc. But before नौं, after आ, व is more commonly found than इ; as in चुरावनौं, 'to steal,' for H. H. चुराना. Further examples are: सदा काऊ सौं रहिबो नाहि, 'there is no remaining always with any one;' तुम मेरे पुत्रनि कौं पंडित करिबे जोग हौ, 'you are competent to make my sons wise men;' राजा कहनि लाग्यौ, 'the king began to say;' तुम सौं कहन कौं आयौ हौं, 'I have come to tell you.'

481. Instead of the High Hindí terminations ता and आ (या) of the Imperfect and Perfect participles, the Braj has तु and यौ. Before तु, roots in आ sometimes take इय or य instead of व, as, e.g., in बैठाइयतु for बैठावतु, 'seating,' पायतु, 'finding.' The य which in High Hindí is inserted in the perf. part. only after open roots, is always inserted in Braj before औ after all roots whatever. Examples of these participles are, होतु, चलतु, मार्‌यौ, बतायौ, for H. H. होता, चलता, मारा, बताया. Braj Imperfect and Perfect Participles.

a. The final उ of the imperfect participle is occasionally dropped even in the singular, and often in the plural. इ is substituted for उ in the feminine. Sometimes for the imperfect participle in तु or त, longer forms in तो or तौ, plur. ते, occur; as, e.g., होतौ, मारतौ, for होता, मारता.

482 The Conjunctive participle is formed by the affixes कै or कि, कर or करि; but, much more commonly than in High Hindí, by the root alone, or by the affix इ. If the root end in a vowel, य is very commonly written instead of इ, but the Braj Conjunct. Participle.

pronunciation is not perceptibly different. Even when कर or कै is added, this इ or य is often retained after the root. Examples are, from मारनौं,—मारि, मारि कै, मारि करि; from आवनौं,—आय, आय कै, etc.

Braj Noun of Agency.

483. The Braj Noun of Agency agrees, in general, with the High Hindí form; except that for आ final, as usual, we find औ; and the suffix वारौ or हारौ is added to one of the dialectic inflected forms of the infinitive. Thus, e.g., from करनौं, come the various forms of the noun of agency, करनेवारौ, करनवारौ, करिवेहारौ, etc.

Braj Conting. Future.

484. The usual Braj terminations of the Contingent Future are: *Sing.* (1) औं, ऑं, ऊं; (2) ऐ; (3) ऐ; *Plur.* (1) ऐं; (2) औ; (3) ऐं. Besides these we also have the older forms of these terminations, in the *Sing.* (2, 3,) हि; *Plur.* (1, 3,) हिं, (2) हु. Both forms are common in the *Prem Ságar.* In the 1st sing., ऊं or उं is used after vowels. For औ, व is also found in the 2nd plur., as in जाव, 'you may go.' हि and हिं often appear, metri gratiâ, as ही and हीं.

Braj Absolute Future.

485. In the Absolute Future the Braj exhibits two classes of terminations.

(1) The first variety of the future is formed as in High Hindí, by adding the syllable गौ, for H.H. गा, duly inflected, to the several persons of the contingent future. Thus, e.g., we have from करनौं, *Sing.* (1) करौंगौ, (2, 3) करैगा; *Plur.* (1, 3) करैंगे, (2) करौगे. This affix गौ is also added to the longer terminations above noted, as, e.g., in the *Plur.* (1) देहिंगे, for H.H. देंगे; (2) पावऊगे, for H.H. पाओगे; आवगे = H.H. आओगे. The short penultimate vowel is often lengthened, metri gratiâ; as, e.g., in देहींगे.

(2) The second variety of the Braj future is formed by adding to the root the following terminations, इ being regularly employed as a vowel of union:—*Sing.* (1) हौं; (2, 3,) है; *Plur.* (1, 3,) हैं; (2) हौ. For हौं, we occasionally have हों, हूं or हुं, and for हौ, हो.

a. Observe that, as in the infinitive, so in the future, after roots ending in आ, इ either becomes य, or more commonly combines with आ to form ऐ. Thus arise, e.g., such forms as मिलायहौं, बतायहै, = H.H. मिलाऊंगा, बतावेगा; and ऐहै, 'he will come,' जैहौ, 'you will go,' for आइहै, जाइहौ, = H.H. आवेगा, जाओगे.

b. More rarely this इ combines also with the short *a* inherent in the final consonant of a close root; giving, e.g., such forms as करैहौ (= कर + इ + हौ) for करिहौं (H.H. करूंगा); सुनैहौ, मारैहैं for सुनिहौ, मारिहैं (H.H. सुनोगे, मारेंगे).

c. The following passages will illustrate these future forms. ऐसे सुंदरी ब्यायहौं, 'so will I bring a beautiful woman;' अबहीं या कौं मारिहौं, 'I will kill this (snake) immediately;' हम सों को करिहै सगाई, 'who will form an alliance with us?;' बरषा ऋतु बीते घर जैहौ, 'when the rains are over, you shall go home;' हम सबै भूखौं मरिहैं, 'we shall all starve to death;' या सों तुम्ह कैसे बैर करिहौ, 'with this (snake) how will you be at enmity;' सरग निवास करैहैं, 'they shall dwell in heaven.'

Rem. 1. In some Braj books, printed under English supervision, these terminations हौं, है, etc., will be found separated from the preceding root. This seems to have arisen from a confusion of these terminations with the substantive verb. Similarly the terminations हि, and हु, of the contingent future, are often printed separate from the root, having apparently been confounded with the emphatic particle. This not infrequent printer's error should be noted.

Rem. 2. Observe that there is no difference of signification whatever, between the two forms of the Braj future here given. They both alike express the absolute and unconditioned futurition of the action.

486. The Imperative, as in High Hindí, agrees in form with the contingent future, except in the 2nd pers. sing. which consists of the root alone. But a form in हि is frequently used in poetry and archaic prose, instead of the root; as, या मैं यतन न करहि, 'labour thou not in this;' चिन्ता मति करहि, 'be thou not anxious.' Braj Imperativ *a.* The Respectful Imperative commonly agrees in form with High Hindí, except that, as usual, ए and ओ final become ऐ and औ. य is occasionally doubled; thus, पीछे मारिय्यौ, 'afterwards kill (me).' Occasionally ज appears instead of य in these forms, and इ before य or ज is sometimes lengthened. Examples are: सोकु छाड़िजै, 'abandon grief;' वा कौं बंधु जाणोजै, 'regard him as a brother;' यो कौं मारि खाईये, 'kill and eat this.'

Rem. These *j* forms are the original of the modern *y* forms. The lengthening of the *i* is in compensation for the loss of the first consonant in the original Prakrit termination, *ijjai.*

Braj Participial Tenses.

487. The Participial Tenses are all formed as in High Hindí, by combining the participles with certain tenses of the substantive verb; i.e., in the tenses of the present, हौं, etc., in those of the past, हो, in the presumptive, होउंगो or ह्वैहौं, etc. Examples are: सर्प कहितु है, 'the snake speaks;' तू काहे ते रोवत है, 'why art thou crying?'; वह वा कौं गोद में बैठारयतु है, 'he is seating him in (his) lap;' काल निकट आवतु है, 'death comes near;' हौं ठौर नाहि पायतु, 'I do not find a place;' रानी रोवति ही, 'the queen was crying;' हौं आयौं हौं, 'I have come;' उह आयौ होय, 'he may have come;' कछु दूरि तें चल्यौ हो, 'he had walked for some distance,' etc.

Passive Construction of Transitives.

488. The passive construction of the perfect tenses of transitives with the case of the agent, is regularly employed in Braj, as in High Hindí. But it should be noticed that while ने is often used with the case of the agent, it is also often omitted, both in poetry and, more rarely, in prose; and the noun or pronoun is used in its oblique form, where such a form exists. Thus, उन इक नगर बसायौ, 'he settled a city;' काग सबद कीयौ, 'the crow cawed.' In a French Braj translation of the *Hitopades*,* a special inflection of the

* Vid. De Tassy's '*Chrestomathie*,' Paris, 1849, and compare the Máṛwáṛí inflected case of the agent, § 169, *a.*

substantive in this construction occurs, as, e.g., सुसि कहि, 'the hare said,' where सुसि is the inflected case of the agent, from सुसा, and कहि, perf. fem. sing., agreeing with बात.

489. A number of common verbs assume peculiar forms in Braj, which the student will do well to notice.

(1) The root of the substantive verb, होनौं, 'to be,' in the 2nd form of the absolute future, in the infinitive in बौ, and in the conjunctive participle, becomes ह्व. Thus, the absolute future becomes ह्वैहौं, ह्वैहै, etc.; the infinitive, ह्वैबौ, and the conjunctive participle, ह्वै, ह्वैकै, etc. In the perfect participle and all its tenses, भयौ, (masc. infl. भये or भए, fem. भयी, or भई,) is the common substitute for हुआ.

Rem. The same form, with only the change of यौ to यो, is universally employed in Kanaují, where it is even shortened to भयो or भो.

a. In one place in a Braj work I have noted a perfect, हुत, (Sk. भूत,) 'was,' for H.H. हुआ. हुगे also occurs, 2nd plur. fut., for होगे.

(2) In the verbs देनौं, 'to give,' and लेनौं, 'to take,' the Sanskrit roots, दा and ला, are substituted for दे and ले, in the 2nd form of the future, the infinitive in बौ, and in the perfect participle. In the participle, the final आ is shortened to अ. In the future and infinitive, the radical आ, combining with the union vowel इ, gives ऐ. Thus, the Braj forms of the above tenses of these verbs are as follows: inf., दैबौ, लैबौ, obl. form, दैबे, लैबे; fut., दैहौं, लैहौं, etc.; perf. part., दयौ, लयौ, obl. forms, दये or दए, लये or लए, etc. Thus, e.g., we read, ता में तें कछु तुम कौं दैहैं, 'we will give some of that to you.' Similar forms occur in Kanaují. Sometimes the vowel of union is omitted in the future of these verbs, and the root of the tense becomes द and ल. Thus, e.g., सब सुख संपति लहैं, 'they will take all joy and wealth away.' Similarly, ठाननौ, 'to appoint,' makes the perfect participle, ठयौ, fem. ठई, as in the following: विधाता नें यह ठई, '*Vidhátá* has appointed this.' In one place in the *Prem Ságar* (Ch. I.),

we find a fut. 1st sing., दूहं, for देहौं, H.H., दूंगा, from देना, 'to give;' thus, मैं उस कौं दूहं स्राप, 'I will curse him.'

a. In a Braj commentary on the *Bhakt Málá*, I have found, in a compound form, an imperative 2nd plur., द्यौ, from देनौं, for देउ or देओ, = H.H. दो; thus, यह सुता तिन कौं बिबाहि द्यौ, 'give this daughter in marriage to him.' The form has evidently arisen by *sandhi* from दिऔ, from the root दि, for दे.

(3) The verb करनौं, 'to do' or 'make,' in Braj often forms its perfect participle regularly as कर्यौ, instead of कियौ, which, however, also occurs. Similarly the Kanaují makes करो, for H.H. किया. In the future of this verb, besides the more common and regular forms, करिहौं, करिहै, etc., the Braj also has कैहौं, कैहै, etc., (for करिहौं, etc.,) from the root का, one of the Prakrit substitutes for कृ.* Thus, राज इंद्र कौ कैहौं, 'I will sway *Indra's* sceptre.'

(4) In the perfect tenses of the three verbs, देना, लेना, करना, we often find, besides the forms already mentioned, the forms दीन्हौ, लीन्हौ, कीन्हौ, or often, with ह dropped, दीनौ, लीनौ, कीनौ. Thus, पूरब जनम सुकृत कोउ कीनौ । सो बिधि यह दरसन फल दीनौ,† 'some one in a former birth has practised virtue, hence *Brahmá* has given this vision as a reward.' From the root की, for कर, we also have a rare infinitive, कीबौं.

Additional Braj Tenses.

490. Besides the regular tenses corresponding with those of the High Hindí, the Braj, as also the Kanaují, the old Baiswáṛí of the *Rámáyan*, and the other eastern dialects, presents, in addition to the common regular analytic present imperfect, formed by means of the participle and auxiliary, also a purely inflectional form of the same tense, exactly agreeing in form with the contingent future. While not infrequent in prose, it is especially common in poetry and

* Vararuchi, Prák. Prak. VIII. 17.

† In Prof. Eastwick's edition of the *Prem Ságar*, Anusvár is added to the final vowel in this passage.

in proverbial expressions. It is occasionally used even in literary Urdú, in such common expressions as خدا جانے *Khudá jáne*, 'God knows,' etc. Examples of the Braj tense are: जु पंडित होइ सो दुख सुख न मानै, 'he who is wise regards neither sorrow nor joy;' उह सब को संग छुड़ावहि, 'he abandons the society of all;' पंडित तहां वेद उचरें, 'there Pundits are reciting the Vedas.' This tense is very common both in literature and in the colloquial of the Ganges Valley. Further examples will be found in the Syntax.

a. With this inflected present is combined occasionally, in Braj, the several persons of the present of the substantive verb, हूं, है, etc. Thus, e.g., the following forms are found in the *Prem Ságar*: मैं पहचानूं हूं, 'I recognize;' दीखै है, 'it appears;' आवें हैं, 'they come.' Further west, in Máṛwáṛ, this becomes the rule. There seems to be no difference in meaning between this and other forms of the present. This idiom is even more common in the colloquial about Kanauj, than in common Braj literature. Thus we often hear, साहिब बुलावें हैं, 'the *Sáhib* is calling;' हम आवें हैं, 'I am coming.'

Rem. Misled by the less common occurrence of the present than of the future sense of this form in modern High Hindí, most grammarians have stated that the contingent future ('aorist' of Forbes and others) is sometimes used in the sense of the present. It is, however, more accurate to regard the present as the original, and the future as the secondary meaning of the tense, which in fact is the worn-out remainder of the Sanskrit pres. *Parasmai.*

491. Besides the above tenses, yet another is found Braj 'Inceptive Imperfect.'
occasionally in Braj prose and poetry, formed by the combination of the imperfect participle with the indefinite perfect, भयो, of the substantive verb, होनौं. The nature of this tense may be best denoted by the term, '*Inceptive Imperfect.*' It indicates the subject as entering upon the action expressed by the verb. Examples are: पीवत भयो दही, 'he began to drink the sour milk;' तो वे यह बात में बिचारत भयो, 'so he

began to think on this matter.' Further illustrations will be given below, in treating of the dialect of the *Rámáyan.*

Braj Causals.

492. The Braj commonly adds आव to the root for the First Causal, and, like High Hindí, वा (or वाव) for the Second Causal. But a long vowel in the root of the primitive is sometimes retained where High Hindí shortens it.

a. Many verbs which, in High Hindí, make the Causal irregularly in आल or ला, take the regular form in Braj. If the root end in a vowel, व or य is inserted before the causal affix, आव. Thus, e.g., भूलनौं, 'to forget,' makes भुलावनौं and भुलवानौं; बोलनौं, 'to speak,' बोलावनौं and बुलवानौं; खानौं, 'to eat,' खवानौं (or खवावनौं), and खिलवानौं (or खिलवावनौं); पीवौं, 'to drink,' पियावनौं and पिलवानौं. आव is very rarely in poetry shortened to अव; thus, in the *Prem Ságar* we have a causative form, पुजवै; को पुजवै हिय हौंस हमारी, 'who will fill the desire of my heart?' where पुजवै is for पुजावै.

The Braj Passive.

493. The Braj forms its passive with the verb जानौं, 'to go,' precisely after the manner of High Hindí.

a. But while this is the common form, we also meet in Braj with fragments of an inflected passive, formed by the addition to the root of the active verb, of the suffix इ or इय. To the new root thus formed, the usual conjugational terminations are then affixed. This chiefly occurs in the inflected present, in which tense it frequently occurs, e.g., in the *Rájníti.* Thus we read, जो विद्या बालअवस्था में सिखाइयै सो भूलति नाहीं, 'the knowledge which is taught in childhood is not forgotten;' where सिखाइयै is 3rd sing. present inflected passive of the causal verb, सिखानौं or सिखावनौं.

Rem. 1. In many instances, doubtless, it will be found possible to render such a form as the above either as a present passive, or as the respectful form of the imperative active. But in this case, as in not a few other instances, the latter rendering seems impossible, and the true passive character of the form appears quite clear.

Rem. 2. The existence of inflectional passive forms in Braj, so far as I know, has been hitherto unrecognized, and all such forms have been regarded as respectful forms of the imperative or contingent future. Careful study will show, however, that it is impossible in all cases so to render them, and that we must recognize as still remaining in Braj, fragments of the old inflectional passive, which in Máṛwáṛí, Naipálí, and some other Hindí dialects, still retains a complete conjugation.*

Kanaují Conjugation

494. Very closely allied to the Braj is the Kanaují conjugation. ओ and ए are preferred to the Braj औ and ऐ; उ final is dropped from the termination of the imperfect participle; य is only inserted before the termination ओ of the perfect tenses of pure verbs. करनो and मरनो form the perfect regularly from the root of the infinitive, making करो and मरो, 'did,' 'died,' for H.H. किया and मुआ. For H.H. हुआ, 'became,' K. has भयो or भओ like the Braj. The remaining details can be learned from the tables.

Baghelkhaṇḍí Conjugation.

495. The dialect exhibited in the Baghelkhaṇḍí N. T.† is related much more closely to the Braj in its conjugation than to eastern Hindí; and exhibits the peculiar construction of the case of the agent with H.H. transitive verbs, which is characteristic of all western Hindí. The infinitive ends in बो, and the noun of agency in बारो or हारो. The future tenses correspond exactly to the Braj, except that ए and ओ are preferred to ऐ and औ: as, e.g., in जैहों, = Br. जैहौं, H.H. जाऊंगा, 'I will go;' पैहे, = Br. पैहै, H.H. पाएगा, etc. The imperfect participle ends in तु, as in Braj, and the perfect in ओ, as in Kanaují. व is however preferred to य before the termination of the perfect, as in E. Hindí. Thus we have, e.g., गवो, दवो, for H.H. गया, 'gone,' and दिया, 'given.' भवो is regularly used for H.H. हुआ, 'become.' Quite peculiar is the termination कनाई, in the conjunctive participle, which is added to the root, like के in H.H. य, however, is inserted before the terminations when the root ends in a vowel; thus we find सुनकनाई, आयकनाई, = H.H. सुनकर, आकर. This termination is evidently connected with the Mewáṛí termination, कणे, of the same participle, to be noticed below.

---

* See § 511, and compare remarks on the H.H. *cháhiye* in the Syntax, in which section will be found additional illustrations of the Braj inflected passive.

† Bapt. Mission Press, Serampore, 1821.

Conjugation in Rajputana Dialects: Infinitive.

496. As one general type of conjugation prevails throughout Rajputana, it will be convenient to treat Máṛwáṛí and Mewáṛí, etc., together, noting local differences as they occur.

Two general forms of the Infinitive prevail, the one in णो or णुं, the other in बो. Between these there appears to be no difference in meaning, but only in usage. Both forms are heard everywhere, but among the Mairs णो and णुं are much the more common. In W. Rajputana the final vowel of णो is usually dropped, giving, e.g., बोलण for बोलणो, etc. But देणो and लेणो retain the final vowel. Both णो and बो are used in an inflected form. बो is regularly inflected to बा, but णो is changed to णि, never to णा, and that only among the Mairs. The dat. postposition, ए, is never used after this inflected infinitive. Elsewhere, if any inflected form be required, the oblique form in बा is used. Thus, the Mairs would say, करणि ऊो, करणि ऊं, = H.H. करने का, करने से, 'of doing,' 'by doing;' but the Máṛwáṛís, करबा को, करबा सूं. So also in the 'Plays' we read, चेलो होबा आयो, = H.H. चेला होने आया, 'I have come to be a disciple.' But the High Hindí inflection of the infinitive is also employed, in the Play of '*Ḍúngar Singh*,' ऐसा (*sic*) नही रहणे की आस, 'there is no hope of your remaining thus.'

a. The infinitive in णुं is used by the Mairs, in the Frequentative form of the verb only, where High Hindí employs the verbal noun in आ. Thus for the Frequentative verbs, आया करना, मारा करना, 'to go often,' 'to beat often,' the Mairs say, आणुं करणो, मारणुं करणो. The Máṛwáṛís also use the infinitive in the frequentative verb, but in the other form, saying, e.g., आबो करणो, मारबो करणो. The infinitive in णु (णूं) is employed in the Máṛwáṛí 'Plays,' in the same manner as the other forms; thus, in the Play of '*Bharatrí*,' मानु कहणु म्हारो, 'believe my word,' lit., 'my saying.' The infinitive in णो is sometimes used adjectively like the Urdú infinitive, and may therefore be inflected to णी to agree with a feminine noun, thus: रोटी पकावणी है, 'bread must be cooked;' and in an imperative sense in '*Ḍúngar Singh*,' देर नहीं करणो, 'make no delay.' But the infinitive in बो is never thus employed.*

497. The Imperfect Participle everywhere in Rajputana ends in तो, and the perfect participle in यो. But when the perfect participle is used adjectively, in Máṛwáṛ the suffix ड़ो is added. Thus, from भणबो, 'to read,' the perf. part. adj. is भण्योड़ो, = H.H. पढ़ा ऊआ; from मारणो, 'to beat,' मार्योड़ो, = H.H. मारा ऊआ, etc., etc. Before this affix ड़ो, य of the termination is sometimes dropped, as in कीधोड़ो, = H.H. किया ऊआ. To the imperfect and perfect participles, when used adjectively, is also optionally added, either the perfect participle, व्हियो, of व्हेणो, 'to be,' or थको, or लगो;† as, म्हें छोरां ने आवतो दीठो, 'I saw the boys coming;' वांको भोला थकां को बाप मर गियो, 'their father died in (their) childhood,' etc. Imperfect and Perfect Part. in Rajputana.

a. Before the termination यो of the perfect participle, इ is often inserted in the 'Plays;' या is also often written for यो. Thus, सूरज ऊगोया, 'the sun has risen;' राज ताकिया, '(I) have forsaken (my) kingdom;' कागद ले ऊं आवियो, 'I have brought a paper (i.e., a letter).'

b. When the participles are used as verbal nouns, or absolutely, ओ final becomes आं in the oblique form. Thus, मुलक में लियां फिरूं, 'I will take (thee) about the country;' so also, म्हारो माल मगावतां घड़ी न करसी जेज, 'he will not make an hour's delay in sending for my property.' But otherwise the oblique form ends in आ, sing., आं, plur.

---

* De Tassy mentions an infin. in दी, as, e.g., करदी, for करना. This looks like a Western form, and is therefore noted here; but I have no further information about it.

† थको is evidently a perfect participle from the root थक्, strengthened from थ (Sk. स्था), which appears in the H.H. था. With this may be compared the Guj. subst. verb, थवूं, and the Mt. strengthened pres. forms, थिकूं, etc. Vid. § 477, (3). लगो is used chiefly in Mewáṛ and Máiṛwáṛá.

c. The various verbal forms are often disguised by meaningless enclitic additions. Thus we find ल्यावतास for ल्यावता, = H.H. लाता; छोड़ियासन for छोड़िया, = H.H. छोड़ा; देवुंर, for H.H. देऊं, etc., etc.

Conjunct. Part. in Rajputana.

498. The Conjunctive Participle exhibits several forms. (1) The root alone is used; or (2), ने is added to the root; as, e.g., करने, मारने, = H.H. करके, मारके. Both of these are used throughout Rajputana. The former often occurs in the 'Plays.' In Mewáṛ, the conjunctive participle is formed (3) by adding ऊने to the root; as, e.g., in सुणूने, मारूने, = H.H. सुनके, मारके; or (4) by adding क्ने to the imperfect participle, as in बाड़तोक्ने, 'having cut,' = H.H. काटके.* (5) Again, in E. Rajputana, this participle is formed by adding र् to the root. Thus we have मारर् = H.H. मारके; व्हैर्, = H.H. होकर; खार्, = H.H. खाकर, etc., etc. This last form occurs in the 'Plays;' as, e.g., षूणै बैठर् षावसी, '(although) thou wilt eat (it), sitting in a corner;' and in '*Randhír aur Prem Mohaní*,' लार, = H.H. ला के; thus, ये तो वाट ताखड़ो लार, 'this (fellow) bringing (his own) weights and scales.' (6) I have also heard repeatedly from a native of Rajputana a conjunctive participle formed by the suffix करियाणा or करियाना, as, e.g., सुणकरियाणा, = H.H. सुनकर, 'having heard,' etc. This is said to be also used in poetry, but I have not met with any example.

Noun of Agency in Rajputana.

499. The Noun of Agency is formed by the suffix वालो, which is added to either form of the inflected infinitive. In this combination the infinitive in णो, inflected to णा, seems to be the more common, but the other form of the infinitive is also used, as in the following: म्हारो माल लूटबावालो, 'the robber of my property.' (Play of *Dúṇgar Singh*.)

---

* Compare the Bagh. conj. part. termination, कनाई, given above, § 495.

500. The Máṛwáṛí tenses may be distributed in the same three groups as those of the High Hindí; though I doubt whether examples can be adduced of each of the twelve participial tenses. व is inserted before the terminations as in High Hindí, but much more freely. Thus, e.g., it is constantly inserted after a vowel in the contingent future, 1st sing. and 2nd plur.: as, लावुं गंगा जल, 'shall I bring Ganges water?;' खबरज लेवो आय, 'go and get tidings (of him):' also before the termination of the imperfect participle, तो, as in होवतो, लावतो, = H.H. होता, लाता: also even after a short vowel in the perfect; as, मैं लिवी फकोरो, 'I had taken up the life of a mendicant.' But in the tenses of the perfect य is more common. Thus, although we find भया in the 'Plays,' = H.H. हुआ, भयो is more frequent, as, e.g., in भयो मुसाण्युं, 'he became a *jogí*.' The common colloquial form of this word is व्हियो or व्हीओ. Máṛwáṛí Tenses.

501. The terminations of the Contingent Future in Máṛwáṛí, Mewáṛí, etc., are, *Sing.* (1) उं or ऊं; (2, 3) ऐ; *Plur.* (1) आं; (2) ओ; (3) ऐ. A single example will suffice, in addition to those given above; मन आवे जठे उतरां, 'we will rest (lit., alight) wherever it may please us,' (lit., 'may come into the mind'). Conting. Fut. in Rajputana.

502. Three forms of the Absolute Future prevail in Rajputana. Absolute Fut. in Rajputana.

(1) Two of these are formed directly from the root, by adding the following terminations, viz.:

	Terminations of the 1st Future.			*Terminations of the 2nd Future.*		
Sing.	1. स्यूं.	2. सी.	3. सी.	1. हूं.	2. ही.	3. ही.
Plur.	1. स्यां.	2. स्यो.	3. सी.	1. हां.	2. हो.	3. हो.

N.B. स्यूं and स्यो are sometimes corrupted to सुं or सूं, and सो.

(2) The 3rd form of the future is formed after the analogy of the future in High Hindí; i.e., by adding a syllable, viz.,

लो (instead of II.II. गा), to the several forms of the contingent future. Like गा, this लो is inflected for gender and number, and therefore becomes ला in the masc. plural; ली, in the fem. singular and plural. But ला is sometimes used for लो in the masc. singular. Thus the full terminations added to the root are as follows:—

Terminations of the 3rd Future.

Sing. 1. ऊंलो. 2. ऐलो. 3. ऐलो. *Plur.* 1. आंला. 2. ओला. 3. ऐला.

Rem. These forms appear to be substantially identical in signification, except that the future in लो is said to express a slight degree of dubiety. This future in लो is especially common about Jodhpúr. Further east, in eastern Máṛwáṛ and Mewáṛ, the 2nd form in हूं, etc., is chiefly used; while in Bundá, Kotah, along the river Chambal, and northward to Jaipúr, the future in स्यूं, etc., is the usual colloquial form. The use of this form of the future, therefore, is territorially co-extensive with that of the substantive verb, छूं, etc. (§ 469), and, like that, appears to be the common literary form; while the other futures are used in the same districts as the substantive verb, हूं, etc.

b. The following illustrations of the literary future in स are from the 'Plays.' पोछे पावां लासुं, 'afterward I will bring (him) to (your) feet;' खूणे बैठर खावसो, 'thou wilt eat (it) sitting in a corner;' गोपी चंद सा पुतर होवसो, 'there shall be (to thee) a son like *Gopí Chand*;' सबी मिल चालस्यां, 'we all will go together;' जिस से होस्यो पार, 'by which you shall succeed.' The final Anusvár in these future forms is often omitted in the text, but I judge it to be a printer's error. The 'Plays' do not, that I have noticed, give any examples of either of the other two futures.

Imperative in Rajputana. **503.** The Imperative, in the 2nd singular, consists of the root alone; and adds ओ to the root for the 2nd plural, as in High Hindí. When the root ends in a vowel, व is inserted before ओ; thus, थे डेरा लेवो उठाय, 'take up the tent;' जावो बाई, 'go, mother!' In a few words, final ए in the root is often hardened to य before ओ; thus, ल्यो तरवारां हाथ में,

'take swords in the hand;' रसता बता चो, 'point out the way.' Occasionally in the 'Plays,' the 2nd sing. terminates in ऊं; thus, कयो हमारो मानूं, 'mind my word.'

504. In the Respectful forms of the Imperative, the 'Plays' exhibit the terminations ज्यो or ज्यो, and जे or ज्ये. These ज forms are added not only to a few verbs, as देना, लेना, etc., as in High Hindí, but to all verbs whatever, even when the root terminates in a consonant. The form in ज्यो or जो, at least, is used even with the singular of the 2nd pers. pronoun. Examples of these forms occur in the following: कागद बांचत आवज्यो, 'immediately on reading the paper, come;' थे सुणज्यो सीरदारां, 'hear ye, chieftains;' तू मत जेज लगाजे, 'make thou no delay;' पावां लाज्ये मारै, 'bring (him) to my feet.'

a. In the colloquial, the respectful forms of the imperative are जै or ईजै, and जो or ईजो. Thus from जीमणो, 'to eat,' the respectful forms are जीमजै or जीमीजे, and जीमजो or जीमीजो. In the 'Plays,' also, ई is sometimes inserted before the termination; thus, थे जेज करीज्यो नाहि, 'make you no delay.'

505. In the tenses of imperfect action, the imperfect participle alone is used, as in High Hindí, for a past contingent tense, and not unfrequently in the 'Plays,' as a present tense; as, e.g., सिध होय सो नहो रवता, 'he who is perfect, dwells not (here).' Tenses of the Imperfect in Rajputana.

506. But the Present Imperfect is regularly formed, both in the colloquial and in literature, by adding the several persons of the present of the substantive verb, either of the छ or the ह series, not to the imperfect participle, as in High Hindi, but to the contingent future forms. Illustrations are: जोगी अलष जगावै है, 'a *jogí* is calling "*Alakh*"!';* तुं क्यूं भेजे छै लिर, 'why dost thou send (me) afterward?;' बाणियां क्यूं

* *Alakh!* is 'O (thou) Invisible.'

घालो छो हाथ, 'why do you lay hands upon the merchant?'; क्युं खावो छो जैहर, 'why do you eat poison?.'

a. The auxiliary is often omitted, especially when several verbs occur in the same construction; so that the present imperfect is often identical in form with the contingent future. Thus, in the following, both the first and the second verbs are to be regarded as in the present imperfect; बीन बजावे नाद सुणावे खड्यो छे मेल के बार, 'he is playing the lute, singing a song, standing without the palace.' Similar is the verb in the following; मुझ कुं क्या फरमावो, 'what do you command me?.'

507. The formation of the Past Imperfect is analogous to that of the present, except that the auxiliary past tense, हो or छो, of the substantive verb, is added both in the singular and plural, to that form of the verb only, which is found in the 3rd sing. of the contingent future. Thus, for the H.H. मैं सुणता था, we have हूं सुणै छो, 'I was hearing;' similarly, for तुम क्या करते थे, 'what were you doing?' थे कांई करै छा or करै हा, etc.

a. These forms are colloquial throughout Rajputana, but the tense is sometimes also formed as in High Hindí, by adding the past tense of the substantive verb (छो or हो) to the imperfect participle.

Tenses of the Perfect in Rajputana.

508. The tenses of the Perfect are all formed with the perfect participle, in combination, when necessary, with the various tenses of हूणो (होना); and transitive verbs construe these tenses with the case of the agent, taking the object either in the nominative or dative, exactly as in High Hindí (§ 412). Thus in the following we have both the active and passive construction: सुपनुं आयो रैण मंझ थांको उड़तो देख्यो सीस, 'a dream came in the night,—I saw (thy) head flying.' The following are illustrations of the more common tenses: मैं थ नै भेज्यो छो, 'I had sent thee;' ऊ घोड़ै चढ्यो हूसो, 'he must have mounted (his) horse;' कुण उण नै मार्‌यो होसो, 'some one must have struck him.'

509. The irregular verbs mentioned at § 391, are irregular also in the Rajputana dialects. In W. Rajputana, करणो, 'to do,' makes the perfect, कीधो, कोद्दो, or कर्‌यो; so लेणो, 'to take,' perf., लीधो and लीद्दो; देणो, 'to give,' perf., दीधो and दीद्दो. So also, खाणो, 'to eat,' makes the perfect, खाधो. मरणो, 'to die,' makes the perfect, मर्‌यो or मूश्रो. But in E. Rajputana, as in the 'Plays,' करणो, लेणो, and देणो, have the perfect in नु, नो, or ना, fem. नी, as in the following passages: भायां कीनी गाफली, 'my brothers have been careless (lit., done carelessness);' लीनी फकोरी, '(I) have taken up the life of a *faqír*;' दुष सुष दीनु राम जी, '*Rám Jí* hath given sorrow and joy;' मैं अपना टाबर नें पोशाल मांहों नहीं जाबैं दीनो छै, 'I have not let my children go to school;' जाईबे धो, 'let it go.' जाणो, 'to go,' makes the perfect गीयो.

Rem. These perfect forms in धो and द्दो are well illustrated by such archaic Hindí perfects as दिद्धिय, 'given,' लद्धिय, 'taken,' cited by Beames from *Chand*, who has also दिद्धो, दीधो, and दिज्जय = दिया, किद्धो and किज्जय = किया. As he observes, करणो and देणो have here oddly borrowed a form properly belonging only to लेणो, which in Sk. makes the perfect passive participle लब्ध, Pr. लद्धो. So also खाधो, which he does not mention. A similar confusion has given rise to the न forms of the perfect participle of करणो and लेणो, in Márwáṛí and other dialects, as also लिया and दिया in High Hindí.*

a. Besides the verbs that are usually irregular in other Hindí dialects, all verbs of which the root terminates in ह, often lose that letter before the various verbal terminations, and thus appear as irregular. Thus the perfects of the verbs कहणो, 'to say,' रहणो, 'to remain,' बहणो, 'to flow,' become कयो, रयो, बयो, as in the following: कयो हमारो मान, 'regard what I have said;' कातिक मास रया अलुणा, 'in the month of *Kátik* we remained without salt;' नीर बयो थारा नैण में, 'water has flowed in your eyes.' Sometimes the य of the termination is doubled, in compensation for the loss of ह; thus, जो मेरा कय्या माने, 'if thou regard my word.' Sometimes, again, व is inserted in the hiatus caused by the elision of ह, giving such forms as कवो = कहा; रवतो = रहता; etc., etc. Thus we have, e.g., कुसी रवो, 'remain in happiness;'

---

* Vid. Beames, *Comp. Gramm.* vol. iii. 144-147.

कवो बात, 'say the word;' सो नहीं रवतो इस नगरी के मांहि, 'that (man) dwells not in this village;' वो बी मरद कवता था, 'that man also was saying.' Sometimes in the imperative, ह being dropped, the concurrent vowels are united, so that we have कौ for कहो, and रौ for रहो. Similarly, कै stands for कहि, and बै for बह or बहि, as, e.g., नदी बै जावे, 'the river flows away.'

Causal Verbs in Rajputana.

510. Causal verbs in Máṛwáṛ and Rajputana generally, are formed as in Braj, by adding आव to the root for the First, and वाव for the Second Causal. A long vowel in the root of the primitive, is shortened as usual before the heavy affix. These forms therefore require no further illustration. But a few verbs with monosyllabic open roots, shorten a final long vowel in the root, and insert र before आव for the 1st causal. Thus देणो, 'to give,' makes its first causal, दिरावणो, and लेणो, 'to take,' लिरावणो; as, e.g., मैं जोग लिरावुं, 'I will cause (him) to take up *jog*;' i.e., 'to become an ascetic.' Alternative forms, दवावणो and लवावणो, also exist.

a. Verbs with ह final in the root drop this ह before the causal terminations, as in the primitive conjugation; thus we have the following examples: बवा दियो पाणी, 'the water caused (all) to flow away;' म्हं राजा कवावतो हं, 'I am called a king:' where बवा दियो, कवावतो हं, respectively = H.H. बहा दिया, कहलाता हूं.

The Máṛwáṛí Inflected Passive.

511. The colloquial Máṛwáṛí west of the Aravallí hills is distinguished by a regular inflectional passive verb, the root of which is formed by adding the syllable ईज to the root of the primitive. Roots containing a long vowel shorten that vowel before this affix. Verbs which take र before the causal, insert it also before the passive affix. Thus, to illustrate, from करणो, 'to do,' is derived the passive, करीजणो = H.H. किया जाना, 'to be done;' from खावणो, 'to eat,' the passive खवीजणो, 'to be eaten;' from लेणो, 'to take,' and देणो, 'to give,' the passives, लिरीजणो, 'to be taken,' and दिरीजणो, 'to be given.' Even neuter verbs may take this passive form. Thus, we have from आवणो, 'to come,' the passive अवीजणो. In the case of such verbs, however, the passive is only used impersonally in the 3rd masc. sing. These passive verbs are conjugated throughout like regular primitive verbs. Thus, म्हैं सूं अवीजै नहीं = H. H. मुझ से आया नहीं जाता, 'it is not come by me,' i.e., 'I cannot come;' म्हूं मरीज्यो, 'I was beaten;' थें सूं नहीं खवीजैलो, 'it will not be eaten by you,' i.e., 'you will not be able to eat it.' These forms are rarely heard east of the Aravallí hills.

512. In the dialects of W. Rajputana the various forms of Intensive Compound verbs, explained §§ 427-432, are but rarely used. Instead of these forms, परो or वरो is prefixed to the verb. Thus, for मार डालना the Máṛwáṛís say, परो मारणो; for चला जाना, 'to go away,' परो जावणो; for उठ जाना, 'to rise up,' परो उठणो. But when the action is regarded as terminating with, upon, near, or for the agent, वरो is used instead of परो. Thus, वरो लेणो, 'to take for one's self' = H.H. ले लेना, etc. These compounds with वरो therefore approximate in use to the Middle Voice in Greek. परो and वरो are inflected to परा and वरा, obl. masc., and परी and वरी, fem., to agree with the subject of neuter verbs, or with the object of transitives. Examples are, थूं वरो जा, or (fem.) थूं वरी जा = H.H. तू चला जा or चली जा. But with a transitive verb, in *any* tense these must agree with the object. Thus, ऊ पोथी वरी लेवै, 'let him take the book (i.e., for himself);' हूं पोथी वरी लेऊं हूं, 'I take the book (for myself);' ऊ पोथी परी देहो, 'he will give the book away;' etc.

Intensive Compounds in Rajputana.

Rem. Hence there will evidently be some verbs which can only be used with one of these prefixes. Thus, while one can say, वरो आणो, परो जाणो, परो आणो or वरो जाणो would be a contradiction in terms.

a. In Máṛwáṛ, when the Imperfect Participle of any verb is combined with रहना, as in Continuative Compounds in High Hindí, the combination has, not a continuative, but a *negative* sense. Thus, in the Rajputana colloquial, गातो रहणो, is not 'to continue singing,' but 'to be kept from singing,' 'not to sing.' So, again, कीवाड़ जड़ दो कै मनष माहै आता रहै, is 'shut the door that the people may not come in,'—not, 'may continue to come in.'

Máṛwáṛí Negative Compounds.

513. Before leaving these Rajputana forms, we may briefly indicate a few peculiar forms of the Rajput bard *Chand*, as noted by Beames. (1) The Imperfect Participle occasionally ends in न्त; as, e.g., हवन्त, रहन्त = H.H. होता, रहता. (2) The Perfect termination, इयो (इयौ), is transformed into व, इव, or एव, as, e.g., दिन्नव, 'gave,' for H.H. दिया; भ्रमेव, 'wandered,' for H.H. भ्रमाया; बुल्लिव, 'spoke,' = H.H. बोला, etc., etc.

Forms used by Chand.

(3) The final या of छया is sometimes shortened, thus, छय; छऐ is used as a conjunctive participle. (4) For दीणो, 'given' and कीणो, 'done,' दिन्नो and किन्नो occur; and for देखा, दिट्ठो. (5) The Conjunctive participle is sometimes made to terminate in इथै, इय or य, as, e.g., in किथै for H.H. करके; सिंचिय, for H.H. सींचके, लय = लइय, for H.H. लेकर.

Gaṛhwálí and Kumaoní Conjugation.

514. The verb in the Himalayan dialects of Gaṛhwál and Kumáon presents in many respects a suggestive resemblance to the Máṛwáṛí conjugation. Thus, the auxiliary substantive verb has छ for its radical consonant; लो (fem. ली), instead of गा, is in many places the termination of the future; न in the infinitive, as elsewhere, is changed to ण. इ final in a root is very commonly rejected and the concurrent vowels combined; but the consequent *sandhi* is to औ and not ऐ; as in G. रौणो for H.H. रहना; so that उ, instead of इ, appears to be preferred as a vowel of union before the infinitive termination. But with these resemblances, there also are some variations from the Máṛwáṛí type. Most noticeable is the Imperfect Participle, which often ends in दो or न्दो, plur. दा or न्दा, instead of तो, ता, thus resembling the Panjábí. The तो forms, however, are also used, also sometimes retaining the ancient न before त, as in बरषन्तो, 'raining,' for H.H. बरसता. In the tenses of the Imperfect Participle of some verbs with a vowel final in the root, Kumáoní rejects the participial termination before the auxiliary, and shortens the final radical vowel, giving, e.g., दि छ, for H.H. देता है, 'he gives.' The future termination, लो, in Gaṛhwálí is often added, not to the contingent future terminations, but to the root. I have sometimes heard the negative particle interposed between the conting. future and this suffix लो, thus: एणी कुईं चोइ न लो = H.H. ऐसी बात नहीं होगी, 'such a thing will not be.' Of the two Gaṛhwálí forms often given in the 'Tables,' the first belongs to Tíri, the second is used further east. The causal affix आव is softened to औ; giving, e.g., from the intransitive verb, पगणो, 'to float,' the causal पगौणो. I should expect that in these dialects there would be an inflected passive conjugation, as in the closely-related Máṛwáṛí, and the Naipálí dialect, contiguous on the east; but I have not been able to secure examples.

Naipálí Conjugation.

515. The Naipálí conjugation, so far as I have been able to procure material, is exhibited in the Tables. In the case of the verb छनु, 'to be,' I have been obliged to supply a number of forms from the analogy of other verbs in the dialect. The following remarks are added in further explication of the peculiarities of Naipálí conjugation, which, as will appear, are numerous and important. The usual termination of the infinitive is नु, which is inflected to ना; as, in पाउनु, obl., पाउना, in चिसो न पाउना ले, 'from not finding moisture.' But both the direct and oblique forms also occur in नऽ; as in जाननऽ, 'to know,' both dir. and obl. This oblique form is preferred to that in ना, in those combinations called Intensives, Permissives, etc., in which an infinitive enters as the first member: as in भननऽ लागनु, 'to begin to say;' जानऽ दिनु, 'to permit to go.' But in cases where High Hindí has the inflected infinitive with the postposition तक, Naipálí adds to the न of the infinitive the affix ज्याल्, which is then followed by सम्म = H. H. तक; as in the following: न पाउन्ज्याल् सम्म खोज्दै न कि, 'doth she not seek until she finds (it)?'

516. The imperfect and perfect participles are formed by the addition to the root, in the former case, of the suffix दो or दऽ, in the latter, of the suffix यो. Thus we have, from जाननु, 'to know,' the imperfect participle, जान्दो or जान्दऽ, the perfect participle, जान्यो. Before the द of the imperfect participle, after a vowel final in the preceding root, Anusvár is commonly inserted; as in जांदो, 'going,' from जानु, 'to go;' आउंदो, 'coming,' from आउनु, 'to come.' Naipálí Imperf. and Perf. Participles.

a. In many verbs, however, तो or तऽ is added instead of दो or दऽ. My list of illustrations is not complete, but the facts gathered seem to show that the choice of one or the other is determined by the character of the final letter of the root as hard or soft. If it be hard, the termination retains the original hard initial, त; but if it be soft, then the त of the termination is changed into the soft द. Thus, from खोजनु, 'to seek,' the imperfect participle is खोजदो or खोजदऽ; from पाउनु, 'to find,' पाउंदो or पाउंदऽ; but from सकनु, 'to be able,' it is सकतो or सकतऽ; from देखनु, 'to see,' देखतो; etc.

517. Both participles inflect the strong termination ओ, to आ, masc., and ई, fem. But the weak form in दऽ or तऽ is unchanged for gender or number. Beside the above-named inflections, very frequent is also an inflected locative of these participles, in ऐ; as, from the verbs, खानु, 'to eat,' and पिनु, 'to drink,' in the following: उ रोटी न खांदै दाख रस न पिंदै आयो, 'he came neither eating bread nor drinking wine.' This form is most common in such statical combinations as the above, and also in the absolute construction combined with हुंदै, 'being,' a locative form of the imperfect participle of हुनु, 'to be,' in which the ऐ of the locative

is shortened to इ; as in उन्हेरु जांदै छंदि, 'while they were going.' But the oblique form in आ is also used in this construction, with no apparent difference of meaning; as in यिरोशलीम तीर जांदा छंदि, 'as they were going toward Jerusalem.'

Adj. Suffix of Perf. Part.

518. When the perfect participle is used adjectively, the suffix को is added to its obl. masc. form. Thus, in the attributive construction, ल मोटाया को बाछो ल्या मार, 'bring (and) kill the fatted calf;' and, in the predicative construction, तेरो यो भाइ मऱ्या को थियो, 'this thy brother was dead.' This को is inflected to की, when referring to a feminine noun; thus, उस को सासु ठुला जरा ले दुख्या की थी, 'his mother-in-law was sick with a great fever;' and to का, when the reference is to a noun in the oblique masc., singular or plural; thus, मेरा बालख मठ संगै बिछ्याउना मा सुत्या का छन्, 'my children are asleep with me in bed.'*

a. The participle thus combined with को, may again be used as a noun, and may then take the plural affix हेरु, which is added to the inflected form, का. In this way the affix हेरु is sometimes appended to whole clauses, which are thus treated as substantives. Examples are: मन चूर्ण भया काहेरु सब गर्न, 'to bind up the broken-hearted;' भूत लागि दुखाया काहेरु आये, 'those (who were) afflicted (by) being possessed with devils came.'

Naipálí Subst. Verb.

519. The substantive verb, हुनु, 'to be' or 'to become,' forms the imperfect participle regularly, but in the perfect participle and the tenses derived from it, it reverts, like many other dialects, to the more primitive form of the root, भउ; so that we have a perfect participle, भयो, and an inflected perfect tense:—1. sing., भयां, 'I became;' 2. sing., भयस; etc. It is to be noted that Naipálí possesses also an imperfect participle, छंदो, 'being,' belonging to the root छ (छक्), which appears in the present of the substantive verb. It chiefly appears in the absolute construction, as in the following: लस्कार न छंदा, 'in the absence of the multitude.'

Naipálí Noun of Agency.

520. In the Naipálí Gospel no instance occurs of the Noun of Agency in वाला or हारा, or of any form that could be connected with these. Instead of these, is used a form derived from the root by the addition of the suffix न्या: as from चरनु, 'to sow,' चर्न्या, 'a sower,' = H.H. बोनेवाला; from उठनु, 'to rise,' उठन्या; etc. The plural is regularly

---

* With this idiom may be compared the exactly analogous use of the affix ड़ो in Máṛwáṛí. Vid. § 497.

formed by the suffix हेरु; as in मुक्ति पाउन्यहेरु, 'those finding salvation.' This appears, however, to have a somewhat broader use than the High Hindí noun in वाला. Thus, we have, Luke xv. 12, मेरो हुन्या अंश मलाइ देउ, 'give me the portion that is to be mine;' where, in High Hindí, होनेवाला would scarcely be used. Other illustrations are: तस को शून्य हुन्या बेला नजिकै आयो, 'the time of its becoming desolate is at hand;' मेरो घर प्रार्थना गर्न्या घर हो, 'my house is a house of prayer.' In these last, as in other instances, this form seems to be used where High Hindí would prefer an inflected form of the infinitive.

Naipálí Conj. Participle.

521. The conjunctive participle in Naipálí is regularly formed by adding to the root इ or ई; to which the suffix कन, H.H. कर or के, is very commonly added. Thus, from हिंड्नु, 'to go,' 'to move,' we have the conjunctive participle, हिंडि, or हिंडि कन; from बटोल्नु, 'to gather,' बटोलि, or बटोलि कन. In the case of a number of common verbs whose roots terminate in इ, the root alone, or with कन added, forms the conjunctive participle; as from लिनु, 'to take,' conj. part., लि or लि कन; दिनु, 'to give,' conj. part., दि or दि कन; etc. In a few monosyllabic roots ending in ă, the इ of the conjunctive participle unites with this final inherent ă, giving forms in ऐ. The most important examples of this are found in the case of the verbs, जानु, 'to go,' and हुनु, 'to be,' in which, respectively, the roots गए and भए, which in other dialects are confined to the perfect participle, are substituted also in the conjunctive participle; giving the forms, गै or गै कन, 'having gone,' and भै or भै कन, 'having been' or 'become.'

Naipálí Conting. Fut. and Imperative.

522. The contingent future and imperative are identical in form, except in the 2nd and 3rd sing., and the 3rd plur. In the imperative, the 2nd sing. consists of the root alone, as in High Hindí, to which in the 3rd sing. the suffix ओस, and in the 3rd plur., the suffix उन, is added.* Thus, from भन्नु, 'to speak,' we have the imper. 2nd sing. भन; 3rd sing., भनोस; 3rd plur., भनुन. The respectful or precative forms of the imperative, so common in other dialects, I have not found in Naipálí. Their place appears to be taken by a combination, in the honorific style, of the infinitive of the verb with the 3rd sing. imperative of the verb हुनु, 'to be,' as in the following: मेरा छोरा लाइ हेर्नु हवस, 'be pleased to look upon my son;' तपाञि मेरा घर हिंड्नु हवस, 'your excellency will be pleased to go to my house.'

---

* So Hoernle (*Comp. Gramm.* p. 333); but in the Naipálí Gospel, I have found both these forms also in the contingent future.

Naipálí Absol. Future.

523. In the absolute future, Naipálí agrees with Kumáoní and Gaṛhwálí, in using the type in ल (ल, इल् or लो); in which, again, ल is optionally changed to न. As will appear from the Tables, these terminations, which in certain cases take personal endings, are added to various forms of the contingent future. To the forms in ने are also added, sometimes, the several forms of the present tense of the substantive verb, छुं, etc.; as in गरने छुं = H.H. करूंगा.

Naipálí Present.

524. Naipálí has three forms of the present, which do not appear to differ in meaning. The first, and most common, is formed by adding to the unchanged root the present of the substantive verb, छुं, छस, etc.; the second, by adding to the weak form of the imperfect participle the several personal endings; the third is formed as in High Hindí, by combining with the imperfect participle the present tense of the substantive verb. In this last case, the weak form of the participle is used, and suffers no change for person, gender or number, which are indicated by the substantive verb alone. In the Gospel, at least, this third form is infrequent. As examples of these three forms of this tense, we thus have, from गरनु, 'to do, 'to make,' the 1st plur., 1st form, गरछुं; 2nd form, गरदौं;* 3rd form, गरद॰ छुं. The full paradigms are given in the Tables.

Naipálí Past Imperfect.

525. The past imperfect in Naipálí exhibits two forms, having no apparent difference in meaning. Of these, the first, and much the most common, is formed after the analogy of the 1st form of the present, by adding to the root the past tense of the substantive verb, थ्यां,† थिस, etc.; the second corresponds to the 3rd form of the present, and, like the imperfect in High Hindí, is formed by combining with the imperfect participle the past tense of the substantive verbs. As in the present, the participle is used unchanged throughout in its weak form. Thus the first form, e.g., of the past imperfect of the verb, भननु, 'to speak,' is as follows:—*Sing.* (1) भनथ्यां, (2) भनथिस, (3) भनथ्यो; *Plur.* (1) भनथ्युं, (2) भनथ्यौ, (3) भनथ्या. The 2nd form of the same is, *Sing.* (1) भनद॰ थियां, (2) भनद॰ थिस, etc., etc.

a. In the periphrastic form of both the present and the past imperfect, for the weak uninflected form of the imperfect participle, is often substituted throughout an inflected loc. form in ए. In some instances it is not easy to see any difference in the meaning of the two forms; but

* I supply this from analogy.

† For थ्यां, Hoernle gives थियें or थें. *Comp. Gramm.* p. 366.

TABLE XIX.—DIALECTIC CONJUGATION OF होना, 'to be.'

		High Hindí.	Kanaují.	Braj.	W. Ráj.	E. Ráj.	Gaṛhwálí.	Kumáoní.	Naipálí.	Old Baiswáṛí.	Avadhí.	Ríwáí.	Bhojpúrí.	Mágadhí.	Maithilí.
INFIN.		होना.	होनो.	होनौं, व्हैवो.	होणो, व्हैणो. होण, व्हैवो.	होणो, व्हैणो. व्हैंणूं, व्हैवो.	होणो.	होणौं. ऊणो.	ऊनु.	होब, होन.	होब.	होब.	होअब, होइब. होनां.	होएब, होइब. होअब.	होअल, होएब, होब.
CONTINGENT FUTURE.	SINGULAR.	होऊं.	होऊं.	होऊं.	व्हेऊं.	व्हेऊं.	होऊं.	ऊणी. ऊंलो.	होउं.	होउं.	होउं.	होऊं.	होओं. *f.* होयूं.	होऊं. *f.* होइयों.	होइअऊ, होइओ,[4] होइहीं. होओं, होओं, होऊं, होआं. होइऐ,[4] होई.
		हो.	होए.	होय.	व्है.	व्है.[1]	होई. होव.	ऊने. होले.	होवस.	होर, होउ. होहि, होसि.	होस.	व्हास.	होअसि, होअस. *f.* होइस. होए, होय. होई.	होही, होअइ. होएं,[3] होअं, हो. *f.* होई.	होइऐ, होई,[3] होही,[4] होइ. होऐ,[3] होए,[3] होअं, हो. *f.* होहि. होई.
		हो.	होए.	होय.	व्है.	व्है.[1]	होव.	ऊम. होलो.	हो.	होर, होउ. होहि, होसि.	होय.	व्हाय.	होअसि, होअस. होअसु, होओ. *f.* होअसि. होए, होअ, होय.	होअस, होअइ. होअउ. होए.	होअथि, होऐ,[4] होए, होअ. होओ,[4] होओ, हो.
	PLURAL.	हों.	होंए.	हौंय.	व्हैंआं. व्हैंहां.	व्हैआं.	होवाऊं. होवन.	ऊना. ऊंला.	होऔं.	होहिं.	होईं.	होन.	होईं.[2] *f.* होयूं.	होइअइ, होई,[3] होइअउ. *f.* होइयों.	होइऐन्हि, होइऐन्ह, होइहैन्ह, होइऊन्ह. होअन्ह, होइएं,[4] होइअ, होई. होइहौन्हि, होइऔन्ह, होइहौन्ह, होइओ.[4] *f.* होऐं. होईं.
		हो.	हो.	हो.	व्हैओ. व्हैहो.	व्हैओ.	होयाई. होवन.	ऊना. होला.	होवौ.	होऊ.	होउ.	व्हाव.	होअह. होअ, हो. *f.* होऊ.	होऊन, होऊ,[3] होहो. होहिन, होहीं, होअ. *f.* होऊ. होई.	होइऐन्हि, होइन. होऊन्ह, होहो,[4] होहो. होऊ, होअह, होअ. *f.* होऊ.
		हों.	होंए.	हौंय.	व्है.	व्है.[1]	होवन.	ऊना. होला.	होउन.	होहिं.	होंय.	व्हांय.	होअन. होएं, होईं. *f.* होइन.	होहिन, होहीं, होइन, होईं. होथिन, होथी, होथुन. होखिन. *f.* होयीन, होयिनी. होखीन, होखिनी.	होअथिन्ह, होथिन्ह, होअथि, होअथ. होथी, होथ, होइएन्ह, होऐन्ह, होहिन्ह. होअन्ह, होहीं, होहिं, होएं, होथुन्हि, होऔन्हि. होऊन्ह, होआ. *f.* होथीन्हि, होथीं. होइन्ह, होई.

[1] Also ऊवै, both here and in the Present, Table XX. [2] य optional after हो throughout the Plur. [3] Anusvar optional. [4] क optionally added.

TABLE XIX. (*Continued*).—DIALECTIC CONJUGATION OF होना, 'to be.'

		H. Hindí.	*Kanaují.*	*Braj.*	*W. Ráj.*	*E. Ráj.*	*Gaṛhwálí.*	*Kumáoní.*	*Naipálí.*	*Old Baiswáṛí.*	*Avadhí.*	*Ríwáí.*	*Bhojpúrí.*	*Mágadhí.*	*Maithilí.*
IMPERF. PART.		होता.	होत.	होतु.	व्हेतो.	व्हेतो.	होंदो.	होंनू हातन. *f.* हातिन.	हुंदो. भयो.	होत.	होत.	होत.	होत, होअत, होइत.	होइत, होअत, होत.	होइत, होत.
PRESENT IMPERFECT.	SINGULAR.	होता हूं.	होत हूं.	होतु हों.	व्हेऊं हूं.	व्हेऊं छूं.	होंदो छौं, होंदू.	हूं छूं. हुनूं.	हुंद्० छु. हुंछु.	हौं. होत (अहउं).²	होत अहेउं.	होत आं.	होत बाटों.	होइत हो.	होइत छो.
		होता है.	होत है.	होतु है.	व्हे है.	व्हे छै.	होंदो छ, होंदी.	हूं छै. हूं छै.	हुंद्० छस. हुंछस.	होइ, होय, हो. होहि, होसि. होत.	होत अहेस.	होते ऐ.	होत बाटस.	होइत हं.	होइत छह. छो.⁴
		होता है.	होत है.	होतु है.	व्हे है.	व्हे छै.	होंदो छ, होंद.	हूं छ. हूं छ.	हुंद्० छऽ. हुंछऽ.	होइ, होय, हो. होहि, होसि. होत.	होत अहै.	होत घा.	होत बाटे.	होइत हइ.	होइत अछि. छथि.⁴
	PLURAL.	होते हैं.	होत हैं.	होतु हैं.	व्हेवां हां. व्हेयां	व्हेयां छां.	होंदा छौं, होंदाऊं.	हुना. हुनु.	हुंद्० छूं. हुंछूं.	होहिं. होत (हहिं).²	होत अहो.	होत्यें हैं.	होत बानीं.	होइत हों.	होइत छिऐन्हि.
		होते हो.	होत हो.	होतु हौ.	व्हेवो हो. व्हेओ	व्हेओ छो.	होंदा छन, होंदाई.	हुना. हूं छा.	हुंद्० छौ. हुंछौ.	होऊ. होत (हऊ).²	होत अहें. अहो.	होत अहेन.	होत बाटऽ.	होइत हऽ.	होइत छहन्हि. छिऐन्हि.⁴
		होते हैं.	होत हैं.	होतु हैं.	व्हे है.	व्हे छै.	होंदा छन, होंदान्.	हुना. हुनौ.	हुंद्० छन. हुंछन.	होहिं. होत (हहिं).² होंइ.	होत अहैं.	होत आं.	होत बाटन.	होइत हई.	होइत छैन्हि. छथुन्हि.⁴
PAST IMPERFECT.	SINGULAR.	होता था.	होत हतो.	होतु हो.	व्हे हो. व्हे तो.	व्हे छो.	होंदो थयो.¹	हूं छियो. हूं छियो.	हुद्० थ्यां. हुंथ्यां.	होत रह.	होत रहेउं.	होत रह्योउं.	होत रहलों.	होइत हलूं.	होइत छलऊं.
		होता था.	होत हतो.	होतु हो.	व्हे हो. व्हे तो.	व्हे छो.	होंदो थयो.	हूं छियो. हूं छिये.	हुंद्० थिस. हुंथिस.	होत रह.	होत रहेस.	होत ते. रहा.	होत रहलस (हऽ).³	होइत हलं.	होइत छलऊं.
		होता था.	होत हतो.	होतु हो.	व्हे हो. व्हे तो.	व्हे छो.	होंदो थयो.	हूं छियो. हूं छियो.	हुंद्० थ्यो. हुंथ्यो.	होत रह.	होत रहा.	होत ते, ता. रहा.	होत रहल (हऽ).³	होइत हल.	होइत छल. छलाह.⁴
	PLURAL.	होते थे.	होत हते.	होतु हे.	व्हे हा. व्हे ता.	व्हे छा.	होंदा थया.	हूं छिया. हूं छियां.	हुंद्० थ्यूं. हुंथ्यूं.	होत रहे.	होत रहे.	होत तें. रहेन.	होत रहलों (हं).³	होइत हलों.	होइत छलिऐन्हि.
		होते थे.	होत हते.	होतु हे.	व्हे हा. व्हे ता.	व्हे छा.	होंदा थया.	हूं छिया. हूं छियां.	हुंद्० थ्यौ. हुंथ्यौ.	होत रहेऊ.	होत रह्यो.	होत तें. रहेन.	होत रहलऽ (हऽ).³	होइत हलऽ.	होइत छलऊन्हि. छलिऐन्हि.⁴
		होते थे.	होत हते.	होतु हे.	व्हे हा. व्हे ता.	व्हे छा.	होंदा थया.	हूं छिया. हूं छियां.	हुंद्० थ्या. हुंथ्या.	होत रहे.	होत रहें.	होत तें, ता. रहेन.	होत रहलन (हं).³	होइत हलन.	होइत छलैन्हि. छलथुन्हि.⁴

¹ The participle alone is also used for the imperfect past. ² The use of the auxiliary is exceptional. ³ Optionally inserted in Sáran. ⁴ Honorific, as regards the subject.

TABLE XIX. (*Concluded*).—DIALECTIC CONJUGATION OF होना, 'to be.'

		High Hindi.	*Kanauji.*	*Braj.*	*W. Rāj.*	*E. Rāj.*	*Garhwāli.*	*Kumāoni.*	*Naipāli.*	*Old Baiswāri.*	*Avadhi.*	*Riwāi.*	*Bhojpuri.*	*Māgadhi.*	*Maithili.*
PERF. PART.		हुआ.	भयो.	भयौ.	व्हियो, हुयो. व्हीओ.	व्हियो, हुवो. व्हीओ, हुयो.	होए, होयो.	भयो. हुइयो.	भयो.	भयउ.	भया.	भा.	भइल, भैला, etc.	होल, भेल.	भेल, होल, होलऽ.
PRESENT PERFECT.	SINGULAR.	हुआ हूं.	भयो हूं.	भयौ हौं.	व्हियो हूं.	व्हियो छूं.	होए छौं. होयूं.	हयूं, हैगयूं, हो छौं.	भयां छु.	भयउं, भयेउं, भएउं, भा. *m.* भइउं. *f.*	भयेउं हौं. *m.* भयिउं हौं. *f.*	भ हौं.	भइलों हा. भइल वाड़ों.[2]	होलूं है.	भेलौं यऽ.
		हुआ है.	भयो है.	भयौ है.	व्हियो है.	व्हियो छै.	होय छ. होई.	है छै, हैगे छै. हो छै.	भये छस. भइस	भयउ, भयेउ, भा. *m.* भइ, भइसि. *f.*	भयेस है. *m.* भयिसि है. *f.*	भ है.	भइलस हा. भइल वाड़स.	होला है.	भेलें यऽ.
		हुआ है.	भयो है.	भयौ है.	व्हियो है.	व्हियो छै.	होए छ. होये.	है छ, हैगे छ. हो छ.	भयो छऽ.	भयउ, भयेउ, भा. *m.* भइ. *f.*	भवा है. *m.* भै है. *f.*	भ है.	भइल हा. भइल बा.	होल है.	भेल यऽ.
	PLURAL.	हुए हैं.	भए हैं.	भये हैं.	व्हिया हां.	व्हिया छां.	होया छौं. होयाऊं.	हयां, हैगयां. हैगयूं.	भयूं छौं. भयौं	भए, भये, भे. *m.* भईं. *f.*	भये हैं. *m.* भै अही. *f.*	भयेन्ह हैं. भयेन	भइलीं हां. भइल बानीं.	होलीं है.	भेली यऽ.
		हुए हो.	भए हो.	भये हौ.	व्हिया हो.	व्हिया छो.	होया छन. होयाई.	है छा, हैगे छा. हो छा.	भयौ छौ.	भए, भयेऊ, भएऊ. *m.* भईं, भईऊ. *f.*	भये हैं. *m.* भयिउ है. *f.*	भयेन अहेन.	भइलऽ हा. भइल बाड़ऽ.	होलऽ है.	भेलऽ यऽ.
		हुए हैं.	भए हैं.	भये हैं.	व्हिया है.	व्हिया छै.	होया छन. होइने.	हैईं, हैगईं. हैगईं.	भया छन.	भए, भये, भे. *m.* भईं. *f.*	भयें हैं. *m.* भयेनि हैं. *f.*	भयेन अहैं.	भइलन हां. भइल बाड़न.	होलन है.	भेला यऽ.
PAST PERFECT.	SINGULAR.	हुआ था.	भयो हतो.	भयौ हो.	व्हियो हो.	व्हियो छो.	होए थयो. होइ छयो.[1]	है छियो. *f.* छी. हो छियो.	भयां थ्यां.	*No instance of this tense noted in this verb.*	भयेउं रहा. *m.* भयिउं रही. *f.*	भयों रहा.	भइले रहलों.	होलूं हल.	भेलौं रहे.
		हुआ था.	भयो हतो.	भयौ हो.	व्हियो हो.	व्हियो छो.	होए थयो. होइ छयो.	है छियो. *f.* हो छिये.	भइस थिस.		भयेस रहा. *m.* भै रही. *f.*	भयेस ते. रहा.	भइले रहलस.	होला हल.	भेलें रहे.
		हुआ था.	भयो हतो.	भयौ हो.	व्हियो हो.	व्हियो छो.	होए थयो. होइ छयो.	है छियो. *f.* हो छियो.	भयो थ्यो.		भवा रहा. *m.* भै रही. *f.*	भ तो, ता. रहा.	भइले रहल.	होल हल.	भेल रहे.
	PLURAL.	हुए थे.	भये हते.	भये हे.	व्हिया हा.	व्हिया छा.	होया थया. होइ छया.	है छिया. *f.* हो छिया.	भयूंथ्यूं.		भ रहे. *m.* भयीं रहीं. *f.*	भयेन्ह तें. रहेंन.	भइले रहलीं.	होलों हल.	भेली रहे.
		हुए थे.	भये हते.	भये हे.	व्हिया हा.	व्हिया छा.	होया थया. होइ छया.	है छिया. *f.* हो छिया.	भयौ थ्यौ.		भये रहे. *m.* भयीं रहीं. *f.*	भयेन ते. रहेंन.	भइले रहलूऽ.	होलऽ हल.	भेलऽ रहे.
		हुए थे.	भये हते.	भये हे.	व्हिया हा.	व्हिया छा.	होया थया. होइ छया.	है छिया. हो छिया.	भया थ्या.		भये रहें. *m.* भयीं रहीं. *f.*	भयेन तें. रहेन.	भइले रहले.	होलन हल.	भेला रहे.
CONJ. PART.		होकर.	होइकरके.	व्है, व्हैकरि. होय कै, etc.	व्हैतोकनै. व्हैर.	व्है, व्हैनै.	होइक. होईक.	हैबेर. होइबेर.	भै. भै कन.	होइ.	होकै.	होकै.	*Wanting.*	*Wanting.*	भै के, भे के. होय के, होइ के, ही के.

[1] Also होइ छि throughout the sing. and plur.

[2] This Conjugation with वाड़ों, etc., in the W. and in Champáran.

commonly this latter form seems to be preferred when it is desired to suggest the action of the verb as a permanent condition; as in the words of the Lord to the messengers of John the Baptist, अंधा देखते छन, 'the blind see,' etc.

b. In the first form of both the present and the past imperfect, roots ending in a vowel take Anusvár before the substantive verb; thus, from जानु, जांछु, 'I go;' from लिनु, लिंछस, 'thou takest;' from हुनु, हुंछौ, 'ye are;' from पाउनु, पाउंछन, 'they find,' etc. So in the past imperfect we have, from दिनु, दिंथ्यो, 'he was giving;' from आउनु, आउंथ्यूं, 'we were coming,' etc. Also रहनु, 'to remain,' and दहनु, 'to burn,' sometimes takes Anusvár under similar conditions; as, e.g., in दहंछन, 'they remain;' दहंछुं, 'I burn.'

526. In the tenses of the *perfect*, Naipálí chiefly uses an inflected perfect, given in Table XXI. But sometimes a periphrastic present and past perfect are used, formed by combining with this inflected indefinite perfect, the present and past tenses, respectively, of the substantive verb. It is to be remembered that in these tenses Naipálí follows the idiom of Eastern Hindí in making the transitive verb always to agree in person, gender, and number, with the subject of the action, even though after the analogy of Western Hindí the postposition is appended to the noun which denotes that subject. The periphrastic definite perfect is given in Table XX; of the past perfect the following is an example, from the verb देखनु, 'to see:'—*Sing.* (1) देख्यां थियां, (2) देखिस थिस, (3) देख्यो थियो; *Plur.* (1) देख्यौं थिऊं, (2) देख्यौ थियौ, (3) देख्या थिया, or देखे थिये. Naipálí Perfect Tenses.

527. Naipálí forms First and Second Causals after the analogy of the other Hindí dialects; adding for the First Causal the suffix आउ (Br. आव, H H. आ), and reduplicating this for the second or double Causal. Instances of irregular formations by internal change of the verbal root are also found, as in High Hindí. Examples are:—from मरनु, 'to die;' मारनु, 'to kill;' मराउनु, 'to cause to be killed;' गरनु, 'to do,' 'make;' गराउनु, 'to cause to make.' But I have met one example of a Causal formed by adding या to the root, in छुट्यायो, 'loosed.' Naipálí Causals.

528. The only passive which is used in the Naipálí Gospel is an inflected passive, formed by the addition of इय to the root of the active verb. From this secondary root the several tenses are formed by adding the same terminations as in the active verb. This इय is reduced to इ Naipálí Inflected Passive.

before the terminations of the perfect participle, and before न in the infinitive and the verbal noun in न्या. Thus, from the infinitive मारनु, 'to beat' or 'to kill,' is formed the passive infinitive, मारिनु, 'to be killed,' and the passive verbal noun, मारिन्या. Other examples are the following:—जब तं फिराइयेलास, 'when thou shalt be turned;' कुटियेला, 'he shall be beaten;' नाशियौला, 'ye shall be destroyed;' म० तिमरो छोरो भनिन्या योग्य छइन०, 'I am not worthy to be called thy son;' त्यो धनी मरि गाडियो, 'that rich man, having died, was buried;' पाइया, 'they were found,' etc., etc.

Naipálí Compound Verbs. **529.** The various forms of compound verbs which are formed in High Hindí with the inflected infinitive, are formed in Naipálí with the uninflected infinitive in its weak form; as in छन लाग्यो, 'it began to be,' etc. But in the formation of the Frequentative, गरनु (H.H. करना) is combined, not with a verbal noun in आ, as in High Hindí, but with the inflected (loc.) form of the imperfect participle in ए, as in the following:—कुकुर खटिरा चाटती गर्थ्यो, 'the dogs were wont to lick his sores.' This same form of the imperfect participle is used in the formation of Continuatives; thus, जागदै रहं थ्यो = H.H. जाग रहा था, 'he was staying awake.' In Continuatives formed from the verb छनु, the root भ is substituted for this, as in तं भै रहे थस = H.H. तू हो रहा था.

530. It is important to note a peculiarity in the use of the negative with certain of the verbal forms, in that, instead of following the verb, it is regularly inserted before the final letter of the terminations. Thus we have मानदैन, 'they believe,' but मानदैनन, 'they believe not;' जानिस, 'thou knewest,' but जानिनस, 'thou knewest not.' So also I have noted देख्तैनस, 'thou seest not;' पायेनन, 'they were not found;' सुंपिनस, 'thou didst not deliver,' etc, etc.

531. For the High Hindí forms, चाहिये, and चाहिये था, 'ought,' Naipálí has, for the former, चाहिये छ०, चाहियो, and चाहिंछ०; for the latter, चाहिं थ्यो, and चाहिंदै थ्यो.

Conjugation in the Eastern dialects.

Conjugation in the *Rámáyan*. **532.** In the old Baiswáṛí of the *Rámáyan*, as in all archaic Hindí poetry, the tense-system is not so fully developed, nor are the distinctive characteristics of the various tenses so uniformly and distinctly marked as in modern High Hindí.

But on the other hand, we find a great variety of terminations, and some tenses which are unknown to High Hindí. We begin with the tenses corresponding in general to those of High Hindí.

533. The Infinitive or Gerund presents two forms, analogous to the two in Braj, viz., one in न, and another in ब. Examples are: अब तेहि कहा देन बैदेही, 'when (he) told him to give up *Vaidehí*;' बिनु सिय राम फिरब भल नाहीं, 'it is not well to return without *Rám* and *Sítá*.' The inflected forms also occur; as, e.g., अस न होने, 'it is not so to be.' = H.H. नहीं होने का; मैं तव दसन तोरिबे लायक, 'I am able to break thy teeth.' Infinitive in the *Rámayan*.

534. The Imperfect Participle is formed by adding त to the root; as from बिलोकन, 'to behold,' बिलोकत, 'beholding.' This is often, though not invariably, inflected to ति for the feminine; as in लगावति, from लगावत = H.H. लगाता. There is no other inflection. In the following we have the longer Braj participle in तो; धेनु मन भावतो पय स्रवहिं, 'the cow drops milk satisfying to the heart.' Imperf. and Perf. Part. in the *Rámáyan*.

535. The Perfect Participle regularly consists of the root alone; inflected in the feminine only to इ. Thus from कहन, सुनन, come the perfect participles, कह, सुन, fem., कहि, सुनि. But the longer H.H. forms in आ and ई are frequently used where the metre may require them. In the case of verbs with roots in आ, the व which in High Hindí has only been retained in the tenses of the future, maintains its place before *a* or *á* in the perfect participle also; thus we have गावा, 'sung,' for H.H. गाया; आव or आवा, 'come,' for H.H. आया. But the common forms in या also occur.

536. The Conjunctive Participle is regularly formed by adding इ to the root; thus, तोहि देखि सीतल भइ छाती, 'seeing thee, (my) breast has become cool.' As in the case of all short final vowels, this इ may be lengthened metri gratiâ. This Conj. Part. in the *Rámayan*.

is especially common at the end of a line; as, बैठेउ सभा असि खबरि पाई, 'receiving such news, the assembly sat down.' Much less frequently we find the Braj form in कै, after इ as a union-vowel; as, मुनीसआयसु पाइकै, 'receiving the great sage's command.' The root alone is occasionally used; and the final inherent *a* may be lengthened metri gratiâ, as in the following, where चीन्हा is not the perfect, but the conjunctive participle; सुफल जन्म माना प्रभु चीन्हा, 'recognizing the lord, he regarded his birth as having borne good fruit.'

537. For the Noun of Agency, the affix वार, (plur. वारे, fem. वारि,) is added to the root, as in the following; ते एहि ताल चतुर रखवारे, 'these are the watchful guardians of this lake.'

Conting. Fut. in the *Rámáyan*.

538. The *Rámáyan* exhibits forms of the Contingent Future identical with the longer and archaic Braj forms; viz., *Sing.* (1) औं or ओं; (2, 3,) हि; *Plur.* (1, 3,) हिं; (2) हु. For the longer forms with इ, ए, ऐ, and एं, ऐं, are sometimes used. Examples are:—पावक जरौं, 'I could burn in the fire;' केहि मग जाहीं, 'by what road shall we go?' को कहै, 'who can tell?' य is sometimes inserted after इ final in a root; as, जौलौं जियौं, 'as long as I live.'

a. But instead of these final diphthongs, their elementary vowels often appear: as, e.g., जौ मैं करउं रसोई, 'when I prepare food;' कीचइ मिलइ, 'it mingles with the mire.' The final vowel of these forms, again, metri gratiâ, is often lengthened; as, जो अपने अवगुन सब कहऊं, 'if I should tell all my faults;' अन्न सो जो जो भोजन करई, 'whoever may eat that food.'

b. Before उं, in the 1st sing., ए *ĕ* is sometimes inserted; thus, तुम्हहिं सुनाएउं सोइ, 'that same I will make known to you.'

c. Or, again, the final diphthongs, ए, ऐ, are reduced to their cognate vowel, इ, as in चाहि for चाहै, and especially in the substantive verb; thus, जो आयसु होइ, 'if the order be.'

. *d.* Again, even this final ए is often dropped, leaving the 2nd and 3rd sing. in form like the root; as, अधम सो नारि जो सेव न तेही, 'base (is) that woman, who will not serve her;' सो किमि सोव, 'how could he sleep?' And this final *a*, again, may be lengthened, metri gratiâ, giving a form identical with the H.H. perfect participle; as, मास दिवस महं कहा न माना, 'if in a month's time thou obey not what is told (thee);' जाकर नाम मरत मुख आवा, 'whose name, (if it) come into the mouth of one dying.'

e. For ए of the 2nd and 3rd sing., य appears sometimes in passive forms; as, सपनेहु सुनिय न वेद पुराना, 'not even in a dream is heard *Ved* (or) *Purán*.' उ is sometimes substituted for ए in the 2nd and 3rd sing.; as, जौ अस होउ, 'if it be so.'

f. Finally, for हि, we often find the still older form, सि; as, जौ तैं चहसि, 'if thou wish;' तेहि न भजसि मन मंद, 'wilt thou not worship him, O dull heart?.' Sometimes सु appears for सि.

539. Besides the above forms, I have found in other archaic literary eastern Hindí, a conjugation of this tense with व as the characteristic letter, to which the regular terminations are then added; thus, *Sing.* (1) वौं, (2, 3,) वे; *Plur.* (1, 3,) वें, (2) वो or वौ. With these *v* or *b* forms, as well as those (to be hereafter noticed) of the absolute future, may be compared the Bangálí future terminations, *ibo, ibá* or *ibe, iben.*

540. It may be observed, finally, that although, very often, the forms above noted indicate, in the *Rámáyan*, a degree of dubiety, and for the certain futurition of the event, the forms of the absolute future, as given in § 541, are preferred, yet now and then these forms are unquestionably used where there is no contingency intimated. Thus, सब दुख मिटहि राम पद देखी, 'beholding the feet of *Rám*, all sorrow will cease;' भरतहि समर सिखावन देऊं, 'I will give *Bharat* instruction in war;' प्रभु भंजहिं दारुण विपति, 'the lord will remove the terrible calamity;' विकल होसि तैं कपि के मारे, 'thou shalt be distressed because of a monkey.' But illustration of this belongs rather to Syntax.

Absol. Fut. in the *Rámáyan.* **541**. The Absolute Future exhibits three varieties of conjugation, of which ग, ह, and ब, are, severally, the characteristic letters.

(1) The ग forms are not often used, and cannot be regarded as belonging properly to the dialect. When borrowed from Western Hindí, the suffixes, गो, etc., are added commonly to the *longer* forms of the contingent future; as, e.g., अभय करहिंगे तोहि, 'he will make thee free from fear;' या को फल पावहुगे आगे, 'of this thou shalt receive the fruit hereafter.' But as these archaic Braj forms will be quite familiar to the student of the *Rámáyan*, further illustration is not required.

(2) The 2nd form of the conjugation of the absolute future exhibits the following terminations: *Sing.* (1) हौं; (2, 3,) हहि; *Plur.* (1, 3,) हहिं; (2) हहु. As in Braj, इ is sometimes used as a union-vowel before these terminations; whence after आ final in a root, we have, by *sandhi*, ऐ. Illustrations of these future forms are:—काज मैं करिहौं तोरा, 'I will do thy work;' लै जैहौं तुम कहँ, 'I will carry you off;' आचरजन मानिहहिं, 'they will believe the wonders;' मोहि राज... दैहहु जबहीं, 'when you shall give me the kingdom;' हँसिहहु सुनि हमारी जड़ताई, 'you will laugh, hearing my foolishness.'

Of this general type of conjugation there are several variations:—

a. An original सि appears for हि; as, पछितैहसि अंत अभागी, 'O luckless (woman)! thou wilt repent it in the end.' Analogous is हेसु for हहि, as in the peculiar form, दिहेसु, = H.H. देगा; thus, तिन्हैं दिखाए दिहेसु तैं सीता, 'to him thou shalt show *Sítá.*'

b. The first ह of the future is sometimes rejected; thus, उभय न देखिअहि, 'if one shall regard neither,' lit., 'not regard both;' where देखिअहि is for देखिहहि.

c. ह having thus been rejected, ब is sometimes inserted; as, कौतुक प्रात देखिबहु मोरा, 'in the morning you shall see my exploits.'

(3) The 3rd variety of the absolute future is formed by simply adding ब *ba* to the root in all persons and numbers. This, it will be observed, is the usual type of the future in the modern eastern colloquial dialects. Examples of its use in the *Rámáyan* are:—चौथे दिवस मैं मिलब आई, 'the fourth day I will come and meet (you);' सुनि सुख लहब राम बैदेही। अनुचित कहब न पंडित केही, 'hearing this, *Rám* and *Vaidehí* will obtain joy, nor will any wise (man) call it wrong.'

Variations from the general type occur as follows;—

a. After आ final in a root, उ or इ is sometimes, but not necessarily, inserted; thus, जाब जहं पाउब तहीं, 'where I shall obtain that same, there shall I go;' तौ तुम दुख पाउब, 'then you will find sorrow;' फुलाइब गालु, 'thou wilt puff out the cheek.' So also, more rarely, after a consonant; as, पुरउब मैं अभिलाष तुम्हारा, 'I will fulfil thy desire.'

b. For ब, बि occasionally occurs; as, मैं मारबि काढ़ि कृपाना, 'drawing the sword I will kill thee.'

542. The Imperative exhibits two forms of conjugation; the one, identical with that of the contingent future; the other, with that of the absolute future in ब. In both the इ and the ब forms, we find many of the same variations as have already been noticed in these tenses. Imperative in the *Rámáyan*.

(1) Examples are, of the इ (स) forms:—पावउं मैं तिन्ह करि गति घोरा, 'may I obtain their terrible fate;' जिय मानसि जनि जना, 'do not lose heart;' करसि जनि चिंता, 'be thou not anxious.' Before सि, ए (*ĕ*) may be substituted for *a*; as, सो रचेसि उपाउ, 'contrive that plan.' एसु *ĕsu*, also occurs; as, परखेसु मोहि एक पखवारा, 'try me for a fortnight.' Or, eliding इ, in the 3rd sing., ई may be the termination; as, आचरज करै जनि कोई, 'let no one wonder.' The most common termination in the 2nd sing. is उ; thus, देखु तैं जाई, 'go thou and see;' lit., 'having gone, see.' The same termination is found in the 3rd sing.; as, राउ कुसल होउ,

'may (mine) be a reign of a hundred *kalpas.*' As in the contingent future, the final vowel may be reduced to *a*, so that the root alone appears in both the 2nd and 3rd sing.; thus, मोहि जान न कोई, 'let no one know me.' In the 2nd plur., हु is the common termination; as, प्रभु चरित सुनायहु मोही, 'tell me the deeds of the lord;' तजहु सोच, 'cease (your) anxiety.' But ए (*ĕ*) is very often substituted for *a*, or inserted before हु; as in पद पंकज गहेहु, 'clasp (his) lotus feet;' मासदिवस महं आयेहु, 'come in a month's time.' And हु is sometimes rejected; as in करउ सो बेगि जो तुम्हहिं सोहाई, 'do quickly, what may seem good to you.' The 1st and 3rd plur. regularly end in हिं (हों); thus, तव चरन हम अनुरागहीं, 'let me love thy feet,' where हम is used for the sing., मैं.

(2) The Imperative may also, like the absolute future, terminate in ब throughout, इ or उ being optionally inserted before this termination. Thus, जो जानब सतसंग प्रभाउ, 'know (that) it (is) from the virtue of good association;' मनोरथ पुरइब मोरी, 'fulfil my desire.' बि or बी may be used for ब; as, करबि पाय परि बिनय, 'make entreaty, falling at his feet;' आनबी जानकी, 'bring *Jánakí.*' More rarely बो is used, in the 2nd plur. only; as, अपराध छिमबो, 'pardon (my) transgressions.' One hears this last also in the colloquial near Allahabad.

Respect. Imperative in the *Rámáyan.* **543.** The Respectful form of the Imperative commonly ends in य or इय; as, बिनय करिय सागर सन जाई, 'go and make entreaty of the ocean;' हम कहं परिपालय, 'be pleased to take care of me.' From this form, the letter य is sometimes omitted; as, तुम नीकि उपाय करिअ, 'devise a good plan.' Sometimes ए or ऐ is added, as in Braj and High Hindí.

a. For the forms in य, the older forms in जे are occasionally used, not only as in High Hindí, after roots ending in ई or ए, but even after consonants, as in Braj and Máṛwáṛí; thus, तेहि अभय करीजे, 'make him free from fear;' जियावे जीजे, '(if he) preserve thee alive, live.' To this termination in जे,

उ is sometimes added; as, रावन कर दीजेउ यह पाती, 'give this letter into the hand of *Rávan*.'

544. The present imperfect, in the dialect of the *Rámáyan*, occurs under two general forms; the one, like the inflected present previously noted (§ 490), is precisely identical in form with the contingent future; the other is formed by the imperfect participle, either alone, or, as in High Hindí, in combination with the present tense of the substantive verb.

The Pres. Imperfect in the Rámáyan.

a. There appears to be no difference in signification between these two forms of the tense, except that the participial form is restricted in use to denote an action as occurring in the actual present; whereas the inflected form is extended, as will fully appear in the Syntax, to comprehend all *imperfect* or *incomplete* action, not only in the present, but also in the past and future.

545. The first or inflected form of the present imperfect, exhibits all the variations from the general type, which have been noted in the case of the contingent future. It will not be necessary to refer to these again in detail; the following examples will abundantly illustrate the various forms.

करउं एक बिस्वास, 'one faith I hold;' बंदौं सब के पद कमल, 'I salute the lotus feet of all;' न जानहि मोहि सुरारी, 'dost thou not know me, the enemy of the gods?' फूलै फलै न बेत, 'the reed neither blossoms nor bears fruit.' सि is especially common as the termination of both the 2nd and 3rd sing., and before this, a short ए may be inserted; thus, करसि पान सोवसि दिन राती, 'thou drinkest and sleepest day and night;' कहेसि संसय, 'he declares (his) doubt.' In the following the 3rd sing. termination is इ (metri gratiâ, ई): देह दिनहि दिन दूबरि होई, 'day by day (his) body becomes thin.' य commonly occurs as the 3rd sing. termination after a radical आ, and also in the following; मन सकुचय न, 'in (her) heart (she) shrinks not.' इ may precede य in the same form. उ also occurs in the 2nd and 3rd sing.; as, जो बर मांगु देउं, 'the gift thou askest, I bestow;' अगम लागु मोहि, 'difficult it is to me.' Finally, the root alone is found in the 2nd and 3rd sing.; thus, तेहि बिनु मोह न भाग, 'without that, illusion flees not away.' The final *a* is lengthened in the following:—जीव नित्य केहि लगि रोवा, 'the soul is immortal,—why weepest thou?' Of the plural the following are examples:—1st pers., विनय हम करहीं, 'we make our supplication;' 2nd pers., करहु कवन कारन तप भारी, 'why are you doing (this) heavy penance?' 3rd pers., जे पर दोष लखहिं, 'who gaze upon another's fault.' In the following, one of the first two verbs must be rendered as a present, the other, as contingent future; जे देखहिं देखहिं जिन्ह देखे, 'who see, shall see, who have seen.'

546. In the following passages, the imperfect participle alone is used as a present tense:—जो अवलोकत लोकपति, 'who beholds the lord of the world;' मनहुँ जरे पर लोन लगावति, 'she, as it were, applies salt to a burn.'

a. But to this the present of the substantive verb is occasionally added, as in High Hindí. Examples are:—धर्म्म मैं जानत अहउँ, 'I understand religion;' निसि दिन देव जपत हऊ जेही, 'whom, O divine one, you worship night and day;' मोरि करत हहिं निन्दा, 'they deride me.'

547. Besides the common form of this participle, we also find the older form in न्त used as a present tense; thus, सब संत सुखी विचरंत मही, 'all the holy walk happy on the earth.' The final vowel is sometimes lengthened; as, सापत ताड़त पुरुष कहंता, 'cursing (and) upbraiding, men say.'

Rem. This is not peculiar to the *Rámáyan*. It is also found in the writings of *Kabír*, as in the following from the *Sákhí*; ज्यों ज्यों नर निधरक फिरे त्यों त्यों काल हसंत, 'by so much as man goes about unconcerned, by so much Death laughs;' and also in the colloquial of interior Gaṛhwál, where, for example, I have heard a villager say, पानी ऊपर तें नाहिं बरसन्तो, lit., 'water rains not from above.' Vid. § 514.

Past Conting. Imperf. in the *Ramáyan*.

548. The *Rámáyán* exhibits a Past Contingent tense derived from the imperfect participle by the addition of abraded fragments of the substantive verb. To form this tense, in the 1st sing., उं, and in the 2nd plur., ऊ, is added to the imperfect participle. I have noted no special terminations for the other persons. Before the above tense-endings ए (ĕ) is commonly inserted; thus, पितहि खाइ खातेउं पुनि तोही, 'having eaten thy father, I could then eat thee.' For ए, इ is employed for the fem., as in the following, where, in the first stanza, इ is omitted before उ in the 2nd plur.; जौ तुम मिलतेउ प्रथम मुनीसा। सुनितिउं सिख तुम्हारि धरि सीसा, 'had you met me first, great sage, I, bowing my head, would have heard your advice.' ए, again, is sometimes hardened to य, and यों or यौं substituted for उं in the 1st sing.; thus, जौं जनित्यौं बिनु भट भुइं भाई। तो प्रण करि होत्यौं न हंसाई, 'had I known that the earth had become destitute of warriors, then I had not (by) making (this) decree become a laughing-stock.' One more example will suffice; जौ तुम अवतेउ मुनि की नाईं। पद रज सिर सिसु धरत गुसाईं, 'had you come like a sage, the youths had placed, O Lord, the dust of your feet upon their heads.'*

549. The Past Imperfect is formed in the *Rámáyan* by combining with the imperfect participle रह, instead of H.H. था; thus, मन जुगवत रह नृपरनिवासू, '(his) heart was keeping guard at the women's apartments.' The tense is much less frequent than in modern Hindí.

550. The tense mentioned under § 491, as an Inceptive Imperfect, is much more common in the *Rámáyan* than in Braj prose. Examples are:—गाड़न खेत मझ तहँ भये, 'they began to bury (it) there in a field;' पूछन भये, 'they began to inquire.' The Inceptive Imperfect.

* This inflected archaic tense, derived from the Sk. present participle, dialectic in Hindí, is much more extensively used, in various senses, in some of the cognate languages, as Sindhí, Maráṭhí, etc. See Beames: *Comp. Gramm.*, vol. iii., pp. 126-131.

Perf. Tenses in the *Rámáyan*.

551. The Indefinite Perfect is commonly employed in the *Rámáyan* to express action completed, whether in the past, present or future. The compound participial forms employed in High Hindí to express the various temporal and modal modifications of such completed action, very rarely occur. The most of them, indeed, are quite unknown. As in the case of the imperfect, two forms of the perfect tense occur, the one, consisting merely of the participle, the other, inflectional.

552. The participial form of the perfect differs from that of High Hindí, precisely in the same manner as the imperfect participle; viz., by the substitution of *ă* for the final long *á*. Thus, for कहा, 'said,' we have कह for रहा, 'remained,' रह, etc. This is inflected to इ for the feminine, giving, e.g., such forms as सुनि, मानि, for H.H. सुनी, मानी. But the final इ is often lengthened for the sake of the metre. Further examples are:—गिरिवरगुहा पैठ सो जाई, 'he went and entered a cave in a great mountain;' कह सुग्रीव सुनहु, '*Sugrív* said, Hear!'

a. In the masc. plural the inflection ए is very often assumed, so that the form of this tense thus frequently becomes identical with that found in High Hindí.

b. Observe, that after roots in आ or ओ, व is commonly inserted; as, मैं काह नसावा, 'what have I destroyed;' महि मारि गिरावा, 'he struck him to the earth.'

553. It will be observed that an exceeding ambiguity characterizes many verbal forms in the *Rámáyan*. What with the extreme attrition of many once distinct forms, and the frequent prosodial modifications of final vowels, one and the same form has come to represent several different parts of the verb. Thus, e.g., मार may be 2nd or 3rd sing., of the cont. or abs. fut., or of the imperf. or pres.; or 1st, 2nd or 3rd sing. perf. Again, कहि may be 2nd or 3rd sing. of the cont. or abs. fut., or of the imper. or pres.; or 1st, 2nd or 3rd fem. perf., or the conj. participle; or, again, it may be used to represent the H.H. perf. part. masc. in the passive conjugation, as, e.g., कछु कहि न जाई, 'it cannot at all be told.' देखी,

again, may be 1st, 2nd or 3rd fem. of the perf., or it may be the conj. part., देखि, with the final vowel lengthened metri gratiâ. This remark will be abundantly illustrated by referring to the citations made in the preceding and the following paragraphs.

554. In the case of active transitive verbs, the passive construction mentioned in § 412 (1), is often employed; i.e., the verb is made to agree, not with the subject, but with the object of the action in gender and number. As the post-position ने does not occur in this dialect, the subject, when a pronoun, is simply put in the inflected form, where such form happens to exist. But as no nouns are inflected in the sing., it comes to pass that very often, (as where, e.g., subject and object are both masc. sing.,) the construction is in outward form identical with the active construction of intransitive verbs. Examples are: जो प्रभु बिपिन फिरत तुम देखा, 'that lord whom you (sc. *Párvatí*) saw wandering in the forest;' भगति तैं मांगी, 'thou hast asked piety;' जिन्ह मोहि मारा ते मैं मारे, 'I have beaten those who have beaten me.'

The Passive Construction in the *Rámáyan*.

555. Besides the more common passive construction of this tense in transitive verbs, the active construction also very often occurs, after the regular idiom of all the modern eastern dialects. Thus, बेलपात . . . तीनि सहस संबत सो खाई, 'for three thousand years she ate *bel** leaves,'— where the reference is to *Umá*, afterward the wife of *Shiv*. Similar is the construction in the following: कोउ कह जियत धरहु, 'one said, take (them) alive;' धन्य जे जाये, 'blessed they who bore them;' ते देखे दोउ भ्राता, 'they beheld the two brothers.'

556. Instead of the above forms of the perfect, which are to be regarded as characteristic of the dialect, the forms (K. and B.) in यो and यी, (यो and यी,) also occur. Thus, कपि चरनन्हि परयौ, 'the monkey fell at (his) feet;' नारद मुनि

* The *Ægle marmelos*, the leaves of which are held sacred to *Shiv*.

गरुड़ पठायो, '*Nárad* the sage sent *Garuṛ*.' देना, 'to give,' and लेना, 'to take,' sometimes make the perf. देवा and लेवा, also दयो and लयो.

Infl. Perf. in the *Rámáyan*.

557. The inflected perfect is formed by adding to the perfect participle, in the *Sing.*, (1) उं; (2, 3,) उ; and in the *Plur.*, (1, 3,) न्ह or न्हि; (2) ऊ. For the feminine, these terminations are added to the fem. form of the participle. Before all these endings, ए *ĕ* is often inserted or takes the place of a final short *a*. This inflected perfect is used in the active construction only. Examples are:—तव दरस निःपाप भइउं, 'through the sight of thee, I *(fem.)* have become free from sin;' तुम जानऊ केहि कारन आयेउं, 'you know for what reason I have come;' अब लगि रहिउं कुमारी, 'until now I have remained a virgin;' भवानी सती सरीर रहिउ, '*Bhavání* remained in the body of *Satí*;' खगपति बिरंचि पहं गएऊ, 'the lord of birds went to *Biranchi*;' निज नाम सुनायउ, 'he declared his own name;' तासु पर डारेन्हि गिरितरुजूह, 'they cast upon him trees (and) mountains;' मारेऊ मोहि व्याध की नाईं, 'you have slain me like a hunter;' भल भूलिऊ, 'you (*O Umá*) have forgotten good.'

a. In the 2nd and 3rd sing., the termination सि is often substituted for उ; thus, रिपु सम मोहि मारेसि, 'he has beaten me like an enemy.' And this sometimes becomes हि, as in the future; thus, अब मोहि आइ जगायेहि काहा, 'now for what hast thou come and waked me?' In the following, ऊ is possibly the emphatic participle; कहि न सकहि जस भयऊ विषाद, 'he could not tell the sorrow as it really was.'

b. Observe that these terminations are in like manner added to the irregular participles noted in § 560. Thus, हरि लीन्हेसि सर्बस अरु नारी, 'he has robbed me of property and wife;' कीन्हेऊ सब काजा, 'you have accomplished all (your) work.'

Other Tenses of the Perfect.

558. As remarked above, the indefinite perfect, in its various forms, commonly takes the place of all the tenses of the perfect in High Hindí. Very rarely, however, we find a contingent perfect, and a past perfect formed by the combination of the perfect participle with the verb रहन as an auxiliary. Thus, द्वौ भाई गये रहे देखन फुलवारी, 'the two brothers had gone to see the garden;' and, again, एक सखी सिय संग विहारे गइ रही, 'one maiden companion, sporting with *Sítá*, had gone.'

Irregular Perfects in the *Rámáyan*.

559. The irregular forms of the perfect of certain verbs, already noticed in Braj and High Hindí, occur also with dialectic variations, in the *Rámáyan*. Thus, from होन, 'to be,' we have in the perfect, *Sing.*, भा, भयउ or भयउं; *Plur.*, भे, भै, etc.; from ठानन, 'to determine,' in the perfect ठयउ. जान, 'to go,' sometimes makes the perfect गयउ, (H.H. गया), plur., गये, etc.; and also, more rarely, गा, plur. गै. Besides these, note also, हये or हिए, 'killed,' perf. plur. from हनन; and लयउ, perf., (for H.H. लगा), from लगन. Examples are:— तब जो दुख भा, 'the sorrow which then was;' बहु रोह वियोगनि लोग हये, 'people were slain by diseases and bereavements.' The *Rámáyan*, besides the common present and future forms from जाना, also exhibits a present formed on the base गव or गवन, from the ultimate root, गम्, of the perf. गया. Thus, देखि सरासन गवहिं सिधारे, 'seeing the bow, they went away.'

560. The verbs करना, देना, लेना, in the *Rámáyan*, present not only such forms of the perfect as किय, लिय, दियो, लियो, etc., but also, as in Braj, कीन्हो, 'did,' 'done;' दीन्हो, 'given,' 'gave;' लीन्हो, 'taken,' 'took;' very often apocopated; as, e.g., चिन्ता केहि न कीन्ह बौराहा, 'whom has not greed made mad?'

a. As elsewhere remarked, the final ह of these forms is dropped by many old writers, whence कीन, लीनो, दीन, etc. Thus, in the *Sabhá Bilás*, बिपत कसौती कीन, '(he) has made affliction a touch-stone.'

b. Similarly, in the *Rámáyan*, and other archaic poetry, the perfect of pure verbs in आ also often terminates in न: as, सुनि दसकंध रिसान, 'hearing (this) the Ten-shouldered was enraged;' सकल हरषाने, 'all rejoiced.' Or the termination may be नो; thus, जगती सकल फिरानो, '(he) went around the whole world.'

561. In one instance, again, in the *Rámáyan*, the perfect is made to terminate in ल, as in the Bhojpúrí, Maithilí and Mágadhí dialects; thus, कोपि गगन पर धायल, 'angrily he rushed toward heaven;' where धायल is for H.H. धाया, from धाना, 'to run,' 'to rush.'

562. In one passage, again, we have a perfect terminating in र (for the ल just mentioned), as in the following;—गरजेर बहुरि दससीस, 'again roared the Ten-headed.'

Sansk. Verbal Forms in the *Rámáyan*.

563. Sometimes, for the modern forms of the perfect, Sanskrit or Prakrit forms are employed. Thus, for H.H. किया, 'done,' and गया, 'gone,' we often find the corresponding Sk. forms, कृत and गत, as in the following:—केहि कै मति इन्ह कृत न मलीनी, 'whose understanding have these not defiled?' (*lit.*, 'made unclean'); इहि प्रकार गत बासर सोऊ, 'in this way passed that day.'

564. Besides the participles, referred to in the last paragraph, various other Sanskrit conjugational forms occur in the *Rámáyan*. It will be sufficient, for the most part, merely to notice them, without giving lengthy examples in each case. Most common (1) is the *Pres. Parasmai*, of the 1st conj.: thus, 1st sing. नमामि or प्रनमामि, 'I salute;' पश्यामि, 'I behold;' जपामि (for जल्पामि), 'I repeat:' 3rd plur. पश्यन्ति, 'they behold;' वदन्ति, 'they speak;' नदन्ति, 'they roar;' निरखन्ति, 'they behold.' Thus, पश्यन्ति यं योगी जतन करि, 'whom ascetics, having toiled, behold;' प्रनमामि निरंतर श्रीरमणं, 'I salute without ceasing the glorious *Rám*.' The 2nd sing. असि, of the Sk. subst. verb, occurs in the following, in combination with the relative and correlative pronouns: योऽसि सोऽसि* तव चरण नमामो, 'thou art that which thou art; thy feet we adore!'

(2) The following forms of the *Pres. Átmane* also occur: 1st plur., नमामहे, 'we salute;' स्मरामहे, 'we remember;' भजामहे, 'we worship.' Examples are:—भवनाथ सो स्मरामहे, 'that lord of existence we remember;' रमेस नित्य भजामहे, '*Rám's* lord we ever worship.'

(3) The following Sk. imperatives, 3rd sing. *Parasmai*, are also found, viz.: तनोतु, 'let him extend;' वसतु, 'let him dwell;' त्रातु, 'let him save.' More frequent is the 3rd sing. imper. of the subst. verb, usually in the formula of permission, एवमस्तु, 'let it be so;' as, एवमस्तु करुणानिधि बोले, 'Let it be so, said the Treasury of Compassion.'

(4) The 2nd sing. *Imper. Parasmai* of two or three words is not infrequent; as, पाहि, 'do thou protect;' त्राहि, 'do thou save;' thus, भवभयमोचन पाहि पाहि, 'Protect, protect (me)! O thou deliverer from the dread of existence!'

565. The following Prakritic verbal forms also occur, viz.:—निर्मयौ, for Sk. निर्मितः, 'composed;' as, रामायण जिन निर्मयौ, 'who composed the *Rámáyan*;' कथै, for H. कहै, Sk. कथयति, 3rd sing. pres., 'he tells;' तिष्ठै, for Sk. तिष्ठति, 3rd sing. pres. from root स्था, 'he stands;' वंदि, 'I salute,' for Sk. वंदे, 1st Sing. *Átmane*; as in बहुरि वंदि खलगन, 'again, I salute the wicked;' नौमि, for Sk. नमामि, 1st sing. pres., 'I adore;' as in नौमि निरंतर श्री रघुवीरं, 'I adore without ceasing the glorious *Raghubír*;' and also नमामयं. Finally, in a single instance, we have a Prakrit reduplicated perfect, विवर्धे, for Sk. ववृधे, from वृध्, 'to increase;' as in the following; सेवत विषय विवर्धे जिमि, 'as sensual enjoyment grows (even) on one serving (the gods).' Prak. Verbal Forms in the *Rámáyan*.

* For the elision of अ initial, see §§ 52, 59.

Passive in the *Ramáyan.*

566. The passive is commonly formed by conjugating the verb जाना, 'to go,' together with the perfect participle, or, more commonly, with the root of the verb combined with the suffix इ. Thus, कल्प कोटि लगि जाहिं न गाये, '(the deeds of *Rám*) cannot be sung in ten million *kalpas*;' कहि जात सो नाहीं, 'that is not told,' i.e., 'cannot be told.'

a. But besides the above, a Prakritic present passive often occurs, which is formed by adding to the root, after इ as a union-vowel, the termination यत, unchanged for gender or number; thus, बेषप्रताप पूजियत तेऊ, 'even these are worshipped in virtue of their disguise;' मायापतिसेवक सन माया करियत, 'with the servant of the lord of deception, deception is employed.'

Causal Verbs in the *Ramáyan.*

567. Causal verbs are formed in the *Rámáyan*, by adding आव or आ to the root of the primitive, for the First, and वा for the Second Causal. Many verbs, however, as in High Hindí, instead of adding these letters to the root, form the First Causal by lengthening or *gunating* the medial vowel of the root. Both Causals occur in the following: नृपतनु वेद-विहित अन्हवावा । परम विचित्र बिमान बनावा, 'he caused the body of the king to be washed according to the *Ved*, (and) made a most beautiful chariot.' देना and लेना make their causals, दिवाना and लिवाना.

a. Observe, that many verbs, which in High Hindí form the Causal by the addition of a syllable, in the *Rámáyan* follow the other method. Thus, e.g., for H.H. जलाना, 'to burn,' and बुलाना, 'to call,' the *Rámáyan* often uses जारन (for जालना) and बोलन: as, e.g., जे महिसुर पुर जारे, 'who have burnt villages of Brahmans;' सुचि सेवक बोले, 'he called his upright servants.'

b. Occasionally the root of the Causal is made to terminate in अव, instead of आव, as in the following, where पुरवऊ, 'fill,' is for पुरावऊ; पुरवऊ . . . मनोरथ मोरि, 'fulfil my desire.'

c. Occasionally, again, the characteristic अय or आव of the Causal, is contracted to औ. Thus, in the following, रिसौहिं is for रिसावहिं; रदपट फरकत नयन रिसौहैं, 'his lips quiver, (and) angry are his eyes.'

d. When a syllable is added to a close root, to form the Causal, the usual shortening of a medial long vowel in the primitive, is not infrequently neglected. Thus, for H.H. बुलाना, 'to call,' and दिखाना, 'to show,' we have sometimes, बोलावन, देखावन; as, e.g., तैं बिप्र बोलाई, 'thou, calling a Brahman.'

568. The various Compound verbs explained §§ 425-465, also occur in the *Rámáyan* and similar poetry. But it is important to notice that the parts of the compound are separated at pleasure, often by many intervening words, or, again, are often inverted in order, as the exigencies of the metre may demand. All these various compounds, moreover, present forms more or less divergent from those of High Hindí. Thus, **Compound Verbs in the *Rámáyan.***

(1) In all such compounds as are formed in High Hindí with the conj. part., the termination इ (or ई) is retained. Examples will be found on almost every page. Thus, कहं चंद्रिका चंद्र तजि जाई, 'how can the moonlight forsake the moon?'; जात पथिक जनु लेत बुलाई, 'calls, as it were, the passing traveller.' So also, सो सुधारि हरिजन जिमि लेहीं, 'as the servants of *Hari* rectify (all) these;' where लेहीं cannot be separately translated, but must be connected with सुधारि as a compound, = H.H. सुधार लेते हैं. In the following, again, the parts are inverted and the final इ of the primary verb lengthened, metri gratiâ; सरिता सुभगता सक को कही, 'the loveliness of the river, who can tell?'; where सक को कही, is for को कहि सक, H.H. कौन कह सकता है.

Rem. **The student will do well to take especial notice of the separation and inversion of the parts of compounds and the frequent lengthening of this final इ; as these are among the marked peculiarities of the poetic**

style, which, until recognized and understood, greatly embarrass the reader who is familiar only with prose Hindí.

(2) इ alone is often appended to the root in participial combinations, where in High Hindí we should have आ or ए. Thus, देखि राम रिपुदल चलि आवा, lit., 'seeing *Rám* and *Ripudal* are coming along;' where High Hindí would have चले आते हैं; the first ए has become इ, and the last is changed to आ, to rhyme with the following stanza.

569. Desiderative, Inceptive, Permissive, and Acquisitive Compounds present in the *Rámáyan* a variety of forms.

(1) The Desiderative is sometimes formed with the perfect participle, as in High Hindí; as, बिबाह मैं चाहौं कीन्हा, 'I wish to marry.'

(2) All these are also often formed, as in High Hindí, with the infinitive in न. Thus, मरन अब चहसी, 'dost (thou) now wish to die?'; मोहि जान दे, 'let me go;' सुग्रीवहि तब खोजन लागा, 'he then began to seek for *Sugrív*.'

(3) But especially common in combination with the secondary verb is an inflected verbal noun in ए or ऐ. Thus, चाहहु सुनै राम गुन गूढा, 'you desire to hear the mysterious attributes of *Rám*;' केहि कारन करै न दीन्हा, 'for what reason didst thou not allow (me) to do (it);' रखवारे जब बरजै लागे, 'when the keepers began to forbid them.' For the final ए, अइ is sometimes written; thus, लाग कहइ, 'he began to tell.'

(4) This ए is sometimes further reduced to इ (metri gratiâ, ई); thus, जौ नहाइ चह एहि सर भाई, 'if thou wish to bathe in this lake, brother;' जासु चरित लखि काउ न पावा, 'whose exploits no one was permitted to behold.' And ए also becomes य; as, राम चंद्र गुन बरनय लागा, 'he began to rehearse the virtues of *Rám Chandra*.' All these forms may suffer separation or inversion like those above mentioned: as, लागेउ बृष्टि करै बहु बाना, 'many arrows began to rain;'

TABLE XX. DIALECTIC CONJUGATION OF मारना, 'to strike.'

		High Hindī.	Kanaujī.	Braj.	W. Raj.	E. Raj.	Gaṛhwālī.	Kumāoni.	Naipālī.
Infin.		मारना.	मारनौ, मारन.	मारबौं. मारिबौं.	मारणो, मारणूं. मारवो.	मारबो, मारबूं. मारबो.	मारणो.	मारणो.	मारनु.
Contingent Future. Singular.	1	मारूं.	मारौं.	मारौं.	मारूं.	मारूं.	मारूं.	मारूं. मारनु.	मारूं. मारें.
	2	मारे.	मारे.	मारे.	मारे.	मारे.	मारी.	मारे. मारले.	मारिस. मारे.
	3	मारे.	मारे.	मारे.	मारे.	मारे.	मार.	मार. मारबो.	मारे.
Contingent Future. Plural.	1	मारें.	मारें.	मारें.	मारां.	मारां.	मारूं,मारौं.	मारौं,मारूं. मारनु.	मारौं. मारें.
	2	मारो.	मारो.	मारो.	मारो.	मारो.	मारा. माऱ्याई.	मारो. मारो.	मारो. मारें.
	3	मारें.	मारें.	मारें.	मारे.	मारे.	मार. मारन.	मारे. मारो.	मारन, मारुन. मारें.

		Old Baiswāṛī.		Awadhī.	Rīwāī.	Bhojpūrī.	Māgadhī.	Maithilī.
Infin.		मारन, मारब.		मारब.	मारब.	मारब, मारिब.	मारब.	मारब (inf. मारबा)
Contingent Future. Singular.	1	मारउं. मारेउं.	मारबौं.	मारउं.	मारउं.	मारीं f. मारूँ.	मारूं. f. मारियौं.	मारिअइ, मारिऔ.[2] f. मारौं, मारूं.
	2	मारइ, मारहि, मारि, मार. मारय, मारिय, मारसि, मारइ.	मारबे.	मारस, मार.	मारस.	मारे, मार. f. मारिस. मारसि.	मारही. मारे. f. मारी.	मरिहें,[1] मारहीं.[2] मारे,[1] मारे, मार. f. मारी.
	3	मारइ, मारहि, मारि, मार. मारय, मारिय, मारसि, मारइ.	मारबै.	मारय.	मारि.	मारे, मारनु. मारसि. f. मारसि.	मारस. मारउ, मारे.	मारथि, मारे.[2] मारौ,[2] मारे.
Contingent Future. Plural.	1	मारइं, मारहिं.	मारबैं.	मारी.	मारन.	मारीं f. मारूँ.	मारिअर, मारी.[1] f. मारियौं.	मारिऐन्हि, मारिऐ.[2] मारिहन्हि, मारग्ह, मारी. f. मारीं. मारें.
	2	मारऊ.	मारबो.	मारउ,मारब.	मारब,मारन.	मारइ. मारउ. f. मारूं.	मारहिन, मारहीं. मारऊन, मारहं.[1] f. मारी. मारूं.	मारिऐन्हि, मारऊन्ह. मारही,[2] मारह, मारउ.
	3	मारइं, मारहिं.	मारबैं.	मारैं.	मारैं.	मारन. f. मारिन.	मारिन, मारीं. मारथिन, मारखिन. f. मारथीन. मारखीन.	मारथिन्ह, मारहिन्ह. मारग्ह, मारा, मारें. f. मारी. मारिन्ह.

[1] Anusvár optional.

[2] क optionally added.

TABLE XX. (*Continued*). DIALECTIC CONJUGATION OF मारना, 'to strike.'

		High Hindī.	*Kanaujī.*	*Braj.*	*W. Raj.*	*E. Raj.*	*Gaṛhwālī.*	*Kumāonī.*	*Naipālī.*	*Old Baiswāṛī.*	*Avadhī.*	*Riwāī.*	*Bhojpūrī.*	*Māgadhī.*	*Maithilī.*
ABSOLUTE FUTURE.	SINGULAR.	मारूंगा.	मारिहौं. मारिहूं. मारोंगो.	मारिहौं, मारैहौं. मारौंगौ.	मारहूं. मारूंलो, मारूंगो.	मारसूं. मारसूं.	मारलो.	मारूंलो. मारसी.	मारूंला. मारनेछुं.	मारिहौं. मारौंगो. मारब. मारिब.	मारबूं.	मारबेउं.	मारबौं. *f.* मारबूं. मारब. मारिबौं.[1]	मारबौं, मारब. *f.*	मारबौं,[4] मारबी.[4] मारबे.
		मारेगा.	मारिहै, मारैगो.	मारिहै, मारैहै. मारैगो.	मारही. मारैलो, मारैगो.	मारसी.	मारलो. मारिख्यो.	मारलै.	मारलास. मारनस.	मारिहहि, मारिबहि (मारहिगा). मारिहसि, मारिहेसु. मारब.	मारबे. मारबेस.	मारिहेस. मारिबेस.	मारबे. *f.* मारबिस.	मारबही,[2] मारबे.[3] *f.* मारबीं.[4] मारबा, मारबं.	मारभें, मारभीं.[4] मारितञ, मारतिऐ.[3] *f.* मारबहि. मारबी.
		मारेगा.	मारिहै, मारेगो.	मारिहै, मारैहै. मारैगो.	मारही. मारैलो, मारैगो.	मारसी.	मारलो.	मारलो.	मारला. मारनेछ.	मारिहहि, मारिबहि (मारहिगा). मारब.	मारे.	मारी.	मारी. मारीत.[2]	मारी, मारत. *f.* मारती. मारतह, मारतव.	मारताह,मारतौ,[3] मारतै.[3] *f.* मारतिहि. मारति.
	PLURAL.	मारेंगे.	मारिहैं, मारैंगे.	मारिहैं, मारैंहैं. मारैंगे.	मारहां. मारांला,मारांगा.	मारसां.	मारला.	मारूंला.	मारूंला. मारूनेछूं.	मारिहहिं. मारहिंगे, मारब.	मारब.	मारिब,मारब. मोरबै.	मारबौं. *f.* मारिब. मारबै. मारबी.	मारबह, मारबउ. *f.* मारबी. मारब.	मारभेन्ह, मारबैन्हि. मरब.
		मारोगे.	मारिहो, मारोगे.	मारिहौ,मारैहौ. मारौगे.	मारहो. मारोला,मारोगा.	मारसो.	मारला. मारिख्या.	मारला.	मारलउ, मारौला. मारनेछौ.	मारिहहि, मारिबहु. मारहुगे, मारब.	मारबो.	मारिबा.	मारबह. *f.* मारबू. मारबउ.	मारबहीं, मारबउ. *f.* मारबी. मारबहं, मारिहउ. मारबू.	मारबैन्हि, मारबह.[1] मारभौ,[3] मारबउ.
		मारेंगे.	मारिहैं, मारैंगे.	मारिहैं, मारैहैं. मारैंगे.	मारही. मारैला, मारैगा.	मारसी.	मारला.	मारला.	मारलान, मारलन. मारनन.	मारिहहिं. मारहिंगे, मारब.	मारिहैं.	मारिहैं.	मारिहैं.[1] मारिहेन.	मारतथी, मारथी. *f.* मारतथीन. मारिहैं, मारखिन. मारथीन.	मारथीन्हि, मारतथि. *f.* मारतिन्ह. मारतन्ह, मारता. मारतीत, मारती.
IMPERATIVE.	SING.	मार.	मार.	मार.	मार.	मार.	मार.	मार.	मार. 3. मारोस.	मारहि, मारसि, मारेसु. मारु, मार. मारब, मारद्व. मारबि.	मार, मारस. मारज.	मारस.	मारसि, मार. *f.* मारी. मारस. मारिस.	मारही, मारे. *f.* मारीं.	मारू, मार. *f.* मारहि. मारी.
	PLUR.	मारो.	मारो.	मारौ.	मारो.	मारो.	मारा.	मारो.	मारौ. 3. मारुन.	मारऊ, मारेऊ. मारब, मारबो.	मारब, मारो.	मारब.	मारह, मारउ. *f.* मारू.	मारहीं, मारहु. *f.* मारू.	मारिएन्हि. मारह्न्हि.
Resp. Forms.		मारियो. मारिये.	मारियो. मारिये.	मारियो, मारियै. मारीजै.	मारुजी, मारीजै. मारज्यो,मारीजो.	मारीज्यो. मारीज्यो.	*Wanting.*	मारियो.		मारिय, मारिअ, मारियै, मारीजै, मारीजेऊ.			*s.* मारिहै. *pl.* मारिहैं.	मारबह, मारिह, मारी.	मारल जाय or जाओ. मारियउ, मारी.

[1] In the W. [2] In Champāran. [3] ऊ optionally added. [4] Anusvār optional.

TABLE XX. (*Concluded*). DIALECTIC CONJUGATION OF मारना, 'to strike.'

		High Hindi.	Kanauji.	Braj.	W. Raj.	B. Raj.	Garhwali.	Kumaoni.	Naipali.	Old Baiswari.	Avadhi.	Riwai.	Bhojpuri.	Magadhi.	Maithili.
IMPERF. AND PERF. PART.		मारता. मारा.	मारत. मारो.	मारतु. मार्यो.	मारतो. मार्‌यो.	मारती. मार्‌यो.	मारदो, मारनो. मारे, मारो.	मारनू. मारियो.	मारदो *infl.* आ, ऐ. मार्‌यो. *f.* ई.	मारत, मारन्त. मार०.	मारता. मारा.	मारत. मार०.	मारित, मारइत, मारत, *obl.* मारते. मारल, *obl.* मारले.	मारइत, मारैत, मारत, *obl.* मारइते, etc. मारल, *obl.* मारले.	मारैत, मारत, मारत०. मारल, *obl.* मरले or मारल०.
PRESENT IMPERFECT.	SINGULAR.	मारता हूं.	मारत हूं.	मारौं. मारतु हौं.	मारूं हूं.	मारूं छूं.	मारदो छौं. मारदू.	मारनु.[1] मारन छूं.	मारद० छु.	मारउं. मारेउं. मारत अहउं.	मारत अहेउं.	मारत थां.	मारत बाटौं. *f.* मारत बाड़ूं. मारतारौं. मारतारयूं.	मार० मारइत ही. *f.* मारइत छियों.	मारैत छों. मारै छों.
		मारता है.	मारत है.	मारै, मारहि. मारतु है.	मारै है.	मारै छै.	मारदो छऊ. मारदो.	मारन छ.	मारद० छस.	मारहि, मारै, मारय. मारसि, मारु, मार. मारत(इहि).	मारत अहेस.	मारते है.	मारत बाटस. *f.* मारत बाटिस. मारतारस. मारतारिस.	मार० मारइत हं. *f.* मारइत हीं.	मारैत छें. मारैछें. मारैसे.
		मारता है.	मारत है.	मारै, मारहि. मारतु है.	मारै है.	मारै छै.	मारदो छऊ. मारद.	मारनो. मारन छऊ.	मारद० छऊ.	मारहि, मारै, मारय. मारसि, मारइ, मार. मारत इहि.	मारत अहै.	मारत था.	मारत बाटे. *f.* मारत बतसि. मारतारे. मारतारसि.	मार० मारइत हइ.	मारैत छि. मारैसे. मारैछि, मारैय०, मारैए.
	PLURAL.	मारते हैं.	मारत हैं.	मारैं, मारहिं. मारतु हैं.	मारां हां.	मारां छां.	मारदा छौं. मारदाऊं.	मारनू, मारनु.	मारद० छूं.	मारहिं. मारत इहिं.	मारत अही.	मारतें हैं.	मारत बानीं. *f.* मारत बाड़ूं. मारतानीं. मारतारयूं.	मार० मारइत हीं. *f.* मारइत छियों.	मारैछी. मारैसी.
		मारते हो.	मारत हो.	मारौ, मारहु. मारतु हौ.	मारो हो.	मारो छो.	मारदा छन. मारदाइ.	मारना. मारन छा.	मारद० छौ.	मारहु. मारत इहु.	मारत अहे.	मारत अहेन.	मारत बाटऽ. *f.* मारत बाटू. मारतारऽ. मारतारू.	मार० मारइत हऽ. *f.* मारइत छी.	मारैछऽ. मारैसऽ.
		मारते हैं.	मारत हैं.	मारैं, मारहिं. मारतु हैं.	मारै है.	मारै छै.	मारदा छन. मारदान.	मारनी.	मारद० छन.	मारहिं. मारत इहिं.	मारत अहैं.	मारत थां.	मारत बाटन. *f.* मारत बाटिन. मारतारन. मारतारिन.	मार० मारइत हईं. *f.* मारइत इथीन.	मारैछैन्ह. मारैसैन्ह. मारैसन.
PRESENT PERFECT.	SINGULAR.	मारा हूं.	मारो हूं.	मार्‌यो हूं.	मार्‌यो हूं.	मार्‌यो छूं.	मारे छऊ.	मार, मारो मारियो छऊ.	(मार्‌यां छु.)	मार. मारउं. मारेउं. *f.* मारिउं.	मारेउं हौं. *m.* मारिउं हौं. *f.*	मार हौं.	मारलों हा.[2] *f.* मारलूं हा. मारले बाड़ों. मारले बाड़ूं.	मारलूं है.	मारलों यऽ. मारले छी.
		मारा है.	मारो है.	मार्‌यो है.	मार्‌यो है.	मार्‌यो छै.	मारे छऊ.	मार, मारो मारियो छऊ.	मारिस छस.	मार. मारउ, मारेउ. मारेसि, मारेहि. *f.* मारिउ.	मारेस है. *m.* मारिसि हैं. *f.*	मारेस है.	मारलस हा.[2] *f.* मारलिस हा. मारले बाड़स. मारले बाड़िस.	मारलें है. *f.* मारली है.	मारलें यऽ. मारले छें.
		मारा है.	मारो है.	मार्‌यो है.	मार्‌यो है.	मार्‌यो छै.	मारे छऊ.	मार, मारो मारियो छऊ.	मार्‌यो मारे छऊ.	मार. मारउ, मारेउ. मारेसि, मारेहि. *f.* मारिउ.	मारेस है. *m.* मारिसि है. *f.*	मारेस है.	मारलस हा.[2] *f.* मारलिस हा. मारले बा. मारले बड़सि.	मारिस है. *f.* मारली है.	मारलक यऽ. मारले छि.
	PLURAL.	मारे हैं.	मारे हैं.	मारे हैं.	मार्‌या है.	मार्‌या छै.	मारा छौं. मारीनै.	मारीं, मारीनै. मारिया छन.	मार्‌यूं मार्‌यौं छौं.	मारे. मारेन्हि. *f.* मारीं.	मारे अहीं. *m. f.*	मार हैं.	मारलीं हां.[3] *f.* (मारलूं हां.) मारले बानीं. (मारले बाड़ूं.)	मारलीं है.	मारली यऽ. मारले छी.
		मारे हो.	मारे हो.	मारे हो.	मार्‌या हो.	मार्‌या छो.	मारा छन. मारीनै.	मारीं, मारीनै. मारिया छन.	मार्‌यौ छौ.	मारे. मारेन्हि. *f.* मारिउ.	मारेउ हैं. *m.* मारिउ हैं. *f.*	मारे मारेन हौ.	मारलऽ हा. *f.* मारलू हा. मारले बाड़ऽ. मारले बाड़ू.	मारलऽ है. *f.* मारली है.	मारलऽ यऽ. मारले छऽ.
		मारे हैं.	मारे हैं.	मारे हैं.	मार्‌या है.	मार्‌या छै.	मारा छन. मारीनै.	मारीं, मारीनै. मारिया छन.	मार्‌या छन.	मारे. मारेन्हि. *f.* मारीं.	मारेन हैं. *m.* मारिनि हैं. *f.*	मारे मारेन अहेन.	मारलन हां.[3] *f.* मारलिन हां. मारले बाड़न. मारले बाड़िन.	मारलन है. *f.* मारलिन है.	मारलन्हि यऽ. मारले छैन्ह.
CONJUNCT. PARTICIPLE.		मारकर, etc.	मारके.	मारि, मारिकै. मारिकरि.	मार, मारने. मारतोकने. मारर.	मार, मारने.	मारिक. मारीक.	मारीबेर.	मारि. मारी मारि कन.	मारि.	मारके.	मारके.	मार के, मारि के. (*poet.*)	मार के, मार कर.	मार के, मार कै. मारि कं, मारि कैकं.

[1] Also मारन लागिरयूं.

[2] Also ह or हैं.

[3] Also हुं or हवस.

TABLE XXI. INFLECTED PRESENT AND INDEFINITE PERFECT OF मारना, 'I beat;' 'I did beat.'

		Kanauj.	Braj.	Mârwâr.	Gaṛhwâlî.	Kumâunî.	Naipâlî.	Old Baiswârî.	Awadhî.	Rîwâî.	Bhojpûrî.	Mâgadhî.	Maithilî.
INFLECTED PRESENT.	SINGULAR.	मारूं.	मारौं.	मारूं.	मारदू.	मारछूं.	मार्दि. मारछु.	मारेउं. मारउं.	Wanting.	Wanting.	(मारलों).[1] f. (मारलू).[1]	मारूं. f. मारियों.	मारिचऊ, मारिचौ.[8] मारौं, मारूं, मारिऊं,[8] मारी.
		मारै.	मारै.	मारै.	मारदी.	मारछै.	मार्दस. मारछस.	मारसि, मारहि, मारइ. मारय, मारै, माइ, मार.			मारले. मारेले. f. मारलिसि.	मारही, मारइ. मारै,[3] मारं, मार. f. मारी.	मारहीं, मारिऐ,[8] मारइ,[8] मारा. मारै,[3] मारे,[3] मार, मारही.[8] f. मारी.
		मारै.	मारै.	मारै.	मारद.	मारछ.	मार्दै. मारछ.	मारैसि, मारहि, मारइ. मारय, मारै, माइ, मार.			मारला. मारेला. f. मारलि.	मारस, मारउ. मारइ, मारे.	मारथि, मारै.[3] मारौ,[1] मारी, मारे.
	PLURAL.	मारैं.	मारैं.	मारा.	मारदाऊं.	मारछौं.	मार्दौं. मारछौं, मारछूं.	मारहिं.			मारीला.[2] मारीले. f. मारलू.	मारिचइ, मारिचउ. मारी.[3] f. मारियों.	मारिऐन्हि, मारिऐ.[3] मारिहीन्हि, मारन्ह, मारी. f. मारी. मारैं.
		मारो.	मारौ.	मारो.	मारदाई.	मारछा.	मार्दौ. मारछौ.	मारऊ.			मारलह. मारलऽ. f. मारलू.	मारहिन, मारहीं, मारऊन. मारऊं,[3] मारहो, मारह, मारऽ. f. मारी. मारू.	मारिऐन्हि, मारऊन्ह. मारहीं,[3] मारह, मारऽ.
		मारैं.	मारैं.	मारै.	मारदान.	मारछन.	मार्देन, मार्दैन. मारछन.	मारहिं.			मारले. मारलन.[3] f. मारली. मारलिन.	मारथिन, मारथी, मारथ, मारथुन. मारथं, मारहिन, मारहीं, मारिन. मारखिन. f. मारथिनी, मारथीन. मारखिनी, मारखीन.	मारथिन्ह, मारहिन्ह, मारहैं. मारन्ह, मारा, मारैं, मारैं. मारथि, मारथ. f. मारिन्ह. मारी.
INFLECTED INDEFINITE PERFECT.	SINGULAR.	Wanting.	Wanting.	Wanting.	Wanting.	Wanting.	मार्यो, मार्यें. मारें.	मारउं. f. मारिउं. मारेउं.	मारेउं. f. मारिउं.	मारेऊं. f. मारी.	(मारलों).[6] f. (मारलूं).[1]	मारलूं. f.	मारलऊं, मारलों, मारलाओं, मारलांव, मारलूं. मारलिअऊ, मारलिओ,[8] मारली,[3] मारलों. मारल, मारले,[3] मारलो, मारलिऐ.[8] f. मारलि.
							मारिस.	मारेसि, मारेहि. f. मारिउ. मारेउ, मारउ.	मारेस. f. मारिस.	मारेइ. f. मारिइ.	मारलस, मारलेस.[4] f. मारलिस. मारले, मारए.[4] f. मारली.[5]	मारलही. मारले,[5] मारल. f. मारलौं.	मारलऊं, मारलह,[8] (मारला),[7] (मारलहे),[7] मारली. मारलही,[8] मारलिऐ, मारलि,[3] मारले,[3] मारल.[8] f. मारिलिहिं, मारली. मारलौहि.
							मार्यो. f. मारी.	मारेसि, मारेहि. f. मारिउ. मारेउ, मारउ.	मारेस. f. मारी.	मारी. f. मारी.	मारलस.[8] मारले, मारए.[4] f. मारलसि. f. मारलि.[1]	मारलकइ, मारलकउ, मारलक. (मारल),[7] मारकइ, मारकउ, मारिस. f. मारली.	मारलन्हि, मारलि,[6] मारले, मारली,[3] (मारलऽ).[7] मारलकि,[8] मारलकी,[3] मारलकऽ, (मारलक),[7] मारल. f. मारलकी.
	PLURAL.						मार्यौं. मार्यूं.	मारेन्हि. f. मारीं.	मारा. f. मारीं.	मारेन. f. मारिन.	मारलीं. मारलईं.[4] f. (मारलूं).	मारलिअइ, मारलिअउ. मारली.[3]	मारलिऐन्हि, मारलिऐन्ह, मारलिहिन्ह, मारलैन्हि. मारलिऐ, मारली, मारलियौन्हि, मारलिहौन्ह. मारलिऔ, मारलिअन्ह, मारलिइन्ह. f. मारलौं.
							मार्यौ.	मारेन्हि. f. मारिउ.	मारेउ. f. मारीं.	मारिइ. f. मारिइ.	मारलह, मारलऽ. f. मारलू. मारलअह,[4] मारलअ.[4] f. मारलऽ.[4]	मारलहं,[3] मारलहीं, मारलहो. मारलऽ, मारलऊन. f. मारली. मारलू.	मारलिऐन्हि, मारलहिन्ह, मारलैन्हि, मारलहन्हि. मारलऊन्ह, मारलही,[3] मारलहो,[3] मारलह. मारलहऽ, मारलह, मारलऽ. f. मारलीं.
							मार्या, मार्ये, मारे. मारेन.	मारेन्हि. f. मारीं.	मारेन. f. मारीं.	मारेन. f. मारिन.	मारलन, मारलें. मारलेन,[5] मारलन.[4] f. मारलिन. मारलन.[4] मारली.	मारलकन, मारलन, मारलथी. मारलथु, मारलहीं, मारलहिन. मारलकथिन, मारलखिन. f. मारलिन, मारलकिन. मारलीन, मारलथिनी. मारलकीन, मारलखिनी.	मारलथुन्हि, मारलथुन्ह, मारलथिन्ह, (मारलात).[7] मारलन्ह, (मारलें),[7] मारलकैन्हि, मारलकिन्ह, मारलथ. मारलथीन्ह, मारलका, मारलकथ, मारलखों. f. मारलथीन्हि, (मारलीत).[7] मारलन्हि. मारलकी.

[1] Plur. usually, instead of sing. In W. Bh., ऐ is the union-vowel throughout the pres. [2] In the W., मारीला. [3] Also, मारेले, मारेलन, and in the W., मारैले. [4] In Sáran. [5] In the W. [6] Cf. § 572: long vowel in antepenult irregularly retained in such causal forms. [7] In neut. verbs only. [8] क optionally added. [9] Anusvár optional.

आपन नाम कहन तब लयज, 'he then began to repeat his own name.'*

570. The Avadhí, it will be observed, in the verb as in the pronouns, closely follows the Old Baiswáṛí of the *Rámáyan*. The dialect of Ríwá does not differ widely from that of Avadh. In both we may notice in some words, the extreme abrasion of the leading verb before the auxiliaries, already noted in Kumáoní. This is well illustrated by such forms as Av. भ रहे, ग रहे, (*fem.* भै रहीं, गै रहीं,) for H.H. हुए थे, गए थे; R. भ है, भ ता, = H.H. हुआ है, हुआ था. In the dialect of Ríwá, ए final in a root is often changed to या before the terminations. Thus, यावस, यावा, यात, = H.H. देगा, दोगे, देता. In both the dialects of Avadh and Ríwá, the verbs देना, लेना, and करना, add the terminations of the perfect to the irregular forms, दीन्ह, लीन्ह, and कीन्ह. In the dialect of Avadh, व is often inserted instead of य before the terminations of the perfect. Thus for H.H. गया, 'gone,' Av. has गवा; for बनाया, 'made,' बनावा, etc., etc. In both Avadh and Ríwá, we find a past contingent imperfect tense analogous to that mentioned at § 548, as occurring in the *Rámáyan*.† As previously remarked, neither in these nor in other Eastern colloquials does the Western Hindí construction with ने occur.

Avadhí and Riwáí Conjugation.

571. In the Bhojpúrí, Mágadhí, and Maithilí dialects, we have a still wider divergence from the High Hindí type of conjugation, and an increasing approximation to the Bangálí conjugational system. Each of these dialects, like the Avadhí, Riwáí, and the Old Baiswáṛí, is marked by a much larger use of inflected forms than we find in High Hindí. Thus, in addition to the periphrastic form of the present, each of these, like many of the western colloquials, has also an inflected present. Similarly, where in western dialects, the perfect participle alone is used for the indefinite perfect, these dialects have all retained for this tense a full set of inflective endings. After the same analogy, the imperfect participle, which in Western Hindí is employed without personal affixes, as a past contingent tense, in these dialects is furnished, for this tense, with a complete set of personal terminations in both genders. Especially noteworthy, again, is the large development of honorific forms of conjugation.

Bhojpúrí Conjugation.

---

* This लयज is a corruption of लगज,—the य marking the place of the elided ग. Compare the remarks in § 99.

† See Table XXII.

While in the western Hindí these are restricted to certain persons of the imperative and, rarely, the future, in these dialects they are employed in all tenses. In Maithilí, indeed, one may say that we have two complete conjugations, the one honorific, the other non-honorific.

a. While singular and plural forms occur, much confusion exists as to their use. In particular, plural forms are constantly used for the singular in an honorific sense, where no special honorific forms exist. The rules as to the shortening of long vowels under certain conditions, with their exceptions, as given in §§ 117, 118, are to be carefully noted. They receive illustration in all the following Tables.

572. The paradigms of the inflected present and preterite, in Bhojpúrí, etc., are given in Table XXI. It is to be observed that the rule for the shortening of an antepenultimate vowel, which is applied in the preterite, is not applied in the present. Thus, we have देखलों, 'I see,' but देखलों, 'I saw.' Besides the forms given in the Tables, the inflected present has honorific forms in ईला and ईले for the 2nd and 3rd persons. In Sáran, besides the forms given in the Tables, the inflected perfect indefinite has the following honorific forms. The 1st person, to express respect to an object in the 3rd person, takes the termination इयइन ; as, हम राजा के देखलियइन, 'I saw the king;' and, to express respect to an object in the 2nd person, it takes the termination इयवऽ; as, हम रउरा के देखलियवऽ, 'I saw your honour.' The 2nd person, to express respect to an object in the 3rd person, takes the termination अऊन ;' as, तूं साहिब के देखलऊन, 'you saw the gentleman.'

a. To form a non-honorific plural, सऽ may be affixed to the plural terminations in the verbal conjugation throughout; this सऽ is written in Grierson's Grammar as a separate word; thus, देखलन सऽ, 'they saw.' Also, in Sáran, the 2nd person plural of the inflected perfect indefinite takes the termination अऊस, when it is intended to show contempt to an object in the 3rd person; as, तूं नउआ के मारलऊस, 'you beat the barber;' where 'the barber' is spoken of with contempt.

573. In the inflected perfect indefinite, neuter verbs commonly, though not invariably, drop the terminations ए and अस in the 3rd masc. singular, and also take इ in the 3rd fem. singular, and ई in the 3rd fem. plural. Thus while the active transitive verb, देखब, has the 3rd masc. singular, देखलस, 'he saw;' 3rd fem. singular, देखलसि, 'she saw;' and 3rd fem. plural, देखलिन, 'they (fem.) saw;' the neuter verb, गिरब, 'to fall,' more commonly has, for each of these respectively, गिरल, गिरलि, and गिरली.

574. The periphrastic present imperfect in आरों, etc. (Table XX), differs only in appearance and not in meaning, from the full periphrastic form with the present participle and auxiliary. It has been formed from it by the omission of the initial ब of बाट्, according to § 89, and the common change of ट to र, and fusion of the auxiliary with the principal verb.

575. Bhojpúrí makes the Noun of Agency by adding to the root either the suffix वैया or हारा; thus, from देखब, 'to see,' we have देखवैया, 'one who sees,' or देखनहारा, also देखनिहारा. Three forms of the verbal noun occur. The first consists of the root alone; the second is formed by the addition of ल्; the third, by the addition of ब् to the root. Of these the oblique forms terminate respectively in ए, ला, and (in the W. only) ऐ, or ले. Thus, from देखब, 'to see,' we have the following forms, viz: देख, obl., देखे, (in the W., देखै,); देखल्, obl., देखला, (in the W., देखले,); देखब, obl., (only in the W.,) देखबै.

a. Beames makes the acc. singular of the verbal noun in ब, बे; giving as examples, सुंबे नऽ कैलन, 'they would not give a hearing;' होबे करि ऐसन, 'it will probably be.' But this idiom, it may be remarked, is not confined to Bhojpúrí, as I have often heard in the Central Doáb such expressions as पिंवे नऽ करे, 'he will not drink;' वे मानिवे नऽ करिहैं, 'they will not mind.' According to Beames, for the conjunctive participle as given in the Tables, Bhojpúrí commonly uses the oblique perfect participle with a postposition; thus, जानिले पर, 'on knowing,' etc.

576. In the present imperfect, besides the periphrastic form with the imperfect participle, common in other Hindí dialects, Mágadhí also substitutes for the imperfect participle, an oblique form of the verbal noun, in combination with the auxiliary; giving such alternative forms as देखइत ही, 'I am seeing,' and देखऽ ही or देखे ही, etc., 'I see.' An analogous periphrastic tense is also formed with the same oblique verbal noun in combination with the past tense of the substantive verb, हलूं, etc.; as, देखऽ हलूं, देखऽ हलं, etc., rendered by Grierson simply, 'I saw,' etc. Mágadhí Conjugation.

577. In the past contingent perfect, हल may be added to emphasize the idea of past time. In the inflected perfect the following differences obtain between active and neuter verbs. In the 2nd singular, besides the terminations used in the active verb,* neuter verbs also have ला and ले, as गिरला or गिरले, 'thou didst fall.' In the 3rd singular, instead of the terminations इस and लकइ, of active verbs, neuter verbs have ल and लइ; as, e.g., मारिस or मारलकइ, 'he struck,' but गिरल or गिरलइ, 'he fell.' In the 3rd plural, neuter verbs do not use the terminations कन and कथिन. In the periphrastic tenses with the perfect participle, where active verbs take the oblique form of the participle, as in देखले होतूं, 'had I seen,' and मारले होव, 'I shall have struck,' neuter verbs use the direct form, as, गिरल होतूं, 'had I fallen;' गिरल होव, 'I shall have fallen.'

578. The Noun of Agency, in Mágadhí, is formed by the addition to the verbal noun in न or नि of the affix हार. The verbal nouns, except that in ब, as in Bhojpúrí, have an oblique form, in ए and आ.

Maithilí Conjugation.

579. The Maithilí is distinguished from all the dialects exhibited in this Grammar, by the extraordinary exuberance of its verbal forms. Although only a part of the tenses are exhibited in full in the Tables, it possesses all the tenses which are found in High Hindí, and in each of these uses a bewildering variety of diverse forms, equalled in no other dialect.

580. As already observed, Maithilí is remarkable among the dialects of North India, for its frequent use of that Prakritic क, of which we have had frequent occasion to speak, and which seems to have had so much influence in determining the form of a large number of Tadbhava words in the dialects of North India. But while in most of the Hindí dialects this क, where once used, has disappeared, giving rise to new combinations of then concurrent vowels, in Maithilí, as to a much more limited extent in Mágadhí, it still maintains its place, and most of all in the verbal forms. In these it is sometimes added to the root, as, e.g., in the substantive verb, छिक for छ; sometimes to the tense stem, as in देखलकै, 'he saw' (tense stem, देखल), मारलकैन्हि, 'they struck;' and sometimes, again, to the personal terminations, especially those in औ and ऐ; as, देखभौक, 'you will see;' गिरलैक, 'he fell;' and occasionally to others, as, सुतहक, 2nd plur. imperative, 'sleep ye;' पैभौक, 'you will obtain.' Rarely त is similarly added; as in the strong form of the present of the defective auxiliary substantive verb, हतू, etc., for हऊ = H.H. हूं.

---

* See Table XXI.

581. In Maithilí conjugation, a long vowel preceding ऐ or औ in a final syllable, is regularly shortened in any tense but the contingent future. Thus, for the Mágadhí inflected perf. 3rd sing., भेलै, 'he became,' Maithilí has भेलैक; so also the imperfect participle of देखब, 'to see,' with a light final syllable, is देखत; but with the heavy termination in ऐत, ए is shortened to ऍ, giving देखैत.

a. In the Tables will be noticed many terminations containing an aspirated mute, as खौं, भो, etc. These have arisen from the union of ह with a preceding smooth mute. Thus, छिखौं, is for छिकहौं; देखभो, for देखबहो; मारथिन्ह, for मारतहिन्ह, etc., etc.

582. All the periphrastic tenses denoting perfect or complete action are formed in Maithilí after a two-fold manner; viz, by the combination of the auxiliary, either with the perfect participle, as in Western Hindí; or with the inflected perfect, peculiar to these eastern dialects. In the former case, the direct form of the participle is used in the neuter verb, the oblique form in the active, and the auxiliary alone is inflected; in the latter case, the inflections attach only to the leading verb, and the auxiliary is used throughout in the 3rd pers. singular. These two forms are used with equal frequency, and appear to have the same meaning.* Examples are:—गिरलौं य०, or गिरल छौं, 'I have fallen;' मारलक य०, or मारले छि, 'he has beaten.'

583. In the inflected perfect, the terminations differ to some extent in the case of active and of neuter verbs, as follows:

In the 2nd masc. singular, besides the terminations of active verbs, neuter verbs may take आ, हूं, and हा.

In the 3rd masc. singular, transitive verbs take the terminations, अक, कैक, कौक; neuters either take no termination, or else ए, ऐ, ऐक, औ, or औक.

In the 3rd masc. plural, transitives take the terminations, का, एं, थिन्ह, खिन्ह, अन्ह, and आत; neuters, अय, अयि, यिन्ह, हिन्ह, अन्ह, एं, आ, and आत.

In the 3rd fem. plural, transitives take the terminations, कों, इन्ह, ईत, and neuters, ई, इन्ह, and ईत.

584. It is to be noted that the majority of Maithilí verbal forms to some extent may be used interchangeably, the difference being merely a matter of local or personal habit. This remark, however, is not of universal application, and the use of certain forms is determined by another principle. While in all the Hindí dialects, different forms are to some

---

* See Table XX.

extent employed, according as it is desired to refer to the *subject* of the verb respectfully, or otherwise; in Maithilí, this distinction is extended so as also to include reference, honorific or non-honorific, also to the *object* of the verb. Grierson gives the following principles as regulating the preference of verbal forms in so far as they are determined by this latter consideration.

(1) When the object, direct or indirect, in any person, is referred to with much respect, the terminations in ऐन्ह, (ऐन्हि or ऐन) are commonly employed. In the 2nd plural, when an object in the 3rd plural is referred to with respect, the termination ऊन्ह is used.

(2) When the object, direct or indirect, is in the 1st or 3rd person and is regarded as inferior, the terminations in ही, हीं, ए, and एक are used.

(3) When the object, direct or indirect, is in the 2nd person, and is regarded as inferior to the speaker, the terminations ending in औ or औक are preferred.

When it is referred to with respect, औन्ह is employed. The same terminations are used with reference to an object in the 3rd person, regarded as inferior, when the subject is in the 2nd person.

In the contingent future, negative contingent imperfect, and the inflected perfect, the 1st personal forms are often used in an honorific sense for the 2nd.*

585. In those conjugational forms which are formed with the imperfect participle and an auxiliary, it is to be observed that the त of the participle is often elided, in which case the participle and auxiliary are written as one word. Thus one may say and write, either देखैत छौं, or देखैछौं, 'I see;' देखैत छलौं, or देखैछलौं, 'I was seeing;' गिरैत रहौं, or गिरैरहौं, 'I was falling,' etc., etc.† In the west, this छ is sometimes changed to स, giving such forms, e.g., as देखैसैक, for देखैछैक, or देखैत छैक, 'he sees.' But this change is not made in the 1st pers. singular.

586. In Maithilí, the Noun of Agency is formed either by the affix वैया added to the root, or by the affixes हार or वाला, added to the

---

* For full explication and illustration of these rules, see *Seven Grammars*, part vi. pp. 32-36.

† Compare the analogous formation of the Bh. pres. imperf., देखतारौं, etc., for देखत बाटौं, etc, where, however, the initial letter of the auxiliary, instead of the त of the participle, suffers elision. Vid. supra., § 574.

verbal noun in न or नि. The Verbal Nouns are formed as in Bhojpúrí, with variants, as in देखि for देख, and देखलऽ for देखल. The first form is inflected to अ, ए, or ऐ, the second, to ला, and the third, to बा. Thus, from देखब, 'to see,' come the verbal nouns, देख or देखि, obl., देखै or देखऽ; देखल, or देखलऽ, obl., देखला; and देखब, obl., देखबा.

Bh., Mg., and Mt. Irregular Verbs.

587. With the possible exception of ठान्ना, 'to determine,'—as to the existence of which in these dialects I have no information—the verbs noted as irregular in High Hindí, § 391, are also irregular in the east. Also धरब, 'to seize,' follows the conjugation of करब. These two in Bhojpúrí, Mágadhí, and Maithilí substitute कऽ and धऽ for कर and धर in the infinitive, and the conjunctive and perfect participles, with their derived tenses, giving such forms as the following: Bh. inf., कइल, perf. 3rd sing., धइलस = H.H. करना, धरा; Mt. conj. part., कऽ कऽ or कै कऽ, = H.H. करके; Mg. perf. 3rd sing., धैलक, = H.H. धरा. The substitution of मु for मर, in the root of मरल, = H.H. मरना, 'to die,' often takes place in Bhojpúrí also in the contingent future, the past conting. imperfect, and the infinitive. The same is true also in N. and W. Maithilí; in central and eastern Maithilí, however, the irregularity is confined to the perfect participle and its derived tenses, and the infinitive; while in the extreme south, the verb is regular throughout. In some parts of the Maithilí area, मऽ is the substitute for मर, giving, e.g., such forms as the perf. part., मइल or मैला, 'dead,' = H.H. मुआ. Other instances of these irregularities are the following: Bh. past conting. imperf. 3rd sing., मुअत, = H.H. मरता, 'had he died;' N. Mt. past conting. imperf. 1st sing., मुइतऊं, 'had I died;' imperf. part., मुइत, 'dying.' जाइल or जाएब, 'to go,' has the root गऽ for जा in the perfect participle and the derived tenses, as in High Hindí. In all these dialects, the verbs देल or देब, 'to give,' लेल or लेब, 'to take,' are extremely irregular throughout; but lack of space forbids the full exhibition of their peculiarities. They are given with abundant fulness in Grierson's Seven Grammars.

Bh., Mg., and Mt. Causals.

588. All the three dialects under present discussion, form First and Second Causals from verbal roots, as in High Hindí. The mode of formation agrees with the Braj; viz., आव is added for the First, and वाव for the Second Causal. The last व is often softened to उ, and this, again, is combined with a preceding vowel, giving, e.g., from देखब, 'to see,' देखाउब, देखौलस, = H.H. दिखाऊंगा, दिखाया. Variations from this type occur in Mágadhí, which also optionally makes Causals by adding आय and वाय; and also in Maithilí, which in some sub-dialects adds आ for the First Causal, as High Hindí; or, again, hardens the व of the causal to ब.

Bh., Mg., and Mt. Passive.

589. All these eastern dialects, like High Hindí, form a periphrastic passive by the combination of the perfect participle with the various dialectic equivalents of the H.H. verb, जाना, 'to go;' which is then conjugated throughout in combination with the participle. In addition to this, Bhojpúrí and Maithilí present also an inflected passive conjugation, formed by the addition of आ to the root of the primitive verb. Hence we have, e.g., from the active देखल, 'to see,' the passive infinitive देखायल, 'to be seen,' as well as the inflected causal, देखावल, 'to be caused to see,' 'to be shown.' It should be noted, however, that this inflected passive is not equivalent to the other periphrastic form, but rather indicates, not that something is done, but that it *can* be done; as in the High Hindí idiom, with the periphrastic passive, यह पोथी मुझ से पढ़ी नहीं जाती, 'this book cannot be read by me;' where Bhojpúrí, e.g., would have the inflected passive form, पढ़ालि, instead of पढ़ी जाती.

Bh., Mg., and Mt. Compound Verbs.

590. In general, Intensive, Potential, and Completive Compound verbs are formed in Bhojpúrí, Mágadhí, and Maithilí, as in High Hindí, by adding the verbs indicated in §§ 427–434 to the root form of the simple verb. But sometimes इ is added to the root, as in the Rámáyan, and also, in S. Maithilí, ए. Also in S. Maithilí, in Potentials, पारल is sometimes used instead of सकल. Completives are commonly formed from the root, with or without the added इ or ए; but Maithilí sometimes uses instead of this, the verbal noun in ल, giving such alternative forms as खाइ चुकल, and खाएल चुकल, 'he has done eating.'

591. Frequentatives are formed as in Western Hindí, by conjugating the verb करल or करब, = H.H. करना, with the verbal noun which agrees in form with the perfect participle. Hence we have, for H.H. आया करो, 'come often,' Bh. आइल कर०; Mg. आवल कर०; Mt. आएल कर०. In some places Maithilí uses in this combination the verbal noun in ब, instead of that in ल. Desideratives are formed, as in High Hindí, after the same analogy, only substituting the verb चाहब or चाहल for करब.

592. All these eastern dialects add the dialectic equivalents of H.H. लगना, देना, and पाना, to the inflected form in ए of the verbal noun of any verb, to form, by means of these severally, Inceptives, Permissives, and Acquisitives. In Maithilí, the verbal noun sometimes takes the

inflection ऐ instead of ए. These forms, it will be observed, are essentially identical with those found in the Rámáyan, noted § 568 (1). Thus, we have, e.g., Bh., कहै लागल, = H.H. कहने लगा, 'he began to say;' Mg., हमरा बोलै दीही, 'please let me speak;' Mt., बैसै पावल, 'to be allowed to sit,' etc., etc. This same form is also sometimes used in all these dialects with चाहब, instead of the verbal noun in ल, to form Desideratives; as in Bh., ऊ मुए चाहता, 'he is about to die.' But in Bhojpúrí, when not immediate futurition but desire is to be expressed, these oblique forms are followed by the postposition के or ला.

593. In many parts of the Maithilí country, Continuatives and Progressives are formed, not only with the imperfect, but also with the perfect participle, after the analogy of, e.g., H.H. चले जाते हैं, 'they are going away.' It is to be noted, however, that this particular combination, although so common in High Hindí, is not used either in Maithilí or in Mágadhí. Its place is taken by the Intensive compound, चलि आएब, or चल आएब.

594. In the Tables of Conjugation which follow, only two of the periphrastic tenses are given under each participle; but it is to be understood that in most of the dialects* the other periphrastic tenses may be formed in the same manner as in High Hindí. The conjugation of the most important tenses of होना, 'to be' or 'to become,' is given first, as this is used in some of its forms as an auxiliary. It has not been thought necessary to give in every instance all the alternative forms in each dialect where such exist. They can be supplied, where wanting, from the preceding paradigms.

N.B. It is to be noted that Bhojpúrí, besides the verb होब, as given in the Tables, has also a strengthened form of the same, होखब, which is regularly conjugated throughout, after the manner of a neuter verb, and may also be used as an auxiliary; also, that in this dialect the nom. masc. plural is used for both genders in both numbers, and that other forms specially assigned to these in the Tables are rare and poetic. It should also be noted that besides the perfect, होलूं, etc., given in Table XIX., Mágadhí has also, like many other dialects, a perfect from the root भऽ, भेलूं, etc., regularly conjugated in both numbers.

* Naipálí seems to be the chief exception; in the Naipálí Gospel, at least, most of the periphrastic tenses do not occur.

Origin of the Verbal Forms.

595. The various parts of the Hindí verb are either directly descended from corresponding Sanskrit or Prakrit forms, or are new modern combinations of such ancient forms.

Origin of Infinitives.

596. The Hindí *Infinitive* appears under two general types, of which the characteristic letters are respectively *n* (*ṇ*) and *v* (*b*). The *n*-terminations are *nauṉ*, *no*, *ṇo*, *ṇúṉ*, *ná* or *náṉ*, *n*; the *v*-terminations, *vau* or *vauṉ*, *vo* or *bo*, *b*. Hoernle has conclusively proved that these two varieties of the Hindí infinitive are respectively derived from the two forms of the Sk. fut. pass. part. neut.; the *n*-forms, from the participle in *aníya*; the *v* (*b*)-forms, from the participle in *tavya*.* Not only may all the dialectic variations of the two types be thus explained, but all the peculiarities of the use of the infinitive as a noun, an adjective, or an imperative, are thus accounted for, as originally exhibited in this Sk. participle.† Thus, e.g., we derive the inf. *karná* as follows:—Sk. (neut.) *karaṇíyam*, Ap. Pr. *karaṇahaṉ*, archaic H. *karaṇayam*, Br. *karnauṉ*, K. *karnoṉ* or *karno*, M. *karṇo*, Me. *karṇúṉ*, H.H. *karná*, E.H. *karan*. And the *v*-forms of the same arise thus:—Sk. *kartavyam*, Pr. *kariavvam*, *kareavvam*, Br. *karivauṉ* or *karavauṉ*, M. *karbo*, E.H. *karab*.

a. An infinitive, *kardau*, mentioned in De Tassy's Grammar, I would explain by reference to another Prakrit form in *davvam* (for *tavyam*) of this same affix.‡

b. We should expect the penultimate vowel in the *v*-forms to be lengthened, as in the corresponding Maráṭhí, *karáve*, but the shortening is probably due to the accent, which rests on the first syllable.

c. Inasmuch as the Sk. fut. pass. part., when used as a noun, was declined like neut. nouns of the 1st Sk. decl., the H. obl. infinitive in *e* or *á* must therefore be explained as a corrupted gen. sing.§ But the Braj inflected infinitive in *i* has probably arisen from the Sk. loc. sing. in *e*, so that, e.g., *karani* presupposes an original Sanskrit form, *karaṇiye*.

---

* Vid. *Journ. As. Soc. Beng.*, Part I, No. 2, 1873; *Comp. Gramm.*, §§ 313, 314, 321.

† Vid. Monier-Williams: *Sk. Grammar*, §§ 902, 905, 908.

‡ Vid. Lassen: *Inst. Ling. Prac.*, § 129, (3).

§ Vid. § 190, *a*, *b*.

597. The *Imperfect Participle* presents two general types; the one, ending in a consonant or short vowel, as, e.g., the archaic *kahant*, Br. *kahtu*, K. *kahat*; the other, ending in a long vowel, e.g., G. *chalanto* or *chaldo*, Br. *chaltau*, M. *chalto*, H.H. *chaltá*. All these forms have arisen from the Sk. pres. part. Par. in *at*; the *n* which in one or two dialects appears before *t*, belongs to the original Sk. base, and in Prakrit was always retained throughout the declension of the participle.* Origin of Imperfect Participle.

a. In accordance with the principles already illustrated, we must attribute the shorter participial forms to the simple Sanskrit participle; and the longer to an augmented participle formed by the Prakritic suffix *ka.*† Thus, in order of derivation, we shall have, e.g., for the Sk. nom. masc. sing., *chalan* (from *chalat*), Pr. *chalanto*, archaic H. *chalant*, K. *chalnú*, Br. *chaltu* or *chalatu*, E.H. *chalat*;‡ and from an augmented Prakrit form, *chalantako*, G. *chalanto* and *chaldo*, Br. *chaltau*, M. *chalto*, and, finally, H.H. *chaltá*. The inflections are explained in § 190, *a*, *b*. The unique Kumáoní form in *nú̱* is connected by Beames with a form in *anto*. This last form I have heard in the adjacent state of Gaṛhwál near the snowy ranges, which confirms Beames' explanation.

598. The *Perfect Participle* occurs under three general forms, of which, the 1st ends in *a*, the 2nd, in a long vowel, *á*, *o*, *au*, or *e*. In the 3rd form, *l* is the characteristic letter of the termination. Origin of Perfect Participle.

(1) The 1st and 2nd forms are derived from the Sk. past pass. participle in *ta*. The 1st form is to be explained, as in the imperf. participle, as having arisen from the simple Sk. part. The longer forms have come from an increased Prakrit participle, ending in *taka* for *ta*.§ The *y* which in Br. and M. precedes the vowel-termination, has arisen from the *i* which, according to Vararuchi, was inserted before the participial termination much more freely in Prakrit than in Sanskrit.‖ To illustrate, the Eastern perf. participle, *chala* or *chal*, (in the passive conjugation, *chali*,) has been reduced from the Sk. participle *chalitaḥ*;

---

* Vid. Monier-Williams: *Sansk. Grammar*, § 141; Lassen: *Inst. Ling. Prac.*, § 127 (1). So also Beames, except that he refers the E.H., inf. in *n* to the Sk. neut. verbal noun in *nam*. See *Comp. Gramm.*, vol. iii., § 74.

† Vid. § 100.

‡ Vid. § 85.

§ So also Beames: *Comp. Gramm.*, vol. iii., p. 124.

‖ Vid. *Prák. Prak.*; vii., 32.

while from a Prakrit participle, *chalitakaḥ*, have come the longer forms, thus:—Pr. *chalitakaḥ, chalitao, chaliao*. Br. *chalyau*, M. *chályo*, K. *chalo*, H.H. *chalá*.

a. In the peculiar adjective form of the Máṛwáṛí participle, formed with the affix *ṛo*, as *chályoṛo*, etc., *ṛo* is identical with the same affix in the pronominal adjectives, and is to be connected with the Sanskrit diminutive affix *r*, which in Prakrit was often added to nouns and adjectives with no suggestion of a diminutive sense. Similarly Sindhí adds to these participles, *ṛo* or *lo*, and Maráṭhí, *lá*, all of which affixes have the same origin.

b. The peculiar Garhwálí participle in *e*, may be explained by the substitution of *a* for *i* as a union-vowel, and the insertion of a euphonic *y*, instead of *sandhi* as in the other dialects; thus:—*chaláo, chalayo, chalaya, chale*.*

(2) It has been common to regard the *l* of the perfect participle in the eastern Hindí dialects,—found also in Gujerátí, Maráṭhí, Bangálí, and Oṛiyá,—as having arisen from the *t* of the Sanskrit participle, through *d*, *ḍ*, and *r*. But inasmuch as the change supposed, of *r* to *l*, is the exact reverse of that which these dialects constantly exhibit in other words, it is highly improbable that the law should have been uniformly reversed in this participle only. Nor has it yet been proved that the use of this form in *l*, (which is found also in the Prakrit dialects, coexistent with those in *ḍ* and *r*,) historically followed the use of the other forms. I am therefore inclined to believe, that in this participle in *l*, we have a form as ancient as the Sanskrit participle in *t*, and having no connexion with it.†

(3) The irregular perfect participle of some verbs, ending in *na, ná*, etc., is to be connected with the Sk. perf. pass. participle in *na*. Many verbs which in Sanskrit formed this participle with *ta*, in Prakrit preferred the affix *na*. Thus, e.g., we have in Prakrit, *diṇṇa*, for Sk. *datta*, whence H. *díná*, etc., for *diyá*.

Origin of Conjunctive Participle.

599. The *Conjunctive Participle*, in most of its forms, at least, must, I think, be connected with the Sk. indecl. past act. participle in *ya* or *tvá*.

* Vid., § 79, *b*.

† Since this was written, the same view has been suggested and argued at length by Beames, who suggests a comparison with the Slavonic *l* of the preterite. See his *Comp. Gramm.*, vol. iii., pp. 135, 136.

(1) The Sk. termination *ya* in Prakrit became *ia*, whence, e.g., from Sk. *chalya*, Pr. *chalia*, Br. etc., *chali*, and *chal*. When the significant termination had thus almost or quite vanished, the corresponding participle of the ever convenient root *kṛi*, 'to do,' viz., *kari* or *kar*, (Sk. *kṛitya*, Pr. *karia*,) was pressed into service, and appended to the remainder of the old participle; whence, Br. *chalikari*, H.H. *chalkar*, etc. The other affix, *ke* or *kai*, is another form of this same participle, and has arisen from *kari*, by the elision of *r*, and *sandhi* of *a* and *i*.* A still further reduction gives us the Gaṛhwálí affix, *k*, for *ke*, as, e.g., in *márik*.

(2) *a*. In the *ú* which is added to the root in Mairwáṛí, to form such conjunctive participles as *marúne*, *suṇúne*, etc., we probably have the remainder of the other Prakrit affix of the past act. participle, viz., *túṇa* or *úṇa*, for the ancient Vedic *tvánam*.† Thus, e.g., for the Sk. *mṛitvá*, Prakrit had *maraúṇa*, whence, by the operation of the regular phonetic laws, *maraúṉ*, *marau*, and *marú*, as in Mair. *marúne*.

b. For the explanation of the syllable *ne*, however, we must look elsewhere. For although one might be tempted at first thought to see in this *n* the *n* of the old Prakrit affix *úna*, as in the *n* of the similar Maráṭhí participle, it is clear that this would not account for the lengthened form in *ne*. The true analogue of this Mairwáṛí participle is to be found, not in this participle in *úna*, but in the Gujerátí participle in *íne*, (*ine*), in which *i* represents the remainder of the other Prakrit affix *ia*, while *ne*, as Beames has correctly observed,‡ is to be identified in origin with the *ne* or *neṉ* which, in Gujerátí and some Hindí dialects, is the sign of the objective; a form derived from the Sk. participle, *lagya*, H.H. *lagi*, through the common change of an initial *l* to *n*, an elision of *g*, and *sandhi* of the then concurrent vowels.§ Both the Gujerátí and Mairwáṛí forms thus rest upon

* This is still used in E. Hindí in some phrases, for H.H. *karke*. Thus, have heard a villager say, *kas ke jáh?* = H.H. *kaisá karke jáoge*, lit., 'doing what, will you go?;' i.e., 'how will you go?.' This succession of forms seems clearly to show that Trumpp, in his excellent Sindhí Grammar, is mistaken in identifying this *ke* with the Sindhí *je*, of the same participle, and so with the Sk. affix. *ya*, Pr. *ia*. Vid. *Sindhí Grammar*, p. 283.

† Vid. Monier-Williams, *Sansk. Grammar*, § 555, *a*.

‡ *Comp. Gramm.*, vol. iii., p. 233.

§ For illustrations, see Beames: *Comp. Gramm.*, vols. i., p. 248, ii., p. 260.

the Sk. indecl. past act. participle; the former on the common form in *ya*, the latter on the Vedic form in *tvánam*; the former yielding the termination *i*, the other, *ú*. Then, where the other dialects added to this abraded form, the conjunctive participle of *kari*, Mairwáṛí, with Gujerátí, took for the same purpose the same participle of *lagná*.*

(3) With another form of this participle in *iyána* (§ 498) may be compared another Prakrit form in *ḍáṇi*; as, e.g., *kariḍáṇi*, whence, if *ḍ* be elided, and *y* inserted, we shall have *kariyáṇi*, *kariyáṇa*. In the suffix *ber* of the Kumaoní form of this participle, unexplained in the former edition, I now recognize, with Beames, the Sk. *belá*, H. *ber*, 'time;' thus, Ku. *kari ber*, = H.H. *karke*, is, lit., 'at the time of doing.'

Origin of Noun of Agency.

600. Of the affixes *wála* and *hárá*, used with the inflected infinitive to form the *Noun of Agency*, *wálá* is the Sk. *pálaka*, and *hárá*, Sk. *káraka*.† This etymology of *wálá* may be illustrated by H. *gwálá*, for Sk. *gopálaka*. The *h* of *hárá*, if not organic, from *kh* for *k*, was inserted to prevent the hiatus caused by the early elision of the *k*; thus, the order of derivation would be, e.g., *chalanikárá*, *chalaniárá*, *chalanihárá*. By a further elision of *r* and hardening of *i*, etc., *chalaniárá* readily yields the Naipálí form, *chalanyá*. The inflected infinitive in this idiom is therefore, in fact, an objective genitive, under the government of a suffix.

Origin of Contng. Future and Infl. Pres.

601. The tense-forms which in High Hindí are used as a *Contingent Future* (and in old Hindí, also as abs. fut. and pres.,), have all arisen from Prakrit modifications of the Sk. present Parasmai. It is to be noted that Prakrit often substituted for the Sk. terminations, in the 1st sing. and plur., the full forms of the substantive verb, viz., sing., *amhi*, = Sk. *asmi*, and plur., *amho*, *amha*, = Sk. *smaḥ*. On the strength of this analogy, I assume a Pr. 3rd sing. in *atthi*, = Sk. *asti*. This will explain, as the regular Pr. form in *di* does not, the Hindí 3rd pres. in *hi*.‡ Similarly, I would postulate for the termination of the 3rd plur., a Prakrit form, *ahanti*, for *asanti* (Sk. *santi*), of the substantive verb, as the original of the Hindí

* In the former edition I expressed a different opinion, failing to see the bearing on the question, of this termination *ine* of the Guj. participle.

† So Trumpp, *Sindhí Grammar*, p. 75, and Beames, *Comp. Gramm.*, vol. iii., p. 238. Others have suggested *dháraka*, as in 1st ed.

‡ Beames supposes the *h* to be inserted to prevent hiatus after elision of the Prakritic *d*.

form in *hiṉ*. The following table, with the appended notes, will enable the student to work out most of the Hindí forms.

PRESENT.

		SANSKRIT.	PRAKRIT.	HINDI FORMS.
SINGULAR.	1.	*chalámi.*	*chalámi.* *chalumhi.*	*chaläúṉ, chalauṉ, chaluṉ,* etc.
	2.	*chalasi.*	*chalasi.*	*chalasi, chalahi, chaläi,* *chalai, chale.*
	3.	*chalati.*	*chaladi.* *chaläi.* (*chalatthi*)? (*chalasati*)?	*chalahi, chaläi, chalai.* *chale.*
PLURAL.	1.	*chalámaḥ.*	*chalama.* *chalamho, -ha.*	*chaláṉ, chalauṉ, chalúṉ,* *chalahiṉ, chalaiṉ, chaleṉ,* *chaliṉ, chalan, chalíṉ.*
	2.	*chalatha.*	*chalámu.* *chaladham.* *chalaha.*	*chalahu, chalàu, chalo.* *chalá.*
	3.	*chalanti.*	(*chalahanti*)? *chalenti.* *chalajja.*	*chalahiṉ, chalan, chaläiṉ,* *chalaiṉ, chaleṉ, chalai, chalíṉ,* *chalayyaṉ, chale.*

Rem. 1. The 1st pers. forms, sing. and plur., present a difficulty of which I can offer no solution better than that suggested by Beames, that they have arisen from an exchange of the sing. and plur. forms, or perhaps by a transfer of the 3rd plur. to the 1st pers., in the speech of the illiterate.*

Rem. 2. In all the above forms the Prakrit optionally substituted *e* for *a* after the root, whence the frequent appearance of *e* before the terminations in Old Hindí. This may give a clue also to the explanation of other Hindí forms.

602. According to Vararuchi,† Prakrit sometimes substituted *jja* and *jjá* for the proper affixes of the present and definite future. Hence have

* Vid. *Comp. Gramm.*, vol. iii., pp. 105, 106.

† *Prák. Prak.*, vii., 20.

arisen the dialectic Hindí pres. and fut. forms in *aya* and *iya*, as *mariya*, *maraya* = *martá hai*, etc. The forms in *yai* and *ye*, are explained by Vararuchi,* who states that *jja* or *jjá* was also inserted before the terminations of the present, future, and imperative.

Origin of Future forms

603. (1) The various inflected forms of the *Absolute Future*, with *s* or *h* as the characteristic letter, are all to be connected, not with the 1st future, as has been suggested, but rather with the 2nd future, of the Sk. verb. The *sh* of the Sk. tense, had already become *h* in the Apabhransic Prakrit.† Space will not allow us to work out all details, but the following tables will suffice for illustration.

FUTURE.

	SANSKRIT.	PRAKRIT.	HINDI FORMS.
SINGULAR.	1. *chalishyámi.*	*chalissámi,-himi,* *chalissam.*	*chálasyún, chálasún,* etc. *chálahún, chalihaun,* *chalaihaun,* etc.
	2. *chalishyasi.*	*chalissasi, -hisi,* *chalihissasi.*‡	*chálasí, chálahí.* *chalihasi, chálihahi,* *chalaihai, chalihai.*
	3. *chalishyati.*	*(chalissatthi)?* *chalissäi.*	*chálasí, chálahí.* *chalihahi, chalihai,* *chalaihai.*
PLURAL.	1. *chalishyámaḥ.*	*chalissámo,* etc. *chalihissámo,*‡etc.	*chálasyán, chálahán.* *chalihahin, chalihain.*
	2. *chalishyatha.*	*chalissadha.* *(chalissadhati)?*	*chálasyo, chálaho.* *chalihahu, chalihau.*
	3. *chalishyanti.*	*chalissanti.* *chalihissanti.*	*chálasí, chálahí.* *chalihahin, chalihain.*

(2) In the former edition I suggested that in the futures of the *b* type we might perhaps recognize a fragment from the Sk. subst. verb, *bhú,*

* *Prák. Prak.*, vii., 21.

† Lassen: *Inst. Ling. Prac.*, §§ 177, 1; 186, 2.

‡ Prakrit sometimes, as here, reduplicated the fut. termination throughout. Hence, doubtless, come the longer inflected forms in the *Rámáyan.*

after the analogy of the Latin future in *bo*. But the considerations urged by Beames in his *Comp. Gramm.*, vol. iii., since published, have led me to change my mind, and I now agree with him in deriving these *b* futures from the Sk. fut. pass. participle in *tavyum*, Pr. *iavvam*, combined in some of the dialects with fragments of the subst. verb, *as*. Against the derivation of this fut. *b* from *bhú*, it is urged (1) that the *bh* of *bhú* in all other cases has become, in the modern dialects, not *b*, but *h*; and (2) that it always retains the characteristic vowel, *o*. To these considerations I would add (3) that the derivation from the Sk. fut. pass. participle is confirmed by the fact that in modern Hindí, the inf. in *ná*, confessedly derived from the other Sk. fut. pass. participle in *aníya*, is used in combination with the subst. verb, to denote futurity (commonly with a suggestion of necessity), after the very manner supposed by Beames' hypothesis.* In Sanskrit, the copula was commonly omitted with this participle, a usage probably represented by the Old Baiswáṛí indeclinable future in *ba*, where, e.g., *máribu*, represents Pr. *máriabba*, for Sk. *márituvyá*. In the Riwáí forms, Sing., (1) *máravyĕuṉ*, (2) *máribes*; Plur. (1) *márubai*, (2) *máriba*, we have the combination, for greater precision, of the participle with fragments of the substantive verb.

(3) In many parts of India, where, for some reason, the Sanskrit future failed to maintain itself, when the old present, which usurped its place, by reason of its great diversity of use, had become quite indefinite in meaning, the people constructed a new future, by adding to the various forms of the present, one of two new terminations. These terminations now exist, the one as *gau*, *go*, or *gá*, the other as *lo*, *lá*, or *lyo*. Of these, the former is the past pass. participle of the Sk. *gam*, 'to go,' *gataḥ*, Pr. *gao*. *Lo* may be connected with the Sk. pass. participle *lagna*, Pr. *laggo*, of the root *lag*.† Their inflections are derived as in Tadbhava nouns of the same terminations.

---

* So in Sanskrit, this participle was already sometimes used to denote simple futurity, with no suggestion of propriety or obligation. See Monier-Williams: *Sansk. Gramm.*, § 907.

† Beames has assigned to these future terminations in *gá* and *lo*, the same origin as above suggested in the former edition. He adds the confirmatory illustration of the latter case, that in all the modern Aryan languages of India, the verb *lagná* is used in combination with other verbs in an inceptive sense. Vid. *Comp. Gramm.*, vol. iii. 160-163. The relation of *gá* to the tense stem is illustrated by the fact that it is even yet occasionally separated from it by the emphatic particle *hí*, as in *karúṉ hí gá*.

Rem. In illustration of this use of a verb of motion to form a future, compare with the *gá* future the English idiom, 'I am *going* to say,' which is nearly equivalent to the future, 'I shall say.'

Origin of Imperative Forms.

604. In the *Imperative* the *b*-forms, *ba, bi, bo*, etc., represent the Sk. future pass. participle, in *tavya*. The 2nd sing. in *su, si*, appears to stand for the Sk. 2nd sing. imp. Átm. in *sva*, Pr. *ssu*. The common 2nd plur. imper. in *o*, Br. *au*, has arisen from the older Hindí termination, *ahu*, which we may, with Lassen, connect with the Sk. 2nd plur. imper. Átm. in *dhvam*; so that the order of derivation would be, e.g., *chaladhvam, chalahuṉ, chalahu, chalau, chalo*. Or it may be connected, like the 2nd plur. present, with the Prakrit termination *dham*. The imp. 2nd sing. in *hi* is to be identified with the Sk. termination *hi* of the same, in verbs of Classes 2, 3, 5, and 9, and the *dhi*, which in Vedic Sanskrit was the universal termination of the 2nd sing. imperative. The 2nd sing. in *si* and the 3rd sing. forms in *si, hi, e, ai*, etc., as also the 1st and 3rd plur. in *eṉ*, etc., have, I suspect, arisen from a Prakritic confusion of the imperative terminations with those of the present. The following table will illustrate the derivation of this tense.

IMPERATIVE.

	Sanskrit.	Prakrit.	Hindi Forms.
Singular.	1. *chaláni*.	*chalámu*.	*chalauṉ, chalúṉ*.
	2. *chala*.	*chalasu, chaláhi*. *chala*.	*chalasu, chalasi, chalahi*. *chalu, chala, chale*, etc.
	3. *chalatu*.	*chaladu, chaläu*.	*chalu, chale*, etc.
Plural.	1. *chaláma*.	*chalámo*, etc.	*chaleṉ*, etc.
	2. *chalata*.	*chalaha, chaladham*.	*chalahu, chalau*. *chalo*.
	3. *chalantu*.	*chalantu*.	*chaleṉ*, etc.

Origin of Respectful Forms

605. The *Respectful* forms of the *Imperative* are to be explained by the above-mentioned Prakrit custom of inserting *jja* before the verbal terminations.* The following comparisons will illustrate the derivation: Pr. 2nd plur. imp. (alternative form), *chalijjadham* (or *chalijjidham*), O.H. *chaliyahu*, Máṛ. etc., *chalijyo* or *challjo*, H.H. *chaliyo*. Or, again, 2nd plur. Pr. *challijjaha*, (*chalijjäa*), Br. *chalijjai* or *challje* (for *chalijjaya*), H.H. *chaliye*.

606. As the remaining tenses in most of the dialects are formed by combination with the auxiliary subst. verb, we may here briefly indicate the origin of its various forms. These have arisen, in High Hindí, from the Sk. radicals, as, *bhú*, and *sthá*; and, besides these, in other dialects, from the radicals, Sk. *rah*, *vṛit*, *lag*, and Pr. *achchh*. Origin of Forms of Subst. Verb.

(1) To *as* must be referred the pres., *húṉ*, *hai*, etc., with its dialectic variants. But, as Beames has truly said, it is impossible to derive these from the Prak. *amhi*, (for Sk. *asmi*),† and they apparently compel us to assume another Pr. form, wherein *as* was conjugated, like most Prakrit verbs, after the model of *bhú*, adding *a* to the root in the present. Assuming this, then the order of derivation, as illustrated in the Hindí dialects, will be as follows:—*Sing*., (1) Sk. *asmi*, Pr. (*ahámi*?) O.B. *ahaún*, A. *ahĕṉuṉ*, Br. *hauṉ*, H.H. *húṉ*, R. *áṉ*. (2) Sk. *asi*, Pr. (*ahasi*?) O.B. *ahasi*, *ahahi*, *áhi*, *ahüi*, *ahai*; A. *ahĕs*, *ahas*, *ahe*, etc., etc., after the analogy of other derivatives from the Sk. present. The suggestion of Beames that to this same root we are probably to refer the Máṛ. past tense, *ho* (for Sk. *santo*), = H.H. *thá*, is corroborated by the fact that this tendency to substitute *h* for *s*, is characteristic of the Máṛwáṛí. To the same root, I am now inclined, with Beames, to assign K. *hato*,‡ for Sk. pres. participle, *santo*; though the change from a present to a past sense, is a difficulty which is hardly yet removed.

---

* On this topic, Lassen's remark is worthy of note. He says: "*Conjicio . . . arctius limitatam fuisse regulam ab aliis, et relatum esse incrementum potissimum ad formas, quae potentiali et precutivo Sanscr. respondeant.*" *Inst. Ling. Prac.*, § 124.

† *Comp. Gramm.*, vol. iii., p. 172.

‡ It is against the derivation of this form from *bhú*—suggested in the 1st ed.—that it fails to explain the substitution of *a* for *ú*, and the retention of the *t* of *bhúta*, which elsewhere in the modern derivatives of this participle is rejected. I therefore accept the above explanation of Beames, till a better can be shown. See Beames: *Comp. Gramm.*, vol. iii., p. 177.

(2) To the root *bhú* must be assigned all other forms of the subst. verb with initial *h*; as also the dialectic forms with initial *bh*. These present little difficulty, and the following illustrations of their derivation will suffice :—Sk. pres. Par., 1 sing., *bhavámi*, Pr. (*huvámi ?*); E. and W. Rajp., *hveún*; other dialects, *hoún*, etc.: Sk. fut. Par., 1 sing., *bhavishyámi*; Pr. (*huvissámi ?*); E. Rajp. *hvesyún*, *hvesún*; Br. *hoihaun*, *hvaihaun*, etc.: Sk. past pass. part., *bhúta*; Pr. (*bhavio ?*); Br. *bhayau*; A. *bhavá*; O.B., R. *bhá*, etc.: Sk. pres. part., *bhavat*; Pr. *huvanto*; archaic W. Hindí of Chand, *hunto*; Br. *hutau*, etc.*

(3) From the Sk. past part., *sthita*, root *sthá*, has arisen the Hindí past tense, *thá*, of the subst. verb. G. gives the earlier form *thayo*, where *y* marks the place of the elided *t*, whence, again, Br. *tho*, and so H.H. *thá*. Naipálí presents this participle, inflected with fragments from the root *as*, thus:—Sing. (1) *thiyán*; (2) *this*; (3) *thiyá*. Plur. (1) *thiyún*; (2) *thiyau*; (3) *thiyá*.† Beames instances as analogous changes, O.B. *gá*, for Sk. *gata*; the affixes *ká*, for Sk. *kṛita*, and *lo* or *lá*, for Sk. *lagna*.

With this same root, *sthá*, and not *achchh*,‡ I prefer to connect the Himalayan and Rajputana forms of the substantive verb with initial *chh*. For the Sindhí,§ contiguous to the Rajputana dialects on the west, forms the present of its subst. verb from this root, thus, *thián*, *thien*, etc.; and the connection of the Gaṛhwálí and Kumáoní mountaineers with the Rajputs of the further South and West is admitted. The transition to the *chh* form scarcely needs exposition; *i* would harden into *y* before the following vowel, and *thya* would pass by a familiar phonetic law into *chha*.

* In the first edition I connected this with *bhúta*; but the intermediate form with Anusvár given by Beames, together with the retention of *t*, seem to justify him in deriving it as above. See *Comp. Gramm.*, vol iii., pp. 202, 203.

† See Beames, *Comp. Gramm.* vol. iii., p. 209.

‡ So in the first edition of this Grammar; as also Beames, *Comp. Gramm.*, vol. iii., pp. 186, 187. But a similar argument from contiguous forms, will, I think, lead us still to postulate this root *achchh*, as the origin of the *chh*-forms as in Eastern Hindí.

§ And also Gujerátí. See *Shápur Edaljí's Grammar*, pp. 72-81.

PRESENT OF SUBST. VERB.

	Sindhí.	Máṛ.	Kumáoní.	Gaṛhwálí.	Naipálí.
SINGULAR.	1. *thiúṉ.*	*chhúṉ.*	*chhyauṉ.*	*chhauṉ.*	*chhuṉ.*
	2. *thieṉ, thíṉ.*	*chhai.*	*chhai.*	*chhai, chha.*	*chhas.*
	3. *thie.*	*chhai.*	*chha.*	*chha.*	*chha, chhe.*
PLURAL.	1. *thiúṉ.*	*chháṉ.*	*chhayúṉ.*	*chhaváúṉ.*	*chhúṉ.*
			chhoṉ.	*chhauṉ.*	*chhauṉ.*
	2. *thio.*	*chho.*	*chhá.*	*chhayaí.*	*chhau.*
				chhau.	*chhan.*
	3. *thiani.*	*chhai.*	*chhan, chhín.*	*chhan.*	*chhain.*

(4) The use of the root *rah*, instead of *sthá*, in this tense, as appears from the tables, is confined to the eastern dialects; the forms call for no special remark.

(5) In the Bh. *báṭíṉ*, *baṭe*, *bá*, appears the Sk. root *vṛit*. These forms appear to be connected with the Sk. pres. A'tm., sing. (1) *varte*, (2) *vartase*, (3) *vartate*; *rt* passing into *ṭ*, and the terminal syllables being contracted into *e*, etc., on the usual principles.

(6) The discussion of the future in *lo*, § 603 (3), gives the key to the Gaṛhwálí present of the subst. verb, Sing., *lo*, Plur., *lá*, in which, again, we must recognize a form derived from Pr. *laggo*, for the Sk. past pass. part., *lagna*, root *lag*. No one familiar with the very diversified use of this verb *lagná* in Hindí, will be surprised to see it doing duty, as here, for the substantive verb.

(7) The Mt. present of the subst. verb, Sing. (1) *chhúṉ*, (2) *chhe*, (3) *achh*, must be considered in connexion with the neighbouring Oṛíyá and Bangálí, which furnish for these the forms, O. *achhi*, *achhu*, *achhi*, etc., and Bang. *áchhi*, *áchhis*, *áchhe*, etc., together with the Bh. *khe*, all which are fully explicated by reference to the root *achchh*, which was substituted in Shaurasenic Prakrit for the Sk. *as*, 'to be.' This root was conjugated like all Prakrit verbs; thus, Pres. Sing. (1) *achchhámi*; (2, 3,) *achchhäi*; Plur , (1) *achchhámo*; (2) *achchhattha*; (3) *achchhanti*.*

---

* See Vararuchi: *Prák. Prak.*, xii. 19, 20; Lassen: *Inst. Ling. Prac.*, p. 346; and consult the full discussion of this root and its derivatives by Beames, *Comp. Gramm.*, vol. iii., pp. 180-187. He suggests that *achchh* may represent the Sk. *akṣh*, 'to seem,' 'to appear.'

Origin of Mâṛ. Present.

607. The formation of the Máṛwáṛí present, by adding the present of the substantive verb to a form which, as has been above shown, was itself a true present, is to be explained by the ambiguity which had come to attach to that tense. As it was often used as a contingent future, and therefore did not, *per se*, any longer denote present time, Máṛwáṛí solved the difficulty by adding again, as of old, but in a modern form, the present of the substantive verb. Most other dialects met the case by dropping the old present as such, and forming a new present with the imperfect participle.

Origin of Inflected Perfect and Present.

608. (1) In the partially inflected *perfect* tense which is used in the *Rámáyan*, the terminations in the sing., (1) *-eu͟n*, (2, 3,) *-asi*, *-esi*, *-ehi*, masc., and *-iú͟n*, *-isi*, fem.; and in the plur., (2) *ehu*, *-ihu*, (3) *-en*, represent abraded fragments of the Sk. subst. verb, *asmi*, *assi*, etc.* The sense of their meaning having been lost, the modern form of the subst. verb has again been added in Riwáí, as in *márĕs hai*, 'he has struck,' just as in Máṛwáṛí it is added to the remainder of the old Sk. present, as in *márai chhai*, 'he strikes.'

(2) Traces of the same inflectional additions to the *present* participle appear in Gaṛhwálí, and in such O.B. forms as *kháteu͟n*, 'I could eat;' *janityau͟n*, 'had I known;' *avatehu*, 'had you come,' etc.; found in the *Rámáyan*, always in the sense of a past conditional.†

Origin of Causal Forms.

609. (1) The Sk. causal affix, *aya*, in Prakrit became *e*. This *e* was sometimes added directly to the root; but very commonly, *p*, which in Sanskrit was added only to certain roots ending in vowels, in Prakrit was added, with *á* prefixed, to many other roots before the causal termination. This *p*, again, was early changed to *b* or *v*, so that, e.g., for the Sk. causal base, *káraya*, from *kṛi*, Prakrit exhibits not only *kárе* but *karáve* (for *karápe*), whence, in succession, the causal bases, Br. *karáva*, G. *karau*, H.H. *kará*. The *o*, which occurs in two or three H.H. verbs, as, e.g., *bhigoná*, is a contraction of *áva*.

a. The Sk. *pá*, 'to preserve,' inserted a euphonic *l*, instead of *p*, before the causal affix, making *pálaya* (whence H. *pálná*). It is probable that in Prakrit this may have been used more extensively, and so may be the

* Compare a similar usage in such Sk. phrases as *ádishṭo smi*, 'I am commanded.' Vid. Monier-Williams: *Sansk. Grammar*, § 895.

† Vid. sup., § 557.

original of the *l* (in many dialects, *r*) which is found in many Hindí Causals, as, e.g., *pilâná*, *biṭhláná*, etc.

(2) The regular form of the Sanskrit Causal in *aya*, Prakrit, *e*, is represented in Hindí by many Causals of the 2nd form (§ 421, 2), in which, although the causal affix *aya* (Pr. *e*), has disappeared, Hindí still retains the ancient *vṛiddhi* or *gun* of the vowel of the radical syllable. Thus, e.g., from the Sk. neuter base, *sphaṇṭ*, 'to burst' (represented in H. *phaṭná*), comes the causal base, *sphâṭaya* (Pr. *phâḍe?*), whence H. *phâṛná*.

610. The Prakrit commonly formed the stem of the passive by adding *ijja* to the root, instead of the Sk. pass. affix, *ya*.* From this Prakrit formation has arisen the modern Máṛwáṛí passive in *íjaṇo*, as, e.g., *karíjaṇo*, 'to be done.'† Similarly are to be explained the Naipálí passive in *inu*, and also the pres. passive participles in *yata*, found in the *Rámáyan* (§ 566, *a*), and certain passive forms in *iye*; as, *saráhiye*, 'it is praised,' for Sk. *shlághyate*, etc. In all these, *ijja* has been softened to *iya*. Origin of Inflected Passive.

a. Sometimes Prakrit assimilated the *y* of the Sk. pass. affix to the final consonant of the root, as, e.g. in *dissäi*, for Sk. *dṛishyate*.‡ From this form of the passive are derived many Hindí verbs with a passive sense; as, e.g., *siṇchná*, 'to be watered,' which is for *sichchaná*, and is properly a passive derived from the Sanskrit root *sich* (*siñch*), of which the passive base is *sichya*, Pr. *sichcha*.

---

* The Mágadhí Prakrit excepted. Vid. Vararuchi: *Prák. Prak.*, vii. 8, 9; Lassen: *Inst. Ling. Prac.*, p. 434.

† So the neighbouring Sindhí regularly forms a passive by adding to the verbal root the termination *ja* or *ija*: as from *karaṇu*, pass. *karijaṇu*.

‡ Vararuchi: *Prák. Prak.*, viii. 57, 58.

CHAPTER X.

OF DERIVATIVE AND COMPOUND WORDS.

I. *Of Derivatives.*

611. The general principles which govern the derivation of Hindí words have been already treated in Chapter III.: where also have been noted the forms under which pure Sanskrit words appear in Hindí. It will be the object of this section to indicate the most common methods by which Tadbhava words of various classes are derived, either from original roots or from secondary formations.

Formation of Abstract Nouns.

612. The following are the most common forms of *Abstract Nouns.*

(1) The roots of very many verbs are used as abstract nouns: as, मार् (vb. मारना), 'a beating;' बोल (vb. बोलना), 'speech.' A short vowel in the verb is often lengthened or *gunated* in these nouns: as, e.g., चाल (vb. चलना), 'walk,' 'behaviour;' मेल (vb. मिलना), 'harmony.'

a. Here we must also place many words ending in आव (आउ, आऊ, or आओ): as, बचाव, 'salvation;' बनाव, 'adornment,' etc.

Rem. 1. In many such words the final व is identical with the व (Sk. प) which is the characteristic of the causal affix. Although this व has disappeared from the Causals in High Hindí, it is retained in almost all the dialects; so that the original Hindí form of the causal root, e.g., of बचाना, was not बचा, but बचाव. Hence appears the propriety of placing such words as the above under this class. It should be remarked, however, that many words with this final labial express the abstract idea, not of the causal, but of its primitive. Such nouns will be explained below (3).

Rem. 2. It must not be supposed that nouns of this class are derived from the infinitives with which they are connected. Both the infinitive and the noun are collateral formations from one primitive root.

(2) न (for Sk. न, forming neuters in नं) is added to verbal roots to form abstract nouns: as, चलन (vb. चलना), 'walk;' मरन (vb. मरना) 'dying.'

(3) आन and आउ are added to primitive verbal roots to form abstract nouns: as, चढ़ाउ (vb. चढ़ना), 'an ascent;' उठान (vb. उठना), 'rising;' लगान (vb. लगना), 'fastening.' ऊ, व, or ओ, is sometimes written for the final उ.

a. आई is sometimes added instead of आउ, giving the same sense; as, चढ़ाई = चढ़ाउ.

Rem. All these formations are to be connected with the Sk. affix, त्व or त्वन्. Sindhí preserves the *t*, hardening it however to *ṭ*.

(4) A large class of abstract nouns is formed with the affixes वत, वट, हत, and हट. These are often added to causal roots: as, from बनाना, 'to make,' बनावट, 'a fabrication,' also बनावत; from बुलाना, 'to call,' बुलाहट, 'calling;' and also to adjectives; as, from कड़वा, कड़वाहट, 'bitterness;' from चिकना, चिकनाहट, 'greasiness.'

a. Here also properly come a number of nouns in औती or or औटी (for आवती or आवटी): as, कसौती or कसौटी, 'a touchstone;' छुड़ौटी, 'deliverance;' which are connected, respectively, with कसाना, छुड़ाना.

Rem. Many of these have their origin in the Sk. वृत्ति, 'state,' 'condition.' In others, the termination represents the Sk. suffix ति.

(5) Very common is the affix ई (Sk. यं), forming abstract nouns from other nouns and adjectives. Thus, from ऊंचा, 'high,' ऊंचाई, 'height;' बुरा, 'bad,' बुराई, 'badness;' गोला, 'a ball,' गोलाई, 'roundness;' लड़का, 'a boy,' लड़काई, 'boyhood.'

a. When added to causal roots, ई (for आनी) forms nouns denoting the price paid for the work denoted by the verb: as, from धुलाना, 'to cause to wash,' धुलाई, 'the price paid for washing;' उतारना, 'to carry over,' उतराई, 'ferriage;' ढुलाई, 'price of carriage,' etc.

(6) Other abstract nouns are formed by adding to adjectives and verbal roots the affix आई: as, from चतुर, चतुराई, 'cleverness;' from ठगना, ठगाई, 'cheating.'

(7) Many Tatsama fem. abstract nouns are formed with the affix ति (sometimes नि): as, मति, 'the mind;' बुद्धि (बुध + ति), 'intelligence;' ग्लानि, 'languor.'

a. In Hindí Tadbhava nouns also, this suffix is added to verbal roots; but इ is either dropped or lengthened. Thus, लागना, 'price' (vb. लगना, the radical *a* being lengthened); बढ़ती (for बढ़तिका, बढ़तिया?), 'increase' (vb. बढ़ना); चढ़ती, 'rise (in price)' (vb. चढ़ना).

(8) Tatsama masc. abstracts are formed from nouns and adjectives, by the affix त्व: as, from ईश्वर, 'God,' ईश्वरत्व, 'divinity;' गुरु, 'heavy,' 'venerable,' गुरुत्व, 'dignity.'

a. This affix, through different Prakritic modifications, has become in Tadbhava words, प, पा, पन, or पना: as, from बुढ़ा, 'old,' बुढ़ापा or बुढ़ापन, 'old age;' लड़का, 'a child,' लड़कपन, or, more rarely, लड़कपना, 'childhood.' प is very rare; examples are: खापप, 'maturity;' बुढ़ाप, 'senility.' पनी also, very rarely occurs; as, लुच्चपनी, 'wantonness.'

(9) A few abstracts are formed from adjectives with क; as, ठंडक, 'coolness.'

(10) Many Tatsama fem. abstracts are formed from adjectives with the affix ता: as, from नम्र, नम्रता, 'courtesy;' from पवित्र, पवित्रता, 'holiness.' Others are formed by affixing to roots आ, and, rarely, ना: as, इच्छा, 'desire;' तृष्णा, 'thirst.'

a. For ता, ताई is often substituted; as, सुंदरताई, for सुंदरता, 'beauty.'

(11) Masc. abstract nouns are formed from Sanskrit roots or nominal bases, by adding इमा (Sk. इमन्): as, लघिमा, 'lightness;' महिमा, 'greatness.'

a. In Hindí, this termination has become आई: as, e.g., in ऊंचाई, 'height;' लंबाई, 'length.'

(12) Other Sanskrit abstracts (neut.) occur in Hindí, formed from nominal bases with the suffix य: as, e.g., राज्य, 'kingdom;' स्वाम्य, 'lordship.' But Hindí very commonly drops this य; as, e.g., in राज.

613. The following terminations are used to form nouns denoting *Agency* or *Occupation*. Formation of Nouns of Agency and Occupation.

(1) वाला (Sk. पालक), as thus used with inflected infinitives, has already been noticed. It is also added to nouns to denote 'occupation:' as, दूधवाला, 'a milkman;' and to verbal roots: as, रखवाला, 'a guard.'

a. But some words terminating in वाला, have come directly from old Sanskrit compounds: as, e.g., ग्वाला, 'a cowherd,' Sk. गोपालक. Dialectic variations of this affix are वारी, वार, etc.

(2) From the Sk. कारक we have हारा or हार, used with verbs to form Nouns of Agency, as has been already noticed. This affix is occasionally added to nouns, when the penult of the noun is sometimes shortened; as in पनहारा, 'a water-carrier.' Variations of this affix are the following.

a. By elision of ह in the foregoing, we have also from the same Sk. affix, nouns in आरा, आर, or र, denoting 'occupation:' as, from सोना, सुनार (Sk. सुवर्णकार), 'a goldsmith;' from बनज, बनजारा, 'a trader (in grain);' सुआर (Sk. सूपकार), 'a cook.'

b. A few nouns of agency end in री or आरी (Sk. कारिन्); as, पूजारी (Sk. पूजाकारिन्), 'a worshipper.'

c. Other nouns of agency are formed with एरी and एरू: as, पूजेरी, for पूजारी, 'a worshipper;' लुटेरू, from लूट, 'a robber,' etc.

Rem. The explanation of these variants is probably to be found in the Prakrit root केर, for Sk कृ. एरी would then stand for Pr. केरिक, and एरू for Pr. केरुक.*

(3) Sanskrit nouns of agency were also formed from roots with the affix अक. These are common in Hindí: as, पूजक, 'a worshipper;' रचक, 'a protector.'

a. अक is often corrupted to आ, whence Hindí nouns of agency in आ; as, भुंजा (for भुंजक), 'a parcher.'

b. In Prakrit, this अक often became इक, whence the Hindí affix इया, denoting 'agency:' as, from लखना, 'to behold,' लखिया, 'a beholder;' from गाडर, 'a sheep,' गड़रिया, 'a shepherd.' This इया, again, became ई, whence many Hindí nouns in ई, denoting 'occupation:' as, e.g., हलवाई, 'a confectioner;' बढ़ई, 'a carpenter.'

c. अक also became उक, whence, again, nouns of agency in उआ or ऊआ; as, मछुआ, 'a fisherman.' And उआ became ऊ, whence, finally, other nouns of agency in ऊ: as बैठू, 'a sitter;' खाऊ, 'a great eater,' 'a glutton.'

(4) वैया, (also वाइया and वय्या,) from the Sk. suffix तव्य,† also forms nouns of agency from verbal roots: as, रखवैया, 'a keeper;' मरवैया, 'one dying.' A long vowel is shortened before the affix; as, लिवैया, 'a taker,' from लेना; गवैया, 'a singer,' from गाना.

(5) A few nouns of agency are formed with हा (for वा?); as, चरवाहा, 'a shepherd,' from चरवाना. This is also added to nouns; as, कबिराहा, 'a follower of *Kabír*.'

(6) From verbal roots, two or three nouns of agency are formed with वा: as, देवा, 'a giver;' लेवा, 'a taker.'

---

* But Hoernle regards these last as originally possessional adjectives, and regards the suffix as derived from the Sk. *drish*. *Comp. Gramm.*, § 251.

† Vid. Hoernle: *Comp. Gramm.*, § 314.

Rem. This is probably derived from the Sk. suffix *tavya*, and is thus cognate with the वैया, above mentioned.

(7) A few nouns of agency are formed with आक (Sk. आकु); as, पैराक, 'a swimmer.'

(8) Very common in Hindí are Sanskrit nouns of agency or relationship in ता: as, कर्त्ता, 'a doer,' दाता, 'a giver;' पिता, 'a father.' All these are Sk. noms. sing., from bases in तृ.

(9) Many Sanskrit nouns of agency are formed with the affix अन (अण). In Hindí, these are chiefly found in poetry, as the last member of compounds: as, सागरशयन, 'a sleeper on the ocean;' दुखहरन, 'a remover of sorrow.'

(10) Finally, Sanskrit formed nouns of agency with अ, after *guṇ* of the root. These are found in Hindí, but only as the last member of compounds: as, from the root धृ, धर = धरनेवाला, 'a supporter,' in धरणीधर, 'a mountain,' lit., 'an earth-supporter.'

614. Nouns denoting the *Instrument* are formed from verbal roots.

Derivation of Instrumental Nouns.

(1) With नी, ना, or न (from Sk. suffix अनीय?): as, from धौंकना, 'to blow,' धौंकनी, 'a bellows;' बेलना, 'to roll out,' बेलन or बेलना, 'a rolling-pin.'

(2) Some nouns with an instrumental sense are formed by the affix आ (Sk. अक); as, घेरा, 'a fence,' from घेरना, 'to surround.'

615. (1) *Possessive* nouns are most commonly formed from other nouns with the affixes वाला or हारा: as, e.g., दाँतवाला, 'one having teeth;' कपड़ेवाला, 'a draper.' वाला may be thus added to a series of words, all of which must then be inflected: as, घोड़े गंडे पट्टे वाले, 'horses having collars and girths,' i.e., 'harnessed;' अपनी सी आखों वाली हरिणयों के संग, 'with deer having eyes like her own.*

Derivation of Possessives.

* For derivation of these suffixes see § 613, (1), (2).

(2) The termination आल or आला, (Sk. आल, Pr. आलक,) is added to a few nouns to form possessives: as, लठियाल, 'one having a stick;' जवाला, 'a mixture of other grain with barley (जौ).'

Rem. But in a few words expressive of place, आल stands for the Sk. आलय: as, ससुराल, 'father-in-law's house.' So also, perhaps, घड़ियाल, 'a gong,' from घड़ी, 'a division of time.'

(3) Here may be noted a large class of Persian nouns, formed with the suffix दार (2nd root of داشتن, 'to have'): as, जमीनदार, 'a landholder;' हवादार, 'ventilated,' lit., 'having air.'

Derivation of Diminutives. **616.** *Diminutives* are formed in Sanskrit by adding the following terminations.

(1) Very common is the affix अक or इक. This same affix is similarly used in Hindí: thus, from ढोल, ढोलक, 'a small drum;' or का (fem.) is added; as in पशुका, 'a small animal,' from पशु; or इका, as in शकटिका, 'a toy-cart,' from शकट; or की, as in टमकी, 'a small drum.'

a. क being elided from such diminutives, य was often inserted, whence a large class of Hindí diminutives (fem.) in इया: as, from डिब्बा, 'a box,' डिबिया, 'a little box,' 'a casket;' from फोड़ा, 'a boil,' फुड़िया, 'a small sore,' 'a pimple.' These diminutives often express 'affection;' as, बेटिया, 'a little daughter,' from बेटी.

b. इया, again, very often became ई; whence a large number of diminutives ending in ई: as, e.g., गाड़ी, 'a carriage;' टोकरी, 'a small basket,' etc., etc.

c. In the east, especially, क being elided, व was inserted instead of य, whence another class of diminutives in वा: as, e.g., from पुर, पुरवा, 'a hamlet;' घोड़वा, 'a small horse,' often used by way of depreciation. व is often softened to उ, whence diminutives in उआ; as, बेटुआ, 'a little son.'

(2) Sanskrit also formed diminutives in र, whence have come (*a*) Hindí diminutives in री; as, तितरी, 'a butterfly;'

and (*b*) in ड़ी: as, टिकड़ी, 'a wafer;' पलंगड़ी, 'a small bedstead;' and, still more common, (*c*) others in ला and ली: as, तितली and टिकली, for तितरी and टिकड़ी; घंटाली, 'a little bell,' from घंटा. For ल (र) इल and उल have been often substituted: as, e.g., in खटोला, 'a small bed;' मुरेला, 'a peachick,' etc.

(3) A very few diminutives are formed with ना: as, from भूत, 'a goblin,' भूतना, 'a sprite;' from मटका, 'a large earthen jar,' मटकना.

Nouns of Nativity and Relationship.

617. Nouns expressing *Nativity* or *Relationship* are formed from other nouns with the affix ई (Sk. ईय, इय). Examples are, माड़वाड़ी, 'a native of Máṛwáṛ;' कबीरी, 'a follower of *Kabír*.'

Miscellaneous Derivatives.

618. क, and also रा, ड़ा, and ला, (Sk. र), with their fem. forms, की, री, ड़ी, and ली, are often added to nouns to form derivatives expressive of various other relations difficult to classify. Sometimes the consonant of the affix is preceded by इ or उ, which is combined with the final vowel of the primitive according to the rules of *sandhi*. Examples are: from मट्टी, 'earth,' मटका, 'an earthen jar,' dim. मटकी; from हाथ, 'hand,' come हथेला, 'a pilferer,' हथेली, 'the palm of the hand,' हथौड़ा, 'a hammer,' dim. हथौड़ी, हथरी, 'a handle,' and हथौली, 'a plough handle.'

a. आ and ई (for अक, इक), are similarly added; as, again, from हाथ, हथा, 'a handle,' हथी, 'a horse-brush.'

Derivation of Adjectives.

619. Hindí *Adjectives* are derived as follows:—

(1) Many adjectives were formed in Sanskrit with the affixes अक, इक, or उक. Before these affixes, medial *a* or a final radical vowel was *vriddhied*, and any other vowel changed to its *guṇ*. Examples are: सांसारिक, 'worldly,' from संसार, 'the world;' तापक, 'inflammatory,' from तप, 'heat.'

a. In Prakrit, क was dropped from these forms, whence, य being inserted, Hindí adjectives in इया; as, दूधिया, 'milky,' from दूध. But more commonly *sandhi* took place; whence, from अक came the Hindí adj. termination, आ: as, from मैल, 'dirt,' मैला, 'dirty;' from मुष्टक, for मुष्ट, मोटा, 'fat,' etc. Similarly, from इक has often come the termination ई: thus, from भार, 'a burden,' भारी, 'heavy;' ऊन, 'wool,' ऊनी, 'woolly.' उक also became ऊ, as in a few modern adjectives, e.g., ढालू, 'sloping.'

(2) Many Sanskrit adjectives were formed with the terminations ल, आलु, इल, उल; र, अर, इर, उर. All of these, perhaps, have been preserved in Hindí. Examples are: from दूध, दूधल, 'milky;' from दया, दयाल, or दयालु, 'merciful;' from दांत, दन्तैल, or दन्तेल, 'toothed;' from बोझ, बोझिल, 'loaded;' from काम, 'work,' कमेरा, 'industrious;' from नोक, नोकीला, 'pointed;' from रस, 'juice,' रसीला, 'juicy.' Adjectives in र (एर) are the less common, but other examples occur: as, दंशेर, 'cruel,' from दंश, 'a bite;' दूधेर, 'milky,' from दूध. And through the change of र to ड़ come a very few adjectives in ड़; as, हंसौड़, 'merry,' (हंस + उर,) from the root of हंसना, 'to laugh.'

(3) A few adjectives or nouns occur, which are formed with the Sanskrit suffix इत्: as, दंगैत (दंग + इत), from दंग, 'seditious;' बर्चैत, lit., 'having a spear,' 'a spearman,' from बर्चा.

(4) The following suffixes are also occasionally used to form adjectives: viz., ई (added as initial); as, दंगई, 'turbulent;' इभ; as, तुन्दिभ, 'corpulent;' and हा; as, कंपहा, 'tremulous.'

(5) Many Tatsama adjectives denoting 'possession,' are formed with ई (Sk. इन्): as, धनी, 'wealthy,' (Sk. धनिन्,) from धन, 'wealth;' and also with वान or वन्त (Sk. वत्): as, from धन, धनवान; 'wealthy;' from बल, बलवान, 'strong;' from कृपा, कृपावन्त, 'merciful,' etc.

(6) Many Sanskrit participles, especially those in त and मान (मत्), are used as adjectives in Hindí: as, e.g., क्रोधित, 'angry,' (from क्रुध्); शोभायमान, 'beautiful,' (from शुभ्).

(7) The Sanskrit affix मय, = Engl. '-ful;' is also often added in Hindí to Tatsama nouns: as, दयामय, 'merciful;' पावकमय, 'fiery.'

(8) Very rarely Tatsama adjectives are found in Hindí, formed with the Sk. affix वत्, expressing 'similitude;' as, विधिवत, 'like the moon.'

(9) A very few adjectives occur, formed with the Sk. desiderative affix, स् + आ; the most common example is पियासा, 'thirsty,' Sk. पिपासित:, perf. pass. desider. part., from the root पा, 'to drink;' रोआसा, 'inclined to weep' (from रोना), also occurs.

620. A very large number of *Onomatopoetic* words occur in Hindí, whose derivation is to be traced to an attempt to imitate or suggest a sound or action by the voice. These often have a reduplicated form. Such, e.g., are: खटखट, 'a knocking;' झनझन, 'a jingling;' चट्टाबट्टा, 'a rattle;' किंकणी, 'a tinkling girdle;' सुनसुनाना, 'to whistle,' etc., etc. From such of these as are nouns, are formed a large number of verbs by the addition of the causal termination: as, e.g., from the above nouns, खटखटाना, 'to knock;' झनझनाना, 'to jingle,' etc. Onomatopoetic Words.

II. Of Compound Words.

621. Hindí admits of the greatest freedom in the use of compound words, the length and complexity of which form a distinguishing feature of Hindí as compared with Urdú. Urdú, indeed, from the side of the Arabic, does not admit of the composition of words, and even in its Persian element cannot compare in this respect with Hindí.

Rem. Long and complex compounds are for the most part confined to poetry; but short compounds are freely admissible in prose and in conversation. Many idioms, moreover, which cannot be strictly termed compound words, can only be explicated on the principles which regulate the formation of compounds. Thorough familiarity with these principles is absolutely essential to the understanding of Hindí poetry.

lassification Compounds.

622. The various compounds admissible in Hindí, are the same as those which we meet in Sanskrit, and therefore may be classified in the same manner. And we cannot do better in treating this subject than adopt, for the most part, the classification of Monier-Williams, as given in his Sanskrit Grammar, which will be found much easier of comprehension than that of the Indian grammarians. We have then five general classes of Compounds: 1*st*, *Dependent* Compounds, in which the relation of the several words is that which is expressed by the cases of a noun; 2*nd*, *Copulatives*, in which the relation of the elements is that expressed by a copulative conjunction; 3*rd*, *Descriptives*, in which an adjective is united with a substantive; 4*th*, *Numerals*, in which the first element is a numeral; 5*th*, *Adverbials*, in which the first element is an adverb.

ependent ompounds.

623. *Dependent Compounds* are of six varieties, corresponding to the six cases of nouns, by means of which dependence is expressed.

(1) *Accusatively Dependent* Compounds are very common; the second member is a verbal root or noun of agency, to which the first member stands in the relation of an *accusative* case. A long vowel in the first member of Tadbhava Compounds is very commonly shortened, and a diphthong reduced to its characteristic vowel.

The following are examples of Tadbhavas: तिलचट्टा (तेल + चट्टा), lit., 'oil-licker,' 'a cockroach;' कठफोड़ा (काठ + फोड़ा), 'wood-borer,' 'a woodpecker;' चिड़ीमार, 'a fowler;' मक्खनचोर, 'butter-stealer' (an epithet of *Krishṇa*). Similar Tatsamas are: जगतार, 'world-saviour;' गुणज्ञाता, 'merit-discerner;' जीवनदाता, 'life-giver;' पतितपावन, 'purifier of the guilty;' त्राहिकार, 'cry for mercy;' मनोहर, (मनस + हर, § 59,) 'heart-ravishing.'

a. In many such compounds, the verbal root consists of a single letter or compound letter: as, e.g., प (*Sk.* पा, 'to protect'), in भूप, lit., 'earth-protector,' 'a king;' or द (*Sk.* दा, 'to give'), in सुखद, 'pleasure-giving;' or ज्ञ, (*Sk.* ज्ञा, 'to know,') as in सर्वज्ञ, 'all-knowing,' etc.

b. Compounds in which गत, 'gone,' is the last member, belong to this class; but गत often appears to have lost its specific meaning, and implies mere connexion or proximity, without any suggestion of motion, as in the following from the *Rámáyan*: सुरसरिगत सलिल, 'water in the divine river;' करतलगत पुष्प, 'a flower lying in the hand.'

c. The accusative member is occasionally last in the compound; as, मर्दनमयन, 'destroyer of *Mayan.*'

(2) *Datively Dependent* Compounds are those in which the first word of the two is equivalent to a *dative* case. These are rare; a common illustration is शरणागत, lit., 'having come for refuge,' 'a refugee.'

(3) *Instrumentally Dependent* Compounds are those in which the first stands to the second in the relation of the case of the *agent*. The last member of these compounds is always a Sanskrit perf. pass. participle. They are comparatively rare, and are all Tatsamas. Most common are those in which कृत (perf. pass. part. of *Sk.* कृ, 'to do'), is the second member; these are chiefly used in the titles of books; as, तुलसीदासकृत रामायन, 'the *Rámáyan* by *Tulsí Dás.*'

(4) *Ablatively Dependent* Compounds are those in which the first word is related to the second as an *ablative* case. Examples are, of Tadbhavas: देसनिकाला, 'banishment;' of Tatsamas: मोहजनित, 'born of ignorance;' रत्नजटित, 'inlaid with jewels;' बुद्धिहीन, 'void of wisdom;' पंचरचित, 'composed of the five (*sc.* elements).'

Rem. It should be observed that many of the functions of the Sanskrit instrumental case are in Hindí assumed by the ablative; so that many compounds which in Sanskrit would be classed as *instrumentally* dependent must be reckoned *ablatively* dependent in Hindí.

(5) *Genitively Dependent* Compounds are those in which the relation of the first member to the second is that of a *genitive* case. These are exceedingly common, both in poetry and in prose. In such compounds, if Tadbhavas, a long vowel or diphthong in the first member is commonly shortened, and the laws of *sandhi* are neglected. Examples are, of Tadbhava compounds: लखपति (लाख + पति), 'a millionaire,' lit., 'owner of a *lákh*;' पनचक्की (पानी + चक्की), 'a water-mill;' घुड़साल, 'a stable (for horses);' of Tatsamas: जगदीस, 'Lord of the world;' जलविहंग, 'water-fowl;' दारुनारि, lit., 'a wood-woman,' i.e., 'a puppet;' रामकाथा, 'the story of *Rám.*'

a. अर्थ, in the second place in these compounds, may be often rendered, 'because of:' as, भयार्थ, 'because of fear;' स्नेहार्थ, 'because of affection.'

b. These compounds are especially common in titles of persons: as, धर्म्मावतार, 'incarnation of virtue;' गोपीनाथ, 'lord of the milkmaids:' and also in proper names: as, रामचरन, lit., 'feet of *Rám*;' देवीदास, lit., 'servant of the goddess:' also in the titles of books: as, प्रेमसागर, 'Ocean of love;' ब्रजबिलास, 'sport of *Braj.*'

c. Under this head come many idiomatic combinations in which a numeral is the last member: as, कालकोटि, lit., 'a death-*kror*,' 'a crore of deaths;' तापत्रय, 'the three penances;' नरसहस्र, 'a thousand men.' Similarly is अनेक to be explained in the compound, कामअनेक छवि, 'the beauty of countless *Kám Devs.*'

d. राज or राउ (राज) occurs as the last member in many such compounds, denoting eminence or superiority: as, e.g., मुनिराज, 'the prince of sages;' तीर्थराज, 'the chief of sacred places;' ऋतुराज, 'the prince of the seasons,' i.e., 'the Indian autumn.'

e. In these compounds, an adjective occasionally occupies the last place; especially, योग्य (जोग), 'worthy,' 'fit;' as, ब्याहनयोग्य, 'marriageable.'

f. The colloquial combinations of वाला (for Sk. पालक), with a preceding noun, are originally genitively dependent compounds: as, e.g., दिल्लीवाला, 'a man of Delhi;' दूधवाला, 'a milkman,' etc.

(6) *Locatively Dependent* Compounds are those in which the relation of the first word to the second is that of a *locative* case: as, घुड़चढ़, lit., 'horse-mounted,' 'a horseman;' स्वर्गवासी, 'dweller in heaven;' आनन्दमगन, 'immersed in joy;' धनुपाणि, 'bow in hand.' Here we may note especially a large number of Tatsama compounds, in which ज, 'born,' is the second member; as, जलज, lit., 'the water-born,' 'the lotus;' also others with चर: as, निशाचर, lit., 'night-walker,' 'a demon;' जलचर, 'aquatic animals;' and a few with ग, 'going;' as, नभग (नभः + ग), 'moving in the atmosphere,' 'a bird.'

624. Occasionally the first member of Dependent Compounds is in the plural: as, भक्तनहित, 'love to worshippers;' दीननबंधु,* 'friend of the afflicted.'

Copulative Compounds.

625. *Copulative* Compounds include all compounds the relation between whose members might be expressed by a copulative conjunction. Under this general class we may notice, especially,

(1) *Complementary Copulative* Compounds, in which the one member may be regarded as *complementing* or supple-

* But much more commonly, दीनबंधु.

menting the other. These are the most common. Examples are: माबाप, 'parents;' अन्नजल, 'food and drink;' lit., 'grain,' 'water;' रामानुज, '*Rám* (and his) younger brother, i.e., *Lakshman*, lit., *Rám*-after-born.'

a. Words of opposite meaning are often thus coupled: as, घटती बढ़ती, 'loss and gain;' चराचर (चर + अचर), 'moveable-immoveable,' i.e., 'animate and inanimate.'

b. Under this head also comes the common colloquial idiom in which a word is repeated, either with its initial letter omitted, or another substituted, or with a different medial vowel, to denote indefinitely the remainder of a class. The repeated word gives a sense exactly equivalent to the Sanskrit इत्यादि, or 'et cetera.' Examples are: डेरे एरे, 'tents, etc.,' i.e. 'tents with all their appurtenances;' घोड़े चोड़े, 'horses, etc.,' as, e.g., 'mules, donkeys, etc.;' कोस कास, '*kos*, etc.'

(2) *Reciprocal Copulative* Compounds are those in which two words of similar or identical meaning, are grouped together with a *reciprocal* force. Often the second word is merely the feminine form of the first. Examples are: कही कहा, 'altercation;' लाठा लाठी, 'mutual beating.' Sometimes the two members of the compound differ in a radical letter only: as, अड़ोस पड़ोस, 'neighbourhood;' आम्हने साम्हने, 'facing one another.'

(3) Many other combinations occur which must be reckoned as copulative compounds; but the second word seems to be added merely for the jingle, and adds nothing to the first. The same varieties of formation occur in these as have been mentioned under (1) and (2). Examples are: भला चंगा, 'well (and) sound;' टोआ टोई, 'groping;' काना कानी, 'whispering;' खोज खाज, 'search;' चाल चलन, 'walk,' 'behaviour;' पूछ पाछ, 'inquiry.'

626. Observe that not only the postpositions, but the substantive inflections, are added only to the last member of a copulative compound: as, भूत प्रेतों को, 'to ghosts and goblins:' रूख पेड़ों और पशु पक्षियों ने भी . . . उदासी मानी है, 'even the trees (and) plants, and beasts (and) birds have become dejected.' लषनरामसीतहि, 'to *Lakshman*, *Rám* and *Sítá*.' Similar is the relation of the first two nouns in the following phrase from the *Prem Ságar*: सब लगे पगड़ी फेंटे मिलाय मिलाय . . . उसे काढ़ने, 'all began, tying turbans and waistbands together, to pull at it;' so also in the *Rámáyan*; हठअविवेकहि भजई, 'he praises obstinacy and stupidity.'

a. In the same way, various suffixes, as वाला, मय, etc., are sometimes attached to the last of a number of nouns, which are then to be regarded as forming a copulative compound: as, वह तीन मूंड नौ पग छह कर वाला, 'that three-headed, nine-footed, six-handed creature;' सियाराममय सब जग जानी, 'regarding the whole world as pervaded by *Sítá* and *Rám*;' जड़चेतनगुनदोषमय बिस्व कीन्ह करतार, 'the Creator (has) made the world to consist (both of) the animate (and) the inanimate, (of) virtue (and) of vice.'

Descriptive Compounds.

627. *Descriptive* Compounds are those in which an adjective, or a word used adjectively, is compounded with a substantive. In these, the one member of the compound is predicated of the other. Examples are: भलमानुस (भला + मनुष्य), 'courteous;' कनफटा, 'ear-split,' 'an ascetic with split ears;' also, all compounds in which महा (for महत्, 'great'), occupies the first place; as, महापाप, 'great sin;' महाराज, 'great king.' Other illustrations are: अल्पबल, '(having) little strength;' परमेश्वर (परम + ईश्वर), 'the supreme God;' मध्यलोक, 'the middle world;' i.e., 'the earth;' बहुमूल्य, 'of much value,' 'precious.'

a. Under this head fall compounds, common in poetry, in which वर or वर्य, 'excellent,' follows a substantive, as the second member of the compound; as, मुनिवर्य, 'noble sage:' स्त्रीवर, 'excellent woman.' The qualifying member also takes the second place in मनमलीन, 'mind defiled,' 'unholy;' and regularly in compounds implying *comparison*; as, सरोरुहश्याम, 'dark as the lotus flower.' Under this head may also be mentioned compounds in which अन्तर, 'another,' is the last member; as, जन्मान्तर, 'another birth.'

b. Sometimes an inseparable prefix takes the place of the adjective; especially, कु (also क, का, कद्, or कव), 'bad;' as in कुसपना, 'a bad dream;' कापूत, 'a bad son;' also सु (Greek, εὐ), 'well,' 'good;' as in सुसंगति, 'good society;' also दुर् (दुष, दुस), (Greek, δυς), 'bad;' as, दुर्वचन, 'abuse;' दुष्कर्म्म, 'crime;' दुस्तर, lit., 'difficult to cross.' सु has sometimes an intensive force; as in सुदूरि, 'a great distance.'

Rem. Regularly, these prefixes can only be joined with Sanskrit words; but in poetry this rule is not always observed. Thus we have in the *Rámáyan*, सुसाहेब, 'the good master,' and even, सुचारिउ भाई, 'the noble four brothers.' I have also noted, in poetry, सुखोरिके (सु + खोरिके, for खोलके), 'well opening.'

c. A noun may supply the place of the adjective; as, राजहंस, lit., 'the king-goose,' 'the flamingo.' So explain such idioms as the following: मथुरापुरी का आहुक नाम राजा, 'a king of *Mathurá* named *A'huk*;' where आहुक नाम is a descriptive compound, in which the proper name, आहुक, takes the place of the adjective. These might be termed *appositional* compounds.

d. Similar is the use of आदि as the second member of compounds: as in ब्रह्मादि, lit., '*Brahmá*, the beginning;' i.e., '*Brahmá* and the other gods, beginning with *Brahmá*;' सुधादि असन, 'nectar and other kinds of food.'

e. Sometimes a Sanskrit word and a Persian word, meaning the same thing, are coupled together; as in तन बदन, 'the body.'

Numeral Compounds.

628. *Numeral* Compounds are those in which the first member is a numeral: as, द्विज, 'a Brahman,' lit., 'a twice-born;' त्रिलोक, 'the three worlds;' सहस्रमुख, 'thousand-mouthed;' चतुष्पथ, 'a place where four roads meet;' पंचप्राण, 'the five vital airs;' शतवर्ष, 'a century.'

629. *Adverbial Compounds* are those in which the first member is an inseparable adverb or preposition; as, e.g., compounds with यथा: as, यथाविधि, 'according to rule;' यथोक्त, (यथा + उक्त), 'as spoken,' 'true;' compounds with सह, abbreviated to स; as, सटीका, 'with commentary;' सानुज, 'with (his) younger brother;' and many others: as, प्रतिदिन, 'every day;' अधिकृत, 'a superintendent.' Adverbial Compounds.

a. Here also may be noted compounds with the negative prefix, अन्, corresponding to the *alpha* privative in Greek. In pure Sanskrit words, अन् becomes अ before consonants, but in Hindí words of modern formation, अन् is used before both vowels and consonants. Examples of Tatsama words are:—अनन्त (अन् + अन्त), 'without end;' अप्रिय (अन् + प्रिय), 'unlovable;' अनीश, lit., 'not-God,' i.e., 'created existence;' अदेय (अन् + देय, *Sk.* fut. pass. part.), 'not to be given.' Modern Hindí Tadbhava compounds are:—अनजान (अन् + जान), 'unknown;' अनगिनत, 'uncounted;' अनभल, 'ill-fortune;' अनइस (अन् + अइस), lit., 'not so,' 'other-like.' अन् is even compounded with a perf. part., as in अनभयउ, in the following:—आगउ नृप अनभयउ बिहाना, 'the king awaked ere it was morning;' lit., 'morning not having been.'

b. Under this head also include परस्पर, 'mutual,' from पर, 'other,' reduplicated with a euphonic स.

630. Many of the above compounds are adjectives, and yield no complete sense in themselves. Many others, although substantives, may also be used in an adjective sense; in which case the adjective termination ी, is often added: as, मृगनैनी, 'gazelle-eyed;' पिकबैनी, 'having a voice like the cuckoo.' But this ी is often omitted, and the compound is used in its original form: as, मेघबरण, 'cloud-coloured;' नररूप, 'having the form of a man.'

Rem. These compounds used thus adjectively are constantly met with in poetry, as the predicates of an implied relative clause; of which the copula, usually, and almost always the relative also, is unexpressed. Examples of this construction will be found on almost every page of the *Rámáyan*.

a. In the very common idiom in which the word नाम, 'name,' follows a proper noun, as designating a person or object, the combination, although its parts are usually separated in Hindí, must be explained as a Dependent Compound noun, used adjectively. Thus, हेमकूट नाम पर्वत, 'a mountain named *Hemakúṭ*,' represents the Sanskrit form, हेमकूटनामा पर्वतः.

b. The word रूप, 'form,' at the end of compounds, often has the sense of 'of,' 'consisting of;' as, मोहरूपी सागर, 'sea of error.' But sometimes it may be rendered literally; as, नररूपहरि, '*Hari* in the form of man.'

Anomalous Compounds. **631.** Anomalous compounds are formed with मात्र and अन्तर; as, अस्थिमात्र, 'mere bone;' देशान्तर, 'another country.' मात्र inflects आ final to ए in a preceding Tadbhava word; as, इन के देखने मात्र से, 'from the mere seeing of these.' पूर्व or पूर्वक is added to nouns to form compounds denoting 'manner;' as, बुद्धिपूर्वक वचन, 'words of wisdom;' स्नेहपूर्वक, 'loving,' 'kindly.'

Complex Compounds. **632.** Compound words are themselves often compounded with other words or with other compounds, thus forming *Complex* Compounds. Examples are:—षट्रसभोजन, 'food of six flavours;' a descriptive, involving a numeral compound; नभजलथलवासी, 'dwellers in air, on earth, and in water;' a locative compound, involving a copulative of three members; भानुकरवारि, lit., 'sunbeams-water,' i.e., 'the mirage;' नानायुधधर (नाना + आयुध + धर), 'bearing various weapons;' an acc. dep. compound, used descriptively, in which the acc. member, नानायुध, is itself a descriptive compound. In the *Prem Ságar*, we have the anomalous *quasi* compound, मोह की चिन्तारूपी, for मोहचिन्तारूपी.

a. In the *Rámáyan* and other poetry, we find complex compounds of great length; as, जनमनमंजुमुकुरमलहरनी, 'cleanser of the filth from the beautiful mirror of the human soul;' an accusatively dependent compound, involving four genitively dependents and a descriptive; नखदसनसैलमहाद्रुमायुध, 'having (their) nails and teeth, rocks, and great trees as weapons.'

Rem. Such long compounds are often explicable by beginning with the last member, and proceeding regularly to the first. They are in imitation of Sanskrit idiom and are not admissible in prose, where the postpositions are commonly preferred even for short phrases. Still, in prose, compounds of simple form are often used, when the two ideas are conceived of as one compound whole: as, प्रभुभक्त, 'worshipper of the Lord;' उषाहरण की कथा, 'the story of the rape of *Ushá*;' जितेंद्री, 'one who has subdued the senses.'

633. As remarked § 623 (5), the laws of *sandhi* are always neglected in all Tadbhava compounds, and very often, even where the elements of the compound are Tatsama. Thus, e.g., we find, हरिइच्छा, 'the will of *Hari*,' for हरीच्छा; हिमउपल, 'hailstones,' for हिमोपल; भयआतुर, 'distracted with fear,' for भयातुर, etc., etc.

634. In poetry, the parts of compounds are often inverted: as, e.g., युतविवेक, lit., 'joined with judgment,' i.e., 'discreet,' for *Sk.* विवेकयुक्त; हीनमनि, 'deprived of the jewel,' for मनिहीन; मर्दनमयन, 'destroyer of *Mayan*,' for मयनमर्दन; दिनप्रति, 'every day,' for प्रतिदिन; विगतविवेक, 'deprived of judgment.' Inversion of Compounds.

635. Before leaving this subject, it is important to observe that a large number of Sanskrit words used in Hindí, are compounds formed with various prepositions. Compounds with Prepositions.

The following list contains the most important:—

(1) अति, 'beyond;' as in अत्यन्त, lit., 'beyond limit,' 'infinite,'

(2) अधि, 'above,' 'over;' as in अधिपति, 'a ruler.'

(3) अनु, 'after;' as in अनुज, lit., 'after-born,' 'younger;' also with nouns, as in अनुदिन, 'daily.'

(4) अन्तर्, 'within;' as in अन्तःकरण, 'the internal sense,' 'the heart.'

(5) अप, 'away,'—usually implies detraction; as in अपवाद, 'blame.'

(6) अभि, 'to,' 'towards;' as in अभिमत, 'desired,' 'chosen.'

(7) अव, 'down,'—often implies disparagement; as, अवगाह, 'bathing;' अवगुण (also औगुन,) the opposite of गुण, 'vice,' 'demerit.'

(8) आ, 'to,' 'towards;' as in आदर्शक, 'a mirror.' With the derivatives of गम्, (and also या and इ,) 'to go,' आ reverses their meaning; as in आगमन, 'coming,' contrasted with गमन, 'going;' so in the verb आना, 'to come,' from (आ + इ, 'to go').

(9) उद्, (उत्, उच्, etc.,) 'up;' as in उत्पन्न, 'born;' उच्चरण, 'pronunciation;' so also उ in उठना (Sk. उत + स्था), lit., 'to stand up,' 'to rise.'

(10) उप, 'near to,' 'down', 'under;' as in उपस्थित, 'prepared,' lit., 'standing under.' It often gives a depreciative sense; as in उपहास, 'ridicule,' from हस्, 'to laugh.'

(11) नि, 'down' (in contrast with उत्), as in निगमन, 'the conclusion (in Logic);' निग्रह, 'subduing.'

(12) निर् (निस्, नि, etc.,) 'out,' commonly has the effect of a negative; as in निष्कलंक, 'without blame;' निर्दोष, 'without fault.'

(13) परि, 'around;' as in परिचारक, 'an attendant,' lit., 'a walker around.' It often has merely an intensive force; as in परिपूरण, 'completely filled.'

(14) प्र, 'before,'—hence often indicates superiority; thus, प्रधान, 'chief;' प्रयोग, 'effort,' etc. Often its force is scarcely appreciable; as in प्राप्त (प्र + आप्त), 'obtained.'

(15) प्रति, 'against,' 'towards,' 'back again;' as in प्रतिवादी, 'a respondent;' प्रतिफल, 'recompense.'

(16) वि, 'apart,' often denotes 'negation,' 'separation,' 'distinction,' etc.; as in वियोग, 'separation;' विवेक, 'discrimination;' व्यर्थ (वि + अर्थ), 'profitless,' 'vain.'

(17) सम्, 'with,' (opposed to वि); as in संयोग, 'conjunction;' संग्राम, 'fighting,' 'war.' But often its force is imperceptible.

(18) Two or three Persian and Arabic inseparable prepositions and other words are also compounded with nouns in High Hindí. Most common are the negative particles बे and ग़ैर (غیر); as in बेकाम, 'without work;' ग़ैर हाज़िर, 'not present.'

CHAPTER XI.

ADVERBS, PREPOSITIONS, CONJUNCTIONS, AND INTERJECTIONS.

I. *Adverbs.*

636. The tables on the following pages exhibit a series of adverbs formed from the five pronominal elements noted in § 255.

637. Of the *temporal* adverbs, all which contain a labial vowel or consonant, have arisen from the combination of the Sanskrit noun, *velá* (H. *ber*), 'time,' with one of the pronominal elements, as appears clearly from the Bhojpúrí forms. The forms containing *d* are connected with the Sanskrit series formed with the suffix *dá*, as given in the table. *Jún*, in the Bhojpúrí series, is for Sanskrit *yoni*, 'womb,' hence 'place' or 'time of birth,' with allusion to the doctrine of transmigration. *Khani*, in the Maithilí series, is for Sanskrit *kshaṇ*, 'a moment.' The Mágadhí and Maithilí time-series, *ĕhiya, ŏhiyá, jahiyá*, etc., I am inclined to connect with the Sk. quantitative series of pronominals, *iyat*, etc., which in Ap. Pr. became *ettio*, etc.;* the *h* in the M. forms being merely euphonic, having been inserted to avoid the hiatus occasioned by the disappearance of the *tt*. These pronominal forms were already used in the obl. sing., in Ap. Pr., as pronominal adverbs of place; and may as easily have been employed to denote time, like the Hindí *itne meṉ*, also used adverbially, both in a locative and a temporal sense. Derivation of Pronominal Adverbs.

Rem. Hoernle derives the series, *ab*, etc., from the Ap. Pr. loc. sing., *emvahiṉ*, etc., of the quantitative pronominals, *emva*, etc.; which were used as adverbs of time and place.† But in view of the modern use of the forms in *berá*, as in Bh., I still incline to prefer the etymology suggested above.

---

* Hoernle: *Comp. Gramm.* §§ 438 (7), 469. † Ib., § 469.

TABLE XXIII. PRONOMINAL ADVERBS.

TIME.					
	Prox. Dem.	*Remote Dem.*	*Relative.*	*Correlative.*	*Interrogative.*
Pron. Base.	अ, इ, ई, ए, य.	उ, ऊ, ओ, व.	ज, जि, (य).	त, ति.	क, कि.
H.H.	अब, 'now.'	*Wanting.*† 'then.'	जब, 'when.'	तब, 'then.'	कब, 'when.'
B.	अबी, अबै.*	„	जबै, जौ, जद.	तबै, तौ, तद.	कबै, कद.
M.	„ अभी.	„	जद, जिद. जदे, जदी.	*Relat. used.*	कद, कदे, कदी.
Me.	„ „	„	जदू, जदां, जवां.	„	कदू, कदां, कवां.
N.	ऐल्हे.	„	जैल्हे.	तैल्हे.	कैल्हे.
Bh.	एहबेरा, एबेर. एहजून.	ओहबेरा. ओहजून.	जेहबेरा, जेबेर. जेहजून.	तेहबेरा, तेबेर. तेहजून.	केहबेरा, केबे. केहजून.
Mg.	अखनी. *Wanting.*	*Wanting.* „	जखनी. जहिआ.	तखनी. तहिआ.	कखनी. कहिआ.
Mt.	एखनि, एखन. एहिया. अबे, अबे, आबे.	ओखनि, ओखन. ओहिया. *Wanting.*	जेखनि, जखन. जहिया. जबे, जबे.	तेखनि, तखन. तहिया. तबे, तबे.	केखनि, कखन. कहिया. कबे, कबे.
Sk.	*Wanting.*	„	यदा.	तदा.	कदा.

* Also, in the Sahâranpúr district, यीब.

† Where any form for the remote demonstrative is wanting, the corresponding correlative is used instead.

TABLE XXIV. PRONOMINAL ADVERBS.

Place.					
	Prox. Dem.	*Remote Dem.*	*Relative.*	*Correlative.*	*Interrogative.*
Pron. Elem.	अ, इ, ई, ए, ऐ, य.	उ, ऊ, ओ, वो.	ज, जि (य).	त, ति.	क, कि.
H.H.	यहां, 'here.'	वहां, 'there.'	जहां, 'where.'	तहां, 'there.'	कहां, 'where.'
B.	इत, इतै, ईतै. यहां, यां.	उत. वहां, वां.	जित. जहां, जां.	तित. तहां, तां.	कित, कत. कहां, कां.
M.	अठे, अठी, ईठे.	उठे, उठी, ऊंठे.	जठे, जठी.	*Relat. used.*	कठे, कठो. कैठे, कोठे.
Me.	अडे, अडी. आडे, आडी.	वठे, वठी, वडे, वडी. वाडे, वाडी.	जडे, जडी. जाडे, जाडी.	"	कडे, कडी. काडे, काडी.
Bún.	इते, या, याञ्जी.	उते, वां, वाञ्जी.	जिते, ज्यां, ज्याञ्जी.	तिते, त्यां, त्याञ्जी.	किते, क्यां, क्याञ्जी.
Ku.	यां.	वां.	जां.	तां.	कां.
N.	याहां.	वाहां.	जाहां.	ताहां, त्याहां.	काहां.
O.B.	इहां, ईहां.	उहां, ऊहां.	जहं, जेहां, जहवां. जहिआ.	तहं, तहउं, तहवां. तहिआ.	कहं.
Av.	एठियां, एठियन. हियां, ईहां.	ओठियां, ओठियन. ऊहां.	जेठियां, जेठियन.	तेठियां, तेठियन.	केठियां, केठियन.
R.	इहंवां.	उहंवां.	जहंवां.	तहंवां.	कहंवां.
Bh.	इंहवां, एठेन. एहिआ, हियां. एठां, एठाईं.	उंहवां, ओठेन. ओहिआ, ऊहां. ओठां, ओठाईं.	जंहवां, जेठेन. जेहिआ. जेठां, जेठाईं.	तंहवां, तेठेन. तेहिआ. तेठां, तेठाईं.	कंहवां, केठेन. केहिआ. केठां, केठाईं.
Mg.	ईठमां. एठवां, हियां.	ओठमां, उठमां. ओठवां, ऊहां.	जेठमां. जेठवां.	तेठमां. तेठवां.	केठमां. केठवां.
Mt.	ऐठियां,* इहां, हियां एतय, एते.*	वैठियां, उहां, ऊंहां. ओतय, ओते.	जैठियां, जहां. जतय, जते.	तैठियां, तहां. ततय, तते.	कैठयां,† कहां. कतय, कते.
Sk.	अत्र, इह.	*Wanting.*	यत्र.	तत्र.	कुत्र.

* I have also met with the following series assigned to Tirhut, though Grierson does not give it in his Maithilí Grammars; viz., एँठाम, ओँठाम, जेँठाम, तेँठाम, केँठाम.

† Is 'to what several places?'.

To face page 374.]

TABLE XXV. PRONOMINAL ADVERBS.

DIRECTION.					
	Prox. Demonstr.	*Remote Dem.*	*Relative.*	*Correlative.*	*Interrog.*
Pron. Elem.	इ, ई, ए, ऍ, य.	उ, ऊ, ओ, ऒ, व.	ज, जि (य).	त, ति.	क, कि.
H.H.	इधर, इदर,* 'hither.'	उधर, उदर, 'thither.'	जिधर, 'whither.'	तिधर, 'thither.'	किधर, 'whither.'
Me.					कीथिदस.†
R.	एहि वीत.‡	ओही वीत.	जेहि वीत.	तेहि वीत.	केहे वीत.
Bh.	एने,§ एहर.	ओने,§ ओहर.	जेने, जेहर.	तेने, तेहर.	केने, केहर.
Mg.	ऍन्ने, ऍहर.	उन्ने, उहर.	जेन्ने, जेहर.	तेन्ने, तेहर.	केन्ने, केहर.
Mt.	इन्ने, इनें, ऍन्ने, एने. इन्दे,§ इन्दऽ. ईम्हर.‖	उन्ने, ओने, ऊनें. उन्दे,§ उन्दऽ. ऊम्हर.	जिन्ने, जिनें. जिन्दे; जिन्दऽ. जेम्हर.	तिन्ने, तनें. तिन्दे, . तिन्दऽ. तेम्हर.	किन्ने, कनें. किन्दे, किन्दऽ. केम्हर.

* अधर is also heard.

† Fallon gives the following western variants of इधर, viz., ईंघे and ईमाईं; and of उधर, उन्घे or ऊन्घे. See *Hindustání-English Dictionary*, sub. voc. cit.

‡ Also कयोत and केती; मुंह is also employed for वीत.

§ ह optionally prefixed.

‖ Fallon gives also the following additional eastern variants of इधर, viz.:—एट्ठे, एम्हर, इम्हर, एहोर, हेमर; and analogous equivalents of उधर, अट्ठे, उम्हर, ओहोर, ऊमर. Corresponding forms presumably exist for the other members of the series, but I have not met with them. See *Hindustání-English Dictionary*, sub. voc. cit.

TABLE XXVI. PRONOMINAL ADVERBS.

Manner.					
	Prox. Dem.	*Remote Dem.*	*Relative.*	*Correlative.*	*Interrogative.*
Pron. Elem.	अ, इ, ई, ए, ऐ, य.	उ, ऊ, ओ, औ, व.	ज, जि (य).	त, ति.	क, कि.
H.H.	यूं, 'thus.'	*Wanting.*	ज्यूं, 'as.'	त्यूं, 'so.'	क्यूं, 'how?'
B.	यौं, यों.	वौं, वों, वूं.	ज्यौं, ज्यों, जौं. जों, जूं, जिय.	त्यौं, त्यों. तौं, तों.	क्यौं, क्यों.
M.	असं, इसं.	वूं.	जिसं.	*Relative used.*	किसं.
Me.	ईंकर, ईंगा.	वोंकर, वींगा.	जींकर, जींगा.	"	कोंकर, कींगा.
N.	यसोरि.	उसोरि.	जसोरि.	तसोरि.	कसोरि.
O.B.	इमि.	*Wanting.*	जिमि.	तिमि.	किमि.*
Mt.	एहनाइ, एहिना. एहन, एना.‡	ओहनाइ, ओहिना. ओहन, ओना.‡	जेहनाइ, जहिना. जेहन, जेना.	तेहनाइ, तहिना. तेहन, तेना.	केहनाइ, कहिना. केहन, केना.†
Sk.	इत्थम.	*Wanting.*	यथा.	तथा.	कथा.

* Chand has इम and केम.

† Bhojpúri and Mágadhí use instead of an analogous series, the pronominal adjectives of manner, thus: Bh. अइसें, वइसें, etc.; and Mg. अइसन, ओइसन, etc.

‡ इ optionally prefixed.

638. Of the pronominal adverbs of place, I formerly connected those containing *t*, as *itai*, *ut*, *jatuya*, etc., with the Sk. series in *tra*. But I now agree with Hoernle * that we must regard these as having arisen from the Ap. Pr. loc. sings., *ettahe*, etc., of the quantitative pronouns, *ettio*, etc., which were used as adverbs of place. This will account for the palatal diphthong in the longer forms, as my earlier explanation did not. On the other hand, however, I would still refer the series in *háṇ*, or *áṇ*, to the union of the pronominal base with the locative *stháne*, instead of referring the termination, with Hoernle, to the Pr. obl. suffix, *haṇ*.† So also I would still refer the Máṛ. series with *ṭh*, *aṭhai*, etc., to the same origin, but not the Me. forms in *ḍai*, etc., which Beames has well illustrated by reference to the Oṛíyá expression, *e áṛe*, 'in this direction,' and the fuller Maráṭhí, *ikaḍe*, = *i* + *kaḍe*, loc. sing. of *kaḍ*, for the Sk. *kaṭ*, 'hip.'‡ In such longer forms as the Av. *ĕṭhiyan*, Bh. *iṉhaváṉ*, etc., I would assume as the second element a loc. sing., *ṭhikáne*, analogous to *stháne*, but derived from the strengthened Prakritic root *ṭhik*, for Sk. *sthá*. Indeed the word *ṭhikáná* from this root, meaning 'a support,' 'a resting-place,' is common in Hindí. It is an analogy which supports the above derivation of these adverbs from *stháne* and *ṭhikáne*, rather than from Prakritic terminations, that Bhojpúri presents an alternative series, *ĕhijá*, *ŏhijă*, etc., in which the Persian noun, *já*, of the same meaning, has been substituted for *stháne*.

639. The adverbs of direction, *idhar*, etc., and their dialectic equivalents, are for the most part difficult of explanation. Hoernle § would derive *idhar*, etc., from a form *idaha*, connected with the Prakrit qualitative pronoun, *edṛiha* (Sk. *ídṛisha*), an old locative suffix, *r*, being added. Beames is inclined to connect them with the Maráṭhí, *mhor*, 'face,' dim. from Sk. *mukha*, whence, by contraction, the second element would become *mhar*, *nhar*, *dhar*, *har*, as in the Mt. *temhar*, *tenhar*, H.H. *idhar*, Bh. *ehar*, etc.‖ But the origin of these forms appears not yet to be

* *Comp. Gramm.* p. 313.

† Ib.

‡ *Comp. Gramm.* vol. iii., 261.

§ *Comp. Gramm.* p. 315.

‖ *Comp. Gramm.* vol. iii., p. 261. Hoernle derives these forms in *mhar*, etc., from the obl. stems *ĕva*, *ema*, *ena*, + *r*, of the Pr. quant. pronominal, *ĕvo*, for the Vedic Sk. *ĭvat*. Vid. *Comp. Gramm.* p. 308.

demonstrated. The Bh., Mg., and Mt. forms, *ene*, *ĕnne*, *inne*, etc., seem, however, to be clearly derived from the Ap. Pr. quantitative pronoun, *emva*, the loc. of which, *emvahiṉ*, was used as a pronom. adverb of manner as well as time. Bangálí supplies the intermediate form, *emane*, 'here,' 'hither.'

640. From the loc. sing. of this same pronominal, I would now agree with Hoernle* in deriving the pron. adverbs of manner, *imi*, *yúṉ*, and their variants. These come most naturally from the Ap. Pr. loc. sing. *emväi* or *emväiṉ*, whence, first, the series, *imi*, *im*, etc., then the Máṛ., *ïúṉ*, *úṉ*, and H.H. *yúṉ*, etc., etc. The Mt. forms, *ĕhandi*, *ĕhaná*, *ĕhan*, *end*, etc., are derived from the loc. sing. of the qualitative pronominal, in the following order, taking the series of the proximate demonstrative as an example: Sk. *ídṛishaḥ*, Pr. *äiso*, or, with the pleonastic suffix *ná* (*lá*) added, *äisaná*, whence, *ĕhaná*, *ĕhan*, *ená*. The *i* of *ĕhanäi* may possibly be the loc. case-ending, but more probably the emphatic particle, *i* or *hi*, so that *ĕhandi* is exactly H.H. *aisáhí*. Similarly are derived the remainder of the series. The Mewáṛí suffixes, *kar* and *gá*, are from the Sk. verbal roots, *kṛi*, 'to do,' and *gam*, 'to go.'

Emphatic Particle with Adverbs.

641 The emphatic suffix, ही or ईं, may be added to any of the adverbs in the table. But ईं is commonly substituted for the final आं of the series in हां.

Examples are:—जभी (जबही), 'immediately;' तभी (तबही), 'just then;' कभी (कबही), 'ever;' यहीं (rarely, यहां ही), 'just here;' कहीं, 'anywhere,' 'somewhere;' यूंहीं, 'just as.'

a. The dialects similarly add इ, उ, or ऊं: as, e.g., *Br.* जबइ,=जभी; कहुं,=कहीं; क्यौंहं,=क्यूंहीं; कधी, and in the *Rámáyan*, काउ,=कभी and कतऊं,=कहीं; *Av.* जौह,=जबही, etc., etc. Máṛ. has for कभी, कदे. In Naipálí, ह disappearing, ही or हि by *sandhi* appears as ऐ; as in कहिल्यै, 'ever;' नजिकै, 'quite near,' etc.

Postpositions with Adverbs.

642. Inasmuch as these adverbs are originally substantive combinations, they may be followed by postpositions, thereby expressing yet other variations of the adverbial idea.

---

* *Comp. Gramm.* pp. 313, 314.

Examples are:—with से, 'from;' अब से, 'henceforth;' जब से, 'since;' कब से, 'since when?;' यहाँ से, 'hence;' वहाँ से, 'thence;' कहाँ से, 'whence?;' with को; कहाँ को, 'to what place?;' with का; अब का, 'of the present time;' कहाँ का, 'of what place?;' with तक or तलक, लों, etc.; अब तक, 'till now;' जब तक, 'till when,' 'as long as;' तब तक, 'so long;' कब तक, 'how long?;' यहाँ तक, 'as far as this,' 'to this degree;' वहाँ तक, 'thus far;' कहाँ तक, 'how far?.' For अब तक, 'till now,' 'by this time,' Mâṛ. has हवीं.

a. These postpositions may also be added to the intensive forms: as, अभी से, 'from this very time;' यहीं का, 'of this very place;' कहीं से, 'from some place,' etc.

643. Various other modifications of the radical meaning of these adverbs, are expressed by their repetition and combination. Combinations of Pronominal Adverbs.

(1) Some of them may be repeated to express *universality*, *distribution*, or indefinite *repetition*: as, जब जब, 'whenever,' followed by तब तब in the correlative clause; जहाँ जहाँ, 'wherever,' regularly followed by तहाँ तहाँ; कभी कभी, 'sometimes;' कहीं कहीं, 'in some few places.'

(2) The relative may be combined with the corresponding indefinite adverb to express *indefiniteness*: as, जब कभी, 'whenever;' जहाँ कहीं, 'wherever.'

(3) Or the negative particle, न, may be interposed between two cognate adverbs to express a certain sort of *indefiniteness*: as, जब न तब, 'now and then;' कभी न कभी, 'at some time or other;' कहीं न कहीं, 'somewhere or other.'

(4) Or the correlative may be combined with the relative adverb followed by the genitive postposition: thus, ज्यों की त्यों, 'in the same way as before.'

644. For the pronominal adverbs of manner, यूं, etc., the oblique forms of the pronominal series, ऐसा, etc., (Table XII.), are often employed.

a. The Sanskrit एवम्, = यूं, 'so,' occurs in poetry in Sanskrit phrases, chiefly in the formula, एवमस्तु, 'let it be so.'

b. The 3rd sing. conting. fut., चाहे, of चाहना, 'to wish,' before pronominal adjectives is equivalent to an indefinite adverb; as, चाहे जितना बड़ा हो, 'howsoever great it be.'

Miscellaneous Adverbs.

645. Besides the above pronominal adverbs, are many others of various derivations. Very many of these, indeed, are, in fact, old locative cases of nouns. The following lists will be found to comprehend the most common.

Adverbs of Time.

(1) Adverbs of *Time*:—

आगे (*Sk.* अग्रे), *Dial.* अगारे, अगाड़ू, आगू, अगु, आगै, *N.* अघि, 'before.'

आज (*Sk.* अद्य), *Dial.* अज, अजु, आजु, अज्जवा, 'to-day.'

कल (*Sk.* कल्य), *Dial.* काल, कालि, काल्हि, काल्ह, कल्ह, 'yesterday,' 'to-morrow.'

तड़के, 'at dawn,' 'early.'

तुरन्त, तुरत (*Sk.* pres. part. from त्वर्), 'immediately.'

परसों (*Sk.* परः + श्वस्), *Dial.* परसौं, परहीं, परौं, परों, 'the day before yesterday,' or 'the day after to-morrow.'

तरसों (*Sk.* त्रि + श्वस्), *Dial.* अतरसों, तरसौं, तरौं, तरों, 'three days ago,' or 'three days hence.'

नरसों (*Sk.* अन्य श्वस्?), *Dial.* नरसौं, नरौं, नरों, 'four days ago,' or 'four days hence.'

निदान (*Sk.* नि + दा), 'at last.'

नित, नित्य (*Sk.* नित्यम्), 'constantly.'

पीछे (*Sk.* पश्चात्), *Dial.* पीछू, पिछाड़ू, पिछारे, पिछाड़ी, पछि, पाछे, पाछें, पाछू, 'after,' 'afterwards.'

फिर or फेर, *Dial.* बहोरि, बहुरि,* बहुरौं; also पुन, पुनि (*Sk.* पुनर्), 'again.'

* This is really a conjunctive participle, from बहोरना or बहुरना, 'to return.'

भोरे, भोर, 'at break of day,' *N.* भोखि.

बारंबार (*Sk.* वारंवारम्), 'repeatedly.'

सवेरे (*Sk.* स + वेलायाम्, fem. gen. sing.), about Meerut सिदौसी or सिदौस, 'early,' 'betimes.'

a. The following are only dialectic; अबौं, 'hitherto;' सकारे (*Sk.* स + काले), 'early,' *N.* चाँडे, 'immediately,' and सधै (contracted from सदाहि), 'always.'

b. Of the pure Sanskrit words denoting time, which are used adverbially in Hindí, the following are among the most common, viz.; certain compounds with the affix दा, as, एकदा, 'once;' सदा, सर्वदा, 'always;' and, with the suffixes चित् and अपि, कदाचित and कदापि, 'sometimes,' also 'perhaps;' तत्काल, तत्क्षण, 'instantly.'

(2) Adverbs of *Place*:— Adverbs of Place.

अनत (*Sk.* अन्यत्र), 'elsewhere.'

निकट (*Sk.* नि + कट), and नेरे, *Dial.* नेरौ and नेरू, 'near.'

पार (*Sk.* पारे), 'over,' 'across.'

पास, *Dial.* पासौं and पाहि, 'near;' and, reduplicated, आस पास, 'on both sides,' 'all around.'

परे (*Sk.* पारे), 'on that side,' 'off.'

वरे (*Sk.* अवारे), *Dial.* उरे, 'on that side;' वारापार, वारपार, 'on both sides.'

बाहिर (*Sk.* वाहिस्), 'without.'

भीतर (*Sk.* अभ्यन्तरे), 'within.'

आगे, 'before,' and पीछे, 'behind,' are also used as adverbs of place.

a. In the colloquial of the Upper Doáb, उली or उरली, and पली or परली are combined with तरफ (*Ar.* طرف) in the sense, respectively, 'on this side,' and 'on that side.'

b. The following Sanskrit adverbs occur, formed with the suffix त्र, viz.; अन्यत्र, 'elsewhere;' एकत्र, 'in one place;' सर्वत्र, 'everywhere.'

Adverbs of Manner.

(3) Adverbs of *Manner*:—

अचानक and अचानचक, 'suddenly.'

जानो (imp. 2nd plur. of जानना), *Br.* जानौ, जानहु, in *Rám.*, जनु, जानिबौ, 'so to speak,' 'as it were.'

झट (*Sk.* झटति), *Dial.* चट; also झट पट (from *Sk.* root, पट्; past act. part. पट्यत?), 'quickly.'

ठीक, reduplicated intensive form, ठीक ठाक (*Sk.* root, स्था), 'exactly.'

दैवी (*Sk.* दैव, 'fate'), 'perchance.'

धीरे (*Sk.* root धृ), 'slowly.'

निपट (*Sk.* नि + पट्?), 'very.'

पैदल (*Sk.* पद्), 'on foot.'

बहुत (*Sk.* बहु), 'much,' 'very;' for dialectic forms, see § 338.

बेग (*Sk.* loc. sing. वेगे), 'quickly,' *Dial.* बेगि.

मानो (imp. 2nd plur. of मानना), *Dial.* मानौ, मानहु, मानु, 'as,' 'so to speak.'

लगातार (from *Sk.* root, लग्), 'incessantly;' also लगतातार.

सच (*Sk.* सत्यम्), 'truly;' intensive form, सचमुच.

सेंत, *Dial.* सेंति, 'freely,' 'gratis;' intensive form, सेंतमेंत.

हौले, *Dial.* हौरे, 'gently.'

a. The following are only dialectic:—*G.* पच्छो or पाच्छो, 'quickly,' and मुचाटे, 'slowly;' सुठि (*Sk.* सुष्ठु), 'very,' 'extremely;' and in the *Rámáyan*, बरु (*Sk.* वरम्), 'rather.'

b. The conjunctive participle, करि, of करना, 'to do,' is often used adverbially, for 'as;' thus, निज जन्म सुफल करि लेखौं, 'I will count my birth as having borne good fruit.' Similar is the use of the Braj form, कै; thus, मानुष कृष्ण देव कै मानै, 'they regard the man *Krishṇa* as a god.'

c. The following Sanskrit words are used as adverbs of manner, viz.:—अकस्मात् (अ + कस्मात्, abl. sing. of किम्), 'suddenly;' अति, 'very;' अनन्त, 'infinitely;' अधिक, 'more;' अर्थात् (abl. sing.), '*id est*;' आनन्द (*Sk.* inst. sing., आनन्देन),

'well,' 'happily;' केवल, 'only;' निरन्तर, 'incessantly;' परस्पर, 'mutually;' यथा, 'as;' तथा, 'so;' वृथा, 'in vain;' शीघ्र, 'quickly;' सहज, lit., 'born with,' hence, 'naturally,' 'easily;' सत्य, 'truly.' Sanskrit adverbs formed with the suffix धा, denoting 'distribution,' 'kind,' occasionally occur; as, in the *Rámáyan*, नवधा, 'of nine kinds.'

d. Here may be noted the Sanskrit particle, इव, 'like,' which approximates the nature of an affix, and always follows the word to which it refers; as, हरिजन इव, 'like the servants of *Hari*.'

(4) Adverbs of *Affirmation* and *Negation*. The common affirmative adverb is हां, *Bún.* हौ and हौं; east of Búndelkhanḍ, often तो, 'yes.' सही (*Pers.* صحی), 'truly,' is also very common in affirmation. The negative adverbs are न, नहीं, and मत, 'no,' 'not.' Of these, मत is regularly used with the imperative only; नहीं, never with the imperative; न, with any part of the verb. Adverbs of Affirmation and Negation.

a. जी is often combined with हां and नहीं in respectful address:* thus, जी हां or हां जी; as, क्यों मित्र, विदूषक आए? जी हां आया, 'how friend, has *Bidúshak* come? Yes, Sir; he has come.'

b. Dialectic variations are:—for नहीं, *Br.* नाहिं, नाहि, नांहीं, नाही; नाहिनें, *Már.* नं; in the *Rám.*, नहि, नहिं; modern eastern form, नाहिनठ. Other variations are, ना, नही, नाइ, and नाउ.† For मत, Kanaují has मति and मती; जिनि or जिन is also used. In Eastern Hindí, जिन is always used for मत, and, like that, with the imperative only. Variants of जिन are जनि and जिनु.

c. तो, 'indeed,' *Dial.* तौ, तउ or तऊ, is common. In the *Rámáyan* धौं is occasionally used with a similar force,

* There is a proverb, जी कहो जी कहलाओ, 'say *Jí* (yourself and) you will be called *Jí*.'

† For the derivation of these forms, vide § 472.

usually with अव; as, अवधौं; or sometimes कि precedes; as, किधौं or कीधौं.

d. Various Sanskrit nouns and adjectives are also used in affirmations: as, अवश्य, *Rám.* अवसि, 'certainly;' निःसंदेह, 'without doubt;' निश्चय, *Dial.* निहचे, निहचै, निहचैं, etc., 'assuredly.'

Adverbs of Citation.

646. Here may be also noted the occasional use of the particles अथ, 'now,' and इति, 'thus.' In Hindí prose these are never used except at the beginning and the end of narratives. Thus, at the beginning of the *Prem Ságar*, we have अथ कथा आरंभ, 'Now, the beginning of the story;' and at the end of each chapter, we find the particle इति, which is scarcely capable of translation, but is similar in force to the marks of quotation in English. In Sanskrit, इति was always written at the end of a citation; and traces of this usage are found in Hindí poetry. Thus, in the *Rámáyan*, महिमा निगम नेति कहि गाई; where नेति is, by *sandhi*, for न इति, and we may literally translate, 'Holy Writ, saying No, has sung his greatness;' इति simply marks the negative as the word, not of the writer, but of 'Holy Writ.'* So also, in prose, इति, as the first member of the compound इत्यादि, refers to the noun or nouns immediately preceding; as, ब्रह्मा महेश इत्यादि, '*Brahmá, Mahesh, et al.*'

Persian and Arabic Adverbs.

647. The following Persian and Arabic words occur now and then as adverbs in modern Hindí.—(1) *Pers.*: जल्द or जल्दी (جلد), 'quickly;' बारहा (plur. of بار, 'time'), 'often;' शायद (شاید), *vulg.*, सायद and साइद, 'perhaps;' हमेशा (همیشه), *vulg.*, हमेश and हमेस, 'always;' (2) *Arab.*: अल्बत्ता (البته), *vulg.*, अल्बत्त, 'certainly,' 'indeed;' खास्स कर (خاص کر), 'especially;' फकत (فقط), and about Meerut, खाली (for Ar. خالي), 'only;' बिलकुल (بالكل), 'altogether;' याने (يعني), 'namely,' 'that is to say.'

Adverbial Phrases.

648. Some adverbs and nouns, compounded, form useful adverbial phrases. Examples are:—और कहीं, 'elsewhere;' कभी नहीं, 'never;' धीरे धीरे, 'slowly,' 'easily;' नहीं तो,

* The meaning of the passage is, that the *Ved*, while attempting to set forth the greatness of *Rám*, declares that it has not yet done so; i.e., that his greatness is ineffable.

'else,' i.e., '(if) not, then.' For नहीं तो, we find in the *Rámáyan*, नाहिंत, नतु, नत, and नतरु. किन also occurs, for क्यों नहीं, 'how not?.'

649. Many adjectives, especially such as denote quantity or quality, are used in their uninflected form as adverbs: as, अच्छा and भला, ('good'), 'well;' थोड़ा, 'a little;' बड़ा ('great'), 'very.' So also is used ऐसा; as, मन ऐसा तरपता है, '(my) mind is so agitated;' and, in *Már.*, इधा, इयांरें,= H.H. ऐसे, ऐसेहो. Adjectives and Participles as Adverbs.

Rem. But in some cases, where the adjective must be rendered in English as an adverb, it is yet inflected as a proper adjective; as in the *Shakuntalá*, where *Máḍhavya* says, हम तो बड़े दुखी हैं, 'I am truly very miserable.'

650. Conjunctive participles are very often equivalent to English adverbs; as, जानके, 'knowingly;' मिलके, 'together;' etc. Here we may also note the use of करके, conj. part. of करना, with nouns, adjectives, and numerals, forming adverbial phrases; as, परिश्रम करके, 'laboriously;' मुख्य करके, 'chiefly;' एक एक करके, 'singly;' नीचे मुंह करके, 'with face downwards.' Further illustrations will be found in the Syntax.

651. Finally, we may here notice the participle ही, which may be placed after any word to render it emphatic. It may sometimes be translated by 'just,' 'very,' or some similar word; often, however, its force can only be expressed by a stress of the voice. The Emphatic Particle.

a. After the pronouns यह and वह, and often after जो and सो, ही becomes ई, and is written as a part of the pronoun; thus, यही, 'this very;' वही, 'that very,' etc. For its usage with pronominal plurals, see § 268, and with the pronominal adverbs, see § 641. Examples are:—मैं यह कहता ही था, 'I was in the very act of saying this;' दोही आए, 'just two came;' मेरा एक ही घोड़ा है, 'I have only one horse;' उस ने

यही बात कही, 'he said this very thing.' For सब ही, सभी is sometimes written; as, रूपवती को सभी सोहता है, 'to a beautiful woman, *everything* is becoming.'

b. For ही or ई, Braj also has हू or ऊ. The final ई or ऊ is often shortened, and Anusvár is occasionally added. In one instance in the *Rámáyan* (*Utt. K.*) ह is hardened to घ; thus, जो मन हूं न समाई. 'that which the very mind contains not.' Sometimes the emphatic ई or ऊ, ह having been elided, combines with the final inherent *a* of the word to which it belongs; giving, e.g., such forms as, O.B., एकौ, for एकहु, 'even one,' 'just one;' *N.* एकै for एकही.

c. In colloquial Máŗwáŗí, हज and ज are used instead of ही; thus, म्हांज, = मैंहीं; वोंज कीधो, = उसी ने किया; वोज हो, = वही था, etc., etc.

PREPOSITIONS.

Nature of Hindí Prepositions.

652. With the exception of those particles termed *post*positions, which are employed in substantive declension to denote the several cases of nouns, and a very few other words, Hindí possesses no words of a strictly prepositional character. The words which, for the sake of convenience, are enumerated below, as the equivalents of English prepositions, are really substantives in the obl. singular. Many of them, as, e.g., पीछे, साम्हने, etc., actually occur in the nominative singular, पीछा, साम्हना, etc.; and when in the oblique singular, they not unfrequently are themselves followed by postpositions, as में, पर, etc. In virtue of this their substantive character, they require the noun they modify to be in the inflected genitive. Nearly all are masculine, and therefore require the preceding genitive in के. The few feminines are noted in the list, and of course inflect a preceding का to की. Many words which have been enumerated as adverbs, are also used as prepositions, and will therefore be found in the following lists.

653. The following take the noun either with or without the postpositions. In the latter case, the noun must take the oblique form :— Prepositions used with Obl. Sing.

तले (*Sk.* तल), *Br.* तर, तरे, 'beneath.'

पार, 'across.'

पास, in *Rám.* पहँ, पाहि, पाहिं, 'near,' 'to.'

पीछे, *Máṛ.* पाछो, *N.* पछि, 'behind.'

बिन or बिना (*Sk.* विना), *Br.* बिनु, बिनू, 'without.'

बीच (*Sk.* and W. Hindí, विच्), 'between,' 'among.'

लगि (*Sk.* लगित्वा), *Br.*, *N.* लागि, 'for the sake of.'

संग (*Sk.* सम्, 'with,' + गम्, 'to go'), 'with.'

समेत, 'together with.'

a. सहित, 'with,' properly a Sanskrit adjective, is used as the last member of a compound, as, प्रेम सहित, 'with love;' but it also appears as a postposition, as, गाड़ियों सहित, 'with the carriages.'

b. पास is also used as a noun; e.g., in the *Rámáyan*, संवारहु चारिहु पासा, 'adorn (her) on every side.'

654. The following commonly require the preceding noun to take the genitive postposition, के, viz. :— Prepositions used with Gen. Postpositions.

आगे, 'before.' For dialectic variants, see § 645 (1).

आस पास, 'around,' 'on both sides.'

ऊपर (*Sk.* उपरि), *Máṛ.* ऊपरै (§ 172), 'over,' 'above.'

ढिग (*Sk.* दिश), 'towards.'

द्वारा (*Sk.* द्वार, 'a door'), 'through,' 'by means of.'

निकट, 'near.'

नीचे (*Sk.* नीच), *Br.* नीचू, 'under.' The Gaṛhwálí form, निस्सो, inflects the preceding substantive as a true postposition; as, ईं डाला निस्सो, 'under this tree.'

नेरे, *N.* निरठ, 'near.'

पलटे and संती, 'instead of.'

बाहर or बाहिर, *N.* बाहरठ, 'without.'

भीतर, *N.* भित्रठ, 'within.'

मारे (perf. part. of मारना), 'in consequence of,' 'because of.'

लिये (perf. part. of लेना), 'for,' *K.* लये, लयें, लए, *Bagh.* लाने, लिगां, *Mt.* लैल, लेल.

साथ, 'with,' *N.* सितठ, सङठ.

साम्हने, *Br.* साम्हो, साम्हू, समुहें, सोंहि, सोंहीं, *Máṛ.* हामो, *N.* सांमु, also मुख्यांजी, 'in front of,' 'before.'

हां (*Sk.* स्थाने), 'at,' 'at the house of,' whence also तईं or ताईं, 'towards,' 'to,' = पास, and sometimes को.

a. नाईं, 'like,' requires the preceding genitive to take the fem. form, की.

b. समान, 'equal to,' 'like,' commonly requires the genitive with के; but I have noted an instance in which it is made to agree in gender with the noun to which it refers; thus, स्त्री माता की समान, 'a woman like a mother.'*

Dialectic Prepositions.

655. Only dialectic are the following:—*K.* etc., कने (*Sk.* कर्णे), 'to,' 'near,' = H.H. पास; this often takes the preceding noun in the oblique form without a postposition; सुधा (*Sk.* सार्धम्), 'with;' in the *Rám.*, सरिस (*Sk.* सदृश), 'like;' काजे, काजि, = कारण, 'for,' 'by reason of;' भावें, 'for,' 'in consideration of;' in eastern Hindí, बरे, = लिये, 'for;' *Máṛ.* हेठो, 'below;' *N.* मुनि, मनि, 'under;' थाञि, 'to,' = H.H. पास; तिरठ, पट्टि, 'towards;' बाहिक, 'except;' माजि, 'in,' 'between;' हां, 'like;' माथि, जांभो, 'above;' भयठौं, कां, 'near.'

656. In Rajputana, these words which in High Hindí are used with the genitive as postpositions, are often construed as predicative adjectives, and made to agree with the subject of the sentence in gender and number. Thus, ऊ म्हां पाछो बेठ्यो है, = H.H. वह मेरे पीछे बैठा है, 'he is

* Compare the Máṛwáṛí usage, § 656.

seated behind me;' but या थां पाछी बैठी है, 'she is seated behind thee,' where High Hindí would have तेरे पीछे. Compare the remarks concerning सुधो, § 172.

657. The following Sanskrit words, with a few others, are often used in Hindí in a prepositional sense:—अनन्तर, 'after;' अनुसार, 'according to;' उपरान्त, 'after;' कारण, 'for,' 'because of;' निमित्त, 'on account of;' विरुद्ध (oftener बिरुद्ध), and विपरीत, 'contrary to,' 'against;' विषय or बिषय, also बिखै, 'in respect to,' 'about;' समीप, 'near;' हेतु, *vulg.* हेत, 'by reason of.' Sanskrit, Persian, and Arabic Prepositions.

658. The following Persian words are often used in modern Hindí as prepositions:—अन्दर (اندر), 'within;' गिर्द (گرد), 'about,' 'around;' नज़दीक (نزدیک), in the Doáb, नगीच; in the Himalayas, नज़ीक or नजिक, 'near.' नगीच is even used in literature, as in the *Shakuntalá*; वन के नगीच डेरा करूंगा, 'I will camp near the grove.' बाबत (*fem.* takes की), 'concerning.'

659. The following Arabic words are also much used as prepositions by Hindí-speaking people:—इवज़ (عوض), 'instead of;' ख़िलाफ़ (خلاف), 'contrary to,' 'against;' बग़ैर (بغیر), 'without;' बदले (بدلے), 'in exchange for;' बाइस (باعث), 'by reason of;' बाद (بعد), 'after;' बिदून (بدون), 'without;' मुवाफ़िक़ (موافق), *vulg.* in the Doáb, माफ़िक़, 'according to;' वास्ते (واسطے), 'for;' सबब (سبب), 'for,' 'by reason of;' सिवा (سوا), 'except,' 'besides.'

a. The following are feminine, and require की with the preceding noun:—ख़ातिर (خاطر), 'for,' 'for the sake of;' तरफ़ (طرف), 'towards;' तरह (طرح), 'like,' 'in the matter of;' निसबत (نسبت), 'concerning.'

CONJUNCTIONS.

660. *Copulative* conjunctions are the following:— Copulative Conjunctions.

और (*Sk.* अपर), *Br.* औ, अरु, रु, वो, *N.* अनि, र०. *O.B.* अवर, *Bagh.* वोर, 'and;' भी, *Máṛ.* बी, *N.* पनि, 'also;' फिर,

'again,' 'moreover.' For भी, 'also' (*Sk.* अपिहि, *Pr.* फिंहि), the Sanskrit अपि, sometimes with elision of अ, ऽपि, is used in poetry only. पुनर्, also पुन and पुनि, is used for फिर, resumptive, 'again,' in eastern Hindí; and in Naipálí, फेरि.

Adversative Conjunctions.

661. The most common *Adversative* conjunctions are परन्तु (*Sk.* परं + तु), in Naipálí, तरठ, 'but;' पर, (*Sk.* परं), *Br.* पै, 'yet;' बरञ्च (*Sk.* वरञ्च), 'but,' 'nay.'

a. But the common people in the N.W. Provinces very commonly use the Arabic لكن, लेकिन, for परन्तु, 'but;' and the Arabic بلكه, बल्कि (also, *vulg.*, बल्किन and बलुक), for बरञ्च, which latter is never used by the common people. Equally rare, and used only in poetry and scientific writing, is the Sanskrit किन्तु, = परन्तु, 'but.' The Persian مگر, मगर, 'but,' 'except,' is often used by Urdú-speaking Hindoos.

Disjunctive Conjunctions.

662. The *Disjunctive* conjunctions are या and अथवा, 'or.' The Arabic يا या is often preferred to these by the common people in the N.W. Provinces. The negative disjunctives, 'neither,' 'nor,' are expressed by repeating the negative participle न with each successive clause. 'Else' or 'otherwise' is expressed in Hindí by the two particles, नहीं तो. Of these, नहीं belongs to the protasis of an unexpressed conditional clause, '(if this is) not (so), then.' In Naipálí, for नहीं तो, we have नतर, or the phrase होइनठ भन्यै.

a. कि is sometimes used as a disjunctive, especially in alternative questions; as, क्या तुम आओगे कि नहीं, 'will you go or not?' The Sanskrit किंवा (or किंवा), 'or,' is occasionally found in literature. कि is the regular disjunctive in Naipálí.

b. The 3rd sing. conting. fut., चाहे, of चाहना, 'to wish,' is often used disjunctively in two successive clauses for 'whether . . . . or;' as, चाहे आवे चाहे न आवे, 'whether he come or not.' For the second चाहे, अथवा may be used.

c. The interrogative क्या, similarly repeated with nouns, must also be rendered 'whether' . . . . 'or,' as, क्या स्त्री क्या पुरुष, 'whether men or women.' So in Naipálí is used की...की.

663. The *Conditional* conjunctions are यदि (*Sk.*) or जदि, and, much more commonly, जो, 'if,' *Dial.* जु and जै. The Persian اگر अगर is often used for जो by Hindoos familiar with Urdú. In Naipálí भन्ने (भन्या) = यदि; it always follows the clause it conditions. Conditional Conjunctions.

664. The *Concessive* conjunctions are तो, 'then,' 'indeed,' यद्यपि, 'although,' and तथापि, 'nevertheless;' both यद्यपि and तथापि are Sanskrit. But, colloquially, जो . . . भी is used for यद्यपि, and तो or तौभी, for तथापि; as, जो आप मुझे त्याग भी करें तो, etc., 'even though you should forsake me, yet,' etc. Concessive Conjunctions.

a. Dialectic variations are, for तो, *Br.* तौ, in *Rám.* तउ and त; for यद्यपि, *Rám.* यद्दपि, जद्दपि, *Br.* जौऊ, *N.* भन्ने पनि (always final); for तथापि, तद्दपि, *N.* तपनि; for तौभी, *Br.* तौऊ, *Máṛ.* तोहो and तो पण.

b. चाहे, sometimes followed by भी in the same clause, is often nearly equivalent to 'although;' पर, 'yet,' or परन्तु, may then introduce the consequent clause. Thus, चाहे वह मुझे मार भी डाले, 'even though he should kill me;' चाहे माल सब जाता रहे, पर धर्म्म रहे, 'though property all go, but virtue remain.' चाहो may be thus used for चाहे.

c. फिर भी sometimes has a concessive force = Eng. 'still.'

d. अगरचि (*Pers.* اگرچه), 'although,' is only heard from Urdú-speaking Hindoos.

665. The *Causal* conjunctions are कि, 'for,' क्यूँकि, *Br.* क्योंकि, क्योंकि, and क्योंऊ, *N.* क्याकन and क्याकन भन्या, किनभने (final), 'because.' The Sanskrit noun, कारण, 'reason,' is also used as a causal conjunction, = 'because.' Causal Conjunctions.

Illative Conjunctions.

666. The common *Illative* conjunction is तो, *N.* तउ, 'then.' After जो in the *protasis* of a compound sentence, सो is often used in the *apodosis* in an illative sense; as, वह जो आया सो मुझे जाना पड़ेगा, 'as he has come, I shall therefore have to go.' Under other conditions, the abl. singular of the prox. dem. pronoun, यह, viz., इस से, *Br.* या तें, has the force of the illative 'therefore.'

Final Conjunctions.

667. The *Final* conjunctions are कि, 'that,' and, more emphatic, the abl. singular of the relative pronoun, जिसतें, 'in order that.' Naipálí uses the conj. part. भनयेरउ, lit., 'saying,' *after* the final clause.

a. No negative final conjunction exists, except in the Naipálí, कोनि; its place is supplied by the 3rd sing. conting. future of the substantive verb, with a negative before कि; as, न हो कि or ऐसा न हो कि. The Persian تاکہ ताकि, = जिसतें, belongs rather to Urdú than to Hindí.

INTERJECTIONS AND ENCLITICS.

Vocative Interjections.

668. Vocative interjections are the following:—

हे, अहो, ओ or हो, होत, अजी, अबे, अरे, रे, 'O.' Of these, हे is the most respectful, and must be used to superiors; ओ, हो, होत and अहो, also अजी, may be used in addressing equals or inferiors when no displeasure is intended. अबे and अरे or रे always indicate some degree of displeasure or disrespect; the final ए of these three is always changed to ई in connection with a feminine noun. ओ, हो and रे (री) follow, and the others mentioned, precede, the noun with which they are connected.

Miscellaneous Interjections.

669. Various emotions are expressed by the following:—

अ expresses pity, आ, despondency, वाह, approbation and surprise, 'bravo,' 'well!' धन्य expresses praise, 'bravo,' 'well done!'; हाए हाए, also हा हा and अहह, 'alas!'; दोहाए ='twice a pity;' त्राहि (also त्राह), is 'mercy!', lit., 'save!'; उह and ओह, 'oh,' express pain or disgust; जय जय, 'hurra!,' lit., 'victory!' 'victory!;' छीछी, 'fie,' expresses disgust. Yet other interjections are, धिक, 'shame,' also धिक्कार; दूर, 'begone!'; चुप, 'hush!'; लो, 'lo!'; फिश, 'pshaw!'; स्वस्ति (*Sk.* सु + अस्ति), 'salutation!'. I have also found स्वस्ति used as an adjective with a noun; as, स्वस्ति बचन, 'a well-said word.'

670. The usual words of salutation among the Hindoos are, to equals or inferiors in caste, राम राम, *Rám! Rám!*; to Brahmans, नमस्कार, 'Obeisance!'; to Europeans or Muhammedans, सलाम, lit., 'peace!'; or, still more respectfully, बन्दगी, lit., 'service!'.

671. The following interjections are also used in the colloquial of some parts of the country: शाबाश (Pers. شاد باش), 'well done!'; थू थू and थुड़ी, express disgust; क्यो calls attention; उड़ानछू हट, and हत तेरो, 'begone!'; हाय दैया and हाय मैया, 'Alas!' 'woe!'; lit., 'Alas! nurse,' or 'mother!'. आहि दइय occurs in the *Rámáyan*; thus, the slave girl *Kubarí* says, आहि दइय मैं काह नसावा, 'Alas! what have I destroyed!'. It occurs also in the *Shakuntalá*.

CHAPTER XII.

SYNTAX.

672. In this chapter will be treated, in the first place, the functions of the several parts of speech under their various modifications in respect of number, case, tense, etc., and, in the second place, the construction of sentences from the material thus exhibited. The former may be termed *Analytic*, the latter, *Synthetic* Syntax.

PART I. ANALYTIC SYNTAX.

Gender and Number.

Gender. **673.** Little needs to be said here as to gender. It is chiefly of importance to observe that occasionally, when a noun denotes an object of a different gender from its own, it is construed as having the gender of that object. Thus, though **मूल** is masculine, we have **मेरी जीवनमूल**, when it refers to *Shakuntalá*, in the drama of that name.

Number. **674.** The singular number denotes *unity*, the plural, *plurality*. To this general rule there are three exceptions.

(1) The singular may be used for the plural in a generic sense, to denote a *class*; as, **तजती हैं पति को अकुलीनी नारी**,

lit., 'base-born women desert the husband;' सुर नर मुनि को अति आनन्द हुआ, 'to god, man, and sage, there was great joy.'

a. This generic singular must not be confounded with those cases in which the plural termination is simply dropped, leaving the noun, although plural, in form like the singular. This takes place regularly when the plurality is already indicated by some attributive of the noun, as in the following: थोड़े दिन में, 'in a few days;' ये दोनों बात असत्य दिखाई देती हैं, 'these two things appear untrue;' अठारह पटरानी, 'eighteen queens.'

Sometimes the plural inflection is also omitted, where the indication of plurality is only in the predicate; as, सखी सेवा में खड़ी हैं, 'her companions are standing in her service;' i.e., 'are waiting upon her.'

Rem. This omission of the plural termination occurs chiefly in the nominative of fem. nouns, and is probably becoming more and more common. But in such cases, where there is an emphasis on the plurality, the plural inflection is retained; as, अपनी दो बेटियां ब्याह दीं, 'he gave his two daughters in marriage.'

(2) The plural is used for the singular to express *respect*; as, तारे in the following: हमारे नैनों के तारे श्री कृष्ण चंद, 'the star of my eyes, *Shrí Krishn Chand*.' Plural of Respect.

(3) A very few Hindí nouns are idiomatically used in the plural, where English would require the singular. Examples are found in phrases formed by भूखों, पियासों, and जाड़ों with मरना, 'to die of hunger, of thirst, of cold.'* So also दाम, 'price,' भाग, in the sense of 'fortune,' 'lot,' दर्शन, 'vision,' and समाचार, 'news,' are very commonly construed as plurals; as, also, sometimes, कल्याण, 'welfare,' and प्राण, 'life,' with allusion to the (supposed) five vital airs.' Idiomatic Plurals.

---

* In such idioms the inflection ओं clearly retains its original sense as a genitive termination = Sk. आनाम्, and is to be explained as a genitive of cause, as in such phrases as पंथ का हारा, 'exhausted because of the way.' Vid. infra, Syntax of the genitive.

Of the Nominative.

675. The *Nominative* is used,

Subject Nominative.

(1) As the grammatical subject of the verb; as, **ऋषि के बचन सत्य होंगे**, 'the words of the sage will become true.'

Predicate Nominative.

(2) It is found as the predicate after many intransitive verbs, as in the following examples:—

बुढ़ापा मनुष्य को कैसी आपदा है, 'what an affliction to a man is old age!'; **यही छड़ी .... मेरे चलने का सहारा बनी है**, 'this *staff* .... is become the support of my walk;' **गोपी नाथ कहावेगा**, 'he shall be called *Gopí Náth*;' **वह अपराधी ठहरा**, 'he was counted a transgressor.'

(3) It is sometimes used for the vocative; thus, **बाणासुर ने बुलायके कहा कि बेटा**, '*Bánásur* called and said, Son!'.

(4) It sometimes stands independent by *anakolouthon*; as, **महाराज वे बैठे हैं**, 'the great king—he is seated;' **शास्त्रविद्या औ शस्त्रविद्या ये दोऊ उच्च पद की देनेवारी हैं**, 'sacred science and military science,—these two confer high rank.'

(5) It is sometimes used for the genitive, absolutely, with the infinitive; as, e.g., in the phrase, **धनुष टूटने का शब्द**, 'the noise of the breaking of the bow.'

Of the Accusative.

Objective Accusative.

676. The *accusative* is used to denote (1) the direct object of a transitive verb; or (2) local or temporal relations.

677. To denote the direct *object* of a transitive verb, we may employ either the inflected accusative with **को**, or that form of the accusative which is like the nominative. Similarly, with the perfect tenses of transitive verbs, the object of the action may either be put in the dative of reference with को, or in the nominative. But these two constructions or the two forms of the accusative are by no means interchangeable.

Rem. The correct use of these two alternative forms and constructions is perhaps the most difficult thing in the Hindí language. Only by extensive and continual reading of native books and long intercourse with the people, can the foreigner become able to use them with idiomatic accuracy. But the following principles and illustrations will, it is hoped, at least throw some light on the subject.

678. The general principle which regulates the use of these two forms and constructions is the following: when it is desired to emphasize the object as specific and individual, the accusative with को must be used; otherwise, the nominative form is to be preferred. **Use of को with Accusative.**

(1) Under this general head, observe, that in the case of nouns denoting rational beings, whether they be (*a*) generic, or (*b*) relative terms, or (*c*) proper names, the accusative with को is more commonly preferred.

a. Under this head examples are: (*a*) of generic terms: साथियों को साथ लिया, 'he took (his) companions with (him);' ऐसे कायुर को क्यौं मानो, 'why will you mind such a coward?': (*b*) of relative terms: हरि मा को देखते ही कहने लगा, '*Hari*, immediately on seeing his mother, began to say;' मंत्री हरि-भक्तों को ढूंढ ढूंढ मारने लगे, 'the councillors, seeking around, began to kill the worshippers of *Hari*:' (*c*) of proper names: बसुदेव ने गर्ग मुनि को बुलाया, '*Basudev* called the sage *Garg*;' कंस ने बकासुर को भेजा, '*Kans* sent *Bakásur*;' सब गोपी कन्हैया को लिए जसोदा पास चलीं, 'all the milkmaids took *Krishn* and went to *Jasodá*.'

N.B. बुलाना, 'to call,' as implying a definite object, almost invariably requires the accusative with को.

(2) Conversely, for nouns denoting (*a*) irrational beings, or (*b*) inanimate things, or (*c*) for abstract terms, **Nom. Form of Accusative.**

the nominative form of the accusative, or, with the perfect of transitive verbs, the nominative case, is much more commonly preferred.

a. Examples are (*a*) of animate, irrational beings: गायें चराने लगे, 'they began to pasture the cows;' बछड़े चरने को हांक दिये, 'they drove off the calves to graze:' (*b*) of inanimate, material objects: श्री कृष्ण ने अपना शरीर बढ़ाया, '*Shrí Krishṇ* enlarged his body;' यहीं छाकें खाय, 'let us eat (our) lunches here:' (*c*) of abstract terms: मेरा दोष चित में न लीजे, 'do not take my fault to heart;' जिस पर मैं अनुग्रह करता हूं उस का सब धन खोता हूं, 'I destroy all the wealth of him to whom I show favour.'

(3) Although the use of the two forms of the accusative or the two alternative constructions of the object with the perfects of the transitive verbs, is regulated to a great extent, especially in the colloquial, by the above principles, still it must be observed that other subordinate considerations often limit and modify their application.

a. When it is specially intended to denote the object of the verb as indefinite, the nominative form is preferred, even when referring to rational beings. Thus in the *Prem Ságar*, *Kans* says, जीती लड़की न दूंगा तुझे, 'a *living* girl I will not give thee;' where the omission of को, making the expression indefinite, adds to the emphasis. Similar is the phrase, आप ने मारे हैं बालक, 'you have killed children;' referring to the general massacre by *Kans*.

b. On the other hand, when it is desired to indicate the object with special *definiteness*, the form with को may be employed even with nouns denoting irrational objects or abstract ideas. The accusative with को will therefore generally be preferred when the object of the verb has just been mentioned, or is well known. Thus, तिन दोनों तरवर के बीच उखल को आड़ा डाल, 'throwing the mortar (i.e., the mortar previously mentioned) obliquely between those two trees.'

Again, we have, सोई इस माया को जीतता है, 'that one overcomes this illusive power.' Here को indicates माया as the माया first mentioned in the previous context,* where, it should be noted, the nominative form of the accusative is employed, thus: अपनी माया दूर करो, 'remove your illusive power.'

c. Again, in the case of plural nouns, when it is desired to denote the object *collectively*, as a class or a totality, the accusative with को is employed; but when it is rather to be denoted *distributively*, as a plurality, the nominative form of construction is preferred. Thus we read, सोलह सहस्र एक सौ आठ स्त्रियों को साथ ले, 'taking (his) 16108 wives with him,'—where को denotes the object collectively; उस ने ज्योतिषियों को बुलाया, 'he called the astrologers,'—where को denotes them as a class. But in the following, the nominative form of the accusative denotes the objects as a *plurality*; आप ने क्या चिन्ह 'what signs has your Majesty seen?'

d. The choice between the two forms for the object of a verbal action is frequently determined merely by a regard to *euphony*. Thus, especially, when an accusative and a dative occur in close proximity, the nominative form is often preferred for the direct object, simply to avoid the disagreeable repetition of को. Thus, मैं ने तुम्हारा पुत्र रोहिणी को दिया है, 'I have given your son to *Rohiní*;' मैं चारुमती जो कृताब्रमा को मांगी है जिसे न दूंगा, '*Chárumatí*, who is betrothed to *Kṛitábramá*, I will not give to him.'

e. So also, again, the one form may be preferred to the other simply out of regard to the *rhythm* and balance of clauses, so much affected, even in prose, by Hindí writers. Even a fancy for a rhyme may determine the choice, not only in poetry, but in prose writing. Thus, वहीं किसी ने देखा

* *Prem Ságar*, Adhy. lxxxvii.

मेरा कुंवर कन्हाई, 'has any one seen anywhere my boy, *Kanhái*?',—where कन्हाई is apparently preferred to कन्हाई को, in order to rhyme with माई, which ends the previous clause. Every page of the *Prem Ságar*, with its artificial, rhyming style, will illustrate this remark.

f. Finally, the accusative with को must always be employed, when otherwise the expression might be ambiguous.

Cognate Accusative.

679. Many verbs, transitive and intransitive, may be used with an accusative derived from the same root.

a. Observe, this *cognate* accusative is invariably used in the nominative form; and rarely, if ever, without an attributive adjunct. Thus, तुम कैसी चाल चलते हो, lit., 'what kind of walk are you walking?'; कोकिल मनभावन बोलियां बोल रहे, 'cuckoos were uttering their pleasing notes;' वह बड़ा बोल बोलता है, lit., he talks a great talk,' i.e., 'he speaks boastfully;' सिपाही ने उस को बड़ी मार मारी, lit., 'the soldier beat him a great beating.'

Verbs with two Accusatives.

680. Many verbs may be preceded by two accusatives. We may here distinguish two cases.

(1) The verb, commonly a causal, may take one accusative of the person, and a second, either of a person or a thing. In accordance with the above principles, the personal accusative regularly takes को, and usually, though not invariably, precedes the other.

(2) Verbs signifying 'to think,' 'to suppose,' 'to make,' 'to name,' 'to appoint,' etc., take a second accusative definitive of the first. The first may be termed the *objective*, and the second, the *predicative* accusative. In this case the objective accusative, as more specific, commonly, though not always, takes को, and the predicative accusative is put in the nominative form.

Examples are, under (1), वह सब को बागे पहिराय देगा, 'he will put vestments on all;' मैं सब को मिठाई खिलाऊंगा, 'I will feed all with sweetmeats;' and under (2), इस को तुम क्या कहते हो, 'what do you call this?'; (तू ने) मिस यह बनाया है, 'thou hast made this a pretext;' मैं इस को दुख जानता हूं, 'I regard this as suffering.'

681. The accusative is used with a verb of motion to denote the *place to which*, as in the following example: Accusative of Time and Place.

हस्तिनापुर को चलिये, 'be pleased to go to *Hastinápur*.'

682. It may also denote absolutely *the time at which*: as,

कार्तिक बदी चौदस को, 'on the 14th of the dark half of the month *Kártik*;' कोई रात को न्हाने न पावे, 'let no one be permitted to bathe at night.'

N.B. The postposition is often omitted from both the local and temporal accusative.

683. The accusative with को and its equivalents, कौं, कहं, etc., is also used in accordance with the principles above indicated, in both early and modern poetry. But in archaic poetry the inflected accusative in हि (हिं) is often used for the analytic accusative with को, subject to the same general conditions. Examples of both forms are as follows: जे निज मित्र भानु कौं माने, 'who regard the sun as their own friend;' राखु राम कहं जेहि तेहि भांती, 'keep *Rám* in whatever way (you may);' कहु केहि रंकहिं करौं नरेसू, 'say! what pauper shall I make a king?'; मुनि रघुबरहि प्रसंस, 'the sage extolled *Raghubar*.' Accusative in Poetry.

684. It is important to observe, however, that in Hindí poetry the laws of grammar often yield to the necessities of the measure. Even agreement in gender and number is often sacrificed to the exigencies of the metre. Moreover, in archaic poetry, the modern analytic accusative is but beginning to appear in literature. Hence the nominative form of the noun is constantly employed for the accusative, with a license which in prose or in the colloquial would be quite inadmissible. Thus, e.g., in the following stanzas, prose usage would have demanded वसिष्ठ को and पुरुष को: आदि पुरुष हम मानुष जान्यो, 'we thought the First Man to be a mortal;'* तब नरनाह वसिष्ठ बुलाये, 'then the lord of men summoned *Vasisht*;'† and so in almost every stanza of the *Rámáyan.*

Inflected Accusatives

685. The inflected form of the noun alone is never used in modern Hindí for the object of a verb. But it should be noted that in Permissive and Acquisitive compound verbs, as also sometimes in Desideratives, the inflected infinitive in ए alone, or, in the *Rámáyan* and other Eastern Hindí, the inflected verbal noun in ऐ, as in चलै लागे, 'he began to go,' is *de facto* an accusative under the government of the following verb. Similarly is to be explained the colloquial Braj and Kanaují idiom, in such phrases as, वह खैवे न करे, 'he will not eat;' where the inflected gerund, खैवे, as the object of करे, must be regarded as an inflected accusative.

The Dative.

686. We may classify the uses of this case as follows.

Objective Dative.

(1) The dative is used to denote the *indirect object* of a transitive verb.

Examples are: बलराम जी सब को आसा भरोसा देते थे, '*Balrám Jí* was inspiring all with hope and confidence;' श्री कृष्ण चंद अपनी माया को आज्ञा की, '*Shrí Krishn Chand* commanded his Illusive Power;' यह मूसा मोहि दुख देतु है, 'this mouse gives me trouble.' So, sometimes, with verbs of 'speaking,' we have a dative of the person addressed; as, श्री कृष्ण चंद ने बलदेव जी को सैन से कहा, '*Shrí Krishn Chand* said with a wink to *Baldev Jí.*'

Rem. 1. कहना, 'to say,' 'to tell,' when used of giving an order or direction, is constructed with the dative of the person addressed; but in other cases it is preceded by the ablative: as, उस ने मुझे बैठने को कहा, 'he told me to sit;' but, उस ने मुझ से यह बात कही, 'he said this thing to me.'

* *Prem Ságar.* † *Rámáyan.*

Rem. 2. It should be observed that the case with *ko* before causal verbs is not to be regarded as a dative, as might often appear from the equivalent of an English idiom, but as an accusative. This will appear, if for the English equivalent to the causal verb, the verb 'cause' be used with the infinitive of the primitive verb. Thus, *wah ghoṛe ko ghás khilátá hai*, 'he feeds grass to the horse,' i.e., 'he *causes* the horse to *eat* grass.'*

(2) The dative of a person often very idiomatically precedes an infinitive with the verb होना or पड़ना, to denote a *certainty*, or a *necessity*, or *obligation*, as resting on that person. The idiom is commonly equivalent to the English 'must,' 'have to,' etc. In like manner, as denoting the subject of an obligation, the dative often precedes an infinitive or perfect participle with चाहिये. Dative of Necessity.

Examples: कल हमें तुम्हें यमदग्नि के यहां जाना है, 'to-morrow you and we have to go to the abode of *Yamadagni*;' पर्ब को पहुंचा चाहिये, '(we) ought to arrive there to the festival;' हमें मरना पड़ेगा, lit., 'it will fall to us to die;' i.e., 'we must die.'

(3) The dative is very commonly used to denote *possession* or *acquisition*. Dative of Possession.

a. The dative of possession is usually followed by the substantive verb: as, उन को तन मन की भी सुध न थी, 'they were not conscious even of soul and body;' सब को त्रास भयो, 'to all was terror.'

b. But often the copula is omitted: as, हमें इतना ज्ञान कहां, 'where have we so much wisdom?;' तिन कौं जैसो सुख है, तैसो असंतोषी कौं नाहिं, 'such happiness as these have, the discontented have not.'

c. Or some other neuter verb may take the place of the copula; thus, दुख नाम को न रहा, 'not the name of sorrow remained,' or, '(even) to the name, sorrow remained not.'

* With the Hindí idiom, compare the Sanskrit construction of causal verbs. Vid. Monier-Williams, *Sansk. Gramm.*, § 847.

d. Here also may be noted the common idiom with मिलना, 'to meet,' 'to be found;' which is always used with the nominative of the thing found, and the dative of the finder. Thus, उन को चारों पदार्थ मिलते हैं, 'they obtain the four blessings;' मुझे कुछ नहीं मिला, 'I obtained nothing.' So also is explained a common idiom with लगना: as, मुझे जाड़ा लगता है, 'I feel cold,' lit., 'cold fastens to me;' यह बात तो मुझे बड़ी प्यारी लगी, 'this story has truly pleased me greatly.'

Dative of Advantage.

(4) This is found in construction with such adjectives as उचित, योग्य, 'proper,' 'right,' भला, 'good,' कठिन, 'difficult,' etc., with their opposites.

Examples: ऐसा साहस करना नारी को उचित नहीं, 'it is not seemly for a woman to be so daring;' स्वामी बिन स्त्री को मरना ही भला है, 'for a woman without a husband, it is well even to die;' मनुष्य को परमेश्वर का सत्यज्ञान प्राप्त करना अत्यन्त कठिन है, 'for man to obtain the true knowledge of God, is extremely difficult.'

Rem. योग्य is often construed with the genitive, with a slightly different meaning, as in § 695 (16).

Dative of Final Cause.

(5) The Dative of Final Cause denotes the *motive*, *purpose*, or *object* of an action, or the *use* for which a thing is designed; as in the following examples:—

पुरी की चौकसी को कौन रहेगा, 'who will remain for the watching of the city?'; हम अभी आश्रम के दर्शन को जाते हैं, 'I am just going to visit the hermitage.'

a. The infinitive, in its capacity of a gerund, is very commonly used in the dative in this sense: as, कुछ फूल फल भेंट को ले आ, 'bring some flowers (and) fruits for an offering;' देखिबे कौं तौ द्वै आंखि हीं, 'for seeing, indeed, were two eyes;' कहीं रहने को ठौर बताइये, 'be pleased to show me somewhere a place to stay.' The postposition is often omitted from this gerundial dative; as, वह पढ़ने आता है, 'he comes to read.'

Rem. For the dative of the final cause, modern Hindí often substitutes the genitive with लिये or वास्ते, and in the east, also बदे or खातिर.

b. Here also may be noticed the peculiar use of this dative of the gerund with the substantive verb, to denote the proximate futurition of the act denoted by the gerund. Thus, वह चढ़ने को हुई, 'she was just about to mount;' वह जाने को था, 'he was about to go.'*

(6) A Dative of Reference is used before a great variety of words, to denote the object with respect to which any affirmation is made. **Dative of Reference.**

Thus it is employed with many neuter verbs: as, बान मोर को लगा, 'the arrow struck the peacock;' दरिद्री कौं संसार सूनौ लागतु है, 'to a poor man the world seems lonely;' वही कहिये जो जिसे सुहाय, 'whatever may be pleasing to any one, that very (thing) say;' अनिरुद्ध जी को बांधे बांधे चार महीने हुए, 'four months passed over *Aniruddh* in bondage.' So we may have the dative of reference after an active verb; e.g., स्त्री को कहा है कि कैसा ही पात होय, 'with regard to the woman, it is said, that of whatever kind (her) husband may be.'

a. Many other verbs are preceded by a dative of reference; and, in particular, the Nominal compound verbs, दिखाई देना, सुनाई देना, etc., mentioned § 463. Thus, क्या तुम को चिन्ह नहीं दिखाई देते हैं, 'do not signs appear to you?'.

b. To this head may be referred the use of the dative to denote the object of an action, in the *impersonal* construction (§ 412) of the perfect tenses of transitive verbs. Thus, e.g., उस ने लड़कों को देखा, is literally, 'by him (it was) seen (with respect) to the boys.'

c. Finally, the dative of reference may be used with some adjectives; as, पियहि पियारी, 'dear to (her) husband;' and also, some nouns, in expressions of praise or blame; as, धन्य है तेरे साहस को, 'praise to thy courage;!' धिक्कार मेरे जीतब को, 'a curse to my life!.'

* Compare the English colloquial idiom, 'he was for going.'

687. The dative with the postposition को (कौं, कहं, etc.), is also used in poetry according to the same general principles, as will appear from the following examples: सज्जन कौं दुख हू दिये, 'from having given even pain to a good man;' तुम कहं बिपति बीज बिधि बयउ, '*Brahmá* has sown for you the seed of trouble.' But very often in the *Rámáyan*, the inflected dative in हि (हिं) is preferred. Thus, मातुपितहिं पुनि यह मत भावा, 'this counsel, again, pleased her parents;' बहु बिधि चेरिहि आदर देई, 'in many a way she showed the bondmaid honour;' राजहि तुम पर प्रीति बिशेषी, 'the king has a special love for you.'

Rem. The postposition is often omitted; as, पर अकाज भट सहस बाहु से, 'for another's injury, warriors with a thousand arms.'

The Case of the Agent.

688. The case of the Agent is used only with the tenses of the perfect participle of transitive verbs, and that only in modern High Hindí and other western dialects, to denote the *agent*. Examples will be found further on, in the sections which treat of the aforesaid tenses.

a. In a Hindí translation of the *Bhágavat Purán* I have found the case of the Agent very commonly used with the Infinitive in the titles of the Chapters. Thus, the title of the 8th *Skandh* reads, हरि अवतार लेकर बचाना प्राण दासी का परमेश्वर ने, lit., 'the saving of the life of (his) handmaid by God, having become incarnate as *Hari*.' Again, in the 2nd *Adhyáya* of the same; कहना शुकदेव जी ने कथा गजेन्द्र औ ग्राह की, 'the narration by *Shukdev Jí* of the story of *Gajendra* and *Gráh*.' Pincott, in his *Hindí Manual*, gives the following additional illustration; जा रे उस पांच पाण्डवों ने मेरा क्या करने का है, 'Go! fellow! what can those five *Páṇḍavs* do against me?'. He thinks that this use of this case is extending; it is, however, still quite rare, and I have never heard it in conversation.

b. In Naipálí, as might be expected from its peculiar use of the case of the agent, its employment with other than the tenses of the perfect, is much more common than in High Hindí. Thus, we have, कोहि योहन कोहि इलियास अरुले पुराना भविष्यबक्ता मा एक फेरि उठो भनि भन्द० छन, 'one is saying, John, one, Elias, another, that one of the old prophets is risen again;' where it is used with the present imperfect. In the following it is used with the future; उन्हेरु ले मन फिराउनन, 'they will repent.' On the other hand, ले is sometimes omitted, even with the tenses of the perfect; as, दूत उन खाइ बल दिंदा दर्शन दियो, 'an angel appeared, strengthening him;' but I have noted this with दर्शन दिनु only.

689. In both Braj prose and poetry, the postposition नें is often omitted. Thus, सन्यासियन मेरे बिल तें सब धन काढ़ि लियौ, 'the *Sanyásís* took out all the store from my hole;' ब्राह्मन कह्यो, 'the Brahman said;' मोही सों तुम प्रीति बढ़ाई, 'you have increased (your) love for me.' Omission of Postposition of Agent.

690. In the *Rámáyan* ने is never used; and in the singular, the case of the agent is thus identical in form with the nominative. In the plural, the oblique form alone denotes the case of the agent. Thus, सीतहि चितइ कही प्रभु बाता, 'looking toward *Sítá*, the lord spoke this word;' हरिचरित सुहाये भांति अनेक मुनीसन गाये, 'the illustrious deeds of *Hari*, the great sages have sung in countless ways.' But, as previously remarked, the nominative with the active construction is very often used where modern High Hindí would have the passive construction with the case of the agent.

The Ablative.

691. Most of the Hindí idioms with the ablative rest upon the idea of 'separation.' We may classify them as follows.

The Local Ablative.

(1) The ablative is used commonly with verbs of motion, to denote the *place from which* the motion proceeds.

Thus, बन से घर को आते थे, 'they were coming from the jungle to the house;' मथुरा से चल दिये, 'they set out from *Mathurá*;' सिंहासन से उठे, 'he rose from the throne.' And sometimes the local ablative occurs with other verbs also; as, दूर से उस ने श्री कृष्ण चंद से कहा, 'from afar he said to *Shrí Krishn Chand*.'

The Temporal Ablative.

(2) It similarly denotes the *time from which*, as in the following:—

आज से चौथे दिन, 'on the fourth day from now;' कुछ दिन से, 'some time ago;' तब से, 'since then;' यह रीति परंपरा से चली आती थी, 'this custom had come on down from the olden time.'

Ablative of Separation.

(3) The ablative is used with all adjectives, verbs, and other words expressing local or ideal *separation*.

Thus, after adjectives: वह हम से अलग हुआ, 'he became separated from me;' मैं ने उन को सब भय से निर्भय किया, 'I made them free from all fear.' It is also used on this principle after a great variety of verbs; especially verbs of *asking*, *refusing*, *forbidding*, *desiring*, *saving*, etc., etc. Thus, तुम अपने पिता से जा पूछो, 'go and inquire of your father;' हम से चाहता है अपनी मोच, 'he desires from me his death;' तुम ने हम को आग औ जल से किस लिये बचाया, 'for what did you save us from fire and water?;' जिस के देने से तू नट गई, 'to give which you refused.' Similarly, the verbal noun बर्जन, 'prohibition,' may be followed by the ablative; का बर्जन ऋषिवरों को हरिभजन करने से, 'what prohibition to the great sages from worshipping *Harí*?'.

Ablative of Source and Cause.

(4) The ablative is used to express the *source*, *origin*, or *cause*.

Examples are: इन्द्र के मानने से कुछ नहीं होता, 'nothing comes from obeying *Indra*;' दुख से अति घबराय, 'greatly agitated with sorrow;' तू किस पाप से अजगर हुआ था, 'for what sin didst thou become a serpent?'; नंद जी से इतनी बात सुन, 'hearing so much as this from *Nand Jí*.' Thus may be explained the ablative before verbs of *fearing*, where the ablative denotes that which is the cause of fear; e.g., मैं अपजस से डरता हूं, 'I fear infamy.' Much more rarely, however, डरना is preceded by the accusative; thus, उधर जाने को जी डरता है, '(my) heart fears to go there.'

(5) Hence, by a natural transition, the ablative comes to denote the *means* or *instrument*, as that from which action immediately proceeds; as, for example: **Ablative of Means.**

तू हाथी से चिरवा डालियो, 'do thou tear them to pieces with an elephant;' खुर सों खोदे नदी करारे, 'with (his) hoof he digs up the banks of the river.' To this head may be referred the ablative with verbs of 'filling,' as denoting that with which the action of filling is performed; as, e.g., सरोवर निर्मल जल से भरे हैं, 'the lakes are filled with pure water.'

(6) Hence, again, the ablative may denote the *agent*. **Ablative of the Agent.**

Rem. Observe, however, that this construction is only found in connection with neuter verbs, or with the passive conjugation. Thus, हम से नहीं बनेगा, lit., 'it will not be made by me,' i.e., 'I cannot make it;' उन का बल मुझ से नहीं संभाला जाता, 'their strength cannot be resisted by me.'

(7) The ablative is used with all words denoting or implying *comparison*. **Ablative of Comparison.**

a. Thus, it is used (*a*) with adjectives: as, मुझ से बड़ा, 'greater than I;' ऐसे पूत होने से वह अपूत क्यों न हुआ, 'why was he not sonless, rather than have such a son?;' वह सब से पहिले जा मिली, 'she went and met him first of all:' (*b*) with verbs: as, कोई मुझ से न जीते, 'no one may conquer me;'

29

बालहत्या से बढ़कर तो कोई पाप ही नहीं, 'there is no sin at all, indeed, greater than child-murder:' (*c*) before some adverbs; as, इस से आगे, 'before this;' घर से बाहर, 'outside of the house.'

Ablative of Price.

(8) The ablative may denote the *price*, as that by means of which a thing is obtained.

Examples: यह पुस्तक मुझे एक रुपये से मिली, 'I got this book for one rupee;' दो आने से कभी बिकता है, 'does it ever sell for two *ánás*?'.

Ablative of Manner.

(9) The ablative is very commonly used to denote the *manner* of an action.

Examples: उलटे वेदमंत्रों से यज्ञ कर, 'sacrificing with the vedic formulas (read) backward;' नख सिख से सिंगार कर, 'adorning (themselves) from head to foot;' उस ने अति प्यार से कहा, 'he said with great love.' This use of the ablative is especially common with such words as प्रकार, भांति, रीति, विधि, etc.: as, इस रीति से, 'in this way:' उस भांति, 'in that manner,' etc. Here also place such phrases as इस पंथ से चलो, 'go by this road.'

Rem. This modal ablative denotes the noun as a *norm* or *standard* from which the action may, in a manner, be regarded as proceeding. Compare the English idiom, 'I made it from this rule;' and the Latin, *nostro more*, *meo consilio*, etc.

Ablative of Use.

(10) The ablative is used after nouns expressing *need* or *use*.

Examples: मुझे औषधि से प्रयोजन है, 'I have need of medicine;' इस से क्या काम, 'what is the use of this?.'

Other Idioms with Ablative.

(11) Finally, the ablative with से is used to express a variety of relations expressed in English by the prepositions 'with,' 'by,' or, more rarely, 'in,' 'to,' or 'for.'

Examples: मुझ से संग्राम कर, 'fight with me;' किसी से कलह न करवाओ, 'do not stir up discord with any one;' जिस

से विधना ने संबंध किया, 'with whom *Brahmá* contracted an alliance;' मुंह से मुंह, 'mouth to mouth;' इस से लता लिपट रहा है, 'to this a vine is clinging;' छूने से ठंडी लगती है, 'it (crystal) feels cold to the touch; *lit.* is cold from touching;' यह बातों से न मानेगा, 'this (boy) will not obey for words;' उसे कृष्ण भेस से देख, 'seeing him in the disguise of *Krishṇ*;' आप की कृपा से, 'by your honour's kindness;' मैं ने यह हंसी से नहीं कही, 'I did not say this in jest.'

a. कहना, 'to say,' is commonly preceded by an ablative of the person addressed. The dative or accusative with को is used, but the sense is then different; as, मैं इस मुंदरी को कुछ बुरा कहा चाहता हूं, 'I wish to call this ring something bad;' but, मुझ से कहो, 'tell me;' किस से कहूं, 'whom shall I tell?;' तुझ से भी माता पुत्र कह कर बोली है, '(my) mother has spoken, calling thee also, Son!' In one place in the *Rámáyan*, however, the object of कहना takes पाहि (पाहिं); thus, तब रघुबीर कहा मुनि पाहीं, 'then *Raghubír* said to the sage.'*

b. Other words and phrases of analogous meaning to कहना, are also followed by the ablative: as, जसोदा से तुम ने यह बचन किया था, 'you made *Jasodá* this promise;' अनुसूया मुझ से बकती है, '*Anusúya* is talking nonsense to me.'

Rem. It has been denied that we can correctly say, in such cases as the above, that the noun is in the ablative; and, indeed, if we restrict the word 'ablative' to its etymological sense, then many words mentioned under (10) (11) are certainly not ablatives. But in no language is the usage of the word thus rigidly restricted. Prakrit and modern Hindí, especially, afford abundant examples of the usurpation by one case of the functions of another. It is quite possible, moreover, that 'with' may be the radical signification of *se*, from which all the modern usages of the word are to be derived.

692. The ablative is used in poetry in the same manner as in prose. Two or three examples will suffice: thus, पद नख तें भू खोदत भईं, 'they began to dig the earth with their toe- Ablative in Poetry.

---

* For a fuller explanation and other illustrations, see § 686, *Rem.* 1.

nails;' जो दृग सों छुटी जलधारा, 'the stream of water which fell from their eyes;' जासु कृपा सु दयालु, 'by whose gracious compassion;' प्राण ते अधिक राम प्रिय मोरे, '*Rám* is dearer than life to me.'

Omission of Ablative Post-position.

693. Even in prose the ablative postposition is often omitted. This idiom, however, is by no means everywhere admissible, but occurs chiefly with the ablative of *manner* or of *cause*, and, occasionally, with the ablative of *place*: as, इस रीति, or इस प्रकार, 'in this way;' सब कुशल क्षेम हैं, 'all are well;' गोपी चारों ओर घिर आईं, 'the milk-maids gathered around him from all four sides.'

a. But in poetry, as usual, the postposition is omitted much more freely; thus, पूछि लोगन्ह काह उछाहू, 'she asked the people, for what was the joy,' etc., etc.

Karke as an Ablative Sign.

694. As has been remarked (§ 173, *a*), the conjunctive participle करके, is sometimes used, instead of से, as an ablative postposition, in the sense of 'from' only. Often, करके can hardly be distinguished in meaning from से; e.g., पाप से रहित and पाप करके रहित, both mean 'free from sin.' But sometimes, when a distinction is intended, से denotes the *source*, and करके, the *means* or *instrument*, as in the following: जिस से और जिस करके .... शुभ अशुभ अपना कर्म होता है, 'from whom, and through whom, ... one's fate, good or evil, comes.'

The Genitive.

695. The genitive in Hindí expresses a very great variety of relations, which may be classified and illustrated as follows.

Genitive of Possession.

(1) It is used to denote *possession*: as, राजा का मंदिर, 'the king's palace;' मैं कंस की दासी हूं, 'I am the handmaid of *Kans*;' यह सब मेरे घोड़े हैं, 'all these are my horses.' So is to be explained the genitive in the following, depending on

क्या; इस का क्या बिगड़ता, 'what of this (fellow's) would have been harmed?'.

(2) Also *relationship*: as, मेरा पिता, 'my father;' उन की माएँ, 'their mothers;' ये भनजे कंस के दोउ, 'these are the two nephews of *Kans*.' Genitive of Relationship.

(3) And *material*: as, कंचन के मंदिर, 'temples of gold;' स्फटिक के चार फाटक, 'four gates of crystal;' मधुमाखियों का झुंड, 'a swarm of bees.' Here also I would place the phrase दिन की रात हो गई, *Angl.*, 'the day was turned into night;' and some reduplications with the genitive; as, दूध का दूध, lit., 'milk of milk;' i.e., *pure* milk. Genitive of Material.

(4) It often denotes *origin* or *source*: as, धूप की सुगंध, 'the fragrance of incense;' धनुष टूटने का शब्द, 'the noise of the breaking of the bow;' जन्म के भिखारी, 'beggars by birth.' Genitive of Origin.

(5) Also *cause* or *reason*: as, पंथ का हारा थका, 'weary and exhausted because of the way;' कपटी के मारने का कुछ दोष नहीं, 'there is nothing wrong in killing a deceiver;' ताप का सताया शरीर, 'a body oppressed by heat.' Genitive of Cause.

(6) And *place*: as, मथुरा की नारियां, 'the women of Mathurá;' देस देस के राजा, 'kings of various countries.' Genitive of Place.

(7) Also, the *age*: as, जब ऊषा सात बरस की भई, 'when *U'shá* became seven years old.' In this case the genitive is used predicatively. Genitive of Age.

(8) And *quality* or *kind*: as, अनेक प्रकार की बातें, 'a countless variety of things;' बड़े अचंभे की बात है, 'it is a matter of great wonder;' दस पंसेरी का बोझ, 'a load of ten *panserí* (100 lbs.).' Genitive of Quality.

a. Here may be noted the idiomatic use of the genitive of the infinitive or gerund, to denote a certainty, as determined by the will or nature of the agent. Thus, मैं जाने का नहीं, 'I will not go;' ऐसी बात नहीं होने की, 'such a thing is not to be.'

Rem. In this idiom, the genitive of the gerund is a predicative adjunct of the subject of the sentence, and is therefore inflected to agree with it in gender and number, as in the above examples.

Genitive of Use.

(9) It may indicate *use*: as, खाने का पदार्थ, 'provision for eating;' पीने का पानी, 'drinking-water;' यह देह किसी काम की नहीं, 'this body is of no use.'

Subjective Genitive.

(10) Or the *subject* of the action denoted by the word it qualifies.

Examples: बानासुर के भागने के समाचार, 'the news of the flight of *Bánásur*;' उस के जाने का कारण, 'the reason of his going;' बिलाव का पकड़ा चूहा, 'a mouse caught by a cat.'

Objective Genitive.

(11) And the *object* of an action, direct or indirect.

Examples: मैं तुम्हारे भरोसे पर रहा, 'I relied upon you;' मुझे डर किस का है, 'whom do I fear?' lit. 'fear of whom is to me?;' मेरे उबटन न मलना, 'do not rub *abṭan* upon me;' उस का बेटा महादेव जी की अति कठिन तपस्या करने लगा, 'his son began to perform a most difficult act of penance to *Mahádev Jí*;' अक्रूर ने प्रभु के चरन का ध्यान धर कहा, '*Akrúr*, fixing his contemplation on the feet of the lord, said;' इस अनूठ चरित के सुनने की अभी और अभिलाषा है, 'there is now more desire of hearing this extraordinary story;' परमेश्वर का पापी, 'a sinner against God.'

Rem. The same word may be accompanied either by the subjective or objective genitive, or even by both, as in the following: उन को मेरी दया कुछ न आई, 'they had no compassion upon me.'

Genitive of Price and Time.

(12) It is used of *price*: as, मुझे दस आने का आटा दो, 'give me ten *ánás* worth of flour;' यह कितने का घोड़ा है, 'what is the value of this horse?'.

(13) And *time*: as, आठ दिन की बात है, lit., 'it is a matter of eight days,' i.e., 'eight days ago;' किसी समय की बात है, 'it is a matter of a certain time;' *Angl.*, 'it once happened.'

Partitive Genitive.

(14) The *partitive* genitive is used when it is intended to denote anything as a *whole*, of which a part is taken.

Examples: सृष्टि का आरंभ, 'the beginning of the creation;' जमीन की चौथाई, 'one fourth of the land.'

a. Here may be classified many reduplicated forms denoting *intensity* or *totality*: as, यह सच का सच है, 'this is very truth;' मीठे का मीठा, 'very sweet,' lit., 'sweet of sweet;' सभा की सभा, 'the entire assembly;' झुंड के झुंड, 'swarms upon swarms,' lit., 'swarms of swarms.'

b. Observe, that when a generic term is accompanied by a noun denoting 'measure' or 'quality,' the partitive genitive is not employed, but the generic term follows the other in apposition with it: as, दो बीघा जमीन, 'two *bíghas* of land;' तीन सेर दूध, 'three *sers* of milk;' एक कटोरा पानी, 'a cup of water;' दो जोड़े कपड़े, 'two suits of clothes.'

(15) Many other combinations of nouns with the genitive might be noted: as, e.g., in *oaths*; thus, गंगा जी की कसम, 'by *Gangá Jí*;' in *interjectional* expressions; as, गंगा माई की जय, 'Victory to Mother Ganges:' in phrases denoting the *contents* of any thing: as, पानी का घड़ा, 'a jar of water,' etc., etc. But the above specifications comprise the most important idioms. Other Idioms with Genitive.

(16) The genitive is used before some adjectives; as, योग्य (जोग), and लाइक or लायक (*Ar.* لائق), 'worthy,' 'fit.' Genitive with Adjectives.

Examples: सिखाने के योग्य, 'fit to teach;' पानी के जोग है, 'it looks like rain;' चलने के लाइक, 'fit to walk;' and, in the *Rámáyan*, तोरिबे लायक, 'able to break;' स्वभाव की संकोचिनी, 'shy of disposition' *(fem.)*; (वह) शरीर की तौ कोमल है, 'she is tender, indeed, of body;' केवल तप के धनी, 'only rich in penance.'

696. In various common phrases in which the noun limited by the genitive can be readily understood, it may be omitted. The inflection of the genitive is determined by the noun which is to be understood. Ellipsis with Genitive.

This ellipsis of the noun is especially common with बात, 'a word,' and its equivalents.

Thus, the noun limited is regularly omitted after सुनना and मानना: as, मैं तेरी न सुनूंगा, 'I will not hear thee,' lit., 'thy,' *sc.* 'words' (*sc.* बात, 'word'); तुम मेरा क्यों नहीं मानते हो, 'why do you not regard my word?' (*sc.* बचन). So also in the following: क्या आप के मन में कुछ कहने को है, 'is there in your honour's mind something to say?' (*sc.* बात); दूसरे की तो क्या चलाई, 'what (thought) has he directed to another?' (*sc.* सुध); and, in the common phrase, घर के, lit., 'they of the house,' i.e., often, 'the wife.'

So also is to be explained the following common idiom; आप मेरे कहने का कुछ बुरा न मानें, 'may your honour take no word of mine amiss;' where बचन is to be understood after कुछ.

a. In such elliptical expressions the genitive itself may be treated as a *Tadbhava* noun in आ, and inflected to ओं for the oblique plural, as in the following: एक बार सब घर कों ने महाभारत की कथा सुनी थी, 'once all the house folk had listened to the story of the *Mahábhárat.*'

Inflected Gen. of Possession.

697. It is important to observe that के and the pronominal genitives in रे, are idiomatically used in many expressions denoting possession, where we might expect का or की, रा or री; उस के बहिन न हुई, 'he had no sister;' मेरे एक पुत्र जन्मा, 'one son was born to me;' टट्टू के भी जीव है, 'a pony, also, has a soul.'

a. The practical rule for the use of this idiom would seem to be this. Whenever, in English idiom, possession must be expressed by a verb, as, e.g., 'to have,' the Hindí genitive in ए must be used, whatever may be the gender of the following noun; but when, in English, the possessive case must be employed, then Hindí idiom demands the genitive with का, के, or की, according to § 695 (1). Thus, 'it is my son' must be rendered in Hindí, मेरा पुत्र है; but, 'I have a son,' मेरे पुत्र है. So also, टट्टू के जीव है, is 'a pony has a soul;' but, टट्टू का जीव है, would mean, 'it is the soul of a pony.' Thus, in the *Rámáyan*, नाथ एक संसय बड़ मोरे, 'Lord, I have one great doubt.'

b. But Hindoo authorities say that in cases where the number one is to be emphasized, the uninflected genitive must be used. Thus, 'I have a son,' is, मेरे पुत्र है; but, 'I have *one* son,' i.e., *one*, not two or more, मेरा एक पुत्र है.

Rem. It has been common to postulate some such word as *pás* or *yahán̤*, after this *ke*; but native grammarians deny that there is any ellipsis. Moreover it may be noted that in Máṛwáṛí, which inflects the genitive postposition, *ro* or *ko*, to *rá* and *ká* (obl. masc.), and *rí* and *kí* (fem.), *re* or *ke* is also used as a *third* inflection before both masc. and fem. nouns, when possession is denoted. I would suggest, therefore, that this *ke* of possession probably only chances to be identical in form with the obl. masc. inflection, *ke*; and, in fact, has arisen from another modification of the Sanskrit participle, *krita*.

698. The genitive postposition is very often omitted, even in prose, when the governing noun immediately follows. The two nouns then become, in fact, a Genitively Dependent Compound (§ 623, 5). In conversation, however, the omission is much less common. Omission of Genitive Postposition.

a. The postposition is often idiomatically omitted in such phrases as the following: सो मुंह मांगा धन पावेगा, 'he shall obtain the wealth his lips shall ask,' lit., 'the mouth's asked wealth;' हाथ लगी वस्तु, 'the acquired article.'

b. In phrases expressing a date, the genitive postpositions are always omitted; as, जेठ सुदी पंचमी, 'on the 5th of the light fortnight of *Jeṭh*.' The order is regularly the reverse of the English.

699. The genitive postposition is occasionally added to a verb or sentence, which is thus treated as a substantive. Thus, in the following, from *Madan Manjarí Náṭak*, the Genitive Postposition with Sentences.

words preceding का are regarded as a substantive, and put in the genitive of apposition, with शब्द; पकड़ो पकड़ो मारो मारो का शब्द, 'a sound of "Catch him! Catch him! Strike him! Strike him!"'

Gen. in Poetry. **700.** The genitive postpositions, का, कौ, कर, केर, etc., as used in poetry, are subject to the same rules as in prose. Thus, देवन हु कौ देव मुरारी, 'of the very gods, *Murári* is the God;' सुरपति की पूजा तजी, '(they) abandoned the worship of the ruler of the gods;' तीन लोक कौ बोझ ले, 'assuming the weight of the three worlds;' चरन कमल बंदौं सब केरे, 'I salute the lotus feet of all;' मिटही दोष दुख भवरजनी के, 'the sins and sorrows of the night of existence vanish;' न आजु लगि अनभल काहु क कीन्हि, 'nor has (he) to this day done harm to any one.'

a. In the following sentence from the *Rámáyan* we have a Márwárí possessive genitive in रे; सियरे बदन सूख गौ, 'the face of *Sítá* withered.'

The Locative Case.

701. The postpositions commonly assigned to the locative case, are (1) में, (2) पर, (3) तक, तलक, लग, लौं, etc. As they differ radically in their meaning, we treat them separately.

Locative with में: Place. **702.** (1) The locative with में denotes, primarily, existence *in* a place.

Examples: उस ने ब्रज में जन्म लिया, 'he became incarnate in Braj;' इस संसार में, 'in this world.'

a. After a verb of motion, में must be rendered by 'into,' or 'to.'

Examples: वह सभा में गये, 'he went into the assembly;' हस्तिनापुर में राजसु यज्ञ में आइये, 'come to *Hastinápur* to the royal sacrifice.'

b. This locative may often be rendered by '*among.*'

Examples: स्त्रियों में इतनी दमक कहां पाइये, 'among women where could so much beauty be found?'; हमों में कौन है, 'who is there among us?'.

c. And sometimes by '*at*:' as, पैरों में गिर पड़ा, 'he fell down at (her) feet;' आप के चरनों में प्रनाम करती हूं, 'at the feet of your Excellency I make (my) obeisance.'

d. The locative with में is used idiomatically after all verbs of '*tying*,' '*fastening*,' '*wearing*,' etc. Loc. in में with Verbs.

Examples: इस में गांठ बांधो, 'tie a knot in this;' गंदे कठले गले में डाले खेलते थे, 'with dirty wooden trinkets hung about the neck, they were playing.' Under this head fall certain idioms with लगना, 'to be attached,' etc.; as, न तौ प्रजा के उपकार में चित्त लगता है, 'neither does he attend to helping (his) subjects.'

e. It is also used with verbs of *filling*.

Thus, इस समुद्र में चिन्ता औ मोह रूपी जल भरा है, 'this ocean is filled with the water of anxiety and vain affection.'

(2) The locative with में naturally also expresses the *time within which* any thing happens. Loc. in में, of Time.

Examples: उन दिनों में, 'in those days;' कितने एक दिनों में पहुंचे, 'in several days they arrived.'.

(3) And it also expresses, tropically, various other relations, as follows: Misc. Uses of Loc. in में.

a. Difference; as, हम तुम में कुछ भेद नहीं, 'there is no difference between you and me.' It may thus follow verbs of *fighting*: as, उन दोनों में युद्ध रहा, 'a battle was waged between them;' or words expressing *union* or *reconciliation*: as, उन में मेल हुआ, 'harmony was made between them.'

b. Sphere of action; as, इस में मेरा कुछ बस नहीं, 'I have not any power in this (matter);' हाथ पैर तो कहने ही में नहीं हैं,

'hands (and) feet are not even to be spoken of,' lit., 'are not within speaking, even.'

c. Subject of discourse; as, उन की स्तुति में मैं क्या कहूं, 'what shall I say in his praise?'; and also, *occupation*; as, वह अपनी पति की सेवा में रही, 'she continued in the service of her husband.'

d. Condition; as, पति के ध्यान में सो गई, 'she went to sleep, thinking of her husband,' lit., 'in thought of her husband.'

e. Cause; as, अल्प ही अपराध में क्रोध कर, 'becoming angry for a very small offence.'

f. Instrument; as, उस ने एक ही तीर में इस अजगर का काम तमाम किया, 'he finished this serpent's work with a single arrow.'

g. It is often used in *comparison*, instead of the ablative:

As, इन तीनों देवताओं में शीघ्र वरदाता कौन है, 'of these three gods, who (most) quickly grants a blessing?'.

h. It is used after certain verbs to denote the *price*.

Examples: चार आने में कितनी घास मिलेगी, 'how much grass will one get for four *ánás*?'; यह गाए मैं ने तीस रुपए में मोल ली, 'I bought this cow for thirty rupees.'

i. It may even express the *object* of an affection, where English idiom requires 'for;'

As, मेरा भी इन वृक्षों में सहोदर का सा स्नेह हो गया है, 'my love also for these trees has become like that of an own sister.'

Rem. The distinction between the genitive, accusative, and locative of price, seems to be as follows. The genitive denotes value *absolutely*, as an attribute of the subject; as, *yah kitne ká hírá*, 'what is the value of this diamond?'; the *accusative* denotes the price *definitely*, as that for which a thing is obtained; as, *yah tum ne kitne ko liyá*, 'for how much did you get this?'; the locative denotes the price under a slightly different aspect, as a limit *within which* a thing is bought; as, *yah mujhe ek rupaye meṉ milá*, 'I got this for (lit., within) one rupee.'

k. The locative with में is sometimes used *partitively*;

As, नव महिं एकौ जिन्ह के होई, 'he who has even one of the nine.'

703. The locative with पर, 'on,' denotes (1) *external* Loc. in पर;
contact. Thus it expresses, of Place.

a. Position *on* or *upon* anything:

As, वह कोठी पर बैठा हुआ था, 'he was seated on the house.' Thus it regularly follows certain verbs; as, घोड़े पर चढ़ो, 'mount the horse.' After verbs it is often to be rendered by 'at,' or 'to;' as, वह द्वार पर खड़ा है, 'he is standing at the door;' उसी अंधे कूए पर गए, 'they went to that same blind well.'

b. Distance; as, काशी से कुछ दूर पर, 'at some distance from *Káshí*;' एक कोस पर, 'at (the distance of) one *kos*.'

c. Addition; as, दिन पर दिन तू दुबली होती जाती है, 'day by day you keep on growing thin.'

(2) It is used to denote the *time at which*: Loc. in पर; of Time.

As, वह ठीक समय पर आया, 'he came at the exact time;' पांचवें दिन पर, 'on the fifth day.'

(3) The locative with पर also denotes a variety of Misc. Uses of
tropical relations, as follows: Loc. in पर.

a. The *object* toward which an action or feeling is directed.

Examples: हम पर दया कीजे, 'be pleased to have mercy upon me;' इस बात पर मन लगाओ, 'apply your mind to this;' सिंहनी तुम पर दौड़ेगी, 'the lioness will rush upon you.'

b. Hence it denotes the *subject of discourse*, as the object to which discussion is directed.

Examples: षड्दर्शणां के मत पर सहस्रों ग्रन्थकर्त्ता हुए हैं, 'there have been thousands of commentators on the doctrines of the six systems;' इस पर यदि तुम कहो, 'as to this, if you say.'

c. It may express *conformity* to a rule or custom:

As, हम अपने धर्म्म पर रहेंगे, 'we will abide by our own religion.'

d. Also, *superiority*:

As, इन्द्र का कुछ तुम पर न बस आया, 'no power of *Indra* prevails over you.'

e. The *reason* of any action, as tropically its foundation:

As, मेरी इस बात पर वह जल गया, 'at this word of mine he fell into a passion.'

f. When followed by भी, 'also,' 'even,' the locative must often be rendered by 'notwithstanding,' lit., 'upon—even:'

Thus, इस दुर्बलता पर भी शरीर कैसा रमणीय है, 'notwithstanding this languor, how beautiful is (her) person.'

g. Very rarely, the locative is used for the ablative with a verb in the passive conjugation. Thus, in the *Rájníti,* मो पै चल्यौ नहीं जातु, 'I am not able to walk.'

Loc. of Limitation.

704. The locative forms with तक, तलक, लग, or लौं, all indicate, literally or tropically, the *limitation* of an action or a statement. There is no difference in the meaning of these postpositions.

Examples are: नाक तक पानी आया, 'the water came up to (his) nose;' लड़के से ले बूढ़े तक, 'from the child to the old man.'

a. Peculiar is the following phrase (*poet.*): हम लौं तू निज पियहि सम्हारे, 'thou mentionest thy own beloved even to us.'

705. The locative postpositions, में and पर, are often omitted in prose and in the colloquial. This omission occurs especially in certain adverbial phrases of time and place. Examples are: उस समय, for उस समय में (पर), 'in,' or 'at that time;' पाओं पड़ि, 'falling at (his) feet;' पूरे दिनों लड़का ऊआ, 'the days being fulfilled, a boy was (born);' वह घर गया, 'he went to the house;' मेरा मन इस के वस ऊआ, 'my heart has come into subjection to this (maiden);' उस का पिता घर नहीं है, 'her father is not at home;' मेरे ज्ञान यह हेतु होगा, 'in my opinion this must be the reason;' so, मेरे जाने, 'in my opinion.'

Omission of Loc. Post-position.

a. में is almost invariably omitted in the combinations of a noun and verb, commonly called 'Nominal verbs;' as, काम आना (for काम में आना), 'to be of use,' lit., 'to come in work;' व्याह करना, 'to marry;' व्याह देना, 'to give in marriage;' दृष्टि आना, 'to appear,' *Angl.* 'to come in sight.' तक and its equivalents are never omitted in prose.

706. When the above locative postpositions are employed in poetry, their usage corresponds to that already noted. A few examples will suffice.

Use of Loc. in Poetry.

(1) उपजहिं एक संग जल माहीं, 'they are produced in the water together;' ते उबरे तेहि काल महं, 'they remained safe in that time;' की तुम तीन देव महं कोऊ, 'are you one of the Three gods?'; राम प्रताप प्रगट इहिं माही, 'in this the glory of *Rám* is manifest;' सुमिरन कर में सुरत न हर में, 'the rosary in the hand, the thoughts not on *Hari*:' (2) कपि डार पर, 'the monkeys on the branches;' भले भलाई पै लहहिं, 'the good lay hold of goodness;' जो तुमहिं सुता पर नेह, 'if you have affection for (your) daughter:' (3) कहउं कहां लगि नाम बड़ाई, 'whereunto shall I declare the greatness of the name?'.

a. In poetry, however, these postpositions are more frequently omitted; but any attributive of the noun in the locative, if capable of inflection, must be inflected. Thus, in the following, माहि (में) is omitted: इहि कर नाम सुमिरि

संसारा, 'remembering the name of this One in the world;' है तुम्हरे सेवा बस राजा, 'the king is subject to your service.' And in the following, पर would have been used in prose: भयिउ सरोजबिपिन हिम राती, 'cold night was on the lotus-bed;' पठइय नाथ काज, 'send me, O lord, upon your service.' And in the following examples, prose usage would have demanded तक (or तलक, etc.): तीनि सहस्र संवत सो खाई, 'these she ate for three thousand years;' गगन चढ़ै रज, 'the pollen ascends to the sky.'

Postpositions Combined.

707. A noun in the locative, whether in poetry, prose, or the colloquial, in addition to its own proper postposition, may take that of another case. Each postposition retains in full its special meaning.

Examples are: हम में से कौन है, 'who of us is there?', lit., 'from among us;' पुर में का एक मनुष्य, 'a man belonging to the town;' कोई राजसभा में तें निकस्यो, 'some one went out from the court;' दिल्ली की गद्दी पर से अहमद शाह को उठाया, 'he removed Ahmad Sháh from the throne of Delhi,' lit., 'from on the throne;' अंगूठी मिल जाने तक का वृत्तान्त, 'the story as far as the finding (of) the ring;' अपने शिष्यों तक को न सिखाय, 'he does not teach so much as his own disciples.' Two postpositions are commonly used after verbs of *falling*, with the noun denoting that from which one falls; as, उस डाली पर से गिरा, 'he fell off that branch.'

a. In Máṛwáṛí, the accusative postposition, नै (= H.H. को), is also in like manner sometimes added to माहि (= H.H. में), when it becomes, literally, 'into.' Thus, in '*Dúngar Singh*,' कूद पड़ो किलाके माहीनै, 'jump into the fort.'

Postpositions with several Nouns.

708. Before leaving the cases which are formed with postpositions, it is to be noted with regard to them all, that, inasmuch as the postpositions still partake more of the nature of the prepositions than of true case-endings, when several nouns follow one another in the same case and construction, the postposition proper to them all is used only after the last. Thus, राजा भीमसेन की कन्या दमयन्ती का रूप, 'the beauty of *Damayantí*, the daughter of Rájá *Bhím Sen*;' फल फूल कंद मूल से गुजारा करने लगा, 'he began to live on fruits, flowers, bulbs, and roots.' But the postposition is repeated with both nouns or pronouns when they are to be taken severally; thus, नंद जसोदा से हम ने तुम ने यह बचन किया था, 'you and I each made this promise to *Nand* and *Jasodá*.'

Of the Vocative.

709. The vocative is used in calling or address, either with or without an interjection. **Use of Vocative.**

Examples: हे बेटे, 'O son!'; सखियो सुनो, 'Companions! hear;' पुत्री ऐसी विकल मत हो, 'Daughter! be not so distressed;' सारथी रथ को हांको, 'Charioteer! drive on the chariot.'

a. Certain words in आई, often make the vocative in इया; as, e.g., from भाई, 'brother,' माई, 'mother,' vocative singular, भाइया, भैया. In Garhwál, ओ is often similarly added to proper names; as, हे पंचमो, 'O *Pancham*!', etc.

b. In poetry, the writer often addresses himself by name in the vocative. Thus, मंगलकरनी कलमलहरनी तुलसी कथा रघुनाथ की, lit., 'joy-inspiring, *Kali-yug*-impurity-removing, O *Tulsí*, is the story of *Raghunáth*!'; तुलसी ऐसे पतित को बार बार धिरकार, '*Tulsí*! to such a sinner, again and again a curse!'.

Adjectives.

710. Little needs to be said here as to the construction of adjectives in the sentence. They may define a noun either (1) *attributively*, or (2) *predicatively*. **Attributive and Predicative Adjectives.**

Examples are, of (1): बड़ा नगर, 'a large town;' मीठी बाणी, 'a sweet voice;' बड़े घोड़े, 'large horses;' and of (2):

वह अति सुन्दर थी, 'she was very beautiful;' यह जल ठंडा है, 'this water is cold;' मैं ने उस को व्याकुल देखा, 'I saw that he was distressed;' यह लाठी सीधी बनी है, 'this staff is made straight.'

a. The rules which govern the agreement of the attributive or predicative adjective with the noun qualified, will be found further on, in the section on 'Agreement.'

Subst. Use of Adjectives.

711. Adjectives are often used as nouns, in which case they are inflected like nouns of the same terminations.

Thus, बड़ों के समय से, 'from the time of the ancients' (lit., 'of the great'); किसी ज्ञानी ने कहा है, 'some wise (man) has said;' समरथ कहं नहिं दोष गुसाईं, 'there is no blame to the powerful, *Gusáīṉ* !'. So also are used as nouns the adjectives formed by the addition of सरीखा to an inflected base (§ 202); as, उस सरीखे को मत मानो, 'do not mind the like of him.'

a. When two adjectives used as plural nouns, and connected by a copulative conjunction, follow one another in the same case, the first may take the singular, and the second only, the plural form; as in the phrase, छोटे वो बड़ों ने कहा, 'small and great said.'

Adjectives as Adverbs.

712. A few adjectives are also in frequent use as adverbs. When so used they are never inflected.

Most common is the use of बड़ा, 'great,' and बहुत, 'much,' in the sense of 'very:' as, यह बड़ा कठोर है, 'this is very hard;' वह तो बहुत सुन्दर पद है, 'that is truly a very beautiful word.'

Comparison of Adjectives.

713. *Comparison* has been explained and illustrated, §§ 207, 210. It may be noted in addition, that a very high degree of any quality may be expressed by repeating the adjective; as, काला काला, 'very black,' मीठे मीठे फल, 'very sweet fruits.'

a. Or, for greater emphasis, the first adjective may be taken as a noun in the ablative or genitive; as, भारी से भारी पाप, 'the very greatest sins;' i.e., 'heavier than the heavy;' उत्तम से उत्तम वस्तु, 'the very best thing:' अच्छे से अच्छे काम, 'the very best works.'

b. The common idiom found in the following sentence is to be noted: दोनों पापों में कौन सा बड़ा है, 'of the two sins which is the greater?'.

714. Agreeably to § 691 (7), all adjectives used comparatively, require the noun with which the comparison is made, to be in the ablative.

Thus, पत्थर से भारी, 'heavier than stone;' राजा से धनी, 'richer than a king;' सब जीवों से श्रेष्ठ, 'the noblest of living creatures;' यह उस से उत्तम है, 'this is superior to that.'

715. Certain adjectives require a noun in an oblique case. Thus, especially, Adjectives Governing Nouns.

(1) Adjectives denoting *advantage* or *fitness*, or their contraries, govern a noun in the ablative.

Thus, स्त्री को उचित है, 'it is proper for a woman;' हम को योग्य है, 'it is right for us.' (Vid. § 686 (4).) But योग्य sometimes takes the noun in the genitive; as, पानी के योग्य है, 'it looks like rain.'

(2) Adjectives denoting *likeness*, *conformity*, *worthiness*, or the contrary, commonly take a noun in the inflected genitive.

Thus, बादल के गरज के समान, 'like the thunder from the cloud;' इस के तुल्य, 'equal to this.' So also, योग्य (Urdú لائق, often written लायक), in the sense of 'worthy,' takes the genitive; as, यह पंडित के योग्य है, 'this is worthy of a wise man.'

a. When such adjectives are preceded by any infinitive or

gerund, the postposition, especially in poetry, is often omitted, and the gerund stands alone in the oblique singular. Thus, तुम मेरे पुत्रनि कौं पंडित करबे जोग हौ, 'you are competent to make my sons wise men;' मैं तव दसन तोरिबे लायक, 'I am able to break your teeth.'

(3) A few verbal adjectives expressing desire or affection, take an objective genitive (§ 695, 11); as, रुपयों का लोभी, 'covetous of money;' वह धन का लालची है, 'he is covetous of wealth.'

Adjective Affixes.

716. The adjective भर, 'full,' is never used by itself; but partakes rather of the character of an affix, like the English 'full,' in such phrases as a 'spoonful,' a 'house-full,' etc. But भर is used much more extensively than the corresponding English '-full.' Any noun taking this affix is regularly inflected before it, as before the postpositions, whenever inflection is possible.

Examples: पियाले भर, 'a cup-full;' हांडी भर, 'a jar-full.' भर is used also with nouns of distance, as, कोस भर, 'as much as a *kos*;' and with expressions denoting time, as, दिन भर, 'the whole day;' मेरे जीवन भर, 'all my life long;' and with the pronominal adjectives, इतना, उतना, etc., when it has an intensive force; as, जितना उस ने मुझे दिया उतना भर मैं उसे फिर देऊंगा, 'I will give him back just as much as he gave me.'

a. When भर is added to a feminine noun, the compound becomes masculine; thus, उसे रात भर जागते बीता है, 'he passed the whole night long, waking,' lit., 'to him the whole night,' etc.

Rem. In examples like the last but one, where the noun or adjective with *bhar* is not inflected, *bhar* may be more correctly regarded as the conjunctive participle of *bharná*, 'to fill.'

717. Adjective formations with the affixes सा and सरीखा have been already explained and illustrated, §§ 201, 202.

718. The common idiom should be noted here in which the noun नाम, 'name,' following a proper noun, is used adjectively.

Examples: यह गन्धर्वों का हेमकूट नाम पर्वत है, 'this is the mountain of the *Gandharvas* called *Hemakúṭ*;' कल्याणकटक नगर में भैरव नाम व्याध था, 'in the city of *Kalyánkaṭak* (was) a hunter named *Bhairav*.' In this idiom the word नाम with the preceding word is really a Dependent Compound.*

NUMERALS.

719. एक, 'one,' may be used for the English indefinite *Use of Cardinals.*
article (§ 165), in cases where that article is equivalent to the phrase 'a certain.'

Examples: एक पुरुष ने मुझ से कहा, 'a (certain) man said to me;' एक दिन की बात है, 'a certain day it happened,' lit., 'it is the thing of a (certain) day.'

Rem. It should be observed, that most Europeans use *ek* for the indefinite article much too freely. In the majority of cases, it should not be translated into Hindí.

720. एक when repeated in the same clause and construction, is equivalent to 'each,' or 'each one.' But when the first एक is in the subjective construction, and the other in the objective, the first must then be rendered 'one,' and the second, 'another.'

Examples of both cases are as follows: एक एक चला गया, 'each one went away;' उस ने एक एक को वहां पहुंचा दिया,

---

* Vid. supr., § 630, *a*.

'he conveyed each one there;' एक एक से लड़ा, 'one fought with another;' एक एक से जुट गया, 'each one was joined to another.' So also when repeated in successive clauses, the first एक may be translated 'one,' the second, 'another;' as, एक आता एक जाता था, 'one was coming, another going.'

721. एक is often used elliptically in the beginning of a sentence; as, एक तुम्हारे ही दुख से हम दुखी हैं, 'one (thing is), I am troubled because of your trouble.' If the enumeration is continued, the ordinal दूसरा may follow in the next sentence; but even more frequently फिर or पुनि, 'again,' introduces the second particular in the enumeration; as, एक मैं मन्दमति .... पुनि प्रभु मोहि बिसारेउ, 'one (thing is), I am of a dull mind; again, the lord forgot me.'

722. एक संग or एक साथ is rendered 'together.' Thus, जनमे एक संग सब भाई, 'all the brothers were born together;' सिंह गाय एक साथ रहते, 'the lion and cow would dwell together.' In this idiom, संग or साथ is to be regarded as a noun in the locative, with the postposition omitted.

723. For the use of the singular and plural form of nouns with numerals, see § 674 (1) *a*, *Rem.*

724. Colloquially, a numeral with the postposition तक is used as equivalent to the English 'as much as,' 'as many as.' This phrase may be treated as a nominative plural; as, दस तक आए, 'as many as ten came;' मैं ने चार हाथी तक देखे, 'I saw as many as four elephants.'

Use of Aggregatives. **725.** The *Aggregative* form of the numerals in ओं (§ 223), is used when it is designed to indicate the noun as a collective whole.

Examples occur in the common phrases, आठों पहर, 'the eight watches;' चऊं दिस, 'the four quarters (of the heavens);' तीनों लोक, 'the three worlds.' Similarly, सो छओं बसुदेव को ब्याह दीं, 'he gave those six in marriage to *Basudev*.'

Pronouns.

726. A Personal pronoun, when the subject of a verb, is very commonly omitted. Omission of Pronouns.

a. This omission is generally allowable when no emphasis is intended, and when it can occasion no ambiguity; as, e.g., in direct address; as, आओ, 'go;' *sc.* तुम; बोलूं, 'may (I) speak?'.

727. Pronouns are to be regarded as of the same gender and number with the nouns to which they refer. Agreement of Pronouns.

Thus, राजकन्यां जो भौमासुर ने घेर रखी थीं, 'princesses whom *Bhaumásur* had kept captive;' वह हमारी भक्ति का प्रभाव महर्षी से कहेगी, 'she (*Shakuntalá*) will tell the great sage the greatness of my piety.'

a. But when it is intended to show respect, the pronoun is put in the plural, even when referring to a singular noun.

Thus, तहां के राजा .... इन्हें ले जाते थे, 'the kings of that place would convey him along,' where इन्हें refers to *Balrám.* And in the following, उन्हों refers to *Krishn*; हम उन्हों का ध्यान किये रहते हैं, 'we remain in meditation upon him alone.'

b. The use of the plural for the singular of the 2nd personal pronouns, has already been explained (§ 259).

c. The use of the plural for the singular of the 1st personal pronoun, 'I,' is characteristic rather of eastern Hindí than western. The usage in High Hindí is not regarded by the best authorities as in good taste, and it is doubtless safer for the speaker to use the singular, Still we often find examples in the best literature of the use of *ham* for the singular; nor is it easy to trace any principle which guides the choice. In the *Shakuntalá*, for instance, examples of this usage occur on almost every page.

728. Usually, when a pronoun is followed by दोनों, 'both,' 'the two,' in an oblique case, referring to the same person or thing it is put in the oblique plural, and the postposition is added only after दोनों; as, हम दोनों का, 'of us two;' तुम दोनों से, 'from both of you.' But exceptionally the plural form is used before दोनों in the genitive; as, तुम्हारी दोनों की परस्पर प्रीति, 'the mutual love of you two.'

Honorific Pronoun.

729. The use of the Honorific pronoun आप, for the 2nd personal pronoun, has been explained in § 277.

730. The usage of the various pronouns referred to in the above paragraphs cannot, in the nature of the case, be adequately illustrated by individual phrases separated from their context. But we may note such passages as the following. *Shakuntalá*, when Rájá *Dushyant* imputes deceit to her, suddenly leaves the आप with which she had been addressing him, and says, तू अपना सा कुटिल हृदय सब का जानता है, 'thou thinkest every one have a deceitful heart like thine own.' But again, when in the *Prem Ságar* one girl says to another, सखी तू कुछ चिंता मत करे, 'friend, do not thou be anxious,' in this instance तू indicates affectionate familiarity. So the court jester, *Mádhavya*, with no intention of contempt, addresses Rájá *Dushyant* in the singular as on equality with him, अहो मित्र तू यहाँ है, 'O! friend! art thou here?'. So it is in keeping with the liberty accorded him as jester, that he uses to the king the 2nd personal pronoun instead of the honorific आप, thus; रानी तुम्हारे सुनाने को अभ्यास कर रही है, 'the queen is practising to make you hear.' A man says to his brother, in the 2nd plural, तुम्हारे साथ पासा खेलें, 'let us play dice with you;' but a son to his father, आप इतना बतला दीजे, 'please inform me so much as this;' and *Balrám* and others to *Krishn*; आप की आज्ञा ले, 'obtaining your honour's permission.'

731. आप, as the subject of a verb, regularly requires the verb to be in the 3rd plural; and if the imperative be used, the respectful form in इये or इयेगा, is invariably required. Exceptions are irregular, and are not to be imitated.

The following examples may be noted: आप कहां जाते हैं, 'where is your honour going?'; महाराज ऐसे आप ने क्या चिन्ह देखे, 'Great king! what such signs has your Excellency seen?'; आप सिधारिये, 'be pleased to depart.' Similarly, all other predicates of आप must be in the plural; as, कन्व इस के पिता ऐसे कहाते हैं, '*Kanva* is in this way called the father of this (maiden).'

a. Rájá Lachhman Siṇh, however, in his translation of the *Shakuntalá*, frequently associates आप with a verb in the 2nd plural; as, आप अगलों की रीति पर चलते हो, 'Your Highness observes the custom of the ancients,' *et passim.* But the foreigner will not safely imitate this laxity of usage.

Rem. In the opinion of the Hindoos, the distinctions which are made in the use of the pronouns, are of great importance; and the foreigner cannot be too careful to observe them in conversation with the people. Indeed, a failure to discriminate, in the use of these different pronominal forms, is often the occasion of much unnecessary dislike and ill feeling on the part of natives of India toward foreign residents of the country.

732. The choice between the two forms of the dative and accusative, which occur in the singular and plural of the pronouns, is regulated to a great extent by euphonic considerations. But in accordance with the principles indicated in § 678 (1), the forms with को are preferred for personal objects. Pronom. Dat. and Acc.

a. But if a dative and accusative both occur in the same simple sentence, the form with को is apparently preferred for the accusative, and that in ए (plur. एं), for the dative.

733. The ablative singular of the proximate demonstrative, यह, is often idiomatically used to introduce a clause expressing a consequence or conclusion; as, इस से अब तुम तीरथ न्हाय आओ, 'do you therefore come when you have bathed at a sacred place.' Idioms with Dem. Pronouns.

734. When यह and वह occur in contrasted clauses, यह may often be rendered 'the one,' and वह, 'the other.' Thus,

ये धरे बनमाल वे मुंडमाल, 'the one wears a necklace of flowers, the other, a necklace of skulls;' and so repeatedly in the context.

Adjective use of Pronouns.

735. The demonstrative, relative, and interrogative may be used adjectively before not only single nouns, but also entire phrases.

Thus, यह हमें बड़ा पाप भुगतना पड़ा, 'this expiating of a great sin has fallen to us;' तैं ने यह क्या किया जो छोरी लोक लाज कान आपनी, 'what is this that you have done, to abandon your family, and shame, and modesty?;' हे समुद्र तू जो लंबी सांस लेता है सो क्या तुझे किसी का वियोग है, 'O ocean! art thou parted from some (loved) one, that thou heavest the long-drawn sigh?.'

a. Hence जो is used to introduce the *protasis* of causal and conditional clauses; and सो, less frequently, the *apodosis*. So also, the relative जो, especially in the locative, जिस में, and ablative, जिस तें or जिस से, is used to introduce final clauses denoting the object or purpose of an action. Illustrations of the above will be found further on, in the sections on adjective and causal adverbial clauses.

Pleonastic use of Pronouns.

736. The demonstratives are sometimes used with the correlative, or with nouns, pleonastically.

Thus, सो हे प्राणप्यारी यह तेरे मिलने को तरसता है, lit., 'that same, O thou, dear as my life, this one is longing to meet thee;' कोटवाल जी तौ वे आते हैं, 'the Chief of Police is coming, to be sure!' In some such cases, the pronoun may slightly emphasize that to which it refers.

Attraction of Pronouns.

737. The relative and interrogative pronouns are often used, by *attraction*, for the indefinite pronoun.

Thus, जो कोई इस से जाकर जो मांगता है, 'whatever any one goes and asks of this (one) that he obtains;' क्या जानिये कि

किस समय क्या करे, 'who knows what he may do at some time?'

a. In poetry, this attraction is often extended to a great length, as in the following: मति कीरति गति भूति भलाई जब जेहि जतन जहां जेहि पाई, 'whoever, at any time, by any effort, in any place, has obtained intelligence, renown, felicity, wealth, prosperity.'

738. जो is often used, especially in the colloquial, pleonastically, with है, 'is;' thus, परमेश्वर जो है सो सर्वशक्तिमान है, where in English idiom we would simply say, 'God is almighty.'

739. The distinction between the two interrogatives, कौन and क्या, and that between the two indefinite pronouns, कोई and कुछ, has been already explained (§§ 274, 275). Use of Interrogative Pronouns.

a. In the oblique singular, कौन से takes the place of किस, when used adjectively before impersonal substantives; as, कौन से राजवंश के भूषण हो, 'of what royal family are you the ornament?'

b. The following idiom with कौन may be noted; हम छुड़ानेवाले कौन हैं, 'who am I, that I should deliver (you)?'

740. The usage of कौन in the plural varies. The Urdú oblique plural form, किन, is used; as, किन लोगों का, 'of what people?' But the common people often use the uninflected singular in the oblique plural; as, कौन लोग से, 'from what people?'

741. क्या is used as both nominative and accusative; the oblique form in को is appropriated to the dative.

Thus, तुम क्या बोलते हो, 'what are you saying?'; but, तुम काहे को बोलते हो, 'why (for what object) are you speaking?'.

a. The ablative of क्या is used commonly for 'why,' in the sense of 'from what cause;' as, सत्य है काहे से कि इन नैनों को नित्य महाराज का दर्शन मिलता है, 'true! (and) why? because your Majesty is ever before these eyes.'

b. क्या is used idiomatically in expressions denoting surprise.

Examples: देखती क्या है कि एक पुरुष सन्मुख आय खड़ा हुआ, 'what does she see (but) that a man has come and stands before her;' घोड़े दौड़े क्या हैं उड़ आए हैं, 'the horses have run—(why!) they have come flying.'

c. क्या is sometimes used absolutely in the accusative, as in the following:

इस के मारने से परलोक क्या बिगड़ेगा, 'from killing this girl, what harm for the life to come?'. Hence it is often used merely as the sign of a question; as, क्या तू ने अब तक नहीं सुना, 'hast thou not yet heard?'. The dialectic किं is also similarly employed (§ 298).

d. For the use of क्या as a conjunction, see § 662, *c*.

e. The postposition is sometimes omitted after काहे; thus, तू काहे रोवति है, 'why art thou crying?'.

Use of Indefinite Pronouns.

742. In further illustration of the distinction between the two indefinite pronouns कोई and कुछ (§ 275), the following points may be noted.

a. कुछ is often used as a plural for कोई.

Thus, 'some book has fallen,' is कोई पुस्तक गिरी है; but, 'some books have fallen,' is कुछ पुस्तकें गिरी हैं. Other examples are: कुछ दिन इस आश्रम की रक्षा करो, 'for some days protect this hermitage;' कुछ स्त्रियों का सा बोल, 'a voice as of some women.'

b. When कोई is used substantively, the inflected form, किसी को, is commonly preferred for the accusative; but when it is used adjectively, if the accompanying noun be in the nominative form of the accusative, कोई also retains the nominative form, as in the following: अपने रहने को कोई ठौर रखोगे, 'will you keep any place for your residence?'.

c. कोई is used with numerals to denote a number approximately, like 'some' in English; as, कोई दस आदमी आए, 'some ten men came.'

d. With proper names, कोई must be translated 'a certain;' as, कोई ऊधो आया, 'a certain *U'dho* (has) come.'

e. कुछ is used adjectively before substantives in any case singular or plural: as, कुछ दूर पर, 'at some distance;' कुछ गाओं में, 'in some villages,' etc.

f. कोई and कुछ in successive clauses must be translated 'one' . . . . 'another:' thus, कोई कुछ कहता था कोई कुछ, 'one was saying one thing, (and) another, another;' thus, किसी को पानी बरसाय बहाया किसी को आग बरसाय जलाया, 'raining water, one he washed away; raining fire, another he burned (to death).'

g. कुछ is added to the relative pronominal, जैसा, 'as (whatlike),' to impart indefiniteness; as, जैसा कुछ हो, 'of whatsoever sort it may be.'

h. कुछ is sometimes used where English requires an adverbial phrase; as, प्रसन्न होने का कुछ यह भी कारण है, 'this, at any rate, is in some measure a reason for being pleased.'

743. The *Reflexive* pronoun, आप, may be used with both nouns and pronouns, when it is equivalent to the English 'self,' 'myself,' 'yourself,' 'himself,' etc., according to the context. Use of Reflexive Pronoun.

Thus, मैं अपने को खिला सकता हूं, 'I am able to feed myself;' वह आप कहता है, 'he himself says.' The ablative, आप से, is often to be translated 'of one's own accord:' कुत्ता आप से चला गया, 'the dog went away of his own accord,' or 'of himself;'

and so, likewise, the fuller expression, आप से आप; thus, तुम्हारे हृदय में आप से आप उत्पन्न हुआ है, 'in your heart it has spontaneously sprung up.'

a. In the following, the plural, आपस में, refers to the persons mentioned in the context; आपस में दुख की चरचा चली, in English idiom, 'they talked with each other of the sorrow.'

b. In the following, अपन is accusative singular; हेतु अपन पुनि जानि, 'regarding himself, again, as the cause (of *Rám's* exile).'

c. The reflexive is repeated in the phrase, अपने आप, 'of myself, himself, itself,' etc. (sc. से): as, क्या यह अपने आप झुका है, 'has this bent of itself?'; also in the idiomatic phrase, अपने आप में होना, lit. 'to be in one's self,' i.e., 'in one's right mind;' as, जिस समय यह शाप हुआ मैं अपने आप में न हूंगी, 'when this curse fell, I must not have been in my right mind.'

d. आप ही आप is used for the English phrase 'to one's self;' as, तू क्या आप ही आप कह रही है, 'what art thou saying to thyself?'. So, by itself, it is used in the drama for the English 'aside,' where it is evidently an abbreviation for आप ही आप से कहता है.

744. The reflexive genitive, अपना, must always be substituted in High Hindí for the genitive, singular or plural, of all pronouns, when the genitive in question refers to the grammatical *subject* of the sentence, or to the *agent* in the passive or impersonal construction (§ 412).

Examples:—तुम अपनी बड़ाई चाहते हो, 'you desire your own greatness;' राजा अपने देश को गये, 'the king went to his own country;' उस ने अपनी जान दी, 'he gave his life.'

a. अपना may also be used when the reference is not to the grammatical subject, but to the *subject* of *discourse*. Thus, अपनी बड़ाई सभी को भाती है, 'to every one, one's own exaltation is pleasing;' इसे अपनी भी सुध नहीं है, 'she has not a thought even of herself;' जिस में अपनी कुशल होय सो कीजे, 'be pleased to do that wherein your safety lies.'

b. अपना is also sometimes employed, when the reference is to the *speaker*; as, अवध अपना देश है, '*Avadh* is my country.' So also when another is associated with the speaker; as, यह सब अपने दिनों का फेर है, 'all this is the change of our times.'

Rem. But in the examples under *a* and *b*, the genitive of the personal pronouns might also have been used; and *must*, in general, be used in such cases, where the use of the reflexive would occasion ambiguity.

c. अपना is used absolutely in such a phrase as the following: अपना दुख है, अपना सुख है, where it is equivalent to हर एक का, 'every one has his own sorrow, every one has his own joy.'

d. अपना, as well as the other pronominal genitives, is idiomatically omitted when the reference is obvious; as, especially, before nouns expressing relationship. Thus, वह स्त्री पति के निकट जाय बोली, 'that woman, approaching (her) husband, said;' मैं घर जाता हूं, 'I am going to (my) house.'

e. अपना is used substantively in the plural, to denote one's own kindred or connexions; as, जो तू अपनों ही को मारेगा, 'if you will kill even your own (friends).'

745. The pronominal इतना is idiomatically used in the locative case with में in expressions denoting 'time,' 'place,' 'price,' etc., as in the following: **Use of Pronominals.**

इतने में क्या हुआ, 'in the meantime what happened?'; इतने जून आऊंगा, 'I will come at this same hour;' तुम्हें इतने में मिलेगा, 'you will get (it) for so much.'

a. इतना and उतना are idiomatically combined in the sense of 'a trifle,' 'a little more or less;' thus, इतने उतने की कुछ परवा नहीं, 'such small matters are of no consequence.'

746. जितना is also used in expressions of time in the same manner as इतना, above. In the following the postposition is omitted: दूसरा आदमी न मिलेगा जितने, 'for so long as I shall not find another man.' जितने में also sometimes has the sense 'inasmuch as.' जितना, preceded by चाहे, is equivalent to the indefinite expression, 'however much' or 'many;' thus, मेरे रनवास में चाहे जितनी रानी हों, 'however many queens I may have in my *zanána.*'

747. The oblique singular pronominals, ऐसे, वैसे, जैसे, तैसे, कैसे, are often used adverbially, and are to be rendered, 'as,' 'so,' 'how.'

Thus, महादेव के कोप की कुछ आंच तझ में ऐसे बनी है जैसे समुद्र में बड़वानल, 'some heat of the fire of *Mahádev's* wrath in thee is become like the submarine fire in the ocean.'

748. ऐसे and जैसे are also colloquially used in the manner of prepositions governing the genitive, in the sense of 'like.'

Thus, कुछ किला के ऐसे दिखाई देता है, 'something like a fort appears;' वह क्या तोप के जैसे सुनाई देता है, 'what is that which sounds like a cannon?'.

749. ऐसे में (and sometimes ऐसों में), is used, after the analogy of इतने में, above, to denote an accompanying circumstance; thus, ऐसे में कठिन धूप कैसे सहेगी, 'in such a condition how wilt thou endure the severe heat?'.

750. ऐसा is sometimes repeated with an indefinite sense; thus, ऐसे ऐसों को मैं समझता क्या हूं, 'what do I understand of anything of this kind?'. ऐसा, combined with वैसा or तैसा, has a disparaging sense which may be variously rendered in English; as, मैं क्या ऐसा वैसा हूं जो दबूं, 'am I one of so little account that I should be crushed?'; ऐसी वैसी बात हो जाएगी, '(if) anything go wrong;' तुम्हारे घर के सब ऐसे वैसे हो जाएं, 'may all of your house go to the bad!'; कोई ऐसा तैसा यां आवे, 'shall such a fellow come here!'.

751. वैसे is sometimes very idiomatically used to describe an object as in its original or ordinary condition; as, वैसे तो

छूने से ठंडी लगती है, 'under its ordinary condition, indeed, (the crystal) feels cold to the touch.' The interrogative pronominal, कैसा, is used in exclamatory expressions, like the English 'how;' thus, आम के पत्ते कैसे हिलते हैं, 'how the leaves of the mango-tree are shaking!'.

752. कैसा is idiomatically used with the indefinite pronoun, कोई, to emphasize the indefiniteness; as, कोई कैसा ही आवे, 'whatsoever sort of person may come.' Sometimes in such expressions the interrogative pronominal adverb क्यों and the negative are combined with कैसा, as in the following: वह कैसा क्यों न हो, 'whatever manner of person he may be;' lit., 'what-like (or) after what manner he may not be.' Sometimes indefiniteness is also expressed with कैसा alone; as स्त्री कैसी ही सुशीलता से रहे, 'with however much virtue a woman may behave.'

Syntax of the Verb.

The Infinitive.

753. The uses of the *Infinitive* may be classified under three heads.

(1) It is most commonly used as a *gerund* or *verbal noun*. Under this head we may note the following particulars. Infinitive as a Verbal Noun.

a. As a *nominative*, it often stands as the subject of a verb: as, e.g., हमें यहां रहना भला नहीं, 'it is not well for us to remain here,' lit. 'for us to remain here is not well;' मैं ने तुम्हारा कहना मान लिया था, 'I (on the former occasion) believed your word.' It is also used idiomatically as a predicate, expressing certain futurition; as, इस अच्छे सगुन का क्या फल होना है, lit. 'of this good omen what is to be the result?'.

b. In accordance with the original use of the Sanskrit future passive participle, whence the Hindí infinitive is derived, it is often used as a subject with the copula, to express *necessity* or *obligation*; as, मनुष्य को मरना है, 'man must die;' तपस्वियों के आश्रम में नम्रता से जाना कहा है, 'it is said (that) one is to enter the retreat of ascetics with humility.'* So it is used as the subject with पड़ना, 'to fall,' expressing *necessity*; as, अब उन के पास जाना पड़ा, 'now I must go to them,' lit., 'it has fallen (to me) to go to them.'

c. Sometimes it expresses certain futurition, as in *a.*, above, where it is used as a predicate nominative: इस अच्छे सगुन से क्या फल होना है, 'what is to be the fruit of this good omen?'.

d. As an accusative, the infinitive is commonly used in the nominative form; as, तुम राम नाम कहना छोड़ दो, 'cease to speak the name of *Rám*!'.

Rem. But in Permissive, Acquisitive, and sometimes in Desiderative Compound verbs, the infinitive in its inflected form, without the postposition, is practically used as an accusative. Examples will be found in §§ 436, 439, 440, and, further on, in the Section on the Syntax of Compound Verbs.

e. The postposition को, of the *dative* of the final cause (§ 686, (5)), is very commonly omitted; as, हम आप से कुछ मांगने आए हैं, 'I have come to ask something from you;' स्त्रियां न्हान आईं, 'the women came to bathe.' So also the genitive postposition is often omitted from the infinitive before certain adjectives, as, लाइक, योग्य, etc., especially in dialectic Hindí; as, e.g., राजा हिरन्यगर्भ के गुन प्रीति करिवे जोग हैं, 'the virtues of the Rájá *Hiranyagarbha* are worthy to be esteemed;' मैं तव दसन तोरिवे लायक, 'I am able to break thy teeth.'

f. The *dative* of the infinitive, as remarked § 686, (5), *b.*, is idiomatically used with the substantive verb, to denote an action as *imminent*. Thus, जब वह चलने को उठा था, 'when

---

* In the Bhojpúrí, Mágadhí, and Maithilí dialects this form in न is only used in this sense. Grierson: *Seven Grammars*; Part i., p. 27.

he was about to go;' वह गहिबे कों भई, 'she was about to clasp (him).' In this idiom को must always be used, as also in phrases like the following; दुर्योधन ने द्रौपदि को जांघ पर बैठने को कहा, '*Duryodhan* told *Draupadi* to sit on his lap.'

g. Occasionally, an action or event about to happen, is also denoted by the infinitive with पर. Thus, जब पांच बरस बीतने पर आए, 'when five years were drawing to a close;' वह अस्त होने पर है, 'he is about to set.'

h. The *genitive* of the infinitive is often used, chiefly in negative clauses, as the predicate of a sentence, to express *certainty* or *resolution*; as, मैं नहीं कहने का, 'I certainly will not tell.' In this idiom, the का of the genitive must be inflected to agree in gender and number with the subject; as, e.g., यह स्त्री नहीं जाने की, 'this woman certainly is not going.' In the *Rámáyan* the same idiom occurs, the postposition, however, being omitted; as, भे न भाइ अहहिं न होने, 'he neither has been, nor, brother, is he, nor will he be.' The same idiom occurs in the following, where the emphatic particle उ or ऊ is added to the infinitive: एन्ह सम कोउ .... है नहिं कतहुं होनेऊ नाहीं, 'like these .... none are, nor even ever are to be;' भयउ न है कोउ होनेउ नाहीं, 'like you, none was, nor is, nor even is to be.'

i. The inflected infinitive without the postposition is used in regimen with certain adjectives; as, यह क्षत्री के ब्याहने योग्य होगी, 'this (maiden) must be worthy to be wedded to a *Kshatri*.'

k. While thus used as a noun, the infinitive may also govern the case proper to it as a verb. Of this, the examples already given, afford abundant illustration.

(2) The infinitive is occasionally used *adjectively*, and is then made to agree with its object in gender and number. **Infinitive as Adjective.**

Thus, स्त्री को पति की सेवा करनी योग्य है, 'a woman is bound to serve her husband;' मुझे ये डाभ ब्राह्मणों को देने हैं, 'I must give this *Kusa* grass to the Brahmans,' where डाभ is plural, as referring to several bundles of grass; जो कुछ कहनी न कहनी बात मेरे मुख से निकली हों, 'whatever word (fit) to be said (or) not (fit) to be said, may have escaped my lips.' In this case, the infinitive preserves unchanged its original sense as a future passive participle.

Infinitive for Imperative.

(3) The infinitive is correctly used for the *imperative*, when it is not intended to insist on the immediate fulfilment of the order, but merely to say that a certain thing *is to be done*.

Thus, (*P. S.* Ch. XLVIII.,) *Jasodá* says to *U'dho* about to go to *Krishṇ*, यह तो तुम श्री कृष्ण बलराम प्यारे को देना, 'this, then, you are to give to dear *Shrí Krishṇ* and *Balrám*.' It is therefore often used when it is intended to speak deferentially, as in *Shakuntalá*, by the hermit maidens to *Rájá Dushyant*; कभी फिर भी दर्शन देना (sc. हमें), 'let us see you yet again some time;' or again, प्रथम मिलाप को भूल मत जाना, 'do not forget the first meeting.'

Rem. This use of the infinitive for the imperative is derived from its original character as the Sanskrit fut. pass. participle.

The Imperfect and Perfect Participles.

754. The essential distinction between these two participles has been already indicated (§ 383*), and will receive abundant illustration from the examples in the following sections. As there is no difference in their use, they are conveniently treated together.

Adjective use of Participles.

(1) They are used *adjectively* with nouns and pronouns, both in the *attributive* and the *predicative* construction. In this case the participle हुआ or भया, of the substantive verb, duly inflected if necessary, is

regularly added to the participle. But when there is no danger of ambiguity, this may be omitted.

a. Examples of the *attributive* use of these participles are as follows: आप को गई प्रतीति मुझ पर आई, 'the lost confidence in me came (back) to your Majesty;' कोई दुष्ट मरा हुआ काला नाग तुम्हारे पिता के कंठ पर डाल गया है, 'some evil person has cast a dead black snake upon your father's neck;' तुम ने दान की हुई गाए फिर दान की, 'a cow already given as alms, you gave in alms again.'

b. In the following examples these participles are used adjectively in the *predicative* construction: तिन के पीछे एक शूद्र मारता आता है, 'a *Shúdra*, beating them, follows;' जरासिंध भी यों कहता हुआ उन के पीछे दौड़ा, '*Jarásindh* also, thus speaking (as he went), ran after them;' जो मैं जीती जाऊंगी, 'if I escape alive;' क्या तैं ने अर्जुन को दूर गया जाना, 'did you suppose *Arjun* to be gone far away?'. So may be explained फूला, 'swollen,' in the common idiom, फूला न समाना; as, मैं अपने तन में फूला नहीं समाता हूं, 'I am not able to contain myself (for joy).' Similarly, in the *Rámáyan*: यह मोहि मांगे देऊ, 'give me this which I have asked,' lit., 'give this to me having asked;' सो मुख कोटिहिं न परै कही, 'that with ten million mouths could not be told,' lit., 'fall told;' चरन परत नृप राम निहारे, '*Rám* beheld the king falling at (her) feet.'

c. Usually, when the noun qualified takes को in the singular or plural, a predicative participle remains uninflected, whatever be the gender or number of the noun; thus, उन दोनों को लड़ता देखि, 'seeing them both fighting.'

d. Under this head are properly explained the so-called Continuative Compound verbs (§ 442). Thus, e.g., in वह स्त्री गाती रही, 'that woman remained singing,' it is plain that the imperfect participle, गाती, is simply a predicative adjunct of the noun स्त्री after रही. The same remark applies to analogous combinations with the perfect participle; as, e.g, in वह भागा जाता था, 'he was fleeing away,' where भागा is a predicative adjunct of वह.

e. Here may also be noted the common phrase, होता चला आना, where both होता and चला are predicative adjuncts; as, e.g., यह परंपरा से होता चला आया है, 'this has come along down from the olden time.' In this, as in the similar phrase, होता चला जाना, होता represents the action as continuously occurring during the time indicated.

Participles Absolute.

(2) The perfect and imperfect participles are very often used *absolutely* in the inflected masculine form, to denote various circumstances of time, manner, etc., accompanying the leading verb.

Examples: अरुण को सारथी किये उदय हुआ चाहता है, 'with the dawn as his charioteer, (the sun) is about to rise;' सिर झुकाये रथ को फिर फिर देखता चौकड़ भरता है, 'with head bent, again and again looking at the chariot, he bounds along;' दर्शन पीछे हुए मनोरथ पहले ही हो गया, 'the desire which came *after* beholding (you) even before (that) was fulfilled.'

a. The so-called '*Adverbial participle*' is but an imperfect participle absolute with the emphatic ही. Thus, तेरी मा तुझे जनते ही मरी थी, 'thy mother died immediately upon giving thee birth.' The perfect participle is, much more rarely, used in the same way; as, रूप देखे ही बन आवे, 'having actually seen (her) beauty (description) may succeed;' गयेऊ मज्जन न पाया, 'even having gone, he could not bathe.' Where another ही has just preceded, the ही may be omitted from the participle; as, विरह का गीत ही सुनते, 'on merely hearing a song of separation;' यह मुझे निगले जाता है, lit., 'this (serpent) is going, having swallowed me,' i.e., 'he is devouring me;' कृष्ण साथ रहते हम क्या डरें, '*Krishn* remaining with (us), what should we fear?'.

b. The perfect participle absolute, लिये, of लेना, 'to take,' is often equivalent to the English preposition 'with;' as, कोई

ब्राह्मण कांख में पोथी लिये आता है, 'some Brahman, with a book under his arm, is coming;' or to some English phrase; as, मेरे धनुष बाण को लिये रहो, 'stay in charge of my bow and arrow.'

c. The perfect participle absolute is especially common in expressions which denote 'time elapsed;' as, पांच बरस हुए वह चला गया, 'five years ago, he went away;' कितने एक दिन बीते राजा फिर गये, 'several days having passed, the king went again.' Very idiomatic is the following: तुम को देस से आए कितने बरस हुए, 'how many years has it been since you came from (your) country?'

d. In these participles absolute, in eastern Hindí, संते* is often used for होते; as, यह अशक्य संते, 'this being impossible.' In the following, संते is redundant: इस देह को त्याग करत संते, 'in leaving this body;' विधवा भए संते पुत्रों के अधीन रहे, 'having become a widow, let her remain subject to her sons.'

e. These participles absolute are even more common in poetry than in prose. Thus, जिअत न करब सवतिसेवकाई, 'while I live, I will not serve a rival wife;' कटत सीस नृप पौतृक तर्यौ, 'king *Pautrik*, on his head being cut off, obtained salvation;' तासु बचन सुनिते सब डरीं, 'on hearing her word, all feared;' तुम तौ . . . धरे देह जनु रामसनेहू, 'you are, indeed, love to *Rám*, as it were, incarnate.'

f. In archaic poetry, the perfect participle absolute is often used where modern Hindí would have the conjunctive participle. Thus, गये भवन पूछहिं पितामाता, 'having gone home, they asked their parents;' यथा नवहिं बुध विद्या पाये, 'as bow the wise, having received knowledge.' And so *Chand*, (as quoted by Mr. Beames); वसि किये भूमियां धूमि खग्ग, 'having subdued the rulers of the land with fire and sword.'

* For the Sanskrit सति, pres. part. loc. absol. of अस्, 'to be.' Vid. Monier-Williams' *Sanskrit Grammar*, § 840.

Rem. It will often be impossible to express in English idiom the distinction between the participle absolute and the predicative participle, and often it is a matter of little consequence which is used. But the distinction appears to be as follows. In the predicative construction the participle describes or defines the *subject* of the verb; in the absolute construction it defines after the manner of an adverb, the *verb* itself. Thus, *wah rotá huá chalá játá thá*, 'he was going along weeping;' but, *wah rote hue chalá játá thá*, is rather, 'he was going along tearfully.'

Emphatic Participles in Compound Forms? (3) The inflected perfect participle is seemingly substituted for the root in Intensive Compounds, with the effect of throwing a special emphasis on the leading verb. This emphasis can scarcely be expressed in English otherwise than by an inflection of the voice.

Examples of this idiom constantly occur in the *Shakuntalá*. Thus, इस लता को क्यों छोड़े जाती है, 'why art thou *leaving* this vine?'; इस सगुन के भरोसे पर मैं कहे देती हूं, 'in the confidence of this omen, I *assure* (thee).

Rem. 1. While the perfect participle in this idiom has the form of the inflected singular, it may perhaps be doubted whether this is more than a coincidence. The form has probably arisen by the elision of ही and *sandhi* of concurrent vowels, from the combination of the emphatic particle ही with the uninflected participle; or, possibly, with the root of the Intensive form; so that, e.g., कहे देता हूं is either for कहा ही देता हूं or कह ही देता हूं.

Rem 2. It will be evident from the above examples that in the so-called Statical compound verb (§ 445), we have simply an imperfect participle absolute in construction with a finite verb.

Subst. use of Participles. (4) In the fourth place, both these participles are often used gerundially as *substantives*, both with and without the postpositions.

Examples: उस सोते का पलंग उठाय, 'lifting the bedstead of the sleeper;' मेरे गये का सोग, 'grief at my departure;' मेरा कहा मानिये, 'obey my word;' सूरज डूबते समय, 'at the time of sunset;' उस के पूछे तें क्या प्रयोजन, 'what is the use of having asked him?'; (तू) अपनी विवाहिता को छोड़ते नहीं लजाता, 'thou art not ashamed of forsaking thy married (wife);' (रातें) सेज पर करवटें लेते कटती हैं, 'the nights are spent in tossing on the bed;' अपने त्याग हुए पर भी, 'notwithstanding her abandonment.'

a. As substantives, these participles are often construed with a preposition: as, ऐसे पाहुने को बिना सत्कार किये छोड़कर, 'leaving such a guest without having shown (him) hospitality;' तुम्हारे बिना सींचे, 'without having watered you;' बैरी के आए पीछे, 'after an enemy has come,' or 'after the advent of an enemy.'

b. The substantive use of these participles is also common in poetry. Thus: सुकृत जाय अस कहत तुम्हारे, 'may your merit perish, for your speaking thus;' रहत न प्रभु चित चूक किये की, 'the defects of (our) work remain not in the mind of the Lord;' देह धरे कर यह फल, 'this is the fruit of having assumed a body.' So is to be explained a common idiom of the imperfect participle with the verb बनना, 'to be made;' thus, भरतमुख बनै न उत्तर देत, lit., 'from the mouth of *Bharat* no reply is made,' i.e., '*Bharat* could frame no reply.'

Rem. In many cases it is impossible to distinguish this substantive use of the participle from the participle absolute. Thus, in the following, *muyai* may be explained in either way: *muyai karai ká sudhá taḍágá*, 'when dead' (or 'to a dead man') 'what avails a lake of nectar?.' In some instances also the true explanation may be that we have not a participle before us, but the verbal noun in *á*, mentioned § 386, *b*.

The Conjunctive Participle.

755. The chief uses of the *Conjunctive* participle may be classified as follows.

(1) It is used to denote an action as merely *preliminary* or *introductory* to the action of the leading verb. Preliminary Participle.

a. As thus employed it is very commonly used where English would have the copulative conjunction. It is, indeed, always idiomatically preferred to the conjunction, except when the two clauses are distinctly of co-ordinate importance. Thus we say, **पाठशाला को जाकर पढ़ा करता है**, 'he goes to school and reads,' because the first verb is merely preliminary to the action of the second. But, again, we must use the conjunction in the following: **वह पढ़ता और लिखता है**, 'he reads and writes,' because the two actions are co-ordinate. Other examples of the preliminary use of the participle are as follows: **वहां जाकर उस से कहो**, 'go and tell him,' lit., 'having gone, tell him;' **कोई भोजन बनाय जिमाए**, 'one would prepare food, and give him to eat;' **वह राजर्षि यज्ञ पूरा करा कर हस्तिनापुर को बिदा हुआ है**, 'that royal sage, having effected the completion of the sacrifice, has departed to *Hastinápur*;' **यह कह कर अन्तर्धान हो गये**, 'saying this, he vanished.'

b. In rendering such English phrases as 'go and see,' 'did you go and call him,' where the leading verb is preceded by the verb 'to go,' Hindí idiom often reverses the English. Thus, 'go and see' may indeed be rendered **जाके देखो**; but also, with a slightly different shade of meaning, **देखि आओ**, lit., 'having seen, come;' **वह ब्राह्मण को बुलाय आया**, 'he has gone and called a Brahman,' lit., 'has come, having called a Brahman.'

Rem. **In this idiom, the participle formed with the affix *i* or *y*, is commonly preferred to that with the affix *kar* or *ke*.**

c. **It is well to note here the distinction between the conjunctive participle, and the perfect and imperfect participles absolute. The conjunctive participle represents the action without any reference to its progress; the two participles absolute add each their own characteristic idea, denoting the action as in progress or completed. Thus, *wah kapṛe pahinke báhar áyá*, is 'having dressed he came out;' *kapṛe pahine báhar áyá*, is 'he came out dressed;' and *kapṛe pahinte báhar áyá*, 'he came out dressing,' i.e. 'in the act of dressing.' But English idiom is often incapable of expressing the distinction between the conjunctive participle and the perfect participle absolute; and, as remarked, § 754 (2) *f*, in old Hindí, the perfect participle often takes the place of the conjunctive.**

(2) By a natural transition, the conjunctive participle, from denoting simple antecedence, comes also to express the *cause* of the action of the leading verb. **Participle of Causation.**

Examples: बाणासुर अति भय खाय भाग गया, '*Báṇásur*, greatly fearing, fled away;' नगर को जलता देख सब यदुबंसी भय खाय पुकारे, 'seeing the city burning, all the family of *Yadu* cried out with fear.'

a. It should be observed, that although the causal relation may thus be expressed by the conjunctive participle, yet when it is intended to give prominence to the causal relation, it is expressed by some tense of the verb in a subordinate clause. Thus, without such emphasis, we may say, यह मनुष्य अति अपवित्र हो नष्ट हो जायगा, 'this man, being very unholy, will perish;' but if we wish to make the cause more prominent, we must say, यह मनुष्य जो अति अपवित्र है नष्ट हो जायगा, 'since this man is very unholy, etc.;' or, again, यह मनुष्य नष्ट हो जायगा क्योंकि अति अपवित्र है, 'this man will perish, because he is very unholy.'

(3) The conjunctive participle may also denote the *means* by which an action is effected. **Participle of Means.**

a. This usage is especially common with करके. Thus, इस पवित्र आश्रम के दर्शन करके हम अपना जन्म सुफल करें, 'let me make my birth fruitful of good by visiting this holy hermitage.'

(4) It sometimes has a *concessive* force. **Concessive Participle.**

a. This is especially the case with the conjunctive participle होकर, etc., of होना, 'to be;' thus, तिस को देख सुन बड़े बड़े मुनीश होकर उठे, 'hearing and seeing him, great and mighty sages though they were, they arose;' ऐसे सूर हो स्त्री पर शस्त्र करो, 'being such a brave, do you raise a weapon against a woman?'.

(5) It is constantly used to express various circumstances accompanying the action of the leading verb. **Circumstantial Participle.**

a. In this *modal* sense, it may often be best rendered into English by an adverb of manner, or by some equivalent phrase. Examples are as follows: उस ने हंसकर कहा, 'he laughingly said;' चित दे सुनो, 'listen attentively!', lit., 'giving attention, hear!'; वह क्रोध कर बोल उठा, 'he spoke up angrily;' तुम ने महा अधर्म्म जानके कियो, 'you have knowingly committed a great wrong.'

b. Under this specification may be noted various idiomatic uses of करके, etc., conjunctive participle of करना, 'to do' or 'make.' Thus, वे दोनों ब्राह्मण मेरी मेरी कर झगड़ने लगे, 'those two Brahmans, crying *Mine*! *Mine*! began to quarrel;' आत्मा अपने को उन के साथ एक करके समझता है, 'the soul regards itself as one with these;' तुम हरि को पुत्र कर मत जानो, 'do not regard *Hari* as a son.' कर or करके is thus often added to nouns so as to give them an adverbial force; as, कृपा करके यह तो कहो, 'now kindly tell me this.' Similarly, it is added to some pronominals: as, रात की बात सब कर सुनाता हूं, 'I am going to tell you in full the affair of the night;' and to numerals, when repeated, as, एक एक कर गिनियो, 'please count (them) one by one.'

c. The conjunctive participle of होना, 'to be,' is sometimes equivalent to 'as,' in such phrases as the following: मैं ब्रह्मा हो बनाता हूं विष्णु हो पालता हूं शिव हो संहारता हूं, 'as *Brahmá* I create, as *Vishṇu*, preserve, as *Shiv*, destroy.' With a word denoting place, it is equivalent to *viá*, 'by way of,' 'through;' as, मेरी जीवनमूल यहीं होकर गई है, 'the Root of my life has gone through just this place.'

Special Idioms with Conj. Participle.

756. The conjunctive participle बढ़कर, is sometimes used as an *adjective*; thus, इस से बढ़कर नहीं है, 'there is none superior to this.'

757. Occasionally, certain conjunctive participles have a *prepositional* force. Thus, e.g., very often, बढ़के, in combination with आगे, as, वह गांव इस से थोड़ा आगे बढ़के है, 'that village is a little beyond this;' also, होके, छोड़के, and many other participles: as, वह पुरवा सड़क से कुछ हटके है, 'that hamlet is somewhat off the road;' इस को छोड़के और कोई नहीं है, 'there is no other besides this;' जिस जिस देश में हो प्रभु जाते थे, 'through whatever country the lord was passing;' यह गाय रुपये ले नहीं दी जाती है, 'that cow is not given for money;' उस ने पियाला भरके दिया, 'he gave him a cupful.'

a. The conjunctive participle, कर or करके, of करना, 'to make,' is especially common in this prepositional sense; as, बल करि हीन, 'deprived of strength;' जिस करके, 'through, or by means of, which,' etc. Very idiomatic is the use of करके in the following: एक पांच तत्त्व करके मृत्यु है, '(there) is one death, pertaining to the five elements,' i.e., 'there is one death, of the body.'*

b. The conjunctive participle, मिलके, 'having met,' must sometimes be rendered 'with,' or 'together.' Thus, ज्ञान ध्यान मिलके बिसरायी, 'he caused them to forget both knowledge and contemplation;' दोनों मिलके गये, 'both went together.'

758. Ordinarily, as in most of the above examples, the conjunctive participle refers to the subject of the leading verb, or, in the passive construction of the perfect tenses (§ 412), to the agent. But sometimes it may refer, instead, to the subject of discourse. Thus, रानी को कुछ सोच समझकर धीरज आया, 'the queen, somewhat reflecting and understanding, became composed.' This is especially frequent in poetry; as, बंधु निधन सुन उपजा क्रोधा, 'hearing of the death of (his) brother, (his) wrath arose.' Sometimes the conjunctive participle refers to the (unnamed) agent of the action of a verb in the passive conjugation: thus, मारके तू निकाला गया, 'thou wast cast out by beating;' वह खोदके जीती निकाली गई, 'she was, by digging, taken out alive.' This idiom is often heard in the colloquial.

Reference of Conj. Participle.

* The Hindoos believe the body to be composed of the five elements, viz., 'earth,' 'fire,' 'air,' 'ether,' and 'water;' and suppose death to consist in the dissolution of these elements.

Diff. Forms of Conj. Participle.

759. There is no difference in meaning between the different forms of the conjunctive participle. The forms in *kar* and *ke* are the most modern, and are preferably employed in modern High Hindí. But in a long succession of participles, where the repetition would be disagreeable, the root-form is often preferred. When two participles of similar meaning follow each other with no word intervening, *kar* or *ke* can be used only after the last: as, *ján bújh kar*, 'knowing;' *soch samajh kar*, 'reflecting and understanding;' *khá pí kar*, 'eating and drinking.' So also when the participle immediately precedes the leading verb, as in certain *quasi* compounds, § 431, the root-form is usually employed: as, *wah uṭh dháyá*, 'he arose and ran;' *Káshí ho áyá hai*, 'he has come by way of Benares.'

760. By means of a series of conjunctive participles, a sentence may be idiomatically sustained to a great length, without any danger of obscurity; thus, वहां से उठ उग्रसेन के पास आय सब समाचार सुनाय उन से बिदा हो बाहर आय बरात की सब सामा मंगवाय मंगवाय इकट्ठी करने लगे, 'rising thence, going to *Ugrasen*, and telling all the news, taking leave of him and going out, they began, sending hither and thither, to gather all the supplies for the marriage procession.'

The Noun of Agency.

Construction of Noun of Agency.

761. With the verbal Noun of Agency in वाला or हारा, the object of the action is most frequently put in the genitive, but occasionally it is made in the accusative, with or without को.

Examples: ऐसे काम का करनेवाला, 'the doer of such a deed;' पापी लोगों का तारनहारा, 'the Saviour of sinners;' प्रेम करनेवाला, 'one who exercises love;' प्रजा को दुख देनेवाला, 'a troubler of the people;' वह गीत गानेवाला है, 'he is a singer of hymns;' मुझे कौन रोकनेवाला है, 'who is there that will hinder me?'; ये ही बात मेरे मन को बढ़ानेवाली है, '*this* word is encouraging to my heart.'

Rem. Native grammarians deny that in such phrases as the third, fourth, and fifth above given, the noun is to be regarded as an accusative. They say that there is *samása*, 'union,' of the noun and verb; so that

the object of the verbal action and the noun of agency, are to be regarded as forming a genitively dependent compound. But this explanation will evidently not apply to the last three illustrations.

b. In many instances the Noun of Agency is a compendious idiomatic equivalent of some English phrase, as in the following: **जाने को आज्ञा देनेवाली तुम कौन हो**, 'who are you, to be ordering me to go?'.

762. As the predicate of a sentence after the substantive verb, the Noun of Agency is often nearly equivalent to a future participle. Thus, **वह यहां से जानेवाला है**, 'he is about to go from here.' So also in other constructions; as, **पिता कन्व हस्तिनापुर के जानेवालों को आज्ञा दे रहे हैं**, 'Father *Kanva* is giving orders to those who are to go to *Hastinápur*.' **Noun of Agency as Fut. Participle.**

Of the Tenses.

763. As already shown (§§ 395, 396), the tenses of the Hindí verb are properly distributed under three heads, as follows: (1) the tenses denoting *future* action; (2) those denoting action as *imperfect* or *incomplete*; (3) those denoting action as *perfect* or *completed*. For a brief statement of the distinction between the several tenses of each group, the student may refer to §§ 397–408. The statements made in those paragraphs, it is believed, will be justified by the illustrations of the use of the several tenses which will be found in the following sections. We begin with the tenses of the *future*. **Tenses Classified.**

The Contingent Future.

764. The Contingent future, in modern High Hindí, denotes a future action as conditioned or contingent. We may specify the following cases.

Conting. Fut. as Potential.

(1) It is used, in simple sentences, to express a *possibility*.

Thus, **कोई कहे**, 'some one may say;' **तुम सहित गिरि तें गिरौं**, 'with you I could drop from a mountain.'

Conting. Fut. in Conditional Clauses.

(2) It may thus express *liberty* or *permission*.

Thus, **आज्ञा हो तो हम घर जांय**, 'if permission be given, then we may go home;' **मार तो डालूं**, 'I might, indeed, kill (her);' and in questions, as, **मैं जाऊं**, 'may I go?'; **हम यहां रहें**, 'may we remain here?'.

(3) It is used in the *protasis* of conditional clauses, when the condition is not regarded as an objective reality, but only as a *possibility*. Also, similarly, it is employed in the *apodosis* of conditional clauses, whenever the conclusion is only affirmed as *possible*.

Thus, in the *protasis*, we have, **जो तुम उस को एक बेर देखो तो फिर ऐसी न कहोगे**, 'if you once see her, then you will not again say such a (thing);' and, in both *protasis* and *apodosis*, **इसी के समान बर मिले तो दें**, '(if) a husband be found (who is) her equal, then we may give (her).'

(4) Similarly, the contingent future is required in *relative* clauses implying a condition, when the condition is merely supposed to exist.

Thus, **मन क्रम बचन कपट तजि जो कर भूसुरसेव**, 'whoever, abandoning deceit, in heart, deed, and word, serves the lords of the earth (i.e., Brahmans).'

Conting. Fut. in Final Clauses.

(5) Hence, again, it is used (*a*) in all *final* clauses denoting *purpose*, and (*b*) in all clauses denoting *result*, when that result is regarded not as a reality, but merely a future possibility.

Thus, under (*a*), **इस बात की चर्चा हम ने इस लिये की है कि... उस का शंका दूर हो जावे**, 'I have mentioned this thing that ... his doubt may be removed;' and, under (*b*), **मुझे ऐसे बची**

कीजे कि कोई मुझे न जीत सके, 'make me so powerful that no one may be able to overcome me;' **ऐसे उपाय करो जिस से वह राजर्षि फिर मिले**, 'contrive some plan by which I may again meet that royal sage.'

(6) It is thus sometimes used in other cases to express an *intention*.

Examples: **जो मैं आज आप से न मिलूं तो आग में जल मरूं**, 'if I be not united with you to-day, then I will burn myself to death;' **जो हम हारें तो तुम्हारे दास होकर रहें**, 'if I am beaten, then I will remain with you as a slave;' **मैं तुझे क्या मारूं**, 'why should I kill thee?'.

Conting. Fut. of Uncertainty.

(7) It must be used in all interrogative phrases relating to the future, which imply *uncertainty* or *perplexity*.

Thus, **हम इस लड़की को किस को दें**, 'to whom shall we give this girl?'; **हम क्या करें**, 'what shall we do?'.

(8) It must be used to denote a future action or event, when the time of its occurrence or continuance is regarded as *indefinite*.

Examples: **जब यह ध्वजा आप से गिरे तब मेरे पास आइयो**, 'whenever this banner shall fall of itself, then come to me;' **जब हम पुकारें तब उत्तर दो**, 'when we call, then answer (us);' **जब तक मैं यहां रहूं**, 'so long as I remain here.'

Conting. Fut. as Optative.

(9) It is used to express a *wish*.

Examples: **किसी दिन मैं आप अपने को न भूल जाऊं**, 'may I not some day forget my own self;' **पावउं मैं तिन्ह करि गति घोरा**, 'may I obtain their fearful fate;' **मोहि संकर देउ**, 'may *Sankar* (i.e., *Shiv*) give me.'

(10) It is thus sometimes used, in the 2nd singular, as a mild *imperative*.

Examples: **तू हमारे चरन मत परसे**, 'do not thou touch our feet;' **मो सों कपट करे जिन पियारी**, 'do not deceive me, beloved!'.

Conting. Fut. in Comparison.

(11) It is used in *comparisons*, denoting that with which the comparison is made, not as an objective reality, but merely as a supposed case.

Examples: बलदेव जी का क्रोध यों बढ़ा जैसे पून्यौ को समुद्र की तुरंग बढ़े, 'the wrath of *Baldev* swelled, as will swell the tide of the sea at full moon;' यों चीर डाला कि जैसे कोई दातन चीर डाले, 'he split him, as one might split a tooth-stick.'

Concessive Conting. Fut.

(12) It may express a *concession*.

Examples: स्त्री अपने पति से जितना कष्ट पावे, 'however much ill-treatment a woman may experience from her husband;' कवि न होउं न चतुर कहाउं, '(though) I be not a poet, nor be called clever.'

Conting. Fut. expressing Duty, etc.

(13) It is employed to express *propriety* or *duty*; and after clauses expressing 'fitness,' 'unfitness,' etc.

Examples: फिर उस को यह भी दिखावे, 'again, it should show him this also;' तुम को कब योग्य है कि बन में बसो, 'when (i.e., how) is it befitting you that you should live in the wilderness?'.

Conting. Fut. in Ellipsis.

(14) The 3rd singular of this tense in a few verbs is used by itself elliptically.

This usage is especially common with जानना and चाहना; thus, तुम्हारे मन में जाने क्या सोच है, 'in your mind (who) knows what thought (there is)?'. The full phrase here would be क्या जाने, 'what can one know,' constantly used in the colloquial. Sometimes the 2nd plural of चाहना is used in the same way; as, अब चाहो सो हो, 'now come what may,' lit., 'now (what) you may wish let that be.'

765. It is important to observe that the accurate discrimination which has appropriated the contingent future almost exclusively to the indication of *contingent* futurition, belongs only to the most modern development of the language. In old Hindí, as, e.g., in the *Rámáyan*, the forms denote not only contingency, but also the certain futurition of an action, and even, as previously remarked, an action in the present. The proverbs of the language afford abundant illustration of the use of this tense in its original character (§ 601) as a present. Thus, e.g., *háth ko háth pahcháne*, 'the hand knows the hand.' Other illustrations from High Hindí will be found in the section on the syntax of the present imperfect.

The Imperative.

766. The Imperative needs little illustration. We may observe,

(1) It is the only tense ordinarily admissible in command and prohibition.

N.B. The future cannot be substituted for the imperative. 'Thou shalt not steal,' in Hindí is *tú chorí na kar*; *chorí na karegá*, would be, 'wilt not steal.'

Use of Negative with Imperative.

(2) In prohibition, न or मत may often be indifferently used. But when the phrase consists only of the imperative and the negative, मत is preferred to न; thus, मत जाओ, 'do not go;' मत दौड़ियो, 'please do not run.' नहीं, as containing the present of the substantive verb (§ 472), cannot be used with the imperative.

(3) The use of the singular and plural forms of the imperative is determined by the pronominal form which is used, or by the degree of respect which it is desired to express. The ordinary form of command to an inferior is the 2nd person plural; as, सारथी घोड़ों को रोको, 'Charioteer! stop the horses!'. The sing. often indicates contempt.

Hortative Imperative.

(4) To the 1st and 3rd persons of the imperative are to be assigned all hortatory phrases.

a. But it is to be noted that whenever the English 'let,' means 'to allow' or 'to permit,' not the imperative, but the permissive compound must be used. Thus, 'let us go,' in the hortatory sense, is हम जाय (or जायें); but if it mean, 'permit us to go,' we must render the phrase, हम को जाने दो.

b. Further examples of the use of the imperative are as follows: शकुन्तला से भी पूछ, 'ask (thou) *Shakuntalá* also;' तुम तो यादवों को मारो, 'do you then destroy the *Yádavs*;' हम भी बैठें, 'let us too sit down;' अब थोड़े से और बीन लें, 'let us now pluck a few more;' तेरे मन की दुख परिहरौं, 'let me remove the sorrow of thy heart.' Poetic examples are: पावक महं करउ निवासू, 'make your abode in the fire;' सो जानब सतसंग प्रभाऊ, 'know, (that it was) in virtue of good association;' ताहि बोइ तू फूल, 'sow thou for him flowers.'

The Respectful Forms of the Imperative.

Use of the Prec. Forms.

767. Of the two Respectful or Precative forms of the Imperative, in यो and ये, the latter is the more respectful. The form in यो is properly used only to equals and inferiors; that in ये, to equals and superiors, but never to inferiors. The less frequent form in येगा does not differ from that in ये.

Thus, in the *Prem Ságar*, *Satraját* says to his wife, तू किसू के सौंहीं मत कहियो, 'do not mention (it) before any one;' and *Krishṇa* to his companions, तुम दस दिन तक यहां रहियो, 'remain here for ten days;' and the Sun-god to *Satraját*, इस को मेरे समान जानियो, 'regard this (person) as equal to me.' But the cowherds say to *Krishṇa*, इस महा भयावनी गुफा में आप भी न आइये, 'into this great (and) dreadful cave neither let your honor enter;' again, to *Krishṇa*, मुझे दास समझकर कृपा रखियेगा, 'regarding me as your servant, be pleased to have mercy;' करिय न संसय अस उर आनी, '(by) raising such questions in your heart, cherish no doubt.' Yet, in the *Shakuntalá*, *Shakuntalá* uses the form in यो to her foster-father, *Kanva*; thus, पिता इस लता को मेरे ही समान गिनियो, 'Father, please count this vine as my very self.'

a. In the following, the respectful form is used in the 1st plural, in a hortative sense: देखिय कपि कहां कर आही, 'let us' (or 'me') 'see the monkey, of what place he is.'

768. Forms outwardly identical with these respectful forms, are often used, especially in poetry, for the contingent future, and even for the present. Thus, जो मर जाइये तो संसार के दुख से छूटिये, 'if one die, then he is released from the sorrow of the world;' बायस पालिय अति अनुरागा, '(though) one bring up a crow with extreme affection;' जाइय बिनु बोलेऊ न संदेहा, 'though you should go even without having been called, there is no apprehension.' In the following, the जे form is used in the 1st singular of the contingent future; as, इस लिये मैं आया हूं कि अपने भाइयों को ले जाय माता को दीजे, 'I have come here for this (purpose) that I may take away my brothers, and give (them) to (my) mother.' Similar Forms of other Tenses.

a. In the following, the form in येगा is used for the absolute future; जद आप कोपियेगा तभी भाग जायगे, 'when your honor shall please to be angry, then at once they will flee away.'

769. The explanation of the use of these forms in *ya*, *ye*, etc., in these various tenses, is to be found in their derivation from the Prakrit affix *jja*, which in Prakrit appears not only in the imperative, but was also added to the root to form a present and future.* It is not therefore correct to say, as many do, that these respectful forms of the imperative and absolute future are used for the present and future. They are true present and future forms, which happen to have the same form with the respectful or precative imperative.

770. In many cases, again, these forms in इये and इय must be interpreted as the remainder of the old Prakrit passive conjugation formed with the suffix *ijja* (§ 610), now almost obsolete. Thus, in particular, I would interpret the common idiom with चाहिये, expressive of 'duty' or 'obligation;' as, हमें वहां जाना चाहिये. Here जाना (sometimes जाया), is evidently the nominative to चाहिये, and we may render, lit., 'with respect to us, to go there is' (or 'should be') 'desired;' thus, तपोवनवासियों का अपमान न होना चाहिये, 'one should Passive Forms like Precative.

* Vid. §§ 602, 605.

not be disrespectful to those who dwell in the sacred grove.' In the following examples also, these forms in य should be explained as passives: न जानिये यह क्यौंकर जिया, lit., 'it is not known how this (man) lived;' मनुष्यजाति की स्त्रियों में इतनी चमक कहां पाइये, 'among women of the human race, where could so much brilliancy (sc. of beauty) be found?'; जितने फूल पूजा के लिये चाहियें उतने बीन चुकीं, 'we have already plucked as many flowers as are desired for worship;' बवा सो लुनिय लहिय जो दीन्हा, 'that is reaped which is sown, that is received which was given;' सुधा सराहिय अमरता गरल सराहिय मीच, 'ambrosia is praised by Immortality, poison is praised by Death.'

a. चाहिये is combined with the past tense of the substantive verb when referring to past time; thus, तेरे इस सुन्दर अंग को तौ अच्छे वस्त्राभरण चाहिये थे, 'for this beautiful body of thine, there ought to have been rich clothes and jewels.'

The Absolute Future.

Future of Certainty.

771. As remarked in § 396, in the absolute future a future action or state of being is either (1) affirmed, or (2) assumed as a *certainty*.

Examples: (1) ऐसा बर घर और कहीं न मिलेगा, 'such a husband (and) house will not be found elsewhere;' मैं काल आऊंगा, 'I will come to-morrow;' अब ऊं या कौं मारिहौं, 'I will kill this (snake) immediately;' भली भांति पछताब पिताहू, 'you, (my) father, will thoroughly repent (of this);' हंसी करैहउ पर पुर जाई, 'you will cause a laugh, going to a strange city;' अब क्यौं जीवहिंगे, 'now how shall we live?;' जहां तुम जाअगे तहां हम हूं जाहिंगे, 'where you go, there I will go.' (2) जो कृष्ण को देंगे तो लोग कहेंगे, 'if we shall give (her) to *Krishṇa*, then people will say—;' ये भाट अब न पावेंगे तो अपकीर्ति करेंगे, 'if these bards shall now receive nothing, then they will give (us) a bad name.'

772. The future of the substantive verb is often very idiomatically used, both alone and as an auxiliary, to denote what is *presumed* to be true. Presumptive Future.

Thus, पिता कन्व को ये तुम से भी अधिक पियारे होंगे, 'to (our) father *Kanva*, these are doubtless dearer than even thou (art).'* In this, as in other similar cases, this future may often be idiomatically rendered by 'must;' as, उस ऋषि का हृदय बड़ा कठोर होगा, 'the heart of that saint must be very hard.'

a. The future 3rd singular, होगा, is thus often used alone, in answers, as equivalent to the adverb 'probably.' Thus, क्या यह नगर बहुत पुराना है? होगा, 'Is this town very old? Probably.'

b. Very rarely, the absolute future is used in this sense for the presumptive perfect, as in the following, where we should have expected हुआ होगा; मेरा चित्त किसी बड़े भ्रम में होगा, 'my memory must have been in a great bewilderment.'

773. Occasionally, in the *Rámáyan*, the future in हौं, इहि, etc., has an optative sense. Thus, होइहहु संतत पियहि पियारी, 'may you ever be dear to (your) husband;' मो से सठ पर करिहहिं दाया, 'may (the prince of *Raghu*) be gracious to a wretch like me.' Optative Future.

Tenses of the Imperfect Participle.

774. The characteristic common to all the tenses of the Imperfect Participle, is the indication of an action, under various modifications of mode and time, as *unfinished* or *incomplete*. We consider, first,

The Indefinite Imperfect.

775. This tense, primarily, denotes an incomplete action, without necessary reference to any time. It may

---

* Compare the German idiom: *sie werden eben theurer sein.*

therefore refer to the past, present, or future. It is moreover employed both in an indicative and a contingent sense.

Indef. Imperf. of Past Repetition.

(1) It is frequently used to denote an action in *past* time as *repeatedly* occurring.

Examples: जब कभी घात पा जाते उस को बिना छेड़े न छोड़ते, 'whenever they would find an opportunity, they would never let him go without having insulted him;' कोई उस के राज भर में भूखा न सोता, 'no one in his whole kingdom would sleep hungry.'

Indef. Imperf. denoting a Single Act.

(2) It is also occasionally used to denote a *single* action in past time, in such sentences as the following:—

अर्जुन की क्या सामर्थ्य थी जो हमारी बहन को ले जाता, 'what was *Arjun's* power that he should carry off our sister?'.

Indef. Imperf. or Present.

(3) It is sometimes apparently, though very rarely, used to denote an action incomplete at the *present* time.

Rem. But in such cases it will very commonly be found that the time is determined as present, by an auxiliary verb, or by some word in the context. Thus, देखते ही तुम्हारी गोद में आ बैठती, 'immediately on seeing (you), she comes and sits in your lap.'

a. It is also used for the present in other cases, when no special stress is laid upon the time; as, मुझ से कुछ नहीं हो सकता, 'nothing can be (done) by me.' This usage is especially common in the *Rámáyan*, where the auxiliary is rare; thus, बहु विधि करति विलाप जानकी, 'in many a way, *Jánakí* laments.'

Rem. It should be noted that in many negative phrases where this tense is apparently used for the present imperfect, the auxiliary is really present in the negative, नहीं, which is compounded of न with the archaic 3rd sing. present, अहि, of the substantive verb;* as, मुझ से कुछ नहीं हो

* See Table xviii., Cols. 9, 10.

सकता, 'nothing can be (done) by me;' मैं नहीं जानता क्या उत्तर देओगे, 'I know not what answer you will give.' In such constructions the usual auxiliary is commonly omitted, and when used, as it is rarely, it is in fact redundant.

(4) It is often used in statements of *general application*, in which no limitation to any time is intended. Indef. Imperf. in General Statements.

Examples: चांद बिन यामिनी सोभा नहीं पाती, 'without the moon, the night has no beauty;' होनेहार कहीं नहीं रुकती, 'that which is to be is never hindered;' कोई नहीं जानता इस का भेव, 'the nature of this (person) no one knows.'

a. In these cases, however, it will be found that in most instances the tense is connected with the negative नहीं, which really contains the substantive verb.

(5) It is used very commonly in the *protasis* and *apodosis* of conditional clauses. As thus employed, it refers to past time, and in the *protasis* denotes the non-fulfilment of the condition; in the *apodosis*, it states what would have been, had the condition been fulfilled. Indef. Imperf. in Conditional Clauses.

Examples: जो मैं उस का नांव गांव ही जानता तो मैं कुछ उपाय करता, 'had I known even his name and village, then I would have devised some plan;' नहीं तो एक भी जीता न रहता, 'else, not even one would have remained alive.'

a. It is also employed in simple sentences implying a condition; as, मैं इसे क्यों न सींचती, 'why should I not water this?'

(6) It is used to express a wish which cannot be realized. In these cases, the optative clause is to be regarded as the *protasis* of a conditional sentence of which the *apodosis* is unexpressed. Indef. Imperf. in Wishes.

Thus, कदाचित आज कन्व घर होते, 'if *Kanva* were by chance at home to-day!' sc. e.g. 'then how good it would be!' In this instance,* *Shakuntalá* herself, in reply to

---

* *Shakuntalá*, Act i. p. 10.

Anasúya's wish, supplies the apodosis, तौ क्या होता, 'what then (if he were)?'

776. It is not to be supposed that in this sense of a past conditional, this tense is really identical in origin with the exactly similar forms which have an indicative sense. The actual existence of an *inflected* past conditional, derived from the imperfect participle, in the eastern Hindí dialects, suggests the opinion that we have here in reality two tenses, the one, indicative, consisting merely of the imperfect participle; the other, a contingent, being an inflected derivative from the imperfect participle; which two tenses, through the processes of phonetic decay, have been reduced in modern High Hindí to one identical form.

Inflected Past Contingent. **777.** The inflected past contingent of the *Ramáyán* and other eastern dialects has already been noted (§ 548). One or two illustrations will illustrate its perfect identity in meaning with the indefinite imperfect in the contingent construction. बूढ़ भयउं न तो करतेउं कछुक सहाय तुम्हार, 'I have become old, else I would render you some assistance;' जौं जनत्यों बन बंधु बिछोहू पिता बचन मनत्यों नहिं ओहू, 'if I had known of this bereavement of my brother in the wilderness, I would not have obeyed that word of (my) father;' नाहित .... मैं आनतेउं सीतहि बरजोरे, 'else, I would have taken away *Sítá* by force.'

The Present Imperfect.

Pres. Imperf. of Present Action or Being. **778.** This tense denotes, primarily and fundamentally, (1) an action in progress, or a state as existing at the present time.

Examples: तुम तपस्वी की कन्या को चाहते हो, 'you desire the hermit's daughter;' तू क्यूं डरता है, 'why dost thou fear?'; मोरि करत हहिं निन्दा, 'they mock me.'

Pres. Imperf. of Repetition. *a.* Hence it also denotes *habitual* or *repeated* action continued up to the present time.

Examples: ये दोनों .... जहां जाते हैं, तहां ही उत्पात मचाते हैं, 'where these two go, there they stir up mischief;' निरा-

कार ब्रह्म को स्तुति वेद किस भाँति करते हैं, 'in what way the *Veds* extol the formless *Brahm*;' निसिदिन देव जपत हउ जेही, 'whom, O deity, you invoke night and day.'

b. It is used, like the indefinite imperfect, to express *general truths*, but commonly with special application to the present time. Pres. Imperf. of General Truths.

Examples: जो नर तीरथ . . . करता है सो . . . परमगति पाता है, 'the man who performs a pilgrimage, obtains supreme felicity;' जो कर्म में लिखा है सोई होता है, 'what is written in fate, that very (thing) comes to pass.'

c. Hence this tense is used in comparisons, when that with which the comparison is made, is represented as a common occurrence. Thus, वह सारे फल जैसे आसमान से ओले गिरते हैं धरती पर गिर पड़े, 'all those fruits fell on the ground, as falls the hail from heaven;' जैसे सूरज का तेज मेंह बरसाकर सुखकारी होता है, 'as the heat of the sun, causing it to rain, becomes a source of pleasure.'

(2) The present imperfect is used for the *future*, to denote that future as *imminent*. The Imminent Present.

Examples: मैं गुफा में जाता हूं, 'I am going into the cave;' मैं तुझे अभी मारता हूं, 'I will kill thee immediately;' हम भी अपने कार्य्य को जाते हैं, 'I (*plur.* for *sing.*) also am going to my work.' This idiom represents a future action, as it were, already begun.

(3) It is also used of *past* time, Pres. Imperf. of Past Action.

a. In vivacious narration, as a *historical present*, when the narrator mentally transfers himself to a past time.

Examples: मारू बाजते हैं कड़खैत कड़खा गाते हैं, 'the drums are beating, the bards are singing their war-songs.' This is especially the case with the idiomatic phrases, क्या देखता हूं, etc.; as, ऊषा क्या देखती है कि चहुं ओर बिजली चमकने लगी, 'what does *U'shá* see, but that on every side the lightning has begun to flash.'

b. When an action begun in the past, is regarded as continuing at the present time.

Examples: जिस दिन से मांगी उसी दिन से मैं दुख उठाती हूं, 'from the very day I asked (it), I have suffered pain;' मैं कई दिन से देखता हूं, 'for some days past I am noticing, etc.'

c. It is also used for a past action, when that action has been just *interrupted*, and is therefore really an action *unfinished* in the present.

Thus, in the *Prem Ságar*, *Shatdhanvá's* speech is interrupted by *Akrúr*, who replies, तू बड़ा मूर्ख है जो हम से ऐसी बात कहता है, 'thou art a great fool, to say (lit., who sayest) such a thing to me.' Similarly we may explain *Akrúr's* words to *Shatdhanvá*; क्या हम तेरी जाति पांति पूछते हैं, 'are we inquiring thy caste (and) rank ?'.

Use of Inflected Present.

779. The use of the inflected present corresponds with that of the analytic present as above explained, but is even more freely used to denote action imperfect in either past, present, or future time. In illustration, we add to the examples of this tense previously given (§§ 490, 506, *a*, 545), the following.

(1) Examples of the *actual* present: न जानूं यह अनसूंघा फूल विधाता किस बड़भागी के हाथ लगावेगा, 'I know not to what fortunate man *Vidháta* will consign this unsmelt flower;' सकौं तोरि अरि अमरऊ मारी, 'I can kill thy enemy, even (though he be) immortal;' केहि आराधऊ का तुम चहऊ, 'whom are you worshipping? what do you wish?;' (2) of the *habitual* present: जासु भजन बिनु जरनि न जाहीं, 'without whose worship, passion departs not;' संतत संत प्रसंसहिं तेहीं, 'the good ever extol that man;' ये मुरली बजावें वे सींगी, 'this one plays the flute, the other, the horn;' (3) of the *imminent* present: बरनौं रघुबर बिमल जस, 'I will set forth the spotless fame of the chief of *Raghu*;' (4) of the *historical* present: देखि शिवहि सुरत्रय मुसुकाहीं, 'seeing *Shiv*, the divine Triad smile;' गये

भवन पूछहिं पितुमाता, 'having gone home, they ask their parents.'

a. Very often in the inflected present the habitual and historical sense are combined. Thus, **कोई मुख धुलावै कोई जिमावै**, 'one would wash (his) face, another would feed (him);' **जिन्हों का गुण गाया करे**, 'she would often sing his praise.'

b. In the following this tense is used for the *presumptive imperfect* (§ 783): **जानहिं सानुज रामहिं मारी**, lit., 'he is probably thinking (thus), having killed *Rám* with his younger brother (I will rule);' where modern High Hindí would have **जानते होंगे** for **जानहिं**.*

c. In the following, the same form occurs twice in the same line, once as an absolute future, once as a present: **जे देखहिं देखहिं जिन्ह देखे**, 'who shall see, do see, or have seen.'*

780. Similar also is the use of the inflected present with **हूं**, etc., (§§ 490, *a*, 506), which occurs not infrequently in the *Prem Ságar*. Thus, **तू हमें नहीं जानती मैं पहचानू हूं**, 'you do not know me, (but) I recognize you;' **एक दुख मुझे जब न तब साले है**, 'one sorrow pierces me now and then;' **नहीं कुछ न कुछ उपद्रव मचावें हैं**, 'they excite some violent act or other.'

The Past Imperfect.

781. This tense is commonly used, (1) to denote an action as in progress at a certain definite past time. Past Imperf. of Past Action Continuing.

Examples: **मैं श्री महादेव के पास पढ़ता था**, 'I was reading with *Shrí Mahádev*;' **ठौर ठौर दुंदुभी बाजते थे**, 'in every place drums were beating;' **एक नारी रोवति ही**, 'a woman was crying.'

(2) This tense is also sometimes used to denote an action as *repeatedly* occurring during a certain period of past time. Past Imperf. of Past Repetition.

* *Rámáyan*, Ay. K.

Examples: **जिस नगर में जाते थे तहां के राजा अति शिष्टाचार कर उन्हें ले जाते थे**, 'into whatever city they were entering, the king of that place would with extreme courtesy escort them (on their way);' **जितने अस्त्र शस्त्र चलाते थे एक भी न लगता था**, 'of all the weapons and missiles they were hurling, not even one would hit.'

The Contingent Imperfect.

Usage of Conting. Imperf.

782. This tense denotes the action of a verb as in progress, not actually, but *possibly* and *contingently*.

Thus, **कदाचित कोई मन में कहता हो**, 'perchance some one may be saying in his mind;' **जिस में हरिणों के झुंड चरते हों**, 'in which herds of deer may be grazing.'

a. It is used in *comparisons*, when the comparison is made, not with an actual event, but with a supposed case.

Examples: **तीनों ऐसे चले कि जैसे तीनों काल देह धरि जाते होंय**, 'the three walked as though the three Times (i.e., Past, Present, Future) were walking incarnate;' **ऐसा शब्द हो रहा था कि जैसे मेघ गरजता हो**, 'there was a continuous sound as if it were thundering.'

The Presumptive Imperfect.

Usage of Presumptive Imperf.

783. This tense differs from the preceding, much as the absolute future differs from the contingent future; i.e., whereas the contingent imperfect represents the action of the verb as *possibly* in progress, the presumptive imperfect represents it as *probably* in progress (§ 407). The absolute future of the auxiliary, however, never denotes the action as an objective reality, but only as assumed to be so.

Thus, **वे हमारे सुरत करते होंगे**, 'they will be (i.e., are probably) thinking of me;' तेरे लिये गौतमी घबराती होगी, '*Gautamí* will be anxious for thee.'

The Past Contingent Imperfect.

784. This extremely rare tense represents an action as conditionally assumed to have been in progress at a certain past time; but invariably implies the negation of the condition. Use of Past Conting. Imperfect.

A single example will suffice; जो तुम उस काल अपना काम करते होते तो तुम मार न खाते, 'had you at that time been doing your work, you would not have got a beating.'

Tenses of the Perfect Participle.

785. The rules for the two constructions of the tenses of the perfect participle of transitive verbs, have been already given (§ 412), and need not be repeated here. The following examples will abundantly illustrate those rules.

(1) The following are examples of the *passive* construction, in which the verb agrees with the object of the action, in gender and number: नंद जसोदा ने बड़ा तप किया था, '*Nand* and *Jasodá* had performed a heavy penance,' lit., 'by *Nand-Jasodá* heavy penance was performed;' श्री कृष्ण ने बांसुरी बजाई, '*Shrí Krishn* played the pipe;' उस ने सहस्र ब्राह्मण जिमाए, 'he fed a thousand Brahmans;' जसोदा ने रस्सियां मंगाईं, '*Jasodá* sent for ropes.' Passive Construction of Perf. Tenses.

a. In the case of pronouns, the gender of the verb is of course determined by that of the noun to which the pronoun may refer. Thus, यह हम ने क्या किया, 'what is this we have done?' (*sc.* काम); and *Sítá* says,* केहि अपराध नाथ हौं त्यागी, 'for what fault, (my) lord, am I deserted?'.

* *Rámáyan*, Sund. K.

b. The verb मारना, when used with the instrument, idiomatically agrees, not with the object struck, but with the instrument of striking, and the object is put in the genitive. Thus, उस ने मेरी तलवार मारी, 'he struck me with a sword;' उस ने उस का थप्पड़ मारा, 'he boxed him' (i.e., 'struck him with the palm of the hand').

Impers. Construction of Perf. Tenses.

(2) The following are examples of the *impersonal* construction, in which the verb is always put in the masculine singular, without reference to the gender or number of either subject or object of the action: प्रभु ने जरासंध को छुड़वाय दिया, 'the lord caused *Jarásandh* to be released;' कंस ने वसुदेव देवकी को एक कोठरी में मूंद दिया, '*Kaṉs* shut up *Basudev* and *Devakí* in one room;' मैं ने उस गाय को देखा, 'I saw that cow;' उस ने अपनी बेटियों को बुलाया, 'he called his daughters.'

a. The pronominal accusative plurals in एं, like those with को, whatever their gender may be, require the verb to be in the impersonal construction, in the masculine singular. Thus, उस ने इन्हें रखा, 'he has kept these;' उस ने उन्हें पकड़ बांधा, 'he caught and bound them.'

Active Construction of Perf. Tenses.

786. As remarked before, the perfect of transitive verbs is often construed actively in the *Rámáyan*. To the examples given in § 555, the following may be added: तुम्ह देखे दयाल रघुराई, 'have you seen the gracious prince of *Raghu*?'.

Inflected Perfect.

a. The inflected perfect of the *Rámáyan*, whether of intransitive or transitive verbs, is always used in the active construction. Besides the examples given in § 557, the following may be noted: जनमत काहे न मारसि मोही, 'why didst thou not kill me at my birth?'; कहेन्हि करिय उतपात आरंभ, 'they (i.e., the monkeys) said, Begin the destruction;' हरि आनेउ सीता जगदंबा, 'you have carried off *Sítá*, the mother of the world.' So in the modern colloquial about

Allahabad, people say, **तुम का कहिन**, = H.H. **तुम ने क्या कहा**, 'What did you say?', etc., etc.

b. So also the perfect in **न** or **ना** (§ 560, *b*) is most commonly used actively. But this termination is chiefly used in verbs which are causals in form, but neuter in sense. Thus, **उर आनंद अधिकान**, 'joy swelled in his breast;' **कपि सकल पराने**, 'all the monkeys fled;' **पाछिल पछिताना**, 'afterward he repented.'

The Indefinite Perfect.

787. The *Indefinite Perfect* (1) simply indicates an action as completed, without reference to any definite time. It thus nearly corresponds to the Greek aorist. **Aoristic Indef. Perfect.**

Examples: **उस ने यह बात कही**, 'he said this thing;' **यह भेद किसी ने नहीं पाया**, 'no one discovered this secret;' **अभय भई**, 'she became free from fear;' **सदा सुमन फल सहित सब द्रुम नव नाना जाति**, 'various sorts of trees ever bent with flowers and fruits.'

(2) It may be used for the *present perfect*, when the time is evident from the context. **Indef. Perf. for Present.**

Example: **तुम बहुत दिन जीते बचे**, 'you have escaped alive for many a day.'

(3) Under similar conditions it is also used, where English idiom would demand the *pluperfect*. **Indef. Perf. for Pluperfect.**

Examples: **किसी ने न जाना कि वह किधर गये**, 'no one knew whither he had gone;' **जब असुरों की बहुत सी सेना कट गई**, 'when much of the army of the demons had been destroyed.'

(4) It is occasionally used where we would use the *present*, in general statements, when these are referred to as a matter of past experience. **Indef. Imperf. in General Statements.**

Examples: **जिस ने संसार में आय तुम्हारा नाम न लिया तिस**

से अमृत छोड़ विष पिया, 'whoever, coming into the world, takes not (lit., did not take) your name, that person, leaving ambrosia, drinks (lit., drank) poison.'

a. So also, when used for the present perfect, it must sometimes be rendered by the present in English: thus, अब मैं ने भी तपोवन के चिन्ह देखे, 'now I too see the marks of a sacred grove;' मैं जान्यो जिय कर निर्मान, 'measuring (you) in (my) mind, I know (that you are not Brahmans).' This usage is especially common with रहना, even in High Hindí; as, अब यहां कोई मक्खी भी नहीं रही, 'now not so much as a fly remains here.'

Indef. Imperf. in Drama. *b.* Idiomatically, it is often used in the drama in announcing the coming and going of the characters, where English idiom requires the present. Thus, दो ढाढ़ी गाते हुए आए, 'two musicians come singing.' This is common in the *Shakuntalá*; but other writers, again, use the present in such cases.

Indef. Imperf. for Future. (5) It is often used colloquially for the *future*, to express prompt and ready action. One gives the order to a servant, पानी लाओ, 'Bring water,' and he answers, लाया, lit., 'Brought;' meaning, 'it shall be brought instantly.' So in the *Shakuntalá*, *Máḍhavya*, going to fulfil the king's command, says, संदेसा दिया, 'the message (is) given.'

Use of Perfect in *Rámáyan*. **788.** In the *Rámáyan* and other archaic poetry, one tense constantly discharges all the functions of the different compound perfect tenses of modern prose Hindí. Thus, सती .... जनमी जाइ हिमाचल गेहा, '*Satí* has gone and been born in the house of *Himáchal*.' Other illustrations will be found in §§ 551, 558.

The Present Perfect.

789. The *Present Perfect* represents the action of a verb as complete, with a reference to the present time.

Examples: हम यहां तुम से मांगने आए हैं, 'I have come to

ask just this of you;' अब से मैं ने आप का नाम सुना है, 'since I have heard your honour's name;' तुम्हारे पिता ने .... मूंद रखा है, '(whom) your father has kept shut up.'

Pres. Perf. for Present.

a. It is thus often used where English idiom would require the *present*.

Thus, तुम निश्चिन्त क्यों बैठे हो, 'why are you sitting unconcerned?'; बार बार में तोरन बंदनवार बंधी हैं, 'in each door wreaths and garlands are fastened.'

Pres. Perf. for Past Perfect.

b. It is more rarely used where we would have expected the *past perfect*.

As, किसी समय राजा हरिश्चंद्र बड़ा दानी हो गया है, 'once the Rájá *Harishchandra* had become (or became) very liberal.'

Pres. Perf. for Indef. Perfect.

c. And in the following we would have expected the *indefinite perfect*:

मुझे कल राजा के यहां से गाए मिली है, 'I got (the cow) yesterday from the Rájá's place.'

Rem. In this case the action is regarded as effecting a result continuing to the present time; whence the use of the present auxiliary.

The Past Perfect.

Past. Perf. and English Pluperfect.

790. The *Past Perfect* differs from the English pluperfect, in that the latter always refers to a certain definite point of past time, prior to which the action or event occurred; while this Hindí tense simply indicates that the action occurred prior to an interval of past time, which is *not*, necessarily, defined. The Hindí past perfect may therefore be employed whenever an interval of time, definite or indefinite, has elapsed since the completion of the action.

It is therefore often necessary to translate this tense by the English indefinite past tense. Thus: मैं तुम्हें सावधान

करने आया था, 'I came to put you on your guard;' जिस समय यह जन्मा था, 'when this person was born;' जब इस का नाल भी नहीं कटा था तब उन को वन में पड़ी मिली थी, 'when even her navel had not been cut, then he found her lying in the jungle,' lit.' 'she lying, met him;' तुम तो अमर है भए, (है भए *Br.* = हुए थे,) 'you had, indeed, been immortal.'

The Contingent Perfect.

791. The *Contingent Perfect* represents a completed action as a mere *hypothesis* or assumption. Thus it may be used,

Cont. Perf. as Hypothetical. (1) In *conditional* clauses, denoting the condition not as a fact, but as a mere assumption.

Thus, जो नल ने कोई निर्दयता का काम भी किया हो, 'if *Nal* have committed some deed even of unkindness.'

As Dubitative. (2) It may express *doubt*.

As, हंसी से न कही हो, 'may she not have spoken in jest?'.

As Concessive. (3) Or a *concession*.

As, जो जो कुछ उस ने रींधा होय, 'whatever he may have cooked.'

As Past Potential (4) It may describe a *past possibility*.

Thus, यदुकुल में ऐसौ नहीं कोय तजके खेत जो भाग्यौ होय, 'in the family of *Yadu* is no one who has abandoned a (battle) field and fled.'

In Comparisons. (5) It is often used in *comparisons* referring to past time, when the comparison is made, not with an actual, but with a supposed case.

Thus, जैसे .... बरण बरण के घटा घिर आई होंय, 'as if clouds of various hues had gathered round.'

a. In the *Rámáyan*, also, this tense occurs, but very rarely. Thus, जौ परिहास कीन्ह कछु होई, 'if he have ridiculed you in any thing.'

Of the Presumptive Perfect.

792. In the *Presumptive Perfect* a completed action is assumed as an objective reality; i.e., the action is denoted as a *probability*. It is thus often to be rendered by the aid of an English adverb. Use of Presumptive Perf.

Examples: बालक की क्या गति हुई होगी, 'what must have been the state of the child!'; आप ने यह दोहा सुना होगा, 'your honour has doubtless heard this couplet;' नदी के प्रवाह से झुका होगा, 'it must have bent by the current of the river.'

a. It is used in questions implying some perplexity; as, कन्व मुनि ने क्या संदेशा भेजा होगा, 'what message can the sage *Kanva* have (probably) sent?'.

The Past Contingent Perfect.

793. The *Past Contingent Perfect* is used only in the *protasis* and *apodosis* of conditional clauses. It always denotes an action or event as a past possibility which was not realized. Past Conting. Perf. in Condit. Clauses.

Examples: जो उठी भी होती तो क्या करती, 'even if I had risen, then what could I have done?'; अपनी लड़की अपने हाथ से न मारी होती, 'had I not killed my daughter with my own hand.' I have noted a single example in the *Rámáyan*: जौ न होति सीता सुधि पाई, 'if I had not obtained intelligence of *Sítá*.'*

a. This tense differs from the Indefinite Imperfect in conditional clauses, only in that it denotes the action as finished; and it may thus often be a matter of indifference which tense is employed. But when the completion of the action is an essential element in the supposition, as in the first clause in the first of the above examples, then this perfect tense should be used in preference to the imperfect.

---

* *Sítá K.*

Of the Passive Conjugation.

Passive, when employed.

794. The *Passive* conjugation is employed in Hindí chiefly in the following cases:—

(1) When the agent is either unknown, or is not to be definitely mentioned.

(2) It is elegantly used with a negative to express *impossibility.* The negative is regularly placed between the verb and the auxiliary.

Examples are, under (1): इस का भेद कुछ जाना नहीं जाता, 'the secret of this is not known;' नतु मारे जैहैं सब राजा, 'else all the kings will be killed.' Under (2): उन का बल अब मुझ से संभाला नहीं जाता, 'his strength is not now to be withstood by me.'

Passive of Neuters.

795. Even neuter verbs may be thus conjugated passively. Thus, हम से आया नहीं जाता, 'I cannot come,' lit., 'it cannot be come by me;' राम कृपा बिना आइ न जाए, 'without *Rám's* favour one cannot come.'

Agent with Passive.

796. The agent with the passive voice is regularly put in the ablative, as in the above examples. But in the following from the *Ráj Níti*, the agent is put in the locative with पै=पर: मो पै चलो नहिं जाए, 'I am not able to walk.' Observe, that the case of the agent is *never* used with the passive conjugation.

797. When the same passive verb in successive coordinated sentences, is used in different tenses, the participle of the principal verb is properly used only with the first auxiliary. Thus, लोग मारे गए भी जाते हैं भी जायंगे, 'people have been, are, and will be killed.'

798. It should be carefully observed that in the majority of cases the English passive is to be rendered into Hindí idiom, not by the passive conjugation, but by the neuter verb. Thus, 'these fields are being irrigated,' is idiomatically rendered ये खेत सिंच रहे हैं; so also, राजा विश्राम को जाने से रुक जांयगे, 'the king will be hindered from going to rest.'

Rem. It will be remembered here, that many of these so-called neuter verbs are in reality corrupted Prakrit or Sanskrit passives (§ 610, *a*).

799. The inflected passive forms found in archaic Hindí have been already illustrated (§§ 493, *a*, 566, *a*). They are used under the same rules as the modern analytic passive. Inflected Passives.

Of Causal Verbs.

800. *Causal* verbs call for little special remark. True causals are regularly followed by two accusatives. Examples will be found in § 421–424. Construction of Causals.

801. Sometimes the causal conveys the sense, not of causing an action, but (1), of allowing it to take place, or (2), of causing an action or state to continue.

Thus, नख केश बढ़ाये .... सब राजा खड़े हो बिन्ती कर रहे थे, 'with nails and hair allowed to grow, all the kings were standing and making supplication;' मारे मरिय जियाये जीजे, 'if he kill thee, die; if he save thee alive, live.'

Of Compound Verbs.

802. In the Syntax of *Compound* verbs, the following points are chiefly to be noted.

(1) In *Intensive* compound verbs, when the conjugated member is intransitive, the compound is always used *actively* in the tenses of the perfect; whether the first member be transitive or intransitive. Construction of Intensives.

Thus in the following examples, although the simple verb, as a transitive, is construed passively with the case of the agent in the tenses of the perfect, yet the compound forms given are construed actively: उस ने रोटी खाई, 'he ate bread,' but वह रोटी खा गया, 'he ate up the bread;' मैं ने उस को देखा, 'I saw it,' but वह देख पड़ा, 'it appeared;' उस ने सुना, 'he heard,' but वह सुन रहा है, 'he is listening.'

a. In compounds in which रहना is the last member, it is important to observe that although it is always used in the form of the first three tenses of the perfect participle, in sense these compounds are always imperfect, emphasizing the continuity of the action. Thus, e.g., सुन रहा है, सुन रहा था, are respectively, 'he is listening,' 'he was listening.'

Construction of Frequentatives and Acquisitives.

(2) On the other hand, in *Frequentative* and *Acquisitive* compounds, although the second conjugated member, when used alone, is always used passively in the tenses of the perfect, yet in this combination it is always treated as active. The same remark applies to the following compounds, in which देना, लेना, or पाना, occur as the second element; viz., चल देना, 'to go away,' हो लेना, 'to accompany,' देख पाना, 'to get a sight.'

Construction of Certain Nominals.

a. Also the following *Nominal* verbs, denoting perception by the senses, although formed with the transitive देना, are always used actively in all tenses: viz., दिखाई देना, 'to appear;' सुनाई देना, 'to sound' (*intr.*): सुंघाई देना, 'to smell' (*intr.*); छुआई देना, 'to be felt.' In like manner is employed, बंधाई देना, 'to be bound.'

Examples:—वह फिरा किया, 'he was wont to go about;' मैं नहीं देखने पाया, 'I was not permitted to see;' वे चल दिये, 'they set out;' वह मेरे पीछे हो लिया, 'he followed after me;' कोई नहीं देख पाया, 'no one obtained a sight;' दो गांव दिखाई दिये, 'two villages appeared;' मुझे कुछ नहीं सुनाई दिया, 'nothing was heard by me;' कोई फूल सुंघाई दिया, 'some flower emitted a perfume;' वह क्या मुझे छुआई दिया, 'what was that which I felt?'.

(3) The similarity in sense of combinations with लेना to the Greek middle voice, has already been noted. A single additional example will suffice: जटों में पंछियों ने घोंसले बना लिये हैं, 'in (his) locks the birds have made nests (for themselves).'

(4) Some of these compounds govern a different case from the single verb. Thus we say, उस ने मुझ से कहा, 'he said to me,' but मुझे कह दिया, 'he told me.'

(5) Permissive Compounds are always preceded by the dative; as, तू मुझे यहां ठहरने न देगी, 'thou wilt not let me stop here.' Permissives.

(6) In literature, the verbs सकना and चुकना, of the Potential and Completive Compounds, are very rarely, if ever, used alone. But in the colloquial they are thus used in some parts of the country, especially when the action referred to may be readily understood. सकना, indeed, occurs alone in the *Rámáyan*; as, e.g., सकहु तो ... मेटहु कठिन कलेस, '(if) you are able, then ... remove this sore trouble.' Completives and Potentials.

a. सकना is usually combined either with the root or the inflected infinitive in ने. But sometimes it is combined with the infinitive in ब, as in the following: राम चाप तोरब सक नाहीं, '*Rám* will not be able to break the bow.'

b. चुकना is most frequently used in composition with another verb, but it also occurs by itself, in the sense of 'to be finished, ended, discharged;' as, तुम्हारे कहने ही से ऋण चुक गया, 'from your mere talking the debt is discharged.' From this a causal, चुकाना, 'to cause to finish,' is formed, which is always used alone.

(7) The idiom of the Desiderative compound with चाहिये, as denoting obligation or duty, has been already explained (§ 437). Of Desideratives.

803. The existence of the Statical combinations has been denied, but they occur in the *Shakuntalá*, as in the following: Of Staticals.

घड़े उठाते उठाते तुम्हारी सखी थक गई है, 'from continuously lifting the jars, your companion has become tired out.' In this idiom the participle may perhaps be explained as used in a substantive sense.

804. In the colloquial, compound verbs are often themselves compounded. Examples of such colloquial expressions are as follows: साहिब लोग अभी चलने लग रहे, 'the gentlemen are just now in the act of starting;' नहीं सक आयगी, 'it will not be possible;' सब खाने लग गये, 'all have set to eating.'

OF ADVERBS.

805. The use of many adverbs as substantives has been already explained (§ 642). But the following additional particulars may be noted.

806. The addition of the gen. postpositions to the pronominal adverbs is especially common; as, अब के बरस, 'in the present year;' अब का हमारा अपराध क्षमा हो, 'may our *present* offence be pardoned;' तुम कहां के हो, 'where do you live?'; lit., 'of where are you,' *sc.* आदमी. जब तक followed by a negative, is to be rendered 'until,' or by an equivalent word; lit., 'as long as . . . not;' but, without the negative, 'as long as.'

Thus, जब तक मैं न आऊं, is 'until I come,' but, जब तक मैं रहूं, 'as long as I remain;' जब तक मर्म न जाने वैद्य औषधि भी नहीं कर सकता है, 'until the physician know the secret,' (or 'as long as the physician knows not, etc.') 'he cannot even treat (the case);' similarly, जब तक मैं फिर आऊं तब तक घोड़ों की पीठ ठंडी कर लो, 'against I come back, cool off the back of the horses.'* In the following, however, जब तक alone, in the

* Mr. Pincott would here translate *jab tak*, 'until,' as if it were *jab tak main phir na áún*; but I see no sufficient reason for disregarding the omission of the negative.

Shakuntalá, seems to mean 'until:' जब तक इस के पुत्र का जन्म हो, 'until a son be born to her;' but, जौ लौं जियौं तौ लौं अनि कछु कहसि बहोरी, 'as long as I live, never say anything again.'

807. तब तक must be rendered 'hitherto' or 'thus far' in the following: ये दुख तौ थे ही तब तक। एक नया घाव और हुआ, 'these then were my troubles *thus far*; (now) one new hurt more has come.' In the following, where no जब तक precedes, तब तक is 'by that time:' तब तक तुम ने आ थामा, 'by that time you came and arrested (me).'

808. A relative adverb used as a substantive in the genitive, is combined with the correlative to denote manner, place, etc., as unchanged; as, ज्यों का त्यों, 'in exactly the same way;' जहां का तहां, 'exactly in the same place.'

809. जहां तक is idiomatically used of *measure* or *extent* in such phrases as, जहां तक तुम से हो सके, 'as far as you may be able.' कहां तक idiomatically denotes a measure as indefinitely large. Thus, जो दान दिया मैं कहां तक कहूं, 'how can I fully tell the alms he gave?'. This idiom cannot be literally translated.

810. कहां (कहं), 'where,' is idiomatically repeated in successive clauses to denote extreme disparity or incongruity. Repetition of Interrog. Local Adverbs.

Examples: कहां ये बालक रूपनिधान कहां ये सबल मल्ल, 'what equality between these beautiful children and these powerful wrestlers?'; कहं कुंभज कहं सिंधु अपारा, 'what was the Jar-born (*Agastya*, who drank the ocean!) in comparison with the boundless ocean?'.

811. The relative and correlative adverbs are conjoined to express *universality*. Conjunction of Relative and Correlative Adverbs.

Examples: जहं तहं देखौं द्रोह भारि, 'everywhere I see the

two brothers;' जिधर तिधर नगरनिवासी लोग प्रभु के चरित्र बखानें, 'in every direction the inhabitants of the town are recounting the exploits of the lord.'

812. कत,—though derived from the Sanskrit कुत्र (कथ), 'where,'—is commonly to be rendered, 'how,' or 'why;' thus, जगतार कत हम गावों, 'Saviour of the world! how shall I sing;' कैकयि कत जननी जग माझा, 'why was *Kekayi* born into the world?'

Idioms with Indef. Local Adverb.

813. The indefinite कहीं, 'somewhere,' is used in comparisons to denote excess as indefinitely great; it is also idiomatically used in expressions of doubt, as equivalent to the phrase, 'by any chance,' 'possibly.'

Examples: वह घर इस से कहीं ऊंचा है, 'that house is ever so much higher than this;' सखी ने ब्याह की बात कहीं हंसी से न कही हो, '(whether her) companion may not possibly have spoken of marriage in jest.' For कहीं, कतहुं is used in the *Rámáyan*; as, कतहुं तम नहीं, 'nowhere is there darkness.'

Adverbs of Direction and Manner.

814. इधर, उधर, 'hither,' 'thither,' as also the dialectic इत and उत, are often used in successive clauses to express a contrast.

Examples: इधर तो अनिरुद्ध जी महाशोक करते थे उधर राजकन्या योग करने लगी, 'here, then, *Aniruddh Jí* was greatly grieving, and there the princess was devoting herself to austerities;' इत हित मित छूटें उतहि बिलोके परम ऊलासा, 'here he parts from friend and loved one, there he beholds supernal joy.'

815. For यूं, 'thus,' the original Sanskrit इथं occurs in the *Rámáyan*, with इदं, 'this;' as, इदमिथम कहि न जाए, lit., 'this is (so)—(it) cannot be said;' i.e., 'it cannot be told just as it is.'

816. For क्यों with the negative, किम is often used in the

Rámáyan and in other poetry; as, **कह लंकेस कहसि किन बाता**, 'said the lord of *Lanká*, Why dost thou not speak a word?'.

817. **बरु**, 'rather,' 'sooner,' I have only met with in poetry; thus, **जिये मीन बरु बारि विहीना**, 'sooner might a fish live deprived of water.'

818. **परे**, 'on that side,' is often used in the sense of 'off,' in commands; as, **परे हो**, 'be off!' **परे हट**, 'move off!'

819. The particle **कि** is elegantly used for an adverb of time, denoting an action as coincident with another mentioned in the foregoing clause. **कि of Coincidence.**

Examples: **मैं सपने में तुझे देख रहा था कि . . . . कोई मुझे उठाय यहां ले आया**, 'in a dream I was gazing on thee, when some one, lifting me up, brought me here;' **वह गाय रही कि शिव जी ने कहा**, 'she was singing away, when *Shiv Jí* said.'

820. The particles **अथ** and **इति** have been already explained and illustrated (§ 646). But after a phrase or quotation, modern Hindí often uses **ऐसा**, where Sanskrit would have had **इति**. Thus, **बिना प्रयोजन क्या यह हुआ ऐसा जानने की इच्छा न करे**, 'what has taken place,—without a motive let him not desire to know this;' **मृत्यु ने हमारे केश को पकड़ा है ऐसा समझ धर्म का आचरण करे**, 'considering that death has seized our hair, let him practice virtue.' In both these sentences, **ऐसा**, like the Sanskrit **इति**, marks the preceding clause as quoted, as it were, from the lips or mind of the subject of the sentence. **Particles of Quotation.**

821. The emphatic particle **हि**, as remarked § 651, may be variously translated. In addition to the illustrations there given, the following may be noted. **The Emphatic Particle.**

बकले का वस्त्र इस मोहिनी की गात को सोभा देता ही है, 'a garment of bark *does* grace the body of this charming creature,' where it is intended to emphasize the contradiction of an opposite expression just preceding. Other examples are: हम ही तुम ही जानें, 'only you and I know;' वह पथ का हारा थका तो था ही, 'he was indeed wearied and exhausted by the journey;' बालक बच रहा सकट ही टूट गया, 'the child was saved, only the cart was broken;' दुख सुख ही जानौं, 'I will regard sorrow as very joy;' ये सिद्धान्त क्या ही अद्भुत हैं, 'how very wonderful are these doctrines!'; मैं ने तुम ही को बुलाया, 'I called *you*!', i.e., *you*, and no one else; जाइय बिन बोलेहु, 'should you go even without having been called;' एक अविनाशी कदम तट पर था सोई था, 'one imperishable *kadam* tree stood on the bank, (and) that only.'

N.B. The emphatic particle *hi* must not be confounded with the *hi* which in the *Rámáyan* and other old poetry is the sign of the dative and accusative cases. In the *Rámáyan*, *hu*, *huṇ*, or *au* is the common form of the emphatic affix. (Vid. §§ 178, 651, *b*.)

OF PREPOSITIONS.

Prepositions with Gen. and Abl.

822. The Syntax of prepositions calls for little remark. Their real nature and construction have been already explained (§§ 652–659).

823. बाहर, 'without,' भीतर, 'within,' आगे, 'before,' are preceded not only by the genitive, as previously noted, but also by the ablative. In the latter case there is always an implied comparison. Sometimes it is of little consequence which is used; but often the two constructions convey a slightly different sense.

Thus, इस के बाहर, is, lit., 'on the outside;' but, इस से बाहर, 'outside of this;' मेरे आगे चलो, is, 'walk before me;' but, वह मुझ से आगे दौड़ा, 'he ran ahead of me,' etc.

a. समेत commonly takes the noun in its oblique form, where such a form exists. In the following from the *Rámáyan*, समेत exceptionally governs the accusative in हि; बैठे आसन ऋषिहि समेता, 'he sat on the seat with the sage.'

Omission of Postpositions.

b. The genitive postposition is sometimes omitted before some prepositions without any difference in the sense; as, प्रिया के दर्शन बिना, 'without the sight of (my) beloved.' But in other cases, the presence or absence of the postposition changes the sense; thus, किस के लिये, is 'for whom?'; किस लिये, 'for what?' 'why?'

824. Many words which, when following a noun in the genitive, must be rendered into English as prepositions, under other circumstances must be regarded as nouns, and often translated accordingly. Such, e.g., are कारण, हेतु, निमित्त, and many others. Thus, मेरे जाने के कारण, 'on account of my going,' but, इस कारण, 'for this reason.' So also, in the following phrase, लिये has a prepositional force: तुम किस के लिये आए, 'for whom have you come?'. But in the following it must be regarded as a substantive, signifying 'object;' तुम किस लिये आए, 'for what object have you come?'.

Inseparable Prepositions.

825. The inseparable preposition स, 'with,' is properly used only with pure Sanskrit nouns. In colloquial Hindí it is not often heard, but it is more common in poetry: as, e.g., सानुज (स + अनुज), 'with his younger brother;' सप्रेम, 'with love;' सपरिवार, 'with attendants.'

OF CONJUNCTIONS.

Copulative Conjunctions.

826. The copulative conjunction और is used much less freely than the equivalent English 'and;' the conjunctive participle is often preferred to a finite verb followed by the conjunction (§ 755 (1) *a*).

Thus, a Hindoo would not be likely to express the phrase, 'he went and saw the town,' by वह गया और नगर को देखा, but rather, उस ने जाकर नगर को देखा.

a. It is also to be noted that Hindí idiom often

requires the omission of the copulative between pairs of words where it would be necessary in English.

Examples: भले बुरे की पहचान, 'knowledge of good (and) evil;' दुख सुख का देनेवाला, 'the giver of joy (and) sorrow;' चलो देखो, 'go! (and) see!'; कृष्ण बलदेव, '*Krishn* (and) *Baldev*;' मेरे हाथ पांव नहीं चलते हैं, 'my hands (and) feet do not move.'

Rem. Such phrases are doubtless conceived in the popular mind as equivalent to copulative compounds (§ 625).

827. भी is to be rendered 'also,' in an enumeration of particulars, but in other cases it must be translated 'even.'

Thus, श्री कृष्ण चंद भी बलराम जी भी द्वारिका में आए, '*Shrí Krishn Chand* and also *Balrám Jí* came to *Dváriká*;' but, श्री कृष्ण चंद भी किसी को कुछ नहीं देते हैं, 'even *Shrí Krishn Chand* gives nothing to any one.'

a. Also, after words implying comparison, भी must be rendered 'still,' 'yet,' 'even;' as, और भी है, 'there is still more;' यह वृक्ष उस घर से भी ऊंचा है, 'this tree is higher even than that house;' फिर भी is also sometimes to be rendered 'yet,' 'still;' as, फिर भी चित्र उस के रूप को कहां पाता है, 'yet, how can a picture equal her beauty?'. Sometimes, again, भी can only be translated into English by some limiting phrase as, 'at all,' 'in the least,' etc.; as, कुछ भी नहीं चौंके, 'they did not start in the least.'

b. Sometimes, again, भी can scarcely be rendered into English except by an emphasis; thus, यह कार्य्य कैसा भी लघु क्यों न हो, 'howsoever trivial this work may be.'

828. The Sanskrit अपि, 'also,' 'even,' is never used in conversation, and only now and then in poetry; thus, अति गोप्यमपि सज्जन करहिं प्रकास, 'even that which is most mysterious, the good make clear.'

829. The phrase तिस पर भी, is often used as a copulative conjunction, equivalent to 'moreover;' as, तिस पर भी यह कहता है, 'moreover he says this.' इस पर भी may often be rendered, 'notwithstanding,' 'nevertheless;' as, इस पर भी तू मुझे प्यारा लगता है, 'nevertheless thou art dear to me.'

830. Of the disjunctive conjunctions, वा or अथवा, and या (Ar.) are the most common; कै and कैतो are dialectic. कि also is often used as a disjunctive. Disjunctive Conjunctions.

a. कि and कै are especially used in short disjunctive phrases; as, भला हो कै बुरा, 'be it good or evil.' But sometimes it is repeated before successive sentences; as, कै हरि ने मेरी प्रीति की प्रतीति न करी कै जरासंध का आना सुन प्रभु न आए, 'has not *Hari* had confidence in my affection? or hearing of the coming of *Jarásandh*, has the lord not come?'.

b. किंवा is rare, but we find it in the *Rámáyan*, as, अभिमान मोह बस किंवा, 'or (being) in the power of pride or love.'

831. Sometimes in brief phrases, where it may be readily understood, the disjunctive may be omitted.

Thus, संपति प्रभुताई जाइ रहो पाई बिनु पाई, 'wealth and authority pass away, obtained (or) not obtained,' i.e., 'they are gone even before we obtain them.'

832. जो is commonly used as a conditional conjunction in the colloquial; यदि—usually pronounced, and often written जद—is Sanskrit, and in conversation is somewhat pedantic. Conditional Conjunctions.

a. जौ पै is sometimes used dialectically as a conditional conjunction. Thus, जौ पै जिय न होति कुटिलाई, 'if there is no treachery in his heart.'

833. The conjunction तो or तौ may be variously rendered, according as it has the force of an illative or or an emphatic particle. The Illative Conjunctions.

(1) As an illative conjunction it regularly introduces the apodosis of a conditional sentence.

Thus, जो मैं नहीं आऊं तो वह नहीं आवेगा, 'if I do not go, then he will not come.'

(2) As an emphatic particle, it is variously rendered into English.

Examples are: हमारी तो सुनो, 'just hear me!'; अपना बचन निबाहे तौ, 'do end your talk now!'; देखो तो, 'pray look!'.

a. The illative तो is only apparently used for the temporal conjunction. Thus, यह समाचार सुनाय नारद जी तो चले गये, 'having told this news, *Nárad Jí* then went away;' where तो suggests the accomplishment of his object in telling the news, as the reason for his departure.'

b. In other cases तो conveys a shade of emphasis which can only be expressed in English by a peculiar stress of voice; as, e.g., त्रिभुवनपति जगत का कर्त्ता तो मैं हूं, 'lord of the three worlds, and creator of the earth am *I*!'.* So also, as used in an enumeration of particulars; as, एक तौ मेरे पांव में दाभ की पैनी अणि लगी है। दूसरे कुरे की डार में अंचल उलझा है, 'for one (thing), a sharp spear of grass is stuck in my foot; for another, (my) veil is entangled in the branch of a barleria.'

c. In the following passage the word occurs in both senses; जो उस से कुछ मांगता तो वे देते तो सही, 'if I had asked anything from him, then he would indeed assuredly have given it.'

Concessive Conjunctions.

834. The concessive conjunction is यद्यपि (यदि + अपि), 'although,' to which तदपि, or तथापि, 'yet,' answers in the principal clause. These are pure Sanskrit and are rarely used in the colloquial, except by pundits. The corrupted form यदपि is employed in the *Rámáyan*. In

* In these cases, तो would be represented in German by '*doch*' or '*nun*.'

the common colloquial, जो भी and तौ भी are usually employed, as also चाहे . . . परन्तु.

835. कदाचित and कदापि, 'perhaps,' like many of the foregoing, are rarely heard in the colloquial, except from those conversant with Sanskrit. The Persian शायद (सायद and साइद) is often heard instead. All these are regularly followed by the contingent future. The verbal forms, जाने, क्या जाने, often take the place of these in the colloquial. Conjunctions of Possibility.

836. कि is radically an explanatory particle; its use as a final, = 'that,' is easily derived from this explanatory sense. The Explanatory Particle.

Thus, वह इस कारन से गया कि देखे, etc., 'for this reason he went, that he might see;' here कि is merely explicatory of the word कारन, 'reason.' And in cases where no such noun occurs in the principal clause, it may yet be understood.

a. Often कि must be rendered by the word 'saying;' as, वह यही मनाता था कि वह पुरुष कब प्रगटे, 'he was propitiating this (deity), saying, When will that man appear?'.

b. Sometimes कि is used pleonastically, after a relative pronoun or adverb; thus, जो बात कि तुम ने कही, 'that thing which you said;' विष्णु का दूसरा पैंड़ था जब कि हरि ने अहंकारी बलि छला था, '(this) was Vishnu's second step when he deceived the self-asserting *Bali*.'

c. But the combination जब कि is often rendered 'since,' in phrases like the following: जब कि परमात्मा क्षणभर भी ऐसा नहीं हो सकता, 'since the Supreme Spirit not even for an instant can be such.' Further illustration of the use of the conjunctions will be found in the section on compound sentences.

Of Interjections.

Interjections with dative.

837. Interjections call for little remark. The following interjectional expressions require a noun in the dative; viz., धन्य, धिक, धिक्कार, or धिरकार.

Thus, परमेश्वर को धन्य, 'praise to God!'; धिक्कार मेरे जीवन को, 'a curse to my life!'.

838. अरे or रे changes final ए to ई after a feminine noun; रे (री) follows the vocative, or if no noun or pronoun be expressed, then, the verb of the sentence.

Thus, कृपायतन कर दास मैं सुनु मातु री, 'I am the servant of the Abode of Compassion; hear! O mother!'; सुनता है रे, 'Hallo! dost thou hear?'.

Of the Repetition of Words.

839. The repetition of words is a marked characteristic of Hindí idiom. Any part of speech, except a postposition or conjunction, may be repeated, to express, as the case may be, the various ideas of *repetition*, *distribution*, *variety*, *intensity*, or *continuance.*

Repetition of Nouns.

840. Nouns when repeated may be taken (1) *distributively*.

Examples: घर घर मंगलाचार हो रहे थे, 'festivities were going on in each house.' Sometimes the noun thus repeated is equivalent to an English adverbial phrase; as, पाँति पाँति, 'in rows.'

a. An attributive genitive or adjective before such nouns is put in the plural; as, मेरे रोम रोम प्रसन्न हो गये हैं, 'my each individual hair is delighted.'

(2) Or the repetition may express *variety*.

Thus, देश देश के राजा, 'kings of various countries.'

(3) The noun is also repeated to express *intensity* or *emphasis*. The emphatic ही often intervenes between the repeated words.

Thus, मन ही मन में कहने लगा, 'in his inmost soul he began to say;' बातों ही बातों में, 'in the very midst of the conversation;' रनवास की स्त्रियों को शकुन्तला ही शकुन्तला कहकर, 'calling the ladies of his zanána just nothing but *Shakuntalá*;' दोनों कार्य दूर दूर पर हैं, 'the two acts are very far apart.'

a. When the first noun is in the plural, ही is not used; as, उन के हाथों हाथ, 'in their very hands;' मारों मार, 'blow on blow.'

b. Sometimes the first noun is put in the genitive; as, मूर्खों का मूर्ख, lit., 'a fool of fools,' i.e., 'a very fool;' भंवरों के झुंड के झुंड, 'swarms upon swarms of bees.'

c. I have also noted the phrase दूधा दूध, 'very milk,' i.e., 'pure milk.'

d. The repetition sometimes suggests *continuance* in a place; as, सड़क के किनारे किनारे चलो, 'walk along by the side of the road.'

841. For the repetition of nouns, etc., with the alteration of a letter, see § 625 (1) *b*.

842. Repetition has the same effect in adjectives. Thus, **Repetition of Adjectives.**

(1) The adjectives may be taken *distributively*.

Thus, सब बड़े बड़े यदुबंसी, 'every one of the great *Yadubansís*.'

(2) Or sometimes the repetition expresses *variety*.

Examples: नये नये सुख, 'various new pleasures;' अनूठे अनूठे खेल खेलने लगे, 'they began to play various unheard-of games.'

(3) They are repeated to express *intensity*.

Thus, मीठी मीठी पवन चल रही है, 'the soft, soft wind is blowing;' सुथरे सुथरे वस्त्र, 'the cleanest clothes.' Sometimes the first adjective takes the genitive postposition; as, भूखे का भूखा, 'extremely hungry.'

Repetition of Numerals.

843. Numerals are repeated in a *distributive* sense.

Thus, उन के दस दस पुत्र भए, 'ten sons were (born) to each one.' To the repeated numeral, the conjunctive participle करके is often added (§ 650), as follows: दो दो करके निकल गये, 'they went out by twos;' एक एक करके आये, 'they came one by one.'

a. When the number is a compound, only the last part is repeated; as, एक रुपिया चार चार आना, 'one rupee and four *ánás* each.'

Repetition of Pronouns.

844. Pronouns, when repeated, are often to be taken *distributively*. Or the repetition may denote *variety*.

Examples: उन्हों ने अपने अपने घर जाय जाय कहा, 'having gone each one to his own house, they said—;' जो जो जिस जिस वस्तु की इच्छा करै सो सो ला दीजो, 'whatever different things each one may desire, that bring and give;' हम क्या क्या दुख पाते हैं, 'what various sorrows do we experience!'.

a. But कोई, repeated, is 'a few;' as, तुम्हारी कृपा पावै कोई कोई, 'some few may gain your favour.'

845. The relative जैसा is idiomatically repeated with the genitive postposition; as, जैसे का तैसा, 'exactly as before;' or, if the noun qualified be feminine, जैसी की तैसी उस की दशा रही, 'his state remained just as it was before.'

Repetition of Particles.

846. Repetition of verbs is confined to the participles. It may indicate

(1) Simple *repetition* of the action.

Examples: छिलके बह बह कर आते हैं, 'pieces of bark keep floating down;' सब गोपी पशु पक्षी द्रुम बेलि से पूछती पूछती ढूंढने

लगी, 'all the milk-maids, repeatedly questioning beast, bird, tree and vine, began to search;' मुख पास भंवर आय आय बैठते थे, 'the bees kept coming and resting on her face.'

(2) The repetition of certain verbs thus expresses *intensity*.

Thus, इन्द्र पछताय पछताय रो रो कहने लगा, '*Indra*, deeply repenting and weeping much, began to say.'

(3) It may sometimes denote the *continuance* or *prolongation* of the action.

It will sometimes be found difficult to render this idiom into English. चलते चलते घर को पहुंचे, 'walking on and on they reached home;' इसी रीति से चले चले राज मंदिर में आ विराजे, 'in this way having gone on, he came and displayed his glory in the palace;' श्री कृष्ण को बंधे बंधे पूर्व जनम की सुधि आई, 'to *Shrí Krishṉ*, as he remained bound, came the recollection of a former birth.'

a. होते होते, is rendered 'gradually,' 'by degrees.' Peculiar is the phrase, हमारे न पहुंचते न पहुंचते, 'my continued non-arrival.'

b. Often the first of the repeated participles is put in the masculine, and the second in the feminine; as, छिपा छिपी, 'secretly;' उन को देखा देखी सब . . . गोपी प्रणाम कर, 'all the milkmaids, making obeisance, with him looking on, etc.' Sometimes the compound has a reciprocal sense, as, मारा मारी, 'mutual beating.'

c. The perfect participles of a neuter and its active or causal are sometimes idiomatically joined together. Often this combination seems to have a certain intensive force; as, यह उपाध बैठे बिठाए में कहां से आई, 'whence came this calamity upon us sitting still?'.

d. Similarly, an active or causal participle is often prefixed idiomatically to a neuter verb with an intervening negative, giving an emphatic force. Thus, सो किसी भांति मेटे न मिटेंगे,

'they cannot in any way be possibly effaced.' Or the reverse order is found, the neuter participle preceding; thus, दनुज महाबल मरै न मारे, 'the demons, mighty in strength, (even when) dead, were not killed;' तनु टर्यो न टार्यो, 'driven back, they not in the least gave way.'

Repetition of Adverbs.

847. The repetition of adverbs has already been noted (§ 643) (1). The following illustrations are added.

जब जब होइ धर्म की हानी तब तब प्रभु धरि विविध शरीरा, 'whenever religion suffers injury, then from time to time the lord, assuming various bodies, etc.;' ज्यौं ज्यौं वह कन्या बढ़ने लगी त्यौं त्यौं उसे अति प्यार करने लगा, 'just in proportion as the girl began to grow, so he began to love her greatly.'

a. An adverb may be repeated with the genitive postposition intervening, for the sake of emphasis; निर्मल होते ही मूर्त्ति ज्यों की त्यों दिखाई देती है, 'immediately on its becoming clear, the image appears exactly as before.' Sometimes the latter may also be in the emphatic form: as, सो (दल) यहां का यहीं ऐसे बिलाय जाएगा, 'that army in this very spot shall so vanish;' जब का तब, 'at that very moment.'

Rem. Observe that in this idiom the genitive postposition is inflected to agree with the noun to which reference is made.

Repetition of Prepositions.

848. Prepositions also are sometimes repeated with a modification of the sense similar to that above noted.

Thus: उन के बीच बीच चारन जस गाते थे, 'all along through the midst, bards were singing (his) renown;' उन्हीं चरणचिन्हों के पास पास, 'close along by those same footsteps;' मेरे पीछे पीछे चले आओ, 'follow along behind me;' हम तुम साथ ही साथ हाट को चलें, 'let us two go *together* to the market.'

Onomatopœia.

849. The fondness of the Hindoos for onomatopoetic words has been already mentioned. This regard for sound extends also to the construction of sentences, and is seen especially in the balanced structure of the language; as in the marked tendency to throw sentences of all kinds into the relative and correlative form; the expression of repeated action by repeating the word expressing the action; the fondness for rhyme, even in prose, etc., etc.

a. The following striking examples of onomatopœia in the choice of words, are from the *Rámáyan.* In the description of the fighting of the monkeys against *Rávan* we read: मर्कट बिकट भट जुटत न लटत तनु जर्जर भये, 'the terrible monkey warriors, fighting, their bodies torn to pieces, are not diminished;' and the fighting of the bears is thus similarly described; जंबुकनिकर कटक्कट कट्टहिं खाहिं ऊंहांहिं अघाइ दपट्टहिं, 'the bear host gnash and grind their teeth; they eat, and howl, and (even) satiated, rush upon (their prey).'

PART II. SYNTHETIC SYNTAX.

OF THE CONSTRUCTION OF SENTENCES.

I.—OF THE SIMPLE SENTENCE.

Of the Parts of a Sentence.

850. As in all languages, the essential elements of a Hindí sentence are two, viz., *subject* and *predicate*, to which may be added the *copula*, as a formal, though not, as will appear, a necessary element of the sentence. We treat first of the simple sentence.

851. The subject in Hindí, may be (1) a noun or pronoun in the nominative case; or (2) two or more nouns or pronouns in the nominative; or pronouns in the nominative; or (3) an adjective or numeral used substantively in the nominative; or (4) an infinitive; or (5) any phrase or sentence. The Subject.

Examples are, of (1): तुलसी दास आया है, '*Tulsí Dás* has come;' ये भले मनुष्य के लक्षण हैं, 'these are the marks of a good man;' (2) तपस्वी और गौतमी दूसरी ओर गये, 'the hermit and *Gautamí* went in another direction' (or 'go'*); मैं और तुम आओगे, 'I and you will go;' (3) दो वहां हैं, 'two are there;' कोई ज्ञानी नहीं कहेगा, 'no wise (man) will say;' (4) तुम को जाना है, 'you must go,' lit., 'to go is for you;' (5) उन्हें बार बार जनम और मरण रूपी इस संसार चक्र में भ्रमना पड़ता है, 'to them it falls to wander in this earthly circle of repeated birth and death.'

a. The cases in which a complete sentence introduced by कि stands as the subject of the verb, will be noticed in the Syntax of the Compound Sentence.

b. Colloquially, the locative with तक, लों, etc., is used as the subject of a sentence in such phrases as the following: एक मनई† तक नहीं आया, 'not so much as one man came;' दो सौ तक इकट्ठे हुए, 'as many as two hundred came.'

Omission of Subject.

852. The subject may sometimes be omitted; (1) when it can be readily supplied from the connection, as, e.g., in questions, or in direct address; or (2) when it is implied in the form of the verb; or (3) in proverbs, where brevity is sought.

Examples: (1) क्या वह आता है हां आता है, 'is he coming? yes (he) is coming;' बेटा यह क्या चाल दिखलाते हो, 'Son! what conduct is this you display?'; (2) ब्राह्मण हूं, '(I) am a Bráhman;' (3) कमा तब खा, 'earn, then eat.'

a. In the phrase बरसता है, the word पानी or मेंह is to be understood as the subject of the verb, and is indeed often expressed.

---

* An explanatory note in a drama, where English idiom would require the present tense.

† मनई is a common word in the Doáb, but is regarded as vulgar by the educated.

853. Sometimes by *anakolouthon*, a nominative, or the case of the agent, stands without a verb, as गोपी in the following: गोपी जो जल भरने को निकली थीं सो रथ दूर से आते देख कहने लगीं, 'the milkmaids, who had gone out to draw water—they, seeing the chariot coming in the distance, began to say—.'

854. The predicate of a sentence may be (1) a verb; (2) a noun or pronoun either in the nominative or some oblique case; (3) an adjective; (4) a numeral; or (5) any word or phrase used as a noun. The Predicate.

Examples: (1) वह जायगा, 'he will go;' (2) उस का नाम आहुक है, 'his name is *A'huk*;' यह राजा का है, 'this is the king's;' वह कोठी पर है, 'he is on the house;' कारण यह है, 'the reason is this;' यह पुस्तक किस की है, 'whose is this book?'; ऐसा सामर्थ किसी में नहीं है, 'in no one is such power;' जो पुत्र मेरे होगा, 'the son whom I shall have;' (3) राजा सिसुपाल बड़ा बली औ प्रतापी है, 'the *Rájá Sisupál* is very mighty and renowned;' (4) मेरे चरण सोलह थे, 'my feet were sixteen;' (5) मैं राजा भीष्मक का पठाया हूं, 'I am the messenger (lit., the sent) of *Rájá Bhíshmak*,' i.e., 'sent by him.'

855. The predicate verb is sometimes omitted when it can be easily supplied from the context. Omission of Predicate.

Thus, दोनों बीरों ने प्रणाम किया एक ने गुरु जान दूसरे ने बंधु मान, 'both heroes saluted him, the one regarding him as a spiritual guide, the other holding him as a brother.'

856. The copula, either explicitly, or as implied in a verbal form, is regularly required to connect the subject and predicate of a sentence. But even in prose the copula may often be omitted in Hindí, where it would be essential in English or even in Urdú. The Copula.

a. Thus, in simple description, where the copula may be readily supplied, Hindí often characteristically omits it; as,

मथुरापुरी का आहुक नाम राजा तिन के दो बेटे एक का नाम देवक दूसरा उग्रसेन, '(there was) a king of the city of *Mathurá*, named *A'huk*, (who had) two sons; the name of one (was) *Devak*, the other (was) *Ugrasen*;' अब नगर का लौटना कैसा, sc. होय or होगा, lit., 'now how is (there) returning to town?' i.e., 'what chance is there of returning to town?'. We should rather have expected here कैसे for कैसा.

b. The copula is also often omitted in comparisons; as, भूमि ऐसी सुहावनी लगती थी कि जैसे सिंगार किये कामिनी, 'the earth looked as fair as a beauty adorned.'

c. Similarly, the copula is very commonly omitted in negative sentences; as, इस को किसी बात का ज्ञान नहीं, 'this (person has) no knowledge of anything.'

Rem. In such phrases the omission of the copula is in fact only apparent. *Nahiṉ*, as remarked § 472, is a compound of the negative *na* with an archaic form of the copula, *áhiṉ*.

d. The copula is also usually omitted in proverbial expressions; as, चोरी का गुड़ मीठा, 'stolen sugar is sweet;' छुछूंदर के सिर में चंबेली का तेल, 'oil of jasmine on the head of a musk-rat.'

e. But when there is any emphasis on the time as to which any affirmation is made, as past, present, or future, the copula must be employed.

857. The omission of the copula is extremely common in poetry; indeed, in the *Rámáyan*, its use is quite exceptional. Examples will be found in almost every line. Thus, सब विधि सब पुर लोग सुखारी, 'in every way, all the people of the city (were) rejoiced;' सतसंगति मुद्मंगलमूला, 'association with the good (is) the root of joy and gladness.'

a. But occasional examples of the use of the copula occur, determined by emphasis, or by the necessities of the metre; as, e.g., दुराराध्य पै अहहिं महेशा, 'but difficult to be worshipped (is) *Mahesh*.'

b. As in all languages, we must distinguish the occasional use of the substantive word, not as a copula, but as an essential word. Thus, ये लोग मानते हैं कि ईश्वर है, 'those people admit that God exists;' भये जे अहहिं जे होइहैं आगे, '(those things) which have been, are, or shall be hereafter.'

858. The predicate may belong to the subject in a greater or less degree as compared with other objects. For illustrations of the syntax of adjectives in such cases, see §§ 207–210, under 'Comparison.' In the case of verbs, the comparison is expressed by prefixing the proper adverb.

859. The subject and predicate may both be ex- Extension of Subject.
tended or defined, as in other languages, by the addition of various words in grammatical dependence upon them. (1) The subject may be defined by a noun or nouns in apposition.

Examples: हस्तिनापुर का रहनेवाला राजा भीष्मक आए हैं, '*Rájá Bhíshmak* of *Hastinápur* (lit., resident of), has come;' कार्तिक महीना आया, 'the month *Kártik* came.'

a. Here note the common idiom with the pronoun क्या, which occurs in the following phrase: सब नगरनिवासी क्या स्त्री क्या पुरुष आपस में यों कहते थे, 'all the inhabitants of the city, whether men or women, were thus talking among themselves.'

b. The common idiom which occurs in such a sentence as the following, must be regarded as an appositive construction: मुझे दो जोड़े कपड़े मिले, 'I got two suits (of) clothes.'

c. In the following from the *Prem Ságar*, बालक is a predicative adjunct of the personal pronoun, मैं: मैं बालक हूं बैरी तेरो, 'I, a child (i.e., although a child), am thy enemy.'

d. When a substantive or any word employed substantively is used simply as a word, without reference to its meaning, it is very often followed by a demonstrative pronoun in apposition. Thus, the phrase '*Ne* is not attached to the subject of an intransitive verb,' must be rendered, अकर्मक धातु के कर्त्ता में ने यह नहीं लगता. So again, जहां कर्म में को यह चिन्ह रहता है, 'where the object has the sign *ko*.' So also where a case other than the nominative is used as a word in the nominative, the same construction is used: as, यहां उस का यही ठीक है, 'here *us ká* is correct.' But the appositive pronoun is sometimes omitted where no ambiguity will follow: as, यहां उस पर ठीक है, 'here *us par* is correct;' करना इस के साथ कहीं को और कहीं का रहता है, 'with (the word) *karná* is connected sometimes *ká*, and sometimes *ko*.'

e. In the following, यह is to be regarded as added in apposition with सो, for the sake of emphasis; सो है प्राणप्यारी यह तेरे मिलने को तरसता है, 'this very same (person), darling, is longing to meet thee.'

(2) The subject may be extended or defined by an adjective. In this case we may distinguish (*a*) the *attributive*, and (*b*) the *predicative* construction.

a. In the attributive construction, the adjective precedes the noun, and forms conjointly with it one complex idea; as, e.g., यह डरावनी मूरत कलि युग है, 'this frightful form is the *Kali Yug*.'

b. In the predicative construction, the adjective follows the noun, and is apprehended separately from it, being, as it were, the predicate of an abridged relative clause. Thus, इस को मारूं तो निर्भय राज करूं, '(if) I kill this (child), then I may reign without fear.' In the following both constructions occur: उस बल का ज्येष्ट पुत्र महापराक्रमी बड़ा तेजस्वी बाणासुर था, 'the youngest son of that *Bal*, very powerful, and greatly renowned, was *Báṇásur*.'

(3) The subject may also be defined by a pronoun used adjectively.

Thus, यह कन्या है भांजी तेरी, 'this girl is thy niece;' जो बात तुम ने कही, 'the thing which you said.'

(4) By a numeral.

Thus, इस बीच दोनों भाई आए, 'in the midst of this, the two brothers came;' दो सहस्र योद्धा दिखाई दिये, 'two thousand warriors appeared.'

(5) By a genitive.

Thus, सब सभा के लोग चुप हो रहे, 'all the people of the assembly held their peace;' अब मेरा मनोरथ पूरा हुआ, 'now my desire has been fulfilled.'

a. Sometimes the defining genitive is omitted, when it is indicated by the context. Thus, बड़ी चिन्ता रहती थी कि तुझे अच्छा पति मिले, 'there continued a great anxiety that you might find a good husband;' where इस की, referring to the following substantive clause, is to be understood before चिन्ता.

Rem. As the genitive is *de facto* an adjective, it admits of the two constructions mentioned above under (2). But as Hindí sometimes imitates the Persian by placing the genitive after the governing noun, its predicative character cannot always be certainly inferred from its position. But it is evidently used as as a predicate in the following: छः बालक तो तिन के कंस ने मार डाला, 'six children of theirs, then, *Kaṉs* has slain.'

(6) By an adjective participle.

Here again, we have both (*a*) the attributive and (*b*) the predicative constructions. Thus, एक मरा सांप वहां पड़ा था, 'a dead snake lay there;' but, in the predicative construction, एक सांप मरा हुआ पड़ा था, 'a snake lay dead;' कंस डरता कांपता उठ खड़ा हुआ, '*Kaṉs*, fearing and trembling, rose and stood up.'

860. The predicate of a sentence may be extended, **Extension of Predicate.**

(1) By a noun, pronoun, or any word or phrase used substantively. This includes several particulars.

a. The direct object of a verb: as, तुम संदेसा कहो, 'declare the message;' राजा भीष्मक कुछ न बोले, '*Rájá Bhíshmak* said nothing.' The object may sometimes be a phrase or sentence; as in the following, after a conjunctive participle: कपिन्ह विध्वंस कृत मख देखि, 'seeing the sacrifice destroyed by the monkeys;' बरात घर के निकट आई सुन, 'hearing that the marriage procession had come near the house;' and, after an imperfect participle, चलिहि बरात सुनत सब रानी, 'all the queens, on hearing (the words), The marriage procession will move.'

Rem. Observe, that the object of the verb may itself again be defined in the same way as the subject noun (§ 859). Thus, मेरा अपराध छमा कीजे, 'pardon my transgression;' इन्हें बन में अकेले न छोड़ियो, 'do not leave them alone in the jungle.'

b. Or the predicate, under the conditions specified in § 412, may be extended by the case of the agent; as, ब्राह्मा ने देवताओं को समझा दिया, '*Brahmá* caused the gods to understand.' And the case of the agent may be further defined by a noun or nouns in apposition: as, स्वर्ग को दो ही ने छुड़ाया है एक तो आगे नरसिंह के नखों ने और अब आप के तीक्ष्ण बाणों ने, 'heaven only by two has been delivered; once before, by the nails of *Narsiṇh*, and now by your Majesty's sharp arrows.'

c. Or by a dative; as, नंद जी ने सब ब्राह्मणों को नौता भेज दिया, '*Nand Jí* sent an invitation to all the Bráhmans.'

d. Or, in short, by any case of any noun or pronoun, defining the predicate in respect of time, place, manner, etc.; as, इन्हों ने गेह में मोहन को आने दिया, 'they allowed *Mohan* to come into the house;' उस के मन से पिछला सब शोक गया, 'all the former grief left his heart;' आग पर्वत की चोटी तक लहकी, 'the fire swept to the top of the mountain.'

e. Or the defining noun may be a nominative in apposition with the predicate; as, षड्दर्शनों के नाम ये हैं न्याय वैशेषिक सांख्य योग्य मीमांसा वेदान्त, 'the names of the six systems are these, *Nyáya, Vaisheshik, Sáṅkhya, Yogya, Mímáṇsá, Vedánt.*' In the following, the nominative defining the predicate is appositive to the subject: तिस का आठवां लड़का तेरा काल उपजेगा, 'her eighth child shall be born (to be) thy death.'

(2) The predicate may be extended by an adjective; or, if a noun, also by a numeral.

Examples: हमारा घर पवित्र कीजे, 'be pleased to purify our house;' ये राजा के चार पुत्र हैं, 'these are the king's four sons;' वह पर्वत ग्यारह योजन ऊंचा था, 'that mountain was eleven *yojans* high.'

(3) Or by a conjunctive participle.

a. Observe that this participle always has the force of an adverbial adjunct of the predicate, expressing the various adverbial relations of time, place, manner, etc., as explained in § 755. Besides the illustrations there given, the following may be noted: नंद जी अति उदास हो लंबी सांसें लेने लगे, '*Nand Jí*, being very sad, began to draw long sighs;' राज ले ढंढोरा दे अपना थाना बैठाया, 'having taken the kingdom, and issued a proclamation, he established his seat.'

(4) Or by an adjective participle absolute (§ 754 (2)).

Examples: कितने एक दिन मथुरा में रहते भये, 'a number of days passed staying in *Mathurá*;' श्री कृष्ण चंद एक सुंदरी नारी संग लिये आये हैं, '*Shrí Krishn Chand* has come in company with a beautiful woman.'

Rem. The conjunctive and adjective participles may, again, themselves be defined in the same way as the tenses of a verb in the predicate of a sentence. For illustrations, see §§ 754–757.

(5) The predicate may also be extended by a preposition with its case.

Thus, उस ने बिन श्री कृष्ण चंद कोई घर न देखा, 'he saw no house without *Shrí Krishn Chand*;' सब गोपी यसोदा के पास चलीं, 'all the milkmaids went to *Yasodá*.'

(6) Or by an adverb.

Thus, वह अति प्रसन्न हुआ, 'he became greatly pleased;' शीघ्र आओ, 'come quickly.'

Agreement.

861. *Agreement* is three fold, viz.; (1) of an adjective used attributively with its noun; (2) of an adjective in the predicative construction with its noun; (3) of the predicate of a sentence, whether verb or adjective, with the subject.

Attributive Agreement.

862. The general rules regulating the agreement of an adjective *attributive* with its subject have been already stated and illustrated (§ 199). The same rules apply to the agreement of the genitive attributive with the noun it defines.

863. But when an adjective or genitive attributive defines several nouns of different genders, usage as to agreement varies.

(1) The attributive may, preferably, agree in gender with the nearest noun.

Examples: **उस की बहू और लड़के**, 'his wife and children;' **तुम्हारी स्त्री और चार पुत्र**, 'your wife and four sons.'

(2) Or the attributive may take the form of the masculine, as the 'more worthy' gender, even though the noun immediately following be feminine.

Examples: **तुम्हारा स्त्रीपुत्रादि**, 'your wife, sons, etc.;' **पुरुषराम जी ने अपने माता और भाइयों को बुलाया**, '*Purusrám Jí* called his mother and brothers;' **अपने स्त्री बालक समेत**, 'with his wife and child.'

Predicative Agreement: Adjectives.

864. When an adjective or adjective participle occurs in the *predicative* construction with its noun, if the noun be in the accusative with **को**, the adjective or participle regularly takes the form of the uninflected masculine singular, irrespective of the gender or case of the noun.

Examples: **मैं त्रिभुवन में ऐसा पराक्रमी किसू को नहीं देखता हूं**, 'in the three worlds I see no one so powerful;' **नगर को जलता देख**, 'seeing the city burning.'

a. But occasionally the predicative adjective or participle takes the feminine termination even after the accusative with को. Thus, in *Damayanti*, मुझ दासी को तुम ने जंगल में अकेली छोड़ा, 'you have left me, your handmaid, alone in the wilderness.'

Rem. Here the construction seems confused; for although the adjective takes the feminine termination, the verb follows the usual rule and retains the masculine form after *ko*.

b. Observe, that when a participle is found inflected after a noun with को, it is to be regarded, not as a predicative adjunct, but as in the absolute construction (754 (2)). Thus, जहां मुनि ऋषि देवताओं को बैठे पाता था, 'where he would find seated, sages, philosophers, and gods.'

865. The same rule as to agreement applies to the pronominal accusatives in ए and एं as to those in को. Thus, हम किसे सच्चा जानें, 'whom shall we regard as the real (one)?.'

a. But in this case, again, we occasionally find a different usage;' as, e.g., in the following; बन में इन्हें अकेले मत छोड़ियो, 'do not leave this (child) alone in the jungle.' Here इन्हें, referring to *Krishna*, is an honorific plural.

866. If the noun be in the nominative or the nominative form of the accusative, the predicative adjective or participle agrees with it in gender and number, as in the attributive construction.

Thus, मन की आस क्यों नहीं पूरी करती, 'why dost thou not fulfil the desire of (my) heart?;' गायें रांभती हाँफती फिरती हैं, 'the cows, panting and lowing, are wandering about;' अपनी गोद मैली करते हैं, 'they soil their laps.'

a. In the following phrase we must supply the 1st personal pronoun; तुम ने इस बन में तजी अकेली, 'you have left (me) alone in this wilderness.'

Inflection of Predicate.

867. The predicate verb, adjective, or noun must be inflected to agree with the subject in number, gender, and person, in so far as they may be capable of such inflection.

Thus, रत्न ही को सब ढूंढते हैं, 'all seek the *jewel*;' लिखने की सामग्री नहीं है, 'there is no material for writing;' शास्त्रविद्या औ शस्त्रविद्या ये दोउ उच्च पद को दैनवारी हैं, 'sacred science and military science—these two procure (men) a high rank.'

a. Observe, that the case of the perfect of transitive verbs, as construed with ने, is no exception to this rule; inasmuch as that which in English is the object, in this passive construction becomes the subject of the verb, with which it therefore agrees according to rule; as, कै (बिहारी ने) . . पिछली प्रीति सब बिसारी, lit., 'or is the old love all forgotten (by *Bihárí*)?;' सो छओं बसुदेव को ब्याह दीं, 'the six (daughters) were given in marriage to *Basudev.*'

868. When the subject of a verb is a sentence, the predicate is always put in the 3rd masculine singular. Thus, in the passive construction, एक गोपी ने कहा सुनो आली, 'one milkmaid said, Listen, dear!'.

Agreement with Honorific Pronoun.

869. When the subject is an honorific pronoun, an honorific plural, or a title of respect, although the reference is to an individual, the predicate or predicates, as also all attributive adjuncts, must agree with it in the plural.

a. It will often happen that the noun or adjective in the predicate nominative, will admit of no distinction in form for plurality. But if, with such a predicate, any inflectible adjunct be joined, it must take the plural inflection, as in the second of the following examples: ये विधाता हैं, 'this is *Vidhátá*;' यही जगत के कर्त्ता हैं, 'this is the Creator of the world;' आप कब तक लौट आंयगे, 'by what time will your honour return?'; हमारे गुरु कण्व ऋषि यहां नहीं हैं, 'our spiritual guide, *Kanva*, the sage, is not here.'

870. When a pronominal nominative plural refers to both masculine and feminine objects, the predicate takes the form of the masculine gender; as, सुदामा की स्त्री बोली ... अब हम महादुःख पाते हैं, '*Sudámá's* wife said (to her husband), Now we are experiencing great trouble.'

Agreement when Two Genders.

871. When the subject consists of two or more nouns or pronouns of different genders, the predicate and copula commonly agree in gender with the nearest noun. The same rule, it should be remarked, applies to an attributive adjunct under similar circumstances.

Thus, इस के तीन नेत्र और चार भुजा थीं, 'this (creature) had three eyes and four arms;' तरुणापन धन प्रभुता अविवेकता ये चारों एक एक अनर्थ की करनिहारी हैं, 'youth, wealth, authority, lack of judgment, these four are each occasions of failure;' आंधी और मेंह आया, 'a dust-storm and shower came.'

a. Some say that occasionally the attributive or predicate takes the masculine gender without reference to the gender of the nearest noun. But I am not able to find any good authority for such usage, and have only noted the following illustration of it in literature: *na purush na strí áyá*, 'neither man nor woman came.'

Agreement when Two 'Persons.'

872. When the subject consists of two or more words of different persons, the verb then preferably agrees with the 1st person, rather than the 2nd or 3rd, and the 2nd, rather than the 3rd.

a. In this case, if the person preferred be in the singular, the verb agrees with it in that number, even though another noun be associated with it. Examples are as follows: यह तुम्हारा कल्पित आत्मा हम तुम नहीं हैं, 'you and I are not that imagined spirit of yours;' आज मैं और तू वहां चलूंगा जहां तू और वह बैठा था, 'to-day thou and I will go to the place where thou and he were seated;' वहां तू और वह न जाने पायगा, 'thou and he will not obtain leave to go there.'

Rem. In the colloquial, however, many people follow the same rule with regard to agreement in the case of different persons, as when there are different genders; i.e., the verb is made to agree in person with the nearest word. Thus many would say, *maiṉ aur tú chalegá, tú aur we chaleṉge.*

Agreement with Generic Words.

873. When the subject denotes, not an individual, but a class, the predicate, although referring to a plurality of individuals, is placed in the singular.

Example: दल चला आता था, 'the army was going along.' So in the following, the subjects are regarded as collectives: ये छः कर्म्म ब्राह्मण के लिये स्थापन किया, 'these six duties were appointed for the Bráhman;' तीन दिन रात बीत गया, 'three days and nights passed.'

a. On the same principle, सब, 'all,' is often treated as a singular; as, सब को सब घबराई, 'all of them were troubled;' यह सब मित्र का दूषण है, 'all these are faults in a friend.'

874. Finally, it should be remarked that the common people, as might be expected, are often very careless of the laws of agreement. Deviations from rule are even found occasionally in literature. Thus we read, in Prof. Eastwick's edition of the *Prem Ságar*, अपने बहन को नौतने गई, 'she went to invite her sister.'

Agreement neglected in Verse.

875. In poetry, moreover, the rules of agreement often give way to the necessities of the metre, as in the following, where जे, (*plur.*) is construed first with a singular verb, and afterwards with a plural: जे यह कथा कपट तजि गावा कहहिं सुनहिं, 'those who, abandoning deceit, sing this tale, hear (it and) tell (it).'

Naipálí Adjective Participle.

876. In Naipálí, the affix को, which is commonly added to participles used adjectively, is also affixed to phrases, thus indicating more clearly their predicative character; thus, त्यो काहाँ बाट को थियो हामीले भनन सक्तौँ नठ, 'we cannot tell whence he was.' This को is then inflected in accord with the above principles.

II.—Of Compound Sentences.

A. Of Co-ordinate Sentences.

877. When two or more connected sentences are grammatically independent of one another, they are called *co-ordinate* sentences; and when one is dependent upon the other, it is called a *subordinate* sentence.

878. *Co-ordinate* compound sentences in Hindí, as in other languages, may be classified as *Copulative*, *Disjunctive*, *Adversative*, and *Causal*.

Copulative Sentences.

879. The conjunctions proper to copulative co-ordination are और and भी. और, 'and,' joins two propositions when they are regarded as of equal importance, and as independent one of the other. और . . . भी, 'and' . . . . 'also,' implies that the affirmation of the former clause is extended either (*a*) in the subject, or (*b*) in the predicate. Copulative Co-ordination.

Examples: वह चला गया और फिर नहीं आया, 'he went away, and did not return;' श्री कृष्ण जी पधारे और बलराम जी भी उन के संग चले गये, '*Shrí Krishṉ* departed, and *Balrám Jí* also went off with him;' यह पुरुष धर्मी है और वह बहुत विद्यामान भी है, 'this man is virtuous, and he is also very learned.'

a. Very often the copula or verb may be omitted from either the first or the second member of the copulative sentence. Thus, यह पुरुष धर्मी औ बहुत विद्यामान भी है, 'this man is both virtuous and also very learned.' The ellipsis of the verb in the second member, is more common in the colloquial speech than in literature.

b. फिर or पुनि is often used as a copulative conjunction, with a resumptive force. Thus, उस ने ऊषा को उठा लिया फिर अनिरुद्ध जी को भी बांध लिया, 'he lifted up *U'shá*; again, he also bound *Aniruddh Jí.*'

c. The pronominal phrase, तिस पर भी, lit., 'upon that also,' is often used as a copulative conjunction, with an *enhancive* force; as, तिस पर भी मनुष्य अधर्म्म करेंगे, 'moreover, men will do unrighteousness.'

Disjunctive Sentences.

Disjunctive Co-ordination. **880.** Disjunctive co-ordinate sentences, when affirmative, are connected by the conjunctions वा or अथवा, या, किंवा, कै and कि, 'or.' Any of these may be repeated in successive clauses, when the first must be rendered 'either,' and the second, 'or.' There is no difference in their meaning: वा is preferred to अथवा to connect single words; अथवा is preferred to connect sentences. The Arabic या appears to be supplanting these. When negative, each member is introduced by the negative particles; न or नहीं before the first member, and न before the second and following clauses.

Examples: हम इन को लेके कुत्ते को हांक सकते हैं अथवा खूंटी बना सकते हैं, 'we can take them and drive away a dog, or make stakes of them;' इन्हें पछाड़ मारो कै मेरे आगे से टालो, 'throw him down, or drive him away from my presence;' धूप लगी है या जैसा मैं समझा हूं, 'has the heat affected (her) or (is it) as I have imagined?'; न वह ठांव है न वह टूटी मढ़ैया, 'neither is there that place, nor that ruined cottage;' धूप नहीं व्यापती न पसीना आता है, 'neither does the heat (of the sun) affect it, nor does the perspiration come.'

a. The second member of a disjunctive sentence may be introduced by नहीं तौ, 'else,' 'otherwise;' as, अब तू या छूट ही जायगा नहीं तौ कुत्तों गिद्धों का भक्षण बनेगा, 'now thou shalt either be released, or else be made food for dogs and vultures.'

b. Sometimes sentences are disjunctively co-ordinated by चाहे .... चाहे; thus, चाहे आवे चाहे न आवे, 'whether he come, or do not come.'

c. The first negative is sometimes omitted; as, इन्हें पाने का हर्ष न जाने का शोक, 'this (man) has neither joy at finding, nor sorrow at losing.' And sometimes the second, as in the common saying: सांच बरोबर तप नहीं झूठ बरोबर पाप, 'neither penance equals truth, (nor does any) sin equal falsehood.'

Adversative Sentences.

881. In adversative co-ordination, two statements are contrasted with one another. These adversative sentences are of three kinds, viz.: (1) the second proposition may be *contradictory* or exclusive of the first; (2) it may be merely *restrictive* of the former statement; or (3) the contrast may be made by *extending* the former statement. Adversative Co-ordination.

a. It is doubtful whether Hindí as yet has strictly appropriated certain adversative conjunctions to introduce restrictive, as distinguished from contradictory, adversative clauses. But, on the whole, the tendency seems to be to introduce a contradictory adversative clause by परन्तु (very rarely, किन्तु), or the equivalent Arabic लेकिन; while पर is commonly employed to introduce a sentence merely restrictive of the other. But an *extensive* adversative clause is regularly introduced by बरन, or the Arabic बल्कि.

b. In the following examples, परन्तु, किन्तु and पर, are used strictly in accordance with the principle above suggested: (1) जीव का बनानेवाला कोई नहीं परन्तु वह आप से आप सदाकाल से बना है, 'of the soul there is no creator, but it has existed of itself from eternity;' दुरात्मा को शास्त्र के पढ़ने से कुछ नहीं होता किन्तु इस विषय में स्वभाव ही बलवान है, 'a man of bad character gains nothing from reading the *Shástra,* but in this matter the nature prevails:' (2) तू ने तो बड़े बड़े बली मारे हैं पर अब मेरे हाथ से जीता न बचेगा, 'thou hast indeed slain many very mighty (men), but now thou shalt not escape alive out of my hand;' मन से तो चाहा कि भागूं पर मारे लाज के भाग न सका, 'in his heart, indeed, he wished to flee, but, for shame, flee he could not.'

c. While these examples seem to sustain the principle suggested, it must be admitted that even good writers often fail to make this distinction in the use of the different adversative conjunctions. Thus, in the following from the *Prem Ságar,* परन्तु is used to express a mere restriction: मैं तेरे आगे कहता हूं परन्तु तू किसू के सोंहीं मत कहियो, 'I am telling it before thee, but do not thou tell it before any one.' And in the following from the *Shaḍ Darshaṇ,* पर introduces a contradictory clause: वेद किसी का बनाया हुआ नहीं है पर आप से आप अनादिकाल से बना हुआ है, 'the *Ved* is not the composition of any one, but has existed of itself from eternity.'

d. Examples (3) of *extensive* adversative clauses are as follows: वे इन के कहने को कुछ ध्यान में न लाये वरन इन की ओर से मुंह फेरा, 'they paid no attention to their speaking, but turned their faces away from them;' ईश्वर के स्थापन करने के लिये नहीं वरन खंडन करने के लिये है, 'it is not for establishing (the doctrine of a) God, but rather for disproving it.'

Causal Sentences.

Causal Co-ordination. **882.** In causal co-ordination, the one sentence denotes either the reason or the consequence, the cause or the effect of the other. A sentence denoting the cause or reason, is commonly introduced by the conjunction क्योंकि, or the noun कारण, used conjunctively; a clause expressing a consequence or effect is introduced by the conjunctive phrases, इस लिये कि, किस लिये कि, इस

वास्ते, or their equivalents. The conjunction पस, 'therefore,' is confined to Urdú.

Examples: हम उन्हें सुख देंगे क्योंकि जिन्हों ने हमारे लिये बड़ा दुख सहा है, 'I will give them happiness, because they have endured great affliction for me;' ऐसा काम न करना ईश्वर के साम्हने अपराध ठहरेगा इस लिये मैं इस आशा का अवलंब करता हूं, 'not to do such a deed, will stand as a sin before God; hence I cherish this hope.'

a. For इस लिये, etc., the pronominal ablatives, इस से, या सों, ता तें, etc., are often used to connect sentences in the causal relation, as, e.g., in the following: यह पाछै दौरि मारैगी या सों या के पास गये ही बने, 'this (vulture) will pursue and kill me, hence one can only succeed by having gone to him.'

b. The connecting conjunction or phrase is sometimes omitted in cases where we must nevertheless recognize the sentences as co-ordinated in the causal relation. Thus, मेरे भक्तों को भीर पड़ी है इस समय चलकर उन की चिन्ता मेटा चाहिये, 'my worshippers are oppressed, (hence) I ought at this time to go and remove their anxiety.'

B. Subordinate Sentences.

883. Subordinate sentences are of three kinds, viz. (1) *Substantive*, (2) *Adjective* or *Relative*, (3) *Adverbial*. These will each be defined and explained in their order below. **Subordinate Clauses Classified.**

884. Before entering upon the consideration of subordinate clauses, it will be convenient to advert to a threefold classification of the tenses of the Hindí verb, as denoting the *possible*, the *impossible*, and the *actual*. I. The following four tenses denote an action, or state of being, contingently, as merely possible, viz., the Contingent Future, the Imperative, the Contingent Imperfect, and the Contingent Perfect. II. The following are used to denote a supposition whose realization has become *impossible*, viz., the Indefinite Imperfect, the Past Contingent Imperfect, and the Past Contingent Perfect. III. The remaining tenses are all indicative; i.e., they all denote an action either as a reality, or as assumed to be such. In all the rules for the use of the tenses in subordinate sentences, it is to be remembered that the tenses of Class I. are required when an action or state is regarded as a mere possibility; those of Class II. are used to denote a past possibility which cannot now be realized;* those of Class III. denote, under various phases, the actual and real. These statements will receive abundant illustration in the following sections.

Substantive Clauses.

885. Those are called substantive clauses which are equivalent to a substantive expanded into a sentence.

a. Thus, in the sentence, परमेश्वर एक है यह धर्म्म की मुख्य बात है, 'that God is one, is a fundamental doctrine of religion,' the phrase परमेश्वर एक है, is evidently equivalent to the substantive phrase, परमेश्वर का एकत्व, 'the Divine unity.' Again, in the sentence कहते हैं कि वह आवेगा, 'the phrase वह आवेगा is evidently equivalent to an accusative case after the verb कहते हैं.

886. Substantive clauses are of two kinds, (1) *Subjective* and (2) *Predicative*. Those are called *subjective* which stand either in the relation of a subject to the leading verb, or in apposition with the subject. Those are called *predicative* which limit or define the predicate of the leading sentence or any adjunct of that predicate.

---

* It should be remarked, however, that the Indefinite Imperfect, in virtue of its double character (§ 775), belongs properly to both Classes I. and II.

887. All subjective substantive clauses are regularly introduced by the particle **कि**, 'that.' Subjective Subst Clauses.

Examples of these are as follows: **खुल जायगा कि मैं राजा हूं**, 'it will be disclosed that I am the king.' Very commonly **यह**, 'this,' stands as the subject of the leading clause, and the following substantive clause then stands in apposition with it; thus, **यह सिद्ध होता है कि मनुष्य को अपनी बुद्धि से परमेश्वर का सत्य ज्ञान प्राप्त करना अत्यन्त कठिन है**, 'this is evident, that for man by his own understanding to obtain the knowledge of God, is extremely difficult.' In the following appositional sentence the substantive clause *defines* the subject, **सोभा**, of the leading verb, as to its elements: **उस समय की सोभा कुछ बरनी नहीं जाती कि सब के आगे बड़े बड़े दंतीले मतवाले हाथियों की पांति**, 'the splendour of that occasion is not to be described, how before all (were) rows of enormous tusked and furious elephants.'

a. Sometimes **कि** is omitted, as in the following: **ऐसा ध्यान बंधता है मानों शिव जी शूकर के पीछे जाते हैं**, 'a thought like this occurs; (It looks) as though *Shiv Jí* were pursuing the boar.'

b. After a leading clause expressing 'fitness,' 'duty,' 'obligation,' etc., the verb of the substantive clause is regularly put in the contingent future, or one of the respectful forms of the imperative. Thus, **उचित है किसी को वहां भेज दीजे**, 'it is fitting that (you) send some one there;' **तुम को अवश्य है कि वहां जाओ**, 'it is necessary that you go there.'

Rem. Sometimes, instead of the contingent future, the infinitive form is used as the nominative of the verb in a simple sentence. This is to be preferred when the action of the verb is conceived as a fact rather than a supposition.

888. *Predicative* substantive clauses are of various forms. Thus, they may stand as the object, either of the verb in the leading clause, or of a participial Predicative Subst. Clauses.

adjunct in the leading clause. In this case they are usually introduced by the particle कि.

Examples: नारद मुनि अनिरुद्ध जी को जाय समझाता था कि तुम किसी बात की चिन्ता मत करो, '*Nárad* the sage went and comforted *Aniruddh Jí* (saying), Do not be anxious about anything;' राजकुमारी मन ही मन यूं कहती फिरती है कि मैं किसे बरूं, 'the princess walks about, saying in her inmost heart, Whom shall I marry?' तुम देखि आओ कि कौन राजा चढ़ आता है, 'go and see what king is coming up against (us).'

a. Occasionally जो introduces the substantive clause, instead of कि. Thus, यही बिचारो जो मथुरा और वृन्दावन में अन्तर ही क्या है, 'consider this, what difference at all is there between *Mathurá* and *Brindában*.'

b. Sometimes, especially before short clauses, कि may be omitted? as, चित्ररेखा बोली सखी इधर आओ, '*Chitrarekhá* said, Friend, come here.'

c. Often the substantive clause precedes, and is then followed by a pronoun, the direct object of the verb, with which the substantive clause stands in apposition. Thus, यह मृग आया वह बराह गया उधर शार्दूल आता है यही कहते, in English idiom, 'Here comes a deer, there went a boar, yonder goes a tiger,'—on saying this; चलो बन को चलो बन को यह चिल्ला चिल्ला कर कान फोड़ते हैं, 'they split (one's) ears, screaming continually, "Go to the wood! Go to the wood."'

Subst. Clauses in Naipálí.

889. In the Naipálí Gospel, I have not found a substantive clause introduced by कि. For कि, in such clauses, is regularly substituted भनि, conjunctive participle of भन्नु, 'to say.' This follows the substantive clause, which is to be regarded as its object. English idiom will most frequently require this भनि to be rendered as 'that,' but in other cases it cannot be transferred in translation. Examples are: ईश्वर को राज्य नजिकै छ भनि जान्नु, 'know that the kingdom of God is near;' उन बार कुन पाठ ले मारौं भनि मत गर्या, 'they took counsel in what way they might kill him,' lit., 'saying, In what way may we kill him?'.

890. It is very important to observe that after verbs of 'saying,' 'thinking,' 'wishing,' etc., Hindí, unlike English, does not admit the *oratio obliqua*. On the contrary, idiom demands that the words or thoughts of the speaker be cited as they pass in his mind. **Oratio Obliqua not used.**

This principle makes it necessary, in translating from English into Hindí, to change both the tense and the person of the verb, as illustrated in the following examples: तू जा हमारी ओर से कह दे कि रानी हम तेरी चितावनी को समझें, 'Go thou, and say from me, "Queen, I (have) understood your admonition,"' where English idiom would have it, 'tell the queen that I have understood,' etc.; ज्यों चाहा कि बलदेव को मारूं, 'as he wished (i.e., was about to) kill *Baldev*,' lit., 'wished, May I kill *Baldev*.'

a. In the *Rámáyan*, we read, भुपति मन माहीं भइ गलानि मोरे सुत नाहीं.* Here there is an ellipsis of a conjunctive participle, as सोचि, 'thinking,' of which the substantive clause, मोरे सुत नाहीं, is the object; and these words, 'I have no son,' are represented as actually passing in the mind of the king. Thus we may render the passage in English idiom, 'sadness entered the heart of the king, as he thought how he had no son.'

891. Predicative substantive clauses, again, may express the *purpose* or *reason* of the action of the leading verb. **Predicative Clauses of Purpose.**

a. In this case, the substantive clause is to be regarded as in apposition to some such word as कारण or हेतु, 'reason,' 'object,' in the principal clause. Such a word is indeed, for the sake of greater clearness, often expressed. The clause denoting the purpose or reason is introduced by the conjunction कि, or the relative जो used as a conjunction. The

* Bál K.

verb of a substantive clause expressing *purpose* must be in the contingent future; but if it state a *reason*, in one of the indicative tenses. Thus, **हम तुम्हें वृन्दावन में भेजा चाहते हैं कि तुम उन का समाधान कर आओ**, 'I wish to send you to *Brindában*, that you may go and comfort them;' **बेग चलो आ जिस से सब एकसंग छेम कुशल से कुटी में पहुंचें**, 'come along quickly, that all together we may reach the hut in safety;' **शकुन्तला मुझे बहुत प्यारी है काहे से कि वह मेरी सहेली की बेटी है**, '*Shakuntalá* is very dear to me, inasmuch as she is the daughter of my confidential friend;' **तू बाबा से समझायकर कहो जो मुझे ग्वालों के संग पठाय दे**, 'do thou coax father that he may send me with the cowherds;' **इस से तेरा नाम प्रियंवदा हुआ है कि तू बात बहुत प्यारी कहती है**, 'for this (reason) has thy name been *Priyamvadá*, that thou speakest words very loving,' lit., 'for what (reason)? that, etc.'

892. A negative clause denoting purpose is introduced by the phrase, **ऐसा न हो कि**, followed by the contingent future. Thus, **वहां न जाइयो ऐसा न हो कि तुम गिरो**, 'do not go there, lest you fall.' **ऐसा** is often omitted.

a. Sometimes the connective must be supplied from the context; as, **नाहिन डर बिगरहि परलोकू**, 'I have no fear lest (my) hereafter should be ruined.'

Predicative Clauses of Result.

893. When the substantive clause denotes the result of an action, if that result is presented (1) merely as a wish or expectation, the verb must be in the contingent future; if (2) as an objective reality, the verb must be in one of the indicative tenses; if (3) as unattainable or inconceivable, the verb must be in the indefinite imperfect.

Thus (1) **एक ऐसी सुन्दर रंगभूमि बनवावें कि जिस की सोभा सुनते ही गांव गांव के लोग उठ धावें**, 'let us cause to be made such a beautiful theatre that the people of each village, immediately on hearing, may rise and run (to see it);' (2) **तुझे**

क्या ऊआ है जो तू ऐसी बातें कहता है, 'what has happened to thee, that thou art saying such things?'; वह बन में इस भांति रो रही थी अकेली कि जिस के रोने की धुन सुन रोते थे पशु पंछी, 'in the wilderness alone, she was weeping away in such a manner that the beasts, and birds, hearing the voice of her weeping, were weeping (too);' (3) अर्जुन को क्या सामर्थ थी जो बहन को ले जाता, 'what power had *Arjun*, that he should carry away (my) sister?'.

Rem. The result of an action is in Hindí more frequently expressed by an adjective clause introduced by a relative pronoun or pronominal, as illustrated in the next paragraph.

Adjective Clauses.

894. Those are called adjective (or relative) clauses which are equivalent to an adjective qualifying some word or clause in the leading sentence.

a. For example, take the compound sentence, श्री कृष्ण ने उन लकीरों को गिना जो उस ने खैंची थीं, '*Shrí Krishn* counted those lines which he had drawn.' Here the phrase introduced by जो qualifies the substantive लकीरों को after the manner of an adjective, and is indeed equivalent to अपनी खींची ऊई लकीरों को.

895. All adjective clauses are regularly introduced by the relative pronoun or a pronominal adjective, to which the corresponding correlative or a demonstrative pronoun regularly answers in the principal clause. The relative clause may be regarded as a simple expansion of the correlative pronoun. Instead of the correlative, one of the demonstratives (as, यह, वह, ऐसा, etc., or the pronominal सब) may be used in the principal clause. **Construction of Adjective Clauses.**

Examples are: जैसी तेरी दशा हो रही है वैसा ही कोई छन्द भी बना दे, 'compose some such verse as shall just correspond to your condition;' जिस ऋषि ने अपनी कन्या ऐसे भेज दी है उस का अपमान मत करो, 'do not treat with disrespect the sage who has thus sent thee his girl.'

a. Where especial distinctness is desired, the noun described by the adjective clause may be repeated in both the principal and subordinate clauses. Thus, राक्षसों का दल जो घिर आया था सो दल बादल सा छाया था, 'the army of demons which had come up around them,—that army cast a shadow as a cloud;' जा घट प्रेम ना बसे ता घट जानौ मसान, 'in whose body love dwells not, regard his body as a burning-ground (of the dead).'

b. But, much more commonly, Hindí idiom, placing the relative clause with the noun first, omits the noun from the principal clause which follows. Thus, जितने शस्त्र हरि पर घाले तितने प्रभु ने सहज ही काट डाले, 'the lord with perfect ease broke in pieces every weapon which was cast at *Hari*;' बारह योजन का नगर जैसा श्री कृष्ण ने कहा था तैसा ही रात भर में बनाया, 'a city twelve *yojans* square, such as *Shri Krishn* had directed, he built in one night.'

c. Sometimes, when the principal clause precedes, the substantive is omitted in the relative clause, as in English. Thus, राजा दुष्यन्त छुटावेगा जो सब तपोवन का रखवाला है, '*Rájá Dushyant* will deliver (you), who is the guardian of the whole sacred grove.'

d. Or the substantive may be omitted in both the principal and subordinate clause, when no particular person is intended, or when the reference is to a subject well known. Thus, जो तेरे योग्य था उसी से आंख लगी, 'thy eye fastened on him who was worthy of thee;' जिस ने सारे संसार को सृजा हम सब उसी के बस हैं, 'we are all in the power of Him who created the world.'

e. Sometimes the correlative may be omitted from the leading clause, especially in poetry; as, मेरे मन का सूल जो खटकता है निकालो, 'take out the thorn which is rankling in my heart;' जे अनिरुद्ध पर परें हथियार अधवर कटें सिला की धार, 'the weapons which fell on *Aniruddh*, were cut in two on the edge of the stone.' In the common formula of assent from an inferior, जो हुक़्म, or जो आज्ञा, there is an ellipsis of the entire principal clause (*sc.* हो सो मैं करूंगा).

f. The relative may be omitted from the subordinate clause. Thus, बचे सो भागे, 'those who escaped, fled;' मीठे बोले ताहि कौन परायौ, 'who is unfriendly to him who speaks kindly?;' उत्तर था सो सुन लिया, '(what) answer there was, that have I heard.' In the following, the relative is omitted in the successive clauses: शकुन्तला के अधर हैं सोई लता के नवीन पल्लव हैं भुजा हैं सोई बेलि हैं और यौवन हैं सोई विकसित फूल हैं, lit., 'those lips (which) are *Shakuntalá's*, they are the young buds of the vine; those arms (which) are (hers) are the tendrils; and those breasts (which) are (hers), they are the opened flowers.' This omission is especially common in these brief expressions; कुछ हो, 'anyhow;' हो सो हो, 'be it as it may;' and in the colloquial style generally; as, तुम करोगी सो अच्छा ही करोगे, 'what thou shalt do, thou wilt do right well.' It is also very frequent in poetry; as, गुरुपदरज मृदु मंजुल अंजन। नयन अमिय दृगदोषविभंजन॥ तेहि करि विमल विवेक विलोचन, 'the soft and beautiful collyrium of the dust of (my) *Guru's* feet; (which is) nectar (to) the eyes, removing (all) defect of vision,—applying this to the clear eyes of the understanding, etc.'

g. Or finally, where the connection is quite plain, both the relative and correlative pronouns are omitted; as, भला किया कंस को मारा, 'you have done well (in that you have) killed *Kaṉs*.'

h. The interrogative pronoun may take the place of the correlative or demonstrative in the principal clause; as, कौन ऐसा है जो इन ऋषिकन्याओं को सताता है, 'who is such (a person) that he is annoying these daughters of a holy sage.'

896. The indicative tenses (Class III. § 884) will appear in adjective clauses whenever the qualification is stated or assumed as a fact. Tenses in Adj. Clauses.

To the illustrations already given, may be added the following:

जितने सुरूप के लक्षण हैं विधाता ने सब उसी मोहिनी में इकट्ठे किये हैं, lit., 'so many as are the marks of beauty, *Vidhátá* has brought them all together in that charming creature.'

897. But when the qualification is not stated as an objective reality, one of the contingent tenses is employed.

a. This is especially the case (1) in adjective clauses, denoting the object, purpose, or result, of an action; also, (2) in all indefinite specifications of number, quantity, quality, etc., where no particular individuals are intended. In this latter case, ऐसा, and इतना or इत्ता, are very commonly found in the principal clause; and the subordinate clause is to be regarded as the expansion of that pronominal. Sometimes the adjective clause is introduced by कि, instead of जो. Examples are as follows: (1) यह ब्राह्मण की बेटी नहीं है जो मेरे ब्याहने योग्य न हो, 'this is not a *Brahman's* daughter, whom it would not be fitting for me to marry;' भांति तेहि राखब राऊ। सोच मोर जेहि करहिं न काऊ, 'keep the king in such a way that he may never feel troubled about me.' (2) जिस शास्त्र में परमेश्वर का शुद्ध वर्णन हो, 'in that Scripture in which there may be a clear account of God;' जितने लोग आए हों सब को नेवोता दो, 'as many people as may have come, invite them all;' ऐसा आनन्द उपजा कि दुख नाम को न रहा, 'such joy arose that sorrow remained not for a name;' i.e., 'not the name of sorrow remained?' ऐसा उपाय करो जो फलदायक हो, 'lay such a plan as may be effective;' किसे इतनी सामर्थ है जो उसे बखाने, 'who has so much ability that (he) might set it forth?'.

b. Under this head come sentences introduced by the words, कि मानो, or often मानो alone; such as, यह भी ऐसा दुर्बल और पीला पड़ गया है मानो . . . उसे रात रात भर जागते बीता है, 'he too is become so thin and sallow that it seems as if he had passed whole nights waking,' lit., '(that) you may believe,' etc.; the remainder of the sentence being really an objective substantive clause dependent on मानो.

c. Sometimes कैसा is used for ऐसा in the principal clause, especially where surprise is expressed; as, कैसी छलांग भरी है कि धरती से ऊपर हो दिखाई देता है, 'it has made what a bound! so that he appears quite above the ground.'

d. In the following the principal clause implies a condition, which not being realized, the result was impossible. Hence the indefinite imperfect (§ 775 (5)) is used in the adjective clause; as, अर्जुन की क्या सामर्थ थी जो हमारी बहन को ले जाता, 'what was *Arjun's* power that he should carry off our sister?'. But in the following the contingent future is employed; नहीं तो उन की क्या सामर्थ थी जो कौरवों से लड़े, 'else what was their power that they should fight with the *Kauravs*?'.

e. Sometimes the adjective clause contains two or more relatives corresponding to as many correlatives in the principal clause. In this case English idiom requires that all, except the leading relative, be translated as indefinites. Thus, जो जेहि भाव नीक तेहि सोई, 'whatever pleases any one, that seems good to him;' जिन के रही भावना जैसी प्रभु मूरति देखी तिन तैसी, 'whatever affection existed with any one, according to that they beheld the lord's form.'

Rem. A similar construction occurs with relative adverbs.

f. Sometimes जैसे, used adverbially, is elegantly substituted for the relative in final clauses, so that they assume the form of adverbial clauses. Thus, जैसे जाय मोह भ्रम भारी करहु सो जतन, 'make such an effort as that vain affection and gross error may depart.'

g. Similarly जहां may take the place of the noun and relative which should appear in the adjective clause; as, धन्य सो नगर जहां तें आये, 'blessed that city whence they came.'

Adverbial Clauses.

Adverbial Clauses Defined

898. The *adverbial* clause is the expansion of an adverb. It therefore defines the predicate of the principal clause in respect of time, place, manner, cause, or any other adverbial idea.

Temporal Adverbial Clauses.

899. *Temporal* abverbial clauses are regularly introduced by जब (जद् or जौ), 'when,' to which the correlative तब (तद् or तौ) regularly corresponds in the principal clause. As remarked in § 642, related adverbial ideas are expressed by the combination of the postpositions से, तक, etc., with the temporal adverb.

Examples are as follows: जब वहां न पाया तब आपस में बोलीं, 'when (they) found (him) not there, then they said among themselves;' भोर जब उठता है तौ सोधी कोई बात मुख से नहीं निकलती है, 'when at daybreak he rises, then no word comes aright from his mouth;' जब तक सांसा तब तक आसा, 'while there is life, there is hope.'

a. For the above adverbs may be substituted various nouns denoting time, as समय, काल, दिन, etc., preceded by the relative pronoun in the subordinate, and the correlative, or a demonstrative, in the principal clause. Thus, e.g., जिस समय अनिरुद्ध जी को बानासुर ले गया उस काल अनिरुद्ध जी बिचारते थे, 'at the time *Bánásur* carried off *Aniruddh*, *Aniruddh* was reflecting.'

b. Occasionally a temporal clause is elegantly introduced by कि, as, वह भूखा बैठा था कि इस में विश्वामित्र ने यह बचन कहा, 'he was sitting hungry, when *Visvámitra* said this word.' When कि is used with जब, the clause, although temporal in form, is causal in sense. Thus, जब कि तू सुख भोगने जाती है रोना उचित नहीं है, 'since thou art going to enjoy pleasure, it is not right to weep.'

c. As in adjective clauses, the relative is often omitted: as, सब गोपियां चारों ओर से घेर कर खड़ी भईं तब श्री कृष्ण उन्हें साथ लिये वहां आए, 'all the milk-maids stood encircling him on every side, then *Shrí Krishṇ*, taking them along, came to that place;' चलेऊ प्रसंग दुरायऊ तबऊं, 'when conversation is actually going on, even then conceal (it).'

900. *Local* adverbial clauses are regularly introduced by the relative adverbs जहां, or जिधर, or their equivalents, combined, when necessary, with various postpositions. The proper correlative or the demonstrative regularly follows in the principal clause. Local Adverbial Clauses.

Thus, जहां लोमस ऋषि थे तहां कितने एक लड़के खेलते हुए आ निकले, 'several children, playing, came out where the sage *Lomas* was;' जहां कंस गया है तहांई तुम्हें भी भेजूंगा, 'where *Kaṇs* has gone, to that very place will I send you too.'

a. When the principal clause precedes the subordinate, वहां is commonly preferred to the correlative तहां; as, रानियां वहां गईं जहां . . . दोनों बीर मृतक लिये बैठे थे, 'the queens went where the two heroes were seated with the corpse;' वहीं गया जहां बसुदेव देवकी थे, 'he went to the very place where were *Basudev* and *Devakí*.'

b. Occasionally, as in temporal clauses, a noun, of locality, combined with the relative or correlative pronoun, takes the place of one or both of the local adverbs; as, धन्य यह ठौर जहां आकर प्रभु ने दर्शन दिया, 'blessed (is) this place, where the lord has come and revealed himself.'

901. *Modal* adverbial clauses are regularly introduced by the modal adverb ज्यूं, or its equivalents, followed by त्यूं, etc., in the principal clause. Modal Adverbial Clauses.

Thus, ज्यौं रथ निकट आया त्यौं गोपियां कहने लगीं, 'as the chariot drew near, the milkmaids began to say.' Or, rarely, the adverbial clause may be introduced by कि, indicating it as the explication of यों in the leading sentence. Thus, यों कह

देवकी को बचाऊं कि जो पुत्र मेरे होगा सो तुम्हें दूंगा, 'speaking thus, I may save *Devakí*, namely; The son which I shall have I will give to you.'

Rem. The latter clause here approximates closely in character to an objective substantive clause; but differs from it in that the sentence is not given as the very words to be spoken, so that it cannot stand in the relation of an accusative to the verb कह.

a. Still more common than the above, is the adverbial use of जैसे or its equivalents to introduce a modal clause. This idiom is used almost invariably in introducing a comparison. Thus, जैसे आप ने कंस को मार भक्तों को सुख दिया तैसे ही मधुपुरी का राज कर प्रजा पालन कीजे, 'as Your Majesty, having destroyed *Kans*, gave joy to your worshippers, even so, reigning over *Madhupur*, be pleased to take care of the people;' जैसे बने तैसे हो ले आते हैं, 'in whatsoever way it may be accomplished, so will we bring him,' where the present is used of an imminent future.

b. When the principal clause precedes the other, the demonstrative is commonly substituted for the correlative pronominal. Thus, ऐसा सुख माना कि जैसे तपी तप कर अपने तप का फल प्राप्त कर सुख माने, 'they rejoice as an ascetic, having done penance, rejoices on receiving the fruit of that penance.'

c. The correlative may be omitted from the principal clause; as, जैस खाल लुहार के सांस लेत बिनु प्रान, 'like the bellows of the blacksmith, it breathes without life.'

d. For जैसे after ऐसे, मानो is often idiomatically substituted; as, ऐसे दीप्तिमान हैं मानो सान का चढ़ा हीरा, '(the king) is as radiant as a polished diamond,' lit., 'as a diamond (which has been) applied to a grindstone.'

e. For जैसे and तैसे, जिमि and तिमि are often substituted in the *Rámáyan.* The correlative, however, is often omitted. Thus, जिमि यह कथा सुनायउ मोही तिमि जनि हरिहि सुनायउ कबहू, 'never tell this story to *Hari*, as you have told it to me.' सहित दोष दुख दास दुरासा दलइ नाम जिमि रवि निस नासा, 'the Name removes the worshipper's despair, with (his) sin and sorrow, as the sun destroys the night.'

f. As in other adverbial clauses, appropriate nouns combined with the relative and correlative pronouns, may take the place of the modal adverb; as, जिहि विधि भा आगे कहब, 'I will tell thee hereafter in what way it happened.'

902. In temporal, local and modal adverbial clauses alike, one principle determines the use of the indicative or contingent tenses. When the adverbial clause is introduced merely as a supposition, without reference to any objective reality, then one of the three contingent tenses, future, imperfect, or perfect, must be used; but when it is presented as an objective reality, one of the indicative tenses. **Tenses in Adverbial Clauses**

a. Thus, the contingent future is used in indefinite statements of time and place; as, जब वह आवे मुझे खबर दीजे, 'when he comes, (then) let me know;' जहां मिले उसे वहां पकड़ लाइयो, 'seize and bring him from wherever you may find him.'

b. Similarly, one of the contingent tenses is commonly employed in comparisons, when the object with which comparison is made, is regarded merely as a *mental conception*. Thus, दोनों वीर ऐसे टूटे जैसे हाथियों के यूथ पर सिंह टूटे, 'the two heroes broke (upon them) as a lion might break upon a herd of elephants.' But when the illustration is regarded as an *objective reality*, one of the indicative tenses is employed. Thus, श्री कृष्ण बलराम ऐसे सोभायमान लगते थे जैसे सघन घन में दामिनी सुहावनी लगती है, '*Shrí Krishṇ* (and) *Balrám* seemed as beautiful as seems the lightning in a dense storm-cloud.'

Rem. The choice of the tense in comparisons is thus obviously determined entirely by the way in which the speaker or writer chooses to regard the object with which comparison is made.

c. In poetry, the copula being omitted, the mode of conception is left undefined. Thus, जो गुनरहित सगुन सो कैसे जल हिमउपल, 'He who is the Unconditioned, how becomes he conditioned? (as) the water (becomes) ice.'

Causal Adverbial Clauses.

903. *Causal* adverbial clauses express (1) the reason, ground, or consequence of the principal clause. They are commonly introduced by जो, used as a conjunction (§ 666), in the sense of 'since,' or 'whereas.' The principal clause is then introduced by सो or तो.

Examples: हम जो ऐसे दुख में हैं हमें कोई छुड़ानेवाला चाहिये, 'since we are in such trouble, we ought to have some deliverer;' जो इस जीव को दुख ही बदा है तो कुछ बस नहीं है, 'since misery alone is fated to this creature, there is nothing in (her) power,' i.e., 'there is no help for it.' Sometimes the subordinate clause is not formally stated; thus, सो ज्ञानी पुरुष मरने के अनन्तर पाषान के समान हो रहता है, 'so intelligent man after death passes into the condition of a stone.'

Conditional Causal Clauses.

(2) Causal adverbial clauses may express the *condition* under which the action of the principal verb takes place, as the *causa sine quâ non* of the event. The subordinate clause is called the *protasis*, and the principal clause the *apodosis*. The *protasis*, expressing the condition, is regularly introduced by जो or यदि, or the Persian अगर, 'if;' and the *apodosis*, by the illative तो, and sometimes तौ भी.

Conditional Clauses in Naipálí.

904. In Naipálí, instead of जो, यदि, and अगर, a conditional clause is indicated by the word भन्या, the inflected perfect participle of भनन्, 'to say.' This भन्या is regularly placed at the end of the conditional clause. Thus, कोहि मठ थाञि आउं छ भन्या, 'if any one comes to me;' तं लाइ कसै ले बिझा मा डाक्यो भन्या, 'if any one calls thee to a feast.' This भन्या is also idiomatically used at the end of clauses which state something, not as a fact, but as a supposition; as, कुन छ जस गधाहा खाडल मा पर्‌यो भन्या, 'who is there whose ass may have fallen into a pit?'. It is also employed instead of जब कि in causal clauses of the 1st class, to denote the ground; reason, or consequence, of the action of the leading verb, as in the following: उन्हेर वे देखते न देखुन भन्या, 'whereas they seeing, see not.'

Rem. The participle भन्या, in these constructions, is to be regarded as in construction with the preceding words after the manner of a case absolute. The idiom may perhaps be illustrated by the English use of the word 'granted;' 'granted that this is so,' i.e., very nearly, 'if this is so.'

905. It is important to give careful attention to the discriminative use of the tenses in compound sentences involving a condition. The following principles are to be noted. The realization of the condition may be (1) possible, (2) actual, or (3) impossible. Hence, three general cases present themselves: Tenses in Conditional Clauses

(1) The condition may be only subjectively assumed as a *possibility*, which may or may not be in accordance with fact. In this case the verb of the *protasis* must be in one of the three contingent tenses, or in the future, imperfect, or perfect. When (*a*) the consequence is regarded as certainly following, if the condition be fulfilled, then the verb of the principal clause will be in one of the indicative tenses; but when the conclusion is presented (*b*) as merely a possible issue, one of the contingent tenses must be employed.

Thus, *a.* कल जो जुरासिंध चढ़ आवे तो प्रजा दुख पावेगी, 'if *Jurásindh* should attack us to-morrow, then the people will have trouble;' यह तुम्हारे ही घर रहे तो भली है, '(if) this (maiden) may abide in *your* house, then it is a good (thing),' sc. बात after भली; जो तेहि आजु बध बिनु आवौं । तौ रघुपतिसेवक न कहावौं, 'if I come to-day without having slain this (demon) then let me not be called the servant of the lord of *Raghu.*' *b.* जो इसी को मारूं तो निर्भय राज करूं, 'if I but kill this woman, then I may reign without fear;'

or, with the respectful form for the contingent future; जो आप इसे खोया चाहिये तो मैं एक उपाय बताऊं, 'if your honour wish to get rid of this, then I may suggest a plan.' Thus the contingent future is used in both apodosis and protasis to express a conceivable hypothesis, with its consequence. Thus, जो दिन प्रति अहार करै सोई विश्व बेगि चौपट होई, 'if he should eat every day, the world might soon be a waste.'

c. For the contingent future in the protasis, the imperative may be substituted; as, सो कृपा कर कहो तो हमारे मन का संदेह जाय, 'kindly tell me that (i.e., if you will tell me), then the doubt of my mind may be removed.'

Rem. 1. Observe that as the Oriental dislikes direct and positive assertion, a contingent tense is often used in Hindí, when English idiom would require the indicative.

Rem. 2. It must also be remembered that in all but the most modern Hindí these nice discriminations are constantly neglected, so that, in poetry especially, e.g., we often find the forms of the *contingent* future, where the letter of these rules would require the absolute future; as, e.g., *jo ihi barai amara so hoí*, where modern idiom would require *hogá*; 'he who marries this girl shall become immortal.'

(2) When the condition is assumed as a reality, either in the future, past or present time, as when its fulfilment is assuredly expected, then the protasis takes the verb in the absolute future or some other of the indicative tenses. In the apodosis, the conditions above specified necessarily regulate the choice of a contingent or indicative tense.

Examples: जो मैं सहारा दूंगी तो भेट के फल में से आधा लूंगी, 'if I help you, then I will take half of the fruit for the present;' जो मैं अब क्रोध करता हूं तो काज बिगड़ेगा, 'if I now get angry, the business will be spoiled;' जो तू ने नहीं लिया तो और कौन ले गया, 'if you did not take him, then who else did carry him off?'.

(3) In the third place, both condition and consequence may be contrary to fact and impossible of realization.

The protasis expresses a condition which was not realized, the apodosis, a consequence which would have followed, had not the condition failed. The verb of the protasis is commonly put in the indefinite imperfect, much less frequently in the past contingent perfect, and very rarely in the past contingent imperfect. The verb of the apodosis is commonly also found in the indefinite imperfect.

Examples: **जो मैं उन से कुछ मांगते तो वह देते**, 'had I asked anything from him, he would have given (it);' **जो यह प्रसंग चलता तो मैं भी सुनता**, 'had this story been going on, then I too should have heard (it).' In the following conditional clause, **जो** is idiomatically omitted from the protasis before **कदाचित**; **कदाचित किसी ने बतलाया न होता तौभी हम जान लेते**, 'if perchance no one had told (us), yet I would have perceived,' etc.

a. Sometimes the past imperfect is used in the apodosis; thus, **जो चाहता तो ला सकता था**, 'he was able to bring it, if he had wished.' The past tense, **था**, of the copula, is sometimes found alone in the apodosis; thus, **जो तुम मेरी सुनते तो अच्छा था**, 'it had been well, if you had heard what I had to say;' **जो इस बात की भनक मेरे कान तक न पहुंची होती तौ मुझ को इस पचायती से क्या काम था**, 'if a rumour of this thing had not reached my ear, then what had been the use of this *pancháyat* decision?'.

b. Sometimes the past contingent perfect is the tense of the apodosis. Thus, **जो तू एक बार भी जी से पुकारा होता तौ तेरी वह पुकार तारों से पार पहुंची होती**, 'if thou hadst even once cried out from the heart, then that cry of thine had reached beyond the stars.'

906. The conditional conjunction is often omitted in all varieties of the conditional sentence. Thus, **इस के समान बर मिले तौ दें**, '(if) a husband be found (who is) her equal, then he may give (her).' In the following, **तौ भी** introduces the apodosis: मैं रत्नों के ढेर उठा डालूं तौ भी उचित हो, '(though) I should take and cast (before them) heaps of jewels, yet it were fitting.' Here may be noted the common idiom, in which a verb is repeated with तो; as, e.g., यह कारण हो तो हो, 'possibly this may be the reason.'

a. In phrases introduced by नहीं तो, or its equivalents, there is an ellipsis of the entire protasis except its negative. Thus, इसी समय जताया चाहिये नहीं तो क्या जानिये पीछे क्या दुख दे, 'I ought to inform (him) at once, (if I do) not, then who knows what pain he may afterwards give?'. Similar are the following passages from the *Rámáyan*; सोइ रघुनाथ तुमहि करनीया नतरु .... मैं न जियब, 'that, O lord of *Raghu*, is to be done by you, else I shall not live;' सुमुखि हो नत जीवन हानी, 'be cheerful, else there is peril of your life;' सहेउं कठोर वचन सठ तोरे नाहिन्त लै जातेउं सीतहि बरजोरे, 'I endure thy hard words, wretch, else I would carry off *Sítá* by force.'

b. The illative conjunction, तो, is also sometimes omitted from the apodosis; and often, as in the following, both the illative and the conditional conjunction are omitted. Thus, काम पड़े अपना बल दिखाते हैं, 'if occasion arise, then they show their strength.' This omission is specially common in poetry; as, एक बार कैसेहुं सुधि जानौं कालहु जीति निमिष महं आनौं, 'could I in any way at all know one trace (of her), I could in a moment conquer and bring captive Death himself.'

907. Sometimes a clause is at once temporal and conditional. In this case, the *protasis* is introduced by जब, but the *apodosis*, by the illative तो; as, जब वह आवे तो मैं कहूं, 'when he comes, then I may tell;' where तो represents the 'telling' as conditioned by the previous clause.

a. Very often the temporal adverb is merely implied, and तो alone in the *apodosis*, marks the conditional character of the *protasis*. Thus, उस का ध्यान छूटा तो उन्हों ने ध्यान कर '(when) his meditation was broken, then, reflecting, he knew;' एक दिन राजा परीक्षित आखेत को गये तो वहां देखा, 'one day (when) *Rájá Paríkshit* went to hunt, then he saw there,' etc.

908. Concessive clauses are a species of conditionals, and are subject to the same rules as to the employment of the tenses. The subordinate clause is introduced by यद्यपि or यद्पि, जो भी, or even जो alone; to which तथापि, तद्पि, or, colloquially, तौ भी, परन्तु, or पर, answer in the principal clause. **Concessive Conditional Clauses.**

Examples: यद्यपि वे पुरुष ज्ञान स्वरूप मानते हैं तथापि उस की ज्ञानस्वरूपता केवल नाममात्र की है, 'although they regard man as intelligent, yet his intelligence is only a mere name;' यद्यपि तपस्वी लोगों में क्षमा बहुत होती है परन्तु जब उन का क्रोध आता है, 'although ascetics are very patient, yet when their anger rises;' यद्पि असमंजस भारी तद्पि बात इक सुनहु हमारी, 'although there is great uncertainty, yet hear a word of mine;' जो अनेक जन्म अवतार ले बहुतेरा कुछ दीजिये तौभी विद्या का पलटा न दिया जाए, 'if one should become incarnate in countless births, and give never so much, yet an equivalent for learning could not be given;' कोई इस देह को पोषे पर यह कभी अपनी न होयगी, 'although one cherish this body, yet it will never become his own.'

a. Sometimes in concessive clauses, चाहे, used as a conjunction, introduces the protasis, followed by परन्तु, or some similar word, in the apodosis; thus, चाहे अपनी सखियों की ओर ही देखा हो परन्तु मैं ने यही जाना, 'though she may have looked *toward* her companions, yet *this* I knew,' etc.

b. The conjunction may be omitted from either clause; thus, क्या हुआ जो अबकी लड़ाई में हारे, 'what though we have been worsted in this present battle?'; यद्यपि इस के फूलने के दिन अभी नहीं आये हैं कैसी कलियों से लद रही है, 'although the blooming time of this (vine) is not just now come, how it is loaded with buds!'.

Of Interrogative Sentences.

Construction of Interrogative Clauses.

909. These present but little that calls for special remark. In the absence of any other interrogative word, a question is often indicated by the interrogative pronoun, क्या (*poet.* कि [की] or किं), which in such cases is incapable of translation. When a question merely implies perplexity, so that a direct answer is not expected, the contingent future may be employed; but when asked for information, one of the indicative tenses is required.

Examples: अब इस गोकुल में रहना कैसे बने, 'now how can one manage to remain in *Gokul*?'; ऐसे लोग क्या कुछ भला कहाते हैं, 'are such people called anything good?'; यह अपमान कैसे सहा जायगा, 'how shall this dishonour be endured?'—where the question is equivalent to a strong negative statement; मैं तुझे क्या मारूं, 'why should I kill thee?'; रामजननि हठ करब कि काउ, 'will the mother of *Rám* ever show obstinacy?'; की तुम्ह हरिदासन्ह महं कोई, 'are you one of the servants of *Hari*?'.

910. The Hindí exhibits a special fondness for interrogative forms. Especially in vivacious conversation, the interrogative is often preferred to the direct form of statement. So also, the interrogative is often substituted for the demonstrative, or correlative pronoun or adverb in the various compound sentences above noted,—especially when surprise is expressed. Thus, जो तू यह न कहती क्या आधा फल न मिलता, 'if you had not said this, would you not have had half of the fruit?'; जो वह नेह ही न रहा तो अब सुध दिलावे क्या होता है, 'if that love has not remained, then if one now recall (it) to (his) mind, what comes (of it)?'; उभय मध्य सिय

सोहति कैसी ब्रह्म जीव बिच माया जैसी, '*Sítá* appeared between the two, like the Illusive Power between *Brahm* and the soul;' राजा युधिष्ठिर कहां आते हैं कि जहां मय दैत्य ने मन्दिर बनाए थे, 'where does Rájá *Yudhishṭir* come, but where the demon *Maya* had built a palace?'.

911. When an affirmative answer is expected or desired to a question, this is very commonly indicated in ordinary conversation by the negative particle न (never नहीं) at the end of the sentence, uttered with a peculiar rising inflection.

Thus, कह राजपुत्र तो कुशल से हैं न, 'tell (me), the prince is certainly well, (is he) not?' अब तो प्रसन्न ऊई न, 'now thou art surely satisfied, (art) thou not?'.

912. In Naipálí, while क्या is sometimes used, as in High Hindí, to introduce an interrogative clause, more commonly the question is indicated as such by कि at the end of the clause. In questions to which an affirmative answer is expected, this कि is regularly preceded by नउ, 'not.' Examples are: तं मसीह होस कि, 'art thou the Messiah?'; यो गालील को मानिस हो कि, 'is this a man of Galilee?'; तिम्हेरु चरा भन्दा बढ़िञा होनउ कि, 'are ye not of more value than the sparrows?'; खर्चउ को लेखा गर्दैनउ कि, 'doth he not take account of the expense?'. In the Gospel, in these cases, as in most negative clauses, नउ is written as a part of the verb which it qualifies. Interrogative Clauses in Naipálí.

Of the Collocation of Words.

913. The normal order of the parts of a simple sentence in Hindí, is (1) subject, (2) predicate, (3) copula, as, मनुष्य पापी है, 'man is a sinner;' राम दास बुद्धिमान है, *Rám Dás* is wise.' But in the passive construction of transitive verbs, the case of the agent takes the first place, the subject nominative or the accusative the second, and the predicate verb the last place; as, उस ने रस्सियां मंगाईं, 'he sent for ropes.' Normal Order of Words.

37

Deviations from Normal Order.

914. Hindí, however, allows the greatest liberty of deviating from this normal order, whether for the sake of emphasis, or to meet the necessities of metre in poetry, and of rhythm even in prose. In general, a word is rendered emphatic in proportion as it is displaced from its normal position in the sentence; as, तजती हैं पति को अकुलीनी नारी, '*base-born women* desert their husbands.' This is the rule with such predicates as धन्य, धिक्कार, etc.; as, धन्य है यह दिन, 'auspicious is this day;' धिक्कार है मुझे, 'a curse to me!'. The predicate is also emphasized by placing it after the copula, last in the sentence; as, तुम्हारा पुण्य है बहुत और पाप है थोड़ा, '*abundant* is your merit, and your sin *little*;' ये हैं ब्रह्मा रुद्र इन्द्र के ईस, 'this is the lord of *Brahmá*, *Rudra*, and *Indra*.' Or the predicate, if emphatic, may take the first place in the sentence; as, सामर्थी वेई हैं जो मा बाप की सेवा करते हैं, 'those are *powerful*, who obey their parents;' यहां सतानेवाला मनुष्य तो कोई नहीं है, 'the trouble here is no *man* (but a bee, etc.).' So, in participial tenses, the participle may for the sake of emphasis be separated from the auxiliary by several works. Thus, in the following, the participle is made strongly emphatic by placing it at the beginning of the sentence, while the auxiliary remains at the end; आये तो मृग के पीछे थे, 'you had *come* indeed after deer.'

Place of Copula

915. The copula receives the greatest emphasis when placed in the beginning of a sentence; as, है तो अच्छा, 'it *is* indeed good.' This is especially common, to heighten the effect of a following adversative clause; as, है तो गरीब पर बुद्धिमान, 'he *is* indeed poor, but wise;' हैं तो कुशल क्षेम से पर . . . निपट भावित हो रहे हैं, 'they *are* indeed well but . . . are in much anxiety.'

Place of the Object.

916. The object of a transitive verb regularly immediately precedes it: as, वह हम को मारता है, 'he is beating me;' but is emphasized when first in the sentence; thus, इस अजीत को मैं कैसे जीतूंगा, 'this unconquerable one, how shall I conquer?'. A less emphatic position is the last; as, जो ब्याहेगा इसे सो मारेगा मुझे, 'he who marries *her*, will kill *me*.' The verb itself, whether transitive or intransitive, is emphatic in the first place; thus, मारिं कहा तोहि हम, 'shall I *kill* thee?' and also in the following; सो देते क्यों नहीं, 'why do you not *give* it?'.

a. If a verb have an indirect object, this regularly immediately precedes the direct object; as, मैं तुम को यह किताब देता हूं, 'I give you this book.' But words denoting the motive or object of an action, are regularly placed immediately before the verb; as, यह हम को बचाने आया, 'he came to save us.' But for emphasis it may follow the verb. Thus, यह असुर आया है प्रजा को दुख देने, 'to afflict the people, this demon has come.'

917. In contrasted clauses, the emphatic words may be placed, the one at the beginning of the first clause, the other, at the end of the second; thus, दुख सहा उस ने हम को दिया सुख, '*sorrow* he endured, to us gave *happiness*.' Order in Contrast.

918. In interjectional phrases, the following is an illustration of the common order; धन्य है परमेश्वर को, 'praise unto God!'. But the copula may sometimes be omitted, and the order inverted; thus, तुलसी ऐसे पतित को बारबार धिरकार, '*Tulsí*! on such a sinner, again and again a curse.' Order in Exclamations.

919. The vocative usually stands first in a sentence, but may come last for emphasis; as, तैं ने यह क्या किया पापिनी, 'what is this thou hast done, thou wicked woman?'.

920. When pronouns of different persons follow one another in the same construction, the order is the reverse of English; i.e., the first person always precedes the 2nd and the 3rd. Thus, हम तुम ने क्या फल पाया, 'what fruit have you and I obtained!' गुरुपत्नी ने हमें तुम्हें ईंधन लेने भेजा, 'the *guru's* wife had sent us and you to get firewood.' Order of Pronouns.

Position of Attributives.

921. Attributive adjuncts, whether adjectives, participles, or genitives, regularly precede the nouns they qualify. When they follow, they are to be taken predicatively, and are thus rendered emphatic. The chief exception to the statement is in the case of the genitive, which, in books written under the influence of Persian, often follows the substantive, in imitation of Persian idiom.

Examples are, वह बड़ी बस्ती है, 'that is a large town;' यह मेरी पुस्तक है, 'this is my book;' मैं ने वहां मरे हुए सिंह को देखा, 'I saw a dead lion there.' But reversing the order, these all become predicative adjuncts. Thus, वह बस्ती बड़ी है, 'that town is large;' यह पुस्तक मेरी है, 'this book is mine;' मैं ने वहां एक सिंह मरा हुआ देखा, 'I saw a lion dead there.' Thus in the following, the position of the genitive indicates it as predicative; हमारा विचार नगर से चले जाने का है, 'it is my purpose to go away from the city.'

922. Appositive adjuncts are regularly treated as attributives, and precede the noun which they define; thus, दशरथ का पुत्र राम, '*Rám* the son of *Dasarath*;' भवानी सुनार, 'the goldsmith *Bhavání*.'

Position and Emphasis.

923. All adjuncts, whether attributive or predicative, are rendered emphatic by separation from the noun which they qualify.

Thus, बिधाता का भी कुछ तुम पर बस न चलेगा, 'even *Brahmá* will not have *any* power over you;' कलि युग में राजा उपजे हैं अभिमानी, 'in the *Kali Yug*, kings have arisen (who are) *proud*;' हाथ में धनुष बाण तो है परन्तु सिर पर बन के फूलों की माला धरी है, '*in* (*his*) *hand* indeed is bow and arrow, but *on* (*his*) *head* is placed a garland of forest flowers.'

Position of Adverbial Adjuncts.

924. Adverbial adjuncts, whether words or phrases, as, e.g., conjunctive participles with their adjuncts, regularly closely precede the word they qualify. They may even come between a verb and its object. In accordance with the general principle above noted, they become emphatic in proportion to their separation from the word. Or emphasis may be expressed by placing them after the word, or between the parts of the periphrastic tenses.

Thus, शीघ्र आओ, 'come quickly!'; वह काशी में रहता था, 'he was living in *Káshí*;' वह हम से हर दिन कहता, 'he would every day say to me;' तुम चलकर देखो, 'go and see.' But with more or less emphasis, हर दिन वह हम से कहता, '*every day* he would say to me;' तुम आओगे कब, '*when* will you come?'; उस का स्वभाव कोमल बहुत है, 'her nature is sensitive, very;' इस गंडे को छूना मत, '*don't* touch that charm;' यह कहो कि तुम ने मुझे रोका क्यों था, 'tell me *why* you *hindered* me.' So, for emphasis, the relative adverb may be transferred from the beginning to the end of a sentence, as often in the drama, *Raṇdhír* aur Prem-*Mohaní*; thus, कोई बात निश्चै न हो जब तक, '*as long as* any matter be not certain.'

a. The emphatic particle, ही, is occasionally inserted in the absolute future, before the terminations गा, गी, etc. It thus appears to give emphasis to the action of the verb, rather than the futurition of the action. This idiom is especially frequent in the *Shakuntalá*; thus, इन से बातें तो करूंहीगा, 'I *will* talk with her;' राजा की आज्ञा तो मानेहींगीं, 'the king's command we will certainly keep.'

b. With the conjunctive participle, ही is regularly added to the verbal stem, but, rarely, is attached to the termination; thus, मैं तो सम्हाल करही लाता था, 'supporting it, indeed, I was bringing it.'

925. When the negative is used with compound verbs, the emphasis of the negation properly falls upon that part of the compound to which it is immediately prefixed; as, e.g., मैं नहीं लिख सकता हूं, 'I am not able to *write*;' but, मैं लिख नहीं सकता हूं, 'I am not *able* to write.' The force of illustrations is indeed lessened when dissevered from the context, Position of Negative.

but the following may be of some value: श्री कृष्ण चंद जी मुख से तो कुछ न बोल सका, पर आँखें डबडबाय ... देख रहे, '*Shrí Krishn Chand* with his mouth indeed was unable to *speak*, but with eyes full of tears stood gazing.' Here the emphasis is on the speaking, but in the following it is the fact of *ability* on which the stress of denial falls: मेरे चरण बीस बिस्वे थे अब कलि युग में चार बिस्वे रहे इस लिये कलि के बीच मैं चल नहीं सकता, 'my feet are twenty in all; now in the *Kali Yug* four out of the twenty are left, hence to walk I am unable.' Again, as appears from the context, with an emphasis on the prohibition: तुम अपनी बहन को ... निकलने न दो, 'do not allow your sister to come out;' but with a different emphasis, ऊषा को मंदिर में उठाय लाया और फिर न जाने दिया, 'he took up and carried *U'sha* to the palace, and did not let her *return*.'

a. Observe that when the passive conjugation is used in strong denials, the negative, in accordance with the above, is almost invariably placed immediately before the auxiliary. Examples are very numerous; thus, उस समय की सोभा कुछ बरनी नहीं जाती, 'to describe the beauty of that time is impossible;' मो पै चल्यो नाहिं जातु, 'for me to walk is impossible.'

b. The parts of a compound verb may be separated, for the sake of emphasis, not only by the negative, but also by one or more other words, as in the following: हो तो ऐसा हो गया हूं, 'I *am*, indeed, become exactly so.'

Position of Conjunctions. **926.** Of conjunctions it is to be observed, that भी must always immediately follow the word which it emphasizes. Thus, मेरा भी एक बेटा पढ़ता था, 'one son of *mine* was also reading;' i.e., of *mine*, as well as of some other person; but, मेरा एक पुत्र भी पढ़ता था, 'one *son*, also, of mine, was reading;' or with yet a different sense, मेरा एक पुत्र पढ़ता भी था, 'one son of mine was *reading*, also.' तो, as a particle of emphasis, regularly follows the word which it emphasizes;

as, मैं तो ज़रूर आऊंगा, 'I indeed, will surely come.' But as an illative particle it commonly takes the first place in the sentence; as, जो आप आज्ञा करें तो हम जन्मभूमि देखि आवें, 'if your honour will give permission, then I will go and see my birth-place.'

a. और (अरु, औ, औ, वो), 'and,' कि, 'that,' परन्तु, पर, किन्तु, 'but,' 'yet,' वा, अथवा, or या, 'or,' must occupy the first place in the sentence they introduce, or immediately precede the phrase they annex. जो or यदि, 'if,' यद्यपि, तथापि, etc., 'although,' regularly take the first place in the sentence; but emphatic words may precede them. Thus, यह आदमी जो आवे भी तौ भी उस से तो क्या काम हो सके, 'this man—even if he come, then of what use can he be?' वह राजा यद्यपि बहुत हो धनवान है तथापि किसी को भी कुछ देता नहीं, 'that *Rájá*, although very wealthy indeed, yet never gives any thing to any one whatever.'

927. As to the arrangement of the various members of a compound sentence, the following points are to be observed:— Arrangement in Compound Sentences.

(1) Final substantive clauses introduced by कि, 'that,' and causal sentences introduced by क्योंकि, 'because,' can never stand first, as sometimes in English. Thus, मैं इस लिये आया हूं कि आप से भेंट होय, 'I have come that I may have an interview with you;' मुझ से इस युग में रहा नहीं जाता क्योंकि शूद्र राजा हो अधिक अधर्म मेरे पर करेंगे, 'it is impossible for for me to remain in this age, because *Shúdras*, becoming kings, will exercise more injustice over me.'

a. But final and causal sentences introduced by the relative pronoun, may emphatically precede the principal clause. Thus, तुम ऐसा उपाय करो जिस से जन्म सुफल होय, 'contrive such a plan that your birth may prove fruitful (of good).'

b. Adjective clauses introduced by the relative जो, regularly precede the correlative clause; but the relative, when emphatic, may be placed last. Thus, वह गुन काम का है

जो दुख हर सके, 'that spiritual guide is of use who is able to remove sorrow;' उस पुष्प बिमान में बैठे जो लंका से आया था, 'he sat in that flower-chariot which had come from *Lanká*.' Or it may be the correlative clause which is emphasized by the reversed position; as in the following; उस ऋषि का हृदय बड़ा कठोर होगा जिस ने ऐसी सुकुमारी को ऐसा कठिन काम सौंपा है, 'very hard must be the heart of that saint who has given such a difficult task to such a fair maiden.'

928. Adverbial clauses, denoting place, time, manner, or the condition of an action, usually precede the principal clause which they follow. But when there is emphasis upon the principal sentence it will precede the subordinate clause.

a. It is to be especially observed that a conditional clause cannot follow the principal clause as freely as in English. The learner should be especially careful in translating such English phrases, as, 'he will go if you will,' to avoid the English order, as in most cases the Hindí will then be obscure. The conditional clause in Hindí very rarely and exceptionally takes the second place in a compound sentence.

b. Examples of the emphatic position of the principal before the adverbial clause are as follows: हम ने तो यह तभी जाना था जब श्री कृष्ण चंद ने . . . ब्रज की रक्षा करी, 'we indeed knew this, at that very time when *Shrí Krishn Chand* protected *Braj*;' प्यारे मनुष्यों को पहुंचाने वहीं तक जाना चाहिये जहां तक जलाशय न मिले, 'one should escort (on their way) those who are dear, until they meet a body of water.'

Arrangement in Poetry.

929. It is important to remark that in poetry, all rules and principles touching the position of words and sentences, give way to the exigencies of the verse. Thus even the order of the parts of compound words is reversed; as, e.g., in मर्दनमयन for मयनमर्दन, 'destroyer of *Mayan*,' to rhyme with सयन in the previous line. Words denoting plurality (§ 164) may precede the noun they modify; as, देहिं गुन गारी, 'they utter abusive words.' Even the postpositions may precede the noun; as, मांझ त्रिवेनी for त्रिवेनी में, 'in the Triple junction.' And an attributive may follow its noun, even at a long distance; as, रेनु भवसागर जिन कीन्ह यह, 'who has made this ocean of life as sand.' And a conditional conjunction may appear in the end of the sentence to which it belongs; as, कोटिसिंधुसोषक तव सायक यद्यपि, 'although thy arrows could dry up ten million oceans.' And the parts of compound verbs are separated and inverted quite at the pleasure of the poet, as illustrated in § 568.

CHAPTER XIII.

PROSODY.

Importance of Prosody. **930.** The Hindí system of prosody, in its fundamental principles, is substantially identical with that of the Sanskrit. In no modern language, probably, has prosody been so elaborately developed as in Hindí. Indeed, prose Hindí until recently has been quite exceptional, and almost owes its existence to the stimulus of a foreign government, or the labours of missionaries, who, as might be expected, are for the most part unable to write a foreign language except in prose. Native writers, left to themselves, have almost without exception written in verse, and their labours have resulted in a system of versification which for inexhaustible variety, as well as for its intrinsic beauty, is probably unsurpassed.

Rem. A general understanding of the principles of Prosody is a prerequisite absolutely necessary to the understanding and interpretation of Hindí poetry. Without this, the student will often be left to uncertain conjecture; nor, again, can any person, without an understanding of this topic, even read properly the simplest Hindí verse. His enunciation, if in public, is sure to be chiefly a matter of amusement to the natives who may hear him.

Quantity and Rhyme. **931.** Hindí prosody knows nothing of metre determined, as in English verse, by the accent. Missionaries have indeed produced many hymns, in accentuated verse, after the manner of English metres; but verse of this kind is entirely a foreign importation, nor is there any reason to believe that the natives of India will ever be led to exchange their own admirable system for the comparatively harsh and inflexible system of English versification, which the exigency of the occasion has called into an existence which is likely to prove but temporary.

932. All Hindí verse is regulated, like that of classic Greek and Latin, by a regard to the quantity of the syllables, as *long* or *short*. In Hindí poetry, however, unlike that of ancient Greek, Latin, and Sanskrit, rhyme (तुक) is almost universally employed; and usage demands that rhyming lines shall always correspond, not in one only, but at least in the two last syllables.

N.B. It should be remembered, however, in order to the correct interpretation of this rule, that the vowel *a*, inherent in all consonants, which in prose is often silent when medial, and always silent when final, in poetry is always counted and commonly pronounced. Thus, e.g., बात, although in prose a monosyllable (*bát*), in poetry is reckoned a dissyllable, *báta*.*

933. *Quantity* is either *long* (गुरु or दीर्घ) or *short* (लघु or ह्रस्व). A long syllable is denoted in Hindí prosodial notation by the mark ऽ, and a short syllable by the mark ।, which signs are thus respectively equivalent to the English marks – and ‿. Quantity is determined by the following rules.

934. Rule I. The vowels अ, इ, उ and ऋ, are *short*, and the remaining vowels, आ, ई, ऊ, ए, ऐ, ओ and औ, are *long*, by nature. Rules for Quantity.

---

* Vid. § 14 (4).

a. It is important to observe that although ए originally denoted a long diphthongal sound only, it has come to represent also, in Hindí, as in Prakrit, a short sound, *ĕ*,* for which reason, in Hindí poetry, ए is sometimes treated as a short vowel.

b. The principle which regulates the quantity of ए seems to be as follows. Whenever ए represents an original radical, as, e.g., in a noun like बेटा, or in a *gunated* causal base, like फेर in फेरना, from फिरना; or has resulted from the combination of two formerly concurrent letters, as in करे for करइ, from करहि, or घोड़े for घोडहि; in such cases ए is invariably long. But in words where ए represents a primitive short vowel, *a* or *i*, as, e.g., in जेहि for जिहि, रहेउं for रहउं, it is usually, though not invariably, counted prosodially short. A good illustration is found in the following half *Dohá* from the *Rámáyan*; जेहि राखेउ रघुबीर ते उबरे तेहि काल महं. This line can only be scanned in accordance with the above principle, by counting ए in जेहि, राखेउ and तेहि, as short, and the remaining *e*'s as long. Otherwise we shall have 27 instants, instead of 24, as required for each line of a *Dohá*. But in the following *Arddha Chaupáí*, ए is short in जेहि, and long in तेहि: सभय हृदय बिनवति जेहि तेही. This Prakritic short, or 'common,' ए appears chiefly in the oblique forms of the various pronouns, and as a union-vowel before verbal terminations; as, तेहि, चलेउ, करेसु, etc., etc.†

935. Rule II. A short vowel before two consonants in the same word becomes long by position. Thus, उ in बुद्धि, and *a* in the first and second syllables of प्रत्यय, are long by position.

* § 3, *b*.

† Compare the remarks in § 3, *b-d*, on the short *e* heard in certain colloquial dialects.

Exc. 1. A short vowel before the plural termination न्ह or न्हि, and sometimes before म्ह and ह्म, as in मुनिन्ह, तुम्ह, and ब्रह्म, remains short.

Exc. 2. A short vowel before a conjunct consonant of which the second element is र, as, e.g., *a* in सप्रेम, may be counted either long or short.

Rem. In Sanskrit prosody, a final short vowel was also lengthened before a conjunct consonant initial in a following word. But Hindí poets commonly neglect this.

936. Rule III. A short vowel before *Anusvár* or *Visarg* followed by a consonant, is long by position. Thus the short vowels in दुःख, संग, सिंग, are all long by position. So also *Anusvár* in the end of a line lengthens a preceding short vowel; as in भयं, नमामयं.

Exc. But when *Anusvár* stands, as is very often the case, for *Anunásik*,* a preceding short vowel remains short. Thus, e.g., in भंवर, बरहिंगे, मुंह, *Anusvár* stands for *Anunásik*; and therefore the vowels अ, इ, and उ, retain their natural short quantity.

937. The unit of metrical quantity is called मात्र *mátra*, 'an instant.' A *mátra* denotes the length of time occupied in the utterance of a short vowel, as अ, इ, or उ. All long vowels and diphthongs are regarded as consisting of two *mátras*. This must be carefully borne in mind, in order to understand the prosodial measurement of verse. The Metrical Unit.

Thus the words तप, ताप, तपस्वी, contain, respectively, 2, 3, and 5 *mátras*, as follows; तप, $\smile + \smile = 2$; ताप, $- + \smile = 3$; तपस्वी, $\smile + - + - = 5$. Similarly the line, काम क्रोध मद लोभ की, contains 13 *mátras*.

---

* § 17.

Rem. For मात्रा, मत्त also occurs in some native works. कल is also used in the same sense.

Prosodial License.

938. The laws of Hindí prosody allow a great degree of liberty in respect of orthography, and even of grammatical construction. The following principles regulate *prosodial license.*

(1) A long may be written for a short vowel, and *vice versâ.*

a. This rule most commonly operates in final letters, especially at the end of lines, either for the sake of rhyme, or to fill out the total quantity of the line; as in हनुमाना for हनुमान (to rhyme with आना); हानी (to rhyme with पहचानी); and (to fill out quantities) बहुता for बहुत, दूता for दूत; छोहु for छोह, etc., etc.

b. But medial and initial radical vowels also are sometimes shortened, even in the middle of a line; as, e.g., in ठकुर for ठाकुर, परसन for परोसन, अनन्द for आनन्द, सुखि गौ for सूखि गौ, अनहिं for आनहिं, कमनीय for कामनीय, etc., etc.

(2) *Anusvár* is inserted or omitted for the sake of rhyme; as in बरायें, सुहावें, to rhyme with बायें and सीवें; and दाउ (for दाँव), to rhyme with काउ.

(3) Diphthongs, medial and final, are resolved into their component vowels; as, भयआतुर for भयातुर; कहइ, मिलइ, करइ, for कहै, मिलै, and करै; पइठिहौं for पैठिहौं, etc., etc. The latter vowel is then very often prolonged; as, e.g., in करई, परई, for करै and परै; and sometimes the former vowel is lengthened: as in the following, where उड़ाउं is written for उड़ौं, to rhyme with खाउं; लरिकाई जहं जहं फिरहिं तहं तहं संग उड़ाउं. More rarely both are lengthened; as in सकाई for सकै, to rhyme with उपाई; thus, जिम धन बिनु रहि न सकाई.

(4) Occasionally a vowel of one organ is exchanged for one of another; as in देयो for देय, in the following: काहि कहै केहि दूषण देयो.

(5) A syllable, most commonly रे, is often added to fill out a line and make a rhyme; as in बड़ेरे, करताह, for बड़े and करता.

(6) A consonant is sometimes doubled, to lengthen a preceding vowel; as in दमक्कहीं, चमक्कहीं, चड्डहिं, दपट्टहिं, for दमकहिं, etc.

(7) For the same reason *Anusvár* is often inserted, as in the following line from *Chand*, given by Beames: प्रथंमं भुजंगी सुधारी ग्रहंनं, where all the *Anusvárs* but the third are *metri gratiá*.

Rem. It is to be remembered, however, that in many of the above cases the variations represent archaic forms of the words in question, chosen *metri gratiá*.

(8) The rules of agreement are often neglected, so that the masculine is used for the feminine, the singular for the plural, and *vice versá*, to meet the exigencies of the rhyme. Thus, we have किये for किया, गावा for गाये, पाये for पायो, etc., etc.*

939. *Pause* (विराम) is of two kinds, *sentential* and *harmonic*. The sentential pause occurs at the end of correspondent lines, and is marked by the signs, ।, *half-pause*, and ॥, *full-pause*. The harmonic pause or *cæsura* varies in different metres, and is marked by no sign. Metrical Pause

940. The simple feet used in Hindí verse are of three kinds, viz., monosyllabic, dissyllabic, and trisyllabic. Varieties of Feet.

---

* Vid. § 875.

Occasionally, compound polysyllabic feet are also employed. Each class of feet contains several varieties, as indicated below.*

		Name.	*Abbrev.*	*Symbol.*	*In English.*	
Mono.	1.	गुरु	ग	S	*Long,*	
	2.	लघु	ल	I	*Short,*	
Dissyllabic.	1.	करण	गग	SS	*Spondee,*	—
	2.	ताल	गल	SI	*Trochee,*	—
	3.	ध्वज	लग	IS	*Iambus,*	⏑
	4.	सुप्रिय	लल	II	*Periambus,*	⏑
Trisyllabic.	1.	मगण	म	SSS	*Molussus,*	— —
	2.	नगण	न	III	*Tribrach,*	⏑ ⏑
	3.	भगण	भ	SII	*Dactyl,*	— ⏑ ·
	4.	यगण	य	ISS	*Bacchic,*	⏑ — ·
	5.	जगण	ज	ISI	*Amphibrach,*	⏑ — ·
	6.	रगण	र	SIS	*Cretic,*	— ⏑ ·
	7.	सगण	स	IIS	*Anapest,*	⏑ ⏑ ·
	8.	तगण	त	SSI	*Antibacchic,*	— — ·

a. The *longus* is in Hindí named *guru,* 'heavy,' (also called *háru,*) and the *brevis, laghu,* 'light,' (also called *meru.*)

b. The eight varieties of trisyllabic feet are often collectively termed गण *gaṇ, par excellence.*

Notation of Feet.

941. It is important to note that in Hindí works on prosody, the symbolic letters are always used to denote the feet. Thus भजन would denote the three feet, भगण, जगण, नगण; सरम = सगण + रगण + मगण, etc., etc.

942. Polysyllabic feet are chiefly used in *Játi Chhand.*† They are formed by various combinations of the above three kinds; and have no specific names.

---

* In the following pages it has been thought wise ordinarily to employ the Hindí names and symbols for the various feet, as until the student is familiar with them, he will be quite unable to read intelligently the simplest page of any native work on this important subject. † Vid. § 944.

943. Hindí verse (छन्द) is of two classes; viz., वृत्त छन्द *Vṛitt Chhand*, and जाति छन्द *Játi Chhand*. Verse Classified

944. I. That is called *Vṛitt Chhand* which is regulated by the number of syllables (वरण) in each *charaṇ* or metrical line. It is therefore also called वरण छन्द *Varaṇ Chhand*.

II. That is called *Játi Chhand* which is measured by the number of *mátras* or metrical instants in each line.

I. *Of Vṛitt Chhand.*

945. In *Vṛitt Chhand* each verse consists of four metrical lines (*charaṇ* or *pád*). *Vṛitt Chhand* is further distinguished as of three Orders, viz., (1) सम *sama*, 'even;' (2) अर्द्धसम *arddhasama*, 'half-even;' (3) विषम *vishama*, 'uneven.' These are distinguished as follows: 'Orders' of *Vṛitt Chhand*.

(1) In *Sama Vṛitt* each *charaṇ* has an *equal* number of syllables.

(2) In *Arddhasama Vṛitt* the first and third *charaṇs* have an equal number of syllables, and also the *second* and *fourth*.

(3) In *Vishama Vṛitt* each *charaṇ* has a different number of syllables.

Rem. Although *Vṛitt Chhand* is measured by the number of syllables in each *charaṇ*, yet in most metres of this class these syllables are not taken indifferently, but in each variety are regulated by a certain sequence of *feet*, as in Latin and Greek verse.

946. Native prosodians divide verse of the 1st Order (*Sama Vṛitt*) of the First Class into twenty-six *Genera*, according to the number of syllables in each of the four *charaṇs*. Each of these *genera* has its own specific name, as given below. Genera of *Sama Vṛitt*.

Thus a verse of this class having three syllables in each *charaṇ*, would belong to the 3rd Genus, named मध्या *Madhyá*; one of fifteen syllables, to the 15th Genus, named अति शर्करी *Atisharkarí*, etc., etc.

947. Under each of the above genera, again, are contained as many *Species* as combinations of long and short syllables are possible with any given number of syllables.

Thus the 2nd Genus comprehends four species, as follows: (1) – – ; (2) ⏑ ⏑ ; (3) ⏑ – ; (4) – ⏑ ; and the 3rd Genus comprehends eight possible species, viz., (1) – – – ; (2) ⏑ ⏑ ⏑ ; (3) – ⏑ ⏑ ; (4) ⏑ – – ; (5) ⏑ – ⏑ ; (6) – ⏑ – ; (7) ⏑ ⏑ – ; (8) – – ⏑ .

Rem. It is plain that in metres of a large number of syllables, the number of possible combinations must be very great. Native prosodians give ingenious rules for determining the possible varieties under each genus, the place of any specified variety in the *prastár* (*udisht*), or, the place in the *prastár* being given, to determine the metre of any required species (*nasht*). But these matters seem to be of no practical importance, and we may wisely refer to native authors the student who is curious in these things.

948. All *Sama Vritt* metres containing more than twenty-six syllables, are classified under a 27th Genus named दण्डक *Daṇdak*, which is fancifully said to comprehend 999 varieties.

949. Finally, it should be observed that in *Sama* metres the 2nd *charaṇ* must rhyme with the 1st, and the 4th with the 3rd.

Examples of *Sama Vritt* Metres.

950. The following are examples of the most common metres under each genus. As the 3rd and 4th *charaṇs* are exactly like the 1st and 2nd, the first two *charaṇs* only, for lack of space, have been given in the examples after Genus V.

CLASS I. वृत्त छंद *Vṛitt Chhand*, or वरण छंद *Varaṇ Chhand.*

ORDER I. सम वृत्त *Sama Vṛitt.*

GENUS I. उक्था.

Species.	*Feet in each charaṇ.*	*Examples.*
श्री	ग	धै ॥ है ॥ श्री ॥ की ॥

GENUS II. अत्युक्था.

काम	गग	दाता ॥ ध्याता ॥ कोई ॥ सोई ॥
मधु	लल	तिय ॥ जिय ॥ बधु ॥ मधु ॥
मही	लग	रमा ॥ समा ॥ गही ॥ मही ॥
सारु	गल	ऐनि ॥ मैनि ॥ चारु ॥ सारु ॥

GENUS III. मध्या.

ताली (नारी)	म	हे स्वामी ॥ हौं कामी ॥ तू दाता ॥ है त्राता ॥
कमल	न	चरन ॥ धरन ॥ अमल ॥ कमल ॥
मंदर	भ	धावत ॥ ध्यावत ॥ चंदर ॥ मंदर ॥
शशी	य	भवानी ॥ सुवानी ॥ सुने जो ॥ कहे सो ॥
नरिंद	ज	सम्हार ॥ सवार ॥ परिंद ॥ नरिंद ॥
मृगी or प्रिया	र	है खरी ॥ पत्थरी ॥ तो हिया ॥ री प्रिया ॥
रमण	स	धरनी ॥ बरनी ॥ रमनी ॥ रमनी ॥
पंचाल	त	नाचन्त ॥ गावन्त ॥ दैताल ॥ पंचाल ॥

GENUS IV. प्रतिष्ठा.

कन्या or तीर्णा	मग	हे कर्त्तारा ॥ मेरे भारा ॥ तूही टालि ॥ मोही पालि ॥
समुही or कला	भग	भामिन जो ॥ कामिनि सो ॥ हानि करे ॥ प्रान हरे ॥
मुद्रा	यल	भजे राम ॥ सरे काम ॥ न छापाहि ॥ न मुद्राहि ॥

Species.	*Feet in each charaṇ.*	*Examples.*
कुमारिका	जग	करो कृपा ॥ दयामया ॥ न छोड़िये ॥ न मारिये ॥
राम	सग	जग माही ॥ सुख नाहीं ॥ तजि कामै ॥ भजि रामै ॥
बुद्धि	जल	धर्मै तजि ॥ प्रभू भजि ॥ टरैं दुख ॥ मिलै सुख ॥
धारी or धार	रल	नाम तोर ॥ मुक्ति मोर ॥ मोर भार ॥ तू उतार ॥
बीर	सल	हरु पीर ॥ भव भीर ॥ वरबीर ॥ रघुबीर ॥

Genus V. सुप्रतिष्ठा.

सम्मोहा	मगग	कांधा की बानी ॥ राधा जू मानी ॥ मानी तो मानी ॥ मेरी का हानी ॥
अमक	नलल	श्रुति कहहि ॥ हरिजनहि ॥ छुवत नहि ॥ अमक वहि ॥
हंसी or पंक्ति	भगग	तारक ईसा ॥ देत असीसा ॥ मारत द्रोही ॥ पालत मोही ॥
बिष्णु	भलल	दास जगत ॥ झूठ लगत ॥ याहि तजहि ॥ यीशु भजहि ॥
विलास	जगग	कृपा अपानो ॥ मुही दिखानो ॥ कुचाल म्हारो ॥ तुही सुधारो ॥
प्रिया	सलग	करहु दया ॥ करुणामया ॥ मनरंजना ॥ दुखभंजना ॥
हारित	तगग	तो मानु भारी ॥ ठाने पियारी ॥ सौति सुखारी ॥ होती हमारी ॥

Genus VI. गायत्री.

शेषराज	मम	क्यौं रे आने दो तो ॥ राधा माधो होती ॥
सोमकुल	मस	क्यौं रे मानत है ॥ आली आनत है ॥
शशिभृता	नम	कहत राधा जू ॥ सुनहु कांधा जू ॥

Species.	*Feet in each charaṇ.*	*Examples.*	
शशिवदना	नय	शरण तिहारी	॥ चरण निहारी ॥
कामलता	भय	भावत न तोरी	॥ बात सुनि गोरी ॥
मालती	जज	करो मत मान	॥ तजो यह बान ॥
विमोहा	रर	आउंगी आन ले	॥ स्याम हे मान ले ॥
तिलक	सस	प्रभु के चरणा	॥ जग के शरणा ॥
तनुमध्या	तय	देखो छवि भारी	॥ सोहै अति सारी ॥
वसुमति	तस	आई शुभ घरी	॥ अबै प्रभु हरी ॥

Genus VII. उष्णिक.

सुभग	मभग	मानो मानो हिय से	॥ जानो जानो जिय से
मधुमति	ननग	जग जनम लियो	॥ नहिं भजन कियो
शीर्षरूप	भभग	मारग है भ्रमणा	॥ क्यों न भजो चरणा
कुमारललिता	जसग	कहां लगि तिहारी	॥ करो प्रभु विचारी
भभानिका	रयग	स्याम आज आए हो	॥ ग्वाल बाल धाए हो
सामानिका	रजग	भक्ति मुक्ति बुद्धिदा	॥ ज्ञान देउ सारदा
हंसमाला	सरग	अब की कलोल हो	॥ तब की भई सही
चूड़ामणि	तभग	आना हमें अब है	॥ लेखा उहां सब है

Genus VIII. अनुष्टुप.

हंसरुत	मनगग	देखो आवत विहारी	॥ कैसो देखत निहारी ॥
संजा	मभगग	जानी जानी मठुराई	॥ देखी देखी चतुराई ॥
तुंगा	ननगग	चरण शरण तेरे	॥ रहत न मन मेरे ॥
विद्युन्माला	ममगग	आवत देखो री प्यारी	॥ लावत माला भी सारी ॥
चित्रपदा	भभगग	मानत क्यों न कंधाई	॥ आवत है नियराई ॥
नाराच	भरलग	क्यौं प्रभु छोड़तो मुझे	॥ क्यौं रिसि भावतो तुझे ॥
माणवक	भतलग	प्रीति करो तू सब से	॥ भक्ति करो तो अब से ॥
प्रमाणिक	जरलग	परेश तोहि मानिके	॥ नमों सुचित्त ठानिके ॥
मल्लिका	रजगल	आन देउ मोहि आज	॥ लाय देउंगी पियाज ॥

GENUS IX. बृहती.

Species.	*Feet in each charaṇ.*	*Examples.*
तोमर	सजज	प्रभु यीसु हे प्रिय नाथ ॥ जग में रहो मम साथ ॥
मणिबंध	भमस	चेत करो प्यारे अबही ॥ वेगि तजो साधो सबही ॥
रूपमाली	ममम	मानो मानो मानो री प्यारी ॥
		जानो जानो जानो री सारी ॥
सारंगिका	नयस	भजन करो तू हिय में ॥
		मद न करो हो जिय में ॥

GENUS X. पंक्ति.

मत्ता	मभसग	देखो देखो कहन न मानो ॥
		आवो आवो हम नहि जानी ॥
मनोरमा	नरजग	धरऊ जेहि हेतु साधना ॥
		करऊ तेहि हेतु याचना ॥
हंसी	मभनग	देखो देखो यसमति चली ॥
		पीछे पीछे सब सखि भली ॥

GENUS XI. त्रिष्टुप्.

भ्रमरविलसिता	मभनलग	बंशी की शब्द सुनि सब चली ॥
		गोपी गोपी सब निकरि मिली ॥
मालती	३म + गग	कांधा की बानी राधा साची जानी ॥
		जानी तो जानी मेरी नाही हानी ॥
रथोद्धता	रनरलग	पूछि लेऊ अब राधिका चली ॥
		स्याम आवत चलो चलो भली ॥
इंद्रवज्रा	ततजगग	राधे तिहारी अब तोरि डारी ॥
		माला बिचारी यह आज रारी ॥

Species.	*Feet in each charaṇ.*	*Examples.*
चपला	भभजलग	कुंजन में सखि चबि चलियो ॥
		बेणु बजावत जहां चलियो ॥
दोधक	भभभगग	आवत आज निहाल बिहारी ॥
		देखत साज निकारि सुधारी ॥

GENUS XII. जगती.

जगधरमाला	मभसम	आली राधे करत विहारी रारी ॥
		देखो २ सब सखि देतो गारी ॥
तोटक	ससस	भुजदंड प्रचंड प्रताप बलं ॥
		खलवृंद निकंद महाकुशलं ॥
प्रभा	ननरर	भजन करज्ञ आज साधो तजो ॥
		रहज्ञ मगन साथ प्यारे सजो ॥
प्रियंवदा	नभजर	तिय सरोजनयनी प्रयंवदा ॥
		रहति सो नयन में अली सदा ॥
भजंग प्रयात	४य	चलो आज देखो भले कांध आयो ॥
		लसे मोर पंखी छबीलो सुहायो ॥
मोदक	४भ	देखज्ञ आज रमापति आवत ॥
		बालन को सब खेल सिखावत ॥
मेनावली	४त	प्यारी तजो मान आवो करो गार ॥
		आली धरो ध्यान पावो बड़ो दान ॥

GENUS XIII. अतिजगती.

एकावली	भनजजल	देखज्ञ समय निहाल भजो अब ॥
		तारक शरण निहारत जो सब ॥
कलिहंस	सजससग	अब देज्ञ कांध सब चीज हमारी ॥
		हम लीन नाहि वह बेणु तुमारी ॥

Species.	*Feet in each charaṇ.*	*Examples.*
प्रभावती	तभसजग	कैसो सुहात सबन को बिसारनो ॥
		देखो न भावत नर को बिचारनो ॥
मंजुभाषिणी	सजसजग	तब को तुमैं मुरलिया दई दई ॥
		अब हो कहा करहुगे लई लई ॥
माया	मतयसग	देखो २ जात कंधाई बृज मे रे ॥
		छोड़ो छोड़ो तो चतुराई मग में रे ॥

GENUS XIV. शर्करी.

अपराजिता	ननरसलग	चरण शरण केहि कारण त्यागिहौ ॥
		जग जगमत सोइ मारन भागिहौ ॥
इंदुवदना	भजसनगग	भक्ति बिनु युक्त नर नाहक पधारो ॥
		शक्ति नहि भक्ति बिनु ज्ञान नहिं भारी ॥
वसंततिलक	तभजजगग	मानो सखी कहत श्याम चलो चलो री ॥
		देखो चलो बचन मान गलो गली री ॥

GENUS XV. अतिशर्करी.

चंद्रलेखा	मरमयय	देखो देखो हमारी बानी सखी ने न मानी ॥
		आओ आओ कुमारी राधा करी बेइमानी ॥
भमरावली	ससससस	रघुनाथ रमापति देहु हमें शरणा ॥
		सब छाड़ि गहों मधुसूदन के चरणा ॥
मालती	ननमयय	करहु अब बिहारी नाथ मेरी बिचारी ॥
		सुनहु मम मुरारी पाप सारी बिसारी ॥

GENUS XVI. अष्टि.

चंचला	रजरजरल	छोड़ि देहु मोहि कांध बार बार मैं पुकारि ॥
		आयके कहों अवश्य कंस राज से विचारि ॥

Species.	*Feet in each charaṇ.*	*Examples.*
नाराच	जरजरजग	गलो गली छिपी फिरै लला चली नहीं मिलो ॥
		रहो रहो इहां सखी कहां गयो भलो छलो ॥
मालिनी	नजभजरग	चलत निहारि माधव तिहारि बात मानो ॥
		समुझि गई सबै कहत आज नाहिं जानो ॥

GENUS XVII. अत्यष्टि.

प्रिथ्वी	जसजसयलग	चलो सकल गोपिका लखन आज आई चली ॥
		करो अवन काम छोड़ि सब साथ आओ चली ॥
मंदाक्रांता	मभनततगग	ब्रह्मा ध्यावैं चरण दिन राती कहां का बिचारी ॥
		ध्यावैं जा के पद कमल योगी यती सो पुरारी ॥
मोहन	यरसरसलग	पुकारी टेरिकै सबरी खाइले नहिं बाघ है ॥
		बिगारो काम को अब सों मारने अब आत है ॥
हरिणी	नसमरसलग	करऊ अब स्वामी दीनानाथ मारग शोधिये ॥
		तजऊ अब मो कौं नाहों प्राणनाथ सुहेरिये ॥

GENUS XVIII. धृति.

चर्चरी	रसजजभर	फाग खेलत आज माधव बाग में सब साथ ले ॥
		गोपिका सब रंग छोड़त कुंकुमा गुल हाथ ले ॥
नाराच	ननरररर	करऊ कवन मैं बिहारी मुरारी बुराई कहो ॥
		कहऊ तुम सप्रेम मेरी सदा ज्यों भलाई चहो ॥
मंजीरा	ममभमसम	सोहै कैसी राधा माधव आली आवत टेरो टेरो ॥
		आगे आगे कांधा झूमत पीछे राजकुमारी मेरी ॥

GENUS XIX. अतिधृति.

शार्दूलविक्रीड़ित	मसजसततग	रानी श्री यसुदा पुकारत अरी राधा कहां तू गई ॥
		राधा हेरत कुंज में सुनु चली काहू न वा को लखी ॥

Species.	*Feet in each charaṇ.*	*Examples.*
झूलना	सजजभरसल	करुणानिधान कृपाल माधव देखिये मम रीत ॥ जग जीवना लखि पाद पंकज सेइ गावत गीत ॥

Genus XX. कृति.

गीत	सजजभरसलग	जग क्षेम कारण भक्तपालन साधु वृंद सदा रमैं ॥ प्रभु देहिंगे अब क्षेम मारग भक्ति मुक्ति सुधी हमैं ॥

Genus XXI. प्रकृति.

स्रग्धरा	मरभनययय	देखो देखो सखी आवत अब असुरारी यशोदा विहारी ॥ आने दे तू न माने अब कहन हमारी भई तू दुलारी ॥

Genus XXII. आकृति.

मदिरा	भभभभभभभग	झूमक भूमि झुमावत कंकण घूमि घुमावत आज सही ॥ बीण बजावत टेरि पुकारत भाव बुझावत ताल लही ॥
हंसी	ममतनननसग	जा के जी में जोई भावै करत सवर मन अति अकुलाई ॥ भावै जी में नाहीं वा को करत नर सुपथ मन बिसराई ॥

Genus XXIII. विकृति.

मालिका	रजरजरजरलग	देखिये छिपत कुंज में सखत राधिका न पथ में सभी रही ॥

Species.	*Feet in each charaṇ.*	*Examples.*
		देखिवी भजत साथ छोड़ि मग में खड़ी कहत घूमिके गही ॥
मालती	७भ + गग	नाहक रारि करो ब्रज मोहन नाहक गागरि तू अब तोड़ी ॥
		नाहक मारग रोकत चंचल नाहक तूं दधि भाजन फोड़ी ॥
ललित	नजभजभजभलग	करऊ कृपा सदा प्रभु सहाय आप अब ही अपान जन के ॥
		तजऊ नहीं अनाथ जन को सनाथ करिये पुकार मन के ॥

GENUS XXIV. सत्कृति or संकृति.

Species.	*Feet in each charaṇ.*	*Examples.*
दुरमिला or मधवी	८स	कबहूं यह बात न मानत री सखि मैं उपकारक आज भई ॥
		समुझावत हौं अब मानु अली लखि हाल भली विसराय दई ॥

GENUS XXV. अतिकृति or अभिकृति.

Species.	*Feet in each charaṇ.*	*Examples.*
चारु	८भ + ग	कुंजन से अब माधव आवत बालन को सब खेल दिखावत री ॥
		मारग में सब झूमि झुमावत ताल मृदंग बजाय नचावत री ॥
सुन्दरी	८स + ग	विनु पंकज सोह तडाग नहीं विनु चंद्र निशा जिमि भावत नाहीं ॥
		विनु पंडित ग्रंथ प्रकाश नहीं तिमि ज्ञान नहीं सब धूरि मिलाहीं ॥

Species.	*Feet in each charaṇ.*	*Examples.*

GENUS XXVI. उत्कृति.

किशोर	८स + लल	समुझावऊ आज अली यदुराजकुमार नहीं यह मागत बातन ॥
		अब फेरि बुलाय कहो व्रजभामिनि तोहि बताय दई हम साधन ॥
विलास	८भ + लल	साधऊ काज हमार महा प्रभु मांगत हौं कर जोरि सदा गति सत ॥
		मागऊ मोर कहावत तारक देऊ हमें अब भक्ति सुधी विलसत ॥

GENUS XXVII. दण्डक.

महीधर	४(जर) + जग	कहा करौं अली गई भली भई नहीं लई चली गई कहा भई अरी अली ॥
		मना कियो नहीं तबै रही बड़ी खुसी हंसी सुना दियो अबै भई दुखी घनी ॥
शंख	नन + १४ र	चरण शरण हौं सदा ताहि के जो दयासिंधु गोपाल गोविंद दामोदरो विष्णु जू माधवो स्याम जू श्री स्भू सर्वदा सर्व है दास को ॥
		सदय हृदय है हमैं पालिहै आपनो जानिकै सोइ विश्वेश विश्वं भरो विष्णू जू राधवो राम जू श्री प्रभू दुःख हा हर्ण है चासको ॥

951. The following, among other metres of this Genus, are classified in the *Pingaládarsha* as कवित्त छंद.

घनाक्षरी छंद has 31 syllables, but the feet are left optional. The pause falls upon the 8th, 16th, and 24th syllables. The last two or three syllables of each line must rhyme.

कबहूं तो नाथ मेरी सुधि न लई है तुम कबहूं तो आप कीजे
दृष्टि अब आनिके ॥
बिनतो तो दीननाथ सुनहू अब यांचनो रहहू मन में सदा
मेरी बात मानिके ॥

रूपकघनाक्षरी छंद has 32 syllables, with pause at the 8th, 16th, and 24th syllables. The feet are optional.

मनाये से न मानोंगी बुलाये से न बोलोंगी देखाये से न देखोंगी
सखी आज ठानी यही ॥
कहां लों सहों रोष की रार एरी चलो देखु भयो जो भयो आनिके
रही हार मानी सही ॥

CLASS I. ORDER II. **अर्द्धसम वृत्त** *Arddhasama Vritt.*

952. No division of this Order into genera and species is practicable. As in *Sama Vṛitt* metres, the 1st *charaṇ* rhymes with the 2nd, and the 3rd with the 4th. In the following examples, only the 1st and 2nd *charaṇs* are given; the 3rd and 4th *charaṇs* contain, respectively, the same feet as the 1st and 2nd. *Arddhasama Vṛitt:* Examples.

पुष्पिताया छंद.

Scheme. { 1st and 3rd *charaṇs*, ननरयग.
2nd and 4th ,, नजजरग.

फिरि फिरि भ्रमिके कहि नहीं वेली ॥ विधि यह कौन प्रकार की चंबेली ॥

द्रुतमध्या छंद.

Scheme. { 1st and 3rd *charaṇs*, भभभगग.
2nd and 4th „ नजजयग.

कौतुक आजु कियो बनमाली ॥ जल बिच कूदि पड़ो सुनियो आली ॥

बेगवती छंद.

Scheme. { 1st and 3rd *charaṇs*, सससग.
2nd and 4th „ भभभगग.

सिगरो तन खेद सनो है ॥ तो उर आवत बेगवती है ॥

हरिणप्लुत छंद.

Scheme. { 1st and 3rd *charaṇs*, सससलग.
2nd and 4th „ नभभर.

ब्रज की बनिता लखि पाइहैं ॥ इकहि को इकईस लगाइहैं ॥

हीरा छंद.

Scheme. { 1st and 3rd *charaṇs*, ननजरग.
2nd and 4th „ नजजरग.

सुनऊ कहन हमार राधिका जो ॥ चलऊ जहां यह आज बेणु बाजी ॥

Class I.: Order III. विषम वृत्त *Vishama Vṛitt.*

Vishama Vṛitt Examples.

953. In this Order, each of the four *charaṇs* is formed on a separate scheme. Like Order II., it admits of no subdivision into genera and species. The following are examples of the more common metres.

अमृतधारा छंद.

1st *ch.* ३न+य रघुपति चरणन चित लाई ॥
2nd „ ४न+सग भव तजऊ सकल विषयन तुम भाई ॥
3rd „ ६न+लग जगत जनमि कुछ सुफल करत नहिं अघ कीन्हो ॥
4th „ २न+लग जनम नहक लीन्हो ॥

ललिता छंद.

1st *ch.* सजसल करुणानिधान रघुराउ ॥
2nd „ नसजग शरण अब नाथ मैं भई ॥
3rd „ ननसस सकल विषय तजि चित्त दई ॥
4th „ २(सज) + ग महिमा अपार हम जानि ना लई ॥

प्रवर्द्धमान छंद.

1st *ch.* मसजभगग मेरी जाति अहीर है अली कि न जानी ॥
2nd „ सनजरग चलना पड़त अरी अली न मानी ॥
3rd „ २(ननस) रहत मगन निसु बासर करत न करनी ॥
4th „ ३न + जय चितवत नहिं अब सखि है मन मानी ॥

सौरभ छंद.

1st *ch.* सजसल करुणा निधान रघुवंश ॥
2nd „ नसजग तिलक हरि दीन नाथ हो ॥
3rd „ रनभग देऊ मोहि पद भक्ति सदा ॥
4th „ २(सज)ग + हित जानि मोर बिसराय पाप हो ॥

CLASS II. जाति छंद *Játi Chhand.*

ORDER I. गण छंद *Gaṇa Chhand.*

954. *Játi Chhand* is divided by native writers into गण छन्द *Gaṇa Chhand* and मात्रा छन्द *Mátrá Chhand.*

955. In *Gaṇa Chhand* the verse is commonly measured by the number of instants in each line; but the order of feet in each line, within certain limits, is fixed and invariable. In *Mátrá Chhand* the order of feet is for the most part left to the option of the composer. *Játi Chhand* Classified.

a. This distinction between *Gaṇa Chhand* and *Mátrá Chhand*, as laid down by native prosodians, cannot, however, be rigidly maintained. In many metres classified as *Mátrá Chhand*, certain requisitions and restrictions are made as to the nature of the feet employed, and, on the other hand, in some *Gaṇa Chhand* metres, many of the feet are left to the option of the writer.

Gaṇa Chhand. **956.** Native writers have divided *Gaṇa Chhand* into six species, explanations and examples of which are given below. Each of these species, again, comprehends many varieties according to the succession of feet in the line. A few illustrations are given under each species.

Gaṇa Chhand. Species 1. **957.** The 1st and most popular species of *Gaṇa Chhand*, is termed आर्य्या *A'ryyá*, गाथा *Gáthá*, or गाहा छन्द *Gáhá Chhand.* In all *A'ryyá* metres each verse consists of two lines (*dal*), the 1st of which contains 30, and the 2nd, 27 *mátrás.* Each line must contain 7½ feet, each of which, again, must contain 4 instants, except the 6th of the 2nd line, which has only one. A *jagan* (⏑–⏑) or a polysyllabic foot, is required in the 6th place in the 1st line; but *jagans* are prohibited in the odd feet of the 2nd line. The cæsural pause falls after the 3rd foot or 12th instant of each line.

958. The following is an example of that variety of *A'ryyádi* metres which is known, *par excellence*, as आर्य्या or गाहा.

1 2 3 4 5 6 7 ½

भ + नल + स । नल + गग + ज + भ + ग = 30 instants.

गग + भ + भ । गग + स + ल + नल + ग = 27 instants.

आज चलहु सब मथुरा रहत जहां दीनबंधु आप सखी ॥

माधो को बंधपावन चाहो चलती पास नहिं सखी ॥

959. **चपला छंद** must have a *jagan* in the 2nd and 4th places each line.

स + ज + स + ज + स + नल + गग + ग = 30.

भ + ज + स + ज + नल + ल + स + ग = 27.

करुणानिधान जगनाथ आन अब मोहि शरण तेरी है ।
देखहु कृपा नयन से निहारि धरत सबन चरी है ॥

960. The 2nd species of *Gana Chhand* is called (from its chief variety) **गीति छंद** *Gíti Chhand.* The principal variety differs from all metres of the 1st species in that *both* lines contain 30 instants. The 6th foot must be a *jagan*, as in the 1st line of *Áryyá Chhand.* The other general laws of the verse are the same as in *Áryyá Chhand.** Examples follow. *Gana Chhand. Species 2.*

गीति छंद

गग + गज + गज । भ + स + ज + स + ग = 30 instants.

गग + स + भ । नल + स + ज + गग + ग = 30 instants.

राधो माधो मेरी बात सुनहु साथ त्यागि मति आओ ॥
मानो हमरी सत्यहि डर नहिं यह आनि बूझि तूं आओ ॥

961. **उपगीति छंद** contains in each line 27 instants, and follows in both lines the rules laid down for the 2nd line in *Áryyá Chhand.*

गग + भ + स । स + स + ल + गग + ग = 27 instants.

नल + स + स । नल + भग + ल + स + ग = 27 instants.

आवो आज चलहु कुंजन में सबरी चहो आली ।
चलत फिरत ढूंढत हैं बिच बिच में सोह बनमाली ॥

* Vid. § 957.

962. उद्गीति छंद is the exact reverse of *A'ryyá Chhand*, having 27 instants in the 1st, and 30 instants in the 2nd line. The same laws regulate the long and short lines as in *A'ryyá* metres.

गग + भ + लल + गग + गग + ल + भ + ग = 27 instants.
गग + गग + स + भ + स + ज + भ + ग = 30 instants.

माधो आज चलऊ तुम मानो मानो कहो हमरी ॥
हहै या की अब की गाइन शुभ कीर्त्ति फैलिहै तुमरी ॥

963. आर्य्यागीति छंद differs from *A'ryyá Chhand* in that it adds one half-foot to each line, making two lines of 8 feet each, instead of 7½. The 1st line therefore contains 32, the 2nd, 29 instants. The other rules for each line are the same as those already given.*

गग + गग + स । भ + स + ज + गग + गग = 32 instants.
गल + गल + गल । गल + गग + ल + गल + गग = 29 instants.

मेरे प्यारे कहना मानऊ अबकी नहीं बिसारो मो कौं ॥
चरण शरण हम तजत न निसु दिन ध्याऊं कवन विधि तो कौं ॥

Gaṇa Chhand. Spec. 3, 4, 5, 6.

964. The various species of *Gaṇa Chhand* classified by some as बैतालीयादि *Baitálíyádi*, शिखादि *Shikhádi*, वक्त्रादि *Vaktrádi*, and अचलधृत्यादि *Achaladhṛityádi*, differ widely from the above *A'ryyá* metres. A few examples are given under each head.

965. The *Baitálíyádi* metres all consist of two lines, each containing six feet, and subdivided into two *charaṇs* of three feet each. The number of instants varies from 28 to 32 in each line. The following are the most common varieties.

966. **बैतालीय छंद.** Two lines of 30 instants each, as follows: 6 + र + लग + 8 + र + लग. The combination of long and short syllables in the polysyllabic feet (the 1st and 4th), is optional. Pause at the 14th instant.

मधु सूदन को सखो सखी   तुम देखो कैसो छिपो नखी ॥
अब माधव राधिका चलो   सबरो ऐहैं हो चलो भलो ॥

967. **चारुहासिनी छंद** differs from the foregoing in substituting 6 instants for 8 in the 4th foot, making 28 instants in each line. The feet in both halves of each line therefore exactly correspond.

चलो चलो बाल साथ री   भलो भलो साज माथ री ॥
लखो लखो आत कांध री   कहो कहो सांस बांध री ॥

968. *Shikhádi* metres are characterized by having all the syllables, except the last two, of the same length. The number of instants varies from 28 to 32. The following are the most common varieties. *Shikhádi Metres.*

969. **अनंगक्रीड़ा छंद** has two lines of 32 instants each. In the 1st line all the syllables are long; in the 2nd all are short. In this metre, therefore, no rhyme is possible. Pause at the 8th syllable of the 1st line, and the 8th and 16th of the 2nd.

आवो आवो जी आवो हो मेरे द्वारे राधा माधो ॥
निसु दिन लखत न कहत अपर कुछ शरण चरण तजि भजत अवर कुछ ॥

970. **अतिरुचिरा छंद** Scheme, २७ल + ग = 29 instants in each line. Pause at the 8th, 16th, and 24th syllables.

भजऊ मन चरण   रहऊ हरि शरण   तजऊ सब विषयन रमना ॥
चलऊ पथ सुगम   करऊ तुम वगम   सुफल निधर अपहि मरना ॥

Vaktrádi Metres.

971. *Vaktrádi* metres all contain two lines, each of which is divided into two *charaṇs*, each of eight syllables. The second, third, and fourth syllables must not form a *nagan* (⏑⏑⏑) or *sagan* (⏑⏑–). The following are the most common varieties.

972. **चपलावक्त्रा छंद** requires, in addition to the above conditions, that the fifth syllable begin a *nagan* (⏑⏑⏑).

घूमि देखो मगन में कैसी सोहत री आज ॥
कांधा आज मथुर में देहैं री सबरो साज ॥

973. **युग्मविपुला छंद** requires, in addition to the general conditions of *Vaktrádi* metres, that the fifth syllable of the even *charaṇs* begin a *jagan* (⏑–⏑).

कहना मानु मेरो री आली चलऊ आज हो ॥
मान ले बऊरी राधे देखो कस न माज हो ॥

Achaladhrityádi Metres.

974. The *Achaladhrityádi* metres consist each of four lines of 16 instants, of which the 1st rhymes with the 2nd, and the 3rd with the 4th. The following varieties may be noted. The 1st and 2nd lines only are given in the examples.

975. **विश्लोक छंद** requires that the fifth instant begin a *jagan* (⏑–⏑) or *nagan* (⏑⏑⏑). The final syllable must be long.

माधो करो सहाय लोक की ॥ साधो सदा सुचेत योग को ॥

976. **चित्रा छंद** requires a short syllable at the 5th, 8th, and 9th instants, and a long syllable as final.

आज चलऊ पगन विहारी जू ॥ देखऊं अब झलक तिहारी जू ॥

977. उपचित्रा छंद requires that the 9th and 10th instant fall on one long syllable, which must be followed by two short.

विना परीक्षा तत्व न प्रगटे ॥ वेष धरे सों नाम नहिं घटे ॥

Class II. जाति छंद *Játi Chhand.*

Order II. मात्रा छंद *Mátrá Chhand.*

978. In *Mátrá Chhand* each *charaṇ* or *dal* is composed of a certain number of instants. Often the *charaṇs* are subdivided into feet, each containing, again, a fixed number of *mátrás* or *instants*, and following each other in an invariable order of succession. But the combination of long and short syllables in the several feet is left, for the most part, to the option of the composer; and the verse is thus regulated, not by any reference to the kind of feet employed, but by the number of instants required for each division of the verse. Thus, e.g., the first foot of the *Dohá* must consist of six instants, but these may be so combined as to form a double tribrach (२ नगण ⏑⏑⏑⏑⏑⏑), or a molossus (मगण – – –) or any other feet possible under the conditions. *Laws of Mátrá Chhand.*

979. It should be particularly noticed that not only the total number of metrical instants in a *charaṇ* or *dal* is fixed, but that also the number of instants in each foot is invariable.

Thus the following half *Chaupáí*, although containing the 16 instants required by rule, is faulty in the composition of its feet; भिन्न कुम्हार माटी ताता. In this, the number of instants in each of the four feet is as follows; 7 + 3 + 4 + 2, whereas it should be, 6 + 4 + 4 + 2.

N.B. Observe that in the above, as in all the schemes given below, each figure denotes a foot or other section of a verse, and indicates also the number of instants which it contains. When any figure is followed by the sign of multiplication, ×, it is to be understood that the foot is to be repeated the number of times which is denoted by the multiplier. Thus (4 × 3) would denote that a foot of four instants was to be repeated three times; i.e., 4 × 3 = 4 + 4 + 4. A comma after any figure will be used to denote the metrical pause; thus, 10, + 8, + 8, + 6 = 32, is to be interpreted as denoting a line of 32 instants, composed of four *charaṇs*, respectively containing 10, 8, 8, and 6 instants, the cæsural pause falling at the 10th, 18th, and 26th instant.

980. Verse in *Mátrá Chhand* may be conveniently distributed into three divisions; viz., I. metres consisting of two lines only (द्विपाद्); II. those consisting of four lines (चतुष्पाद्); III. those consisting of more than four lines (बहुपाद्).

a. Many metres are reckoned *Dvipád* by some prosodians, and *Chatushpád* by others. But this is a matter of no great practical importance.

Examples of *Mátrá Chhand.* **981**. Hindú prosodians have enumerated and described a very great variety of metres in *Mátrá Chhand*, as in *Varaṇ Chhand.* But it will suffice to enumerate and illustrate a number of the most common. The metres under each class are arranged according to the number of *mátrás* in each line (*dal*), beginning with the shorter and proceeding to the longer metres.

I. *Verse of Two Lines* (द्विपाद्).

982. **दोहा** or **दोहरा.** This contains two lines, each of 24 instants; each of which is divided into two *charaṇs* and six feet, as follows: 6 + 4 + 3, 6 + 4 + 1. The last foot (3) in the first *charaṇ* must not be a trochee (— ⏑); i.e., it must be a tribrach (⏑ ⏑ ⏑) or an iambus (⏑ —). The last syllable of each line must be short.

माला फेरत जुग गया   गया न मन का फेर ।
कर का मनका छाड़िकै मन का मनका फेर ॥

Rem. This is at present the most popular and common of all metres. It is much used by *Tulsí Dás, Kabír,* and all the most esteemed poets.

983. सोरठा. This is simply an inverted *Dohá*; i.e., the 2nd and 4th *charaṇs* of the *Dohá,* are made to stand as 1*st* and 3*rd,* and *vice versâ.* The same rules and restrictions as to feet hold as in the *Dohá*; i.e., the final syllable of the short *charaṇs* must be short; and the last foot of the longer *charaṇs* must not be a trochee. The rhyme is not made at the end of the line, but maintains its original place at the end of the short *charaṇs.* The scheme stands, $6+4+1$, $6+4+3$. In the following, *Tulsí Dás* has exceptionally rhymed also the longer *charaṇs.*

कुंदइंदुसम देह   उमारमन करुनाअयन ।
जाहि दीन पर नेह   करौ कृपा मर्दनमयन ॥

984. उल्लाल छंद contains in each line of two *charaṇs,* 28 instants; the 1st and 3rd *charaṇs* each have four feet, $(4 \times 3)+3=15$; and the 2nd and 4th, three feet, $6+4+3=13$ instants.

जो प्रभु कहै गुन अमित तोर   सुचि शक्ति प्रेम अपार ।
जब दिवधाम तजि अवतरियो   कीन्ह तबहि नर निस्तार ॥

985. ललित or **हरिपद छंद** contains in each line $16,+12=28$ instants. The last two syllables of each line must be *long.*

कहा मानु अब बात हमारी   चलो सखी तू आजू ।
सुनो हाल हम आज तुमारी   प्रिया सिधारो काजू ॥

986. **महीधरी** or **हरिगीति छंद** has seven feet in each line; thus $(4\times5)+6+2=28$ instants. Pause at the 16th instant, secondary pause at the 9th. The last syllable of each *charaṇ* must be long.

बिनु दाम आवत काम जो नित ताहि नहीं भजे नरा ।
जगदीश एकहि छाड़ि सेवत देवगण संशय भरा ॥

987. **चूड़ियाला छंद** differs from the *Dohá* only in that a third *charaṇ* of 5 instants is added to each line. Thus the scheme for each line is, $6+4+3$, $6+4+1$, $+3+2=29$.

मैं अब मिलन चहों सखी जसुमति सुत जहं होय कता वज्र ।
झपटि झपटि सब दौरिकै यशुदा नंदन को लखवा वज्र ॥

988. **चौपदी छंद** has in each line, $10, +8, +12, =30$ instants; the last syllable must be long. Pause at the 10th and 18th instants.

अति कूर आकार रूप न चन्हि परम चतुर पद पावे ।
सब देखि जगत में आप भलो है बाहर सुमति बतावे ॥

989. **चौबोला छंद** has in each line 30 instants. Pause at the 16th instant. Thus, $(4\times4), +(4\times3)+2=30$ instants.

अमर हित बिचारि धरो तनु जो भूपति वलि सो कपट करी ॥

Rem. In the *Chhandodípak*, the line is divided thus, $(4\times3)+3=15$, $(4\times3)+3=15$. I have followed the *Pingaládarsh*.

990. **घत्ता** or **घत्तानन्द छंद** has two lines, each of 31 instants; each line has nine feet, with pauses at the 10th and 18th instants, thus, $(4\times2)+2$, $4+4$, $(4\times3)+1$.

मोहन मुख आगे अति अनुरागे मैं जुरही मसिछबि निदरि।
दुख देत सु आली बिनु वनमाली घत्ता लहि चूक तन अरि ॥

II. *Verse of Four lines* (चतुष्पाद).

991. Of the various metres enumerated below, a number, as, e.g., *Tribhangi*, *Durmilá*, *Daṇḍkalá*, *Lílávatí*, *Padmávatí*, *Madanhar*, are reckoned by a few prosodians as verses of two lines (द्विपाद). The second pair is, indeed, in respect of feet, only a repetition of the first pair, and does not rhyme with it, so that the verse is really a compound of two *Dvipád* stanzas. On this account, while following common usage in reckoning these as *Chatushpád*, in many cases I have thought it necessary to give examples only of the first of the two couplets.

992. गमक छंद has in each line 5 short syllables.

श्रम सकल । बल विकल ॥ सुर अमृत । असुर मृत ॥

993. दीपक छंद has in each line 10 short instants.

तुम रहहु प्रियनाथ । निसु समय मम साथ ॥
जग के सुखदायक । प्रेम करै लायक ॥

994. The following have each 14 instants in each line, but differ in respect of the metrical pause, and the feet that are permissible.

(1) गजल छंद, 7, + 7, = 14. Last foot must be a trochee.

अब तो हो तु प्रीय सचेत । मग में पड़ि न रहो अचेत ॥
नयन खोलहु अर्जुन समीप । जागत रहो तू सजि दीप ॥

(2) चम्पक छंद, 8, + 6, = 14. Last foot must be a spondee.

मुरली की धुनि सुनि धाईं । सगरी सखियां उठि आईं ॥
मन मोहन की सुनि बानी । रहि रहि सारी मुसुकानी ॥

(3) **बज्र छंद**, 6, + 8, = 14. First foot, ⏑ ⏑ ⏑; last foot, ⏑ – ⏑.

रहहु सदा रघुबंश नाथ। करहु कृपा अब आञ साथ ॥
जतन करहु अब दीननाथ। धरहु अबै मम कोध हाथ ॥

995. **चोपाई छंद**, 8, + 7, = 15. Final syllable must be short.

करहु कृपानिधि धुर्म्म विकाश। मेरे हिय में ज्ञान प्रकाश ॥
रहहु सदा प्रभु चित में आय। कलिमल राघव पल में जाय ॥

996. The following two contain each 16 instants to the line, but differ in the feet and pauses.

(1) **अडिल्ल** or **अलीला छंद**, 8, + 8, = 16. No *jagans* (⏑ – ⏑) allowed; the last foot must be a *bhagan* (– ⏑ ⏑). All four lines must rhyme.

अब वह आवत बेणु बजावत । ग्वाल बाल को नाच नचावत ॥
लखु अति रावत छवि वह छावत। ठुमकि ठुमकि सब खेल खिलावत ॥

(2) **चौपाई** (also called पादाकुलक and कुलपाई) 6 + 4 + 4 + 2 = 16. The last foot is commonly, though not invariably, a spondee.

उघरहिं विमल विलोचन ही के। मिटहिं दोष दुष भवरजनी के ॥
सूझहिं रामचरित मनिमानिक । गुप्त प्रगट जो जेहि खानिक ॥

Rem. This metre ranks with the *Dohá* in popularity. A large part of the *Rámáyan* of *Tulsí Dás* is composed in sections very commonly of four *Chaupáís*, alternating with one or two *Dohás*.

997. **हंसगति छंद**, 5 + 5, + 5 + 5, = 20. Pause at the 10th instant.

यशोदा लाल तूं रारि काहे करो। कहोंगी आज मैं जार नाहीं टरो ॥
सुनौगो यशोदा बतावैगि तेरो । ढीठ तो भयो है देखियो तु मेरो ॥

998. **रासा छंद**, 12, + 9, = 21 instants.

करहु कृपा जग स्वामी   मेरे साथ हो ॥
रहिहूं सदा अभिलाषी   तेरे हाथ हो ॥

999. **लीला छंद**, 11, + 11, = 22. Last syllable must be long.

धन्य भयों मैं आज   हरि के काज आयो ॥
लखो सखी सब साज कस हरि रूप भायो ॥

1000. **रोला छंद** (also called रसावली), 6, + (4 × 4) + 2, = 24. Last syllable must be long; pause at the 11th instant.

रवि छवि देखत घुसत घूघू जहं तहं भागहीं ॥
चक्रवाक लखि अधिक हिय रवि को अनुरागहीं ॥

1001. **काव्य छंद**, 6 + (4 × 3) + 6, = 24; pause at the 11th instant.

माधव आज निहारि   जात बालन संग कुंजन ॥
देखि देखिके आप   चलत मानहु दलगंजन ॥
आवै अब लों आज   धह मिलि री नंदनंदन ॥
करत बड़ो अनरीत   चलत जिमि सिधुरविभंजन ॥

1002. **दुविया छंद** contains 16, + 12, = 28 instants.

आयो आज यहां यदुनन्दन   लीन्हे कर पट सारो ।
देखु देखु सखि सोहत कैसौ   मानो घनघट कारी ॥

1003. **चौपैया छंद**, 10, + 8, + 12 = 30 instants. Last foot a spondee. Subordinate rhymes fall at the 10th and 18th instant.

तल वितल रसातल   गगन भुवन तल   सृष्टि जिती जग माहीं ।
पुर ग्राम सुथल में   कानन जल में   ताहि रहित कहु नाहीं ॥
पिय मिलहि न रामहि तजि सिय वामहि   नहि बचाउ कहुं भावे ।
सुरपति सुत कावो   सब जग नावो   वा चौपैया लागे ॥

1004. **सवाया छंद**, 16, + 15, = 31 instants. Last foot a trochee.

ऐसो राम नाम को सौदा तोहि न भावत मूढ़ अयान ।
निसि दिन आत मोह बस दौरत बरत सबै काज मम सिरान ॥

1005. The four following metres have each 32 instants to the line, and differ only in the cæsural pause, and the feet which are permitted.

(1) **त्रिभंगी छंद**, 10, + 8, + 8, + 6, = 32. No *jagans* (⏑ – ⏑) allowed. Subordinate rhymes at each pause.

समुझिय जगु जन में को फलु मनु में हरि सुमिरन में दिन भरिये ॥
झगड़ो बखेरो घेर घनेरो मेरो तेरो परिहरिये ॥
मोहन बनवारी गिरवर धारी कुंज बिहारी पगु परिये ॥
गोपिन को संगी प्रभु बजरंगी लाल त्रिभंगी उर धरिये ॥

(2) **पदमावती छंद** differs from the *Tribhangi* only in making two pauses instead of three in each line, thus, 10, + 8, + 14, = 32. But some writers make three pauses, dividing thus, 10, + 8, + 6, + 8, = 32. The final syllable must be long. The remaining rules are the same as for the *Tribhangi*.

ब्यालिनि सो बेनी लषि छबि सेनी तब तन आसा मोरैं जू ।
ससि सों मुष सोभित लषि छबी लोभित आवत टकी चकोरैं जू ॥
निकसत मुष स्वासें पाइ सुबासें संगन छोड़त भौरैं जू ।
बाहिर आवत जब पद्मावति तब भीर सुरहिं चकचौरैं जू ॥

(3) **दुरमिला छंद**, 10, + 8, + 8, + 6 = 32. This differs from the *Tribhangi* only in that the last foot must be a spondee. Secondary rhymes are made in the subordinate divisions of each line.

एक चित्त वृतधारी पर उपकारी नित गुरु आज्ञा अनुसारी ।
निरसंचय दाता सब रस ज्ञाता सदा साधु संगति धारी ॥

a. The दंडकला छंद differs from this only in requiring an iambus instead of the final spondee.

(4) लीलावती छंद. Scheme, 18, + 14, = 32. This differs from all the preceding in admitting only one cæsural pause.

पीतांबर की चटक मटक भ्रु की लटक मटक अरु कुंडल की ॥
मुसुकान विलोकन निरखि निरखि के हरषित होय भानुकुल की ॥

1006. हिंडोल छंद. Scheme, 10, + 10, + 10, + 10, = 40. The last foot must be an iambus; subordinate rhymes may occur at each pause.

प्राण के अपण में नैन में बैन में चित्त अरु कर्ण में सदा बसो जमुना ॥
शयन में चलत में कहत में सुनत में खान अरु पान में करो पाप दमुना ॥

1007. मदनहर छंद has in each line 10, + 8, + 8, + 6, + 8, = 40 instants. The final syllable of each line must be long; but the last three syllables must not form a *ragan* (– ⏑ –). The first two and last two *charaṇs* rhyme. Subordinate rhymes occur at the cæsural pauses.

सखि लखु यदुराई छवि अधिकाई भाग भलाई आनि परे
फल सुकृति फरे ।
अतिरूपसदन मुख होत सघन सुख दास हिये दुख दूरि करे
सुख भूरि भरे ॥

III. *Verse of More than Four Lines* (बहुपाद).

1008. कुण्डलिया छंद. This is a compound metre of six lines, consisting of a *Dohá*, followed by two *Kávyas.* The last *charaṇ* of the *Dohá* must be repeated in the beginning of the *Kávya*, and the last two syllables of the *Kávya* must be the same as the first two of the *Dohá*. This metre is much admired. The best examples are in the poem of *Girdhar Ráe*, which is written in this metre.

बीती ताहि बिसार दे   आगे की सुध लेय ।
जो बनि आवै सहज में   ताही में चित देय ॥
ताही में चित देय   बात जोही बनि आवै ।
दुरजन हंसे न कोइ   चित्त में खेद न पावै ॥
कह गिरधर कविराय   यहै कर मन परतीती ।
आगे कीं सुख होय   समुझ बीती सो बीतो ॥

Rem. Sometimes for the *Kávya*, a *Rolá Chhand* may be substituted. This differs from the *Kávya*, however, only in the division of its feet.

1009. छप्पै छंद consists of a *Kávya* and an *Ullál Chhand* (§ 984).

भाल नैन मुख अधर   चिबुक तिय तुम बिलोकि अति ॥
निर्म्मल चपल प्रसन्न   लाल सुभ वृत्ति थकी मति ॥
उपमा कह शशि पंक   कंज बिंबिय गुलाब बर ॥
कंद याम तिथि प्रात   पक्क प्रफुलित सुशोभ धर ॥
सादर किशोर सुभ गंध मृदु   नय सदास आवत न चित ॥
सु कलंक रहित पुग सरल हित   डार गहित षट पद सहित ॥

1010. रसिक छंद consists of 6 lines, each of 11 instants. The final syllable must be short.

हंसत चखत दधि मुदित ॥ सुकत भजत मुख बदित ॥
चखित तियनि मिलि रहत ॥ रिसियुत विरतिहि गहत ॥
अगनित छवि मुख ससिक ॥ सिसु तवन बरस रसिक ॥

Of Metres used in Songs (Bhajans).

1011. Many of the metres enumerated above, in both *Varaṇ Chhand* and *Mátrá Chhand*, are used in the composition of verse designed to be sung. The only special point to be noted is the custom of continuing the same rhyme throughout all the lines of the *bhajan*. A whole or half stanza is often repeated as a refrain. The following are examples added of common metres. Peculiarities of *Bhajan* Metres.

1012. **तोटक सवैया.** Scheme, ८ स + स. Pause at 4th foot. Examples of *Bhajan* Metres.

जप जोग करै तन साधि मरे नर कोटि उपाय रचे भरमाए ॥
श्रुति चारि पुरान कुरान पढ़े नहिं भेद मिले तन झूठि सताए ॥
गुर पंडित पीर फकीर फिरे बहु भांति के रूप विरूप बनाए ॥ etc.

1013. **ध्रुपद गीत** has in each verse 32 short syllables, with pause and rhyme at 8th, 16th, and 24th.

बह चसन बसन बह सरन सदन ।
दह चघ घन बन बह धरम बचन ॥

1014. **पूर्वी गीत** has two lines, of 6 + 6, 6 + 4 = 22 instants, with pause at the 12th; the last two syllables must be long.

काम लहर उठत तुंद क्रोध पवन जोरे ।
लोभ भौर घुमत ठौर मोह सघन घोरे ॥

1015. **ललिता गीत.** In each line 6 + 6 + 2, + 6 + 4 = 24 instants, with pause at the 14th.

भव भय भंजन जनरंजन गंजन सकल हरन ॥
विपति निवारक सुखदायक सायक पड़न चरन ॥

1016. भैरव गीत. The scheme commonly used to this *Rág*, is as follows; 6+4+4+2, +6+4+2=28 instants, with pause at the 16th instant; the metre is complete in two lines.

भजन करो मन लाई भाई भजन करो मन लाई ।
प्रेम सुधा रस चाखो निरमल रसना रस अपनाई ॥

1017. ठुमरी गीत. To this is sung a verse of two lines, as follows; 6 + 4 + 4 + 2, + 4 + 4 + 4 = 28 instants; or 6+4+4+2, +6+4+4+2=32 instants. Pause, in either, at the 16th instant.

(1) अमरित भोजन छाड़ि विमूढ़े कर नित गरल अहारी ।
कंठहि उतरत तन मन यास्यो कोउ न करे पुकारी ॥

(2) जोति घट गई दौ नैनन की नाहि सुने स्वर नीके काना ।
सूंधि सके नहि फूलन बासा रसना भूले रस रुचि नाना ॥